PETERSON'S
COLLEGES IN
NEW ENGLAND

25ᵗʰ Edition

PETERSON'S

A nelnet COMPANY

About Peterson's

To succeed on your lifelong educational journey, you will need accurate, dependable, and practical tools and resources. That is why Peterson's is everywhere education happens. Because whenever and however you need education content delivered, you can rely on Peterson's to provide the information, know-how, and guidance to help you reach your goals. Tools to match the right students with the right school. It's here. Personalized resources and expert guidance. It's here. Comprehensive and dependable education content—delivered whenever and however you need it. It's all here.

For more information, contact Peterson's, 2000 Lenox Drive, Lawrenceville, NJ 08648; 800-338-3282; or find us on the World Wide Web at www.petersons.com/about.

Stephen Clemente, President; Bernadette Webster, Director of Publishing; Mark D. Snider, Editor; Ward Brigham, Research Project Manager; Cathleen Fee, Research Associate; Phyllis Johnson, Programmer; Ray Golaszewski, Manufacturing Manager; Linda M. Williams, Composition Manager; Janet Garwo, Mimi Kaufman, Karen Mount, Danielle Vreeland, Shannon White, Client Relations Representatives

ISSN 1538-3180
ISBN-13: 978-0-7689-2691-0
ISBN-10: 0-7689-2691-2

Printed in the United States of America

10 9 8 7 6 5 4 3 2 1   11 10 09

Twenty-fifth Edition

By producing this book on recycled paper (40% post consumer waste) 10 trees were saved.

CONTENTS

A Note from the Peterson's Editors

Welcome to the world of choosing a college. You are probably considering at least one college that is relatively near your home. It may surprise you to learn that the majority of all students go to college within a 300-mile radius of where they live. Because of that factor, we publish this series of college guides that focuses on the colleges in each of six regions of the country so that students can easily compare the colleges in their own area. (Two-year public and proprietary colleges are not included because their admission patterns are significantly different from other colleges.)

For advice and guidance in the college search and selection process, just turn the page. "Surviving Standardized Tests" describes the most frequently used tests. Of course, part of the college selection process involves visiting the schools themselves and "The Whys and Whats of College Visits" is just the planner you need to make those trips well worth your while. Next, "Applying 101" provides advice on how best to approach the application phase of the process. If you've got questions about transferring, "Successful Transfer" has got the answers you need. "Who's Paying for This? Financial Aid Basics" and the "Financial Aid Programs for Schools in New England" articles provide you with the essential information on how to meet your education expenses. "Searching for Four-Year Colleges Online" gives you all the tips you'll need to augment your college search using the Internet. Lastly, you'll want to read through "How to Use This Guide" and learn how to use all the information presented in this volume.

Following these articles are the **Profiles of Colleges** sections. The **Profiles** are easy to read and should give you a good sense of whether a college meets your basic needs and warrants further consideration. This consistently formatted collection of data can provide a balance to the individual mailings you are likely to receive from colleges. The **Profiles** appear in geographical order by state.

In a number of the **Profiles** (those marked with a *Sponsor* icon), you will find helpful information about social life, academic life, campus visits, and interviews. These **Special Messages to Students** are written in each case by a college admissions office staff member. You will find valuable insights into what each writer considers special about his or her institution (both socially and academically), what is expected of you during your interview at that college, and how important the interview is there. You will also be alerted to outstanding attractions on campus or nearby so you can plan a productive visit. In many cases, travel information (nearest commercial airport and nearest interstate highway) that will be of help on your campus visit is included.

And if you still thirst for even more information, look for the two-page narrative descriptions appearing in the **Close-Ups of Colleges** sections of the book. These descriptions are written by admissions deans and provide great detail about each college. They are edited to provide a consistent format across entries for your ease of comparison.

The **Indexes** at the back of the book (Majors and Degrees, Athletic Programs and Scholarships, and ROTC Programs) enable you to pinpoint colleges listed in the **Profiles** according to their specific offerings. In addition, there is an Alphabetical Listing of Colleges and Universities to enable you to quickly find a school that you may have already determined meets your criteria.

We hope you will find this information helpful. Our advice is to relax, enjoy high school, and do as well as you can in your courses. Give yourself enough time during the early stages of your search to think about what kind of person you are and what you want to become so you can choose colleges for the right reasons. Read all college materials with an open mind, and visit as many campuses as you can. Plan ahead so you do not rush through your applications. Try to remember that admission directors are as interested in you and the possibility of you attending their college as you are in the possibility of applying. They spend most of their time reaching out to students, explaining their colleges' programs and policies, and simplifying the application process whenever they can. If you think of them as people who like students and if you can picture them taking the time to carefully provide the information in this book for you, it might help to lessen any anxiety you are feeling about applying. In fact, the admission people whose names you will find in this book hope to hear from you.

Peterson's publishes a full line of resources to help guide you and your family through the college admission process. Peterson's publications can be found at your local bookstore or library and at your high school guidance office;

A Note from the Peterson's Editors

you can access us online at **www.petersons.com.** Our Web-based resources for high school students can be found at **www.petersons.com/studentedge,** a personalized online resource center that helps you prepare for life after high school. It combines test preparation, college search, financial aid planning, and career exploration in one convenient location.

We welcome any comments or suggestions you may have about this publication and invite you to complete our online survey at **www.petersons.com/booksurvey.** Or you can fill out the survey at the back of this book, tear it out, and mail it to us at:

Publishing Department
Peterson's, a Nelnet company
2000 Lenox Drive
Lawrenceville, NJ 08648

Your feedback will help us make your education dreams possible. The editors at Peterson's wish you success and happiness wherever you enroll.

The College Admissions Process

Surviving Standardized Tests

WHAT ARE STANDARDIZED TESTS?

Colleges and universities in the United States use tests to help evaluate applicants' readiness for admission or to place them in appropriate courses. The tests that are most frequently used by colleges are the ACT of American College Testing, Inc., and the College Board's SAT. In addition, the Educational Testing Service (ETS) offers the TOEFL test, which evaluates the English-language proficiency of nonnative speakers. The tests are offered at designated testing centers located at high schools and colleges throughout the United States and U.S. territories and at testing centers in various countries throughout the world.

Upon request, special accommodations for students with documented visual, hearing, physical, or learning disabilities are available. Examples of special accommodations include tests in Braille or large print and such aids as a reader, recorder, magnifying glass, or sign language interpreter. Additional testing time may be allowed in some instances. Contact the appropriate testing program or your guidance counselor for details on how to request special accommodations.

THE ACT

The ACT is a standardized college entrance examination that measures knowledge and skills in English, mathematics, reading, and science reasoning and the application of these skills to future academic tasks. The ACT consists of four multiple-choice tests.

Test 1: English

- 75 questions, 45 minutes
- Usage and mechanics
- Rhetorical skills

Test 2: Mathematics

- 60 questions, 60 minutes
- Pre-algebra
- Elementary algebra
- Intermediate algebra
- Coordinate geometry
- Plane geometry
- Trigonometry

Test 3: Reading

- 40 questions, 35 minutes
- Prose fiction
- Humanities
- Social studies
- Natural sciences

Test 4: Science

- 40 questions, 35 minutes
- Data representation
- Research summary
- Conflicting viewpoints

Each section is scored from 1 to 36 and is scaled for slight variations in difficulty. Students are not penalized for incorrect responses. The composite score is the average of the four scaled scores. There is also a 30-minute Writing Test that is an optional component of the ACT.

To prepare for the ACT, ask your guidance counselor for a free guidebook called *Preparing for the ACT*. Besides providing general test-preparation information and additional test-taking strategies, this guidebook describes the content and format of the four ACT subject area tests, summarizes test administration procedures followed at ACT test centers, and includes a practice test. Peterson's publishes *The Real ACT Prep Guide* that includes three official ACT tests.

DON'T FORGET TO . . .

- Take the SAT or ACT before application deadlines.
- Note that test registration deadlines precede test dates by about six weeks.
- Register to take the TOEFL test if English is not your native language and you are planning on studying at a North American college.
- Practice your test-taking skills with *Peterson's Master the SAT, Peterson's Ultimate ACT Tool Kit, The Real ACT Prep Guide* (published by Peterson's), *Peterson's Master TOEFL Reading Skills, Peterson's Master TOEFL Vocabulary,* and *Peterson's Master TOEFL Writing Skills.*
- Contact the College Board or American College Testing, Inc., in advance if you need special accommodations when taking tests.

THE SAT

The SAT measures developed critical reading and mathematical reasoning abilities as they relate to successful performance in college. It is intended to supplement the secondary school record and other information about the student in assessing readiness for college. There is one unscored, experimental section on the exam, which is used for equating and/or pretesting purposes and can cover either the mathematics or critical reading area.

Critical Reading

- 67 questions, 70 minutes
- Sentence completion
- Passage-based reading

Mathematics

- 54 questions, 70 minutes
- Multiple-choice
- Student-produced response (grid-ins)

Writing

- 49 questions plus essay, 60 minutes
- Identifying sentence errors
- Improving paragraphs
- Improving sentences
- Essay

Students receive one point for each correct response and lose a fraction of a point for each incorrect response (except for student-produced responses). These points are totaled to produce the raw scores, which are then scaled to equalize the scores for slight variations in difficulty for various editions of the test. The critical reading, writing, and mathematics scaled scores range from 200–800 per section. The total scaled score range is from 600–2400.

SAT SUBJECT TESTS

Subject Tests are required by some institutions for admission and/or placement in freshman-level courses. Each Subject Test measures one's knowledge of a specific subject and the ability to apply that knowledge. Students should check with each institution for its specific requirements. In general, students are required to take three Subject Tests (one English, one mathematics, and one of their choice).

Subject Tests are given in the following areas: biology, chemistry, Chinese, French, German, Italian, Japanese, Korean, Latin, literature, mathematics, modern Hebrew, physics, Spanish, U.S. history, and world history. These tests are 1 hour long and are primarily multiple-choice tests. Three Subject Tests may be taken on one test date.

Scored like the SAT, students gain a point for each correct answer and lose a fraction of a point for each incorrect answer. The raw scores are then converted to scaled scores that range from 200 to 800.

THE TOEFL INTERNET-BASED TEST (IBT)

The Test of English as a Foreign Language Internet-Based Test (TOEFL iBT) is designed to help assess a student's grasp of English if it is not the student's first language. Performance on the TOEFL test may help interpret scores on the critical reading sections of the SAT. The test consists of four integrated sections: speaking, listening, reading, and writing. The TOEFL iBT emphasizes integrated skills. The paper-based versions of the TOEFL will continue to be administered in certain countries where the Internet-based version has not yet been introduced. For further information, visit www.toefl.org.

WHAT OTHER TESTS SHOULD I KNOW ABOUT?

The AP Program

This program allows high school students to try college-level work and build valuable skills and study habits in the process. Subject matter is explored in more depth in AP courses than in other high school classes. A qualifying score on an AP test—which varies from school to school—can earn you college credit or advanced placement. Getting qualifying grades on enough exams can even earn you a full year's credit and sophomore standing at more than 1,500 higher-education institutions. There are currently thirty-seven AP courses in twenty-two different subject areas, including art history, biology, and computer science. Speak to your guidance counselor for information about your school's offerings.

College-Level Examination Program (CLEP)

The CLEP enables students to earn college credit for what they already know, whether it was learned in school, through independent study, or through other experiences outside of the classroom. Approximately 2,900 colleges and universities now award credit for qualifying scores on one or more of the 34 CLEP exams. The exams, which are 90 minutes in length and are primarily multiple choice, are administered at participating colleges and universities. For more information, check out the Web site at www.collegeboard.com/clep.

TOP 10 WAYS NOT TO TAKE THE TEST

10. Cramming the night before the test.

9. Not becoming familiar with the directions before you take the test.

8. Not becoming familiar with the format of the test before you take it.

7. Not knowing how the test is graded.

6. Spending too much time on any one question.

5. Not checking spelling, grammar, and sentence structure in essays.

4. Second-guessing yourself.

3. Forgetting to take a deep breath to keep from—

2. Losing It!

1. Writing a one-paragraph essay.

WHAT CAN I DO TO PREPARE FOR THESE TESTS?

Know what to expect. Get familiar with how the tests are structured, how much time is allowed, and the directions for each type of question. Get plenty of rest the night before the test and eat breakfast that morning.

There are a variety of products, from books to software to videos, available to help you prepare for most standardized tests. Find the learning style that suits you best. As for which products to buy, there are two major categories—those created by the test makers and those created by private companies. The best approach is to talk to someone who has been through the process and find out which product or products he or she recommends.

Some students report significant increases in scores after participating in coaching programs. Longer-term programs (40 hours) seem to raise scores more than short-term programs (20 hours), but beyond 40 hours, score gains are minor. Math scores appear to benefit more from coaching than critical reading scores.

Resources

There is a variety of ways to prepare for standardized tests—find a method that fits your schedule and your budget. But you should definitely prepare. Far too many students walk into these tests cold, either because they find standardized tests frightening or annoying or they just haven't found the time to study. The key is that these exams are standardized. That means these tests are largely the same from administration to administration; they always test the same concepts. They have to, or else you couldn't compare the scores of people who took the tests on different dates. The numbers or words may change, but the underlying content doesn't.

So how do you prepare? At the very least, you should review relevant material, such as math formulas and commonly used vocabulary words, and know the directions for each question type or test section. You should take at least one practice test and review your mistakes so you don't make them again on the test day. Beyond that, you know best how much preparation you need. You'll also find lots of material in libraries or bookstores to help you: books and software from the test makers and from other publishers (including Peterson's) or live courses that range from national test-preparation companies to teachers at your high school who offer classes.

The Whys and Whats of College Visits

Dawn B. Sova, Ph.D.

The campus visit should not be a passive activity for you and your parents. Take the initiative and gather information beyond that provided in the official tour. You will see many important indicators during your visit that will tell you more about the true character of a college and its students than the tour guide will reveal. Know what to look for and how to assess the importance of such indicators.

WHAT SHOULD YOU ASK AND WHAT SHOULD YOU LOOK FOR?

Your first stop on a campus visit is the visitor center or admissions office, where you will probably have to wait to meet with a counselor. Colleges usually plan to greet visitors later than the appointed time in order to give them the opportunity to review some of the campus information that is liberally scattered throughout the visitor waiting room. Take advantage of the time to become even more familiar with the college by arriving 15 to 30 minutes before your appointment to observe the behavior of staff members and to browse through the yearbooks and student newspapers that will be available.

If you prepare in advance, you will have already reviewed the college catalog and map of the campus. These materials familiarize you with the academic offerings and the physical layout of the campus, but the true character of the college and its students emerges in other ways.

Begin your investigation with the visitor center staff members. As a student's first official contact with the college, they should make every effort to welcome prospective students and project a friendly image.

- How do they treat you and other prospective students who are waiting? Are they friendly and willing to speak with you, or do they try their hardest to avoid eye contact and conversation?
- Are they friendly with each other and with students who enter the office, or are they curt and unwilling to help?
- Does the waiting room have a friendly feeling or is it cold and sterile?

If the visitor center staff members seem indifferent to *prospective* students, there is little reason to believe that they will be warm and welcoming to current students. View such behavior as a warning to watch very carefully the interaction of others with you during the tour. An indifferent or unfriendly reception in the admissions office may be simply the first of many signs that attending this college will not be a pleasant experience.

Look through several yearbooks and see the types of activities that are actually photographed, as opposed to the activities that colleges promise in their promotional literature. Some questions are impossible to answer if the college is very large, but for small and moderately sized colleges the yearbook is a good indicator of campus activity.

- Has the number of clubs and organizations increased or decreased in the past five years?
- Do the same students appear repeatedly in activities?
- Do sororities and fraternities dominate campus activities?
- Are participants limited to one sex or one ethnic group, or is there diversity?
- Are all activities limited to the campus, or are students involved in activities in the community?

Use what you observe in the yearbooks as a means of forming a more complete understanding of the college, but don't base your entire impression on just one facet. If time permits, look through several copies of the school newspaper, which should reflect the major concerns and interests of the students. The paper is also a good way to learn about the campus social life.

- Does the paper contain a mix of national and local news?
- What products or services are advertised?
- How assertive are the editorials?
- With what topics are the columnists concerned?
- Are movies and concerts that meet your tastes advertised or reviewed?
- What types of ads appear in the classified section?

The newspaper should be a public forum for students, and, as such, should reflect the character of the campus and of

the student body. A paper that deals only with seemingly safe and well-edited topics on the editorial page and in regular feature columns might indicate administrative censorship. A lack of ads for restaurants might indicate either a lack of good places to eat or that area restaurants do not welcome student business. A limited mention of movies, concerts, or other entertainment might reveal a severely limited campus social life. Even if ads and reviews are included, you should still balance how such activities reflect your tastes.

You will have only a limited amount of time to ask questions during your initial meeting with the admissions counselor, for very few schools include a formal interview in the initial campus visit or tour. Instead, this brief meeting is often just a nicety that allows the admissions office to begin a file for the student and to record some initial impressions. Save your questions for the tour guide and for students on campus you meet along the way.

HOW CAN YOU ASSESS THE TRUE CHARACTER OF A COLLEGE AND ITS STUDENTS?

Colleges do not train their tour guides to deceive prospective students, but they do caution guides to avoid unflattering topics and campus sites. Does this mean that you will see only a sugarcoated version of life on a particular college campus? Not at all, especially not if you are observant.

Most organized campus visits include such campus facilities as dormitories, dining halls, libraries, student activity and recreation centers, and the health and student services centers. Some may only be pointed out, while you will walk through others. Either way, you will find that many signs of the true character of the college emerge if you keep your eyes open.

Bulletin boards in dormitories and student centers contain a wealth of information about campus activities, student concerns, and campus groups. Read the posters, notices, and messages to learn what *really* interests students. Unlike ads in the school newspaper, posters put up by students advertise both on- and off-campus events, so they will give you an idea of what is also available in the surrounding community.

Review the notices, which may cover either campuswide events or events that concern only small groups of students. The catalog may not mention a performance group, but an individual dormitory with its own small theater may offer regular productions. Poetry readings, jam sessions, writers' groups, and other activities may be announced and show diversity of student interests.

Even the brief bulletin board messages offering objects for sale and noting objects that people want to purchase reveal a lot about a campus. Are most of the items computer related? Or do the messages specify CDs, audio equipment, or musical instruments? Are offers to trade goods or services posted? Don't ignore the "ride wanted" messages. Students who want to share rides home during a break may specify widely diverse geographical locations. If so, then you know that the student body is not limited to only the immediate area or one locale. Other messages can also enhance your knowledge of the true character of the campus and its students.

As you walk through various buildings, examine their condition carefully.

- Is the paint peeling, and do the exteriors look worn?
- Are the exteriors and interiors of the building clean?
- Is the equipment in the classrooms up-to-date or outdated?

Pay particular attention to the dormitories, especially to factors that might affect your safety. Observe the appearance of the structure, and ask about the security measures in and around the dormitories.

- Are the dormitories noisy or quiet?
- Do they seem crowded?
- How good is the lighting around each dormitory?
- Are the dormitories spread throughout the campus or are they clustered in one main area?
- Who has access to the dormitories in addition to students?
- How secure are the means by which students enter and leave the dormitory?

While you are on the subject of dormitory safety, you should also ask about campus safety. Don't expect that the guide will rattle off a list of crimes that have been committed in the past year. To obtain that information, access the recent year of issues of *The Chronicle of Higher Education* and locate its yearly report on campus crime. Also ask the guide about safety measures that the campus police take and those that students have initiated.

- Can students request escorts to their residences late at night?
- Do campus shuttle buses run at frequent intervals all night?
- Are "blue-light" telephones liberally placed throughout the campus for students to use to call for help?
- Do the campus police patrol the campus regularly?

If the guide does not answer your questions satisfactorily, wait until after the tour to contact the campus police or traffic office for answers.

Campus tours usually just point out the health services center without taking the time to walk through. Even if you don't see the inside of the building, you should take a close look at the location of the health services center and ask the guide questions about services.

- How far is the health center from the dormitories?
- Is a doctor always on call?
- Does the campus transport sick students from their dormitories or must they walk?
- What are the operating hours of the health center?
- Does the health center refer students to a nearby hospital?

If the guide can't answer your questions, visit the health center later and ask someone there.

Most campus tours take pride in showing students their activities centers, which may contain snack bars, game rooms, workout facilities, and other means of entertainment. Should you scrutinize this building as carefully as the rest? Of course. Outdated and poorly maintained activity equipment contributes to your total impression of the college. You should also ask about the hours, availability, and cost (no, the activities are usually *not* free) of using the bowling alleys, pool tables, air hockey tables, and other ammenities.

As you walk through campus with the tour, also look carefully at the appearance of the students who pass. The way in which both men and women groom themselves, the way they dress, and even their physical bearing communicate a lot more than any guidebook can. If everyone seems to conform to the same look, you might feel that you would be uncomfortable at the college, however nonconformist that look might be. On the other hand, you might not feel comfortable on a campus that stresses diversity of dress and behavior, and your observations now can save you discomfort later.

- Does every student seem to wear a sorority or fraternity t-shirt or jacket?
- Is everyone of your sex sporting the latest fad haircut?
- Do all of the men or the women seem to be wearing expensive name-brand clothes?
- Do most of the students seem to be working hard to look outrageous with regards to clothing, hair color, and body art?
- Would you feel uncomfortable in a room full of these students?

Is appearance important to you? If it is, then you should consider very seriously if you answer *yes* to any of the above questions. You don't have to be the same as everyone else on campus, but standing out too much may make you unhappy.

As you observe the physical appearance of the students, also listen to their conversations as you pass them. What are they talking about? How are they speaking? Are their voices and accents all the same, or do you hear diversity in their speech? Are you offended by their language? Think how you will feel if surrounded by the same speech habits and patterns for four years.

WHERE SHOULD YOU VISIT ON YOUR OWN?

Your campus visit is not over when the tour ends because you will probably have many questions yet to be answered and many places to still be seen. Where you go depends upon the extent to which the organized tour covers the campus. Your tour should take you to view residential halls, health and student services centers, the gymnasium or field house, dining halls, the library, and recreational centers. If any of the facilities on this list have been omitted, visit them on your own and ask questions of the students and staff members you meet. In addition, you should step off campus and gain an impression of the surrounding community. You will probably become bored with life on campus and spend at least some time off campus. Make certain that you know what the surrounding area is like.

The campus tour leaves little time to ask impromptu questions of current students, but you can do so after the tour. Eat lunch in one of the dining halls. Most will allow visitors to pay cash to experience a typical student meal. Food may not be important to you now while you are living at home and can simply take anything you want from the refrigerator at any time, but it will be when you are away at college with only a meal ticket to feed you.

- How clean is the dining hall? Consider serving tables, floors, and seating.
- What is the quality of the food?
- How big are the portions?
- How much variety do students have at each meal?
- How healthy are the food choices?

While you are eating, try to strike up a conversation with students and tell them that you are considering attending their college. Their reactions and advice can be eye-opening. Ask them questions about the academic atmosphere and the professors.

- Are the classes large or small?
- Do the majority of the professors only lecture or are tutorials and seminars common?
- Is the emphasis of the faculty career-oriented or abstract?
- Are the teaching methods innovative and stimulating or boring and dull?
- Is the academic atmosphere pressured, lax, or somewhere in between?
- Which are the strong majors? The weak majors?

- Is the emphasis on grades or social life or a mix of both at the college?
- How hard do students have to work to receive high grades?

Current students can also give you the inside line on the true nature of the college social life. You may gain some idea through looking in the yearbook, in the newspaper, and on the bulletin boards, but students will reveal the true highs and lows of campus life. Ask them about drug use, partying, dating, drinking, and anything else that may affect your life as a student.

- Which are the most popular club activities?
- What do students do on weekends? Do most go home?
- How frequently do concerts occur on campus? Who has recently performed?
- How can you become involved in specific activities (name them)?
- How strictly are campus rules enforced and how severe are penalties?
- What counseling services are available?
- Are academic tutoring services available?
- Do they feel that the faculty really cares about students, especially freshmen?

You will receive the most valuable information from current students, but you will only be able to speak with them after the tour is over. And you might have to risk rejection as you try to initiate conversations with students who might not want to reveal how they feel about the campus. Still, the value of this information is worth the chance.

If you have the time, you should also visit the library to see just how accessible research materials are and to observe the physical layout. The catalog usually specifies the days and hours of operation, as well as the number of volumes contained in the library and the number of periodicals to which it subscribes. A library also requires accessibility, good lighting, an adequate number of study carrels, and lounge areas for students. Many colleges have created 24-hour study lounges for students who find the residence halls too noisy for studying, although most colleges claim that they designate areas of the residences as "quiet study" areas. You may not be interested in any of this information, but when you are a student you will have to make frequent

use of the campus library so you should know what is available. You should at least ask how extensive their holdings are in your proposed major area. If they have virtually nothing, you will have to spend a lot of time ordering items via interlibrary loan or making copies, which can become expensive. The ready answer of students that they will obtain their information from the Internet is unpleasantly countered by professors who demand journal articles with documentation.

Make a point of at least driving through the community surrounding the college because you will be spending time there shopping, dining, working in a part-time job, or attending events. Even the largest and best-stocked campus will not meet all of your social and personal needs. If you can spare the time, stop in several stores to see if they welcome college students.

- Is the surrounding community suburban, urban, or rural?
- Does the community offer stores of interest, such as bookstores, craft shops, and boutiques?
- Do the businesses employ college students?
- Does the community have a movie or stage theater?
- Are there several types of interesting restaurants?
- Do there seem to be any clubs that court a college clientele?
- Is the center of activity easy to walk to, or do you need other transportation?

You might feel that a day is not enough to answer all of your questions, but even answering some questions will provide you with a stronger basis for choosing a college. Many students visit a college campus several times before making their decision. Keep in mind that for the rest of your life you will be associated with the college that you attend. You will spend four years of your life at this college. The effort of spending several days to obtain the information to make your decision is worthwhile.

Dawn B. Sova, Ph.D., is a former newspaper reporter and columnist, as well as the author of more than eight books and numerous magazine articles. She teaches creative and research writing, as well as scientific and technical writing, newswriting, and journalism.

Applying 101

The words "applying yourself" have several important meanings in the college application process. One meaning refers to the fact that you need to keep focused during this important time in your life, keep your priorities straight, and know the dates that your applications are due so you can apply on time. The phrase might also refer to the person who is really responsible for your application—you.

You are the only person who should compile your college application. You need to take ownership of this process. The guidance counselor is not responsible for completing your applications, and neither are your parents. College applications must be completed in addition to your normal workload at school, college visits, and SAT, ACT, or TOEFL testing.

THE APPLICATION

The application is your way of introducing yourself to a college admissions office. As with any introduction, you want to make a good first impression. The first thing you should do in presenting your application is to find out what the college or university needs from you. Read the application carefully to find out the application fee and deadline, required standardized tests, number of essays, interview requirements, and anything else you can do or submit to help improve your chances for acceptance.

Completing college applications yourself helps you learn more about the schools to which you are applying. The information a college asks for in its application can tell you much about the school. State university applications often tell you how they are going to view their applicants. Usually, they select students based on GPAs and test scores. Colleges that request an interview, ask you to respond to a few open-ended questions, or require an essay are interested in a more personal approach to the application process and may be looking for different types of students than those sought by a state school.

In addition to submitting the actual application, there are several other items that are commonly required. You will be responsible for ensuring that your standardized test scores and your high school transcript arrive at the colleges to which you apply. Most colleges will ask that you submit teacher recommendations as well. Select teachers who know you and your abilities well and allow them plenty of time to complete the recommendations. When all portions of the application have been completed and sent in, whether

> ## FOLLOW THESE TIPS WHEN FILLING OUT YOUR APPLICATION
>
> - **Follow the directions to the letter.** You don't want to be in a position to ask an admissions officer for exceptions due to your inattentiveness.
> - **Proofread all parts of your application,** including your essay. Again, the final product indicates to the admissions staff how meticulous and careful you are in your work.
> - **Submit your application as early as possible,** provided all of the pieces are available. If there is a problem with your application, this will allow you to work through it with the admissions staff in plenty of time. If you wait until the last minute, it not only takes away that cushion but also reflects poorly on your sense of priorities.
> - **Keep a copy of the completed application,** whether it is a photocopy or a copy saved on your computer.

electronically or by mail, make sure you follow up with the college to ensure their receipt.

THE APPLICATION ESSAY

Whereas the other portions of your application—your transcript, test scores, and involvement in extracurricular activities—are a reflection of what you've accomplished up to this point, your application essay is an opportunity to present yourself in the here and now. The essay shows your originality and verbal skills and how you approach a topic or problem and express your opinion.

Some colleges may request one essay or a combination of essays and short-answer topics to learn more about who you are and how well you can communicate your thoughts. Common essay topics cover such simple themes as writing about yourself and your experiences or why you want to attend that particular school. Other colleges will ask that you show your imaginative or creative side by writing about a favorite author, for instance, or commenting on a hypothetical situation. In such cases, they will be looking at your thought processes and level of creativity.

Admissions officers, particularly those at small or mid-size colleges, use the essay to determine how you, as a student, will fit into life at that college. The essay, therefore,

is a critical component of the application process. Here are some tips for writing a winning essay:

- Colleges are looking for an honest representation of who you are and what you think. Make sure that the tone of the essay reflects enthusiasm, maturity, creativity, the ability to communicate, talent, and your leadership skills.

- Be sure you set aside enough time to write the essay, revise it, and revise it *again*. Running "spell check" will only detect a fraction of the errors you probably made on your first pass at writing it. Take a break and then come back to it and reread it. You will probably notice other style, content, and grammar problems—and ways that you can improve the essay overall.

- Always answer the question that is being asked, making sure that you are specific, clear, and true to your personality.

- Enlist the help of reviewers who know you well—friends, parents, teachers—since they are likely to be the most honest and will keep you on track in the presentation of your true self.

THE PERSONAL INTERVIEW

Although it is relatively rare that a personal interview is required, many colleges recommend that you take this opportunity for a face-to-face discussion with a member of the admissions staff. Read through the application materials to determine whether or not a college places great emphasis on the interview. If they strongly recommend that you have one, it may work against you to forego it.

In contrast to a group interview and some alumni interviews, which are intended to provide information about a college, the personal interview is viewed both as an information session and as further evaluation of your skills and strengths. You will meet with a member of the admissions staff who will be assessing your personal qualities, high school preparation, and your capacity to contribute to undergraduate life at the institution. On average, these meetings last about 45 minutes—a relatively short amount of time in which to gather information and leave the desired impression—so here are some suggestions on how to make the most of it.

Scheduling Your Visit

Generally, students choose to visit campuses in the summer or fall of their senior year. Both times have their advantages. A summer visit, when the campus is not in session, generally allows for a less hectic visit and interview. Visiting in the fall, on the other hand, provides the opportunity to see what campus life is like in full swing. If you choose the fall, consider arranging an overnight trip so that you can stay in one of the college dormitories. At the very least, you should make your way around campus to take part in classes, athletic events, and social activities. Always make an appointment and avoid scheduling more than two college interviews on any given day. Multiple interviews in a single day hinder your chances of making a good impression, and your impressions of the colleges will blur into each other as you hurriedly make your way from place to place.

Preparation

Know the basics about the college before going for your interview. Read the college catalog and Web site in addition to this guide. You will be better prepared to ask questions that are not answered in the literature and that will give you a better understanding of what the college has to offer. You should also spend some time thinking about your strengths and weaknesses and, in particular, what you are looking for in a college education. You will find that as you get a few interviews under your belt, they will get easier. You might consider starting with a college that is not a top contender on your list, so that the stakes are not as high.

Asking Questions

Inevitably, your interviewer will ask you, "Do you have any questions?" Not having one may suggest that you're unprepared or, even worse, not interested. When you do ask questions, make sure that they are ones that matter to you and that have a bearing on your decision about whether or not to attend that college. The questions that you ask will give the interviewer some insight into your personality and priorities. Avoid asking questions that are answered in the college literature—again, a sign of unpreparedness. Although the interviewer will undoubtedly pose questions to you, the interview should not be viewed merely as a question-and-answer session. If a conversation evolves out of a particular question, so much the better. Your interviewer can learn a great deal about you from how you sustain a conversation. Similarly, you will be able to learn a great deal about the college in a conversational format.

Separate the Interview from the Interviewer

Many students base their feelings about a college solely on their impressions of the interviewer. Try not to characterize a college based only on your personal reaction, however, since your impressions can be skewed by whether you and your interviewer hit it off. Pay lots of attention to everything else that you see, hear, and learn about a college. Once on campus, you may never see your interviewer again.

In the end, remember to relax and be yourself. Your interviewer will expect you to be somewhat nervous, which will relieve some of the pressure. Don't drink jitters-producing caffeinated beverages prior to the interview, and suppress nervous fidgets like leg-wagging, finger-drumming, or bracelet-jangling. Consider your interview an opportunity to put forth your best effort and to enhance everything that the college knows about you up to this point.

THE FINAL DECISION

Once you have received your acceptance letters, it is time to go back and look at the whole picture. Provided you received more than one acceptance, you are now in a position to compare your options. The best way to do this is to compare your original list of important college-ranking criteria with what you've discovered about each college along the way. In addition, you and your family will need to factor in the financial aid component. You will need to look beyond these cost issues and the quantifiable pros and cons of each college, however, and know that you have a good feeling about your final choice. Before sending off your acceptance letter, you need to feel confident that the college will feel like home for the next four years. Once the choice is made, the only hard part will be waiting for an entire summer before heading off to college!

Successful Transfer

Adrienne Aaron Rulnick

Transfer students need and deserve detailed and accurate information but often lack direction as to where it can be obtained. Few general college guides offer information about transfer deadlines and required minimum grade point averages for transfer admission. College catalogs are not always clear about the specific requirements and procedures for transfer students who may be confused about whether they need to present high school records, SAT or ACT scores, or a guidance counselor's recommendation, particularly if they have been out of high school for several years. Transfer advisers are not available to those enrolled at a baccalaureate institution; at community and junior colleges, the transfer advising function may be performed by a designated transfer counselor or by a variety of college advisers who are less clearly identified.

The challenge for transfer students is to determine what they need to know in order to make good, informed decisions and identify the individuals and resources that can provide that information. An organized research process is at the heart of a successful transfer.

HOW TO BEGIN

Perhaps the most important first step in this process is one of self-analysis. Adopting a consumer approach is appropriate— higher education is a formidable purchase, no matter how it is financed. The reputation of the college from which you obtain your degree may open doors to future jobs and careers; friendships and contacts you make at college can provide a significant network for lifelong social and professional relationships. The environment of a transfer school may be the perfect opportunity for you to test out urban living or the joys of country life, explore a different area of the nation, experience college residential living for the first time, or move out of the family nest into your first apartment. Like any major purchase in your life, there are costs and benefits to be weighed. Trade-offs include cost, distance, rigor of academic work, extra time in school required by a cooperative education program, and specific requirements, such as foreign language competence at a liberal arts institution or courses in religion at an institution with a denominational affiliation.

USE EXPERIENCE AS A GUIDE

The wise consumer reflects on his or her own experience with a product (i.e., your initial college or colleges) and then seeks out people who have firsthand experience with the new product being considered. Talk to friends and family members who have attended the colleges you are considering. Ask college faculty members you know to tell you about the colleges they attended and how they view these schools. Talk to people engaged in the careers you are considering: What are their impressions of the best programs and schools in their field? Make sure you sample a variety of opinions, but beware of dated experiences. An engineering department considered top-notch when Uncle Joe attended college twenty years ago might be very different today!

THE NITTY-GRITTY

Once your list is reduced to a manageable number of schools, it is important to identify academic requirements, requisite grade point averages for admission, and deadline dates. Most schools admit for both the fall and spring semesters; those on a trimester system may have winter and summer admissions as well. Some schools have rolling admission policies and will process applications as they are received; others, particularly the more selective colleges, have firm deadlines because their admission process involves a committee review, and decisions are made on a competitive basis. It is helpful to know how many transfer students are typically accepted for the semester you wish to begin, whether the minimum grade point average is indicative of the actual average of accepted students (this can vary widely), and whether the major you are seeking has special prerequisites and admission procedures. For example, fine arts programs admission procedures usually require portfolios or auditions. For engineering, computer science, and some business majors, there are specific requirements in mathematics that must be met before a student is considered for admission. Many specialized health-care programs, including nursing, may only admit once a year. Some schools have different standards for sophomore and junior transfers or for in-state and out-of-state students.

Other criteria that you should identify include whether college housing and financial aid are available for transfer students. Some colleges have special transfer scholarships that require separate applications and references, while others simply award aid based on applications that indicate a high grade point average or membership in a nationally recognized junior and community college honor society, such as Phi Theta Kappa. There are also scholarships for

transfer students who demonstrate accomplishment in specified academic and performance areas; the latter may be based on talent competitions or accomplishment evidenced in a portfolio or audition.

NONTRADITIONAL STUDENTS

For the nontraditional student, usually defined as anyone beyond the traditional college age range of 18 to 23, there may be additional aspects to investigate. Some colleges award credit based on demonstrated life experience; many colleges grant credit for qualifying scores on the CLEP exams or for participation in the DANTES program. Experience in industry may yield college credit as well. If you are ready and able to pursue further college work but are not in a position to attend regular classes, there are a variety of distance learning options at fully accredited colleges. Other colleges provide specialized support services for nontraditional students and may allow students the opportunity to attend part-time if they have family and work responsibilities. In some cases, usually at large universities, there may be married student housing or family housing available. More and more schools have established day-care facilities, although the waiting lists are often very long.

APPLYING

Once you have identified the schools that meet the needs you have established as priorities, it is time to begin the application process. Make sure you observe all the indicated deadlines. It never hurts to have everything in early, as there can be consequences, such as closed-out majors and the loss of housing and financial aid, if you submit your application late. Make appointments with faculty members and others who are providing references; make sure they understand what is required of them and when and where their references must be sent. It is your responsibility to follow through to make sure all of your credentials are received, including transcripts from all colleges previously attended, even if you only took one summer course or attended for less than a semester. If you have not yet had the opportunity to visit the schools to which you are applying, now is the time to do so. Arrange interviews wherever possible, and make sure to include a tour of the campus and visits to the department and career offices to gain a picture of the facilities and future opportunities. If you have questions about financial aid, schedule an appointment in the financial aid office, and make sure you are aware of all the deadlines and requirements and any scholarship opportunities for which you are eligible.

MAKING YOUR CHOICE

Congratulations! You have been accepted at the colleges of your choice. Now what? Carefully review the acceptance of your previous college credit and how it has been applied. You are entitled to know how many transfer credits you have received and your expected date of graduation. Compare financial aid packages and housing options. The best choice should emerge from this review process. Then, send a note to the schools you will not be attending. Acknowledge your acceptance, but indicate that you have chosen to attend elsewhere. Carefully read everything you have received from the college of your choice. Return required deposits within the deadline, reserve time to attend transfer orientation, arrange to have your final transcript sent from the college you currently attend, and review the financial picture. This is the time to finalize college loan applications and make sure you are in a position to meet all the costs entailed at your new college. Don't forget to include the costs of travel and housing.

You've done it! While many transfer students reflect on how much work was involved in the transfer admission process, those who took the time to follow all of the steps outlined report a sense of satisfaction with their choices and increased confidence in themselves.

_____

Adrienne Aaron Rulnick was formerly a Transfer Counselor at Berkshire Community College.

Who's Paying for This?
Financial Aid Basics

A college education can be expensive—costing more than $150,000 for four years at some of the higher priced private colleges and universities. Even at the lower cost state colleges and universities, the cost of a four-year education can approach $60,000. Determining how you and your family will come up with the necessary funds to pay for your education requires planning, perseverance, and learning as much as you can about the options that are available to you. But before you get discouraged, College Board statistics show that 56 percent of full-time students attend four-year public and private colleges with tuition and fees less than $9000, while 9 percent attend colleges that have tuition and fees more than $33,000. College costs tend to be less in the western states and higher in New England.

Paying for college should not be looked at as a four-year financial commitment. For many families, paying the total cost of a student's college education out of current income and savings is usually not realistic. For families that have planned ahead and have financial savings established for higher education, the burden is a lot easier. But for most, meeting the cost of college requires the pooling of current income and assets and investing in longer-term loan options. These family resources, together with financial assistance from state, federal, and institutional sources, enable millions of students each year to attend the institution of their choice.

FINANCIAL AID PROGRAMS

There are three types of financial aid:

1. Gift-aid—Scholarships and grants are funds that do not have to be repaid.
2. Loans—Loans must be repaid, usually after graduation; the amount you have to pay back is the total you've borrowed plus any accrued interest. This is considered a source of self-help aid.
3. Student employment—Student employment is a job arranged for you by the financial aid office. This is another source of self-help aid.

The federal government has four major grant programs—Federal Pell Grants, Federal Supplemental Educational Opportunity Grants, Academic Competitiveness Grants (ACG), and SMART grants. ACG and SMART grants are limited to students who qualify for a Pell grant and are awarded to a select group of students. Overall, these grants are targeted to low-to-moderate income families with significant financial need. The federal government also sponsors a student employment program called the Federal Work-Study Program, which offers jobs both on and off campus, and several loan programs, including those for students and for parents of undergraduate students.

There are two types of student loan programs: subsidized and unsubsidized. The subsidized Federal Stafford Student Loan and the Federal Perkins Loan are need-based, government-subsidized loans. Students who borrow through these programs do not have to pay interest on the loan until after they graduate or leave school. The unsubsidized Federal Stafford Student Loan and the Federal PLUS Loan Program are not based on need, and borrowers are responsible for the interest while the student is in school. These loans are administered by different methods. Once you choose your college, the financial aid office will guide you through this process.

After you've submitted your financial aid application and you've been accepted for admission, each college will send you a letter describing your financial aid award. Most award letters show estimated college costs, how much you and your family are expected to contribute, and the amount and types of aid you have been awarded. Most students are awarded aid from a combination of sources and programs. Hence, your award is often called a financial aid "package."

SOURCES OF FINANCIAL AID

Millions of students and families apply for financial aid each year. Financial aid from all sources exceeds $143 billion per year. The largest single source of aid is the federal government, which will award more than $100 billion this year.

The next largest source of financial aid is found in the college and university community. Most of this aid is awarded to students who have a demonstrated need based on the Federal Methodology. Some institutions use a different formula, the Institutional Methodology (IM), to award their own funds in conjunction with other forms of aid. Institutional

aid may be either need-based or non-need based. Aid that is not based on need is usually awarded for a student's academic performance (merit awards), specific talents or abilities, or to attract the type of students a college seeks to enroll.

Another source of financial aid is from state government. All states offer grant and/or scholarship aid, most of which is need-based. However, more and more states are offering substantial merit-based aid programs. Most state programs award aid only to students attending college in their home state.

Other sources of financial aid include:

- Private agencies
- Foundations
- Corporations
- Clubs
- Fraternal and service organizations
- Civic associations
- Unions
- Religious groups that award grants, scholarships, and low-interest loans
- Employers that provide tuition reimbursement benefits for employees and their children

More information about these different sources of aid is available from high school guidance offices, public libraries, college financial aid offices, directly from the sponsoring organizations, and on the Web at www.petersons.com and www.finaid.org.

HOW NEED-BASED FINANCIAL AID IS AWARDED

When you apply for aid, your family's financial situation is analyzed using a government-approved formula called the Federal Methodology. This formula looks at five items:

1. Demographic information of the family
2. Income of the parents
3. Assets of the parents
4. Income of the student
5. Assets of the student

This analysis determines the amount you and your family are expected to contribute toward your college expenses, called your Expected Family Contribution or EFC. If the EFC is equal to or more than the cost of attendance at a particular college, then you do not demonstrate financial need. However, even if you don't have financial need, you may still qualify for aid, as there are grants, scholarships, and loan programs that are not need-based.

If the cost of your education is greater than your EFC, then you do demonstrate financial need and qualify for assistance. The amount of your financial need that can be

met varies from school to school. Some are able to meet your full need, while others can only cover a certain percentage of need. Here's the formula:

Cost of Attendance
– Expected Family Contribution
= Financial Need

The EFC remains constant, but your need will vary according to the costs of attendance at a particular college. In general, the higher the tuition and fees at a particular college, the higher the cost of attendance will be. Expenses for books and supplies, room and board, transportation, and other miscellaneous items are included in the overall cost of attendance. It is important to remember that you do not have to be "needy" to qualify for financial aid. Many middle and upper-middle income families qualify for need-based financial aid.

APPLYING FOR FINANCIAL AID

Every student must complete the Free Application for Federal Student Aid (FAFSA) to be considered for financial aid. The FAFSA is available from your high school guidance office, many public libraries, colleges in your area, or directly from the U.S. Department of Education.

Students are encouraged to apply for federal student aid on the Web. The electronic version of the FAFSA can be accessed at http://www.fafsa.ed.gov. Both the student and at least one parent must apply for a federal PIN at http://www.pin.ed.gov. The PIN serves as your electronic signature when applying for aid on the Web.

To award their own funds, some colleges require an additional application, the CSS/Financial Aid PROFILE® application. The PROFILE asks supplemental questions that some colleges and awarding agencies feel provide a more accurate assessment of the family's ability to pay for college. It is up to the college to decide whether it will use only the FAFSA or both the FAFSA and the PROFILE. PROFILE applications are available from the high school guidance office and on the Web. Both the paper application and the Web site list those colleges and programs that require the PROFILE application.

If Every College You're Applying to for Fall 2010 Requires the FAFSA

. . . then it's pretty simple: Complete the FAFSA after January 1, 2010, being certain to send it in before any college-imposed deadlines. (You are not permitted to send in the 2010–11 FAFSA before January 1, 2010.) Most college FAFSA application deadlines are in February or early March. It is easier if you have all your financial records for

the previous year available, but if that is not possible, you are strongly encouraged to use estimated figures.

After you send in your FAFSA, either with the paper application or electronically, you'll receive a Student Aid Report (SAR) that includes all of the information you reported and shows your EFC. If you provided an e-mail address, the SAR is sent to you electronically; otherwise, you will receive a paper copy in the mail. Be sure to review the SAR, checking to see if the information you reported is accurately represented. If you used estimated numbers to complete the FAFSA, you may have to resubmit the SAR with any corrections to the data. The college(s) you have designated on the FAFSA will receive the information you reported and will use that data to make their decision. In many instances, the colleges to which you've applied will ask you to send copies of your and your parents' federal income tax returns for 2009, plus any other documents needed to verify the information you reported.

If a College Requires the PROFILE

Step 1: Register for the PROFILE in the fall of your senior year in high school. You can apply for the PROFILE online at http://profileonline.collegeboard.com/prf/index.jsp. Registration information with a list of the colleges that require the PROFILE is available in most high school guidance offices. There is a fee for using the PROFILE application ($25 for the first college and $16 for each additional college). You must pay for the service by credit card when you register. If you do not have a credit card, you will be billed. A limited number of fee waivers are automatically granted to first-time applicants based on the financial information provided on the PROFILE.

Step 2: Fill out your customized PROFILE. Once you register, your application will be immediately available online and will have questions which all students must complete, questions which must be completed by the student's parents (unless the student is independent and the colleges or programs selected do not require parental information), and *may* have supplemental questions needed by one or more of your schools or programs. If required, those will be found in Section Q of the application.

In addition to the PROFILE application you complete online, you may also be required to complete a Business/Farm Supplement via traditional paper format. Completion of this form is not a part of the online process. If this form is required, instructions on how to download and print the supplemental form are provided. If your biological or adoptive parents are separated or divorced and your colleges and programs require it, your noncustodial parent may be asked to complete the Noncustodial PROFILE.

Once you complete and submit your PROFILE application, it will be processed and sent directly to your requested colleges and programs.

IF YOU DON'T QUALIFY FOR NEED-BASED AID

If you are not eligible for need-based aid, you can still find ways to lessen your burden.

Here are some suggestions:

- Search for merit scholarships. You can start at the initial stages of your application process. College merit awards are increasingly important as more and more colleges award these to students they especially want to attract. As a result, applying to a college at which your qualifications put you at the top of the entering class may give you a larger merit award. Another source of aid to look for is private scholarships that are given for special skills and talents. Additional information can be found at www.petersons.com and at www.finaid.org.

- Seek employment during the summer and the academic year. The student employment office at your college can help you locate a school-year job. Many colleges and local businesses have vacancies remaining after they have hired students who are receiving Federal Work-Study Program financial aid.

- Borrow through the unsubsidized Federal Stafford Student Loan programs. These are generally available to all students. The terms and conditions are similar to the subsidized loans. The biggest difference is that the borrower is responsible for the interest while still in college, although most lenders permit students to delay paying the interest right away and add the accrued interest to the total amount owed. You must file the FAFSA to be considered.

- After you've secured what you can through scholarships, working, and borrowing, you and your parents will be expected to meet your share of the college bill (the Expected Family Contribution). Many colleges offer monthly payment plans that spread the cost over the academic year. If the monthly payments are too high, parents can borrow through the Federal PLUS Loan Program, through one of the many private education loan programs available, or through home equity loans and lines of credit. Families seeking assistance in financing college expenses should inquire at the financial aid office about what programs are available at the college. Some families seek the advice of professional financial advisers and tax consultants.

Financial Aid Programs for Schools in New England

Each state government has established one or more state-administered financial aid programs for qualified students. The state programs may be restricted to legal residents of the state, or they also may be available to out-of-state students who are attending public or private colleges or universities within the state. In addition, other qualifications may apply.

The program descriptions are arranged by state in alphabetical order, along with information about how to determine eligibility and apply. The information refers to awards for 2009–10, unless otherwise stated. Students should write to the address given for each program to request award details for 2010–11 be sent to them as soon as they are available.

CONNECTICUT

AIFS-HACU Scholarships. Scholarships to outstanding Hispanic students to study abroad with AIFS. Available to students attending HACU member schools. Students will receive scholarships of up to 50 percent of the full program fee. Students must meet all standard AIFS eligibility requirements. Deadlines: April 15 for fall, October 1 for spring, and March 15 for summer. *Award:* Scholarship for use in freshman, sophomore, junior, or senior year; not renewable. *Award amount:* $6000–$8000. *Number of awards:* varies. *Eligibility Requirements:* Applicant must be Hispanic; age 17 and over; enrolled or expecting to enroll full-time at a two-year or four-year institution or university and must have an interest in international exchange. Applicant must have 3.0 GPA or higher. Available to U.S. and non-U.S. citizens. *Application Requirements:* Application, essay, photo, references, transcript. *Fee:* $95. *Deadline:* varies. **Contact:** David Mauro, Admissions Counselor, American Institute for Foreign Study, River Plaza, 9 West Broad Street, Stamford, CT 06902-3788. *E-mail:* dmauro@aifs.com. *Phone:* 800-727-2437 Ext. 5163. *Fax:* 203-399-5463. *Web site:* www.aifsabroad.com.

Capitol Scholarship Program. Award for Connecticut residents attending eligible institutions in Connecticut or in a state with reciprocity with Connecticut (Massachusetts, Maine, New Hampshire, Pennsylvania, Rhode Island, Vermont, or Washington, D.C). Must be U.S. citizen or permanent resident alien who is a high school senior or graduate. Must rank in top 20% of class or score at least 1800 on SAT. Must show financial need. *Award:* Scholarship for use in freshman, sophomore, junior, or senior year; renewable. *Award amount:* $500–$3000. *Number of awards:* 4500–5500. *Eligibility Requirements:* Applicant must be enrolled or expecting to enroll full- or part-time at a two-year, four-year, or technical institution or university; resident of Connecticut and studying in Connecticut, District of Columbia, Maine, Massachusetts, New Hampshire, Pennsylvania, Rhode Island, or Vermont. Applicant must have 2.5 GPA or higher. Available to U.S. citizens. *Application Requirements:* Application, financial need analysis, test scores, FAFSA. *Deadline:* February 15. **Contact:** Mrs. Linda Diamond, Senior Associate, Connecticut Department of Higher Education, 61 Woodland Street, Hartford, CT 06105. *E-mail:* csp@ctdhe.org. *Phone:* 860-947-1855. *Fax:* 860-947-1313. *Web site:* www.ctdhe.org.

Connecticut Aid to Public College Students Grant. Award for Connecticut residents attending public colleges or universities within the state. Renewable awards based on financial need. Application deadline varies by institution. Apply at college financial aid office. *Award:* Grant for use in freshman, sophomore, junior, or senior year; renewable. *Award amount:* varies. *Number of awards:* varies. *Eligibility Requirements:* Applicant must be enrolled or expecting to enroll full- or part-time at a two-year or four-year institution or university; resident of Connecticut and studying in Connecticut. Available to U.S. citizens. *Application Requirements:* Financial need analysis, FAFSA. *Deadline:* varies. **Contact:** Mrs. Omerine Marino, Senior Associate, Connecticut Department of Higher Education, 61 Woodland Street, Hartford, CT 06105. *E-mail:* caps@ctdhe.org. *Phone:* 860-947-1855. *Fax:* 860-947-1838. *Web site:* www.ctdhe.org.

Connecticut Army National Guard 100% Tuition Waiver. Program is for any active member of the Connecticut Army National Guard in good standing. Must be a resident of Connecticut attending any Connecticut state (public) university, community-technical college or regional vocational-technical school. The total number of available awards is unlimited. *Award:* Scholarship for use in freshman, sophomore, junior, or senior year; not renewable. *Award amount:* $16,000. *Number of awards:* varies. *Eligibility Requirements:* Applicant must be age 17-65; enrolled or expecting to enroll full- or part-time at a two-year, four-year, or technical institution or university; resident of Connecticut and studying in Connecticut. Available to U.S. and non-U.S. citizens. Applicant or parent must meet one or more of the following requirements: Army National Guard experience; retired from active duty; disabled or killed as a result of military service; prisoner of war; or missing in action. *Application Requirements:* Application. *Deadline:* July 1. **Contact:** Capt. Jeremy Lingenfelser, Education Services Officer, Connecticut Army National Guard, 360 Broad Street, Hartford, CT 06105-3795. *E-mail:* education@ct.ngb.army.mil. *Phone:* 860-524-4816. *Fax:* 860-524-4904. *Web site:* www.ct.ngb.army.mil.

Connecticut Independent College Student Grants. Award for Connecticut residents attending an independent college or university within the state on at least a half-time basis. Renewable awards based on financial need. Application deadline varies by institution. Apply at college financial aid office. *Award:* Grant for use in freshman, sophomore, junior, or senior year; renewable. *Award amount:* $250–$8500. *Number of awards:* varies. *Eligibility Requirements:* Applicant must be enrolled or expecting to enroll full- or part-time at a two-year or four-year institution or university; resident of Connecticut and studying in Connecticut. Available to U.S. citizens. *Application Requirements:* Application, financial need analysis, FAFSA. *Deadline:* varies. **Contact:** Mrs. Omerine Marino, Senior Associate, Connecticut Department of Higher Education, 61 Woodland Street, Hartford, CT 06105. *E-mail:* cics@ctdhe.org. *Phone:* 860-947-1855. *Fax:* 860-947-1838. *Web site:* www.ctdhe.org.

Minority Teacher Incentive Grant Program. Program provides up to $5,000 a year for two years of full-time study in a teacher preparation program for the junior or senior year at a Connecticut college or university. Applicant must be African-American, Hispanic/Latino, Asian American or Native American heritage and be nominated by the Education Dean. Program graduates who teach in Connecticut public schools may be eligible for loan reimbursement stipends up to $2,500 per year for up to four years. *Academic Fields/Career Goals:* Education. *Award:* Grant for use in junior or senior year; renewable. *Award amount:* up to $5000. *Number of awards:* 1–75. *Eligibility Requirements:* Applicant must be American Indian/Alaska Native, Asian/Pacific Islander, Black (non-Hispanic), or Hispanic; enrolled or expecting to enroll full-time at a four-year institution or university and studying in Connecticut. Available to U.S. citizens. *Application Requirements:* Application. *Deadline:* October 1. **Contact:** Mrs. Omerine Marino, Senior Associate, Connecticut Department of Higher Education, 61 Woodland Street, Hartford, CT 06105. *E-mail:* mtip@ctdhe.org. *Phone:* 860-947-1855. *Fax:* 860-947-1838. *Web site:* www.ctdhe.org.

MAINE

American Legion Auxiliary Department of Maine Daniel E. Lambert Memorial Scholarship. Scholarships to assist young men and women in continuing their education beyond high school. Must demonstrate financial need, must be a resident of the State of Maine, U.S. citizen, and parent must be a veteran. *Award:* Scholarship for use in freshman year; not renewable. *Award amount:* $1000. *Number of awards:* up to 2. *Eligibility Requirements:* Applicant must be high school student; planning to enroll or expecting to enroll full-time at a four-year institution or university and resident of Maine. Available to U.S. citizens. Applicant or parent must meet one or more of the following requirements: general military experience; retired from active duty; disabled or killed as a result of military service; prisoner of war; or missing in action. *Application Requirements:* Application, financial need analysis. *Deadline:* May 1. **Contact:** American Legion Auxiliary, Department of Maine. *Web site:* www.mainelegion.org.

American Legion Auxiliary Department of Maine National President's Scholarship. Scholarships to children of veterans who served in the Armed Forces during the eligibility dates for The American Legion. One $2500, one $2000, and one $1000 scholarship will be awarded. Applicant must complete 50 hours of community service during his/her high school years. *Award:* Scholarship for use in freshman year; not renewable. *Award amount:* $1000–$2500. *Number of awards:* 3. *Eligibility Requirements:* Applicant must be high school student; planning to enroll or expecting to enroll full-time at a four-year institution or university and resident of Maine. Applicant or parent of applicant must have employment or volunteer experience in community service. Available to U.S. citizens. Applicant or parent must meet one or more of the following requirements: general military experience; retired from active duty; disabled or killed as a result of military service; prisoner of war; or missing in action. *Application Requirements:* Application, essay, references, test scores, transcript. *Deadline:* March 1. **Contact:** American Legion Auxiliary, Department of Maine. *Web site:* www.mainelegion.org.

American Legion Auxiliary Department of Maine Past Presidents' Parley Nurses Scholarship. One-time award for child, grandchild, sister, or brother of veteran. Must be resident of Maine and wishing to continue education at accredited school in medical field. Must submit photo, doctor's statement, and evidence of civic activity. Minimum 3.5 GPA required. *Academic Fields/Career Goals:* Health and Medical Sciences; Nursing. *Award:* Scholarship for use in freshman, sophomore, junior, or senior year; not renewable. *Award amount:* $300. *Number of awards:* 1. *Eligibility Requirements:* Applicant must be age 18 and over; enrolled or expecting to enroll full-time at a two-year, four-year, or technical institution or university and resident of Maine. Applicant or parent of applicant must have employment or volunteer experience in community service. Applicant must have 2.5 GPA or higher. Available to U.S. citizens. Applicant or parent must meet one or more of the following requirements: general military experience; retired from active

duty; disabled or killed as a result of military service; prisoner of war; or missing in action. *Application Requirements:* Application, photo, references, transcript, doctor's statement. *Deadline:* March 31. **Contact:** American Legion Auxiliary, Department of Maine. *Web site:* www.mainelegion.org.

Early College For ME. Scholarship for high school students who have not made plans for college but are academically capable of success in college. Recipients are selected by their school principal or director. Students must be entering a Maine Community College. Refer to Web site: http://www.mccs.me.edu/scholarships.html. *Award:* Scholarship for use in freshman year; renewable. *Award amount:* $2000. *Number of awards:* 200. *Eligibility Requirements:* Applicant must be high school student; planning to enroll or expecting to enroll full-time at a two-year or four-year institution or university; resident of Maine and studying in Maine. Available to U.S. citizens. *Application Requirements:* Application, financial need analysis, references, transcript. *Deadline:* varies. **Contact:** Charles P. Collins, State Director, Center for Career Development, Maine Community College System, 323 State Street, Augusta, ME 04330. *E-mail:* ccollins@mccs.me.edu. *Phone:* 207-767-5210 Ext. 4115. *Fax:* 207-629-4048. *Web site:* www.mccs.me.edu.

Educators for Maine Forgivable Loan Program. Forgivable loan for residents of Maine who are high school seniors, college students, or college graduates with a minimum 3.0 GPA, studying or preparing to study teacher education. Must teach in Maine upon graduation. Award based on merit. For application information see Web site: http://www.famemaine.com. *Academic Fields/Career Goals:* Education. *Award:* Forgivable loan for use in freshman, sophomore, junior, or senior year; renewable. *Award amount:* $2000–$3000. *Number of awards:* up to 500. *Eligibility Requirements:* Applicant must be enrolled or expecting to enroll full-time at a two-year or four-year institution or university and resident of Maine. Applicant must have 3.0 GPA or higher. Available to U.S. citizens. *Application Requirements:* Application, essay, test scores, transcript. *Deadline:* May 15. **Contact:** Finance Authority of Maine. *Web site:* www.famemaine.com.

Maine Rural Rehabilitation Fund Scholarship Program. One-time scholarship open to Maine residents enrolled in or accepted by any school, college, or university. Must be full time and demonstrate financial need. Those opting for a Maine institution given preference. Major must lead to an agricultural career. Minimum 3.0 GPA required. *Academic Fields/Career Goals:* Agribusiness; Agriculture; Animal/Veterinary Sciences. *Award:* Scholarship for use in freshman, sophomore, junior, senior, graduate, or postgraduate years; not renewable. *Award amount:* $800–$2000. *Number of awards:* 10–20. *Eligibility Requirements:* Applicant must be enrolled or expecting to enroll full-time at a two-year, four-year, or technical institution or university and resident of Maine. Applicant must have 3.0 GPA or higher. Available to U.S. citizens. *Application Requirements:* Application, autobiography, financial need analysis, transcript. *Deadline:* June 15. **Contact:** Jane Aiudi, Director of Marketing, Maine Department of Agriculture, Food and Rural Resources, 28 State House Station, Augusta, ME 04333-0028. *E-mail:* jane.aiudi@maine.gov. *Phone:* 207-287-7628. *Fax:* 207-287-5576. *Web site:* www.maine.gov/agriculture.

Robert C. Byrd Honors Scholarship-Maine. Merit-based, renewable scholarship of up to $1500 annually for graduating high school seniors. Must have a minimum of 3.0 GPA. Must be a resident of Maine. Superior academic performance is the primary criterion. For application, see Web site: http://www.famemaine.com. *Award:* Scholarship for use in freshman year; renewable. *Award amount:* up to $1500. *Number of awards:* up to 30. *Eligibility Requirements:* Applicant must be high school student; planning to enroll or expecting to enroll full-time at a two-year, four-year, or technical institution or university and resident of Maine. Applicant must have 3.0 GPA or higher. Available to U.S. citizens. *Application Requirements:* Application, essay, transcript, high school profile. *Deadline:* May 1. **Contact:** Finance Authority of Maine. *Web site:* www.famemaine.com.

State of Maine Grant Program. Scholarship for residents of Maine, attending an eligible school in Connecticut, Maine, Massachusetts,

New Hampshire, Pennsylvania, Rhode Island, Washington, D.C., or Vermont. Award based on need. Must apply annually. Complete free application for Federal Student Aid to apply. One-time award for undergraduate study. For further information see Web site: http://www.famemaine.com. *Award:* Grant for use in freshman, sophomore, junior, or senior year; not renewable. *Award amount:* $500–$1250. *Number of awards:* up to 13,000. *Eligibility Requirements:* Applicant must be enrolled or expecting to enroll full- or part-time at a two-year, four-year, or technical institution or university; resident of Maine and studying in Connecticut, District of Columbia, Maine, Massachusetts, New Hampshire, Pennsylvania, Rhode Island, or Vermont. Available to U.S. citizens. *Application Requirements:* Application, financial need analysis, FAFSA. *Deadline:* May 1. **Contact:** Finance Authority of Maine. *Web site:* www.famemaine.com.

Tuition Waiver Programs. Provides tuition waivers for children and spouses of EMS personnel, firefighters, and law enforcement officers who have been killed in the line of duty and for students who were foster children under the custody of the Department of Human Services when they graduated from high school. Waivers valid at the University of Maine System, the Maine Technical College System, and Maine Maritime Academy. Applicant must reside and study in Maine. *Award:* Grant for use in freshman, sophomore, junior, or senior year; renewable. *Award amount:* varies. *Number of awards:* up to 30. *Eligibility Requirements:* Applicant must be enrolled or expecting to enroll full- or part-time at a four-year institution or university; resident of Maine and studying in Maine. Applicant or parent of applicant must have employment or volunteer experience in police/firefighting. Available to U.S. citizens. *Application Requirements:* Application, letter from the Department of Human Services documenting that applicant is in their custody and residing in foster care at the time of graduation from high school or its equivalent. *Deadline:* continuous. **Contact:** Finance Authority of Maine. *Web site:* www.famemaine.com.

U.S. Department of Education Fulbright-Hays Project Abroad Scholarship for Programs in China. Scholarships offered to students who are participating in a CIEE Chinese language programs in China or Taiwan. Must be a U.S. citizen enrolled in a CIEE program. Students must have completed the equivalent of two years study in Chinese language (documented). Deadlines: April 1 and November 1. There is also a return requirement for scholarship awardees to submit a program report and evaluation. *Academic Fields/Career Goals:* Asian Studies; Education. *Award:* Scholarship for use in junior or senior year; not renewable. *Award amount:* $1000–$12,000. *Number of awards:* 1–20. *Eligibility Requirements:* Applicant must be enrolled or expecting to enroll full-time at a four-year institution or university and must have an interest in foreign language. Applicant must have 3.0 GPA or higher. Available to U.S. citizens. *Application Requirements:* Application, essay, financial need analysis, references, transcript, copy of passport or birth certificate. *Deadline:* varies. **Contact:** CIEE: Council on International Educational Exchange. *Web site:* www.ciee.org.

Veterans Dependents Educational Benefits-Maine. Tuition waiver award for dependent children or spouses of veterans permanently and totally disabled resulting from service-connected disability; died from a service-connected disability; at time of death was totally and permanently disabled due to service-connected disability, but whose death was not related to the service-connected disability; or member of the Armed Forces on active duty who has been listed for more than 90 days as missing in action, captured or forcibly detained or interned in the line of duty. Benefits apply only to the University of Maine System, Maine community colleges and Maine Maritime Academy. Must be high school graduate. Must submit with application proof of veteran's VA disability along with dependent verification paperwork such as birth, marriage, or adoption certificate and proof of enrollment in degree program. *Award:* Scholarship for use in freshman, sophomore, junior, or senior year; not renewable. *Award amount:* varies. *Number of awards:* varies. *Eligibility Requirements:* Applicant must be enrolled or expecting to enroll full- or part-time at a two-year or four-year institution or university; resident of Maine and studying in Maine. Available to U.S. citizens. Applicant must have general

military experience. *Application Requirements:* Application, see Web site for complete application instructions. **Contact:** Mrs. Paula Gagnon, Office Associate II, Maine Division of Veterans Services, State House, Station 117, Augusta, ME 04333-0117. *E-mail:* mainebvs@maine.gov. *Phone:* 207-626-4464. *Fax:* 207-626-4471. *Web site:* www.maine.gov/dvem/bvs.

MASSACHUSETTS

Agnes M. Lindsay Scholarship. Scholarships for students with demonstrated financial need who are from rural areas of Massachusetts and attend public institutions of higher education in Massachusetts. Deadline varies. *Award:* Scholarship for use in freshman, sophomore, junior, or senior year; not renewable. *Award amount:* varies. *Number of awards:* varies. *Eligibility Requirements:* Applicant must be enrolled or expecting to enroll full-time at a two-year or four-year institution or university; resident of Massachusetts and studying in Massachusetts. Available to U.S. citizens. *Application Requirements:* Application, financial need analysis. *Deadline:* varies. **Contact:** Robert Brun, Director of Scholarships and Grants, Massachusetts Office of Student Financial Assistance, 454 Broadway, Suite 200, Revere, MA 02151. *E-mail:* osfa@osfa.mass.edu. *Phone:* 617-727-9420. *Fax:* 617-727-0667. *Web site:* www.osfa.mass.edu.

Christian A. Herter Memorial Scholarship. Renewable award for Massachusetts residents who are in the tenth and eleventh grades, and whose socio-economic backgrounds and environment may inhibit their ability to attain educational goals. Must exhibit severe personal or family-related difficulties, medical problems, or have overcome a personal obstacle. Provides up to 50 percent of the student's calculated need, as determined by federal methodology, at the college of their choice within the continental United States. *Award:* Scholarship for use in freshman year; renewable. *Award amount:* up to $15,000. *Number of awards:* 25. *Eligibility Requirements:* Applicant must be high school student; planning to enroll or expecting to enroll full-time at a two-year, four-year, or technical institution or university and resident of Massachusetts. Applicant must have 2.5 GPA or higher. Available to U.S. citizens. *Application Requirements:* Application, autobiography, financial need analysis, interview, references. *Deadline:* March 14. **Contact:** Robert Brun, Director of Scholarships and Grants, Massachusetts Office of Student Financial Assistance, 454 Broadway, Suite 200, Revere, MA 02151. *E-mail:* osfa@osfa.mass.edu. *Phone:* 617-727-9420. *Fax:* 617-727-0667. *Web site:* www.osfa.mass.edu.

DSS Adopted Children Tuition Waiver. Need-based tuition waiver for Massachusetts residents who are full-time undergraduate students. Must attend a Massachusetts public institution of higher education and be under 24 years of age. File the FAFSA after January 1. Contact school financial aid office for more information. *Award:* Scholarship for use in freshman, sophomore, junior, or senior year; renewable. *Award amount:* varies. *Number of awards:* varies. *Eligibility Requirements:* Applicant must be age 24 or under; enrolled or expecting to enroll full-time at a two-year or four-year institution and resident of Massachusetts. Available to U.S. and non-Canadian citizens. *Application Requirements:* Application, financial need analysis, FAFSA. *Deadline:* varies. **Contact:** Robert Brun, Director of Scholarships and Grants, Massachusetts Office of Student Financial Assistance, 454 Broadway, Suite 200, Revere, MA 02151. *E-mail:* osfa@osfa.mass.edu. *Phone:* 617-727-9420. *Fax:* 617-727-0667. *Web site:* www.osfa.mass.edu.

Early Childhood Educators Scholarship Program. Scholarship to provide financial assistance for currently employed early childhood educators and providers who enroll in an associate or bachelor degree program in Early Childhood Education or related programs. Awards are not based on financial need. Individuals taking their first college-level ECE course are eligible for 100 percent tuition, while subsequent ECE courses are awarded at 50 percent tuition. Can be used for one class each semester. *Academic Fields/Career Goals:* Education. *Award:* Scholarship for use in freshman, sophomore, junior, or senior year; not renewable. *Award amount:* $150–$3600. *Number of awards:* varies. *Eligibility Requirements:* Applicant must be enrolled or expecting to

enroll full- or part-time at a four-year institution or university. Available to U.S. citizens. *Application Requirements:* Application. *Deadline:* July 1. **Contact:** Robert Brun, Director of Scholarships and Grants, Massachusetts Office of Student Financial Assistance, 454 Broadway, Suite 200, Revere, MA 02151. *E-mail:* osfa@osfa.mass.edu. *Phone:* 617-727-9420. *Fax:* 617-727-0667. *Web site:* www.osfa.mass.edu.

John and Abigail Adams Scholarship. Scholarship to reward and inspire student achievement, attract more high-performing students to Massachusetts public higher education, and provide families of college-bound students with financial assistance. Must be a U.S. citizen or an eligible non-citizen. There is no application process for the scholarship. Students who are eligible will be notified in the fall of their senior year in high school. *Award:* Scholarship for use in freshman year; not renewable. *Award amount:* varies. *Number of awards:* varies. *Eligibility Requirements:* Applicant must be high school student; planning to enroll or expecting to enroll full-time at a two-year or four-year institution or university; resident of Massachusetts and studying in Massachusetts. Applicant must have 3.0 GPA or higher. Available to U.S. citizens. *Application Requirements: Deadline:* varies. **Contact:** Robert Brun, Director of Scholarships and Grants, Massachusetts Office of Student Financial Assistance, 454 Broadway, Suite 200, Revere, MA 02151. *E-mail:* osfa@osfa.mass.edu. *Phone:* 617-727-9420. *Fax:* 617-727-0667. *Web site:* www.osfa.mass.edu.

Massachusetts Assistance for Student Success Program. Provides need-based financial assistance to Massachusetts residents to attend undergraduate postsecondary institutions in Connecticut, Maine, Massachusetts, New Hampshire, Pennsylvania, Rhode Island, Vermont, and District of Columbia. High school seniors may apply. Expected Family Contribution (EFC) should be $3850. Timely filing of FAFSA required. *Award:* Grant for use in freshman, sophomore, junior, or senior year; not renewable. *Award amount:* $300–$2400. *Number of awards:* 25,000–30,000. *Eligibility Requirements:* Applicant must be enrolled or expecting to enroll full-time at a two-year, four-year, or technical institution or university; resident of Massachusetts and studying in Connecticut, District of Columbia, Maine, Massachusetts, New Hampshire, Pennsylvania, Rhode Island, or Vermont. Available to U.S. citizens. *Application Requirements:* Financial need analysis, FAFSA. *Deadline:* May 1. **Contact:** Robert Brun, Director of Scholarships and Grants, Massachusetts Office of Student Financial Assistance, 454 Broadway, Suite 200, Revere, MA 02151. *E-mail:* osfa@osfa.mass.edu. *Phone:* 617-727-9420. *Fax:* 617-727-0667. *Web site:* www.osfa.mass.edu.

Massachusetts Cash Grant Program. A need-based grant to assist with mandatory fees and non-state supported tuition. This supplemental award is available to Massachusetts residents, who are undergraduates at public two-year, four-year colleges and universities in Massachusetts. Must file FAFSA before May 1. Contact college financial aid office for information. *Award:* Grant for use in freshman, sophomore, junior, or senior year; not renewable. *Award amount:* varies. *Number of awards:* varies. *Eligibility Requirements:* Applicant must be enrolled or expecting to enroll full-time at a two-year or four-year institution or university and resident of Massachusetts. Available to U.S. citizens. *Application Requirements:* Application, financial need analysis, FAFSA. *Deadline:* continuous. **Contact:** Robert Brun, Director of Scholarships and Grants, Massachusetts Office of Student Financial Assistance, 454 Broadway, Suite 200, Revere, MA 02151. *E-mail:* osfa@osfa.mass.edu. *Phone:* 617-727-9420. *Fax:* 617-727-0667. *Web site:* www.osfa.mass.edu.

Massachusetts Gilbert Matching Student Grant Program. Grants for permanent Massachusetts residents attending an independent, regionally accredited Massachusetts school or school of nursing full time. Must be U.S. citizen and permanent legal resident of Massachusetts. File the Free Application for Federal Student Aid after January 1. Contact college financial aid office for complete details and deadlines. *Award:* Grant for use in freshman, sophomore, junior, or senior year; not renewable. *Award amount:* $200–$2500. *Number of awards:* varies. *Eligibility Requirements:* Applicant must be enrolled or expecting to enroll full-time at a four-year institution or university; resident of Massachusetts and studying in Massachusetts. Available to U.S. citizens. *Application Requirements:* Financial need analysis, FAFSA.

Deadline: varies. **Contact:** Robert Brun, Director of Scholarships and Grants, Massachusetts Office of Student Financial Assistance, 454 Broadway, Suite 200, Revere, MA 02151. *E-mail:* rbrun@osfa.mass.edu. *Phone:* 617-727-9420. *Fax:* 617-727-0667. *Web site:* www.osfa.mass.edu.

Massachusetts Part-Time Grant Program. Award for permanent Massachusetts residents who have enrolled part-time for at least one year in a state-approved postsecondary school. The recipient must not have a bachelor's degree. FAFSA must be filed before May 1. Contact college financial aid office for further information. *Award:* Grant for use in freshman, sophomore, junior, or senior year; not renewable. *Award amount:* $200–$1150. *Number of awards:* 200. *Eligibility Requirements:* Applicant must be enrolled or expecting to enroll part-time at a two-year, four-year, or technical institution or university and resident of Massachusetts. Available to U.S. citizens. *Application Requirements:* Application, financial need analysis, FAFSA. *Deadline:* varies. **Contact:** Robert Brun, Director of Scholarships and Grants, Massachusetts Office of Student Financial Assistance, 454 Broadway, Suite 200, Revere, MA 02151. *E-mail:* osfa@osfa.mass.edu. *Phone:* 617-727-9420. *Fax:* 617-727-0667. *Web site:* www.osfa.mass.edu.

Massachusetts Public Service Grant Program. Scholarships for children and/or spouses of deceased members of fire, police, and corrections departments, who were killed in the line of duty. Awards Massachusetts residents attending Massachusetts institutions. Applicant should have not received a prior bachelor's degree or its equivalent. *Award:* Grant for use in freshman, sophomore, junior, or senior year; not renewable. *Award amount:* varies. *Number of awards:* varies. *Eligibility Requirements:* Applicant must be enrolled or expecting to enroll full-time at a four-year institution or university and resident of Massachusetts. Applicant or parent of applicant must have employment or volunteer experience in police/firefighting. Available to U.S. and non-U.S. citizens. Applicant or parent must meet one or more of the following requirements: general military experience; retired from active duty; disabled or killed as a result of military service; prisoner of war; or missing in action. *Application Requirements:* Application, financial need analysis, copy of birth certificate, copy of veteran's death certificate. *Deadline:* May 1. **Contact:** Alison Leary, Director of Scholarships and Grants, Massachusetts Office of Student Financial Assistance, 454 Broadway, Suite 200, Revere, MA 02151. *E-mail:* osfa@osfa.mass.edu. *Phone:* 617-727-9420. *Fax:* 617-727-0667. *Web site:* www.osfa.mass.edu.

New England Regional Student Program. Scholarship for residents of New England. Students pay reduced out-of-state tuition at public colleges or universities in other New England states when enrolling in certain majors not offered at public institutions in home state. *Award:* Scholarship for use in freshman, sophomore, junior, or senior year; renewable. *Award amount:* varies. *Number of awards:* 8000. *Eligibility Requirements:* Applicant must be enrolled or expecting to enroll full- or part-time at a two-year or four-year institution or university; resident of Connecticut, Maine, Massachusetts, New Hampshire, Rhode Island, or Vermont and studying in Connecticut, Maine, Massachusetts, New Hampshire, Quebec, or Vermont. Available to U.S. citizens. *Application Requirements:* College application. *Deadline:* continuous. **Contact:** Wendy Lindsay, Senior Director of Regional Student Program, New England Board of Higher Education, 45 Temple Place, Boston, MA 02111. *E-mail:* tuitionbreak@nebhe.org. *Phone:* 617-357-9620 Ext. 111. *Fax:* 617-338-1577. *Web site:* www.nebhe.org.

Paraprofessional Teacher Preparation Grant. Grant providing financial aid assistance to Massachusetts residents, who are currently employed as paraprofessionals in Massachusetts public schools and wish to obtain higher education and become certified as full-time teachers. *Academic Fields/Career Goals:* Education. *Award:* Grant for use in freshman, sophomore, junior, or senior year; not renewable. *Award amount:* $250–$7500. *Number of awards:* varies. *Eligibility Requirements:* Applicant must be enrolled or expecting to enroll full- or part-time at a two-year or four-year institution or university and resident of Massachusetts. Available to U.S. citizens. *Application Requirements:* Application, FAFSA. *Deadline:* August 1. **Contact:** Robert Brun, Director of Scholarships and Grants, Massachusetts Office of

Student Financial Assistance, 454 Broadway, Suite 200, Revere, MA 02151. *E-mail:* osfa@osfa.mass.edu. *Phone:* 617-727-9420. *Fax:* 617-727-0667. *Web site:* www.osfa.mass.edu.

Robert C. Byrd Honors Scholarship-Massachusetts. Scholarship for high school senior who is a resident of Massachusetts for at least one year prior to the beginning of the academic year he/she will enter college. Must have applied or been accepted to an accredited institution of higher education and be a U.S. citizen, national or permanent resident. *Award:* Scholarship for use in freshman year; renewable. *Award amount:* $1500. *Number of awards:* varies. *Eligibility Requirements:* Applicant must be high school student; planning to enroll or expecting to enroll full-time at a four-year institution or university and resident of Massachusetts. Applicant must have 3.5 GPA or higher. Available to U.S. citizens. *Application Requirements:* Application, transcript. *Deadline:* June 1. **Contact:** Sally Teixeira, Scholarship Coordinator, Massachusetts Department of Education, 350 Main Street, Malden, MA 02148-5023. *E-mail:* steixeira@doe.mass.edu. *Phone:* 781-338-6304. *Web site:* www.doe.mass.edu.

NEW HAMPSHIRE

Leveraged Incentive Grant Program. Grants to provide assistance on the basis of merit and need to full-time undergraduate New Hampshire students at New Hampshire accredited institutions. Must be a New Hampshire resident, and demonstrate financial need as determined by the federal formula and by merit as determined by the institution. Must be a sophomore, junior or senior undergraduate student. *Award:* Grant for use in sophomore, junior, or senior year; not renewable. *Award amount:* $250–$7500. *Number of awards:* varies. *Eligibility Requirements:* Applicant must be enrolled or expecting to enroll full-time at a two-year, four-year, or technical institution or university; resident of New Hampshire and studying in New Hampshire. Available to U.S. citizens. *Application Requirements:* Application, financial need analysis. *Deadline:* varies. **Contact:** Judith A. Knapp, Coordinator of Financial Aid Programs, New Hampshire Postsecondary Education Commission, Three Barrell Court, Suite 300, Concord, NH 03301-8543. *E-mail:* jknapp@pec.state.nh.us. *Phone:* 603-271-2555 Ext. 352. *Fax:* 603-271-2696. *Web site:* www.nh.gov/postsecondary.

New Hampshire Incentive Program (NHIP). Grants to provide financial assistance to New Hampshire students attending eligible institutions in New England. Must demonstrate financial need. May be a part- or full-time undergraduate student with no previous bachelor's degree. *Award:* Grant for use in freshman, sophomore, junior, or senior year; renewable. *Award amount:* $125–$1000. *Number of awards:* 4300–4500. *Eligibility Requirements:* Applicant must be enrolled or expecting to enroll full- or part-time at a four-year institution or university; resident of New Hampshire and studying in Connecticut, Maine, Massachusetts, New Hampshire, Rhode Island, or Vermont. Available to U.S. citizens. *Application Requirements:* Application, financial need analysis, FAFSA. *Deadline:* May 1. **Contact:** Judith A. Knapp, Coordinator of Financial Aid Programs, New Hampshire Postsecondary Education Commission, Three Barrell Court, Suite 300, Concord, NH 03301-8543. *E-mail:* jknapp@pec.state.nh.us. *Phone:* 603-271-2555 Ext. 352. *Fax:* 603-271-2696. *Web site:* www.nh.gov/postsecondary.

Scholarships for Orphans of Veterans-New Hampshire. Scholarship to provide financial assistance (room, board, books and supplies) to children of parents) who served in World War II, Korean Conflict, Vietnam (Southeast Asian Conflict) or the Gulf Wars, or any other operation for which the armed forces expeditionary medal or theater of operations service medal was awarded to the veteran. *Award:* Scholarship for use in freshman, sophomore, junior, or senior year; renewable. *Award amount:* up to $2500. *Number of awards:* 1–10. *Eligibility Requirements:* Applicant must be age 16-25; enrolled or expecting to enroll full-time at a two-year or four-year institution or university; resident of New Hampshire and studying in New Hampshire. Available to U.S. citizens. Applicant or parent must meet one or more of the following requirements: general military experience; retired from active duty; disabled or killed as a result of military service; prisoner of war; or missing in action. *Application Requirements:* Application. *Deadline:*

varies. **Contact:** Judith A. Knapp, Coordinator of Financial Aid Programs, New Hampshire Postsecondary Education Commission, Three Barrell Court, Suite 300, Concord, NH 03301-8543. *E-mail:* jknapp@pec.state.nh.us. *Phone:* 603-271-2555 Ext. 352. *Fax:* 603-271-2696. *Web site:* www.nh.gov/postsecondary.

Workforce Incentive Program. The program provides incentive for students to pursue careers in critical workforce shortage areas at appropriate New Hampshire institutions and to encourage students to then seek employment in New Hampshire after completion of their career program. May be a part- or full-time student in an approved program, and should demonstrate financial need as determined by the institution. *Academic Fields/Career Goals:* Education; Foreign Language; Nursing; Special Education. *Award:* Forgivable loan for use in freshman, sophomore, junior, senior, graduate, or postgraduate years; not renewable. *Award amount:* varies. *Number of awards:* varies. *Eligibility Requirements:* Applicant must be enrolled or expecting to enroll full- or part-time at a four-year institution or university; resident of New Hampshire and studying in New Hampshire. Available to U.S. citizens. *Application Requirements:* Application. *Deadline:* varies. **Contact:** Judith A. Knapp, Coordinator of Financial Aid Programs, New Hampshire Postsecondary Education Commission, Three Barrell Court, Suite 300, Concord, NH 03301-8543. *E-mail:* jknapp@pec.state.nh.us. *Phone:* 603-271-2555 Ext. 352. *Fax:* 603-271-2696. *Web site:* www.nh.gov/postsecondary.

RHODE ISLAND

Rhode Island State Grant Program. Grants for residents of Rhode Island attending an approved school in United States. Based on need. Renewable for up to four years if in good academic standing and meet financial need requirements. *Award:* Grant for use in freshman, sophomore, junior, or senior year; renewable. *Award amount:* $300–$900. *Number of awards:* 10,000–12,900. *Eligibility Requirements:* Applicant must be enrolled or expecting to enroll full- or part-time at a two-year, four-year, or technical institution or university and resident of Rhode Island. Available to U.S. citizens. *Application Requirements:* Application, financial need analysis. *Deadline:* March 1. **Contact:** Mr. Michael Joyce, Director of Program Administration, Rhode Island Higher Education Assistance Authority, 560 Jefferson Boulevard, Suite 100, Warwick, RI 02886. *E-mail:* mjoyce@riheaa.org. *Phone:* 401-736-1172. *Fax:* 401-736-1178. *Web site:* www.riheaa.org.

VERMONT

Vermont Incentive Grants. Renewable grants for Vermont residents based on financial need. Must meet needs test. Must be college undergraduate or graduate student enrolled full-time at an approved post secondary institution. Only available to U.S. citizens or permanent residents. *Award:* Grant for use in freshman, sophomore, junior, or senior year; renewable. *Award amount:* $500–$10,800. *Number of awards:* varies. *Eligibility Requirements:* Applicant must be enrolled or expecting to enroll full-time at a two-year, four-year, or technical institution or university and resident of Vermont. Available to U.S. citizens. *Application Requirements:* Application, financial need analysis, FAFSA. *Deadline:* continuous. **Contact:** Grant Program, Vermont Student Assistance Corporation, PO Box 2000, Winooski, VT 05404-2000. *Phone:* 802-655-9602. *Fax:* 802-654-3765. *Web site:* www.vsac.org.

Vermont Non-Degree Student Grant Program. Need-based, renewable grants for Vermont residents enrolled in non-degree programs in a college, vocational school, or high school adult program, that will improve employability or encourage further study. Award amounts vary. *Award:* Grant for use in freshman, sophomore, junior, or senior year; renewable. *Award amount:* varies. *Number of awards:* varies. *Eligibility Requirements:* Applicant must be enrolled or expecting to enroll full- or part-time at a two-year, four-year, or technical institution or university and resident of Vermont. Available to U.S. citizens. *Application Requirements:* Application, financial need analysis. *Deadline:* continuous. **Contact:** Vermont Student Assistance Corporation. *Web site:* www.vsac.org.

Vermont Part-Time Student Grants. For undergraduates carrying less than twelve credits per semester who have not received a bachelor's degree. Must be Vermont resident. Based on financial need. Complete Vermont Financial Aid Packet to apply. May be used at any approved post-secondary institution. *Award:* Grant for use in freshman, sophomore, junior, or senior year; renewable. *Award amount:* $250–$8100. *Number of awards:* varies. *Eligibility Requirements:* Applicant must be enrolled or expecting to enroll part-time at a four-year institution or university and resident of Vermont. Available to U.S. citizens. *Application Requirements:* Application, financial need analysis. *Deadline:* continuous. **Contact:** Grant Program, Vermont Student Assistance Corporation, PO Box 2000, Winooski, VT 05404-2000. *Phone:* 802-655-9602. *Fax:* 802-654-3765. *Web site:* www.vsac.org.

Vermont Teacher Diversity Scholarship Program. Loan forgiveness program for students from diverse racial and ethnic backgrounds who attend college in Vermont with a goal of becoming public school teachers. Preference will be given to residents of Vermont. *Academic Fields/Career Goals:* Education. *Award:* Forgivable loan for use in freshman, sophomore, junior, senior, or graduate year; not renewable. *Award amount:* $4000. *Number of awards:* 4. *Eligibility Requirements:* Applicant must be American Indian/Alaska Native, Asian/Pacific Islander, Black (non-Hispanic), or Hispanic; enrolled or expecting to enroll full- or part-time at a four-year institution or university; resident of Vermont and studying in Vermont. Available to U.S. citizens. *Application Requirements:* Application, resume, references, transcript. *Deadline:* April 5. **Contact:** Ms. Phyl Newbeck, Director, Vermont Teacher Diversity Scholarship Program, PO Box 359, Waterbury, VT 05676-0359. *Phone:* 802-241-3379. *Fax:* 802-241-3369. *Web site:* www.vsc.edu/teacherdiversity/.

Searching for Four-Year Colleges Online

The Internet can be a great tool for gathering information about four-year colleges and universities. There are many worthwhile sites that are ready to help guide you through the various aspects of the selection process, including Peterson's College Search at www.petersons.com/ugchannel.

HOW PETERSON'S COLLEGE SEARCH CAN HELP

Peterson's College Search is a comprehensive information resource that will help you make sense of the college admissions process and is a great place to start your college search-and-selection journey—it's as easy as these three steps:

1. Decide what's important
2. Define your criteria
3. Get results

Decide What's Important

There's no such thing as a best college—there's only the best college *for you*! Peterson's College Search site is organized into various sections and offers you enhanced search criteria—and it's easy to use! You can find colleges by name or keyword for starters, or do a detailed search based on the following:

- The Basics (location, setting, size, cost, type, religious and ethnic affiliation)
- Student Body (male-female ratio, diversity, in-state vs. out-of-state)
- Getting In (selectivity, GPA)
- Academics (degree type, majors, special programs and services)
- Campus Life (sports, clubs, fraternities and sororities, housing)

Define Your Criteria

Now it's time to define your criteria by taking a closer look at some more specific details. Here you are able to answer questions about what is important to you, skip questions that aren't important, and click for instant results. You'll be prompted to think about criteria:

- Where do you want to study?
- What range of tuition are you willing to consider?
- How many people do you want to go to school with?

Get Results

Once you have gotten your results, simply click on any school to get information about the institution, including school type, setting, degrees offered, comprehensive cost, entrance difficulty, application deadline, undergraduate student population, minority breakdown, international population, housing info, freshman details, faculty, majors, academic programs, student life, athletics, facilities/endowments, costs, financial aid, and applying. If the schools you are interested in have provided Peterson's with a **Close-Up**, you will find that here too! Here, schools are given the opportunity to communicate unique features of their programs to prospective students.

Get Free Info

If, after looking at the information provided on Peterson's College Search, you still have questions, you can send an e-mail directly to the admissions department of the school. Just click on the "Get Free Info" button and send your message!

Visit School Site

For institutions that have provided information about their Web sites, simply click on any one of the links at the top of the page (e.g., School Web site, Apply Now, Online Tour) and you will be taken directly to that institution's Web page. Once you arrive at the school's Web site, look around and get a feel for the place. Often, schools offer virtual tours of the campus, complete with photos and commentary.

Add to My Saved Colleges

The "Add to My Saved Colleges" features help your college planning with management tools that create notes and track schools.

WRITE ADMISSIONS ESSAYS

This year, 500,000 college applicants will write 500,000 different admissions essays. Half will be rejected by their first-choice school, while only 11 percent will gain admission to the nation's most selective colleges. With acceptance rates at all-time lows, setting yourself apart requires more than just blockbuster SAT scores and impeccable transcripts—it requires the perfect application essay. Named "the world's premier application essay editing service" by the *New York Times* Learning Network and "one of the best essay services on the Internet" by the *Washington Post*, EssayEdge (www.essayedge.com) has helped more applicants write successful personal statements than any other company in the world. Learn more about EssayEdge and how it can give you an edge over hundreds of applicants with comparable academic credentials.

PRACTICE FOR YOUR TEST

At Peterson's, we understand that the college admissions process can be very stressful. With the stakes so high and the competition getting tighter every year, it's easy to feel like the process is out of your control. Fortunately, preparing for college admissions tests, like the PSAT, SAT, and ACT, helps you exert some control over the options you will have available to you. You can visit Peterson's Prep Central (click on the "Prepare for Tests" tab at the top of the screen) to learn more about how Peterson's can help you maximize your scores—and your options.

USE THE TOOLS TO YOUR ADVANTAGE

Choosing a college is an involved and complicated process. The tools available to you on www.petersons.com can help you to be more productive in this process. So, what are you waiting for? Fire up your computer; your future alma mater may be just a click away!

How to Use This Guide

This article provides an outline of the **Profile** format, describing the items covered. All college information presented was supplied to Peterson's by the colleges themselves. Any item that does not apply to a particular college or for which no current information was supplied may be omitted from that college's **Profile**. Colleges that were unable to supply usable data in time for publication are listed by name and, if available, Web address.

PROFILES OF COLLEGES IN NEW ENGLAND

This section presents pertinent factual and statistical data for each college in a standard format for easy comparison.

General Information

The first paragraph gives a brief introduction to the college, covering the following elements.

Type of student body: The categories are *men's* (100 percent of the student body), *primarily men's*, *women's* (100 percent of the student body), *primarily women's*, and *coed*. A few schools are designated as *undergraduate: women only; graduate: coed* or *undergraduate: men only; graduate: coed*. A college may also be designated as coordinate with another institution, indicating that there are separate colleges or campuses for men and women, but facilities, courses, and institutional governance are shared.

Institutional control: A *public* college receives its funding wholly or primarily from the federal, state, and/or local government. The term *private* indicates an independent, nonprofit institution, that is, one whose funding comes primarily from private sources and tuition. This category includes independent, religious colleges, which may also specify a particular religious denomination or church affiliation. Profit-making institutions are designated as *proprietary*.

Institutional type: A *two-year college* awards associate degrees and/or offers the first two years of a bachelor's degree program. A *primarily two-year college* awards bachelor's degrees, but the vast majority of students are enrolled in two-year programs. A *four-year college* awards bachelor's degrees and may also award associate degrees, but it does not offer graduate (postbachelor's) degree programs. A *five-year college* offers a five-year bachelor's program in a professional field such as architecture or pharmacy but does not award graduate degrees. An *upper-level institution* awards bachelor's degrees, but entering students must have at least two years of previous college-level credit; it may also offer graduate degree programs. A *comprehensive institution* awards bachelor's degrees and may also award associate degrees; graduate degree programs are offered primarily at the master's, specialist's, or professional level, although one or two doctoral programs may also be offered. A *university* offers four years of undergraduate work plus graduate degrees through the doctorate in more than two academic and/or professional fields.

Founding date: This is the year the college came into existence or was chartered, reflecting the period during which it has existed as an educational institution, regardless of subsequent mergers or other organizational changes.

Degree levels: An *associate* degree program may consist of either a college-transfer program, equivalent to the first two years of a bachelor's degree, or a one- to three-year terminal program that provides training for a specific occupation. A *bachelor's* degree program represents a three- to five-year liberal arts, science, professional, or preprofessional program. A *master's* degree is the first graduate degree in the liberal arts and sciences and certain professional fields and usually requires one to two years of full-time study. A *doctoral* degree is the highest degree awarded in research-oriented academic disciplines and usually requires from three to six years of full-time graduate study; the *first professional* degrees in such fields as law and medicine are also at the doctoral level. For colleges that award degrees in one field only, such as art or music, the field of specialization is indicated.

Campus setting: This indicates the size of the campus in acres or hectares and its location.

Academic Information

This paragraph contains information on the following items.

Faculty: The number of full-time and part-time faculty members is given, followed by the percentage of the full-time faculty members who hold doctoral, first professional, or terminal degrees, and then the student-faculty ratio. (Not all colleges calculate the student-faculty ratio in the same way; Peterson's prints the ratio provided by the college.)

Library holdings: The numbers of books, serials, and audiovisual materials in the college's collections are listed.

Special programs: *Academic remediation for entering students* consists of instructional courses designed for students deficient in the general competencies necessary for a regular postsecondary curriculum and educational setting. *Services for LD students* include special help for learning-disabled students with resolvable difficulties, such as dyslexia. *Honors programs* are any special programs for very able students,

offering the opportunity for educational enrichment, independent study, acceleration, or some combination of these. *Cooperative (co-op) education programs* are formal arrangements with off-campus employers, allowing students to combine work and study in order to gain degree-related experience, usually extending the time required to complete a degree. *Study abroad* is an arrangement by which a student completes part of the academic program studying in another country. A college may operate a campus abroad or it may have a cooperative agreement with other U.S. institutions or institutions in other countries. *Advanced placement* gives credit toward a degree awarded for acceptable scores on College Board Advanced Placement tests. *Accelerated degree programs* allow students to earn a bachelor's degree in three academic years. *Freshmen honors college* is a separate academic program for talented freshmen. *English as a second language (ESL)* is a course of study designed specifically for students whose native language is not English. *Double major* consists of a program of study in which a student concurrently completes the requirements of two majors. *Independent study* consists of academic work, usually undertaken outside the regular classroom structure, chosen or designed by the student with departmental approval and instructor supervision. *Distance learning* consists of credit courses that can be accessed off campus via cable television, the Internet, satellite, videotapes, correspondence courses, or other media. *Self-designed major* is a program of study based on individual interests, designed by the student with the assistance of an adviser. *Summer session for credit* includes summer courses through which students may make up degree work or accelerate their program. *Part-time degree programs* offer students the ability to earn a degree through part-time enrollment in regular session (daytime) classes or evening, weekend, or summer classes. *External degree programs* are programs of study in which students earn credits toward a degree through a combination of independent study, college courses, proficiency examinations, and personal experience. External degree programs require minimal or no classroom attendance. *Adult/continuing education programs* are courses offered for nontraditional students who are currently working or are returning to formal education. *Internships* are any short-term, supervised work experience, usually related to a student's major field, for which the student earns academic credit. The work can be full- or part-time, on or off campus, paid or unpaid. *Off-campus study* is a formal arrangement with one or more domestic institutions under which students may take courses at the other institution(s) for credit.

Most popular majors: The most popular field or fields of study at the college, in terms of the number of undergraduate degrees conferred in 2008, are listed.

Student Body Statistics

Enrollment: The total number of students, undergraduates, and freshmen (or entering students for an upper-level institution) enrolled in degree programs as of fall 2008 are given.

With reference to the undergraduate enrollment for fall 2008, the percentages of women and men and the number of states and countries from which students hail are listed. The following percentages are also provided: in-state students, international students, and the percentage of undergraduates who went on to graduate and professional schools.

Expenses

Costs are given in each profile according to the most up-to-date figures available from each college for the 2008–09 or 2009–10 academic year.

Annual expenses may be expressed as a comprehensive fee (the annual cost of attending, including full-time tuition, mandatory fees, and college room and board) or as separate figures for full-time tuition, fees, room and board, and/or room only. For public institutions where tuition differs according to residence, separate figures are given for area and/or state residents and for nonresidents. Part-time tuition and fees are expressed in terms of a per-unit rate (per credit, per semester hour, etc.) as specified by the college.

The tuition structure at some institutions is complex in that freshmen and sophomores may be charged a different rate from that of juniors and seniors; a professional or vocational division may have a different fee structure from the liberal arts division of the same institution; or part-time tuition may be prorated on a sliding scale according to the number of credit hours taken. In all of these cases, the average figures are given along with an explanation of the basis for the variable rate. For colleges that report that the room and board costs vary according to the type of accommodation and meal plan, the average costs are given. The phrase *no college housing* indicates that the college does not own or operate any housing facilities for its undergraduate students.

Financial Aid

This paragraph contains information on the following items.

Forms of financial aid: The categories of college-administered aid available to undergraduates are listed. College-administered means that the college itself determines the recipient and amount of each award. The types of aid covered are *non-need scholarships*, *need-based scholarships*, *athletic grants*, and *part-time jobs*.

Financial aid: This item pertains to undergraduates who enrolled full-time in a four-year college in 2007 or 2008. The figures given are the dollar amount of the average financial aid package, including scholarships, grants, loans, and part-time jobs, received by such undergraduates.

Financial aid application deadline: This deadline may be given as a specific date, as continuous processing up to a specific date or until all available aid has been awarded, or as a priority date rather than a strict deadline, meaning that students are encouraged to apply by that date in order to have the best chance of obtaining aid.

Freshman Admission

The supporting data that a student must submit when applying for freshman admission are grouped into three categories: *required for all*, *recommended*, and *required for some*. They may include an essay, a high school transcript, letters of recommendation, an interview on campus or with local alumni, standardized test scores, and, for certain types of schools or programs, special requirements such as a musical audition or an art portfolio.

The most commonly required standardized tests are the ACT and the College Board's SAT and SAT Subject Tests. TOEFL (Test of English as a Foreign Language) is for international students whose native language is not English.

The application deadline for admission is given as either a specific date or *rolling*. Rolling means that applications are processed as they are received, and qualified students are accepted as long as there are openings. The application deadline for out-of-state students is indicated if it differs from the date for state residents. *Early decision* and *early action* deadlines are also given when applicable. Early decision is a program whereby students may apply early, are notified of acceptance or rejection well in advance of the usual notification date, and agree to accept an offer of admission, the assumption being that only one early application has been made. Early action is the same as early decision except that applicants are not obligated to accept an offer of admission.

Transfer Admission

This paragraph gives the application requirements and application deadline for a student applying for admission as a transfer from another institution. In addition to the requirements previously listed for freshman applicants, requirements for transfers may also include a college transcript and a minimum college grade point average (expressed as a number on a scale of 0 to 4.0, where 4.0 equals A, 3.0 equals B, etc.). The name of the person to contact for

additional transfer information is also given if it is different from the person listed in **For Further Information**.

Entrance Difficulty

This paragraph contains the college's own assessment of its *entrance difficulty* level, including notation of an *open admission policy* where applicable. Open admission means that virtually all applicants are accepted without regard to standardized test scores, grade average, or class rank. A college may indicate that open admission is limited to a certain category of applicants, such as state residents, or does not apply to certain selective programs, often those in the health professions.

The five levels of entrance difficulty are *most difficult*, *very difficult*, *moderately difficult*, *minimally difficult*, and *noncompetitive*.

The final item in this paragraph is the percentage of applicants accepted for the fall 2008 freshman (or entering) class.

For Further Information

The name, title, and mailing address of the person to contact for more information on application and admission procedures are given at the end of the **Profile**. A telephone number, fax number, e-mail address, and Web site are also included in this paragraph. Profiles with a *Sponsor* icon do not contain this information, since it is already available in the **Special Message to Students**.

SPECIAL MESSAGES TO STUDENTS

In addition, a number of college admissions office staff members, as part of a major information-dissemination effort, have supplemented their **Profile** with special descriptive information on four topics of particular interest to students.

Social Life: This paragraph conveys a feeling for life on campus by addressing such questions as the following: What are the most popular activities? Are there active fraternities and sororities? What is the role of student government? Do most students live on campus or commute? Does the college have a religious orientation?

Academic Highlights: This paragraph describes some of the special features and characteristics of the college's academic program, such as special degree programs and opportunities for study abroad or internships.

Interviews and Campus Visits: Colleges that conduct on-campus admission interviews describe the importance of an interview in their admission process and what they try to learn about a student through the interview. For those colleges that do not interview applicants individually, there is information on how a student interested in the college

can visit the campus to meet administrators, faculty members, and currently enrolled students as well as on what the prospective applicant should try to accomplish through such a visit. This paragraph may also include a list of the most noteworthy places or things to see during a campus visit and the location, telephone number (including toll-free numbers if available), and business hours of the office to contact for information about appointments and campus visits. Also included, when available, is travel information, specifically the nearest commercial airport and the nearest interstate highway, with the appropriate exit.

For Further Information: The name and mailing address of the person and/or office to contact for more information on the school are included in this paragraph. A telephone number, fax number, e-mail address, and Web site may also be included.

CLOSE-UPS OF COLLEGES IN NEW ENGLAND

Two-page narrative descriptions appear in this section, providing an inside look at colleges and universities, shifting the focus to a variety of other factors, some of them intangible, that should also be considered. The descriptions presented in this section provide a wealth of statistics that are crucial components in the college decision-making equation—components such as tuition, financial aid, and major fields of study. Prepared exclusively by college officials, the descriptions are designed to help give students a better sense of the individuality of each institution, in terms that include campus environment, student activities, and lifestyle. Such quality-of-life intangibles can be the deciding factors in the college selection process.

The absence from this section of any college or university does not constitute an editorial decision on the part of Peterson's. In essence, this section is an open forum for colleges and universities, on a voluntary basis, to communicate their particular message to prospective college students. The colleges included have paid a fee to Peterson's to provide this information. The descriptions are edited to provide a consistent format across entries for your ease of comparison and are presented alphabetically by the official name of the institution.

PROFILES AND CLOSE-UPS OF OTHER COLLEGES TO CONSIDER

Do you know that schools sometimes target specific areas of the country for student recruitment? In this section, you'll find **Profiles** and **Close-Ups** of schools outside the region of this guide looking to recruit students like you.

The format of both the **Profiles** and the **Close-Ups** in this section matches the format in the previous sections.

INDEXES

Majors and Degrees

This index lists hundreds of undergraduate major fields of study that are currently offered most widely. The majors appear in alphabetical order, each followed by an alphabetical list of the colleges that report offering a program in that field and the degree levels (*A* for associate, *B* for bachelor's) available. The majors represented here are based on the National Center for Education Statistics (NCES) 2000 Classification of Instructional Programs (CIP). The CIP is a taxonomic coding scheme that contains titles and descriptions of instructional programs, primarily at the postsecondary level. CIP was originally developed to facilitate NCES's collection and reporting of postsecondary degree completions, by major field of study, using standard classifications that capture the majority of program activity. The CIP is the accepted federal government reporting standard for classifying instructional programs. However, although the term "major" is used in this guide, some colleges may use other terms, such as "concentration," "program of study," or "field."

Athletic Programs and Scholarships

This index lists the colleges that report offering intercollegiate athletic programs, listed alphabetically. An *M* or *W* following the college name indicates that the sport is offered for men or women, respectively. An *s* in parentheses following an *M* or *W* indicates that athletic scholarships (or grants-in-aid) are offered by the college for men or women, respectively, in that sport.

ROTC Programs

This index lists the colleges that report offering Reserve Officers' Training Corps programs in one or more branches of the armed services, as indicated by letter codes following the college name: *A* for Army, *N* for Navy, and *AF* for Air Force. A *c* in parentheses following the branch letter code indicates that the program is offered through a cooperative arrangement on another college's campus.

Alphabetical Listing of Colleges and Universities

This index gives the page locations of various entries for all the colleges and universities in this book. The page numbers

for the **Profiles** are printed in regular type, those for **Profiles** with **Special Messages** in *italic* type, and those for **Close-Ups** in **boldface** type.

DATA COLLECTION PROCEDURES

The data contained in the **Profiles** and **Indexes** were researched between winter 2008 and spring 2009 through *Peterson's Annual Survey of Undergraduate Institutions* and *Peterson's Annual Survey of Undergraduate Financial Aid*. Questionnaires were sent to the more than 2,200 colleges and universities that met the outlined inclusion criteria. All data included in this edition have been submitted by officials (usually admissions and financial aid officers, registrars, or institutional research personnel) at the colleges. In addition, many of the institutions that submitted data were contacted directly by the Peterson's research staff to verify unusual figures, resolve discrepancies, or obtain additional data. All usable information received in time for publication has been included. The omission of any particular item from an index or profile listing signifies that the information is either not applicable to that institution or not available. Because of Peterson's comprehensive editorial review and because all material comes directly from college officials, we believe that the information presented in this guide is accurate. You should check with a specific college or university at the time of application to verify such figures as tuition and fees, which may have changed since the publication of this volume.

CRITERIA FOR INCLUSION IN THIS BOOK

The term "four-year college" is the commonly used designation for institutions that grant the baccalaureate degree. Four years is the expected amount of time required to earn this degree, although some bachelor's degree programs may be completed in three years, others require five years, and part-time programs may take considerably longer. Upper-level institutions offer only the junior and senior years and accept only students with two years of college-level credit. Therefore, "four-year college" is a conventional term that accurately describes most of the institutions included in this guide, but should not be taken literally in all cases. In addition, some two-year colleges granting associate degrees have been included in this publication. Private nonprofit and religious two-year colleges were selected for inclusion.

To be included in this guide, an institution must have full accreditation or be a candidate for accreditation (preaccreditation) status by an institutional or specialized accrediting body recognized by the U.S. Department of Education or the Council for Higher Education Accreditation (CHEA). Institutional accrediting bodies, which review each institution as a whole, include the six regional associations of schools and colleges (Middle States, New England, North Central, Northwest, Southern, and Western), each of which is responsible for a specified portion of the United States and its territories. Other institutional accrediting bodies are national in scope and accredit specific kinds of institutions (e.g., Bible colleges, independent colleges, and rabbinical and Talmudic schools). Program registration by the New York State Board of Regents is considered to be the equivalent of institutional accreditation, since the board requires that all programs offered by an institution meet its standards before recognition is granted. There are recognized specialized or professional accrediting bodies in more than forty different fields, each of which is authorized to accredit institutions or specific programs in its particular field. For specialized institutions that offer programs in one field only, we designate this to be the equivalent of institutional accreditation. A full explanation of the accrediting process and complete information on recognized, institutional (regional and national) and specialized accrediting bodies can be found online at www.chea.org or at www.ed.gov/admins/finaid/accred/index.html.

Profiles of Colleges
in New England

Map of New England

This map provides a general perspective on New England and shows the major metropolitan areas and capital of each state.

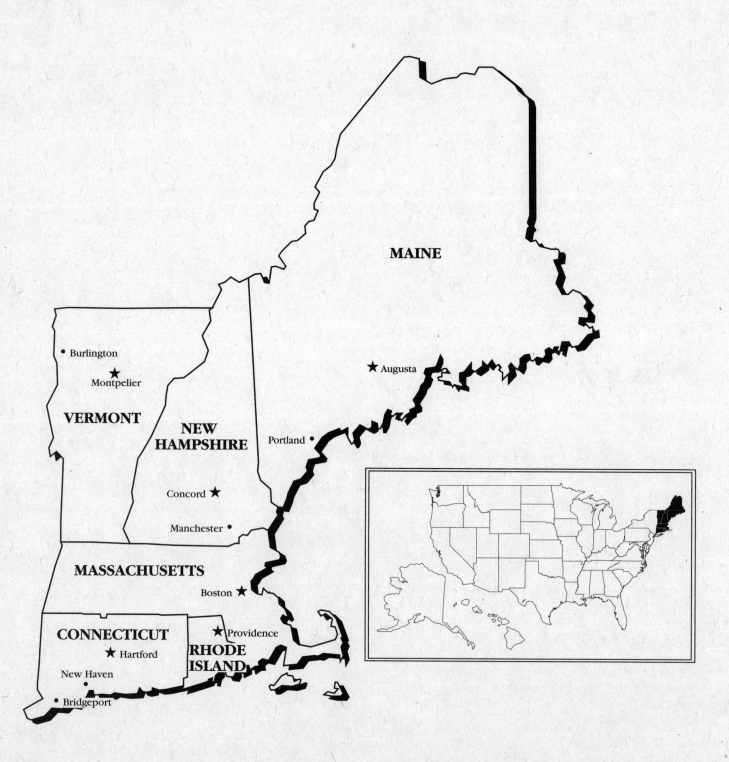

Connecticut

ALBERTUS MAGNUS COLLEGE
New Haven, Connecticut

Albertus Magnus College is a coed, private, Roman Catholic, comprehensive institution, founded in 1925, offering degrees at the associate, bachelor's, and master's levels. It has a 55-acre campus in New Haven near New York City and Hartford.

Academic Information The faculty has 69 members (62% full-time), 70% with terminal degrees. The undergraduate student-faculty ratio is 16:1. Special programs include academic remediation, services for learning-disabled students, an honors program, advanced placement credit, accelerated degree programs, Freshman Honors College, ESL programs, double majors, independent study, distance learning, self-designed majors, summer session for credit, part-time degree programs (evenings, summer), and internships.
Student Body Statistics The student body totals 2,129, of whom 1,714 are undergraduates (188 freshmen). 68 percent are women and 32 percent are men. Students come from 7 states and territories and 3 other countries. 85 percent are from Connecticut. 0.2 percent are international students.
Expenses for 2008–09 *Application fee: $35. Comprehensive fee: $32,066* includes full-time tuition ($21,780), mandatory fees ($844), and college room and board ($9442). Full-time tuition and fees vary according to class time and program. *Part-time tuition: $2178 per course.* Part-time tuition varies according to class time and program.
Financial Aid Forms of aid include need-based and non-need-based scholarships and part-time jobs. The average aided 2008–09 undergraduate received an aid package worth an estimated $9074. The priority application deadline for financial aid is March 15.
Freshman Admission Albertus Magnus College requires a high school transcript, 1 recommendation, SAT or ACT scores, and TOEFL scores for international students. An essay, a minimum 2.5 high school GPA, an interview, and SAT Subject Test scores are recommended. A minimum 2.5 high school GPA is required for some. The application deadline for regular admission is August 20.
Transfer Admission The application deadline for admission is rolling.
Entrance Difficulty Albertus Magnus College assesses its entrance difficulty level as moderately difficult. For the fall 2008 freshman class, 83 percent of the applicants were accepted.
For Further Information Contact Ms. Jessica Van Deren, Dean of Admissions, Albertus Magnus College, 700 Prospect Street, New Haven, CT 06511-1189. *Phone:* 203-773-8501 or 800-578-9160 (toll-free). *Fax:* 203-773-5248. *E-mail:* admissions@albertus.edu. *Web site:* http://www.albertus.edu/.

See page 90 for the Close-Up.

BETH BENJAMIN ACADEMY OF CONNECTICUT
Stamford, Connecticut

For Information Write to Beth Benjamin Academy of Connecticut, Stamford, CT 06901-1202.

BRIARWOOD COLLEGE
Southington, Connecticut

http://www.briarwood.edu/

CENTRAL CONNECTICUT STATE UNIVERSITY
New Britain, Connecticut

Central Connecticut State University is a coed, public, comprehensive unit of Connecticut State University System, founded in 1849, offering degrees at the bachelor's, master's, and doctoral levels and post-master's and postbachelor's certificates. It has a 294-acre campus in New Britain.

Academic Information The faculty has 899 members (48% full-time), 46% with terminal degrees. The undergraduate student-faculty ratio is 19:1. The library holds 717,553 titles, 31,195 serial subscriptions, and 8,851 audiovisual materials. Special programs include academic remediation, services for learning-disabled students, an honors program, cooperative (work-study) education, study abroad, advanced placement credit, ESL programs, independent study, distance learning, self-designed majors, summer session for credit, part-time degree programs, adult/continuing education programs, internships, and arrangement for off-campus study with members of the Inter-Institutional Student Exchange Program. The most frequently chosen baccalaureate fields are business/marketing, education, social sciences.
Student Body Statistics The student body totals 12,233, of whom 9,906 are undergraduates (1,310 freshmen). 48 percent are women and 52 percent are men. Students come from 29 states and territories and 41 other countries. 96 percent are from Connecticut. 1 percent are international students.
Expenses for 2008–09 *Application fee: $50. State resident tuition: $3514* full-time, $334 per credit part-time. *Nonresident tuition:* $11,373 full-time, $334 per credit part-time. *Mandatory fees:* $3528 full-time, $55 per term part-time. Full-time tuition and fees vary according to course level, course load, and reciprocity agreements. Part-time tuition and fees vary according to course level and course load. *College room and board:* $8618. *College room only:* $5020. Room and board charges vary according to board plan.
Financial Aid Forms of aid include need-based and non-need-based scholarships, athletic grants, and part-time jobs. The average aided 2008–09 undergraduate received an aid package worth an estimated $7329. The priority application deadline for financial aid is March 1.
Freshman Admission Central Connecticut State University requires an essay, a high school transcript, a minimum 2.0 high school GPA, SAT scores, and TOEFL scores for international students. A minimum 3.0 high school GPA and 1 recommendation are recommended. An interview is required for some. The application deadline for regular admission is June 1.
Transfer Admission The application deadline for admission is June 1.
Entrance Difficulty Central Connecticut State University assesses its entrance difficulty level as moderately difficult. For the fall 2008 freshman class, 59 percent of the applicants were accepted.
For Further Information Contact Mr. Larry Hall, Director, Recruitment and Admissions, Central Connecticut State University, 1615 Stanley Street, New Britain, CT 06050. *Phone:* 860-832-2285 or 888-733-2278 (toll-free in-state). *Fax:* 860-832-2522. *E-mail:* admissions@ccsu.edu. *Web site:* http://www.ccsu.edu/.

CHARTER OAK STATE COLLEGE
New Britain, Connecticut

Charter Oak State College is a coed, public, four-year college, founded in 1973, offering degrees at the associate and bachelor's levels (offers only external degree programs).

Expenses for 2008–09 *Application fee: $75. State resident tuition: $186 per* credit hour part-time. *Nonresident tuition:* $256 per credit hour part-time. *Mandatory fees:* $40 per term part-time. Part-time tuition and fees vary according to degree level.
For Further Information Contact Ms. Lori Pendleton, Director of Admissions, Charter Oak State College, 55 Paul J. Manafort Drive, New Britain, CT 06053-2150. *Phone:* 860-832-3858. *Fax:* 860-832-3999. *E-mail:* info@charteroak.edu. *Web site:* http://www.charteroak.edu/.

CONNECTICUT COLLEGE
New London, Connecticut

Connecticut College is a coed, private, comprehensive institution, founded in 1911, offering degrees at the bachelor's and master's levels. It has a 702-acre campus in New London.

Academic Information The faculty has 239 members (71% full-time), 73% with terminal degrees. The undergraduate student-faculty ratio is 9:1. The library holds 496,817 titles and 2,279 serial subscriptions. Special programs include study abroad, advanced placement credit, double majors, independent study, self-designed majors, summer session for credit, part-time degree programs, adult/continuing education programs, internships, and arrangement for off-campus study with members of the Twelve College Exchange Program, United States Coast Guard Academy, American University, Trinity College, Wesleyan University, National Theater Institute, Williams College. The most frequently chosen baccalaureate fields are social sciences, biological/life sciences, visual and performing arts.

Student Body Statistics The student body totals 1,852, of whom 1,845 are undergraduates (493 freshmen). 60 percent are women and 40 percent are men. Students come from 46 states and territories and 74 other countries. 81 percent are from Connecticut. 4.5 percent are international students.

Expenses for 2008–09 *Application fee:* $60. *Comprehensive fee:* $49,385. *Part-time tuition:* $1146 per credit hour. Part-time tuition varies according to program.

Financial Aid Forms of aid include need-based scholarships and part-time jobs. The average aided 2008–09 undergraduate received an aid package worth an estimated $31,099. The application deadline for financial aid is February 1.

Freshman Admission Connecticut College requires an essay, a high school transcript, a minimum 2.0 high school GPA, TOEFL scores for international students, and ACT or any 2 SAT Subject Tests required. An interview is recommended. The application deadline for regular admission is January 1, for early decision plan 1 it is November 15, and for early decision plan 2 it is January 1.

Transfer Admission The application deadline for admission is April 1.

Entrance Difficulty Connecticut College assesses its entrance difficulty level as very difficult. For the fall 2008 freshman class, 37 percent of the applicants were accepted.

For Further Information Contact Ms. Martha Merrill, Dean of Admissions and Financial Aid, Connecticut College, 270 Mohegan Avenue, New London, CT 06320-4196. *Phone:* 860-439-2200. *Fax:* 860-439-4301. *E-mail:* admission@conncoll.edu. *Web site:* http://www.conncoll.edu/.

EASTERN CONNECTICUT STATE UNIVERSITY
Willimantic, Connecticut

Eastern Connecticut State University is a coed, public, comprehensive unit of Connecticut State University System, founded in 1889, offering degrees at the associate, bachelor's, and master's levels. It has a 179-acre campus in Willimantic.

Academic Information The faculty has 446 members (45% full-time), 54% with terminal degrees. The undergraduate student-faculty ratio is 16:1. The library holds 239,218 titles and 1,729 serial subscriptions. Special programs include academic remediation, services for learning-disabled students, an honors program, cooperative (work-study) education, study abroad, advanced placement credit, Freshman Honors College, double majors, independent study, distance learning, self-designed majors, summer session for credit, part-time degree programs (daytime, evenings, weekends, summer), adult/continuing education programs, internships, and arrangement for off-campus study with University of Connecticut, Southern Connecticut State University, Central Connecticut State University, Western Connecticut State University. The most frequently chosen baccalaureate fields are business/marketing, psychology, social sciences.

Student Body Statistics The student body totals 5,427, of whom 5,092 are undergraduates (1,017 freshmen). 55 percent are women and 45 percent are men. Students come from 26 states and territories and 34 other countries. 93 percent are from Connecticut. 1 percent are international students.

Expenses for 2008–09 *Application fee:* $50. *State resident tuition:* $3514 full-time, $336 per credit part-time. *Nonresident tuition:* $11,373 full-time, $336 per credit part-time. *Mandatory fees:* $4022 full-time. Full-time tuition and fees vary according to course load, degree level, and reciprocity agreements. Part-time tuition varies according to course load and degree level. *College room and board:* $8855. *College room only:* $4955. Room and board charges vary according to board plan and housing facility.

Financial Aid Forms of aid include need-based and non-need-based scholarships and part-time jobs. The priority application deadline for financial aid is March 15.

Freshman Admission Eastern Connecticut State University requires a high school transcript, SAT or ACT scores, and TOEFL scores for international students. An essay and rank in upper 50% of high school class are recommended. An interview is required for some. The application deadline for regular admission is rolling.

Transfer Admission The application deadline for admission is rolling.

Entrance Difficulty Eastern Connecticut State University assesses its entrance difficulty level as moderately difficult; very difficult for honors program. For the fall 2008 freshman class, 63 percent of the applicants were accepted.

For Further Information Contact Ms. Kimberly M. Crone, Director of Admissions and Enrollment Management, Eastern Connecticut State University, 83 Windham Street, Willimantic, CT 06226. *Phone:* 860-465-5286 or 877-353-3278 (toll-free). *Fax:* 860-465-5544. *E-mail:* admissions@easternct.edu. *Web site:* http://www.easternct.edu/.

FAIRFIELD UNIVERSITY
Fairfield, Connecticut

Fairfield University is a coed, private, Roman Catholic (Jesuit), comprehensive institution, founded in 1942, offering degrees at the associate, bachelor's, and master's levels and post-master's certificates. It has a 200-acre campus in Fairfield near New York City.

Academic Information The faculty has 510 members (49% full-time), 67% with terminal degrees. The undergraduate student-faculty ratio is 12:1. The library holds 351,091 titles, 31,424 serial subscriptions, and 17,983 audiovisual materials. Special programs include services for learning-disabled students, an honors program, study abroad, advanced placement credit, double majors, independent study, distance learning, self-designed majors, summer session for credit, part-time degree programs (daytime, evenings), adult/continuing education programs, and internships. The most frequently chosen baccalaureate fields are business/marketing, communications/journalism, social sciences.

Student Body Statistics The student body totals 5,128, of whom 4,084 are undergraduates (899 freshmen). 58 percent are women and 42 percent are men. Students come from 33 states and territories and 24 other countries. 24 percent are from Connecticut.

Expenses for 2008–09 *Application fee:* $60. *One-time mandatory fee:* $60. *Comprehensive fee:* $46,925 includes full-time tuition ($35,510), mandatory fees ($565), and college room and board ($10,850). *College room only:* $6480. Room and board charges vary according to board plan and housing facility. *Part-time tuition:* $475 per credit hour. *Part-time mandatory fees:* $25 per term. Part-time tuition and fees vary according to course load.

Financial Aid Forms of aid include need-based and non-need-based scholarships, athletic grants, and part-time jobs. The average aided 2008–09 undergraduate received an aid package worth an estimated $23,965. The application deadline for financial aid is February 15.

Freshman Admission Fairfield University requires an essay, a high school transcript, 1 recommendation, rank in upper 20% of high school class, SAT or ACT scores, and TOEFL scores for international students. An interview is recommended. The application deadline for regular admission is January 15 and for early action it is November 15.

Transfer Admission The application deadline for admission is May 1.

Entrance Difficulty Fairfield University assesses its entrance difficulty level as moderately difficult. For the fall 2008 freshman class, 59 percent of the applicants were accepted.

For Further Information Contact Ms. Karen Pellegrino, Director of Admission, Fairfield University, 1073 North Benson Road, Fairfield, CT 06824-5195. *Phone:* 203-254-4100. *Fax:* 203-254-4199. *E-mail:* admis@ mail.fairfield.edu. *Web site:* http://www.fairfield.edu/.

HOLY APOSTLES COLLEGE AND SEMINARY

Cromwell, Connecticut

Holy Apostles College and Seminary is a coed, primarily men's, private, Roman Catholic, comprehensive institution, founded in 1956, offering degrees at the associate, bachelor's, master's, and first professional levels and post-master's, first professional, and postbachelor's certificates. It has a 17-acre campus in Cromwell near Hartford, New Haven.

Academic Information The faculty has 26 members (38% full-time), 88% with terminal degrees. The undergraduate student-faculty ratio is 2:1. The library holds 85,000 titles, 250 serial subscriptions, and 400 audiovisual materials. Special programs include academic remediation, services for learning-disabled students, ESL programs, independent study, distance learning, summer session for credit, part-time degree programs (daytime, evenings, summer), external degree programs, and adult/continuing education programs. The most frequently chosen baccalaureate fields are philosophy and religious studies, social sciences.

Student Body Statistics The student body totals 276, of whom 41 are undergraduates (2 freshmen). 32 percent are women and 68 percent are men. Students come from 7 states and territories and 7 other countries. 65 percent are from Connecticut. 20.5 percent are international students.

Expenses for 2008–09 *Application fee:* $25. *Tuition:* $8640 full-time, $360 per credit part-time.

Financial Aid Forms of aid include need-based and non-need-based scholarships. The application deadline for financial aid is continuous.

Freshman Admission Holy Apostles College and Seminary requires a high school transcript and SAT scores. An interview is required for some. The application deadline for regular admission is rolling and for nonresidents it is rolling.

Transfer Admission The application deadline for admission is rolling.

Entrance Difficulty Holy Apostles College and Seminary has an open admission policy.

For Further Information Contact Very Rev. Douglas Mosey, CSB, Director of Admissions, Holy Apostles College and Seminary, 33 Prospect Hill Road, Cromwell, CT 06416-2005. *Phone:* 860-632-3010 or 800-330-7272 (toll-free). *Fax:* 860-632-3075. *E-mail:* admissions@holyapostles.edu. *Web site:* http://www.holyapostles.edu/.

INTERNATIONAL COLLEGE OF HOSPITALITY MANAGEMENT

Suffield, Connecticut

http://www.ichm.edu/

LYME ACADEMY COLLEGE OF FINE ARTS

Old Lyme, Connecticut

Lyme Academy College of Fine Arts is a coed, private, four-year college, founded in 1976, offering degrees at the bachelor's level and postbachelor's certificates. It has a 3-acre campus in Old Lyme.

Academic Information The faculty has 21 members (38% full-time), 43% with terminal degrees. The student-faculty ratio is 8:1. The library holds 8,686 titles, 60 serial subscriptions, and 14,232 audiovisual materials. Special programs include advanced placement credit, summer session for credit, part-time degree programs (daytime, evenings, summer), adult/

continuing education programs, and arrangement for off-campus study. The most frequently chosen baccalaureate field is visual and performing arts.

Student Body Statistics The student body is made up of 128 undergraduates (11 freshmen). 60 percent are women and 40 percent are men. Students come from 23 states and territories and 2 other countries. 80 percent are from Connecticut.

Expenses for 2009–10 *Application fee:* $55. *Tuition:* $21,792 full-time, $908 per credit part-time. *Mandatory fees:* $1300 full-time, $50 per term part-time.

Financial Aid Forms of aid include need-based and non-need-based scholarships and part-time jobs. The application deadline for financial aid is continuous.

Freshman Admission Lyme Academy College of Fine Arts requires an essay, a high school transcript, 2 recommendations, a portfolio, and SAT or ACT scores. A minimum 2.0 high school GPA and an interview are recommended. An interview is required for some. The application deadline for regular admission is rolling.

Transfer Admission The application deadline for admission is rolling.

Entrance Difficulty Lyme Academy College of Fine Arts assesses its entrance difficulty level as moderately difficult. For the fall 2008 freshman class, 97 percent of the applicants were accepted.

For Further Information Contact Cara Sheridan, Admissions Associate, Lyme Academy College of Fine Arts, 84 Lyme Street, Old Lyme, CT 06371. *Phone:* 860-434-3571 Ext. 119. *Fax:* 860-434-8725. *E-mail:* csheridan@lymeacademy.edu. *Web site:* http://www.lymeacademy.edu/.

MITCHELL COLLEGE

New London, Connecticut

SPONSOR

Mitchell College is a coed, private, four-year college, founded in 1938, offering degrees at the associate and bachelor's levels. It has a 67-acre campus in New London near Hartford and Providence.

Academic Information The faculty has 97 members (35% full-time), 30% with terminal degrees. The student-faculty ratio is 12:1. The library holds 88,500 titles, 106 serial subscriptions, and 1,300 audiovisual materials. Special programs include services for learning-disabled students, cooperative (work-study) education, study abroad, advanced placement credit, ESL programs, double majors, self-designed majors, summer session for credit, part-time degree programs (daytime, summer), and internships. The most frequently chosen baccalaureate fields are liberal arts/general studies, business/marketing, security and protective services.

Student Body Statistics The student body is made up of 936 undergraduates (307 freshmen). 51 percent are women and 49 percent are men. Students come from 25 states and territories and 5 other countries. 0.5 percent are international students.

Expenses for 2009–10 *Application fee:* $30. *Comprehensive fee:* $37,175 includes full-time tuition ($24,035), mandatory fees ($1592), and college room and board ($11,548). *College room only:* $6005. *Part-time tuition:* $275 per credit hour. *Part-time mandatory fees:* $35 per term.

Financial Aid Forms of aid include need-based scholarships, athletic grants, and part-time jobs. The priority application deadline for financial aid is April 1.

Freshman Admission Mitchell College requires an essay, a high school transcript, a minimum 2.0 high school GPA, an interview, and TOEFL scores for international students. The application deadline for regular admission is rolling and for early decision it is November 15.

Transfer Admission The application deadline for admission is rolling.

Entrance Difficulty Mitchell College assesses its entrance difficulty level as moderately difficult.

SPECIAL MESSAGE TO STUDENTS

Social Life Nearly 80 percent of Mitchell College's students live on the campus, making social life an important part of the college experience. Residence hall and campuswide events include dances, movies,

Mitchell College (continued)

recreational and cultural outings to Boston and New York, varsity and intramural sports, student clubs and organizations, and professional entertainers.

Academic Highlights Mitchell College offers a wide array of four- and two-year degrees to accommodate all students' interests. Mitchell College's innovative PG year program, Thames Academy, continues to grow and strengthen. Launched in 2006, Thames Academy is a postgraduate/precollege program offering a year of academic preparation for students between the end of their secondary school/ high school education and the start of their college studies. As one of the country's foremost colleges in promoting student academic success, Mitchell provides a challenging education in a caring and supportive environment, focusing on student asset development, rather than deficit management. Mitchell is particularly known for working with students who have yet to realize their full potential and students who have a diagnosed and documented learning disability and/or ADHD.

Interviews and Campus Visits Student interviews are a requirement of the application process. Open Houses are conducted in October, November, January, February, March, April, and throughout the summer. To schedule a campus visit, prospective students should call the Admission Office, located in Henry Hall, at 800-443-2811 (toll-free), Monday through Friday, 8:30 to 5.

For Further Information Write to Kevin Mayne, Vice President for Enrollment Management and Marketing, Mitchell College, 437 Pequot Avenue, New London, CT 06320. *E-mail:* admissions@mitchell.edu. *Web site:* http://www.mitchell.edu.

See page 102 for the Close-Up.

PAIER COLLEGE OF ART, INC.
Hamden, Connecticut

Paier College of Art, Inc. is a coed, proprietary, four-year college, founded in 1946, offering degrees at the associate and bachelor's levels. It has a 3-acre campus in Hamden near New York City.

Expenses for 2008–09 *Application fee:* $25. *Tuition:* $12,000 full-time, $380 per credit part-time. *Mandatory fees:* $385 full-time, $125 per term part-time.

For Further Information Contact Ms. Lynn Pascale, Secretary to Admissions, Paier College of Art, Inc., 20 Gorham Avenue, Hamden, CT 06514-3902. *Phone:* 203-287-3031. *Fax:* 203-287-3021. *E-mail:* paier.admission@snet.net. *Web site:* http://www.paiercollegeofart.edu/.

POST UNIVERSITY
Waterbury, Connecticut

http://www.post.edu/

SPECIAL MESSAGE TO STUDENTS

Social Life Post University offers small classes and residential living, and a highly engaged student body, faculty, and staff add to the overall quality of the social dynamic of college life. With an average of three campus programs a week, Post University students find plenty to do. Lectures, films, bands, trips, and annual traditions, such as Homecoming, Winterfest, midnight breakfast, Mr. and Ms. Post Competition, and Senior Week keep students entertained. All of the programs are selected and planned by students, so if students want to work with headlining comedians or up-and-coming bands, they can begin arranging it their freshman year. Post's Campus Activities Team (CAT) has won regional awards for its school spirit, designs, and creative programming. Individual students have won national awards for their leadership in guiding these successful activities. At Post, there are more than twenty-five clubs and organizations available, from community

service organizations to clubs focused on majors, and starting a new one is easy. An active Student Government Association provides the student body with resources and advocacy needed to address student concerns. NCAA Division II athletics include men's baseball, basketball, cross-country, golf, soccer, and tennis; women's basketball, soccer, softball, tennis, and volleyball; and coed equestrian.

Academic Highlights The student-faculty ratio of 15:1 permits faculty members to interact with students through small classes and accessibility outside the classroom. The Honors Program challenges academically talented students. The Leever Learning Center helps students improve their basic academic skills. More than 90 percent of the full-time instructional faculty members have doctorates or the highest degree offered in their respective disciplines. Other programs include study abroad, double majors and minors, ACE Scholars (bridge program), and Living and Learning.

Interviews and Campus Visits Visiting Post is an ideal way for each student to form a personal impression of the school and to learn more about the University's offerings. It also gives Post admissions counselors the opportunity to learn more about the student's interests and experiences. Individual visits are recommended but not required. New York City is 90 minutes away and easily accessible by train, bus, or car. Boston is 2 hours from the campus. With a population of 150,000, Waterbury has a fast-moving business economy. It is home to national and international corporations, successful businesses, government agencies, and medical centers. Students benefit from access to these metropolitan areas while studying on a suburban, 58-acre hilltop campus. Student-guided campus tours are available and students are encouraged to call the Office of Admissions at 800-345-2562 (toll-free) to schedule a visit.

For Further Information Write to Jay E. Murray, Director of Admissions, Office of Admissions, Post University, 800 Country Club Road, Waterbury, CT 06723-2540. *E-mail:* admissions@post.edu. *Web site:* http://www.post.edu.

See page 106 for the Close-Up.

QUINNIPIAC UNIVERSITY
Hamden, Connecticut

Quinnipiac University is a coed, private, comprehensive institution, founded in 1929, offering degrees at the bachelor's, master's, doctoral, and first professional levels and postbachelor's certificates. It has a 500-acre campus in Hamden near Hartford.

Academic Information The faculty has 845 members (36% full-time), 66% with terminal degrees. The undergraduate student-faculty ratio is 15:1. The library holds 285,000 titles and 5,500 serial subscriptions. Special programs include services for learning-disabled students, an honors program, study abroad, advanced placement credit, double majors, independent study, distance learning, self-designed majors, summer session for credit, part-time degree programs (daytime, evenings, summer), adult/continuing education programs, and internships. The most frequently chosen baccalaureate fields are business/marketing, communications/journalism, health professions and related sciences.

Student Body Statistics The student body totals 7,434, of whom 5,891 are undergraduates (1,484 freshmen). 62 percent are women and 38 percent are men. Students come from 28 states and territories and 18 other countries. 30 percent are from Connecticut. 1.3 percent are international students.

Expenses for 2009–10 *Application fee:* $45. *Comprehensive fee:* $44,780 includes full-time tuition ($31,100), mandatory fees ($1300), and college room and board ($12,380). *Part-time tuition:* $750 per credit. *Part-time mandatory fees:* $30 per credit.

Financial Aid Forms of aid include need-based and non-need-based scholarships, athletic grants, and part-time jobs. The average aided 2008–09 undergraduate received an aid package worth an estimated $18,306. The priority application deadline for financial aid is March 1.

Freshman Admission Quinnipiac University requires an essay, a high school transcript, 1 recommendation, SAT or ACT scores, and TOEFL scores for international students. A minimum 3.0 high school GPA and an interview are recommended. A minimum 3.0 high school GPA is required for some. The application deadline for regular admission is February 1, for nonresidents it is February 1, and for early action it is November 1. **Transfer Admission** The application deadline for admission is April 1. **Entrance Difficulty** Quinnipiac University assesses its entrance difficulty level as moderately difficult; very difficult for physical therapy, nursing, physician assistant. For the fall 2008 freshman class, 45 percent of the applicants were accepted.

SPECIAL MESSAGE TO STUDENTS

Social Life Quinnipiac has more than seventy-five special-interest and multicultural clubs for student participation. Student government, the newspaper, the Emerging Leaders program, the yearbook, and the student-run TV and radio station are popular, as is a large intramural sports program. About 8 percent of the students are active in fraternities and sororities. Quinnipiac is primarily residential (95 percent of freshmen and 70 percent of all students live on campus) and has no religious affiliation, although the campus benefits from the services of a full-time priest and rabbi, a Hillel House as well as Catholic services.

Academic Highlights Academic life focuses on the Bernhard Library, with automated library systems and more than 150 personal computer workstations. The Financial Technology Center at Quinnipiac University's School of Business is a high-tech, simulated trading floor that provides students an opportunity to access real-time financial data, conduct interactive trading simulations, and develop financial models, preparing them for careers in finance. The School of Business Center contains team study rooms, satellite downlinks for national and international programming, and case-study seminar rooms. The Ed McMahon Mass Communications Center houses a state-of-the-art, fully digital, high-definition television production facility; audio production and video-editing suites; desktop-publishing studios; and a news technology center. All incoming students must purchase a University-recommended laptop, which is supported by a campus wireless network for classroom and residence hall use.

Interviews and Campus Visits Families are encouraged to take time to visit the campus for an open house, group information session, interview, or campus tour. There is an opportunity for discussion with faculty and staff members, including coaches, at the three fall Open House programs for prospective freshmen and transfer students and one spring Open House designed especially for high school juniors and sophomores. The Admissions Office invites accepted students to attend one of two Admitted Student Day programs. Quinnipiac guarantees housing for all full-time undergraduates. The $3-million campus center serves all students, while the gymnasium, with its 28,000-square-foot, $14-million addition and surrounding fields, supplies all the essentials for Division I athletics, intramurals, and fitness. The TD Banknorth Sports Center, with twin 3,500-seat arenas for basketball and ice hockey, opened January 2007 on the nearby 250-acre York Hill campus. For information about appointments and campus visits, prospective students should visit http://www.quinnipiac.edu/visit or call the Admissions Office at 203-582-8600 or 800-462-1944 (toll-free), Monday through Friday, 8 to 5.

For Further Information Write to Mrs. Joan Isaac Mohr, Vice President and Dean of Admissions, Quinnipiac University, 275 Mt. Carmel Avenue, Hamden, CT 06518. *E-mail:* admissions@quinnipiac.edu. *Web site:* http://www.quinnipiac.edu.

See page 108 for the Close-Up.

SACRED HEART UNIVERSITY
Fairfield, Connecticut

Sacred Heart University is a coed, private, Roman Catholic, comprehensive institution, founded in 1963, offering degrees at the associate, bachelor's, master's, and doctoral levels and post-master's and postbachelor's certificates (also offers part-time program with significant enrollment not reflected in profile). It has a 65-acre campus in Fairfield near New York City.

Academic Information The faculty has 565 members (38% full-time), 46% with terminal degrees. The undergraduate student-faculty ratio is 12:1. The library holds 147,098 titles, 1,698 serial subscriptions, and 2,078 audiovisual materials. Special programs include academic remediation, services for learning-disabled students, an honors program, cooperative (work-study) education, study abroad, advanced placement credit, accelerated degree programs, ESL programs, double majors, independent study, distance learning, self-designed majors, summer session for credit, part-time degree programs (daytime, evenings, weekends, summer), adult/continuing education programs, internships, and arrangement for off-campus study. The most frequently chosen baccalaureate fields are business/marketing, health professions and related sciences, psychology.

Student Body Statistics The student body totals 5,958, of whom 4,274 are undergraduates (980 freshmen). 61 percent are women and 39 percent are men. Students come from 32 states and territories and 48 other countries. 32 percent are from Connecticut. 1.1 percent are international students.

Expenses for 2008–09 *Application fee:* $50. *Comprehensive fee:* $40,320 includes full-time tuition ($28,790), mandatory fees ($200), and college room and board ($11,330). *College room only:* $8582. Full-time tuition and fees vary according to program. Room and board charges vary according to board plan and housing facility. *Part-time tuition:* $425 per credit. *Part-time mandatory fees:* $76 per term. Part-time tuition and fees vary according to program.

Financial Aid Forms of aid include need-based and non-need-based scholarships, athletic grants, and part-time jobs. The average aided 2008–09 undergraduate received an aid package worth an estimated $16,757. The priority application deadline for financial aid is February 15.

Freshman Admission Sacred Heart University requires an essay, a high school transcript, 1 recommendation, SAT or ACT scores, and TOEFL scores for international students. A minimum 3.2 high school GPA is recommended. An interview is required for some. The application deadline for early decision it is December 1.

Entrance Difficulty Sacred Heart University assesses its entrance difficulty level as moderately difficult; very difficult for honors program. For the fall 2008 freshman class, 65 percent of the applicants were accepted.

For Further Information Contact Ms. Karen N. Guastelle, Dean of Undergraduate Admissions, Sacred Heart University, 5151 Park Avenue, Fairfield, CT 06825-1000. *Phone:* 203-371-7880. *Fax:* 203-365-7607. *E-mail:* enroll@sacredheart.edu. *Web site:* http://www.sacredheart.edu/.

SAINT JOSEPH COLLEGE
West Hartford, Connecticut

SPONSOR

Saint Joseph College is an undergraduate: women only; graduate: coed, private, Roman Catholic, comprehensive institution, founded in 1932, offering degrees at the bachelor's and master's levels and postbachelor's certificates. It has an 84-acre campus in West Hartford near Hartford.

Academic Information The faculty has 246 members (31% full-time). The undergraduate student-faculty ratio is 9:1. Special programs include services for learning-disabled students, an honors program, study abroad, advanced placement credit, accelerated degree programs, double majors, independent study, distance learning, self-designed majors, summer session for credit, part-time degree programs (daytime, evenings, weekends, summer), adult/continuing education programs, internships, and arrangement for off-campus study with members of the Hartford Consortium for Higher Education, Wesleyan

Saint Joseph College (continued)

University. The most frequently chosen baccalaureate fields are health professions and related sciences, family and consumer sciences, psychology.
Student Body Statistics The student body totals 1,926, of whom 1,062 are undergraduates (226 freshmen). 98 percent are women and 2 percent are men. 93 percent are from Connecticut. 0.2 percent are international students.
Expenses for 2009–10 *Application fee:* $50. *Comprehensive fee:* $39,639 includes full-time tuition ($26,502), mandatory fees ($700), and college room and board ($12,437). *College room only:* $5671. *Part-time tuition:* $595 per credit. *Part-time mandatory fees:* $30 per credit.
Financial Aid Forms of aid include need-based scholarships and part-time jobs. The application deadline for financial aid is continuous.
Freshman Admission Saint Joseph College requires a high school transcript, SAT or ACT scores, and TOEFL scores for international students. An essay, 1 recommendation, an interview, and SAT scores are recommended. The application deadline for regular admission is rolling.
Transfer Admission The application deadline for admission is rolling.
Entrance Difficulty For the fall 2008 freshman class, 82 percent of the applicants were accepted.

SPECIAL MESSAGE TO STUDENTS

Social Life Saint Joseph College (SJC) is a diverse, tightly knit community where faculty members and students know one another by name. Service projects, leadership opportunities, campus ministry, and a wide variety of fun programming activities offer students a chance to become an important part of their campus. On-campus activities, including concerts, performances, multicultural events, dances, service projects, and NCAA Division III sports, draw guests from nearby Trinity College, the University of Hartford, and the Coast Guard Academy. Students also attend events on those campuses and in Hartford's arts and entertainment district. Free shuttle transportation to and from West Hartford Center and the West Farms Mall offers students the opportunity to enjoy time in the bustling local restaurants and shops. Bus trips to nearby Boston, New York City, and other local attractions are very popular. In addition to the undergraduate women's college, there are adult bachelor's degree programs, a graduate school, and continuing studies offerings, all of which are open to both women and men.

Academic Highlights More than thirty majors offer diverse internships and field placements. Success springs from the combination of SJC's liberal arts and sciences curriculum and active mentorship by faculty members, advisers, and alumnae. These opportunities provide students with necessary critical thinking and communication skills that help them to fulfill their potential for professional success. Dual degree programs, study-abroad opportunities, an honors program, and cross-registration with area colleges are available. The Center for Academic Excellence helps students achieve their highest level of education. The College's writing portfolio program has received international acclaim. Students work with faculty members on scholarly research and serve with them on major committees. Qualified students may pursue double and even triple majors.

Interviews and Campus Visits A meeting with an admissions counselor is strongly recommended and easily arranged. Visiting campus is an important part of becoming better acquainted with SJC, and a variety of exciting events are offered each semester for prospective students and their families. While visiting, guests can take student-conducted tours of the 84-acre campus, attend classes, meet with faculty members and academic advisers, and/or learn about financial aid. Guests are encouraged to explore SJC's facilities: The School for Young Children and The Gengras Center; The O'Connell Athletic Center; science labs, including a Freshwater Institute; and The Carol Autorino Center for the Arts and Humanities. For more information, prospective students should call the Office of Admissions at 860-231-5216 or visit the Web site at http://admissions.sjc.edu.

For Further Information Write to Nancy D. Wunderly, Director of Admissions, Saint Joseph College, 1678 Asylum Avenue, West Hartford, CT 06117. *E-mail:* admissions@sjc.edu. *Web site:* http://admissions.sjc.edu.

ST. VINCENT'S COLLEGE
Bridgeport, Connecticut

http://www.stvincentscollege.edu/

SOUTHERN CONNECTICUT STATE UNIVERSITY
New Haven, Connecticut

Southern Connecticut State University is a coed, public, comprehensive unit of Connecticut State University System, founded in 1893, offering degrees at the bachelor's, master's, and doctoral levels and post-master's and postbachelor's certificates. It has a 168-acre campus in New Haven near New York City.

Academic Information The faculty has 1,073 members (42% full-time). The undergraduate student-faculty ratio is 15:1. The library holds 495,660 titles and 3,549 serial subscriptions. Special programs include academic remediation, services for learning-disabled students, an honors program, cooperative (work-study) education, study abroad, advanced placement credit, accelerated degree programs, Freshman Honors College, double majors, independent study, distance learning, self-designed majors, summer session for credit, part-time degree programs (daytime, evenings, weekends, summer), adult/continuing education programs, internships, and arrangement for off-campus study with New England Board of Higher Education. The most frequently chosen baccalaureate fields are business/marketing, liberal arts/general studies, psychology.
Student Body Statistics The student body totals 11,769, of whom 8,496 are undergraduates (1,296 freshmen). 63 percent are women and 37 percent are men. Students come from 32 states and territories and 27 other countries. 94 percent are from Connecticut. 0.7 percent are international students.
Expenses for 2008–09 *Application fee:* $50. *State resident tuition:* $3514 full-time, $357 per credit part-time. *Nonresident tuition:* $11,373 full-time, $357 per credit part-time. *Mandatory fees:* $3665 full-time, $55 per term part-time. *College room and board:* $8966. *College room only:* $4976. Room and board charges vary according to board plan and housing facility.
Financial Aid Forms of aid include need-based and non-need-based scholarships, athletic grants, and part-time jobs. The average aided 2008–09 undergraduate received an aid package worth an estimated $8154. The application deadline for financial aid is March 9.
Freshman Admission Southern Connecticut State University requires an essay, a high school transcript, SAT or ACT scores, and TOEFL scores for international students. The application deadline for regular admission is April 1.
Transfer Admission The application deadline for admission is July 1.
Entrance Difficulty Southern Connecticut State University assesses its entrance difficulty level as moderately difficult. For the fall 2008 freshman class, 63 percent of the applicants were accepted.
For Further Information Contact Ms. Paula Kennedy, Associate Director of Admissions, Southern Connecticut State University, Admissions House, 131 Farnham Avenue, New Haven, CT 06515-1202. *Phone:* 203-392-5651. *Fax:* 203-392-5727. *E-mail:* williamsj11@southernct.edu. *Web site:* http://www.southernct.edu/.

SWISS HOSPITALITY INSTITUTE
CÉSAR RITZ

See International College of Hospitality Management.

TEIKYO POST UNIVERSITY

See Post University.

TRINITY COLLEGE

Hartford, Connecticut

Trinity College is a coed, private, comprehensive institution, founded in 1823, offering degrees at the bachelor's and master's levels. It has a 100-acre campus in Hartford.

Academic Information The faculty has 255 members (72% full-time), 86% with terminal degrees. The undergraduate student-faculty ratio is 10:1. The library holds 904,988 titles, 1,407 serial subscriptions, and 101,249 audiovisual materials. Special programs include an honors program, study abroad, advanced placement credit, accelerated degree programs, double majors, independent study, self-designed majors, summer session for credit, adult/continuing education programs, internships, and arrangement for off-campus study with members of the Twelve College Exchange Program, Hartford Consortium for Higher Education. The most frequently chosen baccalaureate fields are area and ethnic studies, history, social sciences.

Student Body Statistics The student body totals 2,566, of whom 2,388 are undergraduates (589 freshmen). 51 percent are women and 49 percent are men. Students come from 43 states and territories and 41 other countries. 17 percent are from Connecticut. 4.2 percent are international students.

Expenses for 2009–10 *Application fee:* $60. *One-time mandatory fee:* $25. *Comprehensive fee:* $48,624 includes full-time tuition ($36,864), mandatory fees ($1860), and college room and board ($9900). *College room only:* $6400. *Part-time tuition:* $4096 per course.

Financial Aid Forms of aid include need-based and non-need-based scholarships and part-time jobs. The average aided 2008–09 undergraduate received an aid package worth an estimated $35,002. The application deadline for financial aid is March 1 with a priority deadline of February 1.

Freshman Admission Trinity College requires an essay, a high school transcript, and 3 recommendations. An interview and TOEFL scores for international students are recommended. SAT or ACT scores and SAT Subject Test scores are required for some. The application deadline for regular admission is January 1, for early decision plan 1 it is November 15, and for early decision plan 2 it is January 1.

Transfer Admission The application deadline for admission is April 1.

Entrance Difficulty Trinity College assesses its entrance difficulty level as most difficult. For the fall 2008 freshman class, 42 percent of the applicants were accepted.

For Further Information Contact Mr. Larry Dow, Dean of Admissions and Financial Aid, Trinity College, 300 Summit Street, Hartford, CT 06106-3100. *Phone:* 860-297-2180. *Fax:* 860-297-2287. *E-mail:* admissions. office@trincoll.edu. *Web site:* http://www.trincoll.edu/.

See page 116 for the Close-Up.

UNITED STATES COAST GUARD ACADEMY

New London, Connecticut

United States Coast Guard Academy is a coed, public, four-year college, founded in 1876, offering degrees at the bachelor's level. It has a 110-acre campus in New London near Providence and Hartford.

Academic Information The faculty has 124 members (92% full-time), 53% with terminal degrees. The student-faculty ratio is 8:1. The library holds 155,000 titles and 514 serial subscriptions. Special programs include academic remediation, an honors program, double majors, independent study, summer session for credit, internships, and arrangement for off-campus study with Connecticut College. The most frequently chosen baccalaureate fields are engineering, business/marketing, social sciences.

Student Body Statistics The student body is made up of 973 undergraduates (271 freshmen). 27 percent are women and 73 percent are men. Students come from 51 states and territories and 10 other countries. 6 percent are from Connecticut. 1.2 percent are international students.

Expenses for 2008–09 *Application fee:* $0. *One-time mandatory fee:* $3000. *Comprehensive fee:* $0. Tuition, room and board, and medical and dental care are provided by the U.S. government. Each cadet receives a salary from which to pay for uniforms, supplies, and personal expenses. Entering freshmen are required to deposit $3000 to defray the initial cost of computer, uniforms, books and other items.

Freshman Admission United States Coast Guard Academy requires an essay, a high school transcript, 3 recommendations, medical exam, physical fitness exam, SAT or ACT scores, and TOEFL scores for international students. An interview is recommended. The application deadline for regular admission is February 1 and for early action it is November 1.

Entrance Difficulty United States Coast Guard Academy assesses its entrance difficulty level as very difficult. For the fall 2008 freshman class, 22 percent of the applicants were accepted.

For Further Information Contact Capt. Susan Bibeau, Director of Admissions, United States Coast Guard Academy, 31 Mohegan Avenue, New London, CT 06320-4195. *Phone:* 860-444-8500 or 800-883-8724 (toll-free). *Fax:* 860-701-6700. *E-mail:* admissions@uscga.edu. *Web site:* http://www.uscga.edu/.

UNIVERSITY OF BRIDGEPORT

Bridgeport, Connecticut

University of Bridgeport is a coed, private, comprehensive institution, founded in 1927, offering degrees at the associate, bachelor's, master's, doctoral, and first professional levels and post-master's certificates. It has an 86-acre campus in Bridgeport near New York City.

Academic Information The faculty has 552 members (21% full-time). The undergraduate student-faculty ratio is 12:1. The library holds 272,430 titles and 2,117 serial subscriptions. Special programs include academic remediation, services for learning-disabled students, an honors program, cooperative (work-study) education, advanced placement credit, accelerated degree programs, ESL programs, double majors, independent study, distance learning, self-designed majors, summer session for credit, part-time degree programs, adult/continuing education programs, internships, and arrangement for off-campus study with Fairfield University, Sacred Heart University. The most frequently chosen baccalaureate fields are business/marketing, health professions and related sciences, liberal arts/general studies.

Student Body Statistics The student body totals 5,323, of whom 2,028 are undergraduates (453 freshmen). 69 percent are women and 31 percent are men. Students come from 41 states and territories and 49 other countries. 67 percent are from Connecticut. 12.6 percent are international students.

Expenses for 2008–09 *Application fee:* $25. *Comprehensive fee:* $35,070 includes full-time tuition ($22,500), mandatory fees ($1970), and college room and board ($10,600). Full-time tuition and fees vary according to program. Room and board charges vary according to board plan and student level. *Part-time tuition:* $750 per term. *Part-time mandatory fees:* $75 per term. Part-time tuition and fees vary according to program.

Financial Aid Forms of aid include need-based and non-need-based scholarships, athletic grants, and part-time jobs. The average aided 2007–08 undergraduate received an aid package worth $20,803. The priority application deadline for financial aid is April 1.

Freshman Admission University of Bridgeport requires an essay, a high school transcript, a minimum 2.0 high school GPA, SAT or ACT scores, and TOEFL scores for international students. 1 recommendation and an interview are recommended. An interview, portfolio, audition, and SAT Subject Test scores are required for some. The application deadline for regular admission is rolling and for early action it is January 1.

Transfer Admission The application deadline for admission is rolling.

Entrance Difficulty University of Bridgeport assesses its entrance difficulty level as moderately difficult. For the fall 2008 freshman class, 62 percent of the applicants were accepted.

For Further Information Contact Ms. Barbara Maryak, Associate Vice President Admissions, University of Bridgeport, 126 Park Avenue, Bridgeport, CT 06604. *Phone:* 203-576-4552, 800-EXCEL-UB (toll-free in-state), or 800-243-9496 (toll-free out-of-state). *Fax:* 203-576-4941. *E-mail:* admit@bridgeport.edu. *Web site:* http://www.bridgeport.edu/.

UNIVERSITY OF CONNECTICUT

Storrs, Connecticut

University of Connecticut is a coed, public university, founded in 1881, offering degrees at the associate, bachelor's, master's, doctoral, and first professional levels and post-master's and postbachelor's certificates. It has a 4,104-acre campus in Storrs.

Academic Information The faculty has 1,360 members (76% full-time), 76% with terminal degrees. The undergraduate student-faculty ratio is 17:1. The library holds 3 million titles, 17,378 serial subscriptions, and 61,417 audiovisual materials. Special programs include services for learning-disabled students, an honors program, cooperative (work-study) education, study abroad, advanced placement credit, accelerated degree programs, ESL programs, double majors, independent study, distance learning, self-designed majors, summer session for credit, part-time degree programs (daytime, evenings, summer), adult/continuing education programs, internships, and arrangement for off-campus study with other public institutions in Connecticut. The most frequently chosen baccalaureate fields are business/marketing, health professions and related sciences, social sciences.

Student Body Statistics The student body totals 24,273, of whom 16,765 are undergraduates (3,604 freshmen). 50 percent are women and 50 percent are men. Students come from 47 states and territories and 62 other countries. 77 percent are from Connecticut. 1.1 percent are international students.

Expenses for 2008–09 *Application fee:* $70. *State resident tuition:* $7200 full-time, $300 per credit part-time. *Nonresident tuition:* $21,912 full-time, $913 per credit part-time. *Mandatory fees:* $2138 full-time. Part-time tuition varies according to course load. *College room and board:* $9300. *College room only:* $5090. Room and board charges vary according to board plan and housing facility.

Financial Aid Forms of aid include need-based and non-need-based scholarships, athletic grants, and part-time jobs. The average aided 2008–09 undergraduate received an aid package worth an estimated $11,048. The priority application deadline for financial aid is March 1.

Freshman Admission University of Connecticut requires an essay, a high school transcript, SAT or ACT scores, and TOEFL scores for international students. 1 recommendation is recommended. The application deadline for regular admission is February 1 and for early action it is December 1.

Transfer Admission The application deadline for admission is April 1.

Entrance Difficulty University of Connecticut assesses its entrance difficulty level as moderately difficult; very difficult for education, engineering, pharmacy, physical therapy. For the fall 2008 freshman class, 54 percent of the applicants were accepted.

For Further Information Contact Mr. Brian Usher, Associate Director of Admissions, University of Connecticut, 2131 Hillside Road, U-88, Storrs, CT 06269. *Phone:* 860-486-3137. *Fax:* 860-486-1476. *E-mail:* beahusky@uconnvm.uconn.edu. *Web site:* http://www.uconn.edu/.

UNIVERSITY OF HARTFORD

West Hartford, Connecticut

University of Hartford is a coed, private, comprehensive institution, founded in 1877, offering degrees at the associate, bachelor's, master's, and doctoral levels and post-master's and postbachelor's certificates. It has a 320-acre campus in West Hartford near Hartford.

Academic Information The faculty has 928 members (36% full-time). The undergraduate student-faculty ratio is 14:1. The library holds 481,685 titles and 2,424 serial subscriptions. Special programs include academic remediation, services for learning-disabled students, an honors program, cooperative (work-study) education, study abroad, advanced placement credit, ESL programs, double majors, independent study, distance learning, self-designed majors, summer session for credit, part-time degree programs (daytime, evenings, summer), adult/continuing education programs, internships, and arrangement for off-campus study with members of the Hartford Consortium for Higher Education. The most frequently chosen baccalaureate fields are business/marketing, health professions and related sciences, visual and performing arts.

Student Body Statistics The student body totals 7,366, of whom 5,695 are undergraduates (1,469 freshmen). 52 percent are women and 48 percent are men. Students come from 49 states and territories and 47 other countries. 40 percent are from Connecticut. 3.5 percent are international students.

Expenses for 2009–10 *Application fee:* $35. *Comprehensive fee:* $40,308 includes full-time tuition ($27,750), mandatory fees ($1230), and college room and board ($11,328). *Part-time tuition:* $410 per credit.

Financial Aid Forms of aid include need-based and non-need-based scholarships, athletic grants, and part-time jobs. The average aided 2008–09 undergraduate received an aid package worth an estimated $17,441. The priority application deadline for financial aid is February 1.

Freshman Admission University of Hartford requires a high school transcript and SAT or ACT scores. An essay, 2 recommendations, and an interview are recommended. The application deadline for regular admission is rolling.

Transfer Admission The application deadline for admission is rolling.

Entrance Difficulty University of Hartford assesses its entrance difficulty level as moderately difficult. For the fall 2008 freshman class, 57 percent of the applicants were accepted.

For Further Information Contact Mr. Richard Zeiser, Dean of Admissions, University of Hartford, 200 Bloomfield Avenue, West Hartford, CT 06117. *Phone:* 860-768-4296 or 800-947-4303 (toll-free). *Fax:* 860-768-4961. *E-mail:* admissions@hartford.edu. *Web site:* http://www.hartford.edu/.

UNIVERSITY OF NEW HAVEN

West Haven, Connecticut

University of New Haven is a coed, private, comprehensive institution, founded in 1920, offering degrees at the associate, bachelor's, and master's levels and post-master's and postbachelor's certificates. It has a 78-acre campus in West Haven near Hartford, New Haven.

Academic Information The faculty has 503 members (36% full-time). The undergraduate student-faculty ratio is 15:1. Special programs include academic remediation, services for learning-disabled students, an honors program, cooperative (work-study) education, study abroad, advanced placement credit, accelerated degree programs, double majors, independent study, summer session for credit, part-time degree programs (daytime, evenings, weekends, summer), adult/continuing education programs, and internships. The most frequently chosen baccalaureate fields are business/marketing, security and protective services, visual and performing arts.

Student Body Statistics The student body totals 5,233, of whom 3,552 are undergraduates (1,148 freshmen). 50 percent are women and 50 percent are men. Students come from 39 states and territories and 27 other countries. 36 percent are from Connecticut. 2.2 percent are international students.

Expenses for 2009–10 *Application fee:* $75. *Comprehensive fee:* $41,886 includes full-time tuition ($28,250), mandatory fees ($1432), and college room and board ($12,204). *College room only:* $7600. *Part-time tuition:* $471 per credit hour. *Part-time mandatory fees:* $63 per credit hour.

Financial Aid Forms of aid include need-based scholarships, athletic grants, and part-time jobs. The average aided 2008–09 undergraduate received an aid package worth an estimated $17,762. The application deadline for financial aid is March 1.

Freshman Admission University of New Haven requires an essay, a high school transcript, 1 recommendation, SAT or ACT scores, and TOEFL scores for international students. An interview is recommended. The application deadline for regular admission is rolling.

Transfer Admission The application deadline for admission is rolling.

Entrance Difficulty University of New Haven assesses its entrance difficulty level as moderately difficult. For the fall 2008 freshman class, 68 percent of the applicants were accepted.

For Further Information Contact Mr. Kevin Phillips, Director of Undergraduate Admissions, University of New Haven, Bayer Hall, 300 Boston Post Road, West Haven, CT 06516. *Phone:* 203-932-7318 or 800-DIAL-UNH (toll-free). *Fax:* 203-931-6093. *E-mail:* adminfo@newhaven.edu. *Web site:* http://www.newhaven.edu/.

WESLEYAN UNIVERSITY

Middletown, Connecticut

Wesleyan University is a coed, private university, founded in 1831, offering degrees at the bachelor's, master's, and doctoral levels and post-master's certificates. It has a 240-acre campus in Middletown.

Academic Information The faculty has 356 members (92% full-time), 91% with terminal degrees. The undergraduate student-faculty ratio is 9:1. The library holds 2 million titles and 9,812 serial subscriptions. Special programs include services for learning-disabled students, an honors program, study abroad, advanced placement credit, double majors, independent study, self-designed majors, summer session for credit, adult/continuing education programs, and arrangement for off-campus study with members of the Twelve College Exchange Program, American University. The most frequently chosen baccalaureate fields are area and ethnic studies, English, social sciences.

Student Body Statistics The student body totals 3,149, of whom 2,772 are undergraduates (715 freshmen). 49 percent are women and 51 percent are men. Students come from 52 states and territories and 45 other countries. 8 percent are from Connecticut. 7 percent are international students.

Expenses for 2008–09 *Application fee:* $55. *One-time mandatory fee:* $300. *Comprehensive fee:* $49,270 includes full-time tuition ($38,364), mandatory fees ($270), and college room and board ($10,636). Room and board charges vary according to board plan and housing facility.

Financial Aid Forms of aid include need-based scholarships and part-time jobs. The average aided 2007–08 undergraduate received an aid package worth $32,002. The application deadline for financial aid is February 15.

Freshman Admission Wesleyan University requires an essay, a high school transcript, 2 recommendations, SAT and SAT Subject Test or ACT scores, and TOEFL scores for international students. An interview is recommended. An interview is required for some. The application deadline for regular admission is January 1, for early decision plan 1 it is November 15, and for early decision plan 2 it is January 1.

Transfer Admission The application deadline for admission is March 15.

Entrance Difficulty Wesleyan University assesses its entrance difficulty level as most difficult. For the fall 2008 freshman class, 27 percent of the applicants were accepted.

For Further Information Contact Ms. Nancy Meislahn, Dean of Admission and Financial Aid, Wesleyan University, Stewart M Reid House, 70 Wyllys Avenue, Middletown, CT 06459-0265. *Phone:* 860-685-3000. *Fax:* 860-685-3001. *E-mail:* admissions@wesleyan.edu. *Web site:* http://www.wesleyan.edu/.

WESTERN CONNECTICUT STATE UNIVERSITY

Danbury, Connecticut

Western Connecticut State University is a coed, public, comprehensive unit of Connecticut State University System, founded in 1903, offering degrees at the associate, bachelor's, master's, and doctoral levels and postbachelor's certificates. It has a 340-acre campus in Danbury near New York City.

Academic Information The faculty has 537 members (41% full-time). The undergraduate student-faculty ratio is 16:1. The library holds 216,284 titles and 1,010 serial subscriptions. Special programs include academic remediation, services for learning-disabled students, an honors program, cooperative (work-study) education, study abroad, advanced placement credit, accelerated degree programs, ESL programs, double majors, independent study, distance learning, self-designed majors, summer session for credit, part-time degree programs (daytime, evenings, weekends, summer), internships, and arrangement for off-campus study with other units of the Connecticut State University System. The most frequently chosen baccalaureate fields are business/marketing, education, security and protective services.

Student Body Statistics The student body totals 6,462, of whom 5,769 are undergraduates (944 freshmen). 54 percent are women and 46 percent are men. Students come from 21 states and territories and 10 other countries. 91 percent are from Connecticut. 0.3 percent are international students.

Expenses for 2008–09 *Application fee:* $50. *State resident tuition:* $3514 full-time, $319 per credit hour part-time. *Nonresident tuition:* $11,373 full-time, $319 per credit hour part-time. *Mandatory fees:* $3574 full-time. Full-time tuition and fees vary according to reciprocity agreements. *College room and board:* $9158. *College room only:* $5384. Room and board charges vary according to housing facility.

Financial Aid Forms of aid include need-based and non-need-based scholarships and part-time jobs. The average aided 2008–09 undergraduate received an aid package worth an estimated $10,946. The application deadline for financial aid is March 30 with a priority deadline of March 1.

Freshman Admission Western Connecticut State University requires a high school transcript, 2 recommendations, standardized test scores, SAT or ACT scores, and TOEFL scores for international students. An essay and an interview are required for some.

Entrance Difficulty Western Connecticut State University assesses its entrance difficulty level as moderately difficult; minimally difficult for educational achievement program. For the fall 2008 freshman class, 54 percent of the applicants were accepted.

SPECIAL MESSAGE TO STUDENTS

Social Life There are six on-campus residence halls at Western Connecticut State University (WestConn). Students run academic and social clubs and fraternal organizations; publish a newspaper, literary magazine, history journal, and yearbook; run a radio station; and administer their own campus government association. WestConn participates in NCAA Division III men's and women's sports and offers intramural sports, sports clubs, and a premier recreation center that includes a swimming pool, indoor track, and weight-lifting machines.

Academic Highlights Nationally respected, WestConn's faculty members and administrators are continually cited for scholarly achievement; 90 percent of full-time faculty members have doctoral, terminal, or first professional degrees. The student-faculty ratio is 15.4:1. The library holds 200,000 volumes and more than 400,000 bound periodicals, microforms, government documents, music scores, electronic resources, and audiovisual items. Special programs and facilities include services for learning-disabled students, study abroad, the Jane Goodall Center for Excellence in Environmental Studies, and the Meteorology and Weather Center. WestConn is also home to the nation's first program in computer-information-security management and the only licensed meteorology program in Connecticut. The most popular majors include communications, theater arts, education, business, justice and law administration, music, and nursing. WestConn offers its excellent educational programs through five academic units: the Ancell School of Business, the School of Arts and Sciences, the School of Professional Studies, the School of Visual and Performing Arts, and the Division of Graduate and External Programs.

Interviews and Campus Visits Interviews are not required, but candidates are encouraged to attend an information session before they enroll. These sessions provide information about the University and the admissions process, offering an important opportunity to assess how the University can help students meet their long-term educational goals. It also affords the opportunity to meet with professors, other potential students, and current students. Student-guided tours also are available. Touring students and parents visit the library, residence halls, the new "green" Science Building and other classroom buildings, computer laboratories, Midtown Student Center and new Campus Center at Westside, and the recreation center. For more information, students should call the Office of Admissions at 203-837-9000 or 877-837-WCSU (toll-free).

For Further Information Write to Office of University Admissions, Western Connecticut State University, 181 White Street, Danbury, CT 06810. *E-mail:* admissions@wcsu.edu. *Web site:* http://www.wcsu.edu.

YALE UNIVERSITY
New Haven, Connecticut

Yale University is a coed, private university, founded in 1701, offering degrees at the bachelor's, master's, doctoral, and first professional levels and post-master's certificates. It has a 200-acre campus in New Haven near New York City.

Academic Information The faculty has 1,577 members (70% full-time), 85% with terminal degrees. The undergraduate student-faculty ratio is 6:1. The library holds 12 million titles, 85,000 serial subscriptions, and 263,738 audiovisual materials. Special programs include services for learning-disabled students, an honors program, study abroad, advanced placement credit, accelerated degree programs, ESL programs, double majors, independent study, self-designed majors, summer session for credit, part-time degree programs, and internships. The most frequently chosen baccalaureate fields are history, interdisciplinary studies, social sciences.
Student Body Statistics The student body totals 11,445, of whom 5,277 are undergraduates (1,318 freshmen). 50 percent are women and 50 percent are men. Students come from 52 states and territories and 74 other countries. 7 percent are from Connecticut. 8.6 percent are international students.
Expenses for 2008–09 *Application fee:* $75. *Comprehensive fee:* $46,000 includes full-time tuition ($35,300) and college room and board ($10,700).
Financial Aid Forms of aid include need-based scholarships and part-time jobs. The average aided 2008–09 undergraduate received an aid package worth an estimated $37,223. The application deadline for financial aid is March 1.
Freshman Admission Yale University requires an essay, a high school transcript, 3 recommendations, SAT and SAT Subject Test or ACT scores, and TOEFL scores for international students. An interview is recommended. The application deadline for regular admission is December 31 and for early action it is November 1.
Transfer Admission The application deadline for admission is March 1.
Entrance Difficulty Yale University assesses its entrance difficulty level as most difficult. For the fall 2008 freshman class, 9 percent of the applicants were accepted.
For Further Information Contact Admissions Director, Yale University, PO Box 208234, New Haven, CT 06520. *Phone:* 203-432-9300. *Fax:* 203-432-9392. *E-mail:* student.questions@yale.edu. *Web site:* http://www.yale.edu/.

Maine

BATES COLLEGE
Lewiston, Maine

Bates College is a coed, private, four-year college, founded in 1855, offering degrees at the bachelor's level. It has a 109-acre campus in Lewiston.

Academic Information The faculty has 193 members (86% full-time), 87% with terminal degrees. The student-faculty ratio is 10:1. The library holds 620,000 titles, 27,000 serial subscriptions, and 35,000 audiovisual materials. Special programs include services for learning-disabled students, an honors program, cooperative (work-study) education, study abroad, advanced placement credit, accelerated degree programs, double majors, independent study, self-designed majors, internships, and arrangement for off-campus study with American University, Williams College (Mystic Seaport Program), McGill University, Washington and Lee University, Morehouse College, Spelman College. The most frequently chosen baccalaureate fields are English, psychology, social sciences.
Student Body Statistics The student body is made up of 1,776 undergraduates (521 freshmen). 54 percent are women and 46 percent are men. Students come from 46 states and territories and 65 other countries. 11 percent are from Maine. 5.5 percent are international students.
Expenses for 2008–09 *Application fee:* $60. *Comprehensive fee:* $49,350.

Financial Aid Forms of aid include need-based scholarships and part-time jobs. The average aided 2008–09 undergraduate received an aid package worth an estimated $32,955. The application deadline for financial aid is February 1.
Freshman Admission Bates College requires an essay, a high school transcript, 3 recommendations, and TOEFL scores for international students. An interview is recommended. The application deadline for regular admission is January 1, for early decision plan 1 it is November 15, and for early decision plan 2 it is January 1.
Transfer Admission The application deadline for admission is March 1.
Entrance Difficulty Bates College assesses its entrance difficulty level as most difficult. For the fall 2008 freshman class, 29 percent of the applicants were accepted.
For Further Information Contact Mr. Wylie Mitchell, Dean of Admissions, Bates College, Andrews Road, Lewiston, ME 04240-6028. *Phone:* 207-786-6000. *Fax:* 207-786-6025. *E-mail:* admissions@bates.edu. *Web site:* http://www.bates.edu/.

BOWDOIN COLLEGE
Brunswick, Maine

Bowdoin College is a coed, private, four-year college, founded in 1794, offering degrees at the bachelor's level (SAT or ACT considered if submitted. Test scores are required for home-schooled applicants). It has a 205-acre campus in Brunswick near Portland.

Academic Information The faculty has 206 members (84% full-time), 96% with terminal degrees. The student-faculty ratio is 9:1. The library holds 1 million titles, 18,851 serial subscriptions, and 28,762 audiovisual materials. Special programs include services for learning-disabled students, study abroad, advanced placement credit, accelerated degree programs, double majors, independent study, self-designed majors, and arrangement for off-campus study with Twelve College Exchange Program. The most frequently chosen baccalaureate fields are foreign languages and literature, biological/life sciences, social sciences.
Student Body Statistics The student body is made up of 1,723 undergraduates (488 freshmen). 51 percent are women and 49 percent are men. Students come from 51 states and territories and 26 other countries. 13 percent are from Maine. 3 percent are international students.
Expenses for 2008–09 *Application fee:* $60. *One-time mandatory fee:* $100. *Comprehensive fee:* $48,570 includes full-time tuition ($37,790), mandatory fees ($400), and college room and board ($10,380). *College room only:* $4850. Room and board charges vary according to board plan.
Financial Aid Forms of aid include need-based and non-need-based scholarships and part-time jobs. The average aided 2008–09 undergraduate received an aid package worth an estimated $33,139. The application deadline for financial aid is February 15.
Freshman Admission Bowdoin College requires an essay, a high school transcript, 3 recommendations, and TOEFL scores for international students. An interview is recommended. The application deadline for regular admission is January 1, for early decision plan 1 it is November 15, and for early decision plan 2 it is January 1.
Transfer Admission The application deadline for admission is March 1.
Entrance Difficulty Bowdoin College assesses its entrance difficulty level as most difficult. For the fall 2008 freshman class, 19 percent of the applicants were accepted.
For Further Information Contact Peter T. Wiley, Associate Dean of Admissions, Bowdoin College, 5000 College Station, Brunswick, ME 04011-8411. *Phone:* 207-725-3190. *Fax:* 207-725-3101. *E-mail:* admissions@bowdoin.edu. *Web site:* http://www.bowdoin.edu/.

CENTRAL MAINE MEDICAL CENTER COLLEGE OF NURSING AND HEALTH PROFESSIONS
Lewiston, Maine

Central Maine Medical Center College of Nursing and Health Professions is a coed, private, two-year college, founded in 1891, offering degrees at the associate level.

Academic Information The faculty has 18 members (72% full-time), 6% with terminal degrees. The student-faculty ratio is 12:1. The library holds 1,975 titles and 339 serial subscriptions. Special programs include advanced placement credit, summer session for credit, and arrangement for off-campus study.

Student Body Statistics The student body is made up of 150 undergraduates. 87 percent are women and 13 percent are men. Students come from 4 states and territories. 97 percent are from Maine.

Expenses for 2008–09 *Application fee:* $40. *Tuition:* $5865 full-time. *Mandatory fees:* $1210 full-time. *College room only:* $1500.

Financial Aid Forms of aid include need-based scholarships. The priority application deadline for financial aid is May 1.

Freshman Admission Central Maine Medical Center College of Nursing and Health Professions requires an essay, a high school transcript, SAT or ACT scores, and TOEFL scores for international students. The application deadline for regular admission is February 15.

Entrance Difficulty Central Maine Medical Center College of Nursing and Health Professions assesses its entrance difficulty level as moderately difficult.

For Further Information Contact Mrs. Kathleen C. Jacques, Registrar, Central Maine Medical Center College of Nursing and Health Professions, CMMC College of Nursing, 70 Middle Street, Lewiston, ME 04240. *Phone:* 207-795-2858. *Fax:* 207-795-2849. *E-mail:* jacqueka@cmhc.org. *Web site:* http://www.cmmcson.edu/.

COLBY COLLEGE

Waterville, Maine

Colby College is a coed, private, four-year college, founded in 1813, offering degrees at the bachelor's level. It has a 714-acre campus in Waterville.

Academic Information The faculty has 225 members (73% full-time), 81% with terminal degrees. The student-faculty ratio is 10:1. The library holds 814,952 titles, 10,177 serial subscriptions, and 22,344 audiovisual materials. Special programs include services for learning-disabled students, an honors program, study abroad, advanced placement credit, double majors, independent study, self-designed majors, part-time degree programs, internships, and arrangement for off-campus study with Pomona College, Pitzer College, Howard University, Claremont McKenna College, Scripps College, Boston University (Sea Semester), Williams College (Mystic Seaport Program), Clark Atlanta University. The most frequently chosen baccalaureate fields are area and ethnic studies, biological/life sciences, social sciences.

Student Body Statistics The student body is made up of 1,846 undergraduates (482 freshmen). 54 percent are women and 46 percent are men. Students come from 48 states and territories and 59 other countries. 11 percent are from Maine. 5.4 percent are international students.

Expenses for 2008–09 *Application fee:* $65. *Comprehensive fee:* $48,520.

Financial Aid Forms of aid include need-based scholarships and part-time jobs. The average aided 2008–09 undergraduate received an aid package worth an estimated $31,627. The application deadline for financial aid is February 1.

Freshman Admission Colby College requires an essay, a high school transcript, 2 recommendations, and TOEFL scores for international students. An interview is recommended. SAT or ACT scores and SAT Subject Test scores are required for some. The application deadline for regular admission is January 1, for early decision plan 1 it is November 15, and for early decision plan 2 it is January 1.

Transfer Admission The application deadline for admission is March 1.

Entrance Difficulty Colby College assesses its entrance difficulty level as most difficult. For the fall 2008 freshman class, 31 percent of the applicants were accepted.

For Further Information Contact Mr. Steve Thomas, Director of Admissions, Colby College, Office of Admissions and Financial Aid, 4800 Mayflower Hill, Waterville, ME 04901-8848. *Phone:* 207-859-4800 or 800-723-3032 (toll-free). *Fax:* 207-859-4828. *E-mail:* admissions@colby.edu. *Web site:* http://www.colby.edu/.

COLLEGE OF THE ATLANTIC

Bar Harbor, Maine

College of the Atlantic is a coed, private, comprehensive institution, founded in 1969, offering degrees at the bachelor's and master's levels. It has a 35-acre campus in Bar Harbor.

Academic Information The faculty has 38 members (63% full-time), 63% with terminal degrees. The undergraduate student-faculty ratio is 11:1. The library holds 50,000 titles, 30,000 serial subscriptions, and 2,500 audiovisual materials. Special programs include academic remediation, services for learning-disabled students, cooperative (work-study) education, study abroad, advanced placement credit, accelerated degree programs, independent study, self-designed majors, part-time degree programs (daytime), internships, and arrangement for off-campus study with University of Maine, Landing School of Boatbuilding, SEA Education Association, Shoal's Marine Laboratory, Ecoleague consortium: Alaska Pacific University, Antioch College, Green Mountain College, Northland College and Prescott College. The most frequently chosen baccalaureate field is liberal arts/general studies.

Student Body Statistics The student body totals 327, of whom 324 are undergraduates (70 freshmen). 64 percent are women and 36 percent are men. Students come from 37 states and territories and 35 other countries. 18 percent are from Maine. 13.6 percent are international students.

Expenses for 2009–10 *Application fee:* $45. *Comprehensive fee:* $41,550 includes full-time tuition ($32,580), mandatory fees ($480), and college room and board ($8490). *College room only:* $5400. *Part-time tuition:* $3620 per credit. *Part-time mandatory fees:* $160 per term.

Financial Aid Forms of aid include need-based scholarships and part-time jobs. The average aided 2008–09 undergraduate received an aid package worth an estimated $28,020. The priority application deadline for financial aid is February 15.

Freshman Admission College of the Atlantic requires an essay, a high school transcript, 3 recommendations, and TOEFL scores for international students. A minimum 3.0 high school GPA, an interview, and SAT or ACT scores are recommended. An interview is required for some. The application deadline for regular admission is February 15, for early decision plan 1 it is December 1, and for early decision plan 2 it is January 10.

Transfer Admission The application deadline for admission is April 1.

Entrance Difficulty College of the Atlantic assesses its entrance difficulty level as very difficult. For the fall 2008 freshman class, 69 percent of the applicants were accepted.

For Further Information Contact Ms. Sarah Baker, Dean of Admission, College of the Atlantic, 105 Eden Street, Bar Harbor, ME 04609-1198. *Phone:* 207-288-5015 Ext. 233 or 800-528-0025 (toll-free). *Fax:* 207-288-4126. *E-mail:* inquiry@coa.edu. *Web site:* http://www.coa.edu/.

HUSSON UNIVERSITY

Bangor, Maine

Husson University is a coed, private, comprehensive institution, founded in 1898, offering degrees at the associate, bachelor's, master's, and doctoral levels and post-master's and postbachelor's certificates. It has a 170-acre campus in Bangor.

Academic Information The faculty has 88 members (95% full-time), 61% with terminal degrees. The undergraduate student-faculty ratio is 21:1. The library holds 49,036 titles, 500 serial subscriptions, and 22,000 audiovisual materials. Special programs include academic remediation, services for learning-disabled students, cooperative (work-study) education, advanced placement credit, ESL programs, double majors, independent study, self-designed majors, summer session for credit, part-time degree programs (daytime, evenings, weekends, summer), adult/continuing education programs, and internships. The most frequently chosen baccalaureate fields are business/marketing, health professions and related sciences, security and protective services.

Student Body Statistics The student body totals 2,626, of whom 2,257 are undergraduates (479 freshmen). 59 percent are women and 41 percent are men. Students come from 9 states and territories and 9 other countries. 80 percent are from Maine.

Husson University (continued)

Expenses for 2009–10 *Application fee:* $25. *Comprehensive fee:* $19,984 includes full-time tuition ($12,690), mandatory fees ($300), and college room and board ($6994). *Part-time tuition:* $423 per credit hour.

Financial Aid Forms of aid include need-based and non-need-based scholarships and part-time jobs. The average aided 2008–09 undergraduate received an aid package worth an estimated $10,019. The priority application deadline for financial aid is April 15.

Freshman Admission Husson University requires an essay, a high school transcript, 1 recommendation, SAT or ACT scores, and TOEFL scores for international students. An interview is recommended. The application deadline for regular admission is September 1.

Transfer Admission The application deadline for admission is September 1.

Entrance Difficulty Husson University assesses its entrance difficulty level as moderately difficult. For the fall 2008 freshman class, 86 percent of the applicants were accepted.

For Further Information Contact Ms. Carlena Bean, Director of Admissions, Husson University, One College Circle, Bangor, ME 04401-2999. *Phone:* 207-941-7067 or 800-4-HUSSON (toll-free). *Fax:* 207-941-7935. *E-mail:* beanc@husson.edu. *Web site:* http://www.husson.edu/.

MAINE COLLEGE OF ART
Portland, Maine

Maine College of Art is a coed, private, comprehensive institution, founded in 1882, offering degrees at the bachelor's and master's levels and postbachelor's certificates. It is located in Portland near Boston.

Academic Information The faculty has 51 members (41% full-time), 78% with terminal degrees. The undergraduate student-faculty ratio is 10:1. The library holds 33,000 titles, 101 serial subscriptions, and 300 audiovisual materials. Special programs include services for learning-disabled students, study abroad, advanced placement credit, double majors, self-designed majors, part-time degree programs, internships, and arrangement for off-campus study with Association of Independent Colleges of Art and Design Mobility Program. The most frequently chosen baccalaureate field is visual and performing arts.

Student Body Statistics The student body totals 370, of whom 342 are undergraduates (103 freshmen). 66 percent are women and 34 percent are men. Students come from 20 states and territories. 38 percent are from Maine.

Expenses for 2008–09 *Application fee:* $40. *Comprehensive fee:* $36,565 includes full-time tuition ($26,490), mandatory fees ($675), and college room and board ($9400). Room and board charges vary according to board plan and housing facility. *Part-time tuition:* $1104 per credit hour.

Financial Aid Forms of aid include need-based and non-need-based scholarships and part-time jobs. The average aided 2008–09 undergraduate received an aid package worth an estimated $13,894. The priority application deadline for financial aid is March 1.

Freshman Admission Maine College of Art requires an essay, a high school transcript, 2 recommendations, a portfolio, SAT or ACT scores, and TOEFL scores for international students. A minimum 2.0 high school GPA and an interview are recommended. The application deadline for regular admission is rolling.

Transfer Admission The application deadline for admission is rolling.

Entrance Difficulty Maine College of Art assesses its entrance difficulty level as moderately difficult. For the fall 2008 freshman class, 80 percent of the applicants were accepted.

For Further Information Contact Ms. Blaise Maccarrone, Administrative Assistant to Admissions, Maine College of Art, 97 Spring Street, Portland, ME 04101-3987. *Phone:* 207-699-5026 or 800-639-4808 (toll-free). *Fax:* 207-699-5080. *E-mail:* admissions@meca.edu. *Web site:* http://www.meca.edu/.

MAINE MARITIME ACADEMY
Castine, Maine

Maine Maritime Academy is a coed, primarily men's, public, comprehensive institution, founded in 1941, offering degrees at the associate, bachelor's, and master's levels. It has a 35-acre campus in Castine.

Academic Information The faculty has 90 members (77% full-time), 22% with terminal degrees. The undergraduate student-faculty ratio is 12:1. The library holds 427,532 titles, 347 serial subscriptions, and 2,161 audiovisual materials. Special programs include academic remediation, cooperative (work-study) education, study abroad, advanced placement credit, double majors, independent study, distance learning, self-designed majors, adult/continuing education programs, internships, and arrangement for off-campus study with International Association of Maritime Universities. The most frequently chosen baccalaureate fields are engineering, engineering technologies, transportation and materials moving.

Student Body Statistics The student body totals 860, of whom 842 are undergraduates (250 freshmen). 16 percent are women and 84 percent are men. Students come from 35 states and territories and 8 other countries. 69 percent are from Maine. 0.2 percent are international students.

Expenses for 2009–10 *Application fee:* $15. *State resident tuition:* $7900 full-time, $300 per credit hour part-time. *Nonresident tuition:* $15,600 full-time, $550 per credit hour part-time. *Mandatory fees:* $2205 full-time. *College room and board:* $8450. *College room only:* $5250.

Financial Aid Forms of aid include need-based and non-need-based scholarships and part-time jobs. The average aided 2008–09 undergraduate received an aid package worth an estimated $9554. The priority application deadline for financial aid is April 15.

Freshman Admission Maine Maritime Academy requires a high school transcript, 1 recommendation, physical examination, SAT or ACT scores, and TOEFL scores for international students. An interview is recommended. The application deadline for regular admission is July 1 and for early decision it is December 20.

Transfer Admission The application deadline for admission is July 1.

Entrance Difficulty Maine Maritime Academy assesses its entrance difficulty level as moderately difficult. For the fall 2008 freshman class, 67 percent of the applicants were accepted.

For Further Information Contact Mr. Jeffrey C. Wright, Director of Admissions, Maine Maritime Academy, Castine, ME 04420. *Phone:* 207-326-2215, 800-464-6565 (toll-free in-state), or 800-227-8465 (toll-free out-of-state). *Fax:* 207-326-2515. *E-mail:* admissions@mma.edu. *Web site:* http://www.mainemaritime.edu/.

NEW ENGLAND SCHOOL OF COMMUNICATIONS
Bangor, Maine

New England School of Communications is a coed, primarily men's, private, four-year college, founded in 1981, offering degrees at the associate and bachelor's levels. It has a 200-acre campus in Bangor.

Expenses for 2008–09 *Application fee:* $15. *Comprehensive fee:* $17,405 includes full-time tuition ($10,400), mandatory fees ($280), and college room and board ($6725). *Part-time tuition:* $350 per credit.

For Further Information Contact Ms. Louise Grant, Director of Admissions, New England School of Communications, 1 College Circle, Bangor, ME 04401. *Phone:* 207-941-7176 Ext. 1093 or 888-877-1876 (toll-free). *Fax:* 207-947-3987. *E-mail:* info@nescom.edu. *Web site:* http://www.nescom.edu/.

SAINT JOSEPH'S COLLEGE OF MAINE
Standish, Maine

http://www.sjcme.edu/

THOMAS COLLEGE
Waterville, Maine

Thomas College is a coed, private, comprehensive institution, founded in 1894, offering degrees at the associate, bachelor's, and master's levels (associate). It has a 70-acre campus in Waterville.

Expenses for 2008–09 *Application fee:* $50. *Comprehensive fee:* $27,920 includes full-time tuition ($19,230), mandatory fees ($520), and college room and board ($8170). *College room only:* $4130. Room and board charges vary according to board plan and housing facility. *Part-time tuition:* $801 per credit hour.
For Further Information Contact Mr. James Love, Dean of Admissions, Thomas College, 180 West River Road, Waterville, ME 04901. *Phone:* 207-859-1101 or 800-339-7001 (toll-free). *Fax:* 207-859-1114. *E-mail:* admiss@thomas.edu. *Web site:* http://www.thomas.edu/.

UNITY COLLEGE
Unity, Maine
http://www.unity.edu/

UNIVERSITY OF MAINE
Orono, Maine

University of Maine is a coed, public unit of University of Maine System, founded in 1865, offering degrees at the bachelor's, master's, and doctoral levels and post-master's certificates. It has a 3,300-acre campus in Orono.

Academic Information The faculty has 829 members (73% full-time), 61% with terminal degrees. The undergraduate student-faculty ratio is 15:1. Special programs include services for learning-disabled students, an honors program, cooperative (work-study) education, study abroad, advanced placement credit, accelerated degree programs, Freshman Honors College, ESL programs, double majors, independent study, distance learning, self-designed majors, summer session for credit, part-time degree programs (daytime, evenings, summer), internships, and arrangement for off-campus study with Bangor Theological Seminary, other institutions of the University of Maine System.
Student Body Statistics The student body totals 11,818, of whom 9,667 are undergraduates (2,062 freshmen). 48 percent are women and 52 percent are men. Students come from 48 states and territories and 65 other countries. 84 percent are from Maine. 1.1 percent are international students.
Expenses for 2008–09 *Application fee:* $40. *State resident tuition:* $7170 full-time, $239 per credit hour part-time. *Nonresident tuition:* $20,580 full-time, $686 per credit hour part-time. *Mandatory fees:* $1930 full-time. Full-time tuition and fees vary according to reciprocity agreements. Part-time tuition varies according to reciprocity agreements. *College room and board:* $8008. Room and board charges vary according to board plan and housing facility.
Financial Aid Forms of aid include need-based scholarships, athletic grants, and part-time jobs. The average aided 2008–09 undergraduate received an aid package worth an estimated $11,369. The application deadline for financial aid is May 1 with a priority deadline of March 1.
Freshman Admission University of Maine requires an essay, a high school transcript, 1 recommendation, SAT or ACT scores, and TOEFL scores for international students. An interview and audition for music majors are required for some. The application deadline for regular admission is rolling and for early action it is December 15.
Transfer Admission The application deadline for admission is rolling.

Entrance Difficulty University of Maine assesses its entrance difficulty level as moderately difficult; very difficult for engineering, science, wildlife ecology programs, nursing. For the fall 2008 freshman class, 77 percent of the applicants were accepted.
For Further Information Contact Ms. Sharon Oliver, Director of Admissions, University of Maine, 5713 Chadbourne Hall, Orono, ME 04469-5713. *Phone:* 207-581-1561 or 877-486-2364 (toll-free). *Fax:* 207-581-1213. *E-mail:* um-admit@maine.edu. *Web site:* http://www.umaine.edu/.

See page 118 for the Close-Up.

THE UNIVERSITY OF MAINE AT AUGUSTA
Augusta, Maine

The University of Maine at Augusta is a coed, public, four-year college of University of Maine System, founded in 1965, offering degrees at the associate and bachelor's levels and postbachelor's certificates (also offers some graduate courses and continuing education programs with significant enrollment not reflected in profile). It has a 159-acre campus in Augusta.

Academic Information The faculty has 253 members (41% full-time), 16% with terminal degrees. The student-faculty ratio is 18:1. The library holds 94,379 titles, 23,766 serial subscriptions, and 4,860 audiovisual materials. Special programs include academic remediation, services for learning-disabled students, an honors program, study abroad, advanced placement credit, double majors, independent study, distance learning, self-designed majors, summer session for credit, part-time degree programs (daytime, evenings, summer), adult/continuing education programs, internships, and arrangement for off-campus study with other units of the University of Maine System. The most frequently chosen baccalaureate fields are business/marketing, health professions and related sciences, liberal arts/general studies.
Student Body Statistics The student body is made up of 5,202 undergraduates (575 freshmen). 73 percent are women and 27 percent are men. Students come from 16 states and territories and 2 other countries. 97 percent are from Maine.
Expenses for 2008–09 *Application fee:* $40. *State resident tuition:* $5700 full-time, $190 per credit hour part-time. *Nonresident tuition:* $13,800 full-time, $460 per credit hour part-time. *Mandatory fees:* $795 full-time, $26.50 per credit hour part-time. Both full-time and part-time tuition and fees vary according to reciprocity agreements.
Financial Aid Forms of aid include need-based and non-need-based scholarships, athletic grants, and part-time jobs. The average aided 2008–09 undergraduate received an aid package worth an estimated $8467. The priority application deadline for financial aid is March 1.
Freshman Admission The University of Maine at Augusta requires a high school transcript and TOEFL scores for international students. An essay and SAT or ACT scores are recommended. An interview and music audition are required for some. The application deadline for regular admission is August 31.
Transfer Admission The application deadline for admission is rolling.
Entrance Difficulty The University of Maine at Augusta assesses its entrance difficulty level as noncompetitive; minimally difficult for transfers; moderately difficult for allied health, architecture, liberal arts, bachelor's degree programs. For the fall 2008 freshman class, 77 percent of the applicants were accepted.
For Further Information Contact Jonathan Henry, Director of Admissions/Dean of Enrollment, The University of Maine at Augusta, 46 University Drive, Robinson Hall, Augusta, ME 04330. *Phone:* 207-621-3465 or 877-862-1234 Ext. 3185 (toll-free in-state). *Fax:* 207-621-3333. *E-mail:* umaadm@maine.edu. *Web site:* http://www.uma.maine.edu/.

UNIVERSITY OF MAINE AT FARMINGTON
Farmington, Maine

University of Maine at Farmington is a coed, public, comprehensive unit of University of Maine System, founded in 1863, offering degrees at the bachelor's and master's levels. It has a 50-acre campus in Farmington.

University of Maine at Farmington (continued)

Academic Information The faculty has 176 members (75% full-time), 72% with terminal degrees. The undergraduate student-faculty ratio is 15:1. The library holds 98,935 titles, 498 serial subscriptions, and 8,550 audiovisual materials. Special programs include academic remediation, services for learning-disabled students, an honors program, study abroad, advanced placement credit, accelerated degree programs, double majors, independent study, distance learning, self-designed majors, summer session for credit, part-time degree programs (daytime, summer), internships, and arrangement for off-campus study with National Student Exchange, SALT Center for Documentary Field Studies, other institutions of the University of Maine System. The most frequently chosen baccalaureate fields are education, health professions and related sciences, psychology.

Student Body Statistics The student body totals 2,229, of whom 2,194 are undergraduates (516 freshmen). 64 percent are women and 36 percent are men. Students come from 20 states and territories and 8 other countries. 85 percent are from Maine. 0.2 percent are international students.

Expenses for 2008–09 *Application fee:* $40. *State resident tuition:* $7296 full-time, $228 per credit hour part-time. *Nonresident tuition:* $15,072 full-time, $471 per credit hour part-time. *Mandatory fees:* $910 full-time. Full-time tuition and fees vary according to course load, reciprocity agreements, and student level. Part-time tuition varies according to course load, reciprocity agreements, and student level. *College room and board:* $7158. *College room only:* $3810. Room and board charges vary according to board plan and housing facility.

Financial Aid Forms of aid include need-based and non-need-based scholarships and part-time jobs. The average aided 2007–08 undergraduate received an aid package worth $8719. The priority application deadline for financial aid is March 1.

Freshman Admission University of Maine at Farmington requires an essay, a high school transcript, a minimum 2.0 high school GPA, 1 recommendation, and TOEFL scores for international students. An interview is recommended. A minimum 2.5 high school GPA and SAT or ACT scores are required for some. The application deadline for regular admission is rolling and for early action it is December 1.

Entrance Difficulty University of Maine at Farmington assesses its entrance difficulty level as moderately difficult. For the fall 2008 freshman class, 68 percent of the applicants were accepted.

For Further Information Contact Mr. James G. Collins, Associate Director of Admissions, University of Maine at Farmington, 246 Main Street, Farmington, ME 04938-1994. *Phone:* 207-778-7050. *Fax:* 207-778-8182. *E-mail:* umfadmit@maine.edu. *Web site:* http://www.umf.maine.edu/.

UNIVERSITY OF MAINE AT FORT KENT
Fort Kent, Maine

University of Maine at Fort Kent is a coed, public, four-year college of University of Maine System, founded in 1878, offering degrees at the associate and bachelor's levels. It has a 52-acre campus in Fort Kent.

Academic Information The faculty has 72 members (57% full-time), 50% with terminal degrees. The student-faculty ratio is 17:1. The library holds 65,461 titles, 310 serial subscriptions, and 3,209 audiovisual materials. Special programs include academic remediation, services for learning-disabled students, an honors program, cooperative (work-study) education, advanced placement credit, accelerated degree programs, ESL programs, double majors, independent study, distance learning, self-designed majors, summer session for credit, part-time degree programs (daytime, evenings, summer), external degree programs, and internships. The most frequently chosen baccalaureate fields are education, business/marketing, health professions and related sciences.

Student Body Statistics The student body is made up of 1,102 undergraduates (119 freshmen). 68 percent are women and 32 percent are men. Students come from 20 states and territories and 12 other countries. 96 percent are from Maine. 24.7 percent are international students.

Expenses for 2008–09 *Application fee:* $40. *State resident tuition:* $5700 full-time, $190 per credit hour part-time. *Nonresident tuition:* $14,310 full-time, $477 per credit hour part-time. *Mandatory fees:* $713 full-time, $23.75 per credit hour part-time. Both full-time and part-time tuition and fees vary according to course load. *College room and board:* $6940. *College room only:* $4000. Room and board charges vary according to board plan and housing facility.

Financial Aid Forms of aid include need-based and non-need-based scholarships and part-time jobs. The average aided 2008–09 undergraduate received an aid package worth an estimated $8825. The priority application deadline for financial aid is March 1.

Freshman Admission University of Maine at Fort Kent requires an essay, a high school transcript, and TOEFL scores for international students. SAT and SAT Subject Test or ACT scores are recommended. An interview, SAT scores, and SAT and SAT Subject Test or ACT scores are required for some. The application deadline for regular admission is rolling.

Transfer Admission The application deadline for admission is rolling.

Entrance Difficulty University of Maine at Fort Kent assesses its entrance difficulty level as minimally difficult. For the fall 2008 freshman class, 76 percent of the applicants were accepted.

For Further Information Contact Mrs. Jill Cairns, Acting Director of Admissions, University of Maine at Fort Kent, 23 University Drive, Fort Kent, ME 04743. *Phone:* 207-834-7600 or 888-TRY-UMFK (toll-free). *Fax:* 207-834-7609. *E-mail:* umfkadm@maine.edu. *Web site:* http://www.umfk.maine.edu/.

See page 120 for the Close-Up.

UNIVERSITY OF MAINE AT MACHIAS
Machias, Maine

University of Maine at Machias is a coed, public, four-year college of University of Maine System, founded in 1909, offering degrees at the associate and bachelor's levels. It has a 42-acre campus in Machias.

Academic Information The faculty has 76 members (43% full-time), 55% with terminal degrees. The student-faculty ratio is 13.6:1. The library holds 83,819 titles, 15,500 serial subscriptions, and 3,314 audiovisual materials. Special programs include academic remediation, services for learning-disabled students, cooperative (work-study) education, study abroad, advanced placement credit, double majors, independent study, distance learning, self-designed majors, summer session for credit, part-time degree programs (daytime, evenings, summer), internships, and arrangement for off-campus study. The most frequently chosen baccalaureate fields are biological/life sciences, business/marketing, interdisciplinary studies.

Student Body Statistics The student body is made up of 1,023 undergraduates (117 freshmen). 68 percent are women and 32 percent are men. Students come from 24 states and territories and 9 other countries. 76 percent are from Maine. 3.3 percent are international students.

Expenses for 2009–10 *Application fee:* $40. *State resident tuition:* $5700 full-time, $190 per semester hour part-time. *Nonresident tuition:* $15,840 full-time, $528 per semester hour part-time. *Mandatory fees:* $1171 full-time. *College room and board:* $6574. *College room only:* $3308.

Financial Aid Forms of aid include need-based and non-need-based scholarships and part-time jobs. The priority application deadline for financial aid is March 1.

Freshman Admission University of Maine at Machias requires an essay, a high school transcript, 1 recommendation, SAT scores, and TOEFL scores for international students. A minimum 2.5 high school GPA, 2 recommendations, and an interview are recommended. A minimum 2.0 high school GPA and an interview are required for some. The application deadline for regular admission is August 15 and for early action it is December 15.

Entrance Difficulty University of Maine at Machias assesses its entrance difficulty level as moderately difficult. For the fall 2008 freshman class, 83 percent of the applicants were accepted.

For Further Information Contact Mr. Stewart Bennett, Director of Admissions, University of Maine at Machias, 9 O'Brien Avenue, Machias, ME 04654. *Phone:* 207-255-1318, 888-GOTOUMM (toll-free in-state), or 888-468-6866 (toll-free out-of-state). *Fax:* 207-255-1363. *E-mail:* ummadmissions@maine.edu. *Web site:* http://www.umm.maine.edu/.

UNIVERSITY OF MAINE AT PRESQUE ISLE
Presque Isle, Maine

University of Maine at Presque Isle is a coed, public, four-year college of University of Maine System, founded in 1903, offering degrees at the associate and bachelor's levels. It has a 150-acre campus in Presque Isle.

Academic Information The faculty has 119 members (50% full-time), 45% with terminal degrees. The student-faculty ratio is 20:1. Special programs include academic remediation, services for learning-disabled students, an honors program, cooperative (work-study) education, advanced placement credit, accelerated degree programs, double majors, independent study, distance learning, self-designed majors, summer session for credit, part-time degree programs (daytime, evenings, summer), adult/continuing education programs, internships, and arrangement for off-campus study with Tri-Campus Exchange.

Student Body Statistics The student body is made up of 1,460 undergraduates (200 freshmen). 65 percent are women and 35 percent are men. Students come from 15 states and territories and 6 other countries. 98 percent are from Maine.

Expenses for 2008–09 *Application fee:* $40. *State resident tuition:* $5700 full-time, $190 per credit hour part-time. *Nonresident tuition:* $14,310 full-time, $477 per credit hour part-time. *Mandatory fees:* $775 full-time, $16 per credit hour part-time. Both full-time and part-time tuition and fees vary according to course load and reciprocity agreements. *College room and board:* $7096. *College room only:* $3540. Room and board charges vary according to board plan and housing facility.

Financial Aid Forms of aid include need-based and non-need-based scholarships and part-time jobs. The average aided 2007–08 undergraduate received an aid package worth $8770.

Freshman Admission University of Maine at Presque Isle requires an essay, a high school transcript, and a minimum 2.0 high school GPA. 1 recommendation and an interview are required for some. The application deadline for regular admission is rolling and for early action it is October 31.

Entrance Difficulty University of Maine at Presque Isle assesses its entrance difficulty level as minimally difficult; moderately difficult for nursing and medical laboratory technician programs. For the fall 2008 freshman class, 87 percent of the applicants were accepted.

For Further Information Contact Ms. Erin V. Benson, Director of University Relations and Student Enrollment Services, University of Maine at Presque Isle, 181 Main Street, Presque Isle, ME 04769. *Phone:* 207-768-9453. *Fax:* 207-768-9777. *E-mail:* adventure@umpi.maine.edu. *Web site:* http://www.umpi.edu/.

UNIVERSITY OF NEW ENGLAND
Biddeford, Maine

University of New England is a coed, private, comprehensive institution, founded in 1831, offering degrees at the associate, bachelor's, master's, and first professional levels and post-master's and postbachelor's certificates. It has a 410-acre campus in Biddeford.

Academic Information The faculty has 320 members (56% full-time). The undergraduate student-faculty ratio is 13:1. The library holds 156,752 titles, 39,705 serial subscriptions, and 10,656 audiovisual materials. Special programs include academic remediation, services for learning-disabled students, cooperative (work-study) education, study abroad, advanced placement credit, accelerated degree programs, double majors, independent study, distance learning, summer session for credit, part-time degree programs (evenings), internships, and arrangement for off-campus study with Greater Portland Alliance of Colleges and Universities. The most frequently chosen baccalaureate fields are biological/life sciences, health professions and related sciences, psychology.

Student Body Statistics The student body totals 4,267, of whom 2,140 are undergraduates. 73 percent are women and 27 percent are men. 40 percent are from Maine. 0.8 percent are international students.

Expenses for 2009–10 *Application fee:* $40. *Comprehensive fee:* $38,790 includes full-time tuition ($26,940), mandatory fees ($980), and college room and board ($10,870). *Part-time tuition:* $970 per credit hour.

Financial Aid Forms of aid include need-based and non-need-based scholarships and part-time jobs. The average aided 2008–09 undergraduate received an aid package worth an estimated $23,956. The priority application deadline for financial aid is May 1.

Freshman Admission University of New England requires a high school transcript, SAT or ACT scores, and TOEFL scores for international students. An essay and an interview are recommended. An interview is required for some. The application deadline for regular admission is February 15.

Transfer Admission The application deadline for admission is rolling.

Entrance Difficulty University of New England assesses its entrance difficulty level as moderately difficult. For the fall 2008 freshman class, 78 percent of the applicants were accepted.

For Further Information Contact Mr. Robert J. Pecchia, Associate Dean of Admissions, University of New England, Hills Beach Road, Biddeford, ME 04005-9526. *Phone:* 207-283-0170 Ext. 2297 or 800-477-4UNE (toll-free). *Fax:* 207-602-5900. *E-mail:* admissions@une.edu. *Web site:* http://www.une.edu/.

UNIVERSITY OF SOUTHERN MAINE
Portland, Maine

University of Southern Maine is a coed, public, comprehensive unit of University of Maine System, founded in 1878, offering degrees at the associate, bachelor's, master's, doctoral, and first professional levels and post-master's certificates. It has a 144-acre campus in Portland.

Academic Information The faculty has 710 members (57% full-time), 51% with terminal degrees. The undergraduate student-faculty ratio is 13:1. Special programs include academic remediation, services for learning-disabled students, an honors program, cooperative (work-study) education, study abroad, advanced placement credit, accelerated degree programs, ESL programs, double majors, independent study, distance learning, self-designed majors, summer session for credit, part-time degree programs (daytime, evenings, weekends, summer), internships, and arrangement for off-campus study with National Student Exchange. The most frequently chosen baccalaureate fields are business/marketing, health professions and related sciences, social sciences.

Student Body Statistics The student body is made up of 7,879 undergraduates (1,027 freshmen). 57 percent are women and 43 percent are men.

Expenses for 2008–09 *Application fee:* $40. *State resident tuition:* $6540 full-time, $218 per credit hour part-time. *Nonresident tuition:* $18,060 full-time, $602 per credit hour part-time. *Mandatory fees:* $927 full-time. Full-time tuition and fees vary according to course load, degree level, and reciprocity agreements. Part-time tuition varies according to course load, degree level, and reciprocity agreements. *College room and board:* $8344. *College room only:* $4472. Room and board charges vary according to board plan, housing facility, and location.

Financial Aid Forms of aid include need-based and non-need-based scholarships and part-time jobs. The average aided 2008–09 undergraduate received an aid package worth an estimated $10,677. The priority application deadline for financial aid is February 15.

Freshman Admission University of Southern Maine requires an essay, a high school transcript, SAT or ACT scores, and TOEFL scores for international students. A minimum 2.8 high school GPA, 1 recommendation, and an interview are recommended. An interview and auditions for music majors are required for some. The application deadline for regular admission is February 15.

Transfer Admission The application deadline for admission is February 15.

Entrance Difficulty University of Southern Maine assesses its entrance difficulty level as moderately difficult; very difficult for nursing, computer science, engineering, sports medicine, business programs. For the fall 2008 freshman class, 81 percent of the applicants were accepted.

For Further Information Contact Mr. Jonathan Barker, Director of Technology for Admissions, University of Southern Maine, 96 Falmouth Street, PO Box 9300, Portland, ME 04104-9300. *Phone:* 207-780-5724 or 800-800-4USM Ext. 5670 (toll-free). *Fax:* 207-780-5640. *E-mail:* usmadm@usm.maine.edu. *Web site:* http://www.usm.maine.edu/.

WESTBROOK COLLEGE

See University of New England.

Massachusetts

AMERICAN INTERNATIONAL COLLEGE

Springfield, Massachusetts

American International College is a coed, private, comprehensive institution, founded in 1885, offering degrees at the associate, bachelor's, master's, and doctoral levels and post-master's certificates. It has a 58-acre campus in Springfield.

Expenses for 2008–09 *Application fee:* $25. *Comprehensive fee:* $34,250 includes full-time tuition ($24,100) and college room and board ($10,150). Room and board charges vary according to board plan. *Part-time tuition:* $497 per credit.

For Further Information Contact Mr. Peter Miller, Dean of Admissions, American International College, 1000 State Street, Springfield, MA 01109-3189. *Phone:* 413-205-3201. *Fax:* 413-205-3051. *E-mail:* inquiry@aic.edu. *Web site:* http://www.aic.edu/.

AMHERST COLLEGE

Amherst, Massachusetts

Amherst College is a coed, private, four-year college, founded in 1821, offering degrees at the bachelor's level. It has a 1,020-acre campus in Amherst.

Academic Information The faculty has 223 members (91% full-time). The student-faculty ratio is 8:1. The library holds 1 million titles, 12,190 serial subscriptions, and 48,742 audiovisual materials. Special programs include an honors program, study abroad, double majors, independent study, self-designed majors, and arrangement for off-campus study with Five Colleges, Inc., Twelve College Exchange Program. The most frequently chosen baccalaureate fields are English, foreign languages and literature, social sciences.

Student Body Statistics The student body is made up of 1,697 undergraduates (439 freshmen). 51 percent are women and 49 percent are men. Students come from 48 states and territories and 41 other countries. 12 percent are from Massachusetts. 7.2 percent are international students.

Expenses for 2008–09 *Application fee:* $60. *Comprehensive fee:* $47,430 includes full-time tuition ($36,970), mandatory fees ($670), and college room and board ($9790). *College room only:* $5250.

Financial Aid Forms of aid include need-based scholarships and part-time jobs. The average aided 2008–09 undergraduate received an aid package worth an estimated $37,078. The priority application deadline for financial aid is February 15.

Freshman Admission Amherst College requires an essay, a high school transcript, 3 recommendations, SAT and SAT Subject Test or ACT scores, and TOEFL scores for international students. The application deadline for regular admission is January 1 and for early decision it is November 15.

Transfer Admission The application deadline for admission is February 1.

Entrance Difficulty Amherst College assesses its entrance difficulty level as most difficult. For the fall 2008 freshman class, 15 percent of the applicants were accepted.

For Further Information Contact Mr. Thomas H. Parker, Dean of Admission and Financial Aid, Amherst College, PO Box 5000, Amherst, MA 01002-5000. *Phone:* 413-542-2328. *Fax:* 413-542-2040. *E-mail:* admission@amherst.edu. *Web site:* http://www.amherst.edu/.

ANNA MARIA COLLEGE

Paxton, Massachusetts

Anna Maria College is a coed, private, Roman Catholic, comprehensive institution, founded in 1946, offering degrees at the associate, bachelor's, and master's levels and post-master's and postbachelor's certificates. It has a 180-acre campus in Paxton near Boston.

Academic Information The faculty has 179 members (28% full-time), 41% with terminal degrees. The undergraduate student-faculty ratio is 10:1. The library holds 85,117 titles and 176 serial subscriptions. Special programs include academic remediation, services for learning-disabled students, an honors program, cooperative (work-study) education, study abroad, advanced placement credit, accelerated degree programs, double majors, independent study, self-designed majors, summer session for credit, part-time degree programs (daytime, evenings, summer), adult/continuing education programs, internships, and arrangement for off-campus study with Colleges of Worcester Consortium. The most frequently chosen baccalaureate fields are health professions and related sciences, business/marketing, security and protective services.

Student Body Statistics The student body totals 1,333, of whom 1,001 are undergraduates (245 freshmen). 56 percent are women and 44 percent are men. Students come from 16 states and territories and 3 other countries. 88 percent are from Massachusetts. 0.5 percent are international students.

Expenses for 2008–09 *Application fee:* $40. *Comprehensive fee:* $35,200 includes full-time tuition ($23,500), mandatory fees ($2350), and college room and board ($9350). Full-time tuition and fees vary according to program. Room and board charges vary according to board plan. *Part-time tuition:* $783 per credit hour. Part-time tuition varies according to class time, course load, and program.

Financial Aid Forms of aid include need-based and non-need-based scholarships and part-time jobs. The average aided 2008–09 undergraduate received an aid package worth an estimated $17,956.

Freshman Admission Anna Maria College requires a high school transcript, a minimum 2.0 high school GPA, SAT or ACT scores, and TOEFL scores for international students. 1 recommendation and an interview are recommended. An essay and audition for music programs, portfolio for art programs are required for some. The application deadline for regular admission is rolling.

Transfer Admission The application deadline for admission is rolling.

Entrance Difficulty Anna Maria College assesses its entrance difficulty level as minimally difficult; moderately difficult for nursing program. For the fall 2008 freshman class, 89 percent of the applicants were accepted.

For Further Information Contact Ms. Jenna Noel, Admissions Coordinator, Anna Maria College, Box O, Sunset Lane, Paxton, MA 01612. *Phone:* 508-849-3360 or 800-344-4586 Ext. 360 (toll-free). *Fax:* 508-849-3362. *E-mail:* admissions@annamaria.edu. *Web site:* http://www.annamaria.edu/.

See page 92 for the Close-Up.

THE ART INSTITUTE OF BOSTON AT LESLEY UNIVERSITY

Boston, Massachusetts

The Art Institute of Boston at Lesley University is a coed, private, comprehensive institution, founded in 1912, offering degrees at the associate, bachelor's, master's, and doctoral levels and postbachelor's certificates. It has a 1-acre campus in Boston.

Academic Information The faculty has 225 members (32% full-time), 43% with terminal degrees. The undergraduate student-faculty ratio is 10:1. The library holds 100,000 titles, 1,160 serial subscriptions, and 49,943 audiovisual materials. Special programs include academic remediation, services for learning-disabled students, an honors program, study abroad, advanced placement credit, accelerated degree programs, Freshman Honors College, ESL programs, double majors, independent study, distance learning, self-designed majors, summer session for credit, part-time degree programs (daytime, evenings, weekends, summer), external degree programs, adult/continuing education programs, internships, and arrangement for off-campus study with Association of

Independent Colleges of Art and Design, NY studio program, Parsons School of Design. The most frequently chosen baccalaureate fields are liberal arts/general studies, psychology, visual and performing arts.

Student Body Statistics The student body totals 6,686, of whom 1,267 are undergraduates (327 freshmen). 75 percent are women and 25 percent are men. Students come from 56 states and territories and 24 other countries. 58 percent are from Massachusetts. 3.5 percent are international students.

Expenses for 2009–10 *Application fee:* $50. *Comprehensive fee:* $38,990 includes full-time tuition ($25,780), mandatory fees ($810), and college room and board ($12,400).

Financial Aid Forms of aid include need-based and non-need-based scholarships and part-time jobs. The average aided 2008–09 undergraduate received an aid package worth an estimated $15,652. The priority application deadline for financial aid is March 12.

Freshman Admission The Art Institute of Boston at Lesley University requires an essay, a high school transcript, 3 recommendations, an interview, a portfolio, and SAT or ACT scores. The application deadline for regular admission is rolling.

Transfer Admission The application deadline for admission is rolling.

Entrance Difficulty For the fall 2008 freshman class, 65 percent of the applicants were accepted.

For Further Information Contact Bob Gielow, Director of Admission, The Art Institute of Boston at Lesley University, 700 Beacon Street, Boston, MA 02215-2598. *Phone:* 617-585-6710 or 800-773-0494 (toll-free in-state). *Fax:* 617-585-6720. *E-mail:* admissions@aiboston.edu. *Web site:* http://www.aiboston.edu/.

ASSUMPTION COLLEGE
Worcester, Massachusetts

Assumption College is a coed, private, Roman Catholic, comprehensive institution, founded in 1904, offering degrees at the bachelor's and master's levels and post-master's and postbachelor's certificates. It has a 180-acre campus in Worcester near Boston.

Academic Information The faculty has 224 members (69% full-time), 81% with terminal degrees. The undergraduate student-faculty ratio is 12:1. The library holds 139,170 titles, 1,273 serial subscriptions, and 3,313 audiovisual materials. Special programs include services for learning-disabled students, an honors program, study abroad, advanced placement credit, double majors, independent study, self-designed majors, summer session for credit, part-time degree programs (evenings, weekends, summer), adult/continuing education programs, internships, and arrangement for off-campus study with Colleges of Worcester Consortium. The most frequently chosen baccalaureate fields are business/marketing, history, psychology.

Student Body Statistics The student body totals 2,626, of whom 2,169 are undergraduates (607 freshmen). 59 percent are women and 41 percent are men. Students come from 30 states and territories and 12 other countries. 68 percent are from Massachusetts. 0.6 percent are international students.

Expenses for 2008–09 *Application fee:* $50. *Comprehensive fee:* $35,007 includes full-time tuition ($28,686), mandatory fees ($165), and college room and board ($6156). *College room only:* $3620. Full-time tuition and fees vary according to course load and reciprocity agreements. Room and board charges vary according to housing facility. *Part-time tuition:* $956 per credit hour. *Part-time mandatory fees:* $165 per year. Part-time tuition and fees vary according to course load.

Financial Aid Forms of aid include need-based and non-need-based scholarships, athletic grants, and part-time jobs. The average aided 2008–09 undergraduate received an aid package worth an estimated $18,341. The application deadline for financial aid is February 1.

Freshman Admission Assumption College requires an essay, a high school transcript, 1 recommendation, and TOEFL scores for international students. An interview is recommended. The application deadline for regular admission is February 15 and for early action it is November 15.

Transfer Admission The application deadline for admission is July 1.

Entrance Difficulty Assumption College assesses its entrance difficulty level as moderately difficult. For the fall 2008 freshman class, 71 percent of the applicants were accepted.

For Further Information Contact Ms. Kathleen Murphy, Dean of Enrollment, Assumption College, 500 Salisbury Street, Worcester, MA 01609-1296. *Phone:* 508-767-7110 or 888-882-7786 (toll-free). *Fax:* 508-799-4412. *E-mail:* admiss@assumption.edu. *Web site:* http://www.assumption.edu/.

ATLANTIC UNION COLLEGE
South Lancaster, Massachusetts

Atlantic Union College is a coed, private, Seventh-day Adventist, comprehensive institution, founded in 1882, offering degrees at the associate, bachelor's, and master's levels and postbachelor's certificates. It has a 314-acre campus in South Lancaster near Boston.

Academic Information The faculty has 67 members (39% full-time). The undergraduate student-faculty ratio is 9:1. The library holds 153,827 titles and 4,921 audiovisual materials. Special programs include academic remediation, an honors program, cooperative (work-study) education, study abroad, advanced placement credit, Freshman Honors College, ESL programs, self-designed majors, summer session for credit, part-time degree programs (daytime, evenings, summer), external degree programs, adult/continuing education programs, and internships.

Student Body Statistics The student body totals 387, of whom 385 are undergraduates (57 freshmen). 61 percent are women and 39 percent are men. Students come from 15 states and territories and 17 other countries. 55 percent are from Massachusetts.

Expenses for 2009–10 *Application fee:* $25. *Comprehensive fee:* $21,570 includes full-time tuition ($14,960), mandatory fees ($1610), and college room and board ($5000). *Part-time tuition:* $468 per credit.

Financial Aid Forms of aid include need-based and non-need-based scholarships and part-time jobs. The average aided 2007–08 undergraduate received an aid package worth $11,596. The priority application deadline for financial aid is April 15.

Freshman Admission Atlantic Union College requires a high school transcript, a minimum 2.2 high school GPA, 2 recommendations, SAT and SAT Subject Test or ACT scores, and TOEFL scores for international students. An essay and an interview are required for some. The application deadline for regular admission is August 1.

Transfer Admission The application deadline for admission is August 1.

Entrance Difficulty Atlantic Union College assesses its entrance difficulty level as moderately difficult. For the fall 2008 freshman class, 37 percent of the applicants were accepted.

For Further Information Contact Mrs. Rosita Lashley, Director for Admissions, Atlantic Union College, PO Box 1000, South Lancaster, MA 01561-1000. *Phone:* 978-368-2239 or 800-282-2030 (toll-free). *Fax:* 978-368-2015. *E-mail:* rosita.lashley@auc.edu. *Web site:* http://www.auc.edu/.

BABSON COLLEGE
Wellesley, Massachusetts

Babson College is a coed, private, comprehensive institution, founded in 1919, offering degrees at the bachelor's and master's levels and post-master's certificates. It has a 370-acre campus in Wellesley near Boston.

Academic Information The faculty has 247 members (64% full-time), 70% with terminal degrees. The undergraduate student-faculty ratio is 14:1. The library holds 131,436 titles and 626 serial subscriptions. Special programs include services for learning-disabled students, an honors program, study abroad, advanced placement credit, Freshman Honors College, independent study, self-designed majors, summer session for credit, internships, and arrangement for off-campus study with Pine Manor College, Regis College (MA), Brandeis University, Wellesley College, Olin College of Engineering. The most frequently chosen baccalaureate field is business/marketing.

Student Body Statistics The student body totals 3,439, of whom 1,851 are undergraduates (469 freshmen). 42 percent are women and 58 percent

Babson College (continued)

are men. Students come from 44 states and territories and 64 other countries. 30 percent are from Massachusetts. 20.2 percent are international students.

Expenses for 2008–09 *Application fee:* $65. *Comprehensive fee:* $48,116 includes full-time tuition ($36,096) and college room and board ($12,020). *College room only:* $7756. Room and board charges vary according to board plan and housing facility.

Financial Aid Forms of aid include need-based and non-need-based scholarships and part-time jobs. The average aided 2008–09 undergraduate received an aid package worth an estimated $30,627. The application deadline for financial aid is February 15.

Freshman Admission Babson College requires an essay, a high school transcript, 2 recommendations, SAT or ACT scores, and TOEFL scores for international students. An interview is recommended. The application deadline for regular admission is January 15, for early decision it is November 1, and for early action it is November 1.

Transfer Admission The application deadline for admission is April 1.

Entrance Difficulty Babson College assesses its entrance difficulty level as very difficult. For the fall 2008 freshman class, 35 percent of the applicants were accepted.

For Further Information Contact Ms. Adrienne Ramsey, Senior Assistant Director of Undergraduate Admission, Babson College, Lunder Undergraduate Admission Center, Babson Park, MA 02457-0310. *Phone:* 781-239-5522 or 800-488-3696 (toll-free). *Fax:* 781-239-4135. *E-mail:* ugradadmission@babson.edu. *Web site:* http://www.babson.edu/.

BAPTIST BIBLE COLLEGE EAST

See Boston Baptist College.

BARD COLLEGE AT SIMON'S ROCK

Great Barrington, Massachusetts

Bard College at Simon's Rock is a coed, private, four-year college, founded in 1964, offering degrees at the associate and bachelor's levels. It has a 275-acre campus in Great Barrington near Albany and Springfield.

Academic Information The faculty has 78 members (62% full-time), 79% with terminal degrees. The student-faculty ratio is 9:1. The library holds 73,514 titles and 417 serial subscriptions. Special programs include services for learning-disabled students, study abroad, double majors, independent study, self-designed majors, part-time degree programs (daytime), internships, and arrangement for off-campus study with Bard College. The most frequently chosen baccalaureate fields are English, psychology, visual and performing arts.

Student Body Statistics The student body is made up of 436 undergraduates. Students come from 41 states and territories and 11 other countries. 18 percent are from Massachusetts.

Expenses for 2009–10 *Application fee:* $50. *Comprehensive fee:* $51,130 includes full-time tuition ($39,380), mandatory fees ($790), and college room and board ($10,960).

Financial Aid Forms of aid include need-based and non-need-based scholarships and part-time jobs. The average aided 2007–08 undergraduate received an aid package worth $19,500. The priority application deadline for financial aid is April 15.

Freshman Admission Bard College at Simon's Rock requires an essay, a high school transcript, a minimum 2.0 high school GPA, 2 recommendations, an interview, parent application, and TOEFL scores for international students. A minimum 3.0 high school GPA is recommended. SAT or ACT scores and PSAT are required for some. The application deadline for regular admission is May 31.

Transfer Admission The application deadline for admission is July 15.

Entrance Difficulty Bard College at Simon's Rock assesses its entrance difficulty level as very difficult. For the fall 2008 freshman class, 80 percent of the applicants were accepted.

For Further Information Contact Steven Coleman, Director of Admissions, Bard College at Simon's Rock, 84 Alford Road, Great Barrington, MA 01230-9702. *Phone:* 413-528-7312 or 800-235-7186 (toll-free). *Fax:* 413-528-7334. *E-mail:* admit@simons-rock.edu. *Web site:* http://www. simons-rock.edu/.

BAY PATH COLLEGE

Longmeadow, Massachusetts

Bay Path College is an undergraduate: women only; graduate: coed, private, comprehensive institution, founded in 1897, offering degrees at the bachelor's and master's levels and postbachelor's certificates. It has a 48-acre campus in Longmeadow near Boston.

Academic Information The faculty has 223 members (20% full-time), 38% with terminal degrees. The undergraduate student-faculty ratio is 14:1. The library holds 62,023 titles, 1,351 serial subscriptions, and 4,261 audiovisual materials. Special programs include academic remediation, services for learning-disabled students, an honors program, cooperative (work-study) education, study abroad, advanced placement credit, Freshman Honors College, ESL programs, double majors, independent study, distance learning, self-designed majors, summer session for credit, part-time degree programs (daytime, evenings, weekends), adult/continuing education programs, internships, and arrangement for off-campus study with Cooperating Colleges of Greater Springfield. The most frequently chosen baccalaureate fields are business/marketing, liberal arts/general studies, psychology.

Student Body Statistics The student body totals 1,784, of whom 1,409 are undergraduates (208 freshmen). 100 percent are women. Students come from 16 states and territories and 8 other countries. 50 percent are from Massachusetts. 0.8 percent are international students.

Expenses for 2008–09 *Application fee:* $25. *Comprehensive fee:* $33,590 includes full-time tuition ($23,840) and college room and board ($9750). Room and board charges vary according to board plan. *Part-time tuition:* $450 per credit.

Financial Aid Forms of aid include need-based and non-need-based scholarships and part-time jobs. The priority application deadline for financial aid is March 15.

Freshman Admission Bay Path College requires a high school transcript, SAT or ACT scores, and TOEFL scores for international students. An essay, a minimum 2.5 high school GPA, and an interview are recommended. An interview is required for some. The application deadline for regular admission is rolling and for early action it is December 15.

Transfer Admission The application deadline for admission is rolling.

Entrance Difficulty Bay Path College assesses its entrance difficulty level as moderately difficult. For the fall 2008 freshman class, 83 percent of the applicants were accepted.

For Further Information Contact Julie Richardson, Dean of Enrollment Management, Traditional Program, Bay Path College, 588 Longmeadow Street, Longmeadow, MA 01106-2292. *Phone:* 413-565-1000 Ext. 1331 or 800-782-7284 Ext. 1331 (toll-free). *Fax:* 413-565-1105. *E-mail:* admiss@ baypath.edu. *Web site:* http://www.baypath.edu/.

BAY STATE COLLEGE

Boston, Massachusetts

http://www.baystate.edu/

BECKER COLLEGE

Worcester, Massachusetts

Becker College is a coed, private, four-year college, founded in 1784, offering degrees at the associate and bachelor's levels (also includes Leicester, MA small town campus). It has a 100-acre campus in Worcester near Boston.

Academic Information The faculty has 184 members (22% full-time), 27% with terminal degrees. The student-faculty ratio is 16:1. The library holds 75,000 titles and 400 serial subscriptions. Special programs include academic remediation, services for learning-disabled students, cooperative (work-study) education, advanced placement credit, accelerated degree programs, distance learning, summer session for credit, part-time degree programs (daytime, evenings, weekends, summer), adult/continuing education programs, internships, and arrangement for off-campus study with Colleges of Worcester Consortium. The most frequently chosen baccalaureate fields are business/marketing, science technologies, visual and performing arts.

Student Body Statistics The student body is made up of 1,752 undergraduates (347 freshmen). 67 percent are women and 33 percent are men. Students come from 26 states and territories and 5 other countries. 77 percent are from Massachusetts.

Expenses for 2008–09 *Application fee:* $30. *Comprehensive fee:* $37,508 includes full-time tuition ($24,780), mandatory fees ($2968), and college room and board ($9760). Room and board charges vary according to board plan and housing facility. *Part-time tuition:* $1025 per credit hour. Part-time tuition varies according to program.

Financial Aid Forms of aid include need-based and non-need-based scholarships and part-time jobs. The average aided 2008–09 undergraduate received an aid package worth an estimated $13,911. The priority application deadline for financial aid is March 1.

Freshman Admission Becker College requires a high school transcript, a minimum 2.0 high school GPA, SAT or ACT scores, and TOEFL scores for international students. An essay is recommended. A minimum 2.5 high school GPA and an interview are required for some. The application deadline for regular admission is rolling.

Transfer Admission The application deadline for admission is rolling.

Entrance Difficulty Becker College assesses its entrance difficulty level as minimally difficult; moderately difficult for nursing, animal science programs. For the fall 2008 freshman class, 72 percent of the applicants were accepted.

For Further Information Contact Admissions Receptionist, Becker College, 61 Sever Street, Worcester, MA 01609. *Phone:* 508-373-9400 or 877-5BECKER Ext. 245 (toll-free). *Fax:* 508-890-1500. *E-mail:* admissions@beckercollege.edu. *Web site:* http://www.becker.edu/.

BENJAMIN FRANKLIN INSTITUTE OF TECHNOLOGY
Boston, Massachusetts

Benjamin Franklin Institute of Technology is a coed, private, primarily two-year college, founded in 1908, offering degrees at the associate and bachelor's levels. It has a 3-acre campus in Boston.

Academic Information The faculty has 70 members (43% full-time), 3% with terminal degrees. The student-faculty ratio is 12:1. The library holds 10,000 titles and 90 serial subscriptions. Special programs include academic remediation, services for learning-disabled students, cooperative (work-study) education, advanced placement credit, ESL programs, summer session for credit, part-time degree programs (daytime, evenings), adult/continuing education programs, internships, and arrangement for off-campus study with University of Massachusetts—Dartmouth, Boston Architectural College, Wentworth Institute of Technology.

Student Body Statistics The student body is made up of 536 undergraduates (243 freshmen). 11 percent are women and 89 percent are men. Students come from 7 states and territories. 95 percent are from Massachusetts.

Expenses for 2009–10 *Application fee:* $25. *Comprehensive fee:* $23,884 includes full-time tuition ($13,950), mandatory fees ($334), and college room and board ($9600). *Part-time tuition:* $581 per credit.

Financial Aid Forms of aid include part-time jobs. The priority application deadline for financial aid is April 15.

Freshman Admission Benjamin Franklin Institute of Technology requires a high school transcript and TOEFL scores for international students. An essay, a minimum 2 high school GPA, and an interview are recommended. The application deadline for regular admission is August 15.

Transfer Admission The application deadline for admission is rolling.

Entrance Difficulty Benjamin Franklin Institute of Technology has an open admission policy.

For Further Information Contact Ms. Brittainy Johnson, Associate Director of Admissions, Benjamin Franklin Institute of Technology, 41 Berkeley Street, Boston, MA 02116-6296. *Phone:* 617-423-4630 Ext. 122. *Fax:* 617-482-3706. *E-mail:* bjohnson@bfit.edu. *Web site:* http://www.bfit.edu/.

BENTLEY UNIVERSITY
Waltham, Massachusetts

Bentley University is a coed, private, comprehensive institution, founded in 1917, offering degrees at the associate, bachelor's, master's, and doctoral levels and post-master's and postbachelor's certificates. It has a 163-acre campus in Waltham near Boston.

Academic Information The faculty has 484 members (59% full-time), 65% with terminal degrees. The undergraduate student-faculty ratio is 12:1. The library holds 177,000 titles, 30,700 serial subscriptions, and 9,500 audiovisual materials. Special programs include services for learning-disabled students, an honors program, study abroad, advanced placement credit, accelerated degree programs, double majors, independent study, self-designed majors, summer session for credit, part-time degree programs (evenings), adult/continuing education programs, internships, and arrangement for off-campus study with The Bentley-Brandeis-Regis Exchange. The most frequently chosen baccalaureate fields are business/marketing, computer and information sciences, interdisciplinary studies.

Student Body Statistics The student body totals 5,664, of whom 4,259 are undergraduates (974 freshmen). 40 percent are women and 60 percent are men. Students come from 44 states and territories and 78 other countries. 50 percent are from Massachusetts. 9 percent are international students.

Expenses for 2008–09 *Application fee:* $50. *Comprehensive fee:* $45,808 includes full-time tuition ($33,030), mandatory fees ($1458), and college room and board ($11,320). *College room only:* $6770. Room and board charges vary according to board plan and housing facility. *Part-time tuition:* $1581 per course. *Part-time mandatory fees:* $45 per term. Part-time tuition and fees vary according to class time.

Financial Aid Forms of aid include need-based and non-need-based scholarships, athletic grants, and part-time jobs. The average aided 2007–08 undergraduate received an aid package worth $26,584. The application deadline for financial aid is February 1.

Freshman Admission Bentley University requires an essay, a high school transcript, 2 recommendations, SAT or ACT scores, and TOEFL scores for international students. An interview is recommended. The application deadline for regular admission is January 15, for nonresidents it is January 15, for early decision it is November 15, and for early action it is November 15.

Transfer Admission The application deadline for admission is rolling.

Entrance Difficulty Bentley University assesses its entrance difficulty level as very difficult; moderately difficult for transfers. For the fall 2008 freshman class, 38 percent of the applicants were accepted.

For Further Information Contact Admissions Office, Bentley University, 175 Forest Street, Waltham, MA 02452. *Phone:* 781-891-2244 or 800-523-2354 (toll-free). *Fax:* 781-891-3414. *E-mail:* ugadmission@bentley.edu. *Web site:* http://www.bentley.edu.

BERKLEE COLLEGE OF MUSIC
Boston, Massachusetts

Berklee College of Music is a coed, private, four-year college, founded in 1945, offering degrees at the bachelor's level.

Academic Information The faculty has 529 members (45% full-time). The student-faculty ratio is 11:1. The library holds 30,208 titles and 77 serial subscriptions. Special programs include services for learning-disabled students, study abroad, advanced placement credit, ESL programs, double majors, self-designed majors, summer session for credit, internships, and arrangement for off-campus study with Pro Arts Consortium. The most frequently chosen baccalaureate fields are business/marketing, education, visual and performing arts.

Berklee College of Music (continued)

Student Body Statistics The student body is made up of 4,054 undergraduates (634 freshmen). 28 percent are women and 72 percent are men. Students come from 54 states and territories and 73 other countries. 12 percent are from Massachusetts. 22.8 percent are international students.

Expenses for 2009–10 *Application fee:* $150. *Comprehensive fee:* $45,730 includes full-time tuition ($29,700), mandatory fees ($950), and college room and board ($15,080). *Part-time tuition:* $1053 per credit hour. There is a one-time $2,950 charge for laptop purchase required of all entering students.

Financial Aid Forms of aid include need-based and non-need-based scholarships and part-time jobs. The average aided 2008–09 undergraduate received an aid package worth an estimated $12,279. The application deadline for financial aid is May 1.

Freshman Admission Berklee College of Music requires an essay, a high school transcript, 2 recommendations, an interview, 2 years of formal music study and audition, and TOEFL scores for international students. The application deadline for regular admission is January 15 and for early action it is November 1.

Transfer Admission The application deadline for admission is January 15.

Entrance Difficulty Berklee College of Music assesses its entrance difficulty level as moderately difficult. For the fall 2008 freshman class, 44 percent of the applicants were accepted.

For Further Information Contact Mr. Damien Bracken, Director of Admissions, Berklee College of Music, 1140 Boyleston Street, Boston, MA 02215-3693. *Phone:* 617-747-2222 or 800-BERKLEE (toll-free). *Fax:* 617-747-2047. *E-mail:* admissions@berklee.edu. *Web site:* http://www.berklee.edu/.

BOSTON ARCHITECTURAL COLLEGE

Boston, Massachusetts

Boston Architectural College is a coed, private, comprehensive institution, founded in 1889, offering degrees at the bachelor's and master's levels. It has a 1-acre campus in Boston.

Academic Information The faculty has 229 members (5% full-time), 26% with terminal degrees. The undergraduate student-faculty ratio is 4:1. The library holds 27,000 titles, 130 serial subscriptions, and 250 audiovisual materials. Special programs include advanced placement credit, independent study, distance learning, summer session for credit, adult/continuing education programs, internships, and arrangement for off-campus study with Art Institute of Boston at Lesley College, ProArts Consortium. The most frequently chosen baccalaureate field is architecture.

Student Body Statistics The student body totals 1,176, of whom 624 are undergraduates (61 freshmen). 33 percent are women and 67 percent are men. Students come from 25 states and territories and 10 other countries. 49 percent are from Massachusetts.

Expenses for 2008–09 *Application fee:* $50. *Tuition:* $10,600 full-time, $883 per credit hour part-time. *Mandatory fees:* $20 full-time, $10 per term part-time. Both full-time and part-time tuition and fees vary according to course load, degree level, program, and reciprocity agreements.

Financial Aid Forms of aid include need-based and non-need-based scholarships and part-time jobs. The average aided 2008–09 undergraduate received an aid package worth an estimated $5766. The priority application deadline for financial aid is April 15.

Freshman Admission Boston Architectural College requires a high school transcript and resume. The application deadline for regular admission is rolling.

Transfer Admission The application deadline for admission is rolling.

Entrance Difficulty Boston Architectural College assesses its entrance difficulty level as noncompetitive. For the fall 2008 freshman class, 71 percent of the applicants were accepted.

For Further Information Contact Richard Moyer, Director of Admission, Boston Architectural College, 320 Newbury Street, Boston, MA 02115-2795. *Phone:* 617-585-0256 or 877-585-0100 (toll-free). *Fax:* 617-585-0121. *E-mail:* admissions@the-bac.edu. *Web site:* http://www.the-bac.edu/.

BOSTON BAPTIST COLLEGE

Boston, Massachusetts

Boston Baptist College is a coed, private, Baptist, four-year college, founded in 1976, offering degrees at the associate and bachelor's levels. It has an 8-acre campus in Boston near Providence.

Academic Information The faculty has 9 members (44% full-time), 56% with terminal degrees. The student-faculty ratio is 6:1. Special programs include academic remediation, an honors program, summer session for credit, part-time degree programs (daytime, summer), adult/continuing education programs, and internships. The most frequently chosen baccalaureate field is theology and religious vocations.

Student Body Statistics The student body is made up of 121 undergraduates (24 freshmen). 46 percent are women and 54 percent are men. Students come from 24 states and territories and 5 other countries. 35 percent are from Massachusetts. 5.4 percent are international students.

Expenses for 2008–09 *Application fee:* $40. *Comprehensive fee:* $19,444 includes full-time tuition ($10,374), mandatory fees ($1650), and college room and board ($7420). *College room only:* $4570. Room and board charges vary according to board plan. *Part-time tuition:* $432 per hour.

Financial Aid Forms of aid include need-based scholarships. The application deadline for financial aid is continuous.

Freshman Admission Boston Baptist College requires an essay, a high school transcript, 1 recommendation, SAT or ACT scores, and TOEFL scores for international students. An interview is recommended. The application deadline for regular admission is rolling.

Transfer Admission The application deadline for admission is rolling.

Entrance Difficulty Boston Baptist College assesses its entrance difficulty level as moderately difficult. For the fall 2008 freshman class, 88 percent of the applicants were accepted.

For Further Information Contact Mrs. Karen Fox, Director of Admissions, Boston Baptist College, 950 Metropolitan Avenue, Boston, MA 02136. *Phone:* 617-364-3510 Ext. 217 or 888-235-2014 (toll-free out-of-state). *Fax:* 775-522-4803. *E-mail:* kfox@boston.edu. *Web site:* http://www.boston.edu/.

BOSTON COLLEGE

Chestnut Hill, Massachusetts

Boston College is a coed, private, Roman Catholic (Jesuit) university, founded in 1863, offering degrees at the bachelor's, master's, doctoral, and first professional levels and post-master's certificates (also offers continuing education program with significant enrollment not reflected in profile). It has a 379-acre campus in Chestnut Hill near Boston.

Academic Information The faculty has 1,224 members (55% full-time). The undergraduate student-faculty ratio is 13:1. The library holds 3 million titles, 31,664 serial subscriptions, and 171,099 audiovisual materials. Special programs include services for learning-disabled students, an honors program, study abroad, advanced placement credit, accelerated degree programs, double majors, independent study, self-designed majors, summer session for credit, part-time degree programs (evenings, weekends, summer), internships, and arrangement for off-campus study with Boston University, Brandeis University, Hebrew College, Pine Manor College, Regis College (MA), Tufts University. The most frequently chosen baccalaureate fields are business/marketing, communications/journalism, social sciences.

Student Body Statistics The student body totals 13,903, of whom 9,060 are undergraduates (2,167 freshmen). 52 percent are women and 48 percent are men. Students come from 54 states and territories and 58 other countries. 29 percent are from Massachusetts. 2.5 percent are international students.

Expenses for 2008–09 *Application fee:* $70. *One-time mandatory fee:* $425. *Comprehensive fee:* $50,345 includes full-time tuition ($37,410), mandatory fees ($540), and college room and board ($12,395). *College room only:* $7945. Room and board charges vary according to housing facility.

Financial Aid Forms of aid include need-based and non-need-based scholarships, athletic grants, and part-time jobs. The average aided 2008–09 undergraduate received an aid package worth an estimated $29,586. The priority application deadline for financial aid is February 1.

Freshman Admission Boston College requires an essay, a high school transcript, 2 recommendations, SAT and SAT Subject Test or ACT scores, and TOEFL scores for international students. The application deadline for regular admission is January 1 and for early action it is November 1.

Transfer Admission The application deadline for admission is April 1.

Entrance Difficulty Boston College assesses its entrance difficulty level as very difficult. For the fall 2008 freshman class, 26 percent of the applicants were accepted.

For Further Information Contact Office of Undergraduate Admissions, Boston College, 140 Commonwealth Avenue, Devlin 208, Chestnut Hill, MA 02467-3809. *Phone:* 617-552-3100 or 800-360-2522 (toll-free). *Fax:* 617-552-0798. *E-mail:* ugadmis@bc.edu. *Web site:* http://www.bc.edu/.

THE BOSTON CONSERVATORY
Boston, Massachusetts

The Boston Conservatory is a coed, private, comprehensive institution, founded in 1867, offering degrees at the bachelor's and master's levels and post-master's and postbachelor's certificates.

Academic Information The faculty has 189 members (39% full-time). The undergraduate student-faculty ratio is 4:1. The library holds 30,261 titles, 182 serial subscriptions, and 12 audiovisual materials. Special programs include cooperative (work-study) education, advanced placement credit, ESL programs, double majors, independent study, summer session for credit, internships, and arrangement for off-campus study with members of the Pro Arts Consortium. The most frequently chosen baccalaureate field is visual and performing arts.

Student Body Statistics The student body totals 655, of whom 482 are undergraduates (150 freshmen). 61 percent are women and 39 percent are men. Students come from 44 states and territories and 30 other countries. 18 percent are from Massachusetts.

Expenses for 2008–09 *Application fee:* $105. *Comprehensive fee:* $47,870 includes full-time tuition ($30,400), mandatory fees ($1800), and college room and board ($15,670). *College room only:* $10,500. Full-time tuition and fees vary according to course load, degree level, and program. Room and board charges vary according to board plan and housing facility. *Part-time tuition:* $1260 per credit. *Part-time mandatory fees:* $390 per term. Part-time tuition and fees vary according to course load, degree level, and program.

Financial Aid Forms of aid include need-based and non-need-based scholarships and part-time jobs. The average aided 2008–09 undergraduate received an aid package worth an estimated $13,967. The priority application deadline for financial aid is March 1.

Freshman Admission The Boston Conservatory requires an essay, a high school transcript, a minimum 2.7 high school GPA, 4 recommendations, audition, and TOEFL scores for international students. An interview is required for some. The application deadline for regular admission is December 1.

Transfer Admission The application deadline for admission is December 1.

Entrance Difficulty The Boston Conservatory assesses its entrance difficulty level as moderately difficult. For the fall 2008 freshman class, 13 percent of the applicants were accepted.

For Further Information Contact Ms. Halley Shefler, Dean of Enrollment, The Boston Conservatory, 8 The Fenway, Boston, MA 02215. *Phone:* 617-912-9153. *Fax:* 617-536-3176. *E-mail:* admissions@bostonconservatory.edu. *Web site:* http://www.bostonconservatory.edu/.

BOSTON UNIVERSITY
Boston, Massachusetts

Boston University is a coed, private university, founded in 1839, offering degrees at the bachelor's, master's, doctoral, and first professional levels and post-master's, first professional, and postbachelor's certificates. It has a 132-acre campus in Boston.

Expenses for 2008–09 *Application fee:* $75. *Comprehensive fee:* $48,468 includes full-time tuition ($36,540), mandatory fees ($510), and college room and board ($11,418). *College room only:* $7420. Full-time tuition and fees vary according to class time and degree level. Room and board charges vary according to board plan and housing facility. *Part-time tuition:* $1142

per credit. *Part-time mandatory fees:* $40 per term. Part-time tuition and fees vary according to class time, course load, and degree level.

For Further Information Contact Ms. Kelly Walter, Director of Undergraduate Admissions, Boston University, 121 Bay State Road, Boston, MA 02215. *Phone:* 617-353-2300. *Fax:* 617-353-9695. *E-mail:* admissions@bu.edu. *Web site:* http://www.bu.edu/.

BRANDEIS UNIVERSITY
Waltham, Massachusetts

Brandeis University is a coed, private university, founded in 1948, offering degrees at the bachelor's, master's, and doctoral levels and postbachelor's certificates. It has a 235-acre campus in Waltham near Boston.

Academic Information The library holds 1 million titles, 35,125 serial subscriptions, and 40,773 audiovisual materials. Special programs include services for learning-disabled students, an honors program, study abroad, advanced placement credit, ESL programs, double majors, independent study, self-designed majors, summer session for credit, adult/continuing education programs, internships, and arrangement for off-campus study with Tufts University, Babson College, Bentley College, Boston University, Wellesley College, Boston College. The most frequently chosen baccalaureate fields are area and ethnic studies, biological/life sciences, social sciences.

Student Body Statistics The student body totals 5,327, of whom 3,196 are undergraduates (754 freshmen). 56 percent are women and 44 percent are men. Students come from 47 states and territories and 54 other countries. 26 percent are from Massachusetts. 7.6 percent are international students.

Expenses for 2008–09 *Application fee:* $55. *Comprehensive fee:* $47,648 includes full-time tuition ($36,122), mandatory fees ($1172), and college room and board ($10,354). *College room only:* $5808. Room and board charges vary according to board plan and housing facility. *Part-time tuition:* varies with course load.

Financial Aid Forms of aid include need-based and non-need-based scholarships and part-time jobs. The average aided 2008–09 undergraduate received an aid package worth an estimated $29,044.

Freshman Admission Brandeis University requires an essay, a high school transcript, 2 recommendations, SAT or ACT scores, and TOEFL scores for international students. An interview is recommended. The application deadline for regular admission is January 15, for early decision plan 1 it is November 15, for early decision plan 2 it is January 1, and for early action it is December 15.

Transfer Admission The application deadline for admission is April 1.

Entrance Difficulty Brandeis University assesses its entrance difficulty level as most difficult; very difficult for transfers. For the fall 2008 freshman class, 33 percent of the applicants were accepted.

For Further Information Contact Mr. Gil J. Villanueva, Dean of Admissions, Brandeis University, 415 South Street, Waltham, MA 02254-9110. *Phone:* 781-736-3500 or 800-622-0622 (toll-free out-of-state). *Fax:* 781-736-3536. *E-mail:* admissions@brandeis.edu. *Web site:* http://www.brandeis.edu/.

BRIDGEWATER STATE COLLEGE
Bridgewater, Massachusetts

Bridgewater State College is a coed, public, comprehensive unit of Massachusetts Public Higher Education System, founded in 1840, offering degrees at the bachelor's and master's levels and post-master's and postbachelor's certificates. It has a 235-acre campus in Bridgewater near Boston.

Academic Information The faculty has 672 members (46% full-time). The undergraduate student-faculty ratio is 18.6:1. The library holds 577,881 titles and 31,617 serial subscriptions. Special programs include academic remediation, services for learning-disabled students, an honors program, study abroad, advanced placement credit, accelerated degree programs, ESL programs, double majors, independent study, distance learning, summer session for credit, part-time degree programs (daytime, evenings, weekends, summer), adult/continuing education programs,

Bridgewater State College (continued)

internships, and arrangement for off-campus study with 8 members of the Southeastern Association for Cooperation in Higher Education in Massachusetts, 9 members of the College Academic Program Sharing. The most frequently chosen baccalaureate fields are business/marketing, education, psychology.

Student Body Statistics The student body is made up of 8,497 undergraduates. 60 percent are women and 40 percent are men. Students come from 26 states and territories and 19 other countries. 95 percent are from Massachusetts. 1 percent are international students.

Expenses for 2009–10 *State resident tuition:* $910 full-time. *Nonresident tuition:* $7050 full-time. *Mandatory fees:* $5327 full-time. *College room and board:* $6852.

Financial Aid Forms of aid include need-based and non-need-based scholarships and part-time jobs. The average aided 2007–08 undergraduate received an aid package worth $7687. The priority application deadline for financial aid is March 1.

Freshman Admission Bridgewater State College requires an essay, a high school transcript, a minimum 3.0 high school GPA, SAT or ACT scores, and TOEFL scores for international students. Recommendations are recommended. The application deadline for regular admission is February 15 and for early action it is November 15.

Transfer Admission The application deadline for admission is June 1.

Entrance Difficulty Bridgewater State College assesses its entrance difficulty level as moderately difficult. For the fall 2008 freshman class, 62 percent of the applicants were accepted.

For Further Information Contact Mr. Gregg Meyer, Director of Admissions, Bridgewater State College, Gates House, Bridgewater, MA 02325. *Phone:* 508-531-1237. *Fax:* 508-531-1746. *E-mail:* admission@bridgew.edu. *Web site:* http://www.bridgew.edu/.

CAMBRIDGE COLLEGE
Cambridge, Massachusetts

Cambridge College is a coed, private, comprehensive institution, founded in 1971, offering degrees at the bachelor's, master's, doctoral, and first professional levels and post-master's certificates. It is located in Cambridge near Boston.

Academic Information The faculty has 1,093 members (3% full-time), 20% with terminal degrees. The undergraduate student-faculty ratio is 11:1. The library holds 30,000 titles and 21 serial subscriptions. Special programs include services for learning-disabled students, accelerated degree programs, ESL programs, independent study, distance learning, summer session for credit, part-time degree programs (evenings, weekends, summer), adult/continuing education programs, and internships. The most frequently chosen baccalaureate fields are business/marketing, interdisciplinary studies, psychology.

Student Body Statistics The student body totals 6,098, of whom 1,128 are undergraduates (309 freshmen). 72 percent are women and 28 percent are men. Students come from 19 states and territories and 50 other countries. 86 percent are from Massachusetts.

Expenses for 2009–10 *Application fee:* $30. *Tuition:* $10,959 full-time.

Financial Aid Forms of aid include need-based and non-need-based scholarships and part-time jobs. The application deadline for financial aid is continuous.

Freshman Admission Cambridge College requires an essay, a high school transcript, and TOEFL scores for international students. 3 years of work experience is recommended. An interview is required for some. The application deadline for regular admission is rolling.

Transfer Admission The application deadline for admission is rolling.

Entrance Difficulty Cambridge College has an open admission policy. It assesses its entrance difficulty as noncompetitive for transfers.

For Further Information Contact Ms. Farah Ravanbakhsh, Assistant Vice President for Undergraduate Admissions & Enrollment, Cambridge College, 1000 Massachusetts Avenue, Cambridge, MA 02138. *Phone:* 617-873-0124 or 800-877-4723 (toll-free). *Fax:* 617-349-3545. *E-mail:* admit@cambridgecollege.edu. *Web site:* http://www.cambridgecollege.edu/.

CLARK UNIVERSITY
Worcester, Massachusetts

Clark University is a coed, private university, founded in 1887, offering degrees at the bachelor's, master's, and doctoral levels and post-master's and postbachelor's certificates. It has a 50-acre campus in Worcester near Boston.

Academic Information The faculty has 299 members (62% full-time). The undergraduate student-faculty ratio is 10:1. The library holds 289,658 titles and 1,383 serial subscriptions. Special programs include academic remediation, services for learning-disabled students, an honors program, study abroad, advanced placement credit, accelerated degree programs, ESL programs, double majors, independent study, self-designed majors, summer session for credit, part-time degree programs (evenings, weekends, summer), adult/continuing education programs, internships, and arrangement for off-campus study with Worcester Consortium for Higher Education, Howard University. The most frequently chosen baccalaureate fields are psychology, biological/life sciences, social sciences.

Student Body Statistics The student body totals 3,330, of whom 2,380 are undergraduates (591 freshmen). 60 percent are women and 40 percent are men. Students come from 44 states and territories and 72 other countries. 36 percent are from Massachusetts. 8.4 percent are international students.

Expenses for 2009–10 *Application fee:* $55. *Comprehensive fee:* $41,970 includes full-time tuition ($34,900), mandatory fees ($320), and college room and board ($6750). *College room only:* $3900. *Part-time tuition:* $1090 per credit hour.

Financial Aid Forms of aid include need-based and non-need-based scholarships and part-time jobs. The average aided 2008–09 undergraduate received an aid package worth an estimated $27,945. The application deadline for financial aid is January 15.

Freshman Admission Clark University requires an essay, a high school transcript, 2 recommendations, SAT or ACT scores, and TOEFL scores for international students. An interview is recommended. The application deadline for regular admission is January 15 and for early decision it is November 15.

Transfer Admission The application deadline for admission is April 15.

Entrance Difficulty Clark University assesses its entrance difficulty level as moderately difficult. For the fall 2008 freshman class, 56 percent of the applicants were accepted.

For Further Information Contact Mr. Harold Wingood, Dean of Admissions, Clark University, Admissions House, 950 Main Street, Worcester, MA 01610. *Phone:* 508-793-7431 or 800-GO-CLARK (toll-free). *Fax:* 508-793-8821. *E-mail:* admissions@clarku.edu. *Web site:* http://www.clarku.edu/.

COLLEGE OF OUR LADY OF THE ELMS
See Elms College.

COLLEGE OF THE HOLY CROSS
Worcester, Massachusetts

College of the Holy Cross is a coed, private, Roman Catholic (Jesuit), four-year college, founded in 1843, offering degrees at the bachelor's level (standardized tests are optional for admission to the College of Holy Cross). It has a 174-acre campus in Worcester near Boston.

Academic Information The faculty has 318 members (81% full-time). The student-faculty ratio is 10.3:1. The library holds 624,981 titles, 9,668 serial subscriptions, and 29,544 audiovisual materials. Special programs include an honors program, study abroad, advanced placement credit, accelerated degree programs, double majors, independent study, self-designed majors, internships, and arrangement for off-campus study with Colleges of Worcester Consortium of Higher Education. The most frequently chosen baccalaureate fields are English, psychology, social sciences.

Student Body Statistics The student body is made up of 2,898 undergraduates (737 freshmen). 56 percent are women and 44 percent are men. Students come from 46 states and territories and 15 other countries. 38 percent are from Massachusetts. 1.3 percent are international students.

Expenses for 2009–10 *Application fee:* $60. *Comprehensive fee:* $49,342 includes full-time tuition ($38,180), mandatory fees ($542), and college room and board ($10,620). *College room only:* $5440.

Financial Aid Forms of aid include need-based and non-need-based scholarships, athletic grants, and part-time jobs. The average aided 2008–09 undergraduate received an aid package worth an estimated $29,166. The application deadline for financial aid is February 1.

Freshman Admission College of the Holy Cross requires an essay, a high school transcript, 2 recommendations, and TOEFL scores for international students. An interview is recommended. The application deadline for regular admission is January 15 and for early decision it is December 15.

Transfer Admission The application deadline for admission is May 1.

Entrance Difficulty College of the Holy Cross assesses its entrance difficulty level as very difficult. For the fall 2008 freshman class, 34 percent of the applicants were accepted.

For Further Information Contact Ms. Ann Bowe McDermott, Director of Admissions, College of the Holy Cross, 105 Fenwick Hall, 1 College Street, Worcester, MA 01610-2395. *Phone:* 508-793-2443 or 800-442-2421 (toll-free). *Fax:* 508-793-3888. *E-mail:* admissions@holycross.edu. *Web site:* http://www.holycross.edu/.

CURRY COLLEGE

Milton, Massachusetts

Curry College is a coed, private, comprehensive institution, founded in 1879, offering degrees at the bachelor's and master's levels. It has a 131-acre campus in Milton near Boston.

Academic Information The faculty has 463 members (25% full-time). The undergraduate student-faculty ratio is 12:1. The library holds 139,000 titles, 29,800 serial subscriptions, and 2,700 audiovisual materials. Special programs include academic remediation, services for learning-disabled students, an honors program, study abroad, advanced placement credit, accelerated degree programs, double majors, independent study, self-designed majors, summer session for credit, part-time degree programs (daytime, evenings, weekends, summer), external degree programs, adult/continuing education programs, internships, and arrangement for off-campus study. The most frequently chosen baccalaureate fields are health professions and related sciences, business/marketing, security and protective services.

Student Body Statistics The student body totals 3,079, of whom 2,753 are undergraduates (587 freshmen). 59 percent are women and 41 percent are men. Students come from 31 states and territories and 17 other countries. 76 percent are from Massachusetts. 0.8 percent are international students.

Expenses for 2008–09 *Application fee:* $40. *Comprehensive fee:* $38,800 includes full-time tuition ($26,700), mandatory fees ($1020), and college room and board ($11,080). *College room only:* $6500. Room and board charges vary according to board plan and housing facility. *Part-time tuition:* $960 per credit hour. Part-time tuition varies according to course load.

Financial Aid Forms of aid include need-based and non-need-based scholarships and part-time jobs. The average aided 2008–09 undergraduate received an aid package worth an estimated $17,286. The priority application deadline for financial aid is March 1.

Freshman Admission Curry College requires an essay, a high school transcript, a minimum 2.0 high school GPA, 1 recommendation, and TOEFL scores for international students. An interview is recommended. An interview, SAT or ACT scores, are required for some. The application deadline for regular admission is April 1 and for early decision it is December 1.

Transfer Admission The application deadline for admission is July 1.

Entrance Difficulty Curry College assesses its entrance difficulty level as moderately difficult. For the fall 2008 freshman class, 66 percent of the applicants were accepted.

For Further Information Contact Ms. Jane P. Fidler, Dean of Admission, Curry College, 1071 Blue Hill Avenue, Milton, MA 02186. *Phone:* 617-333-2210 or 800-669-0686 (toll-free). *Fax:* 617-333-2114. *E-mail:* curryadm@curry.edu. *Web site:* http://www.curry.edu/.

DEAN COLLEGE

Franklin, Massachusetts

http://www.dean.edu/

See page 96 for the Close-Up.

EASTERN NAZARENE COLLEGE

Quincy, Massachusetts

Eastern Nazarene College is a coed, private, comprehensive institution, founded in 1918, affiliated with the Church of the Nazarene, offering degrees at the associate, bachelor's, and master's levels. It has a 15-acre campus in Quincy near Boston.

Expenses for 2008–09 *Application fee:* $25. *Comprehensive fee:* $29,927 includes full-time tuition ($21,280), mandatory fees ($734), and college room and board ($7913). *College room only:* $3975. *Part-time tuition:* $842 per credit hour.

For Further Information Contact Mr. Jeffrey Wells, Vice President of Enrollment Management, Eastern Nazarene College, 23 East Elm Avenue, Quincy, MA 02170. *Phone:* 800-883-6288 or 800-88-ENC88 (toll-free). *Fax:* 617-745-3992. *E-mail:* admissions@enc.edu. *Web site:* http://www.enc.edu/.

ELMS COLLEGE

Chicopee, Massachusetts

http://www.elms.edu/

EMERSON COLLEGE

Boston, Massachusetts

SPONSOR

Emerson College is a coed, private, comprehensive institution, founded in 1880, offering degrees at the bachelor's, master's, and doctoral levels.

Academic Information The faculty has 404 members (40% full-time), 49% with terminal degrees. The undergraduate student-faculty ratio is 14:1. The library holds 179,380 titles, 31,258 serial subscriptions, and 11,596 audiovisual materials. Special programs include services for learning-disabled students, an honors program, study abroad, advanced placement credit, double majors, independent study, self-designed majors, summer session for credit, part-time degree programs (daytime, evenings, summer), adult/continuing education programs, internships, and arrangement for off-campus study. The most frequently chosen baccalaureate fields are communications/journalism, English, visual and performing arts.

Student Body Statistics The student body totals 4,536, of whom 3,644 are undergraduates (774 freshmen). 59 percent are women and 41 percent are men. Students come from 44 states and territories and 50 other countries. 25 percent are from Massachusetts. 2.8 percent are international students.

Expenses for 2008–09 *Application fee:* $65. *Comprehensive fee:* $40,716 includes full-time tuition ($28,352), mandatory fees ($532), and college room and board ($11,832).

Financial Aid Forms of aid include need-based and non-need-based scholarships and part-time jobs. The average aided 2008–09 undergraduate received an aid package worth an estimated $16,153. The priority application deadline for financial aid is March 1.

Freshman Admission Emerson College requires an essay, a high school transcript, 1 recommendation, SAT or ACT scores, and TOEFL scores for international students. An interview and Performing Arts applicants must submit a theatrical resume and either audition or interview, or submit a portfolio or an essay. Film applicants must submit a sample of creative work. are required for some. The application deadline for regular admission is January 5 and for early action it is November 1.

Transfer Admission The application deadline for admission is March 1.

Emerson College (continued)

Entrance Difficulty Emerson College assesses its entrance difficulty level as very difficult. For the fall 2008 freshman class, 37 percent of the applicants were accepted.

SPECIAL MESSAGE TO STUDENTS

Social Life With dozens of institutions of higher education, Boston is considered one of the country's best-known college towns. The city contains a wealth of diversions ranging from scenic harbor cruises and Boston Pops concerts to baseball's Fenway Park and the legendary Boston Marathon. Emerson's campus is located on Boston Common in the heart of the city's Theatre District—walking distance from the Massachusetts State House, historic Freedom Trail, Chinatown, and numerous restaurants and museums. There are more than sixty student organizations and performance groups, fifteen NCAA teams, and several student publications and honor societies.

Academic Highlights Emerson is one of the premier colleges in the country for the study of communication and the arts. Students may choose from more than two dozen undergraduate and graduate programs, which are supported by state-of-the-art facilities and a nationally renowned faculty. The campus is home to WERS-FM, the oldest noncommercial radio station in Boston; the historic 1,200-seat Cutler Majestic Theatre; and *Ploughshares*, the award-winning literary journal for new writing. Hundreds of internships exist throughout the city and across the country, including exclusive placements through the College's Los Angeles Center and Washington, D.C., program. Emerson also sponsors study-abroad programs in the Netherlands, Taiwan, and summer film study in the Czech Republic as well as course cross-registration with the six-member Boston ProArts Consortium.

Interviews and Campus Visits Student-guided tours and information sessions are conducted on weekdays and specific Saturdays during the academic year (during the summer, weekdays only). Interested students can find available tour dates and times online at http://visit.emerson.edu or by contacting the Office of Undergraduate Admission at 617-824-8600 or admission@emerson.edu.

For Further Information Write to Office of Undergraduate Admission, Emerson College, 120 Boylston Street, Boston, MA 02116-4624. *E-mail:* admission@emerson.edu. *Web site:* http://www.emerson.edu.

EMMANUEL COLLEGE
Boston, Massachusetts

Emmanuel College is a coed, private, Roman Catholic, comprehensive institution, founded in 1919, offering degrees at the bachelor's and master's levels and post-master's certificates. It has a 17-acre campus in Boston.

Academic Information The faculty has 235 members (39% full-time), 50% with terminal degrees. The undergraduate student-faculty ratio is 15:1. The library holds 131,000 titles, 1,063 serial subscriptions, and 800 audiovisual materials. Special programs include academic remediation, services for learning-disabled students, an honors program, study abroad, advanced placement credit, accelerated degree programs, double majors, independent study, distance learning, self-designed majors, summer session for credit, part-time degree programs (evenings, weekends, summer), adult/continuing education programs, internships, and arrangement for off-campus study with College of Notre Dame (CA), Colleges of the Fenway. The most frequently chosen baccalaureate fields are communications/journalism, business/marketing, psychology.
Student Body Statistics The student body totals 1,902, of whom 1,693 are undergraduates (480 freshmen). 72 percent are women and 28 percent are men. Students come from 29 states and territories and 30 other countries. 68 percent are from Massachusetts. 1.1 percent are international students.

Expenses for 2009–10 *Application fee:* $40. *Comprehensive fee:* $41,150 includes full-time tuition ($29,200) and college room and board ($11,950).
Financial Aid Forms of aid include need-based and non-need-based scholarships and part-time jobs. The average aided 2008–09 undergraduate received an aid package worth an estimated $20,291. The priority application deadline for financial aid is April 1.
Freshman Admission Emmanuel College requires an essay, a high school transcript, 2 recommendations, SAT or ACT scores, and TOEFL scores for international students. The application deadline for regular admission is March 1 and for early decision it is November 1.
Transfer Admission The application deadline for admission is April 1.
Entrance Difficulty Emmanuel College assesses its entrance difficulty level as moderately difficult. For the fall 2008 freshman class, 56 percent of the applicants were accepted.
For Further Information Contact Ms. Sandra Robbins, Dean for Enrollment, Emmanuel College, Admissions Office, 400 The Fenway, Boston, MA 02115. *Phone:* 617-735-9715. *Fax:* 617-735-9801. *E-mail:* enroll@emmanuel.edu. *Web site:* http://www.emmanuel.edu/.

ENDICOTT COLLEGE
Beverly, Massachusetts

Endicott College is a coed, private, comprehensive institution, founded in 1939, offering degrees at the associate, bachelor's, and master's levels. It has a 240-acre campus in Beverly near Boston.

Academic Information The faculty has 171 members (43% full-time), 43% with terminal degrees. The undergraduate student-faculty ratio is 16:1. The library holds 120,476 titles and 67,643 serial subscriptions. Special programs include academic remediation, an honors program, study abroad, advanced placement credit, accelerated degree programs, ESL programs, independent study, distance learning, self-designed majors, summer session for credit, part-time degree programs (daytime, evenings, weekends, summer), adult/continuing education programs, internships, and arrangement for off-campus study with 10 members of the Northeast Consortium of Colleges and Universities in Massachusetts. The most frequently chosen baccalaureate fields are business/marketing, parks and recreation, visual and performing arts.
Student Body Statistics The student body totals 3,947, of whom 2,306 are undergraduates (587 freshmen). 56 percent are women and 44 percent are men. Students come from 26 states and territories and 28 other countries. 50 percent are from Massachusetts. 2.5 percent are international students.
Expenses for 2008–09 *Application fee:* $40. *Comprehensive fee:* $35,910 includes full-time tuition ($24,130), mandatory fees ($400), and college room and board ($11,380). *College room only:* $7930. Full-time tuition and fees vary according to student level. Room and board charges vary according to board plan and housing facility. *Part-time tuition:* $740 per credit. *Part-time mandatory fees:* $150 per term. Part-time tuition and fees vary according to student level.
Financial Aid Forms of aid include need-based and non-need-based scholarships and part-time jobs. The average aided 2008–09 undergraduate received an aid package worth an estimated $15,615. The priority application deadline for financial aid is March 15.
Freshman Admission Endicott College requires an essay, a high school transcript, a minimum 2.5 high school GPA, SAT or ACT scores, and TOEFL scores for international students. An interview is recommended. An interview is required for some. The application deadline for regular admission is February 15.
Transfer Admission The application deadline for admission is February 15.
Entrance Difficulty Endicott College assesses its entrance difficulty level as moderately difficult. For the fall 2008 freshman class, 49 percent of the applicants were accepted.
For Further Information Contact Mr. Thomas J. Redman, Vice President of Admission and Financial Aid, Endicott College, 376 Hale Street, Beverly, MA 01915. *Phone:* 978-921-1000 or 800-325-1114 (toll-free out-of-state). *Fax:* 978-232-2520. *E-mail:* admissio@endicott.edu. *Web site:* http://www.endicott.edu/.

FISHER COLLEGE
Boston, Massachusetts

Fisher College is a coed, private, primarily two-year college, founded in 1903, offering degrees at the associate and bachelor's levels.

Academic Information The faculty has 83 members (29% full-time). The student-faculty ratio is 22.9:1. The library holds 30,000 titles and 160 serial subscriptions. Special programs include academic remediation, services for learning-disabled students, study abroad, advanced placement credit, ESL programs, independent study, distance learning, summer session for credit, part-time degree programs (daytime, evenings, summer), adult/continuing education programs, internships, and arrangement for off-campus study.
Student Body Statistics The student body is made up of 1,281 undergraduates (331 freshmen). 70 percent are women and 30 percent are men. Students come from 34 states and territories and 40 other countries. 74 percent are from Massachusetts.
Expenses for 2009–10 *Application fee:* $50. *Tuition:* $22,500 full-time, $250 per credit hour part-time.
Financial Aid Forms of aid include need-based scholarships and part-time jobs. The application deadline for financial aid is continuous.
Freshman Admission Fisher College requires a high school transcript and TOEFL scores for international students. A minimum 2 high school GPA is recommended. An essay, an interview, and SAT or ACT scores are required for some. The application deadline for regular admission is rolling.
Transfer Admission The application deadline for admission is rolling.
Entrance Difficulty Fisher College assesses its entrance difficulty level as minimally difficult. For the fall 2008 freshman class, 66 percent of the applicants were accepted.
For Further Information Contact Mr. Robert Melaragni, Dean of Admissions, Fisher College, 118 Beacon Street, Boston, MA 02116. *Phone:* 617-236-8818, 800-821-3050 (toll-free in-state), or 800-446-1226 (toll-free out-of-state). *Fax:* 617-236-5473. *E-mail:* admissions@fisher.edu. *Web site:* http://www.fisher.edu/.

FITCHBURG STATE COLLEGE
Fitchburg, Massachusetts

Fitchburg State College is a coed, public, comprehensive unit of Massachusetts Public Higher Education System, founded in 1894, offering degrees at the bachelor's and master's levels and post-master's and postbachelor's certificates. It has a 45-acre campus in Fitchburg near Boston.

Academic Information The faculty has 270 members (68% full-time), 63% with terminal degrees. The undergraduate student-faculty ratio is 16:1. The library holds 259,321 titles, 2,967 serial subscriptions, and 2,211 audiovisual materials. Special programs include academic remediation, services for learning-disabled students, an honors program, study abroad, advanced placement credit, accelerated degree programs, double majors, independent study, distance learning, self-designed majors, summer session for credit, part-time degree programs (daytime, evenings, summer), adult/continuing education programs, internships, and arrangement for off-campus study. The most frequently chosen baccalaureate fields are business/marketing, education, liberal arts/general studies.
Student Body Statistics The student body totals 6,761, of whom 4,057 are undergraduates (771 freshmen). 53 percent are women and 47 percent are men. Students come from 15 states and territories and 4 other countries. 91 percent are from Massachusetts. 0.2 percent are international students.
Expenses for 2008–09 *Application fee:* $10. *State resident tuition:* $970 full-time, $40.42 per credit part-time. *Nonresident tuition:* $7050 full-time, $293.75 per credit part-time. *Mandatory fees:* $5430 full-time, $226.25 per credit part-time. Full-time tuition and fees vary according to reciprocity agreements. Part-time tuition and fees vary according to class time, course load, and reciprocity agreements. *College room and board:* $7148. Room and board charges vary according to board plan and housing facility.
Financial Aid Forms of aid include need-based and non-need-based scholarships and part-time jobs. The average aided 2008–09 undergraduate received an aid package worth an estimated $8238. The priority application deadline for financial aid is March 1.

Freshman Admission Fitchburg State College requires an essay, a high school transcript, a minimum 2.0 high school GPA, 16 core courses, SAT or ACT scores, and TOEFL scores for international students.
Entrance Difficulty Fitchburg State College assesses its entrance difficulty level as moderately difficult. For the fall 2008 freshman class, 64 percent of the applicants were accepted.
For Further Information Contact Director of Admissions, Fitchburg State College, 160 Pearl Street, Fitchburg, MA 01420-2697. *Phone:* 978-665-3140 or 800-705-9692 (toll-free). *Fax:* 978-665-4540. *E-mail:* admissions@fsc.edu. *Web site:* http://www.fsc.edu/.

FRAMINGHAM STATE COLLEGE
Framingham, Massachusetts

Framingham State College is a coed, public, comprehensive unit of Massachusetts Public Higher Education System, founded in 1839, offering degrees at the bachelor's and master's levels and postbachelor's certificates. It has a 73-acre campus in Framingham near Boston.

Academic Information The faculty has 266 members (63% full-time). The undergraduate student-faculty ratio is 15:1. Special programs include an honors program, advanced placement credit, ESL programs, double majors, independent study, distance learning, summer session for credit, part-time degree programs (daytime, evenings, summer), internships, and arrangement for off-campus study with College Academic Program Sharing, 8 members of the other Massachusetts State colleges. The most frequently chosen baccalaureate fields are business/marketing, family and consumer sciences, social sciences.
Student Body Statistics The student body totals 6,097, of whom 3,962 are undergraduates (650 freshmen). 65 percent are women and 35 percent are men. Students come from 20 states and territories and 12 other countries. 95 percent are from Massachusetts.
Expenses for 2008–09 *Application fee:* $35. *State resident tuition:* $970 full-time, $162 per course part-time. *Nonresident tuition:* $7050 full-time, $1175 per course part-time. *Mandatory fees:* $5171 full-time, $926.50 per course part-time. Full-time tuition and fees vary according to class time. Part-time tuition and fees vary according to class time and course load. *College room and board:* $7509. *College room only:* $4875. Room and board charges vary according to board plan and housing facility.
Financial Aid Forms of aid include need-based and non-need-based scholarships and part-time jobs.
Freshman Admission Framingham State College requires an essay, a high school transcript, minimum of 16 college preparatory courses in specified areas, SAT or ACT scores, and TOEFL scores for international students. A minimum 3.0 high school GPA is recommended. An essay and an interview are required for some. The application deadline for regular admission is May 15 and for early action it is November 15.
Transfer Admission The application deadline for admission is May 1.
Entrance Difficulty Framingham State College assesses its entrance difficulty level as moderately difficult. For the fall 2008 freshman class, 61 percent of the applicants were accepted.
For Further Information Contact Ms. Elizabeth J. Canella, Associate Dean of Admissions, Framingham State College, 100 State Street, PO Box 9101, Framingham, MA 01701-9101. *Phone:* 508-626-4500. *Fax:* 508-626-4017. *E-mail:* admiss@framingham.edu. *Web site:* http://www.framingham.edu/.

FRANKLIN INSTITUTE OF BOSTON
See Benjamin Franklin Institute of Technology.

FRANKLIN W. OLIN COLLEGE OF ENGINEERING
Needham, Massachusetts

Franklin W. Olin College of Engineering is a coed, private, four-year college, founded in 2002, offering degrees at the bachelor's level.

Franklin W. Olin College of Engineering (continued)

Academic Information The faculty has 38 members (87% full-time), 87% with terminal degrees. The student-faculty ratio is 9:1. The library holds 140,273 titles, 194 serial subscriptions, and 837 audiovisual materials. Special programs include study abroad, independent study, self-designed majors, and internships. The most frequently chosen baccalaureate field is engineering.

Student Body Statistics The student body is made up of 301 undergraduates (75 freshmen). 40 percent are women and 60 percent are men. Students come from 44 states and territories and 10 other countries. 9 percent are from Massachusetts. 3 percent are international students.

Expenses for 2009–10 *Application fee:* $70. *Comprehensive fee:* $51,275 includes full-time tuition ($36,400), mandatory fees ($1645), and college room and board ($13,230). *College room only:* $8500. All students are awarded full-tuition scholarships.

Freshman Admission Franklin W. Olin College of Engineering requires an essay, a high school transcript, 3 recommendations, and SAT or ACT scores. An interview and SAT Subject Test scores are recommended. The application deadline for regular admission is January 1.

Entrance Difficulty Franklin W. Olin College of Engineering assesses its entrance difficulty level as very difficult. For the fall 2008 freshman class, 14 percent of the applicants were accepted.

For Further Information Contact Mr. Charles Nolan, Vice President for External Relations and Dean of Admission, Franklin W. Olin College of Engineering, Olin Way, Needham, MA 02492-1200. *Phone:* 781-292-2250. *Fax:* 781-292-2310. *E-mail:* info@olin.edu. *Web site:* http://www.olin.edu/.

GORDON COLLEGE
Wenham, Massachusetts

Gordon College is a coed, private, nondenominational, comprehensive institution, founded in 1889, offering degrees at the bachelor's and master's levels. It has a 500-acre campus in Wenham near Boston.

Academic Information The faculty has 178 members (55% full-time), 45% with terminal degrees. The undergraduate student-faculty ratio is 15:1. The library holds 142,688 titles and 8,555 serial subscriptions. Special programs include academic remediation, services for learning-disabled students, an honors program, cooperative (work-study) education, study abroad, advanced placement credit, double majors, independent study, self-designed majors, part-time degree programs (daytime, evenings), internships, and arrangement for off-campus study with members of the Christian College Consortium, Northeast Consortium of Colleges and Universities in Massachusetts. The most frequently chosen baccalaureate fields are education, English, social sciences.

Student Body Statistics The student body totals 1,718, of whom 1,590 are undergraduates (421 freshmen). 63 percent are women and 37 percent are men. Students come from 44 states and territories and 23 other countries. 29 percent are from Massachusetts. 2.9 percent are international students.

Expenses for 2008–09 *Application fee:* $50. *Comprehensive fee:* $34,718 includes full-time tuition ($26,132), mandatory fees ($1162), and college room and board ($7424).

Financial Aid Forms of aid include need-based and non-need-based scholarships and part-time jobs. The average aided 2008–09 undergraduate received an aid package worth an estimated $15,936. The priority application deadline for financial aid is March 1.

Freshman Admission Gordon College requires an essay, a high school transcript, 2 recommendations, an interview, pastoral recommendation, statement of Christian faith, SAT or ACT scores, and TOEFL scores for international students. A minimum 3.0 high school GPA and SAT Subject Test scores are recommended. The application deadline for regular admission is rolling, for early decision it is November 15, and for early action it is December 1.

Transfer Admission The application deadline for admission is rolling.

Entrance Difficulty Gordon College assesses its entrance difficulty level as moderately difficult. For the fall 2008 freshman class, 71 percent of the applicants were accepted.

For Further Information Contact Admissions Office, Gordon College, 255 Grapevine Road, Wenham, MA 01984-1899. *Phone:* 978-867-4218 or 866-464-6736 (toll-free). *Fax:* 978-867-4682. *E-mail:* admissions@hope. gordon.edu. *Web site:* http://www.gordon.edu/.

HAMPSHIRE COLLEGE
Amherst, Massachusetts

Hampshire College is a coed, private, four-year college, founded in 1965, offering degrees at the bachelor's level. It has an 800-acre campus in Amherst.

Academic Information The faculty has 164 members (60% full-time), 82% with terminal degrees. The student-faculty ratio is 11.4:1. The library holds 134,695 titles, 28,558 serial subscriptions, and 41,424 audiovisual materials. Special programs include services for learning-disabled students, study abroad, advanced placement credit, accelerated degree programs, independent study, self-designed majors, internships, and arrangement for off-campus study with members of Five Colleges, Inc. The most frequently chosen baccalaureate fields are social sciences, English, visual and performing arts.

Student Body Statistics The student body is made up of 1,428 undergraduates (389 freshmen). 58 percent are women and 42 percent are men. Students come from 46 states and territories and 31 other countries. 18 percent are from Massachusetts. 4.7 percent are international students.

Expenses for 2008–09 *Application fee:* $55. *Comprehensive fee:* $48,629 includes full-time tuition ($37,789), mandatory fees ($760), and college room and board ($10,080). *College room only:* $6428. Room and board charges vary according to board plan.

Financial Aid Forms of aid include need-based and non-need-based scholarships and part-time jobs. The average aided 2008–09 undergraduate received an aid package worth an estimated $32,910. The priority application deadline for financial aid is February 1.

Freshman Admission Hampshire College requires an essay, a high school transcript, 2 recommendations, and TOEFL scores for international students. An interview is recommended. The application deadline for regular admission is January 15, for early decision it is November 15, and for early action it is December 1.

Transfer Admission The application deadline for admission is March 1.

Entrance Difficulty Hampshire College assesses its entrance difficulty level as very difficult. For the fall 2008 freshman class, 53 percent of the applicants were accepted.

For Further Information Contact Ms. Karen S. Parker, Director of Admissions, Hampshire College, 893 West Street, Amherst, MA 01002. *Phone:* 413-559-5471 or 877-937-4267 (toll-free out-of-state). *Fax:* 413-559-5631. *E-mail:* admissions@hampshire.edu. *Web site:* http://www.hampshire.edu/.

HARVARD UNIVERSITY
Cambridge, Massachusetts

Harvard University is a coed, private university, founded in 1636, offering degrees at the bachelor's, master's, doctoral, and first professional levels and post-master's and first professional certificates. It has a 380-acre campus in Cambridge near Boston.

Academic Information The faculty has 2,265 members (81% full-time), 99% with terminal degrees. The undergraduate student-faculty ratio is 6.8:1. The library holds 16 million titles and 110,463 serial subscriptions. Special programs include services for learning-disabled students, an honors program, study abroad, advanced placement credit, accelerated degree programs, double majors, independent study, self-designed majors, summer session for credit, internships, and arrangement for off-campus study with Massachusetts Institute of Technology. The most frequently chosen baccalaureate fields are biological/life sciences, history, social sciences.

Student Body Statistics The student body totals 19,230, of whom 6,678 are undergraduates (1,666 freshmen). 50 percent are women and 50

percent are men. Students come from 54 states and territories and 108 other countries. 16 percent are from Massachusetts. 10.2 percent are international students.

Expenses for 2008–09 *Application fee:* $65. *Comprehensive fee:* $47,215 includes full-time tuition ($32,557), mandatory fees ($3616), and college room and board ($11,042). *College room only:* $6060.

Financial Aid Forms of aid include need-based scholarships and part-time jobs. The average aided 2008–09 undergraduate received an aid package worth an estimated $39,193. The priority application deadline for financial aid is February 1.

Freshman Admission Harvard University requires an essay, a high school transcript, 2 recommendations, an interview, SAT or ACT scores, and SAT Subject Test scores. The application deadline for regular admission is January 1.

Entrance Difficulty Harvard University assesses its entrance difficulty level as most difficult. For the fall 2008 freshman class, 8 percent of the applicants were accepted.

For Further Information Contact Admissions Office, Harvard University, Byerly Hall, 8 Garden Street, Cambridge, MA 02138. *Phone:* 617-495-1551. *E-mail:* college@harvard.edu. *Web site:* http://www.harvard.edu/.

HEBREW COLLEGE

Newton Centre, Massachusetts

Hebrew College is a coed, private, Jewish, comprehensive institution, founded in 1921, offering degrees at the bachelor's, master's, and doctoral levels. It has a 3-acre campus in Newton Centre near Boston.

Academic Information The faculty has 41 members (49% full-time), 73% with terminal degrees. Special programs include distance learning, summer session for credit, part-time degree programs (daytime, evenings, summer), internships, and arrangement for off-campus study with Boston College, Boston University, Northeastern University, Simmons College, University of Massachusetts Boston, Brandeis University, Andover Newton Theological School, Tufts University.

Student Body Statistics The student body is made up of 6 undergraduates (1 freshman). 83 percent are women and 17 percent are men. Students come from 6 states and territories and 1 other country. 99 percent are from Massachusetts.

Expenses for 2008–09 *Application fee:* $50. *Tuition:* $900 per credit part-time. *Mandatory fees:* $100 per term part-time.

Financial Aid Forms of aid include need-based and non-need-based scholarships. The application deadline for financial aid is April 15.

Freshman Admission Hebrew College requires an essay, a high school transcript, 3 recommendations, an interview, and TOEFL scores for international students. GRE, audition is required for some. The application deadline for regular admission is rolling and for early decision it is December 15.

Transfer Admission The application deadline for admission is April 15.

Entrance Difficulty Hebrew College has an open admission policy.

For Further Information Contact Kristin Card, Director of Enrollment Management, Hebrew College, 160 Herreck Road, Newton Centre, MA 02459. *Phone:* 617-559-8610 or 800-866-4814 Ext. 8619 (toll-free). *Fax:* 617-559-8601. *E-mail:* admissions@lhebrewcollege.edu. *Web site:* http://www.hebrewcollege.edu/.

HELLENIC COLLEGE

Brookline, Massachusetts

Hellenic College is a coed, private, Greek Orthodox, four-year college, founded in 1937, offering degrees at the bachelor's level (also offers graduate degree programs through Holy Cross Greek Orthodox School of Theology). It has a 52-acre campus in Brookline near Boston.

Expenses for 2008–09 *Application fee:* $50. *Comprehensive fee:* $29,750 includes full-time tuition ($17,870), mandatory fees ($450), and college room and board ($11,430). *Part-time tuition:* $744 per credit hour.

For Further Information Contact Ms. Sonia Daly, Director of Admissions, Hellenic College, 50 Goddard Avenue, Brookline, MA 02445-7496. *Phone:* 617-731-3500 Ext. 1285 or 866-424-2338 (toll-free). *Fax:* 617-850-1460. *E-mail:* admissions@hchc.edu. *Web site:* http://www.hchc.edu/.

ITT TECHNICAL INSTITUTE

Woburn, Massachusetts

ITT Technical Institute is a coed, proprietary, primarily two-year college of ITT Educational Services, Inc., founded in 2000, offering degrees at the associate and bachelor's levels.

Financial Aid Forms of aid include need-based scholarships and part-time jobs. The application deadline for financial aid is continuous.

Entrance Difficulty ITT Technical Institute assesses its entrance difficulty level as minimally difficult.

For Further Information Contact Director of Recruitment, ITT Technical Institute, 10 Forbes Road, Woburn, MA 01801. *Phone:* 781-937-8324 or 800-430-5097 (toll-free in-state). *Fax:* 781-937-3402. *Web site:* http://www.itt-tech.edu/.

LABOURÉ COLLEGE

Boston, Massachusetts

Labouré College is a coed, private, Roman Catholic, two-year college, founded in 1971, offering degrees at the associate level.

Academic Information The library holds 10,975 titles, 155 serial subscriptions, and 650 audiovisual materials. Special programs include academic remediation, services for learning-disabled students, accelerated degree programs, independent study, summer session for credit, part-time degree programs (daytime, evenings, weekends, summer), and adult/continuing education programs.

Student Body Statistics The student body is made up of 548 undergraduates.

Expenses for 2008–09 *Application fee:* $25. *Tuition:* $21,878 full-time.

Financial Aid Forms of aid include need-based scholarships and part-time jobs. The priority application deadline for financial aid is April 1.

Freshman Admission Labouré College requires a high school transcript, recommendations, and TOEFL scores for international students. The application deadline for regular admission is rolling.

Transfer Admission The application deadline for admission is rolling.

Entrance Difficulty Labouré College assesses its entrance difficulty level as minimally difficult.

For Further Information Contact Ms. Gina M. Morrissette, Director of Admissions, Labouré College, 2120 Dorchester Avenue, Boston, MA 02124. *Phone:* 617-296-8300. *Fax:* 617-296-7947. *E-mail:* admit@laboure.edu. *Web site:* http://www.laboure.edu/.

LASELL COLLEGE

Newton, Massachusetts

Lasell College is a coed, private, comprehensive institution, founded in 1851, offering degrees at the bachelor's and master's levels and postbachelor's certificates. It has a 50-acre campus in Newton near Boston.

Academic Information The faculty has 179 members (37% full-time), 34% with terminal degrees. The undergraduate student-faculty ratio is 13:1. The library holds 55,147 titles, 169 serial subscriptions, and 2,492 audiovisual materials. Special programs include an honors program, cooperative (work-study) education, study abroad, advanced placement credit, ESL programs, double majors, independent study, self-designed majors, part-time degree programs (daytime), and internships. The most frequently chosen baccalaureate fields are business/marketing, communications/journalism, law/legal studies.

Lasell College (continued)

Student Body Statistics The student body totals 1,469, of whom 1,372 are undergraduates (487 freshmen). 69 percent are women and 31 percent are men. Students come from 23 states and territories and 14 other countries. 57 percent are from Massachusetts.

Expenses for 2009–10 *Application fee:* $40. *Comprehensive fee:* $35,800 includes full-time tuition ($24,300), mandatory fees ($1000), and college room and board ($10,500). *Part-time tuition:* $775 per credit. *Part-time mandatory fees:* $280 per term.

Financial Aid Forms of aid include need-based and non-need-based scholarships and part-time jobs. The average aided 2008–09 undergraduate received an aid package worth an estimated $22,029.

Freshman Admission Lasell College requires an essay, a high school transcript, a minimum 2.0 high school GPA, college preparatory program, SAT or ACT scores, and TOEFL scores for international students. An interview is recommended. The application deadline for regular admission is rolling.

Transfer Admission The application deadline for admission is rolling.

Entrance Difficulty Lasell College assesses its entrance difficulty level as moderately difficult. For the fall 2008 freshman class, 61 percent of the applicants were accepted.

For Further Information Contact Mr. James Tweed, Director of Undergraduate Admission, Lasell College, 1844 Commonwealth Avenue, Newton, MA 02466. *Phone:* 617-243-2225 or 888-LASELL-4 (toll-free). *Fax:* 617-243-2380. *E-mail:* info@lasell.edu. *Web site:* http://www.lasell.edu/.

LESLEY UNIVERSITY
Cambridge, Massachusetts

Lesley University is a coed, private, comprehensive institution, founded in 1909, offering degrees at the associate, bachelor's, master's, and doctoral levels and post-master's certificates. It has a 5-acre campus in Cambridge near Boston.

Academic Information The faculty has 225 members (32% full-time), 43% with terminal degrees. The undergraduate student-faculty ratio is 10:1. The library holds 118,729 titles, 1,150 serial subscriptions, and 49,943 audiovisual materials. Special programs include academic remediation, services for learning-disabled students, an honors program, study abroad, advanced placement credit, accelerated degree programs, Freshman Honors College, double majors, independent study, distance learning, self-designed majors, summer session for credit, part-time degree programs (daytime, evenings, weekends, summer), external degree programs, adult/continuing education programs, internships, and arrangement for off-campus study with Harvard University Extension Program, National Audubon Society Expedition Institute. The most frequently chosen baccalaureate fields are liberal arts/general studies, psychology, visual and performing arts.

Student Body Statistics The student body totals 6,686, of whom 1,267 are undergraduates (327 freshmen). 75 percent are women and 25 percent are men. Students come from 56 states and territories and 24 other countries. 56 percent are from Massachusetts. 3.5 percent are international students.

Expenses for 2009–10 *Application fee:* $50. *Comprehensive fee:* $40,860 includes full-time tuition ($28,150), mandatory fees ($310), and college room and board ($12,400).

Financial Aid Forms of aid include need-based and non-need-based scholarships and part-time jobs. The average aided 2007–08 undergraduate received an aid package worth $16,022. The priority application deadline for financial aid is March 15.

Freshman Admission Lesley University requires an essay, a high school transcript, 2 recommendations, SAT or ACT scores, and TOEFL scores for international students. An interview is recommended.

Transfer Admission The application deadline for admission is rolling.

Entrance Difficulty Lesley University assesses its entrance difficulty level as moderately difficult. For the fall 2008 freshman class, 65 percent of the applicants were accepted.

For Further Information Contact Ms. Deborah Kocar, Director of Lesley College Admissions, Lesley University, 29 Everett Street, Cambridge, MA 02138-2790. *Phone:* 617-349-8800 or 800-999-1959 Ext. 8800 (toll-free). *Fax:* 617-349-8810. *E-mail:* lcadmissions@lesley.edu. *Web site:* http://www.lesley.edu/.

MARIAN COURT COLLEGE
Swampscott, Massachusetts

http://www.mariancourt.edu/

MASSACHUSETTS COLLEGE OF ART AND DESIGN
Boston, Massachusetts

Massachusetts College of Art and Design is a coed, public, comprehensive unit of Massachusetts Public Higher Education System, founded in 1873, offering degrees at the bachelor's and master's levels and postbachelor's certificates. It has a 5-acre campus in Boston.

Academic Information The faculty has 259 members (38% full-time). The undergraduate student-faculty ratio is 13:1. The library holds 258,675 titles and 557 serial subscriptions. Special programs include study abroad, double majors, independent study, self-designed majors, summer session for credit, part-time degree programs, internships, and arrangement for off-campus study with members of the Pro Arts Consortium, Association of Independent Colleges of Art and Design, CAPS, Colleges of the Fenway. The most frequently chosen baccalaureate fields are education, architecture, visual and performing arts.

Student Body Statistics The student body totals 2,349, of whom 2,199 are undergraduates (276 freshmen). 68 percent are women and 32 percent are men. Students come from 26 states and territories and 49 other countries. 71 percent are from Massachusetts.

Expenses for 2008–09 *Application fee:* $65. *State resident tuition:* $7900 full-time, *Nonresident tuition:* $23,000 full-time. Full-time tuition varies according to course load and degree level. *College room and board:* $12,060. Room and board charges vary according to housing facility.

Financial Aid Forms of aid include need-based and non-need-based scholarships and part-time jobs. The average aided 2008–09 undergraduate received an aid package worth an estimated $8917. The priority application deadline for financial aid is March 1.

Freshman Admission Massachusetts College of Art and Design requires an essay, a high school transcript, a minimum 3.0 high school GPA, 3 recommendations, a portfolio, SAT or ACT scores, and TOEFL scores for international students. The application deadline for regular admission is February 1 and for early action it is December 1.

Transfer Admission The application deadline for admission is March 1.

Entrance Difficulty Massachusetts College of Art and Design assesses its entrance difficulty level as very difficult; most difficult for out-of-state applicants. For the fall 2008 freshman class, 51 percent of the applicants were accepted.

For Further Information Contact Kathleen Keenan, Assistant VP for Planning and Enrollment, Massachusetts College of Art and Design, 621 Huntington Avenue, Boston, MA 02115. *Phone:* 617-879-7230. *Fax:* 617-879-7250. *E-mail:* admissions@massart.edu. *Web site:* http://www.massart.edu/.

MASSACHUSETTS COLLEGE OF LIBERAL ARTS
North Adams, Massachusetts

Massachusetts College of Liberal Arts is a coed, public, comprehensive unit of Massachusetts Public Higher Education

System, founded in 1894, offering degrees at the bachelor's and master's levels and post-master's certificates. It has an 80-acre campus in North Adams.

Academic Information The faculty has 171 members (53% full-time), 53% with terminal degrees. The undergraduate student-faculty ratio is 12.6:1. The library holds 180,000 titles, 10,000 serial subscriptions, and 7,000 audiovisual materials. Special programs include academic remediation, services for learning-disabled students, an honors program, study abroad, advanced placement credit, accelerated degree programs, double majors, independent study, distance learning, self-designed majors, summer session for credit, part-time degree programs (daytime, evenings, summer), internships, and arrangement for off-campus study with College Academic Program Sharing, Williams College, Berkshire Community College. The most frequently chosen baccalaureate fields are business/marketing, English, social sciences.

Student Body Statistics The student body totals 1,942, of whom 1,584 are undergraduates (332 freshmen). 59 percent are women and 41 percent are men. Students come from 17 states and territories. 76 percent are from Massachusetts.

Expenses for 2008–09 *Application fee:* $25. *One-time mandatory fee:* $140. *State resident tuition:* $1030 full-time, $42.92 per credit part-time. *Nonresident tuition:* $9975 full-time, $415.63 per credit part-time. *Mandatory fees:* $5395 full-time, $183.01 per credit part-time. *College room and board:* $7754. *College room only:* $3278. Room and board charges vary according to board plan and housing facility.

Financial Aid Forms of aid include need-based and non-need-based scholarships and part-time jobs. The priority application deadline for financial aid is March 1.

Freshman Admission Massachusetts College of Liberal Arts requires an essay, a high school transcript, a minimum 2.5 high school GPA, SAT or ACT scores, and TOEFL scores for international students. SAT scores are recommended. An interview is required for some. The application deadline for regular admission is rolling and for early action it is December 1.

Transfer Admission The application deadline for admission is rolling.

Entrance Difficulty Massachusetts College of Liberal Arts assesses its entrance difficulty level as moderately difficult. For the fall 2008 freshman class, 78 percent of the applicants were accepted.

For Further Information Contact Mr. Joshua Mendal, Associate Director of Admission, Massachusetts College of Liberal Arts, 375 Church Street, North Adams, MA 01247-4100. *Phone:* 413-662-5410 or 800-292-6632 (toll-free in-state). *Fax:* 413-662-5179. *E-mail:* admissions@mcla.edu. *Web site:* http://www.mcla.edu/.

MASSACHUSETTS COLLEGE OF PHARMACY AND HEALTH SCIENCES
Boston, Massachusetts

Massachusetts College of Pharmacy and Health Sciences is a coed, private university, founded in 1823, offering degrees at the bachelor's, master's, doctoral, and first professional levels and postbachelor's certificates. It has a 3-acre campus in Boston.

Academic Information The faculty has 199 members (98% full-time), 85% with terminal degrees. The undergraduate student-faculty ratio is 19:1. Special programs include services for learning-disabled students, study abroad, advanced placement credit, accelerated degree programs, double majors, independent study, distance learning, summer session for credit, part-time degree programs (daytime, evenings, weekends, summer), adult/continuing education programs, internships, and arrangement for off-campus study with Colleges of the Fenway. The most frequently chosen baccalaureate field is health professions and related sciences.

Student Body Statistics The student body totals 3,909, of whom 2,746 are undergraduates (604 freshmen). 70 percent are women and 30 percent are men. Students come from 42 states and territories and 34 other countries. 45 percent are from Massachusetts. 2.3 percent are international students.

Expenses for 2008–09 *Application fee:* $70. *Comprehensive fee:* $35,220 includes full-time tuition ($22,900), mandatory fees ($720), and college

room and board ($11,600). Full-time tuition and fees vary according to course load, degree level, location, program, and student level. Room and board charges vary according to housing facility. *Part-time tuition:* $840 per credit. *Part-time mandatory fees:* $180 per term.

Financial Aid Forms of aid include need-based and non-need-based scholarships and part-time jobs. The average aided 2008–09 undergraduate received an aid package worth an estimated $12,564. The application deadline for financial aid is March 15.

Freshman Admission Massachusetts College of Pharmacy and Health Sciences requires an essay, a high school transcript, 2 recommendations, SAT or ACT scores, and TOEFL scores for international students. The application deadline for regular admission is February 1 and for early action it is November 15.

Transfer Admission The application deadline for admission is February 1.

Entrance Difficulty Massachusetts College of Pharmacy and Health Sciences assesses its entrance difficulty level as moderately difficult. For the fall 2008 freshman class, 69 percent of the applicants were accepted.

SPECIAL MESSAGE TO STUDENTS

Social Life The Massachusetts College of Pharmacy and Health Sciences (MCPHS) is located in the academic heart of Boston and is a member of the Colleges of the Fenway. MCPHS students benefit from the proximity of these colleges and the social, cultural, and recreational opportunities of the Fenway neighborhood and the city of Boston. On the campus, there are more than eighty recognized student organizations, such as SGA and the newspaper, *The Dispenser*. The Department of Recreation and Wellness offers students opportunities to participate in clubs, intramurals, and wellness classes and activities.

Academic Highlights The College opened state-of-the-art clinics and laboratories in 2005 for its programs in dental hygiene, nursing, and physician assistant studies. A 93,000-square-foot Academic and Student Center opened in 2004. It houses a professional pharmacy lab and an expanded library and technical center as well as four floors of apartment style residences for 230 students. MCPHS opened a new architecturally arresting academic building on Huntington Avenue in January 2009. The Richard E. Griffin Academic Center contains 49,700 square feet of classrooms, teaching laboratories, a technology center, and a 230-seat auditorium. The College offers a number of innovative, accelerated three-year Bachelor of Science programs in nursing, radiologic sciences, and dental hygiene. The premedical studies major prepares students for advancement into various professional and graduate programs in health care. MCPHS offers a professional six-year degree program in pharmacy and four-year majors in pharmaceutical sciences and marketing/management.

Interviews and Campus Visits Priding itself on the personal approach, the College encourages each student to visit the campus in its Fenway neighborhood of Boston. MCPHS offers a number of different opportunities for visiting: information sessions on a daily basis, individual appointments on and off campus, special information sessions in the summer, and Open Houses in the fall and spring. Visiting students should take special note of the proximity and quality of hospitals and research facilities surrounding the College. The College recognizes the importance of experiential programs and is proud of its partnerships with hospitals and colleges in the world-renowned Longwood Medical and Academic Area of Boston. For information about appointments and campus visits, prospective students should call the Admission Office at 617-732-2850 or 800-225-5506 (toll free) Monday through Friday, 8:30 to 4:30, or e-mail admissions@mcphs.edu.

For Further Information Write to the Admission Office, Massachusetts College of Pharmacy and Health Sciences, 179 Longwood Avenue, Boston, MA 02115. *E-mail:* admissions@mcphs.edu. *Web site:* http://www.mcphs.edu.

MASSACHUSETTS COMMUNICATIONS COLLEGE

See The New England Institute of Art.

MASSACHUSETTS INSTITUTE OF TECHNOLOGY

Cambridge, Massachusetts

Massachusetts Institute of Technology is a coed, private university, founded in 1861, offering degrees at the bachelor's, master's, and doctoral levels. It has a 168-acre campus in Cambridge near Boston.

Academic Information The faculty has 1,835 members (74% full-time), 84% with terminal degrees. The undergraduate student-faculty ratio is 7:1. The library holds 3 million titles, 22,103 serial subscriptions, and 38,798 audiovisual materials. Special programs include services for learning-disabled students, cooperative (work-study) education, study abroad, advanced placement credit, ESL programs, double majors, independent study, internships, and arrangement for off-campus study with Wellesley College, Harvard University, Massachusetts College of Art, School of the Museum of Fine Arts. The most frequently chosen baccalaureate fields are computer and information sciences, engineering, physical sciences.
Student Body Statistics The student body totals 10,299, of whom 4,153 are undergraduates (1,048 freshmen). 45 percent are women and 55 percent are men. Students come from 55 states and territories and 93 other countries. 9 percent are from Massachusetts. 9.4 percent are international students.
Expenses for 2009–10 *Application fee: $75. Comprehensive fee: $49,142* includes full-time tuition ($37,510), mandatory fees ($272), and college room and board ($11,360). *College room only: $6850.*
Financial Aid Forms of aid include need-based scholarships and part-time jobs. The average aided 2007–08 undergraduate received an aid package worth $32,437. The application deadline for financial aid is February 15.
Freshman Admission Massachusetts Institute of Technology requires an essay, a high school transcript, 2 recommendations, SAT or ACT scores, and SAT Subject Test scores. An interview and TOEFL scores for international students are recommended. The application deadline for regular admission is January 1 and for early action it is November 1.
Transfer Admission The application deadline for admission is March 15.
Entrance Difficulty Massachusetts Institute of Technology assesses its entrance difficulty level as most difficult. For the fall 2008 freshman class, 12 percent of the applicants were accepted.
For Further Information Contact Admissions Counselors, Massachusetts Institute of Technology, Building 3-108, 77 Massachusetts Avenue, Cambridge, MA 02139-4307. *Phone:* 617-253-3400. *Fax:* 617-258-8304. *E-mail:* admissions@mit.edu. *Web site:* http://www.mit.edu/.

MASSACHUSETTS MARITIME ACADEMY

Buzzards Bay, Massachusetts

Massachusetts Maritime Academy is a coed, primarily men's, public, comprehensive unit of Massachusetts Public Higher Education System, founded in 1891, offering degrees at the bachelor's and master's levels and first professional certificates. It has a 55-acre campus in Buzzards Bay near Boston.

Academic Information The faculty has 94 members (69% full-time), 39% with terminal degrees. The undergraduate student-faculty ratio is 15:1. The library holds 93,499 titles, 97 serial subscriptions, and 1,221 audiovisual materials. Special programs include academic remediation, services for learning-disabled students, cooperative (work-study) education, advanced placement credit, double majors, distance learning, summer session for credit, part-time degree programs (daytime), adult/continuing education programs, and internships. The most frequently chosen baccalaureate fields are engineering, natural resources/environmental science, transportation and materials moving.
Student Body Statistics The student body totals 1,291, of whom 1,204 are undergraduates (364 freshmen). 9 percent are women and 91 percent

are men. Students come from 25 states and territories and 4 other countries. 78 percent are from Massachusetts. 0.5 percent are international students.
Expenses for 2008–09 *Application fee: $50. One-time mandatory fee: $3206. Area resident tuition:* $1183 full-time, $237 per credit part-time. *State resident tuition:* $2070 full-time, $274 per credit part-time. *Nonresident tuition:* $13,220 full-time, $739 per credit part-time. *Mandatory fees: $4732* full-time. *College room and board: $8607. College room only: $4668.*
Financial Aid Forms of aid include need-based and non-need-based scholarships and part-time jobs. The priority application deadline for financial aid is April 30.
Freshman Admission Massachusetts Maritime Academy requires an essay, a high school transcript, a minimum 2.0 high school GPA, 2 recommendations, physical examination, SAT or ACT scores, and TOEFL scores for international students. An interview is recommended. The application deadline for regular admission is rolling, for nonresidents it is rolling, and for early decision it is November 1.
Transfer Admission The application deadline for admission is rolling.
Entrance Difficulty Massachusetts Maritime Academy assesses its entrance difficulty level as moderately difficult.
For Further Information Contact Roy Fulgueras, Director of Admissions, Massachusetts Maritime Academy, 101 Academy Drive, Blinn Hall, Buzzards Bay, MA 02532. *Phone:* 508-830-5031 or 800-544-3411 (toll-free). *Fax:* 508-830-5077. *E-mail:* fuji@maritime.edu. *Web site:* http://www.maritime.edu/.

See page 100 for the Close-Up.

MERRIMACK COLLEGE

North Andover, Massachusetts

Merrimack College is a coed, private, Roman Catholic, comprehensive institution, founded in 1947, offering degrees at the associate, bachelor's, and master's levels. It has a 220-acre campus in North Andover near Boston.

Academic Information The faculty has 217 members (58% full-time), 65% with terminal degrees. The undergraduate student-faculty ratio is 12:1. The library holds 120,836 titles, 1,895 serial subscriptions, and 2,462 audiovisual materials. Special programs include academic remediation, services for learning-disabled students, an honors program, cooperative (work-study) education, study abroad, advanced placement credit, Freshman Honors College, ESL programs, double majors, independent study, self-designed majors, summer session for credit, part-time degree programs (daytime, evenings), adult/continuing education programs, internships, and arrangement for off-campus study with Northeast Consortium of Colleges and Universities in Massachusetts, American University, Massachusetts Bay Marine Studies Consortium. The most frequently chosen baccalaureate fields are business/marketing, health professions and related sciences, psychology.
Student Body Statistics The student body totals 2,147, of whom 2,087 are undergraduates (599 freshmen). 51 percent are women and 49 percent are men. Students come from 28 states and territories and 9 other countries. 72 percent are from Massachusetts. 1.8 percent are international students.
Expenses for 2009–10 *Application fee: $60. Comprehensive fee: $39,500* includes full-time tuition ($29,310) and college room and board ($10,190). *College room only: $6040.*
Financial Aid Forms of aid include need-based and non-need-based scholarships, athletic grants, and part-time jobs. The average aided 2007–08 undergraduate received an aid package worth $16,035. The application deadline for financial aid is February 1.
Freshman Admission Merrimack College requires an essay, a high school transcript, first quarter senior grades, and TOEFL scores for international students. A minimum 2.8 high school GPA, 1 recommendation, and an interview are recommended. An interview is required for some. The application deadline for regular admission is February 1 and for early action it is November 30.
Transfer Admission The application deadline for admission is December 30.

Entrance Difficulty Merrimack College assesses its entrance difficulty level as moderately difficult; very difficult for engineering, pre-physical therapy programs. For the fall 2008 freshman class, 79 percent of the applicants were accepted.
For Further Information Contact Director of Admissions, Merrimack College, Austin Hall, A22, North Andover, MA 01845. *Phone:* 978-837-5100. *Fax:* 978-837-5133. *E-mail:* admission@merrimack.edu. *Web site:* http://www.merrimack.edu/.

MONTSERRAT COLLEGE OF ART
Beverly, Massachusetts

Montserrat College of Art is a coed, private, four-year college, founded in 1970, offering degrees at the bachelor's level and postbachelor's certificates. It has a 10-acre campus in Beverly near Boston.

For Further Information Contact Mr. Brian Bicknell, Dean of Students, Montserrat College of Art, 23 Essex Street, PO Box 26, Beverly, MA 01915. *Phone:* 978-921-4242 Ext. 1153 or 800-836-0487 (toll-free). *Fax:* 978-921-4241. *E-mail:* bbicknell@montserrat.edu. *Web site:* http://www. montserrat.edu/.

MOUNT HOLYOKE COLLEGE
South Hadley, Massachusetts

Mount Holyoke College is a women's, private, comprehensive institution, founded in 1837, offering degrees at the bachelor's and master's levels and postbachelor's certificates. It has an 800-acre campus in South Hadley near Springfield.

Academic Information The faculty has 240 members (87% full-time), 89% with terminal degrees. The undergraduate student-faculty ratio is 10:1. The library holds 1 million titles, 4,119 serial subscriptions, and 9,470 audiovisual materials. Special programs include services for learning-disabled students, an honors program, cooperative (work-study) education, study abroad, advanced placement credit, double majors, independent study, self-designed majors, part-time degree programs (daytime), adult/continuing education programs, internships, and arrangement for off-campus study with members of the Twelve College Exchange Program, Five Colleges, Inc., Spelman College, Mills College. The most frequently chosen baccalaureate fields are biological/life sciences, English, social sciences.
Student Body Statistics The student body totals 2,241, of whom 2,240 are undergraduates (518 freshmen). Students come from 48 states and territories and 67 other countries. 26 percent are from Massachusetts. 17.2 percent are international students.
Expenses for 2008–09 *Application fee:* $60. *Comprehensive fee:* $48,666 includes full-time tuition ($37,460), mandatory fees ($186), and college room and board ($11,020). *College room only:* $5400. Room and board charges vary according to board plan and housing facility. *Part-time tuition:* $1175 per credit hour.
Financial Aid Forms of aid include need-based and non-need-based scholarships and part-time jobs. The average aided 2008–09 undergraduate received an aid package worth an estimated $31,459. The application deadline for financial aid is March 1 with a priority deadline of February 15.
Freshman Admission Mount Holyoke College requires an essay, a high school transcript, and 2 recommendations. An interview is recommended. SAT Subject Test scores are required for some. The application deadline for regular admission is January 15, for early decision plan 1 it is November 15, and for early decision plan 2 it is January 1.
Transfer Admission The application deadline for admission is May 15.
Entrance Difficulty Mount Holyoke College assesses its entrance difficulty level as very difficult. For the fall 2008 freshman class, 53 percent of the applicants were accepted.
For Further Information Contact Ms. Diane Anci, Dean of Admission, Mount Holyoke College, 50 College Street, South Hadley, MA 01075. *Phone:* 413-538-2023. *Fax:* 413-538-2409. *E-mail:* admission@mtholyoke. edu. *Web site:* http://www.mtholyoke.edu/.

MOUNT IDA COLLEGE
Newton, Massachusetts

Mount Ida College is a coed, private, four-year college, founded in 1899, offering degrees at the associate and bachelor's levels. It has a 72-acre campus in Newton near Boston.

Academic Information The faculty has 174 members (36% full-time), 41% with terminal degrees. The student-faculty ratio is 13:1. The library holds 94,464 titles, 3,735 serial subscriptions, and 3,655 audiovisual materials. Special programs include academic remediation, services for learning-disabled students, an honors program, cooperative (work-study) education, study abroad, advanced placement credit, accelerated degree programs, ESL programs, independent study, distance learning, self-designed majors, part-time degree programs, adult/continuing education programs, and internships. The most frequently chosen baccalaureate fields are business/marketing, health professions and related sciences, visual and performing arts.
Student Body Statistics The student body is made up of 1,460 undergraduates (411 freshmen). 67 percent are women and 33 percent are men. Students come from 31 states and territories and 32 other countries. 60 percent are from Massachusetts. 5.3 percent are international students.
Expenses for 2008–09 *Application fee:* $45. *Comprehensive fee:* $33,600 includes full-time tuition ($22,275), mandatory fees (($225), and college room and board ($11,100). *Part-time tuition:* $600 per credit.
Financial Aid Forms of aid include need-based and non-need-based scholarships and part-time jobs. The average aided 2007–08 undergraduate received an aid package worth $14,294. The priority application deadline for financial aid is May 1.
Freshman Admission Mount Ida College requires a high school transcript, 1 recommendation, SAT or ACT scores, and TOEFL scores for international students. An essay, a minimum 2.0 high school GPA, and extracurricular activities, leadership, and community service are recommended. An interview is required for some. The application deadline for regular admission is rolling.
Transfer Admission The application deadline for admission is rolling.
Entrance Difficulty Mount Ida College assesses its entrance difficulty level as moderately difficult. For the fall 2008 freshman class, 74 percent of the applicants were accepted.
For Further Information Contact Jay Titus, Dean of Admissions, Mount Ida College, 777 Dedham Street, Newton, MA 02459-3310. *Phone:* 617-928-4553. *Fax:* 617-928-4507. *E-mail:* admissions@mountida.edu. *Web site:* http://www.mountida.edu/.

See page 104 for the Close-Up.

NEWBURY COLLEGE
Brookline, Massachusetts

Newbury College is a coed, private, four-year college, founded in 1962, offering degrees at the associate and bachelor's levels. It has a 10-acre campus in Brookline near Boston.

Academic Information The faculty has 107 members (26% full-time), 30% with terminal degrees. The student-faculty ratio is 15:1. The library holds 32,500 titles and 1,115 serial subscriptions. Special programs include academic remediation, services for learning-disabled students, an honors program, cooperative (work-study) education, study abroad, advanced placement credit, accelerated degree programs, Freshman Honors College, ESL programs, double majors, independent study, summer session for credit, part-time degree programs (evenings, weekends, summer), adult/continuing education programs, internships, and arrangement for off-campus study.
Student Body Statistics The student body is made up of 1,202 undergraduates (320 freshmen). 63 percent are women and 37 percent are men. Students come from 20 states and territories and 30 other countries. 70 percent are from Massachusetts.
Expenses for 2008–09 *Application fee:* $50. *Comprehensive fee:* $32,700 includes full-time tuition ($20,900), mandatory fees ($1100), and college room and board ($10,700). Full-time tuition and fees vary according to class time, course load, and program. Room and board charges vary

Newbury College (continued)

according to board plan and housing facility. *Part-time tuition:* $260 per credit hour. Part-time tuition varies according to class time, course load, and program.

Financial Aid Forms of aid include need-based scholarships and part-time jobs. The average aided 2007–08 undergraduate received an aid package worth $4250. The application deadline for financial aid is continuous.

Freshman Admission Newbury College requires an essay, a high school transcript, and TOEFL scores for international students. A minimum 2.0 high school GPA, an interview, and SAT or ACT scores are recommended. SAT or ACT scores are required for some. The application deadline for regular admission is September 1 and for early action it is December 1.

Transfer Admission The application deadline for admission is rolling.

Entrance Difficulty Newbury College assesses its entrance difficulty level as minimally difficult. For the fall 2008 freshman class, 66 percent of the applicants were accepted.

For Further Information Contact Mr. Ken Sawada, Associate Director of Admission, Newbury College, 129 Fisher Avenue, Brookline, MA 02445-5796. *Phone:* 617-730-7007 or 800-NEWBURY (toll-free). *Fax:* 617-731-9618. *E-mail:* info@newbury.edu. *Web site:* http://www.newbury.edu/.

NEW ENGLAND COLLEGE OF FINANCE
Boston, Massachusetts

http://www.finance.edu/

NEW ENGLAND CONSERVATORY OF MUSIC
Boston, Massachusetts

New England Conservatory of Music is a coed, private, comprehensive institution, founded in 1867, offering degrees at the bachelor's, master's, and doctoral levels and postbachelor's certificates. It has a 2-acre campus in Boston.

Academic Information The faculty has 216 members (41% full-time), 10% with terminal degrees. The undergraduate student-faculty ratio is 6:1. The library holds 91,418 titles, 305 serial subscriptions, and 61,416 audiovisual materials. Special programs include services for learning-disabled students, study abroad, advanced placement credit, ESL programs, double majors, independent study, summer session for credit, internships, and arrangement for off-campus study with Simmons College, Tufts University, Northeastern University. The most frequently chosen baccalaureate field is visual and performing arts.

Student Body Statistics The student body totals 714, of whom 356 are undergraduates (83 freshmen). 45 percent are women and 55 percent are men. Students come from 39 states and territories and 16 other countries. 24 percent are from Massachusetts. 23.9 percent are international students.

Expenses for 2008–09 *Application fee:* $100. *Comprehensive fee:* $44,925 includes full-time tuition ($32,900), mandatory fees ($425), and college room and board ($11,600). Room and board charges vary according to board plan. *Part-time tuition:* $1050 per credit.

Financial Aid Forms of aid include need-based and non-need-based scholarships and part-time jobs. The average aided 2008–09 undergraduate received an aid package worth an estimated $21,659. The priority application deadline for financial aid is February 1.

Freshman Admission New England Conservatory of Music requires an essay, a high school transcript, a minimum 2.75 high school GPA, 2 recommendations, audition recording, repertoire list, and TOEFL scores for international students. The application deadline for regular admission is December 1.

Transfer Admission The application deadline for admission is December 1.

Entrance Difficulty New England Conservatory of Music assesses its entrance difficulty level as very difficult. For the fall 2008 freshman class, 31 percent of the applicants were accepted.

For Further Information Contact Ms. Christina Daly, Dean of Admissions, New England Conservatory of Music, 290 Huntington Avenue, Boston, MA 02115-5000. *Phone:* 617-585-1101. *Fax:* 617-585-1115. *E-mail:* admissions@newenglandconservatory.edu. *Web site:* http://www.newenglandconservatory.edu/.

NEW ENGLAND INSTITUTE OF APPLIED ARTS AND SCIENCES

See Mount Ida College.

THE NEW ENGLAND INSTITUTE OF ART
Brookline, Massachusetts

The New England Institute of Art is a coed, proprietary, four-year college of Education Management Corporation, offering degrees at the associate and bachelor's levels. It is located in Brookline near Boston.

Expenses for 2009–10 Tuition cost varies by program. Prospective students should contact the school for current tuition costs. Other charges include a starting kit for all first-quarter students. Kits vary in price, depending on the program of study.

For Further Information Contact Director of Admissions, The New England Institute of Art, 10 Brookline Place West, Brookline, MA 02445-7295. *Phone:* 617-739-1700 or 800-903-4425 (toll-free). *Fax:* 617-582-4500. *Web site:* http://www.artinstitutes.edu/boston.

THE NEW ENGLAND SCHOOL OF ART AND DESIGN AT SUFFOLK UNIVERSITY

See Suffolk University.

NICHOLS COLLEGE
Dudley, Massachusetts

Nichols College is a coed, private, comprehensive institution, founded in 1815, offering degrees at the associate, bachelor's, and master's levels. It has a 210-acre campus in Dudley near Boston.

Academic Information The faculty has 69 members (54% full-time), 39% with terminal degrees. The undergraduate student-faculty ratio is 18:1. The library holds 76,374 titles, 137 serial subscriptions, and 2,016 audiovisual materials. Special programs include academic remediation, services for learning-disabled students, an honors program, cooperative (work-study) education, study abroad, advanced placement credit, accelerated degree programs, double majors, independent study, distance learning, summer session for credit, part-time degree programs (evenings), adult/continuing education programs, internships, and arrangement for off-campus study. The most frequently chosen baccalaureate fields are business/marketing, history, psychology.

Student Body Statistics The student body totals 1,532, of whom 1,308 are undergraduates (391 freshmen). 42 percent are women and 58 percent are men. Students come from 25 states and territories and 6 other countries. 65 percent are from Massachusetts. 0.8 percent are international students.

Expenses for 2008–09 *Application fee:* $25. *Comprehensive fee:* $36,070 includes full-time tuition ($26,670), mandatory fees ($300), and college room and board ($9100). *College room only:* $4800. *Part-time tuition:* $265 per credit hour. Part-time tuition varies according to class time and course load.

Financial Aid Forms of aid include need-based and non-need-based scholarships and part-time jobs. The average aided 2008–09 undergraduate received an aid package worth an estimated $19,549. The priority application deadline for financial aid is March 1.

Freshman Admission Nichols College requires an essay, a high school transcript, 1 recommendation, SAT or ACT scores, and TOEFL scores for international students. An interview is required for some. The application deadline for regular admission is rolling.

Transfer Admission Nichols College requires standardized test scores and a college transcript. The application deadline for admission is rolling.

Entrance Difficulty Nichols College assesses its entrance difficulty level as moderately difficult. For the fall 2008 freshman class, 65 percent of the applicants were accepted.

For Further Information Contact Ms. Marie Keegan, Admissions Assistant, Nichols College, 124 Center Road, Dudley, MA 01571. *Phone:* 508-213-2203 or 800-470-3379 (toll-free). *Fax:* 508-943-9885. *E-mail:* admissions@nichols.edu. *Web site:* http://www.nichols.edu/.

NORTH ADAMS STATE COLLEGE

See Massachusetts College of Liberal Arts.

NORTHEASTERN UNIVERSITY

Boston, Massachusetts

Northeastern University is a coed, private university, founded in 1898, offering degrees at the bachelor's, master's, doctoral, and first professional levels and post-master's certificates. It has a 67-acre campus in Boston.

Academic Information The faculty has 1,378 members (70% full-time). The undergraduate student-faculty ratio is 15:1. The library holds 994,122 titles and 6,773 serial subscriptions. Special programs include academic remediation, services for learning-disabled students, an honors program, cooperative (work-study) education, study abroad, advanced placement credit, accelerated degree programs, ESL programs, double majors, independent study, distance learning, self-designed majors, summer session for credit, part-time degree programs (evenings, weekends, summer), adult/continuing education programs, internships, and arrangement for off-campus study with New England Conservatory of Music, Hebrew College. The most frequently chosen baccalaureate fields are business/marketing, engineering, health professions and related sciences.

Student Body Statistics The student body totals 21,324, of whom 15,521 are undergraduates (2,923 freshmen). 50 percent are women and 50 percent are men. Students come from 50 states and territories and 94 other countries. 33 percent are from Massachusetts. 5.5 percent are international students.

Expenses for 2008–09 *Application fee:* $75. *One-time mandatory fee:* $250. *Comprehensive fee:* $45,661 includes full-time tuition ($33,320), mandatory fees ($401), and college room and board ($11,940). *College room only:* $6340. Room and board charges vary according to board plan and housing facility.

Financial Aid Forms of aid include need-based scholarships, athletic grants, and part-time jobs. The average aided 2008–09 undergraduate received an aid package worth an estimated $17,877.

Freshman Admission Northeastern University requires an essay, SAT or ACT scores, and TOEFL scores for international students. A minimum 2.0 high school GPA and 2 recommendations are recommended. A high school transcript and an interview are required for some. The application deadline for regular admission is January 15 and for early action it is November 15.

Transfer Admission The application deadline for admission is May 1.

Entrance Difficulty Northeastern University assesses its entrance difficulty level as very difficult. For the fall 2008 freshman class, 35 percent of the applicants were accepted.

For Further Information Contact Ronne Turner, Director of Admissions, Northeastern University, 360 Huntington Avenue, 150 Richards Hall, Boston, MA 02115. *Phone:* 617-373-2200. *Fax:* 617-373-8780. *E-mail:* admissions@neu.edu. *Web site:* http://www.northeastern.edu/.

PINE MANOR COLLEGE

Chestnut Hill, Massachusetts

http://www.pmc.edu/

REGIS COLLEGE

Weston, Massachusetts

Regis College is a coed, private, Roman Catholic, comprehensive institution, founded in 1927, offering degrees at the associate, bachelor's, master's, and doctoral levels and post-master's certificates. It has a 131-acre campus in Weston near Boston.

Academic Information The faculty has 129 members (50% full-time), 57% with terminal degrees. The undergraduate student-faculty ratio is 13:1. The library holds 135,458 titles, 607 serial subscriptions, and 7,670 audiovisual materials. Special programs include academic remediation, services for learning-disabled students, an honors program, study abroad, advanced placement credit, accelerated degree programs, double majors, independent study, self-designed majors, summer session for credit, part-time degree programs (daytime, evenings, weekends, summer), adult/continuing education programs, internships, and arrangement for off-campus study with Babson College, Bentley College, Boston College, American University, National Federation of Carondelet Colleges. The most frequently chosen baccalaureate fields are health professions and related sciences, biological/life sciences, social sciences.

Student Body Statistics The student body totals 1,590, of whom 991 are undergraduates (237 freshmen). 86 percent are women and 14 percent are men. Students come from 20 states and territories and 19 other countries. 92 percent are from Massachusetts. 2.2 percent are international students.

Expenses for 2008–09 *Application fee:* $50. *One-time mandatory fee:* $195. *Comprehensive fee:* $39,750 includes full-time tuition ($27,800) and college room and board ($11,950). *College room only:* $6100. Full-time tuition varies according to course load and student level. *Part-time tuition:* varies with class time.

Financial Aid Forms of aid include need-based and non-need-based scholarships and part-time jobs. The average aided 2008–09 undergraduate received an aid package worth an estimated $22,111. The priority application deadline for financial aid is February 15.

Freshman Admission Regis College requires an essay, a high school transcript, a minimum 2.0 high school GPA, 2 recommendations, and SAT or ACT scores. A minimum 3.0 high school GPA, an interview, and rank in upper 50% of high school class are recommended. An interview is required for some. The application deadline for regular admission is rolling.

Transfer Admission The application deadline for admission is rolling.

Entrance Difficulty Regis College assesses its entrance difficulty level as moderately difficult. For the fall 2008 freshman class, 75 percent of the applicants were accepted.

For Further Information Contact Ms. Wanda Suriel, Director of Admission, Regis College, 235 Wellesley Street, Weston, MA 02493. *Phone:* 781-768-7100 or 866-438-7344 (toll-free). *Fax:* 781-768-7071. *E-mail:* admission@regiscollege.edu. *Web site:* http://www.regiscollege.edu/.

SALEM STATE COLLEGE

Salem, Massachusetts

Salem State College is a coed, public, comprehensive unit of Massachusetts Public Higher Education System, founded in 1854, offering degrees at the bachelor's and master's levels and post-master's certificates. It has a 62-acre campus in Salem near Boston.

Academic Information The faculty has 771 members (44% full-time). The undergraduate student-faculty ratio is 15:1. The library holds 277,985 titles, 1,914 serial subscriptions, and 3,811 audiovisual materials. Special programs include academic remediation, services for learning-disabled students, an honors program, study abroad, advanced placement credit, ESL programs, double majors, independent study, distance learning, summer session for credit, part-time degree programs (daytime, evenings, summer), adult/continuing education programs, internships, and

Salem State College (continued)

arrangement for off-campus study with other Massachusetts state colleges, Northeast Consortium of Colleges and Universities in Massachusetts. The most frequently chosen baccalaureate fields are business/marketing, education, health professions and related sciences.

Student Body Statistics The student body totals 10,157, of whom 7,677 are undergraduates (1,151 freshmen). 63 percent are women and 37 percent are men. 97 percent are from Massachusetts. 4 percent are international students.

Expenses for 2008–09 *Application fee:* $25. *State resident tuition:* $910 full-time, $37.92 per credit part-time. *Nonresident tuition:* $7050 full-time, $293.75 per credit part-time. *Mandatory fees:* $5550 full-time, $232 per credit part-time. Both full-time and part-time tuition and fees vary according to class time and course load. *College room only:* $6038. Room charges vary according to housing facility.

Financial Aid Forms of aid include need-based and non-need-based scholarships and part-time jobs. The average aided 2007–08 undergraduate received an aid package worth $8137. The priority application deadline for financial aid is April 1.

Freshman Admission Salem State College requires a high school transcript, a minimum 2.0 high school GPA, SAT or ACT scores, and TOEFL scores for international students. An interview is required for some. The application deadline for regular admission is rolling.

Transfer Admission The application deadline for admission is rolling.

Entrance Difficulty Salem State College assesses its entrance difficulty level as minimally difficult. For the fall 2008 freshman class, 55 percent of the applicants were accepted.

For Further Information Contact Mr. Nate Bryant, Dean of Student Development, Salem State College, 352 Lafayette Street, Salem, MA 01970. *Phone:* 978-542-6200. *Fax:* 978-542-6893. *E-mail:* admissions@salemstate.edu. *Web site:* http://www.salemstate.edu/.

SCHOOL OF THE MUSEUM OF FINE ARTS, BOSTON

Boston, Massachusetts

School of the Museum of Fine Arts, Boston is a coed, private, comprehensive institution, founded in 1876, offering degrees at the bachelor's and master's levels and postbachelor's certificates. It has a 14-acre campus in Boston.

Academic Information The faculty has 114 members (46% full-time), 61% with terminal degrees. The undergraduate student-faculty ratio is 9.5:1. The library holds 1 million titles, 523 serial subscriptions, and 408 audiovisual materials. Special programs include services for learning-disabled students, study abroad, ESL programs, double majors, independent study, self-designed majors, summer session for credit, part-time degree programs (daytime, evenings, weekends, summer), adult/continuing education programs, internships, and arrangement for off-campus study with Pro Arts Consortium, Association of Independent Colleges of Art and Design. The most frequently chosen baccalaureate fields are education, visual and performing arts.

Student Body Statistics The student body totals 750, of whom 656 are undergraduates (129 freshmen). 67 percent are women and 33 percent are men. Students come from 38 states and territories and 40 other countries. 42 percent are from Massachusetts.

Expenses for 2008–09 *Application fee:* $65. *One-time mandatory fee:* $125. *Tuition:* $28,532 full-time, $1195 per credit hour part-time. *Mandatory fees:* $1080 full-time, $480 per term part-time. Full-time tuition and fees vary according to course load, degree level, and program. Part-time tuition and fees vary according to class time, course load, and program. *College room only:* $11,720. Room charges vary according to housing facility.

Financial Aid Forms of aid include need-based and non-need-based scholarships and part-time jobs. The average aided 2008–09 undergraduate received an aid package worth an estimated $18,280. The priority application deadline for financial aid is March 15.

Freshman Admission School of the Museum of Fine Arts, Boston requires an essay, a high school transcript, a portfolio, and TOEFL scores for international students. An interview and SAT or ACT scores are required for some. The application deadline for regular admission is February 1.

Transfer Admission The application deadline for admission is March 1.

Entrance Difficulty School of the Museum of Fine Arts, Boston assesses its entrance difficulty level as moderately difficult. For the fall 2008 freshman class, 82 percent of the applicants were accepted.

For Further Information Contact Jesse Tarantino, Assistant Dean of Admissions, School of the Museum of Fine Arts, Boston, 230 The Fenway, Boston, MA 02115. *Phone:* 617-369-3626 or 800-643-6078 (toll-free in-state). *Fax:* 617-369-4264. *E-mail:* admissions@smfa.edu. *Web site:* http://www.smfa.edu/.

SIMMONS COLLEGE

Boston, Massachusetts

Simmons College is an undergraduate: women only; graduate: coed, private university, founded in 1899, offering degrees at the bachelor's, master's, and doctoral levels and post-master's and postbachelor's certificates. It has a 12-acre campus in Boston.

Academic Information The faculty has 477 members (52% full-time). The undergraduate student-faculty ratio is 13:1. The library holds 207,823 titles, 44,734 serial subscriptions, and 8,785 audiovisual materials. Special programs include academic remediation, services for learning-disabled students, an honors program, cooperative (work-study) education, study abroad, advanced placement credit, accelerated degree programs, Freshman Honors College, ESL programs, double majors, independent study, self-designed majors, summer session for credit, part-time degree programs (daytime, evenings, summer), adult/continuing education programs, internships, and arrangement for off-campus study with members of Colleges of the Fenway, Fisk University, Mills College, Spelman College. The most frequently chosen baccalaureate fields are health professions and related sciences, psychology, social sciences.

Student Body Statistics The student body totals 4,933, of whom 2,060 are undergraduates (391 freshmen). 100 percent are women and 0 percent are men. Students come from 39 states and territories and 30 other countries. 64 percent are from Massachusetts. 3.1 percent are international students.

Expenses for 2008–09 *Application fee:* $55. *Comprehensive fee:* $41,500 includes full-time tuition ($29,120), mandatory fees ($880), and college room and board ($11,500). Full-time tuition and fees vary according to course load and program. Room and board charges vary according to board plan. *Part-time tuition:* $910 per credit. Part-time tuition varies according to course load and program.

Financial Aid Forms of aid include need-based and non-need-based scholarships and part-time jobs. The average aided 2008–09 undergraduate received an aid package worth an estimated $19,758. The priority application deadline for financial aid is February 15.

Freshman Admission Simmons College requires an essay, a high school transcript, 2 recommendations, SAT or ACT scores, and TOEFL scores for international students. A minimum 3.0 high school GPA and an interview are recommended. The application deadline for regular admission is February 1, for nonresidents it is February 1, and for early action it is December 1.

Transfer Admission The application deadline for admission is April 1.

Entrance Difficulty Simmons College assesses its entrance difficulty level as moderately difficult; very difficult for honors, nursing program, physical therapy program. For the fall 2008 freshman class, 55 percent of the applicants were accepted.

For Further Information Contact Catherine Capolupo, Director of Undergraduate Admissions, Simmons College, 300 The Fenway, Boston, MA 02115. *Phone:* 617-521-2057 or 800-345-8468 (toll-free out-of-state). *Fax:* 617-521-3190. *E-mail:* ugadm@simmons.edu. *Web site:* http://www.simmons.edu/.

See page 112 for the Close-Up.

SIMON'S ROCK COLLEGE OF BARD

See Bard College at Simon's Rock.

SMITH COLLEGE

Northampton, Massachusetts

Smith College is a women's, private, comprehensive institution, founded in 1871, offering degrees at the bachelor's, master's, and doctoral levels and post-master's and postbachelor's certificates. It has a 125-acre campus in Northampton near Hartford.

Academic Information The faculty has 309 members (91% full-time), 98% with terminal degrees. The undergraduate student-faculty ratio is 9:1. The library holds 1 million titles, 37,414 serial subscriptions, and 74,858 audiovisual materials. Special programs include services for learning-disabled students, an honors program, study abroad, advanced placement credit, accelerated degree programs, double majors, independent study, self-designed majors, part-time degree programs (daytime, evenings), adult/continuing education programs, internships, and arrangement for off-campus study with Pomona College, Amherst College, Bowdoin College, Connecticut College, Dartmouth College, Mount Holyoke College, Trinity College, Vassar College, Wellesley College, Wesleyan University, Wheaton College, Williams College, several historically black colleges. The most frequently chosen baccalaureate fields are area and ethnic studies, foreign languages and literature, social sciences.
Student Body Statistics The student body totals 3,065, of whom 2,596 are undergraduates (656 freshmen). Students come from 51 states and territories and 62 other countries. 23 percent are from Massachusetts. 6.8 percent are international students.
Expenses for 2008–09 *Application fee:* $60. *Comprehensive fee:* $48,108 includes full-time tuition ($35,810), mandatory fees ($248), and college room and board ($12,050). *College room only:* $6030. *Part-time tuition:* $1120 per credit hour.
Financial Aid Forms of aid include need-based scholarships and part-time jobs. The average aided 2008–09 undergraduate received an aid package worth an estimated $34,370. The application deadline for financial aid is February 15.
Freshman Admission Smith College requires an essay, a high school transcript, 3 recommendations, and TOEFL scores for international students. An interview is recommended. SAT or ACT scores are required for some. The application deadline for regular admission is January 15, for early decision plan 1 it is November 15, and for early decision plan 2 it is January 2.
Transfer Admission The application deadline for admission is May 15.
Entrance Difficulty Smith College assesses its entrance difficulty level as very difficult. For the fall 2008 freshman class, 52 percent of the applicants were accepted.
For Further Information Contact Ms. Debra Shaver, Director of Admissions, Smith College, 7 College Lane, Northampton, MA 01063. *Phone:* 413-585-2500 or 800-383-3232 (toll-free). *Fax:* 413-585-2527. *E-mail:* admission@smith.edu. *Web site:* http://www.smith.edu/.

SPRINGFIELD COLLEGE

Springfield, Massachusetts

http://www.spfldcol.edu/

STONEHILL COLLEGE

Easton, Massachusetts

Stonehill College is a coed, private, Roman Catholic, four-year college, founded in 1948, offering degrees at the bachelor's level. It has a 375-acre campus in Easton near Boston.

Academic Information The faculty has 242 members (61% full-time), 66% with terminal degrees. The student-faculty ratio is 13:1. The library holds 210,000 titles, 9,980 serial subscriptions, and 8,664 audiovisual materials. Special programs include services for learning-disabled students, an honors program, study abroad, advanced placement credit, double majors, independent study, self-designed majors, summer session for credit, part-time degree programs (daytime, evenings, summer), internships, and arrangement for off-campus study with 8 members of the Southeastern

Association for Cooperation of Higher Education in Massachusetts. The most frequently chosen baccalaureate fields are business/marketing, psychology, social sciences.
Student Body Statistics The student body is made up of 2,426 undergraduates (635 freshmen). 60 percent are women and 40 percent are men. Students come from 30 states and territories and 11 other countries. 54 percent are from Massachusetts. 0.5 percent are international students.
Expenses for 2008–09 *Application fee:* $60. *Comprehensive fee:* $41,980 includes full-time tuition ($30,150) and college room and board ($11,830). Room and board charges vary according to board plan. *Part-time tuition:* $1005 per course. *Part-time mandatory fees:* $25 per term. Part-time tuition and fees vary according to course load.
Financial Aid Forms of aid include need-based and non-need-based scholarships, athletic grants, and part-time jobs. The average aided 2008–09 undergraduate received an aid package worth an estimated $19,987. The priority application deadline for financial aid is February 1.
Freshman Admission Stonehill College requires an essay, a high school transcript, and TOEFL scores for international students. Campus visit is recommended. An interview is required for some. The application deadline for regular admission is January 15 and for early decision it is November 1.
Transfer Admission The application deadline for admission is April 1.
Entrance Difficulty Stonehill College assesses its entrance difficulty level as very difficult; moderately difficult for transfers. For the fall 2008 freshman class, 45 percent of the applicants were accepted.
For Further Information Contact Mr. Brian P. Murphy, Dean of Admissions and Enrollment, Stonehill College, 320 Washington Street, Easton, MA 02357-5610. *Phone:* 508-565-1373. *Fax:* 508-565-1545. *E-mail:* admissions@stonehill.edu. *Web site:* http://www.stonehill.edu/.

SUFFOLK UNIVERSITY

Boston, Massachusetts

Suffolk University is a coed, private, comprehensive institution, founded in 1906, offering degrees at the associate, bachelor's, master's, doctoral, and first professional levels and post-master's, first professional, and postbachelor's certificates (doctoral degree in law). It has a 2-acre campus in Boston.

Academic Information The faculty has 1,037 members (41% full-time), 52% with terminal degrees. The undergraduate student-faculty ratio is 12.6:1. The library holds 129,647 titles, 23,183 serial subscriptions, and 699 audiovisual materials. Special programs include academic remediation, services for learning-disabled students, an honors program, cooperative (work-study) education, study abroad, advanced placement credit, accelerated degree programs, Freshman Honors College, ESL programs, double majors, independent study, distance learning, summer session for credit, part-time degree programs (daytime, evenings, weekends, summer), adult/continuing education programs, internships, and arrangement for off-campus study. The most frequently chosen baccalaureate fields are business/marketing, communications/journalism, social sciences.
Student Body Statistics The student body totals 9,435, of whom 5,809 are undergraduates (1,572 freshmen). 57 percent are women and 43 percent are men. Students come from 41 states and territories and 104 other countries. 68 percent are from Massachusetts. 9.6 percent are international students.
Expenses for 2008–09 *Application fee:* $50. *Comprehensive fee:* $39,924 includes full-time tuition ($25,850), mandatory fees ($104), and college room and board ($13,970). *College room only:* $11,630. Room and board charges vary according to board plan and housing facility. *Part-time tuition:* $634 per credit. *Part-time mandatory fees:* $10 per term.
Financial Aid Forms of aid include need-based and non-need-based scholarships and part-time jobs. The average aided 2008–09 undergraduate received an aid package worth an estimated $15,232. The application deadline for financial aid is March 1.
Freshman Admission Suffolk University requires an essay, a high school transcript, 2 recommendations, SAT or ACT scores, and TOEFL scores for international students. A minimum 2.5 high school GPA is recommended. An interview is required for some. The application deadline for regular admission is March 1 and for early action it is November 20.
Transfer Admission The application deadline for admission is March 15.

Suffolk University (continued)

Entrance Difficulty Suffolk University assesses its entrance difficulty level as moderately difficult. For the fall 2008 freshman class, 82 percent of the applicants were accepted.

For Further Information Contact Undergraduate Admissions, Suffolk University, 8 Ashburton Place, Boston, MA 02108. *Phone:* 617-573-8460 or 800-6-SUFFOLK (toll-free). *Fax:* 617-742-4291. *E-mail:* admission@suffolk.edu. *Web site:* http://www.suffolk.edu/.

TUFTS UNIVERSITY
Medford, Massachusetts

Tufts University is a coed, private university, founded in 1852, offering degrees at the bachelor's, master's, doctoral, and first professional levels and post-master's certificates. It has a 150-acre campus in Medford near Boston.

Academic Information The faculty has 944 members (68% full-time), 79% with terminal degrees. The undergraduate student-faculty ratio is 7.4:1. The library holds 2 million titles, 4,341 serial subscriptions, and 40,307 audiovisual materials. Special programs include services for learning-disabled students, an honors program, study abroad, advanced placement credit, double majors, independent study, self-designed majors, summer session for credit, adult/continuing education programs, internships, and arrangement for off-campus study with Boston College, Boston University, Brandeis University, Swarthmore College, American University, Lincoln University. The most frequently chosen baccalaureate fields are engineering, social sciences, visual and performing arts.

Student Body Statistics The student body totals 10,030, of whom 5,044 are undergraduates (1,297 freshmen). 51 percent are women and 49 percent are men. Students come from 52 states and territories and 78 other countries. 25 percent are from Massachusetts. 5.9 percent are international students.

Expenses for 2008–09 *Application fee:* $70. *Comprehensive fee:* $49,358 includes full-time tuition ($37,952), mandatory fees ($888), and college room and board ($10,518). *College room only:* $5428. Room and board charges vary according to board plan.

Financial Aid Forms of aid include need-based and non-need-based scholarships and part-time jobs. The average aided 2008–09 undergraduate received an aid package worth an estimated $30,363. The application deadline for financial aid is February 15.

Freshman Admission Tufts University requires an essay, a high school transcript, 1 recommendation, SAT and SAT Subject Test or ACT scores, and TOEFL scores for international students. An interview is recommended. The application deadline for regular admission is January 1, for early decision plan 1 it is November 1, and for early decision plan 2 it is January 1.

Transfer Admission The application deadline for admission is March 1.

Entrance Difficulty Tufts University assesses its entrance difficulty level as most difficult. For the fall 2008 freshman class, 26 percent of the applicants were accepted.

For Further Information Contact Mr. Lee Coffin, Office of Undergraduate Admissions, Tufts University, Bendetson Hall, Medford, MA 02155. *Phone:* 617-627-3170. *Fax:* 617-627-3860. *E-mail:* admissions.inquiry@ase.tufts.edu. *Web site:* http://www.tufts.edu/.

UNIVERSITY OF MASSACHUSETTS AMHERST
Amherst, Massachusetts

University of Massachusetts Amherst is a coed, public unit of University of Massachusetts, founded in 1863, offering degrees at the associate, bachelor's, master's, and doctoral levels and post-master's and postbachelor's certificates. It has a 1,463-acre campus in Amherst near Hartford.

Academic Information The faculty has 1,356 members (85% full-time), 87% with terminal degrees. The undergraduate student-faculty ratio is 18:1. The library holds 3 million titles, 57,233 serial subscriptions, and 25,230 audiovisual materials. Special programs include academic remediation, services for learning-disabled students, an honors program, cooperative (work-study) education, study abroad, advanced placement credit, Freshman Honors College, ESL programs, double majors, independent study, distance learning, self-designed majors, summer session for credit, part-time degree programs (daytime, evenings, summer), adult/continuing education programs, internships, and arrangement for off-campus study with members of the National Student Exchange, Five Colleges, Inc., other units of the University of Massachusetts System. The most frequently chosen baccalaureate fields are business/marketing, communications/journalism, social sciences.

Student Body Statistics The student body totals 26,359, of whom 20,539 are undergraduates (4,270 freshmen). 50 percent are women and 50 percent are men. Students come from 52 states and territories and 45 other countries. 81 percent are from Massachusetts. 1 percent are international students.

Expenses for 2009–10 *Application fee:* $70. *State resident tuition:* $1714 full-time. *Nonresident tuition:* $9938 full-time. *Mandatory fees:* $10,203 full-time. *College room and board:* $8276. *College room only:* $4612.

Financial Aid Forms of aid include need-based and non-need-based scholarships, athletic grants, and part-time jobs. The average aided 2007–08 undergraduate received an aid package worth $12,593. The priority application deadline for financial aid is February 14.

Freshman Admission University of Massachusetts Amherst requires an essay, a high school transcript, SAT or ACT scores, and TOEFL scores for international students. A minimum 3.0 high school GPA is recommended. The application deadline for regular admission is January 15 and for early action it is November 1.

Transfer Admission The application deadline for admission is April 15.

Entrance Difficulty University of Massachusetts Amherst assesses its entrance difficulty level as moderately difficult. For the fall 2008 freshman class, 64 percent of the applicants were accepted.

For Further Information Contact Mr. Kevin Kelly, Director, Undergraduate Admissions, University of Massachusetts Amherst, 37 Mather Drive, Amherst, MA 01003. *Phone:* 413-545-0222. *Fax:* 413-545-4312. *E-mail:* mail@admissions.umass.edu. *Web site:* http://www.umass.edu/.

UNIVERSITY OF MASSACHUSETTS BOSTON
Boston, Massachusetts

University of Massachusetts Boston is a coed, public unit of University of Massachusetts, founded in 1964, offering degrees at the bachelor's, master's, and doctoral levels and post-master's and postbachelor's certificates. It has a 177-acre campus in Boston.

Academic Information The faculty has 913 members (51% full-time), 62% with terminal degrees. The undergraduate student-faculty ratio is 16:1. The library holds 600,000 titles and 26,500 serial subscriptions. Special programs include academic remediation, services for learning-disabled students, an honors program, cooperative (work-study) education, study abroad, advanced placement credit, accelerated degree programs, Freshman Honors College, ESL programs, double majors, independent study, distance learning, self-designed majors, summer session for credit, part-time degree programs (daytime, evenings, weekends, summer), adult/continuing education programs, internships, and arrangement for off-campus study with members of the National Student Exchange, New England Regional Student Exchange, Boston Five Course Exchange Program. The most frequently chosen baccalaureate fields are business/marketing, health professions and related sciences, social sciences.

Student Body Statistics The student body totals 14,117, of whom 10,478 are undergraduates (1,020 freshmen). 57 percent are women and 43 percent are men. Students come from 41 states and territories and 139 other countries. 95 percent are from Massachusetts. 3.1 percent are international students.

Expenses for 2008–09 *Application fee:* $40. *State resident tuition:* $1714 full-time, $71.50 per credit hour part-time. *Nonresident tuition:* $9758 full-time, $406.50 per credit hour part-time. *Mandatory fees:* $7397 full-time, $308 per credit hour part-time. Both full-time and part-time tuition and fees vary according to class time, course load, program, reciprocity agreements, and student level.

Financial Aid Forms of aid include need-based and non-need-based scholarships and part-time jobs. The average aided 2007–08 undergraduate received an aid package worth $11,852. The priority application deadline for financial aid is March 1.

Freshman Admission University of Massachusetts Boston requires a high school transcript, a minimum 2.75 high school GPA, SAT or ACT scores, and TOEFL scores for international students. An essay is recommended. An essay and an interview are required for some. The application deadline for regular admission is June 1.

Transfer Admission The application deadline for admission is rolling.

Entrance Difficulty University of Massachusetts Boston assesses its entrance difficulty level as moderately difficult. For the fall 2008 freshman class, 63 percent of the applicants were accepted.

For Further Information Contact Mrs. Liliana Mickle, Director of Undergraduate Admissions, University of Massachusetts Boston, 100 Morrissey Boulevard, Boston, MA 02125-3393. *Phone:* 617-287-6000. *Fax:* 617-287-5999. *E-mail:* enrollment.info@umb.edu. *Web site:* http://www.umb.edu/.

UNIVERSITY OF MASSACHUSETTS DARTMOUTH

North Dartmouth, Massachusetts

University of Massachusetts Dartmouth is a coed, public unit of University of Massachusetts, founded in 1895, offering degrees at the bachelor's, master's, and doctoral levels and post-master's and postbachelor's certificates. It has a 710-acre campus in North Dartmouth near Boston and Providence.

Academic Information The faculty has 611 members (60% full-time). The undergraduate student-faculty ratio is 18:1. The library holds 463,000 titles, 2,783 serial subscriptions, and 8,200 audiovisual materials. Special programs include academic remediation, services for learning-disabled students, an honors program, cooperative (work-study) education, study abroad, advanced placement credit, double majors, independent study, distance learning, self-designed majors, summer session for credit, part-time degree programs (daytime, evenings, weekends, summer), internships, and arrangement for off-campus study with members of the Southeastern Association for Cooperation in Higher Education in Massachusetts. The most frequently chosen baccalaureate fields are business/marketing, health professions and related sciences, social sciences.

Student Body Statistics The student body totals 9,155, of whom 7,982 are undergraduates (1,786 freshmen). 48 percent are women and 52 percent are men. Students come from 25 states and territories and 16 other countries. 96 percent are from Massachusetts. 0.3 percent are international students.

Expenses for 2008–09 *Application fee:* $40. *State resident tuition:* $1417 full-time, $59.04 per credit part-time. *Nonresident tuition:* $8099 full-time, $337.46 per credit part-time. *Mandatory fees:* $7441 full-time, $310.04 per credit part-time. Full-time tuition and fees vary according to program and reciprocity agreements. Part-time tuition and fees vary according to course load, program, and reciprocity agreements. *College room and board:* $8716. *College room only:* $5954. Room and board charges vary according to board plan and housing facility.

Financial Aid Forms of aid include need-based and non-need-based scholarships and part-time jobs. The average aided 2007–08 undergraduate received an aid package worth $11,562. The priority application deadline for financial aid is March 1.

Freshman Admission University of Massachusetts Dartmouth requires an essay, a high school transcript, a minimum 3.0 high school GPA, SAT or ACT scores, and TOEFL scores for international students. The application deadline for regular admission is rolling and for early decision it is November 15.

Transfer Admission The application deadline for admission is rolling.

Entrance Difficulty University of Massachusetts Dartmouth assesses its entrance difficulty level as moderately difficult. For the fall 2008 freshman class, 66 percent of the applicants were accepted.

For Further Information Contact Dr. Carnell Jones Jr., Interim Director of Admissions, University of Massachusetts Dartmouth, 285 Old Westport Road, North Dartmouth, MA 02747-2300. *Phone:* 508-999-8605. *Fax:* 508-999-8755. *E-mail:* admissions@umassd.edu. *Web site:* http://www.umassd.edu/.

See page 122 for the Close-Up.

UNIVERSITY OF MASSACHUSETTS LOWELL

Lowell, Massachusetts

SPONSOR

University of Massachusetts Lowell is a coed, public unit of University of Massachusetts, founded in 1894, offering degrees at the associate, bachelor's, master's, and doctoral levels and post-master's certificates. It has a 100-acre campus in Lowell near Boston.

Academic Information The faculty has 690 members (60% full-time). The undergraduate student-faculty ratio is 13:1. The library holds 11,870 titles, 1,119 serial subscriptions, and 385 audiovisual materials. Special programs include services for learning-disabled students, an honors program, cooperative (work-study) education, study abroad, advanced placement credit, accelerated degree programs, double majors, distance learning, summer session for credit, part-time degree programs, adult/continuing education programs, internships, and arrangement for off-campus study with Northeast Consortium of Colleges and Universities in Massachusetts. The most frequently chosen baccalaureate fields are business/marketing, engineering, security and protective services.

Student Body Statistics The student body totals 10,075, of whom 7,316 are undergraduates (1,528 freshmen). 40 percent are women and 60 percent are men. Students come from 32 states and territories and 19 other countries. 86 percent are from Massachusetts. 0.8 percent are international students.

Expenses for 2008–09 *Application fee:* $40. *State resident tuition:* $1454 full-time, $60.58 per credit part-time. *Nonresident tuition:* $8567 full-time, $356.96 per credit part-time. *Mandatory fees:* $7727 full-time, $328.17 per credit part-time. Part-time tuition and fees vary according to course load. *College room and board:* $7519. *College room only:* $4902. Room and board charges vary according to board plan and housing facility.

Financial Aid Forms of aid include need-based and non-need-based scholarships, athletic grants, and part-time jobs. The average aided 2007–08 undergraduate received an aid package worth $9609. The priority application deadline for financial aid is March 1.

Freshman Admission University of Massachusetts Lowell requires an essay, a high school transcript, a minimum 3.0 high school GPA, 1 recommendation, audition for music students, SAT or ACT scores, and TOEFL scores for international students. An interview is required for some. The application deadline for regular admission is rolling.

Transfer Admission The application deadline for admission is rolling.

Entrance Difficulty University of Massachusetts Lowell assesses its entrance difficulty level as moderately difficult. For the fall 2008 freshman class, 75 percent of the applicants were accepted.

SPECIAL MESSAGE TO STUDENTS

Social Life There are more than 100 campus organizations to choose from at University of Massachusetts Lowell (UML), including academic, recreational, social, and special-interest groups; musical ensembles; the student newspaper; an FM radio station; and The Off-Broadway Players. Campuswide events include University Week and Spring Carnival, and residence hall associations regularly sponsor social and recreational events. Students are involved in a wide variety of community service activities, the fourteen intercollegiate sports teams, and a lively recreational sports program.

University of Massachusetts Lowell (continued)

Academic Highlights UML offers more than seventy different undergraduate concentrations in five colleges, including recent popular choices such as meteorology, sound recording technology, exercise physiology, criminal justice, plastics engineering, a new forensic science concentration in chemistry, and an entrepreneurship concentration in the College of Management. Most courses incorporate some kind of practical component that gives students hands-on experience in their field. A wide range of resources, including a University-wide honors program, multimedia computer labs, and an active peer tutoring program, ensure that all students have access to the programs and services that support their success.

Interviews and Campus Visits Individual interviews are recommended but not required. Students desiring interviews are asked to call the Office of Undergraduate Admissions to schedule appointments and to arrange a tour. There is a University-wide open house in mid-October, and a number of weekend snapshot programs are scheduled throughout the year. Students should visit the University's campuses, which cover more than 100 acres on both sides of the beautiful Merrimack River. Some fifty buildings house the residential, administration, and instructional centers, which contain modern laboratory facilities and equipment and several comprehensive computer centers. In 1998, the campus opened a nearby hockey arena and an on-campus baseball stadium, both built in partnership with the city of Lowell and shared by University and professional teams. Students enjoy a new campus center that provides expanded recreational and social areas. Lowell is an exciting place in which to live. The National Historical Park was established to illustrate the importance of Lowell as the birthplace of the Industrial Revolution in America. Now Lowell's historic buildings house museums, performance spaces, shops, and restaurants. For information about appointments and campus visits, prospective students should call the Office of Undergraduate Admissions at 978-934-3931, Monday through Friday, 8:30 to 5. The office is located in Dugan Hall on UML South.

For Further Information Write to Office of Undergraduate Admissions, University of Massachusetts Lowell, 883 Broadway Street, Suite 110, Lowell, MA 01854-5104. *Web site:* http://www.uml.edu.

See page 124 for the Close-Up.

UNIVERSITY OF PHOENIX–BOSTON CAMPUS

Braintree, Massachusetts

University of Phoenix–Boston Campus is a coed, proprietary, comprehensive institution, founded in 2001, offering degrees at the bachelor's and master's levels.

Academic Information The faculty has 107 members (8% full-time), 6% with terminal degrees. The library holds 16,781 serial subscriptions. Special programs include services for learning-disabled students, advanced placement credit, accelerated degree programs, independent study, distance learning, external degree programs, and adult/continuing education programs. The most frequently chosen baccalaureate fields are business/marketing, computer and information sciences.
Student Body Statistics The student body totals 361, of whom 265 are undergraduates (20 freshmen). 54 percent are women and 46 percent are men. 5.3 percent are international students.
Expenses for 2008–09 *Application fee:* $0. *Tuition:* $13,500 full-time. Full-time tuition varies according to course level and course load.
Financial Aid Forms of aid include need-based and non-need-based scholarships. The average aided 2007–08 undergraduate received an aid package worth $6432. The application deadline for financial aid is continuous.
Freshman Admission University of Phoenix–Boston Campus requires 1 recommendation and TOEFL scores for international students. A high school transcript is required for some. The application deadline for regular admission is rolling.
Transfer Admission The application deadline for admission is rolling.

Entrance Difficulty University of Phoenix–Boston Campus has an open admission policy.
For Further Information Contact Ms. Audra McQuarie, Registrar/Executive Director, University of Phoenix–Boston Campus, 4035 South Riverpoint Parkway, Mail Stop CF-L101, Phoenix, AZ 85040. *Phone:* 480-557-6151 or 800-228-7240 (toll-free). *Fax:* 480-643-3068. *E-mail:* audra.mcquarie@phoenix.edu. *Web site:* http://www.phoenix.edu/.

UNIVERSITY OF PHOENIX–CENTRAL MASSACHUSETTS CAMPUS

Westborough, Massachusetts

University of Phoenix–Central Massachusetts Campus is a coed, proprietary, comprehensive institution, founded in 2003, offering degrees at the bachelor's and master's levels.

Academic Information The faculty has 80 members (6% full-time), 26% with terminal degrees. The library holds 3,000 audiovisual materials. Special programs include services for learning-disabled students, advanced placement credit, accelerated degree programs, independent study, and distance learning. The most frequently chosen baccalaureate fields are business/marketing, computer and information sciences.
Student Body Statistics The student body totals 148, of whom 117 are undergraduates (11 freshmen). 52 percent are women and 48 percent are men. 9.4 percent are international students.
Expenses for 2008–09 *Application fee:* $0. *Tuition:* $13,500 full-time. Full-time tuition varies according to course level and course load.
Financial Aid Forms of aid include need-based and non-need-based scholarships. The average aided 2007–08 undergraduate received an aid package worth $5991. The application deadline for financial aid is continuous.
Freshman Admission University of Phoenix–Central Massachusetts Campus requires 1 recommendation. A high school transcript is required for some. The application deadline for regular admission is rolling.
Transfer Admission The application deadline for admission is rolling.
Entrance Difficulty University of Phoenix–Central Massachusetts Campus has an open admission policy.
For Further Information Contact Ms. Audra McQuarie, Registrar/Executive Director, University of Phoenix–Central Massachusetts Campus, 4035 South Riverpoint Parkway, Mail Stop CF-L101, Phoenix, AZ 85040. *Phone:* 480-557-6151, 800-776-4867 (toll-free in-state), or 800-228-7240 (toll-free out-of-state). *Fax:* 480-643-3068. *E-mail:* audra.mcquarie@phoenix.edu. *Web site:* http://www.phoenix.edu/.

URBAN COLLEGE OF BOSTON

Boston, Massachusetts

http://www.urbancollegeofboston.org/

WELLESLEY COLLEGE

Wellesley, Massachusetts

Wellesley College is a women's, private, four-year college, founded in 1870, offering degrees at the bachelor's level (double bachelor's degree with Massachusetts Institute of Technology). It has a 500-acre campus in Wellesley near Boston.

Academic Information The faculty has 326 members (77% full-time), 92% with terminal degrees. The student-faculty ratio is 8:1. The library holds 873,897 titles, 19,653 serial subscriptions, and 32,490 audiovisual materials. Special programs include services for learning-disabled students, an honors program, study abroad, advanced placement credit, double majors, independent study, self-designed majors, summer session for credit, part-time degree programs, adult/continuing education programs, internships, and arrangement for off-campus study with Brandeis University, Babson College, Massachusetts Institute of Technology, members of the Twelve College Exchange Program, Spelman College,

Mills College. The most frequently chosen baccalaureate fields are foreign languages and literature, area and ethnic studies, social sciences.

Student Body Statistics The student body is made up of 2,344 undergraduates (596 freshmen). Students come from 53 states and territories and 82 other countries. 14 percent are from Massachusetts. 7.7 percent are international students.

Expenses for 2008–09 *Application fee:* $50. *Comprehensive fee:* $47,976 includes full-time tuition ($36,404), mandatory fees ($236), and college room and board ($11,336).

Financial Aid Forms of aid include need-based scholarships and part-time jobs. The average aided 2008–09 undergraduate received an aid package worth an estimated $33,843. The priority application deadline for financial aid is January 15.

Freshman Admission Wellesley College requires an essay, a high school transcript, 3 recommendations, Midyear Report, and SAT and SAT Subject Test or ACT scores. An interview and TOEFL scores for international students are recommended. An interview is required for some. The application deadline for regular admission is January 15, for nonresidents it is January 15, for early decision plan 1 it is November 1, and for early decision plan 2 it is January 1.

Transfer Admission The application deadline for admission is March 1.

Entrance Difficulty Wellesley College assesses its entrance difficulty level as most difficult. For the fall 2008 freshman class, 36 percent of the applicants were accepted.

For Further Information Contact Ms. Heather Ayres, Director of Admission, Wellesley College, 106 Central Street, Green Hall 240, Wellesley, MA 02481-8203. *Phone:* 781-283-2253. *Fax:* 781-283-3678. *E-mail:* admission@wellesley.edu. *Web site:* http://www.wellesley.edu/.

WENTWORTH INSTITUTE OF TECHNOLOGY

Boston, Massachusetts

Wentworth Institute of Technology is a coed, private, four-year college, founded in 1904, offering degrees at the associate and bachelor's levels. It has a 35-acre campus in Boston.

Academic Information The faculty has 295 members (49% full-time), 25% with terminal degrees. The student-faculty ratio is 18:1. The library holds 72,000 titles, 500 serial subscriptions, and 2,700 audiovisual materials. Special programs include academic remediation, services for learning-disabled students, cooperative (work-study) education, study abroad, advanced placement credit, summer session for credit, part-time degree programs, and internships. The most frequently chosen baccalaureate fields are computer and information sciences, architecture, engineering technologies.

Student Body Statistics The student body is made up of 3,816 undergraduates (851 freshmen). 20 percent are women and 80 percent are men. Students come from 40 states and territories and 47 other countries. 58 percent are from Massachusetts. 2.9 percent are international students.

Expenses for 2009–10 *Application fee:* $30. *Comprehensive fee:* $32,300 includes full-time tuition ($21,800) and college room and board ($10,500). *Part-time tuition:* $680 per credit.

Financial Aid Forms of aid include need-based scholarships and part-time jobs. The average aided 2007–08 undergraduate received an aid package worth $11,261. The priority application deadline for financial aid is March 1.

Freshman Admission Wentworth Institute of Technology requires an essay, a high school transcript, 1 recommendation, and SAT or ACT scores. A minimum 2.0 high school GPA, an interview, and TOEFL scores for international students are recommended. The application deadline for regular admission is rolling.

Transfer Admission The application deadline for admission is rolling.

Entrance Difficulty Wentworth Institute of Technology assesses its entrance difficulty level as moderately difficult. For the fall 2008 freshman class, 63 percent of the applicants were accepted.

SPECIAL MESSAGE TO STUDENTS

Social Life Wentworth's active Student Government serves as the official representative of the student body. Student activities include chapters of professional associations, hobby and social clubs, and club, intramural, and varsity sports. An extensive calendar of events is coordinated each semester. Fraternities and sororities are not available at Wentworth. More than 50 percent of all full-time students live on the campus. Wentworth does not maintain any religious affiliations.

Academic Highlights Wentworth's degree programs specialize in architecture, biomedical engineering technology (beginning fall 2010), computer science, construction management, design, engineering, engineering technology, and management. The curriculum combines theory learned in the classroom, laboratory training, and on-the-job experience received through the cooperative education program, the largest of its kind in the Northeast. Majors are offered in fourteen technical disciplines. Wentworth is recognized by business, industry, and academic leaders as an innovator in the training of engineering technologists.

Interviews and Campus Visits Prospective students are invited to visit Wentworth. Tours of the facilities, including classrooms, residence halls, studios, and laboratories, are available. Appointments for informational sessions and tours are requested. While on campus, visitors can see Wentworth's varied educational resources, including state-of-the-art laboratories and design studios, the Alumni Library, and the Computer Center. Also of interest are Wentworth's athletic, recreational, and residential facilities. For information about informational sessions and tours, prospective students should visit http://www.wit.edu or call the Office of Admissions at 617-989-4000 or 800-556-0610 (toll-free), Monday through Friday, 8:15 to 4:45. The office is located in Wentworth Hall, the main administration building.

For Further Information Write to Ms. Maureen Dischino, Director of Admissions, Wentworth Institute of Technology, 550 Huntington Avenue, Boston, MA 02115-5998. *E-mail:* admissions@wit.edu. *Web site:* http://www.wit.edu.

See page 126 for the Close-Up.

WESTERN NEW ENGLAND COLLEGE

Springfield, Massachusetts

Western New England College is a coed, private, comprehensive institution, founded in 1919, offering degrees at the associate, bachelor's, master's, doctoral, and first professional levels. It has a 215-acre campus in Springfield.

Academic Information The faculty has 305 members (59% full-time). The undergraduate student-faculty ratio is 15:1. The library holds 131,350 titles, 155 serial subscriptions, and 4,220 audiovisual materials. Special programs include services for learning-disabled students, an honors program, study abroad, advanced placement credit, accelerated degree programs, double majors, independent study, distance learning, self-designed majors, summer session for credit, part-time degree programs (daytime, evenings, weekends, summer), adult/continuing education programs, internships, and arrangement for off-campus study with Cooperating Colleges of Greater Springfield. The most frequently chosen baccalaureate fields are business/marketing, engineering, security and protective services.

Student Body Statistics The student body totals 3,722, of whom 2,796 are undergraduates (739 freshmen). 39 percent are women and 61 percent are men. Students come from 32 states and territories and 3 other countries. 35 percent are from Massachusetts. 0.3 percent are international students.

Expenses for 2008–09 *Application fee:* $50. *Comprehensive fee:* $38,024 includes full-time tuition ($25,556), mandatory fees ($1914), and college room and board ($10,554). Full-time tuition and fees vary according to

Western New England College (continued)

program. Room and board charges vary according to board plan and housing facility. *Part-time tuition:* $481 per credit. Part-time tuition varies according to location and program.

Financial Aid Forms of aid include need-based and non-need-based scholarships and part-time jobs. The average aided 2008–09 undergraduate received an aid package worth an estimated $17,604. The priority application deadline for financial aid is April 15.

Freshman Admission Western New England College requires a high school transcript, 1 recommendation, and SAT or ACT scores. An essay, an interview, and TOEFL scores for international students are recommended. The application deadline for regular admission is rolling.

Transfer Admission The application deadline for admission is rolling.

Entrance Difficulty Western New England College assesses its entrance difficulty level as moderately difficult. For the fall 2008 freshman class, 73 percent of the applicants were accepted.

For Further Information Contact Dr. Charles R. Pollock, Vice President of Enrollment Management, Western New England College, 1215 Wilbraham Road, Springfield, MA 01119. *Phone:* 413-782-1321 or 800-325-1122 Ext. 1321 (toll-free). *Fax:* 413-782-1777. *E-mail:* ugradmis@wnec.edu. *Web site:* http://www.wnec.edu/.

See page 128 for the Close-Up.

WESTFIELD STATE COLLEGE
Westfield, Massachusetts

Westfield State College is a coed, public, comprehensive unit of Massachusetts Public Higher Education System, founded in 1838, offering degrees at the bachelor's and master's levels and post-master's and postbachelor's certificates. It has a 227-acre campus in Westfield.

Academic Information The faculty has 421 members (47% full-time). The undergraduate student-faculty ratio is 16.7:1. The library holds 150,121 titles and 4,426 audiovisual materials. Special programs include services for learning-disabled students, an honors program, cooperative (work-study) education, study abroad, advanced placement credit, double majors, independent study, distance learning, self-designed majors, summer session for credit, part-time degree programs (daytime, evenings, weekends, summer), adult/continuing education programs, internships, and arrangement for off-campus study with National Student Exchange, New England Student Exchange Program. The most frequently chosen baccalaureate fields are liberal arts/general studies, business/marketing, security and protective services.

Student Body Statistics The student body totals 5,548, of whom 4,867 are undergraduates (1,126 freshmen). 53 percent are women and 47 percent are men. Students come from 19 states and territories and 6 other countries. 93 percent are from Massachusetts. 0.1 percent are international students.

Expenses for 2008–09 *Application fee:* $35. *State resident tuition:* $970 full-time, $85 per credit part-time. *Nonresident tuition:* $7050 full-time, $95 per credit part-time. *Mandatory fees:* $5545 full-time, $100 per credit part-time, $145 per term part-time. *College room and board:* $7204. Room and board charges vary according to board plan, housing facility, and location.

Financial Aid Forms of aid include need-based and non-need-based scholarships and part-time jobs. The average aided 2007–08 undergraduate received an aid package worth $7294. The priority application deadline for financial aid is March 1.

Freshman Admission Westfield State College requires a high school transcript, SAT or ACT scores, and TOEFL scores for international students. The application deadline for regular admission is February 1.

Transfer Admission The application deadline for admission is March 1.

Entrance Difficulty Westfield State College assesses its entrance difficulty level as moderately difficult. For the fall 2008 freshman class, 62 percent of the applicants were accepted.

For Further Information Contact Emily Gibbings, Director of Admissions, Westfield State College, 577 Western Avenue, Westfield, MA 01086. *Phone:* 413-572-5218 or 800-322-8401 (toll-free in-state). *Fax:* 413-572-0520. *E-mail:* admission@wsc.ma.edu. *Web site:* http://www.wsc.ma.edu/.

WHEATON COLLEGE
Norton, Massachusetts

Wheaton College is a coed, private, four-year college, founded in 1834, offering degrees at the bachelor's level. It has a 385-acre campus in Norton near Boston.

Academic Information The faculty has 181 members (78% full-time), 81% with terminal degrees. The student-faculty ratio is 10:1. The library holds 378,078 titles, 14,282 serial subscriptions, and 16,519 audiovisual materials. Special programs include an honors program, study abroad, advanced placement credit, accelerated degree programs, double majors, independent study, self-designed majors, part-time degree programs (daytime), internships, and arrangement for off-campus study with members of the Twelve College Exchange Program, American University, Williams College, Brown University, members of the Southeastern Association for Cooperation in Higher Education in Massachusetts, Connecticut College (National Theatre Institute), SALT Center for Documentary Field Studies, Marine Biological Laboratory (Woods Hole, MA). The most frequently chosen baccalaureate fields are psychology, area and ethnic studies, social sciences.

Student Body Statistics The student body is made up of 1,655 undergraduates (420 freshmen). 62 percent are women and 38 percent are men. Students come from 43 states and territories and 36 other countries. 33 percent are from Massachusetts. 3.5 percent are international students.

Expenses for 2008–09 *Application fee:* $55. *One-time mandatory fee:* $50. *Comprehensive fee:* $48,010 includes full-time tuition ($38,585), mandatory fees ($275), and college room and board ($9150). *College room only:* $4830.

Financial Aid Forms of aid include need-based and non-need-based scholarships and part-time jobs. The average aided 2008–09 undergraduate received an aid package worth an estimated $30,159. The application deadline for financial aid is February 1.

Freshman Admission Wheaton College requires an essay, a high school transcript, 2 recommendations, and TOEFL scores for international students. An interview is recommended. The application deadline for regular admission is January 15, for early decision plan 1 it is November 15, and for early decision plan 2 it is January 15.

Transfer Admission The application deadline for admission is March 1.

Entrance Difficulty Wheaton College assesses its entrance difficulty level as very difficult. For the fall 2008 freshman class, 43 percent of the applicants were accepted.

For Further Information Contact Ms. Gail Berson, Vice President For Enrollment and Dean of Admission and Student Aid, Wheaton College, 26 East Main Street, Norton, MA 02766. *Phone:* 508-286-8251 or 800-394-6003 (toll-free). *Fax:* 508-286-8271. *E-mail:* admission@wheatoncollege.edu. *Web site:* http://www.wheatoncollege.edu/.

WHEELOCK COLLEGE
Boston, Massachusetts

Wheelock College is a coed, primarily women's, private, comprehensive institution, founded in 1888, offering degrees at the bachelor's and master's levels and post-master's and postbachelor's certificates. It has a 7-acre campus in Boston.

Academic Information The faculty has 93 members (70% full-time), 67% with terminal degrees. The undergraduate student-faculty ratio is 11:1. The library holds 80,763 titles, 23,498 serial subscriptions, and 4,375 audiovisual materials. Special programs include services for learning-disabled students, an honors program, study abroad, advanced placement credit, Freshman Honors College, double majors, independent study, part-time degree programs (daytime), internships, and arrangement for off-campus study with 5 other members of Colleges of the Fenway. The most frequently chosen baccalaureate fields are education, family and consumer sciences, public administration and social services.

Student Body Statistics The student body totals 1,109, of whom 824 are undergraduates (238 freshmen). 92 percent are women and 8 percent are men. 60 percent are from Massachusetts. 1.2 percent are international students.

Expenses for 2009–10 *Application fee:* $35. *Comprehensive fee:* $39,360 includes full-time tuition ($27,150), mandatory fees ($1010), and college room and board ($11,200). *Part-time tuition:* $850 per credit.

Financial Aid Forms of aid include need-based and non-need-based scholarships and part-time jobs. The average aided 2008–09 undergraduate received an aid package worth an estimated $18,541. The priority application deadline for financial aid is February 15.

Freshman Admission Wheelock College requires an essay, a high school transcript, 1 recommendation, SAT or ACT scores, and TOEFL scores for international students. A minimum 2.0 high school GPA and an interview are recommended. The application deadline for regular admission is March 1 and for early action it is December 1.

Transfer Admission The application deadline for admission is April 15.

Entrance Difficulty Wheelock College assesses its entrance difficulty level as moderately difficult. For the fall 2008 freshman class, 74 percent of the applicants were accepted.

For Further Information Contact Ms. Lisa Slavin, Dean of Admissions, Wheelock College, 200 The Riverway, Boston, MA 02215. *Phone:* 617-879-2206 or 800-734-5212 (toll-free out-of-state). *Fax:* 617-879-2449. *E-mail:* undergrad@wheelock.edu. *Web site:* http://www.wheelock.edu/.

WILLIAMS COLLEGE

Williamstown, Massachusetts

Williams College is a coed, private, comprehensive institution, founded in 1793, offering degrees at the bachelor's and master's levels. It has a 450-acre campus in Williamstown near Albany.

Academic Information The faculty has 315 members (85% full-time), 90% with terminal degrees. The undergraduate student-faculty ratio is 7:1. The library holds 932,000 titles, 12,063 serial subscriptions, and 38,076 audiovisual materials. Special programs include services for learning-disabled students, study abroad, advanced placement credit, double majors, independent study, self-designed majors, internships, and arrangement for off-campus study with members of the Twelve College Exchange Program, Bennington College, Rensselaer Polytechnic Institute, California Institute of Technology, Dartmouth College, Massachusetts College of Liberal Arts, Columbia University. The most frequently chosen baccalaureate fields are social sciences, English, visual and performing arts.

Student Body Statistics The student body totals 2,045, of whom 1,997 are undergraduates (540 freshmen). 50 percent are women and 50 percent are men. Students come from 45 states and territories and 63 other countries. 14 percent are from Massachusetts. 7.2 percent are international students.

Expenses for 2008–09 *Application fee:* $60. *Comprehensive fee:* $47,530 includes full-time tuition ($37,400), mandatory fees ($240), and college room and board ($9890). *College room only:* $5030. Room and board charges vary according to board plan.

Financial Aid Forms of aid include need-based scholarships and part-time jobs. The average aided 2008–09 undergraduate received an aid package worth an estimated $37,857. The application deadline for financial aid is February 1.

Freshman Admission Williams College requires an essay, a high school transcript, 2 recommendations, and SAT and SAT Subject Test or ACT scores. TOEFL scores for international students are recommended. The application deadline for regular admission is January 1 and for early decision it is November 10.

Transfer Admission The application deadline for admission is March 15.

Entrance Difficulty Williams College assesses its entrance difficulty level as most difficult. For the fall 2008 freshman class, 17 percent of the applicants were accepted.

For Further Information Contact Mr. Richard L. Nesbitt, Director of Admission, Williams College, 33 Stetson Court, Williamstown, MA 01267. *Phone:* 413-597-2211. *Fax:* 413-597-4052. *E-mail:* admission@williams.edu. *Web site:* http://www.williams.edu/.

WORCESTER POLYTECHNIC INSTITUTE

Worcester, Massachusetts

Worcester Polytechnic Institute is a coed, private university, founded in 1865, offering degrees at the bachelor's, master's, and doctoral levels and post-master's and postbachelor's certificates. It has an 80-acre campus in Worcester near Boston.

Academic Information The faculty has 314 members (80% full-time), 87% with terminal degrees. The undergraduate student-faculty ratio is 14:1. The library holds 272,022 titles, 56,300 serial subscriptions, and 1,941 audiovisual materials. Special programs include services for learning-disabled students, cooperative (work-study) education, study abroad, advanced placement credit, accelerated degree programs, ESL programs, double majors, independent study, self-designed majors, summer session for credit, part-time degree programs (daytime, summer), internships, and arrangement for off-campus study with Colleges of Worcester Consortium. The most frequently chosen baccalaureate fields are biological/life sciences, computer and information sciences, engineering.

Student Body Statistics The student body totals 4,561, of whom 3,252 are undergraduates (907 freshmen). 27 percent are women and 73 percent are men. Students come from 43 states and territories and 61 other countries. 55 percent are from Massachusetts. 8.4 percent are international students.

Expenses for 2008–09 *Application fee:* $60. *One-time mandatory fee:* $200. *Comprehensive fee:* $47,810 includes full-time tuition ($36,390), mandatory fees ($540), and college room and board ($10,880). *College room only:* $6635. Room and board charges vary according to board plan and housing facility. *Part-time tuition:* $1011 per credit hour. Part-time tuition varies according to course load.

Financial Aid Forms of aid include need-based and non-need-based scholarships and part-time jobs. The average aided 2008–09 undergraduate received an aid package worth an estimated $25,876. The application deadline for financial aid is February 1.

Freshman Admission Worcester Polytechnic Institute requires an essay, a high school transcript, 2 recommendations, and TOEFL scores for international students. An interview, SAT or ACT scores, and IELTS are required for some. The application deadline for regular admission is February 1 and for early action it is November 10.

Transfer Admission The application deadline for admission is April 15.

Entrance Difficulty Worcester Polytechnic Institute assesses its entrance difficulty level as very difficult; moderately difficult for transfers. For the fall 2008 freshman class, 67 percent of the applicants were accepted.

For Further Information Contact Mr. Edward J. Connor, Director of Admissions, Worcester Polytechnic Institute, 100 Institute Road, Worcester, MA 01609-2280. *Phone:* 508-831-5286. *Fax:* 508-831-5875. *E-mail:* admissions@wpi.edu. *Web site:* http://www.wpi.edu/.

WORCESTER STATE COLLEGE

Worcester, Massachusetts

Worcester State College is a coed, public, comprehensive unit of Massachusetts Public Higher Education System, founded in 1874, offering degrees at the bachelor's and master's levels and post-master's and postbachelor's certificates. It has a 58-acre campus in Worcester near Boston.

Academic Information The faculty has 386 members (48% full-time), 37% with terminal degrees. The undergraduate student-faculty ratio is 16:1. The library holds 174,299 titles, 523 serial subscriptions, and 13,008 audiovisual materials. Special programs include academic remediation, services for learning-disabled students, an honors program, study abroad, advanced placement credit, accelerated degree programs, ESL programs, double majors, independent study, distance learning, self-designed majors, summer session for credit, part-time degree programs (daytime, evenings, weekends, summer), adult/continuing education programs, internships, and arrangement for off-campus study with Worcester Consortium for Higher Education, other Massachusetts state colleges. The most frequently chosen baccalaureate fields are business/marketing, health professions and related sciences, psychology.

Student Body Statistics The student body totals 5,378, of whom 4,643 are undergraduates (682 freshmen). 59 percent are women and 41 percent are men. Students come from 15 states and territories and 19 other countries. 97 percent are from Massachusetts. 1.1 percent are international students.

Expenses for 2008–09 *Application fee:* $20. *State resident tuition:* $970 full-time, $40.42 per credit part-time. *Nonresident tuition:* $7050 full-time, $293.75 per credit part-time. *Mandatory fees:* $5200 full-time, $206.25 per credit part-time. Both full-time and part-time tuition and fees vary according to class time, course load, degree level, and reciprocity

Worcester State College (continued)

agreements. *College room and board:* $8527. *College room only:* $5877. Room and board charges vary according to board plan and housing facility.

Financial Aid Forms of aid include need-based scholarships and part-time jobs. The average aided 2007–08 undergraduate received an aid package worth $9086. The application deadline for financial aid is May 1 with a priority deadline of March 1.

Freshman Admission Worcester State College requires a high school transcript, a minimum 2.0 high school GPA, SAT or ACT scores, and TOEFL scores for international students. Recommendations are recommended. An essay and SAT Subject Test scores are required for some. The application deadline for regular admission is June 1.

Transfer Admission The application deadline for admission is June 1.

Entrance Difficulty Worcester State College assesses its entrance difficulty level as moderately difficult; most difficult for Nursing, Occupational Therapy. For the fall 2008 freshman class, 54 percent of the applicants were accepted.

For Further Information Contact Ms. Kim Albro, Clerk of Admissions, Worcester State College, 486 Chandler Street, Administration Building, Worcester, MA 01602-2597. *Phone:* 508-929-8040 or 866-WSC-CALL (toll-free). *Fax:* 508-929-8183. *E-mail:* admissions@worcester.edu. *Web site:* http://www.worcester.edu/.

ZION BIBLE COLLEGE

Haverhill, Massachusetts

Zion Bible College is a coed, private, four-year college, founded in 1924, affiliated with the Assembly of God Church, offering degrees at the bachelor's level.

Student Body Statistics The student body is made up of 265 undergraduates.

Expenses for 2008–09 *Application fee:* $35. *Comprehensive fee:* $13,340 includes full-time tuition ($7050), mandatory fees ($590), and college room and board ($5700). *Part-time tuition:* $235 per credit hour.

Freshman Admission Zion Bible College requires TOEFL scores for international students.

Entrance Difficulty Zion Bible College has an open admission policy.

For Further Information Contact Helen Brouillette, Admissions Director, Zion Bible College, 320 S. Main Street, Haverhill, MA 01835. *Phone:* 800-356-4014 or 800-356-4014 (toll-free). *E-mail:* admissions@zbc.edu. *Web site:* http://www.zbc.edu/.

New Hampshire

CHESTER COLLEGE OF NEW ENGLAND

Chester, New Hampshire

http://www.chestercollege.edu/

COLBY-SAWYER COLLEGE

New London, New Hampshire

Colby-Sawyer College is a coed, private, four-year college, founded in 1837, offering degrees at the associate and bachelor's levels. It has a 200-acre campus in New London.

Expenses for 2008–09 *Application fee:* $45. *Comprehensive fee:* $39,960 includes full-time tuition ($29,620) and college room and board ($10,340). *Part-time tuition:* $990 per credit hour. Part-time tuition varies according to course load.

For Further Information Contact Director of Admissions and Financial Aid, Colby-Sawyer College, 541 Main Street, New London, NH 03257-4648. *Phone:* 603-526-3700 or 800-272-1015 (toll-free). *Fax:* 603-526-3452. *E-mail:* admissions@colby-sawyer.edu. *Web site:* http://www.colby-sawyer.edu/.

COLLEGE FOR LIFELONG LEARNING

See Granite State College.

DANIEL WEBSTER COLLEGE

Nashua, New Hampshire

Daniel Webster College is a coed, private, comprehensive institution, founded in 1965, offering degrees at the associate, bachelor's, and master's levels. It has a 50-acre campus in Nashua near Boston.

Academic Information The faculty has 62 members (56% full-time), 42% with terminal degrees. The undergraduate student-faculty ratio is 14:1. Special programs include services for learning-disabled students, cooperative (work-study) education, advanced placement credit, accelerated degree programs, double majors, independent study, distance learning, summer session for credit, part-time degree programs (daytime, evenings, weekends, summer), external degree programs, adult/continuing education programs, internships, and arrangement for off-campus study with members of the New Hampshire College and University Council.

Student Body Statistics The student body totals 1,007, of whom 885 are undergraduates. 26 percent are women and 74 percent are men. Students come from 17 states and territories and 14 other countries. 37 percent are from New Hampshire.

Expenses for 2009–10 *Application fee:* $35. *Comprehensive fee:* $38,313 includes full-time tuition ($27,690), mandatory fees ($925), and college room and board ($9698). *College room only:* $4761. *Part-time tuition:* $1050 per credit. *Part-time mandatory fees:* $275 per credit.

Financial Aid Forms of aid include need-based and non-need-based scholarships and part-time jobs. The priority application deadline for financial aid is March 1.

Freshman Admission Daniel Webster College requires a high school transcript, SAT or ACT scores, and TOEFL scores for international students. An essay, 2 recommendations, and an interview are recommended. The application deadline for regular admission is rolling.

Transfer Admission The application deadline for admission is rolling.

Entrance Difficulty Daniel Webster College assesses its entrance difficulty level as moderately difficult. For the fall 2008 freshman class, 74 percent of the applicants were accepted.

For Further Information Contact Mr. Daniel Monahan, Dean of Admissions and Financial Assistance, Daniel Webster College, 20 University Drive, Nashua, NH 03063. *Phone:* 603-577-6600 or 800-325-6876 (toll-free). *Fax:* 603-577-6001. *E-mail:* admissions@dwc.edu. *Web site:* http://www.dwc.edu/.

See page 94 for the Close-Up.

DANIEL WEBSTER COLLEGE–PORTSMOUTH CAMPUS

Portsmouth, New Hampshire

http://www.dwc.edu/gcde/portsmouth/

DARTMOUTH COLLEGE

Hanover, New Hampshire

Dartmouth College is a coed, private university, founded in 1769, offering degrees at the bachelor's, master's, doctoral, and first professional levels. It has a 265-acre campus in Hanover.

Academic Information The faculty has 647 members (76% full-time), 87% with terminal degrees. The undergraduate student-faculty ratio is 8:1. Special programs include services for learning-disabled students, an honors program, study abroad, advanced placement credit, double majors, independent study, self-designed majors, summer session for credit, internships, and arrangement for off-campus study with members of the Twelve College Exchange Program, University of California, San Diego, McGill University, Morehouse College, Spelman College, Stanford University. The most frequently chosen baccalaureate fields are history, psychology, social sciences.
Student Body Statistics The student body totals 5,848, of whom 4,147 are undergraduates (1,096 freshmen). 50 percent are women and 50 percent are men. Students come from 54 states and territories and 47 other countries. 4 percent are from New Hampshire. 6.9 percent are international students.
Expenses for 2009–10 *Application fee:* $70. *Comprehensive fee:* $49,224 includes full-time tuition ($38,445) and college room and board ($10,779). *College room only:* $6444.
Financial Aid Forms of aid include need-based scholarships and part-time jobs. The average aided 2008–09 undergraduate received an aid package worth an estimated $35,966. The application deadline for financial aid is February 1.
Freshman Admission Dartmouth College requires an essay, a high school transcript, 2 recommendations, peer evaluation, SAT or ACT scores, SAT Subject Test scores, and TOEFL scores for international students. An interview is recommended. The application deadline for regular admission is January 1 and for early decision it is November 1.
Transfer Admission The application deadline for admission is March 1.
Entrance Difficulty Dartmouth College assesses its entrance difficulty level as most difficult. For the fall 2008 freshman class, 13 percent of the applicants were accepted.
For Further Information Contact Maria Laskaris, Dean of Admissions and Financial Aid, Dartmouth College, 6016 McNutt Hall, Hanover, NH 03755. *Phone:* 603-646-2875. *E-mail:* admissions.office@dartmouth.edu. *Web site:* http://www.dartmouth.edu/.

FRANKLIN PIERCE UNIVERSITY

Rindge, New Hampshire

Franklin Pierce University is a coed, private, comprehensive institution, founded in 1962, offering degrees at the associate, bachelor's, master's, and doctoral levels and post-master's certificates (profile does not reflect significant enrollment at 6 continuing education sites; master's degree is only offered at these sites). It has a 1,000-acre campus in Rindge.

Academic Information The faculty has 244 members (40% full-time), 43% with terminal degrees. The undergraduate student-faculty ratio is 18:1. The library holds 137,458 titles, 19,414 serial subscriptions, and 14,635 audiovisual materials. Special programs include academic remediation, services for learning-disabled students, an honors program, study abroad, advanced placement credit, ESL programs, double majors, independent study, distance learning, self-designed majors, summer session for credit, part-time degree programs (daytime, summer), adult/continuing education programs, internships, and arrangement for off-campus study with 12 members of the New Hampshire College and University Council. The most frequently chosen baccalaureate fields are business/marketing, communications/journalism, security and protective services.
Student Body Statistics The student body totals 2,601, of whom 2,102 are undergraduates (477 freshmen). 51 percent are women and 49 percent are men. Students come from 34 states and territories and 15 other countries. 27 percent are from New Hampshire. 2.6 percent are international students.

Expenses for 2009–10 *Application fee:* $40. *Comprehensive fee:* $38,500 includes full-time tuition ($27,700), mandatory fees ($1000), and college room and board ($9800). *College room only:* $5600. *Part-time tuition:* $923 per credit hour.
Financial Aid Forms of aid include need-based and non-need-based scholarships, athletic grants, and part-time jobs. The average aided 2008–09 undergraduate received an aid package worth an estimated $18,733. The priority application deadline for financial aid is March 1.
Freshman Admission Franklin Pierce University requires an essay, a high school transcript, 1 recommendation, SAT or ACT scores, and TOEFL scores for international students. A minimum 2.0 high school GPA and an interview are recommended. The application deadline for regular admission is rolling.
Entrance Difficulty Franklin Pierce University assesses its entrance difficulty level as moderately difficult. For the fall 2008 freshman class, 77 percent of the applicants were accepted.
For Further Information Contact Office of Admissions, Franklin Pierce University, 20 College Road, Rindge, NH 03461. *Phone:* 603-899-4050 or 800-437-0048 (toll-free). *Fax:* 603-899-4394. *E-mail:* admissions@fpc.edu. *Web site:* http://www.franklinpierce.edu/.

GRANITE STATE COLLEGE

Concord, New Hampshire

Granite State College is a coed, primarily women's, public, four-year college of University System of New Hampshire, founded in 1972, offering degrees at the associate and bachelor's levels and postbachelor's certificates (offers primarily part-time degree programs; courses offered at 50 locations in New Hampshire).

Academic Information The faculty has 147 members. The student-faculty ratio is 10.1:1. The library holds 21 serial subscriptions. Special programs include academic remediation, services for learning-disabled students, cooperative (work-study) education, advanced placement credit, accelerated degree programs, double majors, independent study, distance learning, self-designed majors, summer session for credit, part-time degree programs (daytime, evenings, weekends, summer), adult/continuing education programs, internships, and arrangement for off-campus study with other units of the University System of New Hampshire and the New Hampshire College and University Council. The most frequently chosen baccalaureate fields are business/marketing, interdisciplinary studies, liberal arts/general studies.
Student Body Statistics The student body totals 1,543, of whom 1,365 are undergraduates (47 freshmen). 73 percent are women and 27 percent are men. Students come from 21 states and territories and 1 other country. 92 percent are from New Hampshire.
Expenses for 2008–09 *Application fee:* $45. *State resident tuition:* $5712 full-time, $238 per credit part-time. *Nonresident tuition:* $6048 full-time, $252 per credit part-time. *Mandatory fees:* $195 full-time, $65 per term part-time.
Freshman Admission Granite State College requires an essay, self-certify high school grad or GED, and TOEFL scores for international students. The application deadline for regular admission is rolling.
Transfer Admission The application deadline for admission is rolling.
Entrance Difficulty Granite State College has an open admission policy.
For Further Information Contact Ms. Tessa McDonnell, Dean of Learner Services, Granite State College, 8 Old Suncook Road, Concord, NH 03301. *Phone:* 603-513-1308 or 800-582-7248 Ext. 313 (toll-free in-state). *Fax:* 603-513-1386. *E-mail:* tessa.mcdonnell@granite.edu. *Web site:* http://www.granite.edu/.

HESSER COLLEGE, CONCORD

Concord, New Hampshire

http://www.concord.hesser.edu/

HESSER COLLEGE, MANCHESTER

Manchester, New Hampshire

http://www.manchester.hesser.edu/

HESSER COLLEGE, NASHUA

Nashua, New Hampshire

http://www.nashua.hesser.edu/

HESSER COLLEGE, PORTSMOUTH

Portsmouth, New Hampshire

http://www.portsmouth.hesser.edu/

HESSER COLLEGE, SALEM

Salem, New Hampshire

http://www.salem.hesser.edu/

KEENE STATE COLLEGE

Keene, New Hampshire

Keene State College is a coed, public, comprehensive unit of University System of New Hampshire, founded in 1909, offering degrees at the associate, bachelor's, and master's levels and post-master's and postbachelor's certificates. It has a 160-acre campus in Keene.

Academic Information The faculty has 422 members (44% full-time). The undergraduate student-faculty ratio is 19:1. The library holds 324,561 titles, 969 serial subscriptions, and 11,776 audiovisual materials. Special programs include services for learning-disabled students, an honors program, cooperative (work-study) education, study abroad, advanced placement credit, ESL programs, double majors, independent study, self-designed majors, summer session for credit, part-time degree programs (daytime, evenings, weekends, summer), internships, and arrangement for off-campus study with members of the New Hampshire College and University Council. The most frequently chosen baccalaureate fields are education, psychology, social sciences.
Student Body Statistics The student body totals 5,271, of whom 5,147 are undergraduates (1,298 freshmen). 56 percent are women and 44 percent are men. Students come from 28 states and territories and 7 other countries. 53 percent are from New Hampshire. 0.3 percent are international students.
Expenses for 2008–09 *Application fee:* $40. *State resident tuition:* $6600 full-time, $275 per credit part-time. *Nonresident tuition:* $14,450 full-time, $602 per credit part-time. *Mandatory fees:* $2178 full-time, $86 per credit part-time. Part-time tuition and fees vary according to course load. *College room and board:* $7796. *College room only:* $5256. Room and board charges vary according to board plan and housing facility.
Financial Aid Forms of aid include need-based and non-need-based scholarships and part-time jobs. The average aided 2007–08 undergraduate received an aid package worth $8492. The application deadline for financial aid is March 1.
Freshman Admission Keene State College requires an essay, a high school transcript, 1 recommendation, SAT or ACT scores, and TOEFL scores for international students. The application deadline for regular admission is April 1.
Transfer Admission The application deadline for admission is rolling.

Entrance Difficulty Keene State College assesses its entrance difficulty level as moderately difficult. For the fall 2008 freshman class, 72 percent of the applicants were accepted.
For Further Information Contact Ms. Margaret Richmond, Director of Admissions, Keene State College, 229 Main Street, Keene, NH 03435-2604. *Phone:* 603-358-2273 or 800-KSC-1909 (toll-free). *Fax:* 603-358-2767. *E-mail:* admissions@keene.edu. *Web site:* http://www.keene.edu/.

MAGDALEN COLLEGE

Warner, New Hampshire

http://www.magdalen.edu/

NEW ENGLAND COLLEGE

Henniker, New Hampshire

New England College is a coed, private, comprehensive institution, founded in 1946, offering degrees at the associate, bachelor's, and master's levels. It has a 225-acre campus in Henniker near Boston.

Academic Information The faculty has 109 members (57% full-time), 58% with terminal degrees. The undergraduate student-faculty ratio is 13:1. The library holds 106,625 titles and 261 serial subscriptions. Special programs include academic remediation, services for learning-disabled students, an honors program, study abroad, advanced placement credit, accelerated degree programs, ESL programs, double majors, independent study, distance learning, self-designed majors, summer session for credit, part-time degree programs (daytime, evenings, summer), external degree programs, adult/continuing education programs, internships, and arrangement for off-campus study with members of the New Hampshire College and University Council. The most frequently chosen baccalaureate fields are business/marketing, parks and recreation, visual and performing arts.
Student Body Statistics The student body totals 1,752, of whom 1,061 are undergraduates (299 freshmen). 47 percent are women and 53 percent are men. Students come from 27 states and territories and 20 other countries. 36 percent are from New Hampshire. 5.2 percent are international students.
Expenses for 2009–10 *Application fee:* $30. *Comprehensive fee:* $37,076 includes full-time tuition ($27,200), mandatory fees ($250), and college room and board ($9626). *College room only:* $5000. *Part-time tuition:* $1133 per credit.
Financial Aid Forms of aid include need-based and non-need-based scholarships and part-time jobs. The average aided 2008–09 undergraduate received an aid package worth an estimated $23,858.
Freshman Admission New England College requires an essay, a high school transcript, 3 recommendations, and TOEFL scores for international students. An interview is recommended. The application deadline for regular admission is rolling.
Transfer Admission The application deadline for admission is rolling.
Entrance Difficulty New England College assesses its entrance difficulty level as moderately difficult; minimally difficult for transfers. For the fall 2008 freshman class, 76 percent of the applicants were accepted.
For Further Information Contact Diane Raymond, Director of Admission, New England College, 24 Bridge Street, Henniker, NH 03242. *Phone:* 603-428-2223 or 800-521-7642 (toll-free). *Fax:* 603-428-7230. *E-mail:* admission@nec.edu. *Web site:* http://www.nec.edu/.

NEW HAMPSHIRE COLLEGE

See Southern New Hampshire University.

NEW HAMPSHIRE INSTITUTE OF ART

Manchester, New Hampshire

New Hampshire Institute of Art is a coed, proprietary, four-year college, founded in 1898, offering degrees at the bachelor's level. It is located in Manchester near Boston.

Academic Information The faculty has 69 members (19% full-time), 58% with terminal degrees. The student-faculty ratio is 10:1. The library holds 12,659 titles, 198 serial subscriptions, and 634 audiovisual materials. Special programs include study abroad, advanced placement credit, summer session for credit, and part-time degree programs (daytime, evenings, summer).

Student Body Statistics The student body is made up of 391 undergraduates (103 freshmen). 69 percent are women and 31 percent are men. Students come from 2 states and territories and 2 other countries. 51 percent are from New Hampshire.

Expenses for 2009–10 *Application fee:* $25. *Tuition:* $15,400 full-time, $1542 per course part-time. *Mandatory fees:* $1730 full-time, $233 per course part-time, $165 per term part-time. *College room only:* $7000.

Financial Aid Forms of aid include need-based and non-need-based scholarships and part-time jobs. The priority application deadline for financial aid is May 1.

Freshman Admission New Hampshire Institute of Art requires an essay, a high school transcript, a portfolio, and TOEFL scores for international students. An interview is recommended. The application deadline for regular admission is rolling.

Transfer Admission The application deadline for admission is rolling.

Entrance Difficulty New Hampshire Institute of Art has an open admission policy.

For Further Information Contact Ms. Amanda Abbott, Assistant Director of Enrollment, New Hampshire Institute of Art, 148 Concord Street, Manchester, NH 03104-4158. *Phone:* 603-623-0313 Ext. 576 or 866-241-4918 (toll-free in-state). *E-mail:* aabbott@nhia.edu. *Web site:* http://www.nhia.edu/.

PLYMOUTH STATE UNIVERSITY

Plymouth, New Hampshire

Plymouth State University is a coed, public, comprehensive unit of University System of New Hampshire, founded in 1871, offering degrees at the bachelor's and master's levels and post-master's and postbachelor's certificates. It has a 170-acre campus in Plymouth.

Academic Information The faculty has 426 members (44% full-time). The undergraduate student-faculty ratio is 17:1. The library holds 347,390 titles and 40,975 serial subscriptions. Special programs include services for learning-disabled students, an honors program, study abroad, advanced placement credit, accelerated degree programs, double majors, independent study, self-designed majors, summer session for credit, part-time degree programs (daytime, evenings, summer), internships, and arrangement for off-campus study with members of the New Hampshire College and University Council. The most frequently chosen baccalaureate fields are business/marketing, education, parks and recreation.

Student Body Statistics The student body totals 6,562, of whom 4,300 are undergraduates (1,090 freshmen). 47 percent are women and 53 percent are men. Students come from 29 states and territories and 17 other countries. 58 percent are from New Hampshire.

Expenses for 2008–09 *Application fee:* $40. *State resident tuition:* $6600 full-time, $275 per credit hour part-time. *Nonresident tuition:* $14,450 full-time, $602 per credit hour part-time. *Mandatory fees:* $1824 full-time. Full-time tuition and fees vary according to reciprocity agreements. Part-time tuition varies according to course load and reciprocity agreements. *College room and board:* $8350. *College room only:* $5850. Room and board charges vary according to board plan and housing facility.

Financial Aid Forms of aid include need-based and non-need-based scholarships and part-time jobs. The average aided 2007–08 undergraduate received an aid package worth $7944.

Freshman Admission Plymouth State University requires an essay, a high school transcript, 1 recommendation, SAT or ACT scores, and TOEFL scores for international students. An interview is required for some. The application deadline for regular admission is April 1.

Transfer Admission The application deadline for admission is April 1.

Entrance Difficulty Plymouth State University assesses its entrance difficulty level as moderately difficult. For the fall 2008 freshman class, 74 percent of the applicants were accepted.

For Further Information Contact Mr. Eugene Fahey, Senior Associate Director of Admission, Plymouth State University, 17 High Street, MSC #52, Plymouth, NH 03264-1595. *Phone:* 800-842-6900 (toll-free). *Fax:* 603-535-2714. *E-mail:* plymouthadmit@plymouth.edu. *Web site:* http://www.plymouth.edu/.

RIVIER COLLEGE

Nashua, New Hampshire

Rivier College is a coed, private, Roman Catholic, comprehensive institution, founded in 1933, offering degrees at the associate, bachelor's, and master's levels and post-master's and postbachelor's certificates. It has a 68-acre campus in Nashua near Boston.

Academic Information The faculty has 178 members (40% full-time), 38% with terminal degrees. The undergraduate student-faculty ratio is 14:1. Special programs include services for learning-disabled students, an honors program, advanced placement credit, accelerated degree programs, ESL programs, double majors, independent study, part-time degree programs (daytime, evenings, weekends), internships, and arrangement for off-campus study with members of the New Hampshire College and University Council. The most frequently chosen baccalaureate fields are education, health professions and related sciences, social sciences.

Student Body Statistics The student body totals 2,231, of whom 1,472 are undergraduates (255 freshmen). 81 percent are women and 19 percent are men. Students come from 10 states and territories and 7 other countries. 59 percent are from New Hampshire. 0.1 percent are international students.

Expenses for 2009–10 *Application fee:* $25. *One-time mandatory fee:* $175. *Comprehensive fee:* $33,444 includes full-time tuition ($23,490), mandatory fees ($800), and college room and board ($9154). *Part-time tuition:* $793 per credit.

Financial Aid Forms of aid include need-based and non-need-based scholarships and part-time jobs. The average aided 2008–09 undergraduate received an aid package worth an estimated $16,294. The priority application deadline for financial aid is March 1.

Freshman Admission Rivier College requires an essay, a high school transcript, 1 recommendation, SAT or ACT scores, and TOEFL scores for international students. A minimum 2.3 high school GPA and an interview are recommended. An interview and nursing exam are required for some. The application deadline for regular admission is rolling, for early decision it is November 15, and for early action it is November 15.

Transfer Admission The application deadline for admission is rolling.

Entrance Difficulty Rivier College assesses its entrance difficulty level as moderately difficult. For the fall 2008 freshman class, 77 percent of the applicants were accepted.

For Further Information Contact David Boisvert, Vice President of Enrollment, Rivier College, 420 South Main Street, Nashua, NH 03060. *Phone:* 603-897-8507 or 800-44RIVIER (toll-free). *Fax:* 603-891-1799. *E-mail:* rivadmit@rivier.edu. *Web site:* http://www.rivier.edu/.

See page 110 for the Close-Up.

SAINT ANSELM COLLEGE

Manchester, New Hampshire

http://www.anselm.edu/

SOUTHERN NEW HAMPSHIRE UNIVERSITY

Manchester, New Hampshire

Southern New Hampshire University is a coed, private, comprehensive institution, founded in 1932, offering degrees at the associate,

Southern New Hampshire University (continued)

bachelor's, master's, and doctoral levels and postbachelor's certificates. It has a 288-acre campus in Manchester near Boston.

Academic Information The faculty has 388 members (34% full-time), 25% with terminal degrees. The undergraduate student-faculty ratio is 16:1. The library holds 94,580 titles, 42,135 serial subscriptions, and 2,792 audiovisual materials. Special programs include academic remediation, services for learning-disabled students, an honors program, cooperative (work-study) education, study abroad, advanced placement credit, accelerated degree programs, ESL programs, double majors, independent study, distance learning, summer session for credit, part-time degree programs (daytime, evenings, weekends, summer), adult/continuing education programs, internships, and arrangement for off-campus study with members of the New Hampshire College and University Council. The most frequently chosen baccalaureate fields are business/marketing, education, psychology.

Student Body Statistics The student body totals 4,211, of whom 2,037 are undergraduates (599 freshmen). 54 percent are women and 46 percent are men. Students come from 27 states and territories and 29 other countries. 45 percent are from New Hampshire. 4.4 percent are international students.

Expenses for 2009–10 *Application fee:* $40. *Comprehensive fee:* $36,618 includes full-time tuition ($26,112), mandatory fees ($330), and college room and board ($10,176). *College room only:* $7276. *Part-time tuition:* $1088 per credit.

Financial Aid Forms of aid include need-based scholarships, athletic grants, and part-time jobs. The average aided 2007–08 undergraduate received an aid package worth $15,514.

Freshman Admission Southern New Hampshire University requires an essay, a high school transcript, a minimum 2.0 high school GPA, 1 recommendation, SAT or ACT scores, and TOEFL scores for international students. An interview is recommended. 2 recommendations are required for some. The application deadline for regular admission is rolling and for early action it is November 15.

Transfer Admission The application deadline for admission is rolling.

Entrance Difficulty Southern New Hampshire University assesses its entrance difficulty level as moderately difficult; very difficult for 3-year honors program in business. For the fall 2008 freshman class, 86 percent of the applicants were accepted.

For Further Information Contact Mr. Steve Soba, Director of Admission, Southern New Hampshire University, 2500 North River Road, Manchester, NH 03106-1045. *Phone:* 603-645-9611 or 800-642-4968 (toll-free). *Fax:* 603-645-9693. *E-mail:* admission@snhu.edu. *Web site:* http://www.snhu.edu/.

See page 114 for the Close-Up.

THOMAS MORE COLLEGE OF LIBERAL ARTS
Merrimack, New Hampshire

Thomas More College of Liberal Arts is a coed, private, four-year college, founded in 1978, affiliated with the Roman Catholic Church, offering degrees at the bachelor's level. It has a 14-acre campus in Merrimack near Boston.

Expenses for 2008–09 *Application fee:* $0. *Comprehensive fee:* $22,000 includes full-time tuition ($13,200) and college room and board ($8800). *Part-time tuition:* $600 per credit hour.

For Further Information Contact Teddy Sifert, Director of Admissions, Thomas More College of Liberal Arts, 6 Manchester Street, Merrimack, NH 03054-4818. *Phone:* 603-880-8308 Ext. 14 or 800-880-8308 (toll-free). *Fax:* 603-880-9280. *E-mail:* admissions@thomasmorecollege.edu. *Web site:* http://www.thomasmorecollege.edu/.

UNIVERSITY OF NEW HAMPSHIRE
Durham, New Hampshire

University of New Hampshire is a coed, public unit of University System of New Hampshire, founded in 1866, offering degrees at the associate, bachelor's, master's, and doctoral levels and post-master's and postbachelor's certificates. It has a 2,600-acre campus in Durham near Boston.

Academic Information The faculty has 976 members (63% full-time), 58% with terminal degrees. The undergraduate student-faculty ratio is 18:1. The library holds 2 million titles, 50,043 serial subscriptions, and 39,508 audiovisual materials. Special programs include services for learning-disabled students, an honors program, cooperative (work-study) education, study abroad, advanced placement credit, ESL programs, double majors, independent study, self-designed majors, summer session for credit, part-time degree programs (daytime, evenings, summer), external degree programs, adult/continuing education programs, internships, and arrangement for off-campus study with National Student Exchange, New Hampshire College and University Council Exchange, New England Land Grant Universities Exchange, University of California, Santa Cruz Exchange, The Washington (D.C.) Center Internship. The most frequently chosen baccalaureate fields are business/marketing, health professions and related sciences, social sciences.

Student Body Statistics The student body totals 14,964, of whom 12,218 are undergraduates (2,692 freshmen). 56 percent are women and 44 percent are men. Students come from 47 states and territories and 24 other countries. 63 percent are from New Hampshire. 0.6 percent are international students.

Expenses for 2008–09 *Application fee:* $50. *State resident tuition:* $9402 full-time, $393 per credit hour part-time. *Nonresident tuition:* $22,900 full-time, $954 per credit hour part-time. *Mandatory fees:* $2336 full-time, $584 per term part-time. Part-time tuition and fees vary according to course load. *College room and board:* $8596. *College room only:* $5306. Room and board charges vary according to board plan and housing facility.

Financial Aid Forms of aid include need-based and non-need-based scholarships, athletic grants, and part-time jobs. The average aided 2007–08 undergraduate received an aid package worth $17,910. The priority application deadline for financial aid is March 1.

Freshman Admission University of New Hampshire requires an essay, a high school transcript, 1 recommendation, SAT or ACT scores, and TOEFL scores for international students. A minimum 3.0 high school GPA is recommended. The application deadline for regular admission is February 1, for nonresidents it is February 1, and for early action it is November 15.

Transfer Admission The application deadline for admission is March 1.

Entrance Difficulty University of New Hampshire assesses its entrance difficulty level as moderately difficult; very difficult for biological sciences, nursing, athletic training, environmental conservation, wildlife management, occupational therapy and business. For the fall 2008 freshman class, 65 percent of the applicants were accepted.

For Further Information Contact Admissions Office, University of New Hampshire, 4 Garrison Avenue, Durham, NH 03824. *Phone:* 603-862-0077. *Fax:* 603-862-0077. *E-mail:* admissions@unh.edu. *Web site:* http://www.unh.edu/.

UNIVERSITY OF NEW HAMPSHIRE AT MANCHESTER
Manchester, New Hampshire

University of New Hampshire at Manchester is a coed, public, comprehensive unit of University System of New Hampshire, founded in 1967, offering degrees at the associate, bachelor's, and master's levels. It has an 800-acre campus in Manchester near Boston.

Academic Information The faculty has 36 full-time members. The undergraduate student-faculty ratio is 12:1. The library holds 31,147 titles, 202 serial subscriptions, and 3,349 audiovisual materials. Special programs include academic remediation, services for learning-disabled students, study abroad, advanced placement credit, double majors, independent study, self-designed majors, summer session for credit, part-time degree programs

(daytime, evenings, weekends, summer), adult/continuing education programs, internships, and arrangement for off-campus study with 12 members of the New Hampshire College and University Council. The most frequently chosen baccalaureate fields are business/marketing, communications/journalism, engineering technologies.

Student Body Statistics The student body is made up of 792 undergraduates (109 freshmen). 56 percent are women and 44 percent are men. Students come from 4 states and territories and 5 other countries. 98 percent are from New Hampshire.

Expenses for 2008–09 *Application fee:* $45. *State resident tuition:* $8980 full-time, $374 per credit part-time. *Nonresident tuition:* $22,740 full-time, $948 per credit part-time. *Mandatory fees:* $921 full-time. Full-time tuition and fees vary according to course load and program. Part-time tuition varies according to course load and program.

Financial Aid Forms of aid include need-based and non-need-based scholarships and part-time jobs. The average aided 2007–08 undergraduate received an aid package worth $9326. The priority application deadline for financial aid is March 1.

Freshman Admission University of New Hampshire at Manchester requires an essay, a high school transcript, 1 recommendation, SAT or ACT scores, and TOEFL scores for international students. An interview is recommended. The application deadline for regular admission is June 15.

Transfer Admission The application deadline for admission is June 15.

Entrance Difficulty University of New Hampshire at Manchester assesses its entrance difficulty level as moderately difficult. For the fall 2008 freshman class, 72 percent of the applicants were accepted.

For Further Information Contact Ms. Susan Miller, Administrative Assistant, University of New Hampshire at Manchester, 400 Commercial Street, Manchester, NH 03101. *Phone:* 603-641-4150. *Fax:* 603-641-4125. *E-mail:* unhm@unh.edu. *Web site:* http://www.unhm.unh.edu/.

WHITE PINES COLLEGE

See Chester College of New England.

Rhode Island

BROWN UNIVERSITY
Providence, Rhode Island

Brown University is a coed, private university, founded in 1764, offering degrees at the bachelor's, master's, doctoral, and first professional levels. It has a 140-acre campus in Providence near Boston.

Academic Information The faculty has 828 members (83% full-time), 96% with terminal degrees. The undergraduate student-faculty ratio is 9:1. The library holds 3 million titles and 17,000 serial subscriptions. Special programs include services for learning-disabled students, an honors program, study abroad, advanced placement credit, accelerated degree programs, double majors, independent study, self-designed majors, summer session for credit, part-time degree programs (daytime, summer), adult/continuing education programs, internships, and arrangement for off-campus study with Rhode Island School of Design, Tougaloo College, Wheaton College (MA), Dartmouth Medical School. The most frequently chosen baccalaureate fields are biological/life sciences, physical sciences, social sciences.

Student Body Statistics The student body is made up of 6,095 undergraduates (1,548 freshmen). 52 percent are women and 48 percent are men. Students come from 52 states and territories and 116 other countries. 4 percent are from Rhode Island. 8.4 percent are international students.

Expenses for 2008–09 *Application fee:* $70. *Comprehensive fee:* $47,740 includes full-time tuition ($36,928), mandatory fees ($790), and college room and board ($10,022). *College room only:* $6216. Room and board charges vary according to board plan. *Part-time tuition:* $4616 per course.

Financial Aid Forms of aid include need-based scholarships and part-time jobs. The average aided 2008–09 undergraduate received an aid package worth an estimated $33,521. The application deadline for financial aid is February 1.

Freshman Admission Brown University requires an essay, a high school transcript, SAT and SAT Subject Test or ACT scores, and TOEFL scores for international students. 3 recommendations are required for some. The application deadline for regular admission is January 1 and for early decision it is November 1.

Transfer Admission The application deadline for admission is March 1.

Entrance Difficulty Brown University assesses its entrance difficulty level as most difficult. For the fall 2008 freshman class, 14 percent of the applicants were accepted.

For Further Information Contact Mr. James Miller, Dean of Admission, Brown University, Box 1876, Providence, RI 02912. *Phone:* 401-863-2378. *Fax:* 401-863-9300. *E-mail:* admission_undergraduate@brown.edu. *Web site:* http://www.brown.edu/.

BRYANT UNIVERSITY
Smithfield, Rhode Island

Bryant University is a coed, private, comprehensive institution, founded in 1863, offering degrees at the bachelor's and master's levels. It has a 420-acre campus in Smithfield near Boston and Providence.

Academic Information The faculty has 260 members (62% full-time). The undergraduate student-faculty ratio is 18:1. The library holds 143,393 titles, 26,451 serial subscriptions, and 1,208 audiovisual materials. Special programs include services for learning-disabled students, an honors program, study abroad, advanced placement credit, ESL programs, double majors, independent study, summer session for credit, part-time degree programs (daytime, evenings, summer), adult/continuing education programs, and internships. The most frequently chosen baccalaureate fields are business/marketing, computer and information sciences, social sciences.

Student Body Statistics The student body totals 3,800, of whom 3,515 are undergraduates (911 freshmen). 43 percent are women and 57 percent are men. Students come from 31 states and territories and 32 other countries. 16 percent are from Rhode Island. 3.9 percent are international students.

Expenses for 2009–10 *Application fee:* $50. *Comprehensive fee:* $44,043 includes full-time tuition ($31,974), mandatory fees ($312), and college room and board ($11,757). *College room only:* $7038. *Part-time tuition:* $1347 per credit hour.

Financial Aid Forms of aid include need-based and non-need-based scholarships, athletic grants, and part-time jobs. The average aided 2008–09 undergraduate received an aid package worth an estimated $20,281. The priority application deadline for financial aid is February 15.

Freshman Admission Bryant University requires an essay, a high school transcript, 1 recommendation, senior year first-quarter grades, SAT or ACT scores, and TOEFL scores for international students. A minimum 3.3 high school GPA is recommended. The application deadline for regular admission is February 1 and for early decision it is November 15.

Transfer Admission The application deadline for admission is April 1.

Entrance Difficulty Bryant University assesses its entrance difficulty level as moderately difficult. For the fall 2008 freshman class, 45 percent of the applicants were accepted.

For Further Information Contact Ms. Michelle Beauregard, Director of Admission, Bryant University, 1150 Douglas Pike, Smithfield, RI 02917. *Phone:* 401-232-6100 or 800-622-7001 (toll-free). *Fax:* 401-232-6741. *E-mail:* admission@bryant.edu. *Web site:* http://www.bryant.edu/.

JOHNSON & WALES UNIVERSITY
Providence, Rhode Island

Johnson & Wales University is a coed, private, comprehensive institution, founded in 1914, offering degrees at the associate, bachelor's, master's, and doctoral levels and post-master's certificates (branch locations in Charleston, SC; Denver, CO; North Miami, FL; Norfolk, VA; Gothenberg, Sweden). It has a 47-acre campus in Providence near Boston.

Johnson & Wales University (continued)

Expenses for 2008–09 *Application fee:* $0. *Comprehensive fee:* $31,477 includes full-time tuition ($21,297), mandatory fees ($1288), and college room and board ($8892). *Part-time tuition:* $394 per quarter hour.
For Further Information Contact Ms. Maureen Dumas, Dean of Admissions, Johnson & Wales University, 8 Abbott Park Place, Providence, RI 02903-3703. *Phone:* 401-598-2310, 800-598-1000 (toll-free in-state), or 800-342-5598 (toll-free out-of-state). *Fax:* 401-598-2948. *E-mail:* admissions.pvd@jwu.edu. *Web site:* http://www.jwu.edu/.

NEW ENGLAND INSTITUTE OF TECHNOLOGY

Warwick, Rhode Island

http://www.neit.edu/

PROVIDENCE COLLEGE

Providence, Rhode Island

Providence College is a coed, private, Roman Catholic, comprehensive institution, founded in 1917, offering degrees at the associate, bachelor's, and master's levels. It has a 105-acre campus in Providence near Boston.

Academic Information The faculty has 387 members (76% full-time), 79% with terminal degrees. The undergraduate student-faculty ratio is 12:1. The library holds 424,229 titles and 43,632 serial subscriptions. Special programs include services for learning-disabled students, an honors program, cooperative (work-study) education, study abroad, advanced placement credit, double majors, independent study, self-designed majors, summer session for credit, part-time degree programs (evenings, weekends, summer), adult/continuing education programs, and internships. The most frequently chosen baccalaureate fields are business/marketing, education, social sciences.
Student Body Statistics The student body totals 4,673, of whom 3,938 are undergraduates (988 freshmen). 56 percent are women and 44 percent are men. Students come from 38 states and territories and 19 other countries. 13 percent are from Rhode Island. 1.3 percent are international students.
Expenses for 2008–09 *Application fee:* $55. *Comprehensive fee:* $42,204 includes full-time tuition ($30,800), mandatory fees ($594), and college room and board ($10,810). *College room only:* $6160. Room and board charges vary according to board plan and housing facility. *Part-time tuition:* $1027 per credit.
Financial Aid Forms of aid include need-based and non-need-based scholarships, athletic grants, and part-time jobs. The average aided 2008–09 undergraduate received an aid package worth an estimated $18,500. The application deadline for financial aid is February 1.
Freshman Admission Providence College requires an essay, a high school transcript, 2 recommendations, and TOEFL scores for international students. The application deadline for regular admission is January 15 and for early action it is November 1.
Transfer Admission The application deadline for admission is April 1.
Entrance Difficulty Providence College assesses its entrance difficulty level as very difficult. For the fall 2008 freshman class, 45 percent of the applicants were accepted.
For Further Information Contact Mr. Christopher Lydon, Associate Vice President for Admission and Enrollment Planning, Providence College, River Avenue and Eaton Street, Providence, RI 02918. *Phone:* 401-865-2535 or 800-721-6444 (toll-free). *Fax:* 401-865-2826. *E-mail:* pcadmiss@providence.edu. *Web site:* http://www.providence.edu/.

RHODE ISLAND COLLEGE

Providence, Rhode Island

Rhode Island College is a coed, public, comprehensive institution, founded in 1854, offering degrees at the bachelor's, master's, and doctoral levels and post-master's and postbachelor's certificates. It has a 180-acre campus in Providence near Boston.

Academic Information The faculty has 705 members (43% full-time). The undergraduate student-faculty ratio is 16:1. The library holds 650,538 titles and 6,558 audiovisual materials. Special programs include academic remediation, services for learning-disabled students, an honors program, study abroad, advanced placement credit, ESL programs, double majors, independent study, self-designed majors, summer session for credit, part-time degree programs (daytime, evenings, weekends, summer), adult/continuing education programs, internships, and arrangement for off-campus study with Community College of Rhode Island, Providence College, University of Rhode Island. The most frequently chosen baccalaureate fields are business/marketing, education, psychology.
Student Body Statistics The student body totals 9,085, of whom 7,601 are undergraduates (1,190 freshmen). 68 percent are women and 32 percent are men. Students come from 27 states and territories and 2 other countries. 87 percent are from Rhode Island. 0.4 percent are international students.
Expenses for 2008–09 *Application fee:* $50. *State resident tuition:* $4889 full-time, $208 per credit part-time. *Nonresident tuition:* $13,600 full-time, $570 per credit part-time. *Mandatory fees:* $882 full-time, $24 per credit part-time, $68 per term part-time. Part-time tuition and fees vary according to course load. *College room and board:* $8250. *College room only:* $4600. Room and board charges vary according to board plan and housing facility.
Financial Aid Forms of aid include need-based and non-need-based scholarships and part-time jobs. The average aided 2008–09 undergraduate received an aid package worth an estimated $7817. The priority application deadline for financial aid is March 1.
Freshman Admission Rhode Island College requires an essay, a high school transcript, SAT or ACT scores, and TOEFL scores for international students. An interview is required for some. The application deadline for regular admission is May 1 and for nonresidents it is May 1.
Transfer Admission The application deadline for admission is June 1.
Entrance Difficulty Rhode Island College assesses its entrance difficulty level as moderately difficult. For the fall 2008 freshman class, 71 percent of the applicants were accepted.

SPECIAL MESSAGE TO STUDENTS

Social Life There are six residence halls on campus that provide a close community for nearly 1,200 students. Commuters and residents alike may join any of nearly eighty student organizations, including a completely student-run FM radio station, a student newspaper, service and departmental clubs, multicultural organizations, and more. The College's Division III athletics program fields ten varsity sports for women and nine for men. Student Activities and the various residence organizations plan monthly events and programs. The College's 180-acre suburban campus is located 10 minutes from downtown Providence, Rhode Island's capital city.

Academic Highlights Nearly half of Rhode Island College students pursue the College's well-known preprofessional programs in education, nursing, and social work. The other half are in liberal arts and business programs. The most popular of these majors includes psychology, management (business), communications, accounting, justice studies, and the fine and performing arts. The average class size is 24, and all classes are taught by faculty members rather than graduate or teaching assistants. The College Honors Program provides exceptional educational opportunities for academically talented students with smaller class sizes for even greater faculty-student interaction. Studying abroad is encouraged, and the College has various affiliations and programs

available. The Ridgway F. Shinn Study Abroad Fund helps students subsidize international study. Students have easy access to state-of-the-art computer facilities.

Interviews and Campus Visits Interviews are not required, but candidates are encouraged to attend an information session or meet with a staff member during their senior year. These sessions provide students with information about the College and the admissions process as well as an opportunity to tour the campus. Student-guided tours of the campus are available by appointment. An annual open house is held the second Saturday in November, which offers students and their families a chance to meet RIC faculty and staff members and students and to tour the campus. For further information, prospective students should call the Office of Undergraduate Admissions at 800-669-5760 (toll-free, voice or TDD), Monday through Friday, 8:30 to 4:30. The office is located in the Forman Center.

For Further Information Write to Dr. Holly L. Shadoian, Director of Admissions, The Forman Center, Rhode Island College, 600 Mt. Pleasant Avenue, Providence, RI 02908. *E-mail:* admissions@ric.edu. *Web site:* http://www.ric.edu.

RHODE ISLAND SCHOOL OF DESIGN
Providence, Rhode Island
http://www.risd.edu/

ROGER WILLIAMS UNIVERSITY
Bristol, Rhode Island

Roger Williams University is a coed, private, comprehensive institution, founded in 1956, offering degrees at the associate, bachelor's, master's, and first professional levels and postbachelor's certificates. It has a 140-acre campus in Bristol near Boston.

Academic Information The faculty has 584 members (36% full-time), 54% with terminal degrees. The undergraduate student-faculty ratio is 12:1. The library holds 224,278 titles, 31,904 serial subscriptions, and 96,138 audiovisual materials. Special programs include services for learning-disabled students, an honors program, cooperative (work-study) education, study abroad, advanced placement credit, Freshman Honors College, ESL programs, double majors, independent study, distance learning, self-designed majors, summer session for credit, part-time degree programs (evenings, summer), adult/continuing education programs, and internships. The most frequently chosen baccalaureate fields are business/marketing, psychology, security and protective services.

Student Body Statistics The student body totals 5,159, of whom 4,345 are undergraduates (954 freshmen). 48 percent are women and 52 percent are men. Students come from 42 states and territories and 43 other countries. 18 percent are from Rhode Island. 2.3 percent are international students.

Expenses for 2008–09 *Application fee:* $50. *Comprehensive fee:* $39,598 includes full-time tuition ($25,968), mandatory fees ($1750), and college room and board ($11,880). *College room only:* $6390. Full-time tuition and fees vary according to class time, course load, and program. Room and board charges vary according to board plan and housing facility. *Part-time tuition:* $1082 per credit. Part-time tuition varies according to class time.

Financial Aid Forms of aid include need-based and non-need-based scholarships and part-time jobs. The average aided 2008–09 undergraduate received an aid package worth an estimated $17,017. The application deadline for financial aid is February 1.

Freshman Admission Roger Williams University requires an essay, a high school transcript, a minimum 2.0 high school GPA, and SAT or ACT scores. TOEFL scores for international students are recommended. Portfolio/audition is required for some. The application deadline for regular admission is February 1 and for early action it is November 1.

Transfer Admission The application deadline for admission is rolling.

Entrance Difficulty Roger Williams University assesses its entrance difficulty level as moderately difficult; very difficult for architecture, marine biology programs. For the fall 2008 freshman class, 61 percent of the applicants were accepted.

SPECIAL MESSAGE TO STUDENTS

Social Life Roger Williams University (RWU) is an independent, coeducational, residential, and nonsectarian institution, accredited by the New England Association of Schools and Colleges. *U.S. News and World Report's* "Best Colleges Guide" has once again listed the University in the regional top tier of its category. Situated on 140 acres overlooking Mount Hope Bay, the Roger Williams campus takes advantage of New England's natural beauty. Located in historic Bristol, Rhode Island, Roger Williams is located just 30 minutes from both Providence and Newport, Rhode Island; an hour's drive from Boston, Massachusetts; and just under 4 hours from New York City. With more than seventy student-run clubs and organizations, there's always something to do on campus. Students participate in everything from surf and scuba club to Model United Nations to environmental and animal rights organizations. RWU also boasts nineteen varsity NCAA Division III athletics teams as well as club sports and intramural and recreational athletics.

Academic Highlights Undergraduate academic programs combine a traditional liberal arts education with preparation for professional careers and future study. All students complete an interdisciplinary core curriculum, a major, and a liberal arts concentration or minor, resulting in a well-rounded education. Roger Williams offers thirty-nine majors from accounting and architecture to psychology and visual arts studies. Other programs offered include English as a second language, pre-law, premed, pre-vet, and the 3+3 program offered in conjunction with the Roger Williams University School of Law (the only law school in the state). Roger Williams University also offers graduate degree programs in criminal justice, education, law, literacy education, architecture, public administration, and forensic psychology. Roger Williams believes in educating students to be global citizens and offers extensive opportunities to study abroad. In fact, RWU recognizes forty-five study-abroad programs in twenty-six different countries. Students have studied on every continent but Antarctica.

Interviews and Campus Visits Roger Williams University encourages prospective students to tour the University's campus and take part in an information session. Students learn about academics and social life on campus, while the University staff members hope to learn about students' interests and ambitions. The University hosts on-campus events, including open houses and Junior Jumpstart Days. Tours are given daily, Monday through Friday, at 9, 11, and 1 and on Saturdays at 10 and 12 (April through August). Prospective students can reach the Office of Undergraduate Admission at 401-254-3500 or 800-458-7144 Ext. 3500 (toll-free).

For Further Information Write to Roger Williams University, Office of Undergraduate Admissions, One Old Ferry Road, Bristol, RI 02809. *E-mail:* admit@rwu.edu. *Web site:* http://www.rwu.edu.

SALVE REGINA UNIVERSITY
Newport, Rhode Island

Salve Regina University is a coed, private, Roman Catholic, comprehensive institution, founded in 1934, offering degrees at the associate, bachelor's, master's, and doctoral levels and post-master's and postbachelor's certificates. It has a 70-acre campus in Newport near Boston and Providence.

Academic Information The faculty has 255 members (47% full-time), 52% with terminal degrees. The undergraduate student-faculty ratio is 14:1. Special programs include services for learning-disabled students, an honors program, study abroad, advanced placement credit, accelerated degree programs, ESL programs, double majors, independent study,

Salve Regina University (continued)

distance learning, summer session for credit, part-time degree programs (daytime, evenings, summer), internships, and arrangement for off-campus study. The most frequently chosen baccalaureate fields are business/marketing, education, health professions and related sciences.

Student Body Statistics The student body totals 2,691, of whom 2,127 are undergraduates (556 freshmen). 70 percent are women and 30 percent are men. Students come from 29 states and territories and 8 other countries. 15 percent are from Rhode Island. 1.3 percent are international students.

Expenses for 2008–09 *Application fee:* $50. *One-time mandatory fee:* $2350. *Comprehensive fee:* $39,850 includes full-time tuition ($28,950), mandatory fees ($200), and college room and board ($10,700). Room and board charges vary according to board plan and housing facility. *Part-time tuition:* $965 per term. *Part-time mandatory fees:* $40 per term. Part-time tuition and fees vary according to course load.

Financial Aid Forms of aid include need-based and non-need-based scholarships and part-time jobs. The average aided 2008–09 undergraduate received an aid package worth an estimated $19,602. The priority application deadline for financial aid is March 1.

Freshman Admission Salve Regina University requires an essay, a high school transcript, 2 recommendations, SAT or ACT scores, and TOEFL scores for international students. A minimum 2.7 high school GPA is recommended. The application deadline for regular admission is February 1 and for early action it is November 1.

Transfer Admission The application deadline for admission is rolling.

Entrance Difficulty Salve Regina University assesses its entrance difficulty level as moderately difficult; very difficult for nursing program. For the fall 2008 freshman class, 59 percent of the applicants were accepted.

For Further Information Contact Ms. Colleen Emerson, Dean of Undergraduate Admissions, Salve Regina University, 100 Ochre Point Avenue, Newport, RI 02840-4192. *Phone:* 401-341-2908 or 888-GO SALVE (toll-free). *Fax:* 401-848-2823. *E-mail:* sruadmis@salve.edu. *Web site:* http://www.salve.edu/.

UNIVERSITY OF RHODE ISLAND

Kingston, Rhode Island

University of Rhode Island is a coed, public unit of Rhode Island Board of Governors for Higher Education, founded in 1892, offering degrees at the bachelor's, master's, doctoral, and first professional levels and postbachelor's certificates. It has a 1,200-acre campus in Kingston.

Academic Information The faculty has 699 members (98% full-time), 89% with terminal degrees. The undergraduate student-faculty ratio is 16.5:1. The library holds 1 million titles, 7,926 serial subscriptions, and 11,671 audiovisual materials. Special programs include academic remediation, services for learning-disabled students, an honors program, cooperative (work-study) education, study abroad, advanced placement credit, double majors, independent study, distance learning, summer session for credit, part-time degree programs, adult/continuing education programs, internships, and arrangement for off-campus study with National Student Exchange, New England Land Grant University Exchange Program. The most frequently chosen baccalaureate fields are business/marketing, communications/journalism, health professions and related sciences.

Student Body Statistics The student body totals 15,904, of whom 12,793 are undergraduates (3,042 freshmen). 56 percent are women and 44 percent are men. Students come from 55 states and territories and 64 other countries. 61 percent are from Rhode Island. 0.3 percent are international students.

Expenses for 2008–09 *Application fee:* $65. *State resident tuition:* $7454 full-time, $311 per credit hour part-time. *Nonresident tuition:* $23,552 full-time, $981 per credit hour part-time. *Mandatory fees:* $1474 full-time, $27 per credit hour part-time, $49. Both full-time and part-time tuition and fees vary according to course load, location, and reciprocity agreements. *College room and board:* $8826. *College room only:* $5316. Room and board charges vary according to board plan and housing facility.

Financial Aid Forms of aid include need-based scholarships, athletic grants, and part-time jobs. The average aided 2008–09 undergraduate received an aid package worth an estimated $12,654.

Freshman Admission University of Rhode Island requires an essay, a high school transcript, SAT or ACT scores, and TOEFL scores for international students. A minimum 3.0 high school GPA, 2 recommendations, and an interview are recommended. A minimum 3.0 high school GPA is required for some. The application deadline for regular admission is February 1 and for early action it is December 1.

Transfer Admission The application deadline for admission is May 1.

Entrance Difficulty University of Rhode Island assesses its entrance difficulty level as moderately difficult; very difficult for pharmacy program. For the fall 2008 freshman class, 77 percent of the applicants were accepted.

For Further Information Contact Ms. Joanne Lynch, Assistant Dean of Admissions, University of Rhode Island, Undergraduate Admission Office, Newman Hall, 14 Upper College Road, Kingston, RI 02881. *Phone:* 401-874-7110. *Fax:* 401-874-5523. *E-mail:* lynch@uri.edu. *Web site:* http://www.uri.edu.

Vermont

BENNINGTON COLLEGE

Bennington, Vermont

Bennington College is a coed, private, comprehensive institution, founded in 1932, offering degrees at the bachelor's and master's levels and postbachelor's certificates. It has a 470-acre campus in Bennington near Albany.

Academic Information The faculty has 92 members (67% full-time), 61% with terminal degrees. The undergraduate student-faculty ratio is 9:1. The library holds 121,500 titles, 26,801 serial subscriptions, and 5,681 audiovisual materials. Special programs include services for learning-disabled students, study abroad, accelerated degree programs, ESL programs, double majors, independent study, self-designed majors, part-time degree programs, and internships. The most frequently chosen baccalaureate fields are English, foreign languages and literature, visual and performing arts.

Student Body Statistics The student body totals 759, of whom 618 are undergraduates (190 freshmen). 66 percent are women and 34 percent are men. Students come from 41 states and territories and 12 other countries. 4 percent are from Vermont. 3.9 percent are international students.

Expenses for 2008–09 *Application fee:* $60. *Comprehensive fee:* $48,950 includes full-time tuition ($37,280), mandatory fees ($990), and college room and board ($10,680). *College room only:* $5720. *Part-time tuition:* $1165 per credit hour.

Financial Aid Forms of aid include need-based and non-need-based scholarships and part-time jobs. The average aided 2008–09 undergraduate received an aid package worth an estimated $30,918. The priority application deadline for financial aid is March 1.

Freshman Admission Bennington College requires an essay, a high school transcript, 2 recommendations, graded analytic paper, and TOEFL scores for international students. An interview is recommended. The application deadline for regular admission is January 5, for early decision plan 1 it is November 15, and for early decision plan 2 it is January 5.

Transfer Admission The application deadline for admission is March 15.

Entrance Difficulty Bennington College assesses its entrance difficulty level as very difficult. For the fall 2008 freshman class, 62 percent of the applicants were accepted.

For Further Information Contact Mr. Ken Himmelman, Dean of Admissions and Financial Aid, Bennington College, One College Drive, Bennington, VT 05201-6003. *Phone:* 802-440-4312 or 800-833-6845 (toll-free). *Fax:* 802-440-4320. *E-mail:* admissions@bennington.edu. *Web site:* http://www.bennington.edu/.

BURLINGTON COLLEGE
Burlington, Vermont

Burlington College is a coed, private, four-year college, founded in 1972, offering degrees at the associate and bachelor's levels. It has a 1-acre campus in Burlington.

Academic Information The faculty has 64 members (14% full-time), 30% with terminal degrees. The student-faculty ratio is 5:1. The library holds 13,000 titles, 70 serial subscriptions, and 1,497 audiovisual materials. Special programs include services for learning-disabled students, study abroad, advanced placement credit, double majors, independent study, distance learning, self-designed majors, summer session for credit, part-time degree programs (daytime, evenings, weekends, summer), external degree programs, internships, and arrangement for off-campus study with University of Vermont, Champlain College, Saint Michael's College, Community College of Vermont, Institute for Social Ecology. The most frequently chosen baccalaureate fields are interdisciplinary studies, psychology, visual and performing arts.

Student Body Statistics The student body is made up of 168 undergraduates (20 freshmen). 46 percent are women and 54 percent are men. Students come from 18 states and territories and 5 other countries. 60 percent are from Vermont. 1.8 percent are international students.

Expenses for 2008–09 *Application fee:* $50. *One-time mandatory fee:* $200. *Tuition:* $19,640 full-time, $650 per credit hour part-time. Both full-time and part-time tuition varies according to course load and program. *College room only:* $6750. Room charges vary according to housing facility.

Financial Aid Forms of aid include need-based and non-need-based scholarships and part-time jobs. The average aided 2008–09 undergraduate received an aid package worth an estimated $12,490. The application deadline for financial aid is continuous.

Freshman Admission Burlington College requires an essay, 2 recommendations, and TOEFL scores for international students. Will be considered if submitted is recommended.

Entrance Difficulty Burlington College assesses its entrance difficulty level as moderately difficult. For the fall 2008 freshman class, 54 percent of the applicants were accepted.

For Further Information Contact Ms. Laryn Runco, Admissions Director, Burlington College, 95 North Avenue, Burlington, VT 05401-2998. *Phone:* 802-862-9616 Ext. 104 or 800-862-9616 (toll-free). *Fax:* 802-660-4331. *E-mail:* admissions@burlington.edu. *Web site:* http://www.burlington.edu/.

CASTLETON STATE COLLEGE
Castleton, Vermont

Castleton State College is a coed, public, comprehensive unit of Vermont State Colleges System, founded in 1787, offering degrees at the associate, bachelor's, and master's levels and post-master's certificates. It has a 160-acre campus in Castleton.

Academic Information The faculty has 215 members (41% full-time), 51% with terminal degrees. The undergraduate student-faculty ratio is 14:1. The library holds 179,764 titles, 802 serial subscriptions, and 6,679 audiovisual materials. Special programs include academic remediation, services for learning-disabled students, an honors program, cooperative (work-study) education, study abroad, advanced placement credit, double majors, independent study, self-designed majors, summer session for credit, part-time degree programs (daytime, evenings, summer), internships, and arrangement for off-campus study with Green Mountain College, other Vermont state colleges. The most frequently chosen baccalaureate fields are business/marketing, communications/journalism, parks and recreation.

Student Body Statistics The student body totals 2,089, of whom 1,953 are undergraduates (463 freshmen). 55 percent are women and 45 percent are men. Students come from 29 states and territories and 2 other countries. 63 percent are from Vermont. 0.1 percent are international students.

Expenses for 2009–10 *Application fee:* $35. *One-time mandatory fee:* $200. *State resident tuition:* $7992 full-time, $333 per credit part-time. *Nonresident tuition:* $17,232 full-time, $718 per credit part-time. *Mandatory fees:* $828 full-time. *College room and board:* $7808.

Financial Aid Forms of aid include need-based and non-need-based scholarships and part-time jobs. The priority application deadline for financial aid is April 15.

Freshman Admission Castleton State College requires an essay, a high school transcript, a minimum 2.5 high school GPA, 2 recommendations, SAT or ACT scores, and TOEFL scores for international students. An interview is recommended. The application deadline for regular admission is rolling.

Transfer Admission The application deadline for admission is rolling.

Entrance Difficulty Castleton State College assesses its entrance difficulty level as moderately difficult. For the fall 2008 freshman class, 68 percent of the applicants were accepted.

For Further Information Contact Mr. Maurice Ouimet, Admissions Director, Castleton State College, Seminary Street, Castleton, VT 05735. *Phone:* 802-468-1213 or 800-639-8521 (toll-free). *Fax:* 802-468-1476. *E-mail:* info@castleton.edu. *Web site:* http://www.castleton.edu/.

CHAMPLAIN COLLEGE
Burlington, Vermont

Champlain College is a coed, private, comprehensive institution, founded in 1878, offering degrees at the associate, bachelor's, and master's levels. It has a 21-acre campus in Burlington near Montreal.

Academic Information The faculty has 313 members (28% full-time), 32% with terminal degrees. The undergraduate student-faculty ratio is 14:1. The library holds 94,008 titles, 34,916 serial subscriptions, and 1,262 audiovisual materials. Special programs include services for learning-disabled students, an honors program, cooperative (work-study) education, study abroad, advanced placement credit, Freshman Honors College, double majors, independent study, distance learning, summer session for credit, part-time degree programs (daytime, evenings, summer), internships, and arrangement for off-campus study. The most frequently chosen baccalaureate fields are business/marketing, computer and information sciences, visual and performing arts.

Student Body Statistics The student body totals 2,857, of whom 2,740 are undergraduates (608 freshmen). 43 percent are women and 57 percent are men. Students come from 28 states and territories and 26 other countries. 20 percent are from Vermont. 0.2 percent are international students.

Expenses for 2008–09 *Application fee:* $40. *Comprehensive fee:* $35,565 includes full-time tuition ($24,355) and college room and board ($11,210). *College room only:* $6770. Full-time tuition varies according to course load. Room and board charges vary according to board plan and housing facility. *Part-time tuition:* $1015 per credit hour. Part-time tuition varies according to course level, course load, and degree level.

Financial Aid Forms of aid include need-based and non-need-based scholarships and part-time jobs. The average aided 2007–08 undergraduate received an aid package worth $13,850. The priority application deadline for financial aid is March 1.

Freshman Admission Champlain College requires an essay, a high school transcript, SAT or ACT scores, and TOEFL scores for international students. A minimum 2.0 high school GPA, 1 recommendation, and an interview are recommended. SAT Subject Test scores are required for some. The application deadline for regular admission is January 31 and for early decision it is November 15.

Transfer Admission The application deadline for admission is rolling.

Entrance Difficulty Champlain College assesses its entrance difficulty level as moderately difficult. For the fall 2008 freshman class, 73 percent of the applicants were accepted.

For Further Information Contact Ian Mortimer, Director of Admissions, Champlain College, 163 South Willard Street, Burlington, VT 05401. *Phone:* 802-860-2727 or 800-570-5858 (toll-free). *Fax:* 802-860-2767. *E-mail:* admission@champlain.edu. *Web site:* http://www.champlain.edu/.

COLLEGE OF ST. JOSEPH
Rutland, Vermont

College of St. Joseph is a coed, private, Roman Catholic, comprehensive institution, founded in 1950, offering degrees at the associate, bachelor's, and master's levels and postbachelor's certificates. It has a 90-acre campus in Rutland.

Academic Information The faculty has 59 members (24% full-time), 27% with terminal degrees. The undergraduate student-faculty ratio is 9:1. The library holds 58,648 titles, 104 serial subscriptions, and 5,114 audiovisual materials. Special programs include academic remediation, services for learning-disabled students, advanced placement credit, accelerated degree programs, double majors, independent study, summer session for credit, part-time degree programs (daytime, evenings, summer), and internships. The most frequently chosen baccalaureate fields are business/marketing, liberal arts/general studies, psychology.
Student Body Statistics The student body totals 428, of whom 250 are undergraduates (46 freshmen). 54 percent are women and 46 percent are men. Students come from 12 states and territories and 3 other countries. 67 percent are from Vermont.
Expenses for 2009–10 *Application fee:* $25. *Comprehensive fee:* $25,900 includes full-time tuition ($17,200), mandatory fees ($350), and college room and board ($8350). *Part-time tuition:* $250 per credit. *Part-time mandatory fees:* $45 per term.
Financial Aid Forms of aid include need-based and non-need-based scholarships and part-time jobs. The average aided 2007–08 undergraduate received an aid package worth $14,452. The application deadline for financial aid is continuous.
Freshman Admission College of St. Joseph requires an essay, a high school transcript, a minimum 2.0 high school GPA, 2 recommendations, and SAT or ACT scores. An interview is recommended. The application deadline for regular admission is rolling.
Transfer Admission The application deadline for admission is rolling.
Entrance Difficulty College of St. Joseph assesses its entrance difficulty level as minimally difficult. For the fall 2008 freshman class, 43 percent of the applicants were accepted.
For Further Information Contact Susan Englese, Dean of Admissions, College of St. Joseph, 71 Clement Road, Rutland, VT 05701-3899. *Phone:* 802-773-5900 Ext. 3227 or 877-270-9998 (toll-free in-state). *Fax:* 802-776-5258. *E-mail:* admissions@csj.edu. *Web site:* http://www.csj.edu/.

GODDARD COLLEGE
Plainfield, Vermont

Goddard College is a coed, private, comprehensive institution, founded in 1938, offering degrees at the bachelor's and master's levels. It has a 250-acre campus in Plainfield.

Expenses for 2008–09 *Application fee:* $40. *One-time mandatory fee:* $125. *Comprehensive fee:* $12,752 includes full-time tuition ($11,504), mandatory fees ($160), and college room and board ($1088).
For Further Information Contact Rachel Keach, Admissions Counselor, Goddard College, 123 Pitkin Road, Plainfield, VT 05667-9432. *Phone:* 802-454-8311 Ext. 262 or 800-906-8312 Ext. 243 (toll-free). *Fax:* 802-454-1029. *E-mail:* admissions@goddard.edu. *Web site:* http://www.goddard.edu/.

GREEN MOUNTAIN COLLEGE
Poultney, Vermont

Green Mountain College is a coed, private, comprehensive institution, founded in 1834, offering degrees at the bachelor's and master's levels. It has a 155-acre campus in Poultney.

Academic Information The faculty has 84 members (58% full-time), 61% with terminal degrees. The undergraduate student-faculty ratio is 13.5:1. The library holds 97,800 titles, 318 serial subscriptions, and 900 audiovisual materials. Special programs include services for learning-disabled students, an honors program, cooperative (work-study) education, study abroad, advanced placement credit, accelerated degree programs, ESL programs, double majors, independent study, self-designed majors,

summer session for credit, part-time degree programs (daytime, evenings, summer), adult/continuing education programs, internships, and arrangement for off-campus study with Castleton State College. The most frequently chosen baccalaureate fields are business/marketing, education, visual and performing arts.
Student Body Statistics The student body totals 867, of whom 780 are undergraduates (219 freshmen). 51 percent are women and 49 percent are men. Students come from 26 states and territories and 18 other countries. 15 percent are from Vermont. 0.3 percent are international students.
Expenses for 2008–09 *Application fee:* $30. *One-time mandatory fee:* $200. *Comprehensive fee:* $35,360 includes full-time tuition ($24,938), mandatory fees ($900), and college room and board ($9522). *College room only:* $5704. Full-time tuition and fees vary according to course load. Room and board charges vary according to housing facility. *Part-time tuition:* $832 per credit. *Part-time mandatory fees:* $900 per year. Part-time tuition and fees vary according to course load.
Financial Aid Forms of aid include need-based and non-need-based scholarships and part-time jobs. The average aided 2008–09 undergraduate received an aid package worth an estimated $20,134.
Freshman Admission Green Mountain College requires an essay, a high school transcript, 1 recommendation, and TOEFL scores for international students. A minimum 2.5 high school GPA, an interview, and SAT or ACT scores are recommended. An interview is required for some. The application deadline for regular admission is rolling.
Transfer Admission The application deadline for admission is rolling.
Entrance Difficulty Green Mountain College assesses its entrance difficulty level as moderately difficult. For the fall 2008 freshman class, 71 percent of the applicants were accepted.
For Further Information Contact Dr. Sandra Bartholomew, Dean of Enrollment, Green Mountain College, One Brennan Circle, Poultney, VT 05764. *Phone:* 802-287-8207 or 800-776-6675 (toll-free out-of-state). *Fax:* 802-287-8099. *E-mail:* admiss@greenmtn.edu. *Web site:* http://www.greenmtn.edu/.

JOHNSON STATE COLLEGE
Johnson, Vermont

Johnson State College is a coed, public, comprehensive unit of Vermont State Colleges System, founded in 1828, offering degrees at the associate, bachelor's, and master's levels. It has a 350-acre campus in Johnson near Montreal.

Academic Information The faculty has 146 members (38% full-time), 38% with terminal degrees. The undergraduate student-faculty ratio is 17:1. The library holds 100,053 titles and 522 serial subscriptions. Special programs include services for learning-disabled students, an honors program, cooperative (work-study) education, study abroad, advanced placement credit, accelerated degree programs, ESL programs, double majors, independent study, distance learning, summer session for credit, part-time degree programs, external degree programs, internships, and arrangement for off-campus study with Vermont State Colleges System, National Student Exchange. The most frequently chosen baccalaureate fields are business/marketing, liberal arts/general studies, psychology.
Student Body Statistics The student body totals 1,898, of whom 1,619 are undergraduates (305 freshmen). 62 percent are women and 38 percent are men. Students come from 15 states and territories and 17 other countries. 64 percent are from Vermont. 0.4 percent are international students.
Expenses for 2009–10 *Application fee:* $37. *State resident tuition:* $8088 full-time, $337 per credit part-time. *Nonresident tuition:* $17,448 full-time, $727 per credit part-time. *Mandatory fees:* $951 full-time, $32 per credit part-time. *College room and board:* $7810. *College room only:* $4650.
Financial Aid Forms of aid include need-based and non-need-based scholarships and part-time jobs. The priority application deadline for financial aid is March 1.
Freshman Admission Johnson State College requires an essay, a high school transcript, a minimum 2.0 high school GPA, 1 recommendation, SAT or ACT scores, and TOEFL scores for international students. A minimum 2.5 high school GPA and an interview are recommended. The application deadline for regular admission is rolling.
Transfer Admission The application deadline for admission is rolling.

Entrance Difficulty Johnson State College assesses its entrance difficulty level as moderately difficult. For the fall 2008 freshman class, 82 percent of the applicants were accepted.

For Further Information Contact Patrick Rogers, Assistant Director of Admissions, Johnson State College, 337 College Hill, Johnson, VT 05656-9405. *Phone:* 802-635-1219 or 800-635-2356 (toll-free). *Fax:* 802-635-1230. *E-mail:* jscadmissions@jsc.edu. *Web site:* http://www.johnsonstatecollege.edu/.

LANDMARK COLLEGE

Putney, Vermont

Landmark College is a coed, private, two-year college, founded in 1983, offering degrees at the associate level. It has a 125-acre campus in Putney.

Academic Information The faculty has 96 members (97% full-time), 12% with terminal degrees. The student-faculty ratio is 5:1. The library holds 32,786 titles, 165 serial subscriptions, and 1,535 audiovisual materials. Special programs include academic remediation, services for learning-disabled students, study abroad, advanced placement credit, and summer session for credit.

Student Body Statistics The student body is made up of 486 undergraduates (108 freshmen). 28 percent are women and 72 percent are men. Students come from 43 states and territories and 16 other countries. 5 percent are from Vermont.

Expenses for 2009–10 *Application fee:* $75. *Comprehensive fee:* $53,900 includes full-time tuition ($45,300), mandatory fees ($500), and college room and board ($8100). *College room only:* $4050.

Financial Aid Forms of aid include need-based scholarships and part-time jobs. The priority application deadline for financial aid is March 1.

Freshman Admission Landmark College requires an essay, a high school transcript, 2 recommendations, an interview, diagnosis of LD and/or ADHD and cognitive testing, TOEFL scores for international students, and Wechsler Adult Intelligence Scale III and Nelson Denny Reading Test. The application deadline for regular admission is rolling.

Transfer Admission The application deadline for admission is rolling.

Entrance Difficulty Landmark College assesses its entrance difficulty level as moderately difficult. For the fall 2008 freshman class, 79 percent of the applicants were accepted.

For Further Information Contact Admissions Main Desk, Landmark College, 1 River Road South, Putney, VT 05346. *Phone:* 802-387-6718. *Fax:* 802-387-6868. *E-mail:* admissions@landmark.edu. *Web site:* http://www.landmark.edu/.

LYNDON STATE COLLEGE

Lyndonville, Vermont

Lyndon State College is a coed, public, comprehensive unit of Vermont State Colleges System, founded in 1911, offering degrees at the associate, bachelor's, and master's levels. It has a 175-acre campus in Lyndonville.

Academic Information The faculty has 167 members (35% full-time), 60% with terminal degrees. The undergraduate student-faculty ratio is 15:1. The library holds 109,629 titles and 16,468 serial subscriptions. Special programs include academic remediation, services for learning-disabled students, an honors program, cooperative (work-study) education, study abroad, advanced placement credit, accelerated degree programs, double majors, independent study, self-designed majors, summer session for credit, part-time degree programs (daytime, evenings, summer), adult/continuing education programs, and internships. The most frequently chosen baccalaureate fields are business/marketing, health professions and related sciences, psychology.

Student Body Statistics The student body totals 1,385. 60 percent are from Vermont.

Expenses for 2008–09 *Application fee:* $36. *State resident tuition:* $7488 full-time, $312 per credit hour part-time. *Nonresident tuition:* $16,152 full-time, $673 per credit hour part-time. *Mandatory fees:* $196 full-time. Full-time tuition and fees vary according to course load. Part-time tuition varies according to course load. *College room and board:* $7509. *College room only:* $4472. Room and board charges vary according to board plan and housing facility.

Financial Aid Forms of aid include need-based scholarships. The priority application deadline for financial aid is February 15.

Freshman Admission Lyndon State College requires a high school transcript, a minimum 2.0 high school GPA, 1 recommendation, SAT or ACT scores, and TOEFL scores for international students. A minimum 3.0 high school GPA and an interview are recommended. An essay and a minimum 3.0 high school GPA are required for some. The application deadline for regular admission is rolling.

Transfer Admission The application deadline for admission is rolling.

Entrance Difficulty Lyndon State College assesses its entrance difficulty level as moderately difficult; very difficult for meteorology.

For Further Information Contact Ms. Donna "Dee" Gile, Admissions Assistant, Lyndon State College, 1001 College Road, PO Box 919, Lyndonville, VT 05851. *Phone:* 802-626-6413 or 800-225-1998 (toll-free). *Fax:* 802-626-6335. *E-mail:* admissions@lyndonstate.edu. *Web site:* http://www.lyndonstate.edu/.

See page 98 for the Close-Up.

MARLBORO COLLEGE

Marlboro, Vermont

Marlboro College is a coed, private, comprehensive institution, founded in 1946, offering degrees at the bachelor's, master's, and first professional levels. It has a 350-acre campus in Marlboro.

Academic Information The faculty has 42 members (76% full-time). The undergraduate student-faculty ratio is 8:1. Special programs include services for learning-disabled students, study abroad, advanced placement credit, accelerated degree programs, double majors, independent study, self-designed majors, part-time degree programs (daytime), internships, and arrangement for off-campus study with Brattleboro School of Music, School for International Training. The most frequently chosen baccalaureate fields are English, social sciences, visual and performing arts.

Student Body Statistics The student body totals 330, of whom 329 are undergraduates (77 freshmen). 50 percent are women and 50 percent are men. Students come from 35 states and territories and 2 other countries. 20 percent are from Vermont.

Expenses for 2009–10 *Application fee:* $50. *Comprehensive fee:* $42,880 includes full-time tuition ($32,550), mandatory fees ($1110), and college room and board ($9220). *College room only:* $5080. *Part-time tuition:* $1038 per credit.

Financial Aid Forms of aid include need-based and non-need-based scholarships and part-time jobs. The average aided 2008–09 undergraduate received an aid package worth an estimated $19,062. The application deadline for financial aid is March 1.

Freshman Admission Marlboro College requires an essay, a high school transcript, 2 recommendations, expository essay, and TOEFL scores for international students. An interview is recommended. An interview is required for some. The application deadline for regular admission is March 1, for early decision it is December 1, and for early action it is February 1.

Transfer Admission The application deadline for admission is April 1.

Entrance Difficulty Marlboro College assesses its entrance difficulty level as moderately difficult. For the fall 2008 freshman class, 64 percent of the applicants were accepted.

For Further Information Contact Mr. Mark Crowther, Associate Director of Admission, Marlboro College, PO Box A, South Road, Marlboro, VT 05344-0300. *Phone:* 800-343-0049 (toll-free). *Fax:* 800-451-7555. *E-mail:* admissions@marlboro.edu. *Web site:* http://www.marlboro.edu/.

MIDDLEBURY COLLEGE

Middlebury, Vermont

Middlebury College is a coed, private, comprehensive institution, founded in 1800, offering degrees at the bachelor's, master's, and doctoral levels. It has a 350-acre campus in Middlebury.

Academic Information The faculty has 311 members (80% full-time), 89% with terminal degrees. The undergraduate student-faculty ratio is 9:1.

Middlebury College (continued)

The library holds 853,000 titles, 2,908 serial subscriptions, and 45,024 audiovisual materials. Special programs include services for learning-disabled students, an honors program, study abroad, advanced placement credit, accelerated degree programs, double majors, independent study, self-designed majors, summer session for credit, internships, and arrangement for off-campus study with Swarthmore College, Berea College, Bucknell University, Eckerd College, St. Olaf College, American University, Williams College (Mystic Seaport Program), Institute for Architecture and Urban Studies. The most frequently chosen baccalaureate fields are English, social sciences, visual and performing arts.

Student Body Statistics The student body is made up of 2,455 undergraduates (576 freshmen). 51 percent are women and 49 percent are men. Students come from 52 states and territories and 75 other countries. 6 percent are from Vermont. 11.1 percent are international students.

Expenses for 2008–09 *Application fee:* $65. *Comprehensive fee:* $49,210.

Financial Aid Forms of aid include need-based scholarships and part-time jobs. The average aided 2007–08 undergraduate received an aid package worth $32,896. The application deadline for financial aid is February 1 with a priority deadline of November 15.

Freshman Admission Middlebury College requires an essay, a high school transcript, 3 recommendations, and three tests to include: a writing test, a quantitative test, and an area of the applicant's choice. An interview is recommended. The application deadline for regular admission is January 1 and for early decision it is November 1.

Transfer Admission The application deadline for admission is March 1.

Entrance Difficulty Middlebury College assesses its entrance difficulty level as most difficult. For the fall 2008 freshman class, 17 percent of the applicants were accepted.

For Further Information Contact Mr. Robert Clagett, Dean of Admissions, Middlebury College, Emma Willard House, Middlebury, VT 05753-6002. *Phone:* 802-443-3000. *Fax:* 802-443-2056. *E-mail:* admissions@middlebury.edu. *Web site:* http://www.middlebury.edu/.

NEW ENGLAND CULINARY INSTITUTE

Montpelier, Vermont

http://www.neci.edu/

NEW ENGLAND CULINARY INSTITUTE AT ESSEX

Essex Junction, Vermont

http://www.neci.edu/

NORWICH UNIVERSITY

Northfield, Vermont

Norwich University is a coed, primarily men's, private, comprehensive institution, founded in 1819, offering degrees at the bachelor's and master's levels and postbachelor's certificates. It has a 1,125-acre campus in Northfield near Burlington.

Expenses for 2008–09 *Application fee:* $35. *Comprehensive fee:* $35,096 includes full-time tuition ($24,722), mandatory fees ($1342), and college room and board ($9032). Full-time tuition and fees vary according to program. *Part-time tuition:* varies with course load.

For Further Information Contact Ms. Shelby Wallace, Director of Admissions, Norwich University, 27 I.D. White Avenue, Northfield, VT 05663. *Phone:* 802-485-2658 or 800-468-6679 (toll-free). *Fax:* 802-485-2032. *E-mail:* nuadm@norwich.edu. *Web site:* http://www.norwich.edu/.

SAINT MICHAEL'S COLLEGE

Colchester, Vermont

Saint Michael's College is a coed, private, Roman Catholic, comprehensive institution, founded in 1904, offering degrees at the bachelor's and master's levels and post-master's and postbachelor's certificates. It has a 440-acre campus in Colchester near Montreal.

Academic Information The faculty has 209 members (74% full-time), 74% with terminal degrees. The undergraduate student-faculty ratio is 12:1. The library holds 270,000 titles, 2,560 serial subscriptions, and 8,340 audiovisual materials. Special programs include services for learning-disabled students, an honors program, study abroad, advanced placement credit, ESL programs, double majors, independent study, distance learning, self-designed majors, summer session for credit, part-time degree programs (daytime, evenings, summer), internships, and arrangement for off-campus study with Washington Semester. The most frequently chosen baccalaureate fields are business/marketing, psychology, social sciences.

Student Body Statistics The student body totals 2,460, of whom 2,008 are undergraduates (543 freshmen). 53 percent are women and 47 percent are men. Students come from 37 states and territories and 12 other countries. 20 percent are from Vermont. 1.3 percent are international students.

Expenses for 2009–10 *Application fee:* $50. *Comprehensive fee:* $41,495 includes full-time tuition ($32,940), mandatory fees ($275), and college room and board ($8280). *Part-time tuition:* $1100 per credit.

Financial Aid Forms of aid include need-based and non-need-based scholarships, athletic grants, and part-time jobs. The average aided 2008–09 undergraduate received an aid package worth an estimated $20,879. The priority application deadline for financial aid is February 15.

Freshman Admission Saint Michael's College requires an essay, a high school transcript, SAT or ACT scores, and TOEFL scores for international students. A minimum 3.0 high school GPA, 3 recommendations, and an interview are recommended. The application deadline for regular admission is February 1 and for early action it is November 1.

Transfer Admission The application deadline for admission is March 15.

Entrance Difficulty Saint Michael's College assesses its entrance difficulty level as moderately difficult. For the fall 2008 freshman class, 69 percent of the applicants were accepted.

For Further Information Contact Ms. Jacqueline Murphy, Director of Admission, Saint Michael's College, One Winooski Park, Colchester, VT 05452. *Phone:* 802-654-3000 or 800-762-8000 (toll-free). *Fax:* 802-654-2906. *E-mail:* admission@smcvt.edu. *Web site:* http://www.smcvt.edu/.

SOUTHERN VERMONT COLLEGE

Bennington, Vermont

Southern Vermont College is a coed, private, four-year college, founded in 1926, offering degrees at the associate and bachelor's levels. It has a 371-acre campus in Bennington near Albany.

Expenses for 2008–09 *Application fee:* $30. *Comprehensive fee:* $26,460 includes full-time tuition ($17,960) and college room and board ($8500). *College room only:* $4250. Room and board charges vary according to board plan. *Part-time tuition:* $610 per credit.

For Further Information Contact Mr. Joel Wincowski, Dean of Enrollment Management, Southern Vermont College, 982 Mansion Drive, Bennington, VT 05201. *Phone:* 802-447-6304 or 800-378-2782 (toll-free). *Fax:* 802-447-4695. *E-mail:* admis@svc.edu. *Web site:* http://www.svc.edu/.

STERLING COLLEGE

Craftsbury Common, Vermont

Sterling College is a coed, private, four-year college, founded in 1958, offering degrees at the bachelor's level. It has a 430-acre campus in Craftsbury Common.

Academic Information The faculty has 30 members (53% full-time), 30% with terminal degrees. The student-faculty ratio is 5:1. The library holds 14,095 titles, 15,874 serial subscriptions, and 730 audiovisual

materials. Special programs include services for learning-disabled students, study abroad, advanced placement credit, independent study, self-designed majors, summer session for credit, internships, and arrangement for off-campus study. The most frequently chosen baccalaureate fields are liberal arts/general studies, agriculture, parks and recreation.

Student Body Statistics The student body is made up of 99 undergraduates (27 freshmen). 42 percent are women and 58 percent are men. Students come from 24 states and territories and 1 other country. 23 percent are from Vermont.

Expenses for 2008–09 *Application fee:* $35. *Comprehensive fee:* $28,847 includes full-time tuition ($21,280), mandatory fees ($375), and college room and board ($7192). Full-time tuition and fees vary according to course load. Room and board charges vary according to board plan. *Part-time tuition:* $650 per credit. Part-time tuition varies according to course load.

Financial Aid Forms of aid include need-based and non-need-based scholarships and part-time jobs. The application deadline for financial aid is continuous.

Freshman Admission Sterling College requires an essay, a high school transcript, 2 recommendations, and TOEFL scores for international students. A minimum 2.0 high school GPA and an interview are recommended. The application deadline for regular admission is February 15 and for early action it is December 15.

Transfer Admission The application deadline for admission is rolling.

Entrance Difficulty Sterling College assesses its entrance difficulty level as moderately difficult. For the fall 2008 freshman class, 78 percent of the applicants were accepted.

For Further Information Contact Gwyn Harris, Director of Admissions, Sterling College, PO Box 72, Craftsbury Common, VT 05827. *Phone:* 802-586-7711 Ext. 100 or 800-648-3591 Ext. 100 (toll-free). *Fax:* 802-586-2596. *E-mail:* admissions@sterlingcollege.edu. *Web site:* http://www.sterlingcollege.edu/.

UNIVERSITY OF VERMONT

Burlington, Vermont

University of Vermont is a coed, public university, founded in 1791, offering degrees at the bachelor's, master's, doctoral, and first professional levels and post-master's and postbachelor's certificates. It has a 425-acre campus in Burlington.

Academic Information The faculty has 765 members (80% full-time), 73% with terminal degrees. The undergraduate student-faculty ratio is 16:1. The library holds 3 million titles, 18,891 serial subscriptions, and 44,095 audiovisual materials. Special programs include services for learning-disabled students, an honors program, cooperative (work-study) education, study abroad, advanced placement credit, Freshman Honors College, ESL programs, double majors, independent study, distance learning, self-designed majors, summer session for credit, part-time degree programs (daytime, evenings, summer), internships, and arrangement for off-campus study. The most frequently chosen baccalaureate fields are business/marketing, health professions and related sciences, social sciences.

Student Body Statistics The student body totals 12,800, of whom 10,937 are undergraduates (2,468 freshmen). 56 percent are women and 44 percent are men. Students come from 47 states and territories and 20 other countries. 35 percent are from Vermont. 1 percent are international students.

Expenses for 2008–09 *Application fee:* $55. *State resident tuition:* $11,048 full-time, $460 per credit part-time. *Nonresident tuition:* $27,886 full-time, $1162 per credit part-time. *Mandatory fees:* $1796 full-time. Part-time tuition varies according to course load. *College room and board:* $8534. *College room only:* $5752. Room and board charges vary according to board plan and housing facility.

Financial Aid Forms of aid include need-based and non-need-based scholarships, athletic grants, and part-time jobs. The average aided

2007–08 undergraduate received an aid package worth $16,809. The priority application deadline for financial aid is February 10.

Freshman Admission University of Vermont requires an essay, a high school transcript, SAT or ACT scores, and TOEFL scores for international students. 2 recommendations are recommended. The application deadline for regular admission is January 15 and for early action it is November 1.

Transfer Admission The application deadline for admission is April 1.

Entrance Difficulty University of Vermont assesses its entrance difficulty level as moderately difficult. For the fall 2008 freshman class, 65 percent of the applicants were accepted.

For Further Information Contact Beth A. Wiser, Director of Admissions, University of Vermont, Office of Admissions, 194 South Prospect Street, Burlington, VT 05401-3596. *Phone:* 802-656-3370. *Fax:* 802-656-8611. *E-mail:* admissions@uvm.edu. *Web site:* http://www.uvm.edu/.

VERMONT TECHNICAL COLLEGE

Randolph Center, Vermont

Vermont Technical College is a coed, public, four-year college of Vermont State Colleges System, founded in 1866, offering degrees at the associate and bachelor's levels. It has a 544-acre campus in Randolph Center.

Academic Information The faculty has 229 members (34% full-time), 41% with terminal degrees. The student-faculty ratio is 10:1. The library holds 59,167 titles, 30,000 serial subscriptions, and 6,002 audiovisual materials. Special programs include academic remediation, services for learning-disabled students, an honors program, cooperative (work-study) education, advanced placement credit, accelerated degree programs, ESL programs, double majors, independent study, distance learning, summer session for credit, part-time degree programs (daytime, summer), and internships. The most frequently chosen baccalaureate fields are business/marketing, architecture, engineering technologies.

Student Body Statistics The student body is made up of 1,651 undergraduates (293 freshmen). 41 percent are women and 59 percent are men. Students come from 15 states and territories and 8 other countries. 86 percent are from Vermont. 0.6 percent are international students.

Expenses for 2008–09 *Application fee:* $37. *One-time mandatory fee:* $200. *Area resident tuition:* $9288 full-time, $387 per credit part-time. *State resident tuition:* $13,920 full-time, $580 per credit part-time. *Nonresident tuition:* $17,712 full-time, $738 per credit part-time. *Mandatory fees:* $696 full-time, $29 per credit part-time. *College room and board:* $7510.

Financial Aid Forms of aid include need-based and non-need-based scholarships and part-time jobs. The average aided 2008–09 undergraduate received an aid package worth an estimated $9900. The priority application deadline for financial aid is March 1.

Freshman Admission Vermont Technical College requires a high school transcript and TOEFL scores for international students. A minimum 3.0 high school GPA, 2 recommendations, and an interview are recommended. An essay, 2 recommendations, an interview, and SAT or ACT scores are required for some. The application deadline for regular admission is rolling.

Transfer Admission The application deadline for admission is rolling.

Entrance Difficulty Vermont Technical College assesses its entrance difficulty level as moderately difficult; very difficult for nursing, dental hygiene, veterinary tech, equine studies. For the fall 2008 freshman class, 62 percent of the applicants were accepted.

For Further Information Contact Mr. Dwight A. Cross, Assistant Dean of Enrollment, Vermont Technical College, PO Box 500, Randolph Center, VT 05061. *Phone:* 802-728-1244 or 800-442-VTC1 (toll-free). *Fax:* 802-728-1390. *E-mail:* admissions@vtc.edu. *Web site:* http://www.vtc.edu/.

Close-Ups
of Colleges
in New England

ALBERTUS MAGNUS COLLEGE
NEW HAVEN, CONNECTICUT

The College

Founded in 1925 by the Dominican Sisters of St. Mary of the Springs, Albertus Magnus College educates men and women to become leaders in all walks of life. The College is committed to providing a liberal arts education rooted in the Dominican tradition of scholarship. Professors at Albertus strive to help their students develop in all areas; as much attention is paid to the nurturing of a student's aesthetic, physical, and moral capacities as to his or her intellectual capabilities. In 1992, the College began offering its first graduate-level course of study through the Master of Arts in Liberal Studies program. More recently, the College has expanded its graduate-level offerings to include the Master of Science in Management, the Master of Arts in Art Therapy, the Master of Arts in Leadership, and the Master of Business Administration.

The traditional undergraduate program has a student body of approximately 500 students, who live and learn on the beautiful 50-acre campus in the Prospect Hill neighborhood of New Haven. Another 1,500 students attend graduate programs or accelerated programs for adults. These students come from various parts of the United States (largely the New England area), Europe, Africa, Asia, and South and Central America. About 60 percent of the students live on campus in student dormitories that are renovated mansions from the early 1900s. The housing program fosters a strong sense of community spirit, and students often plan workshops, parties, and other social and learning events in their residence halls.

The Campus Center is a hub of student activities, such as comedy shows, live music, contests, and other unique functions. The variety of on-campus organizations includes the Student Government Association, the Campus Activities Board, the multicultural student union, a dance team, the Psychology Club, the Art Club, the Business Club, and numerous creative writing options, such as *Breakwater* literary magazine and the English Club. Albertus has recently added a new cyber lounge, the Common Ground, where students can check e-mail, work on homework, and enjoy a cup of coffee.

Students may also share in the excitement of live drama through the College's professionally managed ACT 2 Theatre, providing a number of artistic, academic, and recreational possibilities. In addition, students are encouraged to become part of the New Haven community through extracurricular and volunteer activities. The active Campus Ministry provides opportunities to volunteer, organize campus events, and participate in community service projects.

The Cosgrove, Marcus, Messer Athletic Center houses a 25-yard pool, a Jacuzzi, three racquetball courts, a weight and cardio room, a dance studio, and a gymnasium. In addition to this facility, there are soccer and softball fields, an outdoor track, and several tennis courts. Albertus fields intercollegiate athletic teams in baseball, basketball, cross-country, soccer, tennis, and volleyball for men and basketball, cross-country, soccer, softball, tennis, and volleyball for women. Albertus's teams compete in the NCAA Division III/Great Northeast Athletic Conference (GNAC) and the Eastern College Athletic Conference (ECAC). The Athletic Department also offers an intramural program in some sports.

Location

New Haven is a multicultural city with a population of more than 130,000 people. The city hosts approximately 16,000 students attending the seven colleges and universities in the greater New Haven area. This concentration of students creates exciting choices for social, recreational, and cultural activities for Albertus students. The city has some of the finest theaters in the country, including the Long Wharf and Shubert theaters. There are many fantastic art collections, museums, and movie theaters. Large shopping facilities, excellent restaurants, and several recreational areas are only a short distance from the Albertus Magnus College campus.

Majors and Degrees

The Albertus Magnus College traditional undergraduate program confers the Bachelor of Arts (B.A.), Bachelor of Science (B.S.), Bachelor of Fine Arts (B.F.A.), and Associate of Arts (A.A.) degrees. The areas of study include accounting, art (history and studio), art therapy, biology, business administration, chemistry, child development and mental health, communications, computer information systems, creative writing, criminal justice, drama, education (grades 4–12), English, finance, general studies, graphic design, history, humanities, human services, industrial and organizational psychology, international business, marketing, mathematics, performing communications, philosophy/religion, photography, physical sciences, political science, prelaw, premedicine, psychology, Spanish, sports communications, social science, social work, sociology, urban studies, and visual arts.

Academic Programs

Albertus Magnus College is committed to providing a liberal arts education that promotes the pursuit of truth in all its dimensions. The College recognizes the importance of cultivating core competencies and knowledge if students are to meet the challenges and opportunities they encounter in their communities and workplaces. Albertus has recently developed the Insight Program, which serves as the College's core curriculum. Through this program, students build a thinking framework that supports them throughout their lives as they realize their goals. In addition, the Insight Program helps students improve their capabilities in critical and creative thinking; grasp the methods of scientific, quantitative, mathematical, and philosophical reasoning; and appreciate and assess perspectives different from their own. The B.A. and B.S. degrees require 120 credits for graduation, the B.F.A. requires 127 credits, and the A.A. requires 60 credits. The College's Office of Career Services helps graduating students prepare for career direction and job placement. The Academic Development Center and Writing Center provide personal instruction to students who may benefit from additional help with their schoolwork. The centers also provide services to those students with learning disabilities. Students who show strong academic potential may pursue a course of study through the College's honors program. Students may relate academic study to work experience through a system of academically credited internships. Through the College's system of internships for juniors and seniors, Albertus students have become increasingly involved in the New Haven community and gain valuable, practical, professional training. Often, internships lead to permanent positions with local companies and corporations.

Academic Facilities

Rosary Hall, the College's first building, now houses a library collection of 110,000 volumes, 600 periodicals, 4,400 pieces of microfilm, and full access to the Internet, including LexisNexis, EBSCOhost, and PsycINFO. The interlibrary loan program has

access to materials at academic and public libraries across the country. The Media Center has equipment that students may use to produce new materials as well as review older materials. Interlibrary services with other local universities are also available. The New Center for Science, Art and Technology provides the most modern scientific equipment available for students majoring in biological and physical sciences, along with state-of-the-art broadcasting technology for communication students. Aquinas Hall houses the academic computer labs, which are equipped with personal computers, digital scanners, laser printers, and full Internet access. Every classroom in Aquinas Hall is laptop compatible, and the entire campus is engineered for wireless use.

Costs

The costs for the 2008–09 school year are $21,780 for tuition and $9442 for room and board (nineteen meals per week). Expenses for books, travel, and personal supplies vary.

Financial Aid

Albertus Magnus College offers a variety of merit-based scholarships to students who have achieved high academic standing in high school or in their two-year college programs. In addition to scholarships based solely on academics, the College offers scholarships for students who attend Catholic high schools, students who are valedictorians or salutatorians of their high schools, students who live in the New Haven area, and students who have shown a commitment to community service. Interested students should contact the Office of Admission for specific information regarding these and other scholarship opportunities. Scholarships are awarded to eligible students who apply and are accepted to the College prior to March 15.

Approximately 85 percent of the College's students receive financial aid in some form. The College requires that students file the Albertus Magnus College financial aid application form and the Free Application for Federal Student Aid (FAFSA) to be considered for Albertus scholarships and grants, Federal Perkins Loans, Federal Supplemental Educational Opportunity Grants, and Federal Work-Study Program awards. The College awards financial aid on a rolling basis; however, students who are accepted and submit their FAFSA forms by February 28 are given priority.

Faculty

Faculty members at Albertus come from leading universities in the United States and abroad and are one of the College's greatest assets. Ninety percent of the full- and part-time faculty members hold a Ph.D. or the equivalent. Their primary concern is teaching, although the work of many faculty members has been published. Students find faculty members accessible for academic or personal counseling and for campus sports and activities.

Student Government

Through the Student Government Association (SGA), Albertus students have the primary responsibility for governing their own residential and social life. All full-time matriculated students are members of the SGA and, through its committees and officers, manage student government and social affairs and participate in the campus judicial system. Students serve on faculty committees, the Academic Policy Committee, and the Library Committee.

Admission Requirements

Albertus Magnus College welcomes applications from students of all ages, nationalities, and ethnic, cultural, racial, and religious groups. Applicants may be admitted as freshmen or as transfer, provisional, or special students.

In evaluating freshman candidates, the Office of Admission considers a student's application, counselor recommendation, high school transcript, essay, extracurricular activities, and scores on the SAT or ACT. Emphasis is placed on the student's record of performance rather than on the results of standardized tests.

Transfer students are welcome at the College. They must submit high school records, SAT or ACT scores, and college records for evaluation, in addition to the application and the recommendation. Interviews are recommended for freshman and transfer applicants.

More information is available on the College's Web site: http://www.albertus.edu.

Application and Information

The College accepts students for entrance on a rolling admission basis. Students may also apply online at http://www.albertus.edu. As soon as all of a candidate's admission materials have been received, his or her application is considered and notification is made as soon as a decision has been reached.

Application forms, recommendation forms, and information may be obtained by contacting:

Office of Admission
Albertus Magnus College
700 Prospect Street
New Haven, Connecticut 06511-1189
Phone: 203-773-8501
      800-578-9160 (toll-free)
Fax: 203-773-5248
E-mail: admissions@albertus.edu
Web site: http://www.albertus.edu

Beautiful Rosary Hall.

ANNA MARIA COLLEGE
PAXTON, MASSACHUSETTS

The College

Anna Maria College (AMC), a private, four-year, coeducational Catholic college, was founded in 1946 by the Sisters of Saint Anne in Marlboro, Massachusetts. In 1952, AMC moved to its current 190-acre campus in Paxton, Massachusetts. Originally a women's college, AMC has been coeducational since 1973. The 800 full-time undergraduate students come from fifteen states and several countries.

Anna Maria College is a close-knit community. Small class sizes allow for mentor relationships to develop between faculty members and students. Freshman and sophomore classes generally have between 15 and 20 students; some upper-level classes have as few as 5 students. Faculty members teach and advise students based on their knowledge of each person as an individual, and classes are never taught by graduate assistants.

A five-year strategic plan calls for the College to change and enhance its core curriculum and extracurricular activities to ensure that students have access to the programs and services that will help develop their mind, body, and spirit so they can become strong leaders in their communities. A new honors program with unique study abroad options has been added and other academic programs are currently being explored. In addition, the College has added five new sports teams, including lacrosse, tennis, and football, which will kick-off in 2009. AMC has also unveiled a master plan to double the size of its campus footprint to include new residence halls, new academic facilities, and a new all-purpose athletic field.

Anna Maria College is accredited by the New England Association of Schools and Colleges, the Council on Social Work Education, the National League for Nursing Accrediting Commission (RN-B.S.N. program) and is approved by the Board of Registration in Nursing in Massachusetts. AMC is also approved by the Massachusetts Department of Education.

Approximately 50 percent of Anna Maria College's undergraduates reside on campus in the residence halls. Students enjoy a full social life both on campus and within the college-city atmosphere of nearby Worcester. Annual events enjoyed by all students include Winterfest, Harvest and Spring Weekends, President's Christmas Dinner, a semiformal dinner/dance, and Senior Ball.

Anna Maria College's NCAA Division III athletic program offers intercollegiate competition for men (baseball, basketball, cross-country, golf, and soccer and lacrosse, tennis, and football in 2009) and women (basketball, field hockey, soccer, softball, and volleyball and lacrosse and tennis in 2009). Intramural athletics and the coed club sport of cheerleading are also available to students who do not wish to participate on competitive sports teams.

Anna Maria College is linked to the Internet. More than 500 computer hookups link classrooms, offices, the Academic Computing Center, computer labs, the library, and all residence hall rooms. In addition to College-owned computers, students have the opportunity to access the College network to gain access to the Internet from any location on campus through the use of the College wireless network and their personally owned computer.

Location

Anna Maria College is located on a 190-acre wooded campus in Paxton, Massachusetts, 8 miles from Worcester's vibrant downtown. The city offers numerous professional, cultural, and entertainment opportunities, and Boston, Providence, and Hartford are only an hour away.

Local attractions include big-name entertainment and minor league sports teams at the DCU Center; art, history, and science museums; classical music performances at Mechanics Hall; theater; and day and night skiing at Wachusett Mountain.

Majors and Degrees

Anna Maria College offers a four-year curriculum of undergraduate instruction leading to bachelor degrees in the following areas: art, art and business, art therapy, business administration, business administration/management information systems, criminal justice, early childhood education, elementary education, English, environmental science, fire science, graphic design, health science, history, human development/human services, humanities (interdisciplinary program), legal studies, liberal arts/general studies, media communications, modern languages, music, music education, music performance, music therapy, nursing, paralegal studies, political science, psychology, public policy, social science, social work, sociology, sport management, studio art, teacher preparation/licensure, teacher of visual art, and theology. Associate Degrees are available in nursing, business administration, and paralegal studies.

Art therapy, business, criminal justice, fire science, education, social work, and psychology are the most popular majors. The Fifth Year Option allows undergraduate students in good academic standing a unique opportunity to earn both their undergraduate and graduate degrees in five years. Fifth-year master's options are available in business administration, counseling psychology, criminal justice, education, emergency management, fire science, pastoral studies/counseling, and visual art.

Academic Programs

When the Sisters of St. Anne founded Anna Maria College in 1946, their mission was to increase access to high-quality education, educational innovation, and respect for service to others through the development of the total human being. That mission has not changed in more than fifty years. As a Catholic college, the relationship between faith and reason is looked at closely. An AMC education is distinct because of its integration of rich tradition, diversity of knowledge, and the understanding of human history, institutions, and societies with Catholic teachings and traditions. The cornerstone of AMC's academic programs is the core curriculum, which integrates the Catholic character with a commitment to liberal arts education.

The academic programs are grouped into five divisions: Division I: Humanities, Arts, and International Studies; Division II: Business, Law, and Public Policy; Division III: Human Development and Human Services; Division IV: Environmental, Natural, and Technological Sciences; and Division V: Fine Arts. Each division serves to illuminate and explore links between related areas of study so that the educational experience is broad-based and interdisciplinary. Students are encouraged to travel beyond their immediate interests to disciplines that may be connected by similar methods, history, theory, or application. The end result is a strong liberal arts foundation with a focused knowledge and professional preparation in a chosen area of concentration. AMC also encourages students to explore their own areas of interest and design their own majors.

While at AMC, students can gain practical experience and explore career options through internship programs, fieldwork, academic seminars, and summer programs. They also learn through required practicums, part-time work, and community service.

Off-Campus Programs

Anna Maria College is a member of the Colleges of Worcester Consortium, a group of thirteen area colleges (Anna Maria College, Assumption College, Atlantic Union College, Becker College, Clark University, College of the Holy Cross, Massachusetts College of Pharmacy and Allied Health, Nichols College, Quinsigamond Community College, Tufts University School of Veterinary Medicine, University of Massachusetts Medical School, Worcester Polytechnic Institute, and Worcester State College). Students may enroll in non-major courses at any of the member institutions and have credits transferred at no additional cost.

AMC offers several off-campus opportunities for which academic credits are awarded. There are opportunities for study abroad as well as an Urban Seminar course with travel to various locations worldwide. Students are also eligible to apply for Army and Air Force ROTC programs, available through the Colleges of Worcester Consortium. A Washington, D.C., internship is offered for students in all majors, and a Disney internship is also available.

Academic Facilities

The Mondor-Eagan Library houses Anna Maria College's volumes, stacks, periodicals, study rooms, computer center, resource centers, and language laboratory. The library also houses the main computer terminal, which links the combined material resources of central and western Massachusetts libraries, making more than 4 million books and periodicals accessible to students. Classrooms are located in Trinity Hall, Cardinal Cushing Hall, and Foundress Hall, which also houses the Zecco Performing Arts Center. Trinity Hall also houses the learning center. Other facilities include Madore Chapel, St. Joseph's Hall for sciences, and Miriam Hall for music, performance, and art. A new Master Plan for the College calls for a new academic facility, which will allow AMC to expand both its academic offerings and student population while maintaining small class sizes.

Costs

Tuition and fees for the 2008–09 academic year include tuition, $23,500; fees, $2350; and room and board, $9350. Tuition is slightly higher for music majors.

Financial Aid

Ninety-three percent of the most recent freshman class received financial aid in the form of scholarships, grants, loans, and work-study program awards. Some available sources of funds are the Federal Pell Grant, Federal Supplemental Educational Opportunity Grant, and Federal Perkins Loan programs. To apply for aid, students should submit the Free Application for Federal Student Aid (FAFSA), which can be found at http://www.fafsa.ed.gov. Aid is awarded on the basis of need. Non-need-based scholarships are also available. For further information, students should call 508-849-3366.

Faculty

Anna Maria College has 150 full- and part-time faculty members, 95 percent of whom are lay and 5 percent of whom are religious personnel. Faculty members have a deep respect for scholarship and research and are dedicated to teaching and to the success of the student.

Student Government

The Student Government Association (SGA) is the official representative of the student body, serving as the link between students and the administration. There are more than twenty clubs and organizations under the SGA, offering many activities and opportunities to participate in the extracurricular life of AMC.

Admission Requirements

At Anna Maria College, every application is considered individually and weighed on its own merits. Emphasis is placed on the applicant's transcript, recommendations, and SAT or ACT scores. Extracurricular activities and leadership positions are also important. Successful completion of a four-year college-preparatory program is required. Application for admission to AMC is encouraged for all academically qualified candidates regardless of race, religion, age, gender, or creed.

Application and Information

To apply, students should submit a completed application form and an optional personal essay with the required $40 fee, which is waived for online applications; request that an official high school transcript be sent to the Office of Admission; forward the scores from the SAT or ACT; and, if desired, schedule a personal interview. AMC is on rolling admissions; however, the application priority deadline for financial aid is March 1. Students who apply after March 1 do not receive priority for financial aid. Transfer students must submit official transcripts of all postsecondary courses.

Anna Maria College invites students to learn more about AMC's community by visiting the campus. Students should call the Undergraduate Office of Admission to schedule an appointment. For detailed information about Anna Maria College's distinctive programs and campus community, prospective students should contact:

Elaine Lapomardo
Dean of Enrollment
Anna Maria College
50 Sunset Lane
Paxton, Massachusetts 01612-1198
Phone: 508-849-3360
       800-344-4586 Ext. 360 (toll-free)
Fax: 508-849-3362
E-mail: admissions@annamaria.edu
Web site: http://www.annamaria.edu

Socquet House, built in 1750, currently houses the President's Office as well as other administrative offices.

DANIEL WEBSTER COLLEGE

NASHUA, NEW HAMPSHIRE

DANIEL
WEBSTER
COLLEGE
www.dwc.edu

The College

Founded in 1965 as the New England Aeronautical Institute, Daniel Webster College prepares its students for individual excellence through a commitment to individual attention. The College's innovative curricula in aviation, business, computer science, engineering, information systems, and social science equip students with the knowledge and skills necessary to become tomorrow's industry leaders. Daniel Webster College attains this goal through a "hands-on" experience. The College blends theory and practice to give the student the opportunity to hit the ground running from day one.

Daniel Webster College is accredited by the New England Association of Schools and Colleges (NEASC) and is a member of the New Hampshire College and University Council (NHCUC). The College holds Federal Aviation Administration Air Agency Certification PSE 15-21 as an approved pilot school. Courses are operated under Part 141 and Part 61 of the FAA regulations. Daniel Webster College's Air Traffic Management Program is one of thirteen recognized by the FAA as part of their Collegiate Training Initiative (CTI) and is currently ranked number 4 in the country. Daniel Webster College is located between two of the largest-volume airports in the country, Logan International Airport and Manchester-Boston International Airport. This allows the College's students to receive an invaluable, exciting experience.

The student population at Daniel Webster College is quite diverse, with twenty-six states and thirteen countries currently represented. A variety of living options are available to students during their experience at Daniel Webster to promote comfort and enjoyment. Residential students are housed in six residence halls and in contemporary town house–style apartments on campus. Eighty percent of the total student body currently lives on campus, housed in both coeducational and traditional residence halls.

The multipurpose College Center houses the dining hall, Campus Safety, and the Student Affairs Offices. The Residence Life Office is in Fremont Hall, one of the residence halls on campus, conveniently located for student access. Movies, concerts, and other special events are held at the Common Thread, which contains a piano and pool tables and houses a late-night grille, snacks, and coffee bar. The Thread is also home to the campus post office and the Student Activities Board.

There are more than twenty-five student-run clubs and organizations. These extracurricular activities include the Student Activities Board, the student yearbook, Student Senate, the Gaming Guild, the Jazz Band, Theater Group, Outdoor Adventure Klub, Film Society, a variety of intramural athletics, and other exciting programs. The Leadership Initiative and Student Life Office annually bring nationally renowned speakers and visual and performing artists to the campus. A rigorous two- and four-year Air Force ROTC program is also available.

Home of the Eagles, Daniel Webster College's men's and women's sports teams compete in the Great Northeast Athletic Conference at the NCAA Division III level. The Mario J. Vagge Gymnasium has facilities for volleyball and basketball, a weight room, and an aerobics facility. Men's sports include baseball, basketball, cross-country, lacrosse, and soccer. Women compete in basketball, cross-country, field hockey, lacrosse, soccer, softball, and volleyball. Men's ice hockey is currently available as an intercollegiate sport in the ACHA league.

Location

The College is conveniently located in Nashua, New Hampshire, the state's second-largest city, with more than 87,000 people and twice named "The Best Place to Live in America." The city's municipal airport, Nashua Airport/Boire Field, is adjacent to the campus. Nashua, Native American for "river with pebbly bottom", is home to

a symphony orchestra, indoor rock-climbing, a theater guild, Pride baseball, an arts center, a sky-diving simulator, and several fine restaurants, shopping areas, and craft centers. Several Fortune 500 companies are nearby, providing employment and internships.

Boston is just 46 miles to the south, and Manchester, New Hampshire, is 18 miles to the north. Excellent skiing, snowboarding, hiking, and boating and the scenic New Hampshire seacoast are all within an hour's drive.

Majors and Degrees

Daniel Webster College awards Bachelor of Science degrees in aeronautical engineering, aviation flight operations (professional pilot training), aviation management, aviation/air traffic management, business management, computer systems engineering, computer science, gaming simulation and robotics, homeland security, management information systems, marketing management, mechanical engineering, psychology, social science, and sport management.

Associate in Science degrees are awarded in aeronautical engineering, aviation operations, business management, engineering science, and general studies.

Academic Programs

The College operates on a semester system. Courses are designed to provide the highest-quality educational opportunities. Independent study, a customized internship program, and advanced-placement programs are available to qualified students. The College is known for its commitment to individual attention. Daniel Webster College is a STEM institution, meaning that the College has an educational and practical focus on science, technology, engineering, and mathematics. This focus allows the student to be well prepared for the work-force by giving them a unique college learning experience.

The College's Aviation Division provides one of the country's most innovative and respected aviation programs and is one of only a few to introduce aerobatic flight into its educational programs. Students can qualify for private single-engine, instrument, commercial, multiengine, and instructor ratings. A student instructor internship is available to qualified juniors and seniors.

Academic Facilities

Daniel Webster Hall is the oldest building on campus. It currently houses several classrooms, laboratories, the College Store, and administrative and faculty offices. The Anne Bridge-Baddour Library and Success Center houses the College's extensive library collections, multipurpose computer labs, and the offices of the Academic Support Center and Career Resource Center. There are also several conference and seminar rooms, audiovisual labs, classrooms, and staff offices within the 25,000-square-foot building. The Eaton-Richmond Center, Daniel Webster's newest academic building, houses faculty offices, numerous multimedia classrooms, and a 350-seat auditorium, and it features five new, state-of-the-art Windows computer labs.

The Tamposi Aviation Center is adjacent to Nashua Airport/Boire Field, an FAA Class-D airport with a 5,500-foot paved and lighted runway, operating control tower, and ILS, VOR, GPS, and NDB instrument approaches. The College's fleet of aircraft includes Cessna 172 trainers, Piper PA-28 Arrow complex aircraft, and multiengine Piper PA-44 Seminoles. The Center is fully equipped with a flight dispatch area, classrooms, offices, and flight-planning stations. The Flight Simulation Lab is equipped with new Elite iGATE 500 flight simulators configurable to the single-engine Cessna 172 and Piper Arrow and the multiengine Piper Seneca IV. The simulation lab also contains the new Precision Flight Controls' (PFC) jet trainer flight simulator/procedures trainer that represents a Boeing 737-800 or next generation–style cockpit. It is used for Part 121 airline simu-

lation, advanced systems, and cockpit resource management training. The Air Traffic Control Lab features the Adacel MaxSim tower-control simulator, the UFA radar control simulators that are used for TRACON, and Center ATC simulations for en-route and approach control.

Costs

Tuition for 2008–09 is $26,357. Residence costs, including room and board, are $9369. Books, supplies, and miscellaneous personal expenses are estimated at $3500. First-year flight students can expect to pay approximately $10,500 in flight fees.

Financial Aid

The College is committed to helping students make a Daniel Webster College education a reality. It offers more than $8 million annually in institutional funds through a variety of financial assistance programs based on analysis of the Free Application for Federal Student Aid (FAFSA), which can be obtained through high school guidance offices. Daniel Webster College also offers four-year renewable academic performance scholarships to students exhibiting high academic achievement through high school GPA and other test scores. These scholarships range from $500 to full-tuition scholarship opportunities. More than 90 percent of the students at Daniel Webster College receive some form of financial assistance.

In addition to providing aid through its own scholarship and work programs, the College administers both federal and local financial assistance programs. For more information, students should call or write the Director of Financial Assistance at the College.

Faculty

The student-faculty ratio at Daniel Webster College is 13:1. This provides the opportunity for individual attention and instruction, tutoring, and advising. While scholarship is encouraged and applauded, the prime focus of the faculty is high-quality teaching.

Student Government

The Student Activities Board (SAB) and Office of Student Life coordinate a wide variety of student activities. SAB coordinates campus-wide activities, student clubs and organizations, and travel to events in Nashua and beyond. Student Senate represents students' views and facilitates meaningful dialog between the students and the College administration. The Student Senate represents all full-time day students. The Student Senate strives to construct and promote a common voice; encourage the continuous exchange of ideas between students, faculty members, and administrators; make recommendations regarding college policies and procedures concerning students' academic and social environments; and promote the welfare of the student body. The Student Senate works very closely with recognized student organizations by allocating and monitoring funds generated by the student activity fee.

Admission Requirements

A student who has graduated from an accredited high school program is considered for admission. The SAT or ACT is required for all students interested in earning a Bachelor of Science degree. Consideration is based on high school performance, letter of recommendation, and personal essay. Students may be admitted to the September and January semesters. Admission decisions are made without regard to race, color, creed, sex, physical handicap, or national origin.

Although not required for acceptance, a personal admission interview is strongly recommended. A campus visit, including an optional tour by air for students interested in the flight program, provides an important opportunity to gain valuable firsthand knowledge of the college atmosphere and see if Daniel Webster College is the right fit for the prospective student.

Application and Information

The application fee is $35. The College operates on a rolling admission basis, and students are notified of a decision within two weeks after their file is complete. Interested students are urged to arrange a campus visit while the College is in session.

For further information, students should contact:

Daniel Webster College
20 University Drive
Nashua, New Hampshire 03063-1300

Phone: 800-325-6876 (toll-free)
Fax: 603-577-6001
E-mail: admissions@dwc.edu
Web site: http://www.dwc.edu

Daniel Webster College is located in Nashua, New Hampshire—the only city in America twice rated "Best Place to Live in America" by *Money* magazine.

DEAN COLLEGE
FRANKLIN, MASSACHUSETTS

The College

Dean College, accredited by the New England Association of Schools and Colleges, is a private residential college located on 100 pristine acres in Franklin, Massachusetts. Dean College is committed to fostering the academic and personal success of students by offering a variety of associate degree programs, transfer preparation for four-year institutions, and baccalaureate degrees in dance and arts and entertainment management. Students further benefit from the high quality of teaching, personalized academic support, and leadership development opportunities that promote a lifetime of learning and achievement.

The College has 1,000 full- and 500 part-time students. Its diverse student body includes representation from twenty-eight states and sixteen countries. Dean College offers a variety of housing options, with approximately 90 percent of full-time students living in residence halls.

Students can choose from over twenty-five active clubs and activities, eleven athletic programs, a thriving theater arts scene, and a renowned dance school. The College also offers dances, concerts, comedy nights, and provocative speakers. Varsity league play and intramural sports are available, with 9 acres of playing fields, a 900-seat gym, a 1,500-seat football arena, and lots of screaming fans.

Location

Franklin, Massachusetts, is a quiet, charming New England town ideally situated between Boston, Massachusetts, and Providence, Rhode Island. As a result, Dean students enjoy the best of both worlds: a small-college atmosphere where there is ample solitude for learning, combined with access to a wealth of cultural and recreational opportunities located in the big city just a 40-mile car or train ride away—not to mention the joys of Cape Cod and New Hampshire, also within easy range.

Day trips from Dean include New England Patriots, Boston Red Sox, Bruins, and Celtics games; Cambridge and Harvard Square; Boston's theater district; the Museum of Fine Arts in Boston; the museum of the Rhode Island School of Design; Newbury Street in Boston's Back Bay; shopping at Wrentham Outlets; concerts at the Providence Dunkin' Donuts Center; Tweeter Center concerts at Great Woods; New York City; Vermont's Green Mountains; and the Maine seacoast.

Majors and Degrees

Dean College offers associate degree programs in fifteen majors, designed to prepare students for baccalaureate degree programs and for transfer to, major four-year institutions. Associate degrees are offered in business (with concentrations in business administration and business technology), communications, criminal justice, dance, early childhood education, English, health sciences, history, liberal studies, math/science, philosophy, psychology, sociology, sport/fitness studies (with concentrations in athletic training, exercise science, physical education, and sports management), and theater arts (with concentrations in musical theater and theater).

Dean College also offers Bachelor of Arts degrees in dance and arts and entertainment management. The B.A. in dance provides specialized education in the four main dance disciplines—ballet, jazz, modern, and tap—within a broad liberal arts environment. The B.A. in arts management focuses on study related to the business side of the arts and entertainment world.

In addition, students who have satisfied their associate degree requirements may further seek a Bachelor of Science degree in one of five majors—communications/public relations, general studies, psychology, sociology/crime and justice,, and sociology/general sociology—through the SUFFOLK/DEAN Partnership, an on-campus program that allows students to continue living at Dean while benefiting from the wide range of courses available through Suffolk University in Boston.

Academic Programs

A full-time student is required to register for a minimum of 12 credits of academic work per semester. For graduation, associate degree candidates must maintain a 2.0 cumulative grade point average (GPA), must take a minimum of 60 credits, and demonstrate competency in reading/writing, mathematics, and computers.

Transfer credit toward a Dean degree may be earned by successfully completing courses at another regionally accredited college or university. Students may also earn credits through Advanced Placement (AP) tests and the College Level Examination Program (CLEP). For an associate degree, a maximum of 30 credits may be transferred; however, 24 of a student's last 36 credits must be earned at Dean College. For a Bachelor of Arts degree in dance or arts and entertainment management, a maximum of 70 credits may be transferred; however, 24 of a student's last 36 credits must be earned at Dean College. In addition, all dance and arts and entertainment management courses must be approved by the department.

The First-Year Seminar (FYS), a course taken during the first semester, helps students make a successful transition to college by teaching the academic and personal strategies necessary for success at Dean and beyond. Students enroll jointly in a section of FYS, which is paired with a liberal arts course. The FYS instructor, a learning specialist, attends the liberal arts course with the students and then directly models effective learning strategies for that course with the students. In addition, FYS students participate in campus events that address critical issues facing college students.

The Honors Program offers academically talented students an opportunity to engage in stimulating and challenging courses, seminars, and colloquia during their tenure at Dean College. Open to students who meet the entrance criteria, honors scholars enroll in honors sections of specific courses and may enhance nonhonors courses through additional intensive reading and analysis with instructors. Exciting academic and cultural activities outside the traditional class environment are also available.

Academic Facilities

The newly renovated Library-Learning Commons at Dean serves as the hub of the College's academic support efforts. Here, academic coaches provide one-on-one professional tutoring through the Personalized Learning Services program. Students also have access to peer tutors and can participate in

weekly faculty drop-in sessions where group tutoring takes place across various disciplines.

In addition, as part of this facility, the E. Ross Anderson Library has a comprehensive collection of print and online resources to support research needs. The library houses more than 44,000 books and 200 periodical subscriptions, including extensive reference and legal materials.

The A. W. Pierce Technology and Science Building houses academic computer labs, science labs, and classrooms. The Dean College Children's Center, a laboratory preschool, offers a developmental approach to learning, a wide variety of indoor and outdoor activities, and special annual events.

Costs

In 2008–09, Dean College tuition and fees were $26,944. Room and board totaled $11,616.

Financial Aid

In 2007–08, Dean provided students with more than $12 million of merit-based aid, with the average Dean financial award ranging from $6000 to $15,000. These awards, which are based solely on the information students provide on their admission application, not on financial need, help to reduce their average cost of attendance by more than 30 percent.

Approximately 90 percent of all full-time students at Dean College receive a scholarship that is not based on demonstrated financial need. Since the mission of Dean College is to nurture the potential within its students, these scholarships focus on current performance as well as future potential. They are based on academic or athletic performance, performing arts talent, place of residence, and academic potential. In addition, most students apply for—and receive—federal and state financial aid, which is separate from (and can be added to) Dean's scholarship awards.

Student financial aid packages are generally a combination of grants, loans, and work-study, contingent upon demonstrated financial need and the availability of funds. Dean College participates in all federal Title IV aid programs and the Federal Family Education Loan Programs. Residents of Massachusetts and other reciprocal states may also be eligible for state scholarships, grants, or loans. In order to be considered for need-based financial aid, students must submit the Free Application for Federal Student Aid (FAFSA). After receipt of a valid FAFSA, full-time students are considered for all of the financial aid programs that Dean administers.

Faculty

Dean's dedicated faculty members, advisers, and educational specialists—some of the best in their respective fields—offer direct, personal involvement to help students obtain the full value of their college experience. The student-faculty ratio is 19:1.

Student Government

The Student Government Association (SGA) at Dean College is the voice of the students. The organization provides a liaison between the student body and the administration through which information regarding Dean policies is channeled, seeks out student opinion, speaks for the student body, allocates funds collected from the student activities fee to clubs and organizations through a budget request process, and coordinates College activities by planning and helping various College clubs and organizations to plan individual, group, and campuswide activities.

Admission Requirements

Every application to Dean College is carefully reviewed by the Admission Committee. In addition to the completed application, students must submit the $35 paper application fee ($15 if submitted online), an official high school transcript, a letter of recommendation from a guidance counselor or teacher, a written statement or essay, and SAT or ACT scores. Interviews are not required for admission to the College, but they are strongly recommended. Students applying for the B.A. in Dance Program must also submit a resume, a 3-minute video (including 1 minute of barre, in DVD format), and a recent full-length photograph in dance attire. Students applying for the B.A. in Arts and Entertainment Management Program must also submit either a 200-word personal statement that addresses their interest and involvement in the field of arts and entertainment management (in lieu of essay); or a creative, artistic, or performance piece (presented in the form of a DVD, publication clipping, portfolio, etc.) that relates to media arts or performing arts.

Application and Information

Dean College accepts applications on a rolling basis. Once a completed file is received, a decision is made within two weeks.

Office of Admission
Dean College
99 Main Street
Franklin, Massachusetts 02038
Phone: 508-541-1508
       877-TRY-DEAN (toll-free)
E-mail: admission@dean.edu
Web site: http://www.dean.edu

LYNDON STATE COLLEGE
LYNDONVILLE, VERMONT

The College

Big things are happening in this small place called Lyndon. For the 1,400 students who come here from Vermont, New England, and around the world, Lyndon's intimate, personal atmosphere offers a renowned, experiential, professional, and liberal arts education that prepares them to enter directly into careers or to pursue graduate study.

The hallmark of a Lyndon education is experience. The College offers hands-on learning along with the traditionally structured lecture/discussion courses to give students optimum career preparation. New students participate in the First-Year Experience, a one- or two-day field trip that serves as an introduction to their major. This provides them with confidence that they are pursuing the major that is appropriate for them.

Lyndon graduates are recruited on campus for careers at top corporations and organizations. There are 25 grads (and counting) at ESPN. Lyndon grads are famously found everywhere there's weather, including Antarctica, the White House, and The Weather Channel. The College's Music Business and Industry students may be assisting the road manager for the summer European tour of a legendary musician.

Employers seek out Lyndon students because they experience applied theory, by participating in fieldwork as early as their sophomore year. Some might be in a psychology/human services program that combines theoretical and clinical practice; others could travel to Africa with America's foremost polygamy scholar to assist with research; while others learn about bad weather on site at Mount Washington, home of the most complex weather in the country and right down the road from campus. Lyndon's broadcast journalism students have a strong liberal arts foundation that helps them to contextualize and write the news on which they are reporting.

Many students come to Lyndon because they love small town life. Students who come from the "neighborhood" around the College build on their community relationships and go on to outstanding careers in local and regional businesses and organizations. Some students find ways to combine small town life with big world ideas. One Lyndon grad is a local entrepreneur who developed a mobile medical unit that he markets overseas for use in refugee camps and other heath care challenged areas. He grew up in the area. He still lives here. But his real world is a large as his imagination.

Lyndon students win prestigious national awards in their fields, such as Erica Kelleher, who was named *Ski Area Management* (SAM) magazine's Recruit of the Year. Lyndon's meteorology students regularly take first place in national weather forecasting competitions. The television studies students win Emmy awards for their daily live news broadcasts.

Students at Lyndon combine play and work in academic areas such as mountain recreation management with concentrations in adventure-based program management and ski resort management. These majors allowed students to use their knowledge and love of outdoor fun by helping to design and create Kingdom Trails, one of the most famous 100 miles of hiking, biking, and cross country skiing in the country. Other students are participating in the AT&T/Lyndon-sponsored Rural Broadband Project, which analyzes the possibility of introducing broadband Internet into rugged areas around the world.

Campus events range from the intellectual to the physical, with abundant opportunities for learning and fun. Recent activities include visits from U.N. ambassadors; a lecture and arts series featuring master classes with luminaries such as U.S. Poet Laureate Ted Kooser; plays and first-run films in the on-campus theater; ice climbing up the frozen fountain; canoeing in the campus ponds and kayaking in neighboring rivers; skiing and snowboarding on nearby Burke Mountain and Jay Peak; NCAA Division III athletics; and traditional Vermont events such as Sugar on Snow.

Lyndon was established in 1911 as a normal school—a one-room teacher-training college—and has grown to a comprehensive four-year college. It still offers a strong education major but remains progressive in its development of new programs, such as animation and

illustration (B.F.A.); philosophy and film; music business and industry; a media major (new for fall 2009) that will integrate journalism studies with all media forms; a fully online business major; and sustainability studies, the only undergraduate program of its kind in Vermont and one that reflects the Lyndon commitment to an evolving sustainable campus.

There are ten residences halls, including the new Rita L. Bole Complex, a 132 unit, apartment-style hall for upperclassmen. Each residence hall room is equipped with Internet connections, cable TV connections, and telephone lines. Students who live on campus eat at the Stevens Dining Hall and the Hornet's Nest Snack Bar. All students are allowed to have vehicles on campus.

More than twenty-five clubs and organizations include the campus radio station (91.5 FM The Impulse), the student newspaper (*The Critic*), sports clubs, and numerous social and academic clubs. Intercollegiate sports include baseball, basketball, cross-country, lacrosse, soccer, softball, tennis, and volleyball. Intercollege competitive sports include hockey and rugby. Lyndon's intramural program attracts the majority of the student body. Lyndon has a theater which presents films and plays, and a 6,700-square-foot fitness center which is available to students and faculty and staff members. Outdoor recreational activities and sports facilities are available within minutes of the campus.

Fifty-five percent of the 1,400 students at Lyndon are Vermonters.

Lyndon is accredited by the New England Association of Schools and Colleges. Lyndon's three degree programs in recreation and ski resort management are accredited by the National Recreation and Park Association. Lyndon is a member of the Consortium of Vermont State Colleges.

Location

The 174-acre campus is located in Lyndonville, Vermont, high on a hillside overlooking magnificent Burke Mountain and the picturesque Passumpsic Valley in the heart of Vermont's scenic Northeast Kingdom, a *National Geographic*-designated geotourism area. It is located 1 mile west of Lyndonville and 9 miles north of St. Johnsbury and is easily accessible from all points by Interstate 91. Lyndon is a 3-hour drive from Boston and Springfield, Massachusetts, and 2 hours from Montreal.

Majors and Degrees

Lyndon State College offers degrees in the following majors: accounting, adventure-based program management, business administration, computer information systems, education, English, environmental science, exercise science, global studies, interdisciplinary studies, liberal studies, mathematics, media communications, meteorology, music business and industry, natural science, philosophy and film, physical education K–12, psychology/human services, ski resort management, small business management and entrepreneurship, social sciences, sustainability studies, television studies/broadcast journalism, and visual arts (including animation and illustration B.F.A., graphic design, and digital media). For the 2009–10 academic year, Lyndon is adding a new media major that integrates journalism with all media forms, including Internet, television, and print.

Associate degrees are offered in the areas of: business administration, computer science, digital media, general studies, geographic information systems/meteorology, graphic design, nursing and prenursing (offered jointly with Vermont Technical College), special education, television production, television studies, and visual arts.

Academic Programs

Lyndon operates on a two-semester calendar and a six-week summer-session schedule. To graduate with a bachelor's degree, a student must complete 122 semester hours of credit and meet College and program requirements. Sixty-two semester hours are required for an associate degree. Each student is tested for competence in writing and mathematics at entry to Lyndon; any deficiencies must be made up in noncredit classes during the first two semesters. Lyndon has a general education distribution requirement of 42 semester hours.

For two-year programs, students are accepted into a concentration upon admission; for four-year programs, in the fourth semester. Academic departments advise and plan the student's core courses within the concentration. In bachelor's degree programs, most concentrations require at least 42 credits of junior- and senior-level course work. Lyndon requires that 30 of the last 39 hours toward any degree be spent in residence. Leaves of absence are granted to students in good academic standing.

Lyndon recognizes learning acquired from previous experience through an assessment course that documents nontraditional learning. The College offers fieldwork and practicums in most academic programs through the Cooperative Education Office.

Lyndon's Academic Support Center, Career Planning and Placement Office, Financial Aid Office, Student Life, and Health Services are just some of the entities that serve the needs and promote the well-being of students.

Off-Campus Programs

A key component of a Lyndon State education is the variety of opportunities for off-campus study for credit, on either a full-time or part-time basis. Students can apply professional theories and principles through practicums and internships in all majors.

Lyndon grants credit for study in other countries through an approved program such as the Experiment in International Living or the American Institute for Foreign Study. For students who prefer not to study abroad, but who would still enjoy experiencing another culture, Lyndon offers faculty- and staff-accompanied trips each semester to places such as Greece, Russia, Ecuador, England, China, and many other countries of personal and academic interest.

Academic Facilities

Lyndon State College's Academic Center features state-of-the-art academic and computer classrooms and laboratories, including a fully equipped computer laboratory that is linked to the College's expanding computer information network.

The library maintains a collection of more than 110,000 circulating volumes as well as periodicals, audio and video materials, and microfiche collections. The library also participates in the Inter-Library Loan System, which allows students more extensive access to reference materials. The library's electronic catalog allows access to the collections of many other Vermont colleges, the Vermont Department of Libraries, and the University of Vermont.

The state-of-the-art meteorology laboratory, staffed by a technician, prepares weather information and forecast information that is broadcast over Vermont radio and television stations. Meteorology students also operate a 24-hour weather-reporting telephone line.

Operated daily by students, Lyndon TV/News 7 is a noncommercial, public-service television facility that provides local news and educational, cultural, and public-service programs. Radio station WWLR 91.5 FM, The Impulse, is staffed by student DJs.

Costs

The 2008–09 tuition for Vermont residents was $7488 per year; for nonresidents, it was $16,152. Room and board (twenty-one-meal plan) for one academic year were $7509. Required College fees, including health and accident insurance, totaled $1445. Total expenses for a Vermont resident living on campus were $16,442; for a nonresident, $25,106. Miscellaneous expenses were estimated at $1100.

Financial Aid

Financial aid is available in the form of loans, grants, and campus employment under the Federal Work-Study Program. Approximately 80 percent of the student population receives some type of financial aid from institutional and outside sources. Approximately 35 percent of the students are employed by either the Federal Work-Study Program or the Lyndon dining hall.

Applicants for aid are required to complete the Free Application for Federal Student Aid (FAFSA). In addition to filing the FAFSA, transfer students are required to have a financial aid transcript completed by the financial aid officer of each college they attended. For a student to be considered an on-time applicant, the FAFSA should be filed in early February in order to reach the Lyndon's Financial Aid Office by the March 15 deadline.

Faculty

Lyndon's faculty consists of 155 members, 95 percent of whom hold the highest degree in their field from research institutions such as Harvard, Columbia, Yale, and USC. Many of Lyndon's professors have come to Lyndon to teach following prestigious careers at corporations and organizations such as CNN, National Public Radio, and Hewlett-Packard. Some are successful entrepreneurs, offering real world expertise to back up their classroom teaching.

Faculty members serve as academic advisers and mentors to students and student organizations. Student evaluation of teaching is a formal process and is used in personnel decisions.

Student Government

Students actively represent Lyndon on the Vermont State Colleges' Board of Trustees, in the Vermont State Colleges' Student Association, and on many campus committees. The Student Senate heads the student organizations.

Admission Requirements

Lyndon is an SAT-optional college. Lyndon emphasizes academic success as reflected on high school or college transcripts, and social and academic potential as reflected in letters of recommendation. Lyndon seeks applicants whose academic record reveals maturity and motivation as well as a sense of responsibility and leadership.

Entrance requirements include 4 years of English and 2 to 3 years each of mathematics, science, and history. Foreign language is desired. International students seeking to attend Lyndon can find detailed information on the College's Web site.

Students wishing to be considered for early action must apply by November 1. Admission decisions for first-year students are determined on the basis of the student's application, a copy of the secondary school transcript, one to three recommendations from secondary school guidance counselor(s) or teacher(s) that speak to the academic readiness and social preparedness of the applicant, and an interview either in person or by phone. An optional essay on the applicant's motivation to succeed can strengthen an application.

Applicants who have completed examinations taken through the College Board's Advanced Placement Program with a grade of 3 or higher are granted both advanced placement and course credit after evaluation by the Registrar's Office. Advanced standing is awarded for successful performance on the tests of the College-Level Examination Program. Lyndon grants up to 60 college credits for scores above the 40th percentile on the five general examinations in English composition, humanities, mathematics, natural science, and social science/history and for scores at or above the minimum score established by the College Board for a wide variety of subject examinations.

Admission requirements for transfer students are the same as those for freshman applicants, but an official transcript must also be obtained from each college-level institution that the applicant has attended. Transcripts are required even if no credit is being transferred from a particular institution. Transfer credit may be given at Lyndon for courses completed with the equivalent of a grade of C or better at accredited or officially approved institutions.

Lyndon may permit candidates to defer their enrollment for a period of two semesters.

Application and Information

A nonrefundable $37 fee (paper) or $25 (online) must accompany each application. First-year applicants who are unable to afford the application fee should complete the paper application and ask their guidance counselor to sign a College Board Fee Waiver, or print a copy of the NACAC Application Fee Waiver and ask their counselor to complete it. When these forms are ready, prospective students should mail them to Lyndon, along with their application, all transcripts of academic work completed, and their board scores.

For further information, students should contact:

Office of Admissions
Lyndon State College
P.O. Box 919
Lyndonville, Vermont 05851

Phone: 800-225-1998 (toll-free)
Fax: 802-626-6335
E-mail: admissions@lyndonstate.edu
Web site: http://www.lyndonstate.edu

MASSACHUSETTS MARITIME ACADEMY
CAPE COD, MASSACHUSETTS

The Academy

As the oldest continuously operating maritime academy in the United States, Massachusetts Maritime Academy (MMA) is a coeducational state college with both maritime and nonmaritime curricula. Graduates of Massachusetts Maritime Academy have traditionally been recognized for their excellence. Naval admirals and government and business leaders are prominent among the Academy's alumni.

In addition to a Bachelor of Science degree and a professional license, students achieve a sense of self-confidence and competence—qualities that are important to success in any career.

A clear statement of approval regarding the Academy is made by employers within both maritime and shoreside industries. Nearly 100 percent of the senior class find high-paying employment within a few months of graduation.

The approximately 1,000 men and women who are attending MMA have in common an interest in hands-on activities, an aptitude for mathematics and science, leadership potential, and an interest in, or experience on, the ocean. They recognize the value of a regimented campus lifestyle for developing decision-making skills, discipline, and the ability to assume responsibility. The Academy attracts most of its students from the Northeastern states, with Massachusetts residents making up two thirds of the total. However, students from across the nation as well as seven other countries are in attendance. The great majority of students live in traditional college dormitories and are proud members of the Regiment of Cadets. Some students commute to the campus as participants in the Facilities Engineering Program.

The Regiment of Cadets is divided into companies and is administered by student leaders as well as by full-time staff members. All students wear uniforms daily and participate in various activities, such as flag formation (morning colors) and inspection of quarters.

MMA has a fine athletics complex, including artificial turf fields, and a highly competitive athletics program. The Academy fields varsity teams in baseball, crew, cross-country, football, lacrosse, rifle marksmanship, sailing, soccer, softball, spring track, and volleyball. Academy teams have won All–New England titles in baseball and football. A vigorous intramural athletics program spans the academic year. The Academy also has active programs through the Catholic Newman, floor hockey, multi-cultural, photography, pistol and rifle, propeller, rugby, scuba, swimming, and yachting clubs.

Massachusetts Maritime Academy is for the well-directed, environmentally conscientious, motivated young man or woman who loves the ocean and travel and who desires a thorough education to prepare for engineering, business, and maritime-related professions or for the armed forces. For students who are talented in mathematics and science, mature, and self-disciplined and who enjoy travel, the Academy can provide tradition, a fine education, and optimum hands-on training.

Location

The Academy is located on Cape Cod, at the western mouth of the scenic Cape Cod Canal where it joins Buttermilk Bay. Cape Cod is one of the most beautiful resort areas of the United States. Massachusetts Maritime Academy is less than an hour from Boston; Providence, Rhode Island; and the Cape Cod National Seashore.

Majors and Degrees

Massachusetts Maritime Academy provides graduates with a fully accredited Bachelor of Science degree and the option of a professional license, which enables graduates to seek employment within the various maritime industries and within the stationary power-plant industry. To achieve this end, students can major in emergency management, facilities engineering, international maritime business, marine engineering, marine safety and environmental protection, or marine transportation. A five-year dual-major program allows students to obtain both marine transportation and engineering licenses. The marine safety and environmental protection major is designed to present the opportunity for preparation in the scientific, management, and legal foundations of environmental protection. A variety of minor concentrations in such areas as business management, commercial fisheries, environmental/facilities engineering, and mechanical engineering also broaden employment options for graduates.

Academic Programs

Two academic terms on campus separated by a winter Sea Term make up the ten-month academic year. Approximately six months of sea time aboard the Academy's training ship or six months of cooperative education are required. The Sea Term is divided into four cruises of approximately seven weeks each. Countries visited during Sea Term have included Barbados, England, Ireland, Italy, Mexico, Panama, Portugal, and Spain; cadets cruise to twelve to fifteen countries before graduating. During Sea Term, cadets apply classroom lessons to the operation of a large oceangoing vessel. The cadets have the opportunity to ship commercially with a variety of shipping companies or participate in paid co-op programs and internships throughout the world. Cadets have the summer off.

The academic program involves extensive study and emphasizes a blend of mathematics and sciences with technical and professional studies. Each career program provides a solid foundation in mathematics, physical science, humanities, and social studies in addition to a core of required professional subjects. Maritime majors are eligible to sit for U.S. Coast Guard license examinations as a Third Mate (Deck Officer) or Third Assistant Engineer of steam and motor vessels of unlimited tonnage. Facilities engineering majors are eligible for state licensure.

Although there is no military obligation, some students select service in the U.S. Navy, U.S. Army, Coast Guard, or Marine Corps or in other military branches. Courses offered through the Department of Naval Science qualify cadets to apply for an officer's commission in the U.S. Naval or Coast Guard Reserve upon graduation.

Graduates hold positions throughout the maritime industry as well as in government administration and land-based industries, and they have had great success in many fields that are unrelated to the maritime profession, such as power-plant operations and industrial and mechanical engineering.

Academic Facilities

Massachusetts Maritime Academy has facilities representing state-of-the-art technology in order to provide cadets with the finest training available. An All Weather Navigation and Radar Training Simulator coupled with a prototype of a "Schoolship" Full-Function Video Shiphandling Simulator is the most modern instruction device for commercial marine navigation available in the world today. The system features not only video but also realistic radar, loran C, and depth-finding and radio-direction-finding capabilities. The Center for Marine Environmental Protection and Safety provides state-of-the-art emergency response management and tanker liquid cargo simulators for student and industry training. The library computer lab makes personal-application equipment, along with modems, databases, and a wide variety of popular software applications, available to faculty and staff members and cadets.

Costs

For 2007–08, tuition, fees, room, and board were $13,668 for residents of Massachusetts, Connecticut, and Rhode Island. Costs for students from Vermont, New Hampshire, Delaware, Florida, Maryland, New Jersey, North Carolina, Pennsylvania, South Carolina, Virginia, Georgia, and Washington, D.C., were $14,029. Out-of-region tuition and fees came to $24,338. These figures did not include uniforms, books, or incidental personal expenses.

Financial Aid

Massachusetts Maritime Academy offers its 1,000 students more than $500,000 per year in merit awards based on academic achievement, leadership, and community activities. Most of these awards are renewable for four years.

In addition, the Academy assists families with federal and state need-based programs, which include grants, scholarships, work opportunities, and student loan programs. Students apply for the need-based programs by completing the Free Application for Federal Student Aid (FAFSA). Prospective students should contact the Financial Aid Office at 508-830-5087 with any questions concerning the financial aid process.

Faculty

The faculty is known for its high academic standards. Seventy-five percent of the academic faculty members have doctoral degrees or top professional licenses. In the marine transportation department, there are 8 Ship Masters; in the marine engineering department, there are 8 Chief Engineers and 3 Ph.D.'s. These figures compare favorably with those at any similar academy in the country. The student-faculty ratio is a low 14:1 to ensure that all students receive personal attention commensurate with their academic and professional needs. The Academy also provides a strong support and tutorial program to ensure that every student may have an optimum opportunity for success.

Student Government

A student government is elected to help meet the extracurricular needs of the student body, and its members participate with faculty members and administrators on various all-Academy committees. Students are also represented on the Massachusetts Maritime Academy Board of Trustees.

Admission Requirements

Massachusetts Maritime Academy seeks applicants who have demonstrated an aptitude for mathematics and science. SAT or ACT scores are required of all applicants. In making admission decisions, the admission committee considers important criteria to be the applicant's class standing, SAT or ACT scores, and high school average, stressing college-preparatory mathematics and laboratory sciences (such as chemistry and physics). The rest of the evaluation considers the student's leadership potential, athletics or extracurricular participation, church and community involvement, employment, maritime experience, and letters of recommendation. At least two letters of recommendation are required. A personal interview is strongly recommended.

Application and Information

The application should be submitted as soon as possible but no later than June 1 for the class entering in September. The early decision deadline is November 1. Throughout the year, applicants and their families are invited to visit the Academy. Successful applicants receive a timely decision as well as follow-up communication throughout the year.

Application forms may be obtained by contacting:

Office of Admissions
Massachusetts Maritime Academy
101 Academy Drive
Buzzards Bay, Cape Cod, Massachusetts 02532
Phone: 508-830-5000
       800-544-3411 (toll-free)
Fax: 508-830-5077
E-mail: admissions@maritime.edu
Web site: http://www.maritime.edu

Located at the gateway to Cape Cod, Massachusetts Maritime Academy is the oldest continuously operating maritime academy in the United States.

MITCHELL COLLEGE
NEW LONDON, CONNECTICUT

The College

Mitchell is a private, coeducational four-year residential college. With 936 students and a 12:1 student-faculty ratio, the College provides a supportive student-centered learning environment that addresses the educational needs of all students, including those with learning disabilities. Mitchell is especially proud of its success in working with students who have yet to reach their full academic potential. To that end, the College maintains access for students with varied academic abilities who are highly motivated to succeed.

To help guide students, Mitchell College's mission is connected to five distinctive values: Character, Achievement, Respect, Engagement, and Self-Discovery (CARES). The CARES model provides a learning foundation that emphasizes character development, personal and social responsibility, respect for others, and community service. CARES is a comprehensive hands-on partnership that keeps students on course toward their goal of graduation and beyond.

Mitchell College's innovative PG year program, Thames Academy, continues to grow and strengthen. Launched in 2006, Thames Academy is a postgraduate/precollege program—a year of academic preparation for students between the end of their secondary school/high school education and the start of their college studies. As one of the country's foremost colleges in promoting student academic success, Mitchell provides a challenging education in a caring and supportive environment, focusing on student asset development, rather than deficit management.

Nearly all full-time students are of traditional college age, 18 to 22, and come from throughout the country and around the globe. Most students come from New England states, with about 60 percent from Connecticut, 30 percent from other New England states, and the remaining 10 percent from throughout United States and other countries. International students and representatives of multicultural groups make up approximately 31 percent of the student population. About 150 part-time students, many of whom are adult commuters, enhance the classroom experience.

Nearly 80 percent of full-time students live in three traditional residence halls, each housing 100 students. Each building has three floors with double rooms and common baths. The College also offers four historic Victorian and Colonial waterfront residence halls accommodating between 20 and 35 students each. One waterfront residence is dedicated to Thames Academy, the postgraduate/precollege transitional program. In addition to the traditional resident halls, Mitchell has themed, apartment-style living, accommodating 16 students. A new suite style, 120 bed residence hall opened in fall 2008. Facilities include a fully equipped gymnasium, a new fitness center, new dining hall and café, athletic fields, a sailing dock, and indoor recreation areas.

Biking, business, communications, community service, choir, Hillel, music, the newspaper, the yearbook, skiing, multicultural affairs, psychology, and history are among the clubs that bring together students with similar interests. Weekends are filled with guest comedians, bands, formal and casual dances, lectures, and organized trips to Boston and New York City.

The tradition of the scholar-athlete is strong at Mitchell. A provisional member of the NCAA Division III, Mitchell College recently joined the New England Athletic Conference. Other colleges in this conference include Wheelock College, Newbury College, Lesley University, Elms College, Bay Path College, Becker College, and Daniel Webster College.

Mitchell College fields ten intercollegiate teams. Men play baseball, basketball, cross-country, golf, lacrosse, sailing, soccer, and tennis; women play basketball, cross-country, golf, sailing, soccer, softball, tennis, and volleyball. The College has a history of athletic excellence, winning many national and New England championships. A full schedule of intramural sports is organized for students of all athletic experience and ability.

Location

New London, Connecticut, where Mitchell College makes its home, is a major center of activity in southeastern Connecticut, a region rich in historic significance. This small but sophisticated city, also home to Connecticut College and the U.S. Coast Guard Academy, is a maritime and resort center located midway between Boston and New York City on the main rail line.

The campus is situated in the city's most scenic residential section. Bordered by a long stretch of sandy beach, the campus consists of 68 acres of gently sloping hillside and forest. Places for shopping, banking, dining, and fun are within easy walking distance or can be accessed by buses that pass the College entrance. Major shopping malls, factory outlets, and fine and casual dining are minutes from the campus. The region is also home to major tourist attractions, such as the U.S.S. Nautilus and Submarine Museum, Mystic Marinelife Aquarium, Mystic Seaport, Olde Mystic Village, Ocean Beach Park, Stonington Vineyards, Foxwoods Resort and Casino, the Mohegan Sun Casino, and the Essex Steam Train.

Majors and Degrees

Baccalaureate degrees are offered in business administration, communication, criminal justice, early childhood education, environmental studies, homeland security, global studies, hospitality and tourism, human development and family studies, liberal and professional studies, psychology, and sport management. Associate degrees are offered in early childhood education, graphic design, liberal arts, and physical education.

Students undecided about their academic majors are enrolled in the Discovery Program, which is specially designed to provide special courses, additional advising, and services to explore their full potential and assistance in choosing a major.

Academic Programs

The academic calendar consists of two full semesters that run from September to December and from January to May. In addition to five summer sessions, Mitchell College also offers STEP, a five-week bridging program for incoming freshmen.

All students must complete the core curriculum, which consists of expository writing, composition and literature, effective speaking, introduction to computer and information systems, an introductory psychology or sociology course, a mathematics course, a lab science, and either U.S. history I and II or Western civilization I and II.

If a student is having difficulty, it is recognized early. Mitchell grades at four, seven, and fifteen-week intervals. If a student is experiencing a problem, faculty members and the student's academic adviser work with the student to get back on course. Mitchell's Tutoring Center provides free, unlimited individualized tutoring by trained professionals (not peer tutors) in almost every academic discipline. It also offers assistance in improving writing, research, and computer skills as well as test and exam preparation and study skills development. Some of Mitchell's most successful students are regular users of the Tutoring Center, and they attribute much of their success to its programs.

Students with diagnosed learning disabilities may enroll in the College's nationally recognized Learning Resource Center, which provides instruction and support to complement a student's regular academic program. Each student is assigned two learning specialists to work one-on-one with the student and in small-group settings. The program is designed to teach the learning strategies a student needs to gain independence.

Off-Campus Programs

When not in class, Mitchell students gain the skills and experience they need to succeed in their careers and to make a difference in their communities. Nearly all academic programs require or encourage students to participate in volunteer opportunities, internships, or practical experiences as part of their curriculum.

Some of the opportunities include exploring the seacoast with a nationally recognized scientist, teaching at a local elementary school, partnering with a local police officer, helping to negotiate a bill through the state legislature, assisting with advertising campaigns, coaching developmentally challenged athletes and practicing the skills of injury prevention, and sparking the imagination of local school children through storytelling sessions.

Academic Facilities

Mitchell's unique 68-acre waterfront campus includes a 73,590-volume library and two primary classroom buildings. Students have full use of Mitchell's state-of-the-art computing facilities with high-speed Internet access. The Mitchell College Library, dining hall, residence hall lounges, and most classrooms are equipped with wireless network and Internet access. Computer access is also available seven days a week in the library and computer labs. Campus computers are fully equipped for e-mail, scanning, network printing, and secure access to each student's individual network server storage. Students have access to extensive online information resources (including journal databases, music databases, and eBooks) via the library Web site. High-speed Internet is also available to each student living in the residence halls. For those who do not own a computer, Mitchell offers a computer purchasing plan through Dell and additional service agreements through a local authorized Dell service provider.

Costs

Tuition, room and board, and fees for the 2008–09 year were $35,335. Additional annual miscellaneous expenses, including books, were estimated at $1500 per year. Students enrolled in the Learning Resource Center paid an additional $6500 per year.

Financial Aid

Mitchell annually awards more than $4 million in financial aid, both in need-based and merit-based scholarships and in grant programs designed to recognize academic and leadership abilities. Accepted students may qualify for grants and scholarships that do not need to be repaid. They include the Connecticut Independent College Student Grant Program, Federal Pell Grants, Federal Supplemental Educational Opportunity Grants, and Mitchell Scholarships. Self-help aid in the form of loans is also available. They include Federal Stafford Student Loans (subsidized and unsubsidized), Federal PLUS Loans, and Federal Perkins Loan programs. On-campus job opportunities are plentiful for students regardless of their financial aid status.

Mitchell Valued Potential (MVP) scholarships are awarded based on an individual student's ability to contribute to the College. They may be given to students who demonstrate potential in leadership, volunteerism, and involvement in school activities. Various payment plans are available.

Faculty

Thirty-four full-time and 58 part-time faculty members teach in Mitchell's classrooms. The student-faculty ratio is 12:1.

Student Government

The Student Government Association (SGA) is made up of officers and senators who represent the residents and commuters. It addresses issues with campus administration, organizes community projects, serves as the active voice for the student body, and sponsors at least one campuswide program each semester. The SGA also works in tandem with the Student Activities Office concerning club funding and overall programming.

Student involvement is not only encouraged but also expected of all Mitchell students. An active student leads to a well-rounded person. Students enhance their life with self-discipline skills, demonstrate selfless service, and become happier members of the College family through involvement in student activities, athletics, campus employment, and community service opportunities.

Admission Requirements

Each student is evaluated individually as soon as the completed application, along with the official transcript, is received. Admission is based on academic preparation, scholastic aptitude, personal character, and potential for academic success. Other important factors taken into consideration include the student's motivation, initiative, maturity, seriousness of purpose, and leadership potential. SAT or ACT test scores are optional. Campus visit and admissions interviews are required. Open houses are held in October, November, February, March, and April and throughout the summer.

Application and Information

Mitchell uses a rolling admission policy. Students can expect to be notified of decisions within weeks of the College's receipt of completed applications and official transcripts sent directly from the students' high schools.

For more information, students should contact:

Kevin Mayne
Vice President for Enrollment Management and Marketing
Mitchell College
437 Pequot Avenue
New London, Connecticut 06320-4498

Phone: 800-443-2811 (toll-free)
Fax: 860-444-1209
E-mail: admissions@mitchell.edu
Web site: http://www.mitchell.edu

Mitchell is known for its sense of community and commitment to students' academic success.

MOUNT IDA COLLEGE
NEWTON, MASSACHUSETTS

The College

Mount Ida College, founded in 1899, is an affordable private liberal arts college with more than 1,450 students from over twenty-five states and twenty-five countries around the world and offering degree programs in more than twenty-five fields of study. Mount Ida College is a comprehensive college that combines professional education with a solid liberal arts foundation. Mount Ida campus life offers a supportive learning environment and a diverse, welcoming community.

Mount Ida takes a multidisciplinary approach to learning that emphasizes professional preparation. The All-College Curriculum helps students integrate what they learn in all of their courses, inside and outside of their major. Students learn to think critically and creatively. These transferable skills become the foundation for a lifetime of personal and professional success.

Many of the College's programs offer internships or culminate in a senior capstone project. The veterinary technology program, for instance, requires a minimum of six internships to ensure the widest range of practical knowledge possible. This real-world experience helps Mount Ida students quickly land jobs in their fields upon graduation. Mount Ida graduates understand today's world and how to succeed in it.

The result is quite amazing. Several degree programs have an impressive 100 percent job placement rate within a year of graduation, including interior design, liberal studies, business administration, equine management, funeral home management, and veterinary technology. College-wide, 88 percent of Mount Ida graduates work in a field related to their major within one year of earning a degree, and more than 92 percent have positions that require a bachelor's degree.

At Mount Ida, learning takes place both in and out of the classroom. The College offers a full array of leadership opportunities. For instance, 25 percent of incoming students compete at the NCAA Division III level in one of several varsity sports that foster teamwork and leadership. Plus, Mount Ida students have the opportunity to participate in a variety of intramural programs, clubs, and campus organizations to enrich their education

Location

Beyond its unique approach to learning, Mount Ida literally offers students the best of both worlds. The picturesque, 72-acre campus is located in Newton, Massachusetts, which has twice been named the nation's "safest city." At the same time, Mount Ida is just 8 miles (13 kilometers) from downtown Boston, one of the world's greatest college towns, giving Mount Ida's students easy access to the inexhaustible wealth of cultural resources, internships and professional opportunities, community service opportunities, sports, and

nightlife a major city has to offer. The College shuttle bus connects students with the Newton Centre subway service to Boston.

Majors and Degrees

Mount Ida grants B.A., B.S., B.L.S., A.A., and A.S. degrees. Majors and areas of study include American studies, applied forensic science, bereavement studies, biology, business administration, child development, computer animation, criminal justice, dental hygiene, English, equine management, fashion design, fashion merchandising and marketing, funeral home management, funeral service, general studies, graphic design, hotel and tourism management, human services, interior design, liberal studies, management, psychology, sport management, and veterinary technology. Mount Ida also offers a pre-law concentration, pre–dental hygiene studies, and minors in American studies, art/design history, business, coaching, criminalistics, criminal justice, English, forensic psychology, human services, leadership studies, legal studies, marketing, psychology, sociology, and studio art.

Academic Programs

Mount Ida students have access to exceptional academic services, all of which are designed to help them move from potential to achievement. Mount Ida's commitment to its students' success—both at Mount Ida and beyond—is absolute.

In the Academic Success Center, students find content-area tutoring offered by professional and student tutors. In addition, professional writing associates in the comprehensive Writing Center can help students write and revise papers for any of their classes. Students with documented learning disabilities can enhance their academic experience through the Learning Opportunities Program, which provides weekly strategy-based tutorial sessions with a professional learning specialist. The federally funded Learning Circle Program, available to first-generation college students who meet eligibility guidelines, offers academic coaching, financial counseling, topic-based workshops, social events, and cultural opportunities. Altogether, these academic support programs provide an invaluable resource for Mount Ida students.

Students also find support in the Career Services Center, where they find help with resume and cover letter writing, interviewing skills, job research, and identification of their career goals. The Career Services Center also assists with internship and job placements and holds career fairs.

Costs

Tuition for the 2008–09 academic year is $22,275. Room and board charges are $11,100, with books and supplies costing between $500 and $1000, depending on the program of study.

Financial Aid

Need-based and merit-based assistance, including scholarships, grants, loans, and work-study, are available to qualified students. For the 2007–08 school year, $8.5 million in institutional aid was awarded. Mount Ida has a financial aid priority application deadline of May 1.

Faculty

With approximately 190 full- and part-time faculty members, Mount Ida offers a student-faculty ratio of 13:1, with faculty members available to give each and every student the personalized attention they need to turn their potential into lasting achievement.

Mount Ida's faculty members are well-respected practitioners in their fields of expertise—business, computer animation, veterinary technology, funeral service, and more. As such, the professors bring an invaluable expert perspective to the classroom that adds depth and scope to the learning process

Admission Requirements

A composite evaluation is made of each applicant. Official high school and college transcripts (the latter where applicable) are required, as are SAT or ACT test scores, recommendations, and a personal statement/essay. Transfer students must submit official transcripts of all completed college course work. Transfer credit for fashion design, graphic design, and interior design studio courses may depend on a portfolio review. The TOEFL may be required for students for whom English is not their native language; those applicants should check with the admissions office for more information.

Application and Information

Mount Ida has a rolling admissions policy. Although there is no deadline for the submission of applications, applicants are encouraged to apply as early as possible. The priority deadline for admissions is May 1. Applications are considered as long as there is space in the desired program of study. Applicants are notified within three to four weeks after all credentials have been received

The best way to discover what makes Mount Ida so unique is to visit the campus and see that Mount Ida is a truly special learning community. For more information, to apply for admission, or to schedule a visit, students should contact the admissions office or visit the Web (http://www.mountida.edu).

For further information, students should contact:

Jerry C. Titus, Dean of Admissions
Mount Ida College
777 Dedham Street
Newton, Massachusetts 02459

Phone: 617-928-4553
Fax: 617-928-4507
E-mail: admissions@mountida.edu
Web site: http://www.mountida.edu

Carlson Center at Mount Ida College.

POST UNIVERSITY
WATERBURY, CONNECTICUT

The University

Post University was founded in 1890. Its mission is to provide students with the knowledge, personal skills, and experiences required to become leaders in tomorrow's careers. Post University prepares each student, every day, to be a confident, competent, and competitive participant in a global marketplace. The intimate campus, NCAA Division II athletics, a curriculum focus on career and self-awareness, and interdisciplinary leadership core classes provide a lively, challenging, and fun environment to help graduates transition into the world of advanced studies and, eventually, work. At Post, students learn how to think, and they experience how education impacts the world of work.

Approximately two thirds of Post University's students live on campus in one of the six residence halls. More than 70 percent of undergraduates participate in activities that include student government, the campus activities team, clubs and organizations, and intramural sports or NCAA Division II athletics. Students also enjoy the nearby cultural and social activities in Waterbury and West Hartford, as well as trips to New York City and Boston.

Post students participate in a year-round schedule of intercollegiate and intramural athletic activities. The Post University Eagles are members of the National Collegiate Athletic Association (NCAA) Division II and the Central Atlantic Collegiate Conference (CACC). Men's intercollegiate sports teams include baseball, basketball, cross-country, golf, soccer, and tennis. Women's athletic teams include basketball, cross-country, soccer, softball, tennis, and volleyball. The University also sponsors an active, coeducational equestrian team. Intramural sports are diverse, ranging from softball and volleyball to basketball and flag football. Students enjoy the facilities of the Drubner Conference and Fitness Center, including a gymnasium, a swimming pool, tennis and racquetball courts, a fitness club, and weight-training rooms. The Drubner Conference and Fitness Center also houses the campus bookstore.

Location

Located midway between New York City and Boston, Post University occupies a 58-acre hilltop residential campus in the suburbs of Waterbury, Connecticut. Post's campus and the surrounding community offer a safe, scenic, friendly, and convenient home for students. Its location in the heart of Connecticut provides convenient service from Amtrak's Northeast Corridor as well as airline service to Hartford.

The residence halls range from single rooms to suites consisting of private rooms around a shared living and eating facility. This is in addition to the campus's large dining rooms.

Majors and Degrees

The academic programs at Post University are accredited by the New England Association of Schools and Colleges using the same standards that are applied to other universities, such as Harvard and Yale. Post is licensed by the state of Connecticut to grant associate, baccalaureate, and master's degrees in a number of areas, including business, information technology, health sciences and human services, entertainment and sports industries, equine business management, security and justice, and education. In addition, Post has a number of certificate programs that prepare students for the practice of specific specialties and that can be integrated into either an associate or baccalaureate degree.

Academic Programs

For the bachelor's degree, students must complete a minimum of 120 credit hours. To receive an associate degree from Post, students must complete a minimum of 60 credit hours. All programs offer opportunities for cooperative education. The University has a two-semester calendar.

Off-Campus Programs

Post University offers students the opportunity to study abroad through a University-sponsored program and/or an approved study/internship-abroad program at another institution. The equine business management program offers a study-abroad option in England. Through these programs, students have an opportunity to broaden their perspectives and experiences. Courses taken abroad are accepted for degree credit at Post University.

To qualify for study abroad, a student must have a cumulative grade point average of 2.5 or better at the time of attendance.

Academic Facilities

All classroom buildings are equipped with the facilities that are necessary for the applied arts and sciences, business, and liberal arts curricula. The Academic Computer Center houses computers to serve all components of the academic curriculum. The center is open to all students, who use the facility for course assignments, simulations, and special projects. The Leever Learning Center provides learning systems that are structured to meet the needs of individual students. Post's Writing Center is staffed with experienced writing coaches, who work with students at all levels of ability. The Traurig Library and Learning Resource Center has a capacity of more then 84,000 volumes and a growing media collection. As a government document depository, the library houses an extensive government publications collection. University-wide Internet access is available. Students majoring in the equine area use several nearby facilities.

Costs

For 2009–10, full-time resident students pay a comprehensive fee of $32,425, covering tuition, room, and board. For commuting students, the comprehensive fee is $23,425 per year. Equine and laboratory fees, the $40 application fee, and an estimated $500 per year for books and supplies are not included in this basic comprehensive fee.

Financial Aid

Post offers financial assistance through the Federal Work-Study, Federal Supplemental Educational Opportunity Grant, Federal Stafford Student Loan, and Federal Perkins Loan programs. Aid is awarded upon evidence of financial need, as determined by the Free Application for Federal Student Aid (FAFSA). In addition, the University has its own scholarship and grant programs, both academic and athletic, and participates in all state programs that are applicable. In order to apply for financial assistance, a student must apply for admission and be accepted to Post and then submit the FAFSA.

Faculty

The Post faculty has 30 full-time and 122 part-time members, the majority of whom hold advanced degrees in their respective fields. Faculty members focus on instruction and are involved in all facets of student life. All full-time faculty members serve as academic advisers and maintain weekly office hours for student consultation. The student-faculty ratio is 15:1.

Student Government

Students play active roles in the day-to-day functioning of Post University. The students' official voice at the University is the Student Government Association (SGA), which expresses recommendations pertaining to student life, oversees the operations of each active student group, and decides on funding for each group. The Student Activities Committee participates in the scheduling and programming of campus events. A large percentage of Post University's standing committees include student representatives.

Admission Requirements

Post University welcomes applicants who are motivated to succeed academically and in life. Admission to Post University is based upon an evaluation of the candidate's qualifications and the recommendation of an admissions representative. All decisions are made without regard to race, creed, color, religion, national origin, handicap, or sexual orientation.

Criteria for admission are objective as well as subjective. The applicant's academic experience, standardized test scores, personal qualities, recommendations, and individual characteristics are considered. Post has a rolling admissions policy. The Admissions Committee makes a decision with respect to a candidate's admission to the University as soon as the candidate's file is complete. The minimum requirements to make an admissions decision are official high school transcripts and standardized test scores. International students are required to earn a minimum score of 500 on the paper-based version or 173 on the computer-based version of the TOEFL and adhere to the above requirements.

Campus visit appointments may be scheduled Monday through Friday at 11:00, 1:00, and 3:00 and on select Saturdays from 10 to 2. Post periodically offers Group Information Sessions, on-site and off-site Open Houses, and live Internet chats. To schedule a campus visit, students should call the Office of Admission at 800-345-2562 (toll-free) or send an e-mail message to admissions@post.edu.

Transfer candidates must have a minimum GPA of 2.0 and must file transcripts from all other colleges and universities attended. Grades of C or higher may receive transfer credits. The maximum number of transfer credits allowed for bachelor's candidates is 90; the maximum for associate candidates is 30.

Application and Information

To apply, students should submit the application form, the nonrefundable $40 application fee, a recommendation, SAT or ACT scores, and the applicable transcripts. A file must be completed before an admissions decision is made. Post employs a system of rolling admissions. However, each student should attempt to file the application packet as soon as possible. This gives the Admissions Committee the opportunity to carefully review the application and grants the student a chance to begin preparation for life at college. Online applications are available through the University's Web site: http://www.post.edu.

For additional information, students should contact:

Office of Admission
Post University
800 Country Club Road
P.O. Box 2540
Waterbury, Connecticut 06723-2540
Phone: 203-596-4520
        800-345-2562 (toll-free)
Fax: 203-756-5810
E-mail: admissions@post.edu
Web site: http://www.post.edu

The Post University campus is lovely year-round.

QUINNIPIAC UNIVERSITY
HAMDEN, CONNECTICUT

QUINNIPIAC
UNIVERSITY

The University

Quinnipiac offers four-year and graduate-level degree programs leading to careers in health sciences, business, communications, natural sciences, education, liberal arts, and law. A curriculum that combines a career focus with a globally oriented liberal arts background prepares graduates for the future, whether they start their careers right after commencement or opt to pursue advanced study.

Quinnipiac is coeducational and nonsectarian and currently enrolls 5,630 full-time undergraduates, 805 full-time graduate and law students, and 921 part-time students in its undergraduate, graduate, professional, and continuing education programs. Twenty-five percent of the students are residents of Connecticut; the rest represent primarily the northeast corridor, in all a total of twenty-eight states and several countries. The emphasis at Quinnipiac is on community. Students, faculty members, and staff members interact both in and out of the classroom and office. Quinnipiac is big enough to sustain a wide variety of people and programs but small enough to keep students from getting lost in the shuffle. Life on campus emphasizes students' personal, as well as academic, growth. The approximately seventy-five student organizations and extracurricular activities, including intramural and intercollegiate (NCAA Division I) athletics, give students a chance to exercise their talents, muscles, and leadership skills. The University has a student newspaper, TV station, and an FM radio station (WQAQ) and twenty-one intercollegiate teams in men's baseball, basketball, cross-country, ice hockey, lacrosse, soccer, tennis, and track and in women's basketball, cross-country, field hockey, ice hockey, lacrosse, soccer, softball, tennis, track, and volleyball. Teams compete in the Northeast Conference (NEC); men's and women's ice hockey teams are members in the ECAC.

Quinnipiac's 300-acre Mount Carmel (main) campus has fifty buildings. In addition to its academic facilities, the University has twenty-five residence halls of different styles—traditional two-, three-, and four-person rooms; suites; and multilevel suites with kitchens—all with functional furnishings and decor. The residence halls currently house 3,600 men and women, about 95 percent of all freshmen and 70 percent of the total undergraduate population. Housing is guaranteed for three years to incoming freshmen. Construction on the nearby 250 acre York Hill section of the campus will add 1,800 beds plus an additional student center and multilevel parking garage to accommodate seniors as space becomes available in suite-style housing beginning in 2010. The Carl Hansen Student Center, containing recreational facilities, meeting rooms, and offices for student organizations, is adjacent to Alumni Hall, a large multipurpose auditorium used for concerts, lectures, films, and various University and community events.

Facilities for athletic activities are found in and around the gymnasium and recreation center plus the TD Banknorth Sports Center on York Hill, which includes twin 3000-plus-seat arenas for basketball and ice hockey. The Recreation Center includes a 24,000-square-foot recreation/fitness facility with a large free-weight room; an exercise machine center; aerobics studios; basketball, volleyball, and tennis courts; and a suspended indoor track. There are also lighted tennis courts, playing fields, and miles of scenic routes for running and biking.

Career Planning begins in each of the schools with assistance from the deans' offices in health sciences, communications, business, and liberal arts. It begins with faculty advisement, along with career exploration, a focus on internships and clinical placements, exploring various major and job fields, and exposure to prospective employers and job preparation.

Graduate programs lead to the Master of Science degree in accounting, computer information systems, interactive communications, journalism, and molecular and cell biology; the Master of Health Science in medical lab sciences, cardiovascular perfusion, pathologist assistant studies, and physician assistant studies; the Master of Science in Nursing in nurse practitioner studies; the Master of Business Administration; the Master of Business Administration in Health Care Management, the Master of Business Administration–Chartered Financial Analyst, and the Master of Arts in Teaching. A $22-million, on-campus facility houses the Quinnipiac University School of Law and its library.

The school offers full-time and part-time programs leading to a J.D. degree or J.D./M.B.A. degree in combination with the School of Business.

Location

Situated at the foot of Sleeping Giant Mountain in Hamden, Connecticut, Quinnipiac provides the best of the suburbs and the city. The University is only 8 miles from New Haven, 30 minutes from Hartford (the state capital), and less than 2 hours from New York City and Boston. Bordering the campus is the 1700-acre Sleeping Giant State Park, for walking and hiking. The campus shuttle takes students to shopping and restaurants in nearby Hamden and North Haven, plus to New Haven, where they can visit the acclaimed Yale Center for British Art, attend a performance at the Schubert or Long Wharf Theater (which hosts productions by Quinnipiac's Theater Department), marvel at the dinosaurs in the Peabody Museum of Natural History, dine in fine restaurants, or find easy access to Metro North and Amtrak at the New Haven train station. Quinnipiac's New England location also makes it convenient to enjoy a day in the surf or on the slopes. The beaches on Long Island Sound are easy to reach, and several ski resorts are only an hour's drive from campus.

Majors and Degrees

The School of Health Sciences grants bachelor's degrees in athletic training/sports medicine, biomedical science, diagnostic imaging, microbiology/molecular biology, nursing, occupational therapy (5½-year entry-level master's), physical therapy (6½-year entry-level doctorate), and physician assistant studies (6-year freshman entry-level master's). Students who wish to prepare for entry into medical, dental, chiropractic, veterinary, or other medical schools work with a premed adviser and take classes that prepare them to sit for the various entrance exams.

The School of Business (accredited by AACSB International) offers bachelor's degree programs in accounting, advertising, biomedical marketing, entrepreneurship, finance, information systems management, international business, management, and marketing. The school also offers a five-year combined-degree program in which students may be awarded the B.S. degree in business and a graduate degree in accounting, business administration, or computer information systems (M.S. or M.B.A.).

The College of Arts and Sciences offers bachelor's degree programs in biochemistry, biology, chemistry, computer science, criminal justice, English, gerontology, history, interactive digital design, legal studies (paralegal), liberal studies, mathematics, political science, psychobiology, psychology, social services, sociology, Spanish, and theater. Students can also design their own majors. Certification for teaching elementary and secondary education is offered through a five-year program with the School of Education, resulting in a Master of Arts in Teaching (accredited by NCATE). Students can also continue their study in graduate programs in business, law, journalism, or interactive communications.

The School of Communications offers undergraduate majors in journalism, media studies, production (video, film, and interactive media), and public relations and graduate programs in journalism and interactive communications for writing and design in the journalistic community.

Academic Programs

All degree programs at Quinnipiac University are offered through one of the five academic schools. The academic year consists of two 15-week fall and spring semesters and two summer sessions. All baccalaureate candidates are required to complete the University Curriculum, which consists of up to 46 of the 120 semester hours of credit generally needed for graduation at the bachelor's degree level. The University Curriculum promotes the achievement of college-level competence in English and mathematics and requires study in fine arts, humanities, social sciences, and natural sciences. The foundation of the University Curriculum is three university seminars, which focus on the broad theme of community: individual, national, and global in

scope. The Writing Across the Curriculum initiative (WAC) stresses the improvement in writing skills in all subject areas. The University honors program addresses the needs and interests of the most academically talented and committed students. Honors students take a minimum of 21 credits in their existing core curriculum or major courses. Academically talented students are identified during the admission process and are invited to participate in the University honors program. Approximately 60 full-time freshmen enter the honors program each fall.

Advanced placement, credit, or both are given for appropriate scores on Advanced Placement tests and CLEP general and subject examinations as well as for scores of 4 or higher in the International Baccalaureate higher-level subjects.

Off-Campus Programs

Students in any of the five undergraduate schools can get hands-on experience in their field through off-campus internships. The University is affiliated with outstanding health and scientific institutions—such as Children's Hospital (Boston), Yale–New Haven Hospital, Hartford Hospital, Gaylord Rehabilitation Hospital (Wallingford), and the University of Connecticut Health Center—throughout the state and the nation. Opportunities for internships also exist in industry, large and small businesses, media outlets, and social and governmental agencies. Academic credit is available for internships and affiliations, which are often part of degree requirements.

Academic Facilities

Academic life focuses on the Bernhard Library, which opened in the fall of 2000. This attractive facility provides users with 600 seats, arranged as individual carrels and small rooms for group study and is open 24/7 during the fall and spring semesters. A wireless network provides access to automated library systems and extensive Web-based resources. In addition, students use the workstations in the library's Cyber Café for online research and classroom assignments. The library houses an extensive collection of books, periodicals, government documents, films, tapes, and microforms. Members of the Quinnipiac University community may also draw on resources from local and statewide institutions through interlibrary loans and shared electronic resources.

Quinnipiac University was identified as one of the top ten most-wired campuses in the country by *PC Magazine* in January 2007. All incoming students must purchase a University-recommended laptop computer for use in the classroom, residence halls, and library. A 'help desk' offers support to the laptop program. Students can register online, access library resources, course-related materials, complete assignments, and view their grades.

More specialized student-computing facilities are located in classrooms throughout the campus. Tator Hall has five computer classrooms and four teaching laboratories containing approximately 200 computers. The multimedia and video laboratories in the Ed McMahon Mass Communications Center each have fourteen Apple MacIntosh G5 and G4 workstations. The computer cluster in the Financial Technology Center at the School of Business is a high-tech, simulated trading floor providing students with the opportunity to access real-time financial data, conduct interactive trading simulations, and develop financial models in preparation for careers in finance.

The Echlin Health Sciences Center houses physical and occupational therapy, nursing, and related fields of study. Many of the science labs are located in Buckman Center. A clinical skills lab, for use by nursing students and the physician assistant program, simulates a critical care hospital center. Also in the center is the Buckman Theatre, which holds plays, concerts, and lectures. The Lender School of Business has satellite capabilities and the Ed McMahon Mass Communications Center, which contains a state-of-the-art, fully digital, high-definition TV production studio; audio production, print journalism, and desktop publishing laboratories; and a news technology center.

Costs

The basic 2008–09 cost is $42,700, of which tuition and fees (12–16 credits per semester) are $30,900, and room and board average $11,800. Other expenses, estimated at $1200 per year, included books, laboratory and course fees associated with specific courses, and personal travel expenses.

Financial Aid

Quinnipiac designs financial aid packages to include grants and scholarships that do not have to be repaid, self-help financial aid programs such as federal and University-based work study, and loans. Quinnipiac uses the Free Application for Federal Student Aid (FAFSA) to determine need. Transfer students are eligible for the same need-based financial aid consideration as first-time freshmen. Quinnipiac also offers a number of renewable scholarships to new, full-time freshmen and transfer students, awarded on the basis of academic merit.

Faculty

The faculty is characterized by its teaching competence and outstanding academic qualifications. Of the 290 full-time faculty members, 75 percent have earned a Ph.D. or the appropriate terminal degree in their field. The faculty also includes a number of part-time teachers who are practicing professionals and experts in their fields. Classes are taught by these scholars and professionals and not by student instructors, and a low student-faculty ratio promotes close associations among faculty members and students.

Student Government

The Student Government is the student legislative body of Quinnipiac. It represents student opinion, promotes student welfare, supervises student organizations, appropriates funds for student groups, and provides voting student representation on the Board of Trustees.

Admission Requirements

Quinnipiac seeks students from a broad range of backgrounds. Candidates are reviewed for admission once their application is complete. On average, freshman students have a 3.4 GPA or better average in college preparatory courses (transfer students have a 3.0 GPA or better), rank in the top 30 percent of their high school class, and have an average combined score of 1120 on the SAT (critical reading plus math). Visits to the campus for either an interview, open house, group information session, or a campus tour are strongly encouraged. Transfer students are welcome to make an appointment to discuss requirements and the transfer of credit from previous institutions. Quinnipiac sponsors four open house programs during the year and several Saturday morning information sessions followed by a campus tour.

Application and Information

Quinnipiac generally receives between 14,000 and 15,000 applications for admission and admits just under 45 percent, to enroll an incoming class of 1,500 freshmen and 200 transfer students. Quinnipiac has a rolling admission policy for its undergraduate programs but recommends that freshman applicants submit their application materials well before the deadline of February 1 and that students applying to the physical therapy, nursing, and physician assistant studies programs submit their applications by November 1. Applications can be filed early in the fall of the senior year of high school. Applications begin to be reviewed as soon as they are complete, and the University begins notifying students of decisions in early January. For most programs, a completed application consists of a Quinnipiac application form; a transcript of completed high school courses, including grades for the first quarter of the senior year; a score report for either the SAT or ACT; a personal statement (250-word minimum essay); letter(s) of recommendation; and the application fee: $45. Quinnipiac is a member of the Common Application. Students placed on a waiting list are notified of any openings by June 1. When reviewing applications, the University uses the results of the critical reading and the mathematics sections of the SAT and/or the composite score on the ACT for admission and scholarship purposes. Transfer students must forward a transcript of college course work undertaken. Quinnipiac subscribes to the May 1 Candidates Reply Date Agreement. For information about full-time undergraduate study, students should contact:

Office of Undergraduate Admissions
Quinnipiac University
Hamden, Connecticut 06518-1940
Phone: 203-582-8600
    800-462-1944 (toll-free)
Fax: 203-582-8906
E-mail: admissions@quinnipiac.edu
Web site: http://www.quinnipiac.edu

For information regarding transfer and part-time study:

Office of Transfer and Part-time Admissions
Quinnipiac University
Hamden, Connecticut 06518-1940
Phone: 203-582-8612
Fax: 203-582-8906
E-mail: transferadmissions@quinnipiac.edu

RIVIER COLLEGE
NASHUA, NEW HAMPSHIRE

The College

Rivier College, a private Catholic college founded in 1933, has gained a reputation for academic excellence in more than forty programs. The College has adapted to changing needs by developing liberal arts/career-oriented programs designed to prepare graduates in many fields.

The programs in the School of Undergraduate Studies enroll approximately 1,500 students, including 900 full-time day students. With a 14:1 student-faculty ratio, students have plenty of opportunities to connect with faculty members and become active members of the academic community.

Most full-time undergraduate traditional day students are between 18 and 22 years old. The majority are residents of New England, although other states are represented, including Texas and Virginia. International students represent countries in Africa, Asia, Europe, the Middle East, and South America. Students who live on campus reside in four modern residence halls. Most rooms are doubles, with some triples, quads, and singles available. Rivier also provides substance-free housing in Presentation Hall. The newest hall offers suite-style living, with several double and triple rooms sharing a kitchenette and common area. The Dion Center houses the dining room, the commuter lounge, the mail room, a campus store, student development offices, and meeting rooms. All students are permitted to have cars on the campus.

Orientation sessions for new students are sponsored by the Office of Student Development. Academic and personal counseling are available throughout the year. A full-time chaplain and Campus Ministry team coordinate spiritual activities and service opportunities, while a comprehensive career development service helps students prepare for employment after graduation. Students' health needs are met by a Health Services Center. The Office of Student Development, the Student Government Association, and more than twenty-five student clubs and organizations provide a calendar of social, cultural, and recreational activities, including concerts, live entertainment, films, and sporting events. The College and student organizations frequently organize outings, including trips to Boston and New York and abroad. Students also enjoy a variety of performances by the Rivier Theater Company.

Rivier offers a wide range of team and individual sports, including NCAA Division III men's baseball, basketball, cross-country, lacrosse, soccer, and volleyball; and women's basketball, cross-country, field hockey, lacrosse, soccer, softball, and volleyball. The men's volleyball team has been nationally ranked every year since 2001. The Muldoon Health and Fitness Center is home to Rivier's varsity athletics and to many intramural sports and fitness activities, including volleyball, floor hockey, basketball, weight training, aerobics, self-defense, and more. The campus also has soccer and softball fields, as well as a beach volleyball court and cross-country trail. Student athletes and others can take advantage of an on-campus rehabilitation clinic offering free injury assessment, physical and occupational therapy, and athletic training.

Location

Nashua (population 87,000) is located in southern New Hampshire. The city of Boston lies within easy access 40 miles to the south. Local access to public transportation provides for easy travel to and from the campus. Recreational activities abound year-round at nearby lakes and ski areas, in the White Mountains to the north, and at the seacoast, just an hour's drive to the east.

Majors and Degrees

Rivier College awards Bachelor of Arts and Bachelor of Science degrees in the following areas of concentration: art (studio art, graphic design, and photography and digital media); biology (allied health and environmental science) and biology education; business (business management, information technology management, and marketing); communications (advertising/public relations, journalism, photojournalism, scriptwriting, video production, and Web design/online publishing); education (early childhood/special education, elementary education/special education, and human development/interdisciplinary); English and English education; finance, history, law, and political science (criminal justice, history, political science, and social studies education); human development; international studies; liberal studies; mathematics and mathematics education; modern languages (modern languages education and Spanish); nursing; psychology; and sociology. Five-year combined bachelor's/master's degree programs are available in business, English (teacher certification), and psychology. Preprofessional programs are offered in law, dentistry, medicine, and veterinary medicine. Associate degrees are offered in art, business management, early childhood education, information technology management, liberal studies, and nursing.

Academic Programs

Rivier College takes special pride in its curriculum, which offers both professional studies and liberal arts in order to prepare students for a fast-changing, highly technological society. The curriculum is broad-based, with emphasis on preparing students for challenging and rewarding careers and furthering their personal growth. Core curriculum requirements may vary slightly, depending on the degree to be obtained, but generally include courses in the areas of English, mathematics and/or natural sciences, modern language and literature, philosophy, religious studies, social science, and Western civilization. No fewer than ten courses must be taken in the major field. Electives may be chosen according to the student's interests. For the bachelor's degree, a minimum of 120 credits with a grade point average of at least 2.0 is required. For the associate degree, the student must complete a minimum of 60 credits with a grade point average of at least 2.0.

All departments encourage qualified students to pursue internships in their field of study during their junior or senior year. Education specialists student teach in local schools. Nursing majors complete clinical rotations in health-care facilities throughout southern New Hampshire and northern Massachusetts. History, law, and political science majors may work in a law office, business, legal-assistance agency, or government agency. Sociology and psychology majors work with local social service agencies. English and communications majors work in public relations, broadcasting, or corporate communications positions. Art majors work in advertising or graphic design or at local galleries. Business majors work in such areas as marketing, management, and technology.

Honors awards include placement on the dean's list, membership in Kappa Gamma Pi, listing in *Who's Who Among Students in American Universities and Colleges*, listing in *The National Dean's List*, and degrees with honors. Academically talented students may also apply to the four-year honors program.

The college year is divided into two 15-week semesters, with first-semester examinations held before Christmas recess. Students usually take five courses each semester. Academic credit may be granted to incoming freshmen on the basis of scores on Advanced Placement tests and CLEP examinations. Students may also "challenge" courses and receive credit by special examination.

Off-Campus Programs

Through Rivier College's membership in the New Hampshire College and University Council, a sixteen-member consortium of senior and two-year colleges, Rivier students may register for courses at any of the member colleges and receive transfer credits.

Academic Facilities

Academic facilities include Memorial Hall, which houses fourteen classrooms, faculty offices, a lecture hall, a fully equipped digital imaging studio, a communications lab offering the most recent software and video/sound editing equipment, a behavioral science lab, the studio of community television station tv13 Nashua (WYCN), and art department facilities that include a gallery, a slide library, and studios. The Academic Computer Center features up to sixty-eight workstations with a full range of cutting-edge software and Internet/e-mail access. Regina Library houses more than 100,000 volumes and provides access to more than 3 million volumes in twelve area libraries, as well as online access to licensed databases in virtually every academic subject. The Writing and Resource Center is staffed by professional writing consultants as well as student tutors. Other academic facilities include nursing and science laboratories; a physical assessment lab and nursing skills simulation lab, which provide nursing students with practical experience using blood pressure cuffs, ophthalmoscopes, IV pumps, patient simulators, and more; the McLean Center for Finance and Economics; the BAE Student Research Lab; electronic classrooms offering multimedia learning tools; and the Education Center, which houses an eight-classroom Early Childhood Center, observation rooms, and an educational resource center.

Costs

Tuition and fees for the academic year 2008–09 were $22,800; room and board, $8718; and books and supplies, approximately $700. Students should expect to pay a $100 activities fee and a $25 registration fee each semester.

Financial Aid

Financial aid is awarded on the basis of the financial need of the student and family. Approximately 80 percent of Rivier's students receive financial aid from the College or from government or private sources. Federal aid includes Federal Pell Grants, Federal Supplemental Educational Opportunity Grants, Federal Perkins Loans, Federal Stafford Student Loans, the Federal PLUS loan program, and the Federal Work-Study Program. To be considered for financial aid, a student must file the Free Application for Federal Student Aid (FAFSA) with the federal government as soon as possible after January 1 for the coming year. FAFSA results should be on file with the College Financial Aid Office prior to March 1 for the following academic year. Each applicant is assessed individually to determine the best combination of grant, work, scholarship, and loan amounts to meet the need of the student. The College awards more than $5 million worth of merit-based scholarships and grants, ranging in value from $1000 to full tuition. For more information, students should contact the Office of Financial Aid.

Faculty

The College employs 71 full-time faculty members. The full-time student–faculty ratio is 11:1. Part-time instructors in specialized areas are working professionals who bring current knowledge and expertise in their field to their classes. All classes are taught by faculty members, and department chairs serve as academic advisers to students in their major programs.

Student Government

Every full-time day student automatically becomes a member of the Student Government Association (SGA) upon registration and payment of the student activity fee. The main goals of the SGA are to stimulate active participation in all College functions, to establish and maintain effective channels of communication among members of the College community and the community at large, and to foster a mutual trust, encourage a spirit of cooperation, and initiate new endeavors. The SGA also supervises student clubs and organizations and oversees their finances. The SGA Executive Board serves as the channel of communication through which the views of the students on institutional policies reach the College administration.

Admission Requirements

Applicants for admission should ordinarily have completed, in an accredited high school, a minimum of 16 academic units, including 4 in English, 2 in a modern foreign language, 3 in mathematics, 2 in social science, 2 in science, and 3 in electives. The most successful candidates are in the upper half of their class, with at least a B average. Combined SAT scores average 1410–1500. A personal interview is strongly recommended but not required.

Rivier welcomes applications from qualified transfer candidates from accredited institutions, as well as applications from international students. Transfer students must forward transcripts of all previous college work and a high school transcript. International students must fulfill the requirements for general admission; they may also be required to submit Test of English as a Foreign Language (TOEFL) scores. Deferred admission may be granted to students who wish to postpone entrance for up to one year, provided they have not been enrolled full-time at another postsecondary institution.

Application and Information

Applications must be accompanied by a nonrefundable $25 application fee, SAT scores, one letter of recommendation, and a high school transcript. The School of Undergraduate Studies employs a system of rolling admission that allows qualified students to be admitted approximately one month after their application is completed. Transfers should apply by June 1 for fall admission and by December 1 for spring admission. Those applying for financial aid should observe the March 1 deadline. Interviews are arranged through the Admissions Office. Students may apply online at the College's Web site.

More specific information and application forms can be obtained by contacting:

Director of Undergraduate Admissions
Rivier College
420 South Main Street
Nashua, New Hampshire 03060
Phone: 603-897-8507
      800-44-RIVIER (toll-free)
Fax: 603-891-1799
E-mail: rivadmit@rivier.edu
Web site: http://www.rivier.edu

SIMMONS COLLEGE

BOSTON, MASSACHUSETTS

The College

Decades before women gained the right to vote, Boston businessman John Simmons had a revolutionary idea: women should be able to earn independent livelihoods and lead meaningful lives. Simmons College was the result. Founded in 1899, Simmons was the first college in the nation to offer women a liberal arts education integrated with professional preparation. Today, Simmons provides a strong liberal arts education for undergraduate women that is integrated with professional career preparation, interdisciplinary study, and global perspectives. Simmons offers the many benefits of a small university: an innovative undergraduate women's college, renowned coeducational graduate programs and the world's first MBA program designed for women. Exceptional internship and research opportunities provide hands-on experience and career exposure. It is the Simmons faculty that makes the educational experience unique by challenging students to reach their full potential while providing individual support and mentoring. Furthermore, the Simmons community encourages dialogue, respect and collaboration—making the Simmons experience as thoughtful as it is thought-provoking.

Simmons's interdisciplinary approach offers great advantages: a broader education and view of the world; personalized plans of study; and a chance to develop a range of professional skills and strengths needed for graduate school and an increasingly competitive job market. This is reflected by the large percentage of students employed or attending graduate school shortly after graduation. Every student explores a variety of subjects while gaining an in-depth theoretical and practical understanding of her major. First-year core courses emphasize critical thinking and writing skills, while integrating two or more subjects—ranging from bioethics and Buddhist studies to computational linguistics and visual communication.

Students fulfill their independent learning requirement through internships, fieldwork, and research projects. In doing so, they develop skills, confidence, impressive resumes, and a network of professional contacts. Some students co-publish research with faculty in nationally recognized academic journals as undergraduate students. Many students spend one or more semesters interning for businesses and organizations, ranging from Boston Public Schools and *The Boston Globe* to the Museum of Fine Arts, Smash Advertising, and the World Affairs Council. Simmons's Longwood Medical Area partnerships provide outstanding clinical opportunities at Boston's world-renowned hospitals. On campus, students conduct research using state-of-the-art equipment in areas such as materials science, gene splicing, and computer modeling. In addition, professors frequently invite undergraduates to collaborate on professional research projects, articles, and presentations.

Acquiring a global outlook is integral at Simmons—including an understanding of languages, cultures, and international politics. Programs such as Africana studies, East Asian studies, international relations, and modern languages offer a direct route to cross-cultural immersion. Simmons encourages students to spend an entire semester or year abroad. Short-term international courses provide unique opportunities to study topics such as journalism in South Africa, music in Austria, or history and civilization in Japan. Students also take part in local and international service-learning projects, ranging from education initiatives in Boston to health care in Nicaragua.

Approximately 55 percent of Simmons undergraduates live in college housing two blocks from the main campus. The "quintessential New England" residence campus features nine brick residence halls and a private, landscaped quad, as well as Bartol Dining Hall, the state-of-the-art Holmes Sports Center, a student-run cafe, and the campus health center.

Students say that Simmons's location offers the best of both words—an intimate college experience in the heart of a vibrant city. Simmons's 2,060 undergraduates love the fact that they can easily access the city's rich social and cultural resources but also come home to a safe, friendly campus.

Location

Considered by many to be the best college town in the nation, Boston has more than fifty colleges and universities and approximately 300,000 students. Boston is big league in every sense but size—just like Simmons. The historic, tree-lined Simmons campus is located in Boston's eclectic Fenway neighborhood, which is alive with music and fine arts, medical care and research, action and activism, and the resounding cheers of baseball fans at legendary Fenway Park. From campus, it's a safe, easy stroll to other colleges and universities as well as shops, cafes, clubs, museums, movie theaters, parks, and public transportation. Students hop aboard the "T" (Boston's public transportation system) and head to destinations such as Downtown Crossing, the Italian North End, Chinatown, Harvard Square, and Greater Boston's many other diverse neighborhoods.

Majors and Degrees

Simmons offers more than 40 majors and programs. Popular majors include psychology, nursing, biology, political science, and communications. Faculty advisors help each student create a plan that fulfills requirements and satisfies her personal and professional goals. A number of integrated degrees and accelerated programs allow students to go directly from an undergraduate program to earning a graduate degree in areas such as education, health care, liberal arts, physical therapy, and science information technology. Simmons also offers individually designed preprofessional programs for dentistry, law, medicine, and veterinary medicine. Simmons students typically declare a major by the end of their sophomore year, and nearly a third choose to double major.

Academic Programs

Simmons offers a strong liberal arts education integrated with professional preparation, interdisciplinary study, and global perspectives. A minimum of 128 semester hours is required for graduation. Students must demonstrate competence in math and foreign language, complete a core curriculum in the liberal arts and sciences (40 semester hours), complete the courses required for the selected major(s) (20 to 40 semester hours for each major), fulfill an independent learning requirement (8 to 16 semester hours), and round out their program with appropriate electives. Other special academic opportunities include Simmons' outstanding honors, service-learning, and study-abroad programs. The Dorothea Lynde Dix Scholars option is available for women who are 24 years or older, or who hold a previous bachelor's degree.

Off-Campus Programs

Simmons is a member of the Colleges of the Fenway consortium, which allows students to cross-register with neighboring colleges, including Emmanuel College, Massachusetts College of

Art, Massachusetts College of Pharmacy and Allied Health Sciences, Wentworth Institute of Technology, and Wheelock College. A domestic exchange program allows juniors to spend a semester at Belmont University, Mills College, Spelman College, or Fisk University. Students interested in international study may elect to spend one semester or one year at an approved university exchange or participate in intensive study-abroad programs during the spring semester. Many students take advantage of the over 20 short term study abroad programs which bring students to another location for three weeks, typically following the spring semester.

Qualified students, usually juniors, also may apply for the Washington Semester at American University in Washington, D.C. Other opportunities include Success Connection, a mentoring program that matches select seniors with highly successful Simmons alumnae, and the Barbara Lee Internship Fellows program, which places students in Massachusetts legislators' offices and policy advocacy groups for one semester.

Academic Facilities

The beautiful Simmons campus offers an attractive, practical mix of historic and modern architecture, including state-of-the-art facilities and conveniences. The Main College Building houses a dining area and coffee bar, lecture halls and classrooms, administrative and faculty offices, the bookstore, the Student Activities Center, art studios, music practice rooms, and the Trustman Art Gallery.

Park Science Center offers technologically advanced learning environments, including faculty and student research facilities, fully equipped science laboratories, environmental rooms, observation rooms for psychological testing, and food science kitchens.

One Palace Road, the home of Simmons's School of Social Work and Graduate School of Library and Information Science, features electronic classrooms and also houses the centers for academic support, counseling, career education and resources, media, and technology. The newly renovated Beatley Library offers a number of high-tech services, including a wireless network, laptop loans, sophisticated online library service, technology-equipped group study rooms, and more. In January 2009, Simmons will open a state-of-the-art LEED-certified 'green' building to house the School of Management.

Costs

Undergraduate tuition and fees for the 2008–09 academic year were $14,560 per semester; room and board charges were $5750 per semester. Total costs, not including books, supplies, and personal expenses, were $41,490.

Financial Aid

More than 90 percent of Simmons students receive some form of financial aid. Scholarships, grants, loans, and federal work-study are determined by the Free Application for Federal Student Aid (FAFSA). Simmons also awards academic merit scholarships, ranging from $2000 to $15,000 awards, renewable for four years.

Faculty

Simmons offers a learning experience that is highly collaborative and much more personal than that of large universities. The Simmons faculty includes noted researchers, authors, and experts in their respective fields—yet professors passionately uphold their primary obligation to teach. Students say the small classes, intellectual focus, and welcoming environment contribute to their confidence and success. Simmons has 206 full-time and 340 part-time faculty members; 72 percent are women. A

13:1 student-teacher ratio ensures that every student receives individual attention, and reinforces the strong tie between students and professors.

Student Government

The Student Government Association (SGA) coordinates the policies and activities of various student organizations, allocates the student activities funds, and promotes the interests of the student body by working closely with the Simmons faculty and administration. In addition, every academic department has a student liaison that participates in department evaluations and helps promote educational and social activities for students, faculty members, and staff members. Simmons has more than 50 student organizations, clubs and academic liaisons, including 10 NCAA Division III varsity teams, honor societies, cultural organizations, volunteer programs, and a literary magazine.

Admission Requirements

There isn't one "type" of Simmons student, but there are common qualities. Simmons women are intellectually motivated and open-minded. They are serious about their personal and professional goals, and they are determined to make a difference in the world. With this in mind, the Simmons admission team reviews applications to see not only what applicants have accomplished, but also who they are and what kind of person they hope to become.

The admission team also evaluates high school performance, SAT or ACT scores, recommendations, and the application essay. If English is not the applicant's first language, the TOEFL, IELTS, or a comparable exam score is required. Additional English language proficiency exams are accepted on a case by case basis.

Simmons welcomes applications from prospective freshmen, transfer students, international students, and students who are beyond the traditional college age.

Although not required, an interview is highly recommended. This gives admission officers better perspective about an applicant's abilities, interests, and personality—and at the same time, allows the applicant to evaluate Simmons and decide if it's the right place for her.

Application and Information

Students may apply online at www.Simmons.edu, use the Common Application, or submit a print application, along with the $55 fee and all supporting credentials. Simmons waives the application fee for students who apply online. The Early Action deadline is December 1 and is a nonbinding deadline. The deadline for freshman applicants is February 1. Transfer students are evaluated on a continual basis; the preferred filing date for applications is April 1. Students applying for the semester beginning in January should apply by December 1.

Simmons encourages prospective students and their families to attend an admission event or request an individual visit. They are welcome to tour the campus, sit in on a class, talk to current students, and interview a professor, department chair, or program director.

For further information, interested students should contact:

Office of Undergraduate Admission
Simmons College
300 The Fenway
Boston, Massachusetts 02115
Phone: 800-345-8468 (toll-free)
Fax: 617-521-3190
E-mail: ugadm@simmons.edu
Web site: http://www.simmons.edu

SOUTHERN NEW HAMPSHIRE UNIVERSITY

MANCHESTER, NEW HAMPSHIRE

The University

At Southern New Hampshire University (SNHU), there are no limits to what students can achieve. With a culture that inspires every person, every day, to do more, learn more, try harder, and exceed expectations, the University is dedicated to helping students realize their potential. SNHU blends the best elements of its small-college heritage with the power and prestige that come with university status.

The University has approximately 1,900 traditional, full-time undergraduate day students, with a total enrollment in all divisions (day, evening, weekend, and online undergraduate and graduate students) of about 9,400. Programs are offered on campus, on location at the University's centers in New Hampshire and Maine, and online. SNHU offers undergraduate programs in business, culinary arts, education, hospitality management, and liberal arts and graduate programs in business, community economic development, education, and hospitality.

SNHU is the first carbon-neutral school in New Hampshire. The wireless campus features new dorms and apartment buildings, a simulated stock trading room, multimedia classrooms, an auditorium, the museum-quality McIninch Art Gallery, virtual science labs, technology-ready buildings, a library with resources that can be accessed via the Internet, a fitness center that rivals members-only gyms, athletic fields, cooking labs, a bakery, and an award-winning, student-run restaurant.

Students can participate in one of the University's more than forty student clubs or start new ones. Intercollegiate teams compete in Division II of the NCAA, the Eastern College Athletic Conference, and the Northeast-10 Conference. Sports include baseball, men's and women's basketball, cheerleading, men's and women's cross-country, golf, ice hockey, men's and women's lacrosse, men's and women's soccer, softball, men's and women's tennis, and volleyball. Intramural sports, including basketball, flag football, cricket, and volleyball, also are extremely popular. SNHU's powerful athletic teams dominate on the field—and in the classroom. The University's student-athletes earned honors from the NCAA and *USA Today* for high grades and 100 percent graduation rates. In 2001, SNHU was the only Division II school in the country with a perfect graduation rate.

Athletic facilities include an indoor, 25-meter, competition-size swimming pool; a racquetball court; an aerobic studio; cardiovascular equipment; four outdoor lighted tennis courts; a soccer/lacrosse turf field; baseball and softball fields; and two indoor gymnasiums with four basketball courts and areas for indoor soccer, indoor tennis, volleyball, and many other activities. The fitness center features 4,000 square feet of strength equipment and a 1,500-square-foot cardio deck.

The Wellness Center provides short-term health care, health education, and counseling services for students, and the buildings and facilities are accessible to the physically handicapped. A well-qualified student-services staff provides personal, career, and academic counseling; counselors are available on campus. Lifetime career services and counseling are available to all current students and to alumni.

Location

The University is ideally located, with easy access to downtown Manchester, New Hampshire's largest city and the most livable city in the East, according to *Money* magazine. Public transportation is available, and students may keep cars on campus. The mountains, beaches, and Boston are only an hour away. In 2005, Morgan Quinto Press named New Hampshire the nation's most livable state for the second straight year.

Majors and Degrees

The University has five schools: the School of Business, the School of Community Economic Development, the School of Education, the School of Liberal Arts, and the School of Professional and Continuing Studies. The University offers associate, bachelor's, master's, and doctoral degrees. Undergraduate programs provide students with a strong liberal arts foundation and the knowledge and skills they need to succeed in their careers.

The School of Business majors include accounting, accounting/finance, accounting/information systems, advertising, business administration, business studies, computer information technology, fashion merchandising, finance, finance/economics, game design and development, hospitality administration, hospitality business (with concentrations in conventions management, hotel management, and restaurant management), international business, management advisory services, marketing, retailing, sport management, technical management, and the unique 3-Year Honors Program in Business Administration—the only three-year program of its kind in the country. Students save a full year of tuition by acquiring a bachelor's degree in just three years. Customized and outcomes-based, it is not a condensed four-year degree program and does not require night, weekend, or summer course work. The six-semester, 120-credit program features an interdisciplinary course of study.

The School of Education majors include child development, early childhood education, elementary education, English education, justice studies, and social studies education.

The School of Liberal Arts offers degrees in advertising; communication; creative writing; digital media; English language and literature; environment, ethics, and public policy; game design and development; graphic design; history; liberal arts; political science; psychology; psychology/child and adolescent development; public service; and social science. Students in any major within the School of Liberal Arts may participate in the prelaw program.

The School of Continuing and Professional Studies offers degrees in baking and culinary arts and a bachelor's degree in culinary arts that emphasizes industry experience and provides an opportunity for study abroad.

An honors program, a prelaw program, and a pre-M.B.A. program are also available for students seeking additional challenges.

Academic Programs

At Southern New Hampshire University, undergraduate students receive a broad education in the liberal arts and intense practice in oral and written communication, coupled with the specific knowledge and skills they need to succeed in their chosen fields.

Recognizing that successful leaders must be able to view problems from a variety of perspectives, the University mandates that all students complete courses in writing, the fine arts, the social sciences, mathematics, science, and public speaking. First-year students must take SNHU 101, a critical-thinking seminar to help them make the transition to University life. Students also have the opportunity to take elective courses in whatever areas capture their curiosity and may elect to concentrate their electives to earn a minor. The University curriculum offers both structure and flexibility.

Off-Campus Programs

Southern New Hampshire University is adept at mixing academic theory with practical experience inside and outside the classroom. Half of the undergraduates participate in off-campus cooperative education experiences/internships, earning 3 to 12 academic credits. Such opportunities are based on a student's major and career goals and typically are taken during a student's junior or senior year. Students work with faculty members and the Career Development Office to find appropriate assignments. About 70 percent of those who complete co-ops/internships are offered positions by their employers.

Students also work with real-world off-campus partners in their courses. For example, advertising students have created media campaigns for area businesses, marketing students have conducted market research for external groups, and education students assist local teachers in their classrooms. The University's graduates are in demand because businesses know they have been prepared to contribute to their employers and their communities.

Opportunities for studying abroad are available at partnering institutions, which include Huron University in London, SIT in Malaysia, Christelijke Hogesschool in the Netherlands, and Trinity International Hospitality Studies in Crete. Students may choose from thirty-six schools

in twenty-six countries. Closer to home, students are eligible to take courses at New Hampshire College and University Council–member institutions during the regular academic year. Courses must be approved in advance by the registrar and are subject to available space. Participating schools include Colby-Sawyer College, Daniel Webster College, Franklin Pierce College, Keene State College, New England College, Plymouth State University, Rivier College, Saint Anselm College, the University of New Hampshire, and the University of New Hampshire–Manchester.

Academic Facilities

The main campus features new dormitory and apartment buildings, state-of-the-art classrooms, wireless Internet access, auditoriums, technology labs, multimedia rooms, computer labs, a graphic arts lab, a student-run gourmet restaurant, a student-run bakery, a simulated stock trading room, a museum-quality art gallery, and more. Construction of a new academic building and a new dining hall is scheduled to begin during summer 2008.

The University is home to a novel outdoor experiential learning facility called Camp Synergy, which is primarily used for teamwork and leadership training sessions. The Harry A. B. and Gertrude C. Shapiro Library features the Education Resource Center, networked computers, conference rooms, a career and placement resource center, and a growing collection of bound volumes, microfilm, microfiche, and ultrafiche; materials are available online as well. A recording studio, a listening room, and a closed-circuit television network that covers the entire campus are among the school's audiovisual assets.

Costs

Undergraduate tuition for the 2008–09 academic year was $24,624. Typical room and board charges were an additional $8620. Students must pay $330 in student activity fees each year and should plan to budget funds for books, supplies, travel, and personal expenses.

All students are required to bring wireless laptop computers. Culinary arts students are required to purchase uniforms and knife sets.

Financial Aid

More than 90 percent of the University's students receive some form of financial aid, which may include need-based grants, academic and commuter scholarships, work-study funds, and loans. Aid packages range from $250 to the full cost of attending the University. The average aid package has a value of more than $17,500 and includes a combination of scholarships, grants, loans, and employment sources.

The University participates in the Federal Work-Study Program, the Federal Perkins Loan Program, and the Federal Supplemental Educational Opportunity Grant Program. The school is also eligible under the Federal Stafford Student Loan Program and the Federal Pell Grant Program. Aid applicants must complete the Free Application for Federal Student Aid (FAFSA). The Office of Financial Aid can provide the appropriate forms, or students can go online to http://www.fafsa.ed.gov. Academic, athletic, and leadership scholarships are available for students who qualify.

Faculty

The University has more than 128 full-time faculty members and more than 200 part-time instructors. The student-faculty ratio is 15:1. Nearly 75 percent of the full-time faculty members hold Ph.D.'s or the equivalent in their areas of expertise.

The instructional programs blend theory with practice to stimulate students' professional development and personal growth. Faculty members bring extensive academic, work, travel, and life experiences to their classrooms. Although their primary goal is teaching, faculty members remain current in their disciplines. Outside the classroom, faculty members are management consultants, CPAs, analysts, small-business owners, economists, accountants, marketing professionals, entrepreneurs, innkeepers, chefs, world travelers, artists, poets, novelists, and much more.

Student Government

The Student Government Association is led by 25 students, including 5 officers, who represent all the students at the University. Its primary function is to represent the student body in campus affairs and to dispense student activity funds. One student is appointed to represent the student body on the Board of Trustees. Students are also appointed to most other standing committees, including the Financial Aid Advisory Committee, the Curriculum Advisory Committee, the Library Committee, and judiciary committees.

Admission Requirements

Applicants for admission are evaluated individually on the basis of academic credentials and personal characteristics. When reviewing applicants, primary emphasis is placed on a student's academic record, as demonstrated by the quality and level of college-preparatory course work and achievement attained. Most successful candidates admitted to SNHU present a program of study consisting of sixteen college-preparatory courses, including 4 years of English, 3 or more years of mathematics, 2 or more years of science, and 2 or more years of social science. Separate consideration is given to admission decisions for freshman, transfer, culinary arts, 3-Year Honors Program, nontraditional, and international applicants. Students may complete a paper application for admission or apply online.

Application and Information

Applicants for undergraduate day programs must submit an application for admission, an up-to-date official high school transcript, a personal essay, and high school recommendations. SAT or ACT scores are required of freshman applicants. Test scores are optional for students applying to the culinary arts programs. Candidates for the 3-Year Honors Program are also required to have an interview. Transfer students must also submit official transcripts from all schools previously attended. International students whose native language is other than English must prove proficiency in the English language through the TOEFL examination. Admission decisions are based on the quality of academic performance, but a campus visit and interview are strongly recommended for all candidates. The University operates on a rolling admission basis, and applicants can expect a decision within one month of the receipt of their complete credentials. Applicants may also apply as Early Action candidates by submitting their application prior to November 15. SNHU is a member of the Common Application. There is a $40 application fee.

For more information about Southern New Hampshire University, students should contact:

Office of Admission
Southern New Hampshire University
2500 North River Road
Manchester, New Hampshire 03106-1045
Phone: 603-645-9611
      800-642-4968 (toll-free)
Fax: 603-645-9693
Web site: http://www.snhu.edu

Students on the campus of Southern New Hampshire University.

TRINITY COLLEGE
HARTFORD, CONNECTICUT

The College

Since its founding in 1823, Trinity has provided an undergraduate education of uncommon quality. Widely acknowledged as one of the top liberal arts colleges in the country, Trinity has been recognized by a panel of national education editors for its bold and innovative ideas to advance the cause of higher education and ensure greater access.

In its commitment to the rigorous pursuit of the liberal arts and to instruction that is personal and conversational, Trinity is an ideal college. At the same time, Trinity is in close touch with the world beyond its campus. In that respect and in terms of the outstanding opportunities Trinity's capital city location offers students, a Trinity education is indeed a real education.

While remaining faithful to the classic liberal arts tradition, Trinity offers a distinctive educational experience that prepares students for the challenges and opportunities of the twenty-first century. Building on its traditional strengths in arts and humanities and exceptional offerings in science and engineering, Trinity engages students in a conversation with the world through its study-abroad programs, interdisciplinary programs, and innovative, rigorous programs that draw on the rich cultural, educational, and professional assets of Hartford. State-of-the-art electronic facilities support Trinity's pioneering use of information technology in classrooms. The heart of a Trinity education, however, remains the personal encounter between professor and student, the intellectual partnership that discovers a world of ideas and ignites a passion for learning.

Trinity's students come from forty-three states and thirty countries. The College believes that a diverse community makes learning flourish. Trinity's undergraduate enrollment of more than 2,200 students is about equally composed of men and women. More than 90 percent of undergraduates live on campus in College housing. Trinity is engaged in continuing campus revitalization programs that preserve its impressive Gothic buildings as it also develops a campus for the twenty-first century.

Trinity offers a rich array of extracurricular activities—films, plays, concerts, musical theater, sports, academic symposia, and visits by nationally and internationally known writers, speakers, and performers. Participation is an important word on campus, and Trinity students have abundant opportunities to lead and to be involved in numerous student clubs; special interest groups; theater, dance, and music groups; debate; academic programs; campus cinema; Trinity's radio station; and many student publications. With 19 acres of playing fields, Trinity also offers an extensive athletic program. About 40 percent of the student body participate on twenty-nine men's and women's varsity teams (Division III) and even more participate in twelve intramural sports. The Ferris Athletic Center features a swimming pool, a fully equipped fitness center, crew tanks, eight international-size squash courts, basketball courts, and an indoor track.

Location

Situated on a beautiful 100-acre campus in the center of Hartford, the capital of Connecticut, Trinity offers the best of both worlds—a supportive and active campus community located in a city that provides students with myriad opportunities for internships, community service, and cultural exploration. Hartford's businesses, governmental agencies, cultural organizations, and nonprofit institutions offer Trinity students hundreds of opportunities to explore careers through the College's extensive internship program. Hartford has a number of cultural institutions, including the Wadsworth Atheneum (the oldest public art museum in the nation), Mark Twain House, Harriet Beecher Stowe Center, Connecticut Opera, Hartford Symphony, Hartford Stage, and a number of smaller theaters and clubs that provide a cultural stew of dance, theater, and music. The shopping districts of Hartford and surrounding suburbs are nearby. The impressive Connecticut coast is easily accessible, and Boston and New York are each about 2 hours from campus. Off campus, Trinity students have access to a field station in Ashford, Connecticut, dedicated to research in the natural sciences and a wide range of environmental educational endeavors.

Majors and Degrees

The College offers a Bachelor of Arts degree and a Bachelor of Science degree. Majors offered include American studies; anthropology; art history; biochemistry; biology; chemistry; classical civilization; classics; computer science; economics; educational studies; engineering; English; environmental science; history; international studies; Jewish studies; mathematics; modern languages: Chinese, French, German, Italian, Japanese, Russian, and Spanish; music; neuroscience; philosophy; physics; political science; psychology; public policy and law; religion; sociology; studio arts; theater and dance; and women, gender, and sexuality. Trinity also offers a computer coordinate major, and interdisciplinary majors may be individually constructed. Trinity offers a five-year program in engineering and computer science, which leads to a bachelor's degree from Trinity and a master's degree from Rensselaer Polytechnic Institute through Rensselaer at Hartford.

Academic Programs

Featuring more than 900 courses, Trinity's curriculum provides a framework within which students may explore the many dimensions of an undergraduate education. At the same time, the curriculum offers each student flexibility to experiment, to deepen old interests and develop new ones, and to acquire specialized training in a major field. Students must demonstrate proficiency in writing, mathematics, and a second language and fulfill a five-part distribution requirement that consists of at least one course in each of the following categories: arts, humanities, natural sciences, numerical and symbolic reasoning, and social sciences. They must also take a first-year seminar and at least one course that focuses on global engagement.

Off-Campus Programs

More than 50 percent of Trinity students study abroad for a semester or a year at Trinity's Rome Campus, at Trinity in Spain, or in other approved study programs in more than forty countries on six continents. Several Trinity-sponsored global learning sites operate in Austria, Chile, France, Spain, South Africa (Cape Town), and Trinidad. Through the theater and dance department, Trinity offers the Trinity/La MaMa Performing Arts Program in New York City, an extraordinary program that provides intensive study in theater, dance, and performance.

Academic Facilities

The Raether Library and Information Technology Center is home to the Raether and Watkinson Libraries, as well as the Computing Center. It is a place where students and faculty members come together for the serious work of scholarship, where researchers can pore over a book or conduct investigations through a wide selection of online databases. The Raether Library houses nearly 1 million print volumes and approximately 700,000 non-

print materials, including slides, microforms, sound recordings, and other materials in audiovisual and electronic formats. In addition, an online catalog linked with Wesleyan University and Connecticut College provides access to more than 2 million titles. The Watkinson Library, with its impressive collection of rare books, manuscripts, and other unique resources, supports a broad range of research interests.

The campus is fully wired, with every student room connected to the College network and the Web. Public access computers are also available 24 hours a day in select facilities.

Costs

Costs for the 2008–09 academic year are $36,864 for tuition, $9900 for room and board, and $1860 for fees.

Financial Aid

Each student admitted to Trinity who qualifies for aid receives a package that fully meets his or her demonstrated need. While need status is occasionally a factor, the vast majority of admissions decisions are made on a need-blind basis. Students must file the Free Application for Federal Student Aid (FAFSA) as well as the Financial Aid PROFILE of the College Scholarship Service. Admissions applications are due by January 1; FAFSA and PRO-FILE applications are due by February 1. Students are notified of admission and aid decisions by the first week of April. Normally, need is met with a financial aid package that includes grant assistance, work-study, and federal student loans. Federal funds for which accepted students are eligible include Pell Grants, Federal Supplemental Educational Opportunity Grants (FSEOG), Perkins Loans, Stafford Loans, and PLUS Loans. The College administers a large student employment program, and most students who demonstrate need are granted an on-campus job as part of their financial aid package. The ratio of grant assistance to loans and work-study aid is sometimes affected by the academic strength of the student's record. Trinity continues to expand its aid budget to keep pace with the College's goal to increase the socioeconomic and ethnic diversity on campus. Forty percent of the students receive financial aid.

Faculty

The distinctive strength of a Trinity education has always been the close interaction between students and a faculty of devoted teacher-scholars. A student-faculty ratio of 11:1 enables supportive yet challenging educational experiences that establish a foundation for lifetime learning and enables students to pursue academic interests with passion. Students have numerous opportunities to collaborate with faculty members in conducting research; many students have made joint presentations at international, national, or local symposia or have published jointly prepared papers. All courses are taught by Trinity faculty members and not by graduate assistants.

Although the first calling of Trinity's professors is teaching, they are also active publishing scholars of national and international distinction. History professor Joan Hedrick, for example, won the Pulitzer Prize for her biography of Harriet Beecher Stowe. Other notable professors include Henry DePhillips, distinguished chemist and researcher on art restoration; Dan Lloyd, acclaimed philosopher and author of *Radiant Cool;* Lesley Farlow, accomplished dancer and choreographer; Samuel Kassow, distinguished historian; and Joseph Bronzino, an authority on biomedical engineering. Trinity professors pride themselves on their accessibility and keen interest in helping students.

Student Government

Trinity fosters the growth of future leaders by providing students with many opportunities to exercise and test their leadership skills. The Student Government Association (SGA), for example, provides students a strong voice in social, cultural, and—through membership on faculty committees—academic matters. Composed of elected class representatives, the SGA constantly seeks the expertise and insights of all interested students, and its committees offer enterprising students many chances to participate and to develop leadership skills.

Admission Requirements

Trinity seeks an ethnically and geographically diverse group of highly motivated students who have completed a rigorous course of study in secondary school and have demonstrated energy, talent, and leadership in a variety of extracurricular activities. Trinity has no specific GPA minimums or test-score cutoffs. The College is highly selective, and its candidates typically have an A– high school average. At least 16 academic units of college-preparatory course work are recommended, including a minimum of 4 years of English, 3 years of foreign language, 2 years of laboratory science, 2 years of algebra, 1 year of geometry, and 2 years of history. Last year, over 5,000 men and women from all over the nation and world applied for admission to the College, which enrolls an entering class of 575 students. Transfer students with a 3.0 GPA in a strong course of study at another accredited college or university are considered for admission to the sophomore or junior classes.

Admissions officers review each application individually; decisions are based on each candidate's academic record (course of study and GPA), recommendations from secondary school teachers and counselors, test scores, personal strengths, talents, activities, and application and supplemental essays.

Application and Information

Students must submit completed applications to the Admissions Office. Application deadlines are November 15 for early decision I applicants (with notification by December 15), January 1 for early decision II applicants (with notification by February 15), and January 1 for regular decision applicants (with notification by April 1). Transfer applicants must submit applications by April 1 for admission in the following fall semester (with notification by early June) and by November 15 for admission in the following spring semester (with notification by early January). Students may submit an electronic Common Application at http://www.commonapp.org.

Inquiries should be made to:

Larry Dow
Dean of Admissions and Financial Aid
Admissions Office
Trinity College
Hartford, Connecticut 06106-3100
Phone: 860-297-2180
Fax: 860-297-2287
E-mail: admissions.office@trincoll.edu
Web site: http://www.trincoll.edu/admissions

The Long Walk at Trinity College.

UNIVERSITY OF MAINE
ORONO, MAINE

The University

The University of Maine, the land-grant university and sea-grant college of the state of Maine, has a mission to provide teaching and public service and to carry out research for the state of Maine and the country. The University was established in 1865 as the Maine State College of Agriculture and the Mechanic Arts. When the institution opened its doors in 1868, it had 12 students and 2 faculty members. Today, the University of Maine has approximately 740 faculty members and 12,000 students who represent forty-eight states and sixty-five countries. The University of Maine is a participant in the New England Regional Program sponsored by the New England Board of Higher Education.

The University of Maine is the flagship institution of the seven-member University of Maine System. Two hundred four buildings sit on the University of Maine's 660-acre central campus. Forests, botanical gardens, and other "green" spaces make up the rest of the 5,500-acre campus, overlooking the Stillwater River. Ivy-covered buildings and pathways shaded by evergreens create a campus that is inviting and picturesque during all four seasons. Students living on campus may select from a variety of housing options, from residence halls to apartment-style complexes to fraternity and sorority houses.

The University has more than 235 student organizations, including honor and professional societies, fraternities, and sororities. Ten women's and nine men's intercollegiate NCAA Division I athletic programs are part of the campus community. Numerous intramural and club sports give all students an opportunity to be physically active. Two gymnasiums, a field house, an indoor pool, a sports arena, a domed field, and a 10,000-seat athletic stadium are used for NCAA Division I athletics. A 14,000-square-foot recreation center, which opened in fall 2007, and the Maine Bound Center, with a climbing wall, provide opportunities for recreational sports. For students' creative interests, there are two theaters, excellent music facilities, recital halls, and studios for dance and the visual arts. Community services include a newspaper, a radio station, a police and safety department, and a health facility.

Location

The town of Orono is situated in central Maine, 8 miles north of Bangor, Maine's third-largest city. The University of Maine is 240 miles north of Boston and 306 miles from Montreal. The Bangor area is served by daily air and bus transportation. The local area offers many opportunities for a wide range of recreational activities. Within an easy drive of the campus are many sites of great natural beauty such as Acadia National Park, Mount Katahdin and Baxter State Park, as well as several ski resorts, including Sugarloaf/USA and Sunday River.

Majors and Degrees

The University of Maine offers more than eighty baccalaureate degree programs through five colleges: the College of Business, Public Policy, and Health; the College of Education and Human Development; the College of Engineering; the College of Liberal Arts and Sciences; and the College of Natural Sciences, Forestry, and Agriculture. The Division of Lifelong Learning also offers a Bachelor of University Studies degree for part-time adult learners.

Academic Programs

The University of Maine is a year-round educational institution. The academic year is divided into two 15-week semesters, from early September to early May; a three-week May term; a summer session with two- to eight-week sessions; and a summer field session. The University offers evening as well as day classes.

All students in baccalaureate degree programs must meet the University's General Education requirements. In addition, each academic college sets its own requirements in terms of grades and the number of credits and specific courses required for graduation. Information concerning specific graduation requirements can be found in the undergraduate catalog (http://catalog.umaine.edu). Academic advisers assist all students with completing their degree requirements and fulfilling their personal educational objectives.

The University of Maine provides many opportunities to encourage intellectual curiosity and recognize exceptional achievement. Outstanding entering first-year students are offered the opportunity to participate in the Honors College, one of the country's oldest. Those who successfully complete the honors curriculum and the honors thesis graduate with Honors, High Honors, or Highest Honors. Many academic colleges and majors also offer membership in various honor societies. Students and faculty members on campus are members of thirty-nine such societies, including Phi Beta Kappa, Phi Kappa Phi, Tau Beta Pi, Xi Sigma Pi, Kappa Delta Pi, Beta Gamma Sigma, and Alpha Zeta. The University also recognizes top graduates as cum laude, magna cum laude, or summa cum laude.

ROTC programs are available in the Army and Navy/Marine Corps.

Off-Campus Programs

At least forty departments of the University offer field-based learning programs, including internships, cooperative education programs, and field experience. Students are given academic credit and/or compensation for on-the-job experience in their major field.

The University of Maine offers a number of international student exchanges through the Council on International Education Exchange (CIEE), the College Consortium for International Studies (CCIS), and the International Student Exchange Program (ISEP). The University also sponsors reciprocal exchanges between the University of Maine and such countries as Australia, France, Germany, Ireland, and Japan and sponsors a Junior Year Abroad Program in Salzburg, Austria. The Canada Year program, which is coordinated by the University's Canadian-American Center, offers students the opportunity to study at various Canadian universities.

Academic Facilities

Fogler Library, which is located at the center of the campus, was built in 1942 and an addition was completed in 1976. It is Maine's largest library collection and the eighteenth-largest library in New England. It contains 1,094,622 volumes and more than 1.64 million microforms, subscribes to 12,412 periodicals, and is a regional depository for more than 2 million government

documents. Its departments include Reference Services, the Science and Engineering Center, Special Collections, the Learning Materials Center, Government Documents, and the Listening Center.

All departments on campus provide the necessary laboratories and equipment to support student and faculty research. Undergraduates have access to computer facilities through the University's widespread wireless network as well as through computers located throughout the campus. All classroom buildings are wireless and all residence halls are connected to the University's computer system which provides access to a variety of software programs and network services.

Among the other facilities on campus are the newly renovated Collins Center for the Arts, which includes the Hutchins Concert Hall (seating capacity of 1,435) and the Hudson Museum, an ethnographic and archeological museum with a permanent collection of 8,000 pieces of pre-Hispanic Mexican, Central American, and Native American artifacts. The University of Maine Museum of Art, located in downtown Bangor, is the only museum owned by the citizens of the state of Maine housing a permanent fine arts collection. Art Department Galleries, a public observatory, a planetarium, and the Page Home and Farm Museum are all part of the University of Maine campus community. Recently completed or renovated buildings include the Advanced Engineered Wood Composites Building, the Wes Jordan Athletic Training Center, and art galleries and studios in Lord Hall. Renovations on the Collins Center for the Arts were completed in February of 2009.

Costs

Costs are adjusted annually by the University of Maine System Board of Trustees. For the 2008–09 academic year, tuition for undergraduate state residents was $239 per credit hour; for nonresident students, it was $686 per credit hour. (The average credit load for full-time students is 15 credit hours per semester, or 30 credit hours for the academic year.) Canadian and nonresident students who qualify for the New England Regional Program pay $359 per credit hour. Required University fees ($1900 per year for a full-time student) include the Unified Fee, which provides a variety of health-care services and admission to cultural, recreational, and athletic events. Books and supplies average about $1100 for the academic year. Room and board (nineteen meals per week) charges for the academic year were $8008. These costs are subject to change.

Financial Aid

The University requires all financial aid applicants to file the Free Application for Federal Student Aid (FAFSA) and encourages students to file online. The priority deadline to apply for aid is March 1. Awards usually consist of a combination of several types of aid, ranging from grants and scholarships to work-study jobs and student loans.

Faculty

The University of Maine has approximately 829 full- and part-time faculty members and a student-faculty ratio of 15:1. A number of faculty members teach both undergraduate and graduate courses. Graduate students serve as teaching assistants in some departments. Faculty members are involved in both teaching and research and also serve as academic advisers to undergraduate students. In addition, the faculty takes an active part in the education of students outside of the classroom through seminars, workshops, and discussion groups and by serving as advisers to student organizations. Many faculty members also serve on the Student Advisory Committee, the Student Conduct Committee, and other organizations on campus that serve the needs of students.

Student Government

An elected president, vice president, and vice president of financial affairs direct and coordinate Student Government programs at the University of Maine. Student Government works closely with the Office of the Vice President for Student Affairs and appoints 200 student representatives to the various University committees. These committees are involved with the planning and implementation of residence hall programs, student discipline, athletics, and cultural activities on campus. The work of the executive budgetary committee of Student Government includes the budgeting of approximately $400,000 in student activity fees. Student Government comprises five governing boards and the General Student Senate.

Admission Requirements

Admission to the University of Maine is a selective process. Successful applicants are those whose scholastic achievement, intellectual curiosity, and established study habits promise success in a comprehensive university environment. The admission committee reviews the strength of the high school curriculum, the grades received, the counselor recommendation, and either SAT or ACT scores as the primary criteria for admission. Student essays and information regarding the applicant's school and community activities provide additional information that may help the committee evaluate potential for success.

The University recognizes advanced work completed in secondary schools by means of Advanced Placement tests. Also, students who demonstrate advanced knowledge may be exempted from certain courses and requirements if they pass examinations specially developed by the University's academic departments.

Application and Information

An application form, which is available online, from the Admission office, or any Maine high school guidance office, should be submitted with the nonrefundable application fee. Electronic submission is preferred. The University of Maine is a member of the Common Application, which may be submitted electronically or by paper copy, and the online-only Universal College Application. Additional required documents include official high school transcripts along with counselor recommendations. Traditional-age applicants are required to submit scores from either the SAT or ACT.

Students are encouraged to submit their admission applications and all supporting documents by February 1. In addition, the University of Maine has an early action deadline of December 15. Students whose complete applications are postmarked by December 15 are reviewed by the end of January. Early action candidates are given first consideration for merit scholarships awarded by the Admissions Office. Students applying for the spring semester are encouraged to submit applications by December 1. Applications after these dates are processed on a space-available basis. Applications and all supporting documents should be sent to UMS Processing, P.O. Box 412, Bangor, Maine 04402-0412.

Office of Admission
5713 Chadbourne Hall
University of Maine
Orono, Maine 04469-5713
Phone: 207-581-1561
         877-486-2364 (toll-free)
Fax: 207-581-1213
E-mail: um-admit@maine.edu
Web site: http://www.go.umaine.edu/

UNIVERSITY OF MAINE AT FORT KENT

FORT KENT, MAINE

The University

The University of Maine at Fort Kent (UMFK) offers the combination of high-quality education and personalized attention today's students are looking for. The small campus population of 1,300 ensures that professors know their students by name. The favorable student-faculty ratio of 18:1 provides many opportunities for interaction. At the same time, the University is large enough to offer a wide variety of academic and extracurricular opportunities. The University's diverse student body includes individuals from small towns and big cities across the United States and Canada, as well as from Europe, Africa, South America, and Asia.

UMFK was founded in 1878 as the Madawaska Training School to educate teachers for what was known as the Madawaska Territory. Over the next century, the school evolved and refined its program into a comprehensive liberal arts–based institution. In 1970, it became part of the seven-campus University of Maine System.

The University's three residence halls, Crocker Hall, Powell Hall, and the Lodge, offer housing; the dining facility, Nowland Hall, provides meal service for the student body. Computer, cable TV, and phone hookups are provided in every room, and the halls also have lounges, game rooms, and free laundry facilities. Resident students and commuters alike participate in a variety of campus activities, including theatrical and musical performances, intercollegiate and intramural athletics, and numerous student organizations.

Location

The town of Fort Kent is situated on the banks of the Fish and St. John Rivers in an area originally settled by French-speaking Acadians from Maritime Canada. The St. John Valley community is noted as one of the country's few truly international, bilingual-bicultural regions, and the University of Maine at Fort Kent is known as a great place to learn and grow within that community.

The campus has convenient access to numerous areas of scenic natural beauty, as well as recreational opportunities, including ski areas and resorts, Baxter State Park, the Allagash Wilderness Waterway, and the Gaspé Peninsula in Canada's Quebec Province.

The University of Maine at Fort Kent is in proximity to the Maine Winter Sports Center, which is the home to Olympic biathlon training. The facility typically offers on-snow training from Thanksgiving to Easter and also offers summer training on its paved roller ski–training and advanced-training loops and cross-country running trails. Mountain-biking trails are also available at the site. The center features a three-story lodge with showers, locker rooms, and waxing facilities. Former Olympians provide world-class coaching in cross-country skiing and biathlon.

Majors and Degrees

The University of Maine at Fort Kent is a four-year baccalaureate-granting institution that offers the Bachelor of Arts in English and French; the Bachelor of Science in behavioral science, biology, business management, computer applications, e-commerce, education (K–12), environmental studies, nursing, rural public safety administration, social sciences, teacher certification (both elementary and secondary education), and University studies; the Associate of Arts in business, computer science, criminal justice, general studies, and human services; and the Associate of Science in forest technology.

Academic Programs

Dedicated to providing a solid liberal arts education within programs designed to equip students for the twenty-first century, the University of Maine at Fort Kent divides the academic year into two 16-week semesters. Both day and evening classes run from early September through early May. Summer classes and workshops are also offered, beginning in May and usually ending in late July. All students, regardless of degree program and major, are required to complete a general education core curriculum and meet certain requirements for graduation. Each degree program and major also has a number of specific requirements that are described in the University catalog.

Entering freshmen are assigned an adviser who is a member of a special advising team devoted to ensuring the success of every student's first year at UMFK.

After the first year, students choose a faculty academic adviser in their field of study, who guides them toward completion of their program requirements.

Off-Campus Programs

UMFK offers opportunities for students to study abroad, including exchange programs with Canadian and European universities. A cooperative agreement between the University of Maine at Fort Kent and Université de Moncton's Edmundston Campus provides students with a unique opportunity for cross-registration at either campus. The French branch of the Université de Moncton is located only 22 miles from Fort Kent in Edmundston, New Brunswick. The universities celebrate the heritage of the original settlers of the Upper St. John River Valley.

Along with approximately 130 other public universities across the United States, the University of Maine at Fort Kent is a member of the National Student Exchange Program as well as the New England–Quebec and the New England–Nova Scotia Student Exchange Programs. These programs allow full-time students to pursue course work at other universities in the United States, Quebec, or Nova Scotia to satisfy part of the credit requirements for a degree at UMFK.

Bachelor of Science in environmental studies students also benefit from a cooperative program that allows them to spend a semester or a year studying at either the University of Maine at Presque Isle or the University of Maine at Machias. In addition, practical field experience is available to UMFK environmental studies students through an agreement with the National Audubon Expedition Institute. Through this program, students in good standing can spend a year on an excursion that takes them across the country and requires that they encounter and deal with an array of environmental issues.

Academic Facilities

UMFK is home to the state-of-the-art Northern Maine Center for Rural Health Sciences and Northern Aroostook Technology

Center. The facilities serve as a home for the University's nursing program and also house the most modern classrooms and teleconferencing center in northern Maine.

Additional buildings on UMFK's 54-acre campus include the Cyr Hall classroom complex and computer laboratory, Fox Auditorium, the Sportscenter, the Old Model School, the Computer Center, and Nadeau Hall, which houses an e-commerce lab, faculty offices, a nursing lab, a music lab, an on-campus health clinic, and a satellite conference center. In addition to its own collections, Blake Library provides students with a variety of available databases and electronic access to more than 1 million volumes in libraries of the University of Maine System. A recently completed construction project is the Acadian Archives Building, which preserves, celebrates, and disseminates information about the region's history and houses documents and artifacts. This building contains a conference room, reading room, work room, reference desk, a bank of computers, and research materials stacks as well as personnel space, a collections area, and an accessioning room.

The University also owns or has access to a number of off-campus facilities that are available to students, and enhance academic programs by providing opportunity for hands-on study. The Elmer Violette Wilderness Camp, located on the Allagash Wilderness Waterway in the famed North Maine Woods, is frequently used by the Environmental Studies and Forestry Programs to conduct fieldwork. The wilderness camp includes housing and classroom facilities. Other academic programs also use the camp at various times throughout the year.

Other off-campus UMFK facilities include a 1,000-acre wooded lot bordering St. Froid Lake, a biological park near the campus, and access points to the Fish and St. John Rivers.

Costs

In 2007–08, tuition was $5100 per year for Maine residents and $12,780 per year for out-of-state students. Nonresident students who qualify for the New England Regional Program paid $7710 per year for tuition. Room and board costs for 2007–08 were $6620. Required University fees for new students were $653, which include application, matriculation, orientation, student activity, and technology fees. Tuition and fee figures listed are based on 15 credit hours per semester.

Financial Aid

The University of Maine at Fort Kent Office of Financial Aid administers scholarships, grants, loans, and work assistance to more than 80 percent of enrolled students. The University requires all applicants for financial aid to file the Free Application for Federal Student Aid (FAFSA), which is available from the UMFK Office of Financial Aid, from high school guidance offices, and online at http://www.fafsa.cd.gov. UMFK has a preferred filing date of March 1. Consideration is given at any time during the year; however, early application is recommended because awards depend on the availability of funds.

Faculty

Excellence has always been the goal of the 38-member UMFK faculty. Its members include accomplished scholars who hold the highest degree in their professional field. Faculty members are active in professional activities, research, and continuing education. Their top priority, however, is always teaching. Classes are generally small, and every faculty member teaches and advises students.

Student Government

UMFK has a long tradition of strong student government. The Student Senate, which represents all students, is a member of the University of Maine Organization of Student Governments.

Admission Requirements

The UMFK Office of Admissions considers each applicant on an individual basis. Consideration is given to academic preparation, maturity, personal motivation, and goals. Particular attention is given to secondary school performance, especially in the junior and senior years. SAT or ACT scores are not required for admission to the University of Maine at Fort Kent.

Application and Information

Application for admission is made by completing a University of Maine System application form or by applying online at the University's Web site. A nonrefundable fee of $40 must be submitted to the UMFK Office of Admissions. The University follows a rolling admissions schedule and accepts applications at any time during the year. Students are usually accepted for entry in either September or January.

Applications and additional information are available from:

Office of Admissions
University of Maine at Fort Kent
23 University Drive
Fort Kent, Maine 04743
Phone: 207-834-7600
      888-TRY-UMFK (879-8635; toll-free)
Fax: 207-834-7609
E-mail: umfkadm@maine.edu
Web site: http://www.umfk.maine.edu

Students enjoy the close, family-like atmosphere that the University of Maine at Fort Kent provides. The low student-teacher ratio, personalized attention, and numerous campus events and activities all create the ideal setting for a top-quality learning and life experience.

UNIVERSITY OF MASSACHUSETTS DARTMOUTH

NORTH DARTMOUTH, MASSACHUSETTS

UMass | Dartmouth

The University

The University of Massachusetts Dartmouth traces its roots to 1895 when the Massachusetts legislature chartered the New Bedford Textile School and the Bradford Durfee Textile School in Fall River. As the region's economic base shifted from textiles to more diverse manufacturing and service industries, the program of the colleges changed. Courses were developed to respond to the needs of new generations of students, stimulated by the clear economic and social advantages of a well-educated citizenry. In 1962, Southeastern Massachusetts Technological Institute (SMTI) was created, and in 1969, out of a need and a clear demand for a comprehensive public university, SMTI became Southeastern Massachusetts University. Then, in 1988, the Swain School of Design merged with the University's College of Visual and Performing Arts.

In 1991, a new University of Massachusetts system was created, which combined the Amherst and Boston campuses with the University of Lowell, Southeastern Massachusetts University, and the Medical Center in Worcester. Today, UMass Dartmouth provides educational programs, research, extension, and continuing education and cyber education in the liberal and creative arts and sciences and in the professions. A broad range of bachelor's, master's, and doctoral degrees are offered. Graduate programs lead to the Master of Arts, Master of Business Administration, Master of Arts in Teaching, Master of Fine Arts, Master of Art Education, and Master of Science. A Ph.D. is offered in electrical engineering, chemical engineering, biomedical engineering, marine science, and physics.

UMass Dartmouth enrolls approximately 9,500 students; 90 percent are from Massachusetts, with a growing number from other states and countries outside the United States. A residential campus with a variety of student organizations, athletic programs, cultural opportunities, and interest groups, the University fosters personal development, diversity, and responsible citizenship.

Location

Located in historic and scenic southeastern Massachusetts, which includes the nearby cities of Fall River and New Bedford and the Cape Cod region to the east, the campus is situated on 710 acres. The dramatic campus is the work of architect Paul Rudolph, former dean of the Yale University School of Art and Architecture. Metropolitan areas, with libraries, museums, theaters, and numerous educational institutions, are within an hour's drive: Boston to the north and Providence, Rhode Island, to the west. Recreational sites are minutes away and include beaches, hiking, and cultural and nightlife opportunities. New York City is 4 hours by car; the mountains of New Hampshire and Vermont are 3 to 4 hours away. Students can walk to homes and shops in the immediate area of the campus, while public transportation is available to nearby communities.

Majors and Degrees

There are five colleges within the University: College of Arts and Sciences (nineteen majors); Charlton College of Business (seven majors); Engineering (eight majors); Nursing (one major); and Visual and Performing Arts (twelve majors). In addition, honors programs, interdisciplinary studies, prelaw, premedical advising, and a number of different minors and options are available within various departments. The University offers Bachelor of Arts, Bachelor of Fine Arts, Bachelor of Science, and Bachelor of Science in Nursing degrees at the undergraduate level.

Academic Programs

The University operates on a two-semester calendar, with the fall semester beginning the first week of September and concluding in mid-December and the spring semester beginning in late January and concluding in late May. A five-week intersession is offered between semesters. Summer-term courses are offered in June, July, and early August. Undergraduate students usually enroll in four or five courses each semester, and a typical course earns 3 credits. An undergraduate degree requires a minimum of 120 credits (there are a few majors that require 135 credits); a student can complete degree requirements for a specified major within a department or an approved interdepartmental major (30 credits). Students must also complete requirements according to the degree being sought.

Other learning opportunities include independent study, contract learning, and directed study; study abroad; study at a nearby university through cross-registration; and credit by examination. UMass Dartmouth is a member of SACHEM (Southeastern Association for Cooperation in Higher Education in Massachusetts), allowing for cross-registration at Bridgewater State College, Bristol Community College, Cape Cod Community College, Dean College, Massachusetts Maritime Academy, Massasoit Community College, Stonehill College, and Wheaton College. The University has formal exchange agreements with, among others, the University of Grenoble (France), the Lycée du Grésivaudan at Meylan and the Lycée Aristide Berges, Nottingham Trent University (England), the Baden-Württemberg Universities (Germany), Centro de Arte e Comunicação (Portugal), Nova Scotia College of Art and Design, the École Nationale Supérieure des Industries Textiles, Université de Haute Alsace (France), and Minho University (Portugal). Students may also take initiative in finding other programs in addition to the exchange-agreement institutions.

The College of Engineering provides majors in any of the engineering fields and offers students work experience through cooperative education or internships.

Academic Facilities

Computing is an integral part of the curriculum. All academic buildings, including student residences, are connected to a campuswide network. Computing clusters, located in the library and in most classroom buildings, support the classwork of students. More than 200 microcomputers (Apple Macintosh and IBM) or terminals are readily available. The University library supports all programs of instruction and research with 455,323 volumes and 2,925 periodicals. A large interlibrary loan network and delivery system makes millions of volumes available to the students. Each of the five colleges within the University is housed in academic facilities designed for its purposes with classrooms, laboratories, studies, galleries, faculty offices, and lounges.

Costs

In-state tuition and fees for 2008–09 are $8858; non-Massachusetts resident tuition and fees are $18,561. Room and

board expenses range from approximately $8000 to more than $9500, depending on the residence and meal plan chosen. Books and supplies cost approximately $1200 a year depending on a student's courses. Specific fees may be assessed, depending on a student's course of study.

Financial Aid

Nearly all students are eligible for some type of financial aid. UMass Dartmouth awards financial aid based on federal, state, and institutional guidelines; students must submit the Free Application for Federal Student Aid (FAFSA). In determining need, the Financial Aid Services Office considers the total costs of attending the University (tuition, fees, books, room and board, the cost of commuting, and an allowance for living and personal expenses). The difference between total University cost and the estimate of expected family contribution is the amount that the financial aid staff considers to be financial need.

Faculty

The faculty, numbering 350 full-time members, is distributed over twenty-nine departments in the five colleges. More than two thirds of the faculty members have a Ph.D., with a significant number holding the terminal degree in their chosen discipline (e.g., business, fine arts, education). A student-faculty ratio of 16:1 ensures that classes are reasonably sized, with an average class size of 30 students. Faculty members are actively engaged in advising students, providing guidance throughout a student's academic career.

Student Government

The Student Senate is the governing body offering a forum for debate on matters of importance to the student body. The Student Judiciary, a system of courts or judicial agencies, provides students and organizations with the protection of due process in all disciplinary matters. A student is also elected to the University of Massachusetts Board of Trustees. Students serve on the Board of Governors, policy makers for the Campus Center; the Resident Hall Congress; and the Student Activities Board. Students are active, voting participants on policymaking committees that regulate both academic and social aspects of the University.

Admission Requirements

Admission is selective. Applicants are evaluated both by the general standards of the University and by the special standards of the academic areas that they request. In addition, the Board of Higher Education sets guidelines governing admission standards for the University. Admission to some colleges or majors may be limited by spaces available. Students are admitted on a rolling basis with no set deadline. Qualified candidates are accepted until the capacity has been reached in the program of choice. Each applicant's record is assessed on the basis of the depth and rigor of the secondary school program, rank in class and grade point average, SAT or ACT results, college-level records for transfer applicants, and other appropriate measures.

The University realizes its commitment to equal access through standard, as well as alternative, admission programs. For College Now, the alternative program, applicants must meet at least one of three eligibility criteria: low-income status, limited English background, or first generation in the family to attend college.

All applicants for freshman admission to the University are required to submit an application form with the appropriate fee ($40 in state and $60 out of state), a transcript of the secondary school record, SAT or ACT results, and any other information that candidates consider important for the admissions committee to review. Transfer students, who compose approximately one third of the new student population every year, are required to submit records for all college-level work completed in addition to the application form. The admission process is virtually the same for transfer candidates, with primary emphasis on the student's previous college/university record.

Application and Information

Students are invited to visit the University for a campus tour and a meeting with an admissions officer; interviews are not required. Some majors, such as nursing, may close early due to enrollment capacity. Admission is rolling except for early decision (freshmen). The early decision deadline is November 15, with notification by December 15. All other decisions are made within three weeks of the completion of an application. For application forms and related information, students may call, write, or e-mail the admissions office.

Office of Admissions
UMass Dartmouth
285 Old Westport Road
North Dartmouth, Massachusetts 02747-2300
Phone: 508-999-8605
Fax: 508-999-8755
E-mail: admissions@umassd.edu
Internet: http://explore.umassd.edu/

UMass Dartmouth Engaged, Embedded, Evolving.

UNIVERSITY OF MASSACHUSETTS LOWELL

LOWELL, MASSACHUSETTS

University of Massachusetts Lowell
UMASS Lowell

The University

Throughout its 100-year history, the University of Massachusetts (UMass) Lowell has excelled at providing innovative programs that meet both the needs of its students for a high-quality education and the needs of the region for skilled leadership. The University is part of the five-campus University of Massachusetts system.

Two types of learning communities help students make the transition to college. In academic learning communities, groups of 25 students in three shared courses are assigned a senior faculty member/mentor to guide them through discussions around a shared academic interest. In living learning communities, residence hall assignments cluster students into suites and provide activities and discussions around a theme such as arts and culture, politics in the media, or science and technology.

The UMass Lowell education focuses on putting the lessons of the classroom into practice. Students have multiple opportunities for co-ops, internships, service learning activities and knowledge discovery through research, all of which give them hands-on experience in solving the issues of the real world. The real-world focus is also reflected in the interdisciplinary nature of academic initiatives. In the Artbotics Project, art and computer science students collaborated on the development of robots; and during the Urban Village Arts Series, design, English, and sound recording technology majors worked together to produce a CD of the eight multimedia performances. Students graduate with the hands-on experience and practical problem-solving skills employers seek.

UMass Lowell offers dozens of Plus 1 programs that allow students to stay an extra year to earn both bachelor's and master's degrees, giving them a competitive advantage as they enter the workplace. The undergraduate experience is enhanced by the diverse and international campus community and the extensive opportunities for studying abroad. UMass Lowell offers a robust honors program for those students who want to take academics to the next level, and the Centers for Learning, which offer a range of tutoring and other programs designed to help students succeed. The University maintains a student-faculty ratio of 14:1.

The University campus covers 100 acres on both sides of the Merrimack River and includes classroom and laboratory buildings, two libraries, a student center, two gymnasiums, three dining halls, a Center for the Performing Arts, two art galleries, and numerous residence halls. A campus recreation center provides additional social and recreational facilities. State-of-the-art laboratories include such special interest facilities as the six Sound Recording Technology Program studios, an interactive video lab that enables nursing students to simulate medical emergencies, and a manufacturing lab where engineering and management students team up to produce microelectronic components.

UMass Lowell's 6,000 undergraduate students are ethnically, culturally, and economically diverse. Students are active in a wide variety of community service activities, including athletics-based programs for local high school students; the Adaptive Technology Program, in which students create modified devices for the disabled; and community-based initiatives linked to academic programs. There are more than 100 campus organizations to choose from: academic, recreational, and special interest groups; the women's center; marching band; the student newspaper; an FM radio station; and the Off-Broadway Players. A vibrant campus life includes rallying for the nationally ranked Division I River Hawks hockey team and taking part in an active recreational sports program. In conjunction with the five colleges, the Graduate School enrolls nearly 3,000 students in thirty-two master's degree and fifteen doctoral programs.

Location

The University is located in Lowell, a city of 110,000 that has gained national attention by successfully leveraging its history, ethnic diversity, and entrepreneurial spirit to create a vital urban center. The site of a National Historical Park that honors the city as the birthplace of the industrial revolution, Lowell is also home to an acclaimed professional theater company, annual Kerouac and folk festivals, and museums that include the Museum of American Textile History and the Whistler House Museum. Located 25 miles from the cultural and educational riches of Boston and Cambridge, Lowell is also within an hour of ocean beaches and the lakes and mountains of New Hampshire via major highways and regional train and bus service.

Majors and Degrees

The College of Arts and Sciences offers baccalaureate programs in American studies, art, biological sciences, chemistry with an option in forensics science, computer science, criminal justice, design, economics, English, environmental studies, history, liberal arts, mathematics, modern languages, music business, music performance, music studies, philosophy, physics, political science, psychology, sociology, and sound recording technology. Dual majors are permitted. Dual B.A./B.S. and an array of bachelor's to master's degree programs are available in liberal arts, science, and engineering fields. Predental and premedical programs are available.

The James B. Francis College of Engineering offers baccalaureate day programs in chemical, civil and environmental, electrical and computer, mechanical, and plastics engineering. Engineering programs are accredited by the Accreditation Board for Engineering and Technology, Inc. (ABET). Combined bachelor's/master's programs, internships, and co-op opportunities are available in the College of Engineering.

The School of Health and Environment offers baccalaureate day programs in clinical laboratory sciences, which is accredited by the National Accrediting Agency for Clinical Laboratory Sciences (NAACLS); health education; exercise physiology; medical technology; nursing, which is accredited by the National League for Nursing Accrediting Commission (NLNAC); and nutritional science.

The College of Management offers baccalaureate day programs, all of which are accredited by AACSB International–The Association to Advance Collegiate Schools of Business, in business administration (B.S.B.A.), with concentrations in accounting, entrepreneurship, finance, management, management information systems, and marketing.

The University's Graduate School of Education offers widely respected master's and doctoral programs, as well as a range of Plus 1 initial certification courses.

The University's Division of Continuing Studies and Corporate Education offers evening programs through all six colleges. Through the College of Arts and Sciences, baccalaureate programs in applied mathematics, criminal justice, information technology, and liberal arts are offered. Through the College of Engineering, associate and baccalaureate degrees are offered in civil engineering technology, electronic engineering technology,

and mechanical engineering technology. Through the College of Management, an associate degree program in accounting and a baccalaureate degree program in business administration are available. Certificate programs are offered in accounting, computer-assisted manufacturing, computer engineering technology, data/telecommunications, electrooptics, environmental technology, graphic design and digital imagery, hazardous-waste management, Internet technology, land surveying, manufacturing technology, multimedia applications, nutrition, paralegal studies, plastics engineering technology, quality assurance, Spanish, technical writing, UNIX, wastewater treatment, water treatment, and Web site design and development.

Academic Programs

The University operates on a calendar of two semesters, a three-week intersession in January, and a summer term (with two sessions). Full-time undergraduates generally take five courses each semester. A minimum of 120 credits is required for baccalaureate degrees; the minimum credits required for professional degree programs are generally higher. A University general education requirement is imposed for all baccalaureate programs. Majors require 30–60 credits. Elective course options vary widely according to the degree program and major area. Professional degree program options and requirements follow specific accreditation guidelines. Maximum curricular freedom is permitted in B.A. programs. The academic climate is serious and competitive and requires self-motivation.

Academic Facilities

The University has two comprehensive libraries with online capabilities that can be accessed from anywhere a student can log on. Most of the campus, including outside spaces, has wireless access. The University offers an opt-in emergency notification system and a Web self-service system for registration, bill payment, and checking grades.

Costs

The annual costs for 2008–09 for full-time undergraduate residents of Massachusetts were $9181 per year; for nonresidents of Massachusetts, they were $21,201 per year. Residence hall charges were $4742 per year. A full meal plan was $2617 per year. Accident insurance is covered by fees; major medical insurance is optional. Books and supplies are estimated at $400 to $600, depending on the program. Quoted rates are subject to change.

Financial Aid

The University is committed to making higher education accessible to all qualified students. The University participates in federal and state programs, assisting students through grants-in-aid, loans, employment opportunities, and scholarships. The amount of an award is determined by need, as indicated by the Free Application for Federal Student Aid (FAFSA), which should be filed by March 1. The University awards a growing number of merit-based scholarships. In fiscal 2008, the campus awarded $60 million in financial aid and made offers to meet an average of 93 percent of each student's need.

Faculty

Faculty members are respected researchers who value their commitment to teaching and extend the learning experience beyond the classroom. The full-time resident faculty members number 406. The part-time day faculty members number 279. In addition, 175 part-time faculty members are employed in continuing education programs. Most faculty members teach and conduct research in their disciplines. Graduate teaching assistants also hold part-time instructional positions, particularly as discussion section leaders and laboratory teaching assistants.

Student Government

The Student Government Association and the Residence Hall Association provide opportunities in student government at the all-campus level. Leadership opportunities are provided in residence halls and student organizations. Students also participate in the disciplinary system and in most University committees.

Admission Requirements

All undergraduate day applicants must have a high school diploma or a general equivalency diploma and satisfactory SAT scores. The incoming freshmen class for fall 2008 had an average GPA of 3.2 and the average SAT score was 1085. Students whose high school average is below the required minimum may be considered for admission if they present SAT verbal and mathematics scores that are higher than those specified for the admission of degree candidates by the college or program to which they wish to apply.

Transfer students are considered for fall- or spring-semester admissions. Transcripts of completed work must be on file prior to acceptance. Depending on the number of transfer credits and college GPA, transfer students who seek admission as matriculating day students may be asked to provide a high school record and SAT scores.

Application and Information

For day programs, the University practices rolling admissions, which means that applications are evaluated as soon as they are complete. Entering freshmen are admitted for the fall or spring semester. The preferred deadline for freshman applications is February 15 for the fall semester and December 1 for the spring semester. The preferred deadline for transfer applications is August 15 for the fall semester and January 7 for the spring semester.

For application forms and further information, students should contact:

Office of Undergraduate Admissions
University of Massachusetts Lowell
883 Broadway Street
Suite 110
Lowell, Massachusetts 01854-5104
Phone: 978-934-3931
Web site: http://www.uml.edu

The main administration building makes a convenient gathering spot between classes.

WENTWORTH INSTITUTE OF TECHNOLOGY

BOSTON, MASSACHUSETTS

The Institute

Wentworth Institute of Technology was founded in 1904 to provide education in the mechanical arts. Today, it is one of the nation's leading technical institutes, offering study in a variety of disciplines. Wentworth has a current undergraduate day enrollment of approximately 3,500 men and women (3,000 full-time) and graduates more engineering technicians and technologists each year than any other college in the United States. The technical education acquired at Wentworth enables graduates to assume creative and responsible careers in business and industry. Wentworth is located on a 35-acre campus on Huntington Avenue in Boston.

Wentworth provides dormitory and suite-style residence halls on campus for men and women. Students residing in the residence halls are on a full meal plan. Upperclass students have the option of living in on-campus apartments. Students residing in the apartments may prepare their own meals. A cafeteria, snack bar, and convenience store are available for those wishing to purchase their meals.

Career counseling and placement assistance are available to all alumni and to students who have completed at least one semester of study at the Institute. While many graduates of Wentworth are employed in the Boston area, alumni have secured positions throughout the United States and abroad.

Location

Boston is the educational center of New England. It is a city of charm, tradition, and elegance—a major center of art, science, music, history, medicine, and education. Wentworth is situated near the heart of Boston and is surrounded by institutions that provide the cultural advantages for which the city is famous. The Museum of Fine Arts, with its store of art treasures, is diagonally across the street, and admission is free to any student with a Wentworth ID card. Symphony Hall is just a few blocks away. The Harvard Medical School, the New England Conservatory of Music, Emmanuel College, Simmons College, Massachusetts College of Pharmacy and Allied Health Sciences, Massachusetts College of Art and Design, Roxbury Community College, and Northeastern University are among the many educational institutions within a few blocks of the campus.

Majors and Degrees

Wentworth Institute of Technology is a technical college of great diversity. Degree programs are offered in the fields of architecture, biomedical engineering technology (beginning in fall 2010), computer science, construction management, design, engineering, engineering technology, and management. Specifically, bachelor's degrees are awarded in the following majors: the Bachelor of Architecture and the Bachelor of Science in civil engineering technology, computer engineering technology, computer network and information systems, computer science, construction management, electromechanical engineering (optional concentration in biomedical systems engineering), electronic engineering technology, facilities planning and management, industrial design, interior design, management (optional concentrations in communication, project leadership, and technology management), and mechanical engineering technology. Baccalaureate degrees in architecture and interior design are designated as first professional degrees. Completion of a Wentworth baccalaureate degree requires four or five years, depending on the program.

Academic Programs

At Wentworth Institute of Technology, college-level study in technological fundamentals and principles is combined with appropriate laboratory, field, and studio experience. Students apply theory to practical problems, and they acquire skills and techniques by using, operating, and controlling equipment and instruments that are particular to their area of specialization. In addition, study in the social sciences and humanities provides a balanced understanding of the world in which graduates work. Wentworth's programs of study are more practical than theoretical in approach, and the Institute's academic requirements demand extensive time and effort.

During the first two years of study in a degree program at Wentworth, students lay the foundation for more advanced study in the third and fourth (and fifth, where applicable) years. While nearly all majors allow continuous study from the freshman through the senior year, the architecture major requires a petition for acceptance to the baccalaureate program during the sophomore year.

All bachelor's degree programs are conducted as cooperative (co-op) education programs: upon entering their third year, students alternate semesters of academic study at Wentworth with semester-long periods of employment in industry. Two semesters of co-op employment are required; one additional (summer) semester of co-op is optional. Both students and the companies that hire them are enthusiastic about the co-op program and agree that it is a mutually valuable experience.

Academic Facilities

Wentworth's twenty-seven buildings house classrooms, laboratories, studios, administrative offices, and other facilities. Beatty Hall houses the Alumni Library, computer center, classrooms, dining areas, and office space. State-of-the-art laboratories, such as the Richard H. Lufkin Technology Center and the Davis Center for Advanced Graphics and Interactive Learning, are situated throughout the campus.

Costs

For 2009–10, tuition is $21,800, books and supplies are approximately $1000, and room and board are about $10,500 (this figure varies according to accommodation). Tuition includes a brand new laptop that is outfitted with the complete suite of software used in the student's academic program.

Financial Aid

Scholarships are available to students who demonstrate need and academic promise. Merit-based scholarships are also available. Wentworth also provides federal and state financial assistance, such as Federal Pell and Federal Supplemental Educational Opportunity Grants, Federal Perkins Loans, Federal Work-Study Program awards, Gilbert Matching Grants, and Massachusetts No-Interest Loans, to students with financial need in accordance with federal and state guidelines.

Wentworth participates in the Federal Direct Lending program. As a result, students are eligible to borrow under the Federal

Direct Stafford Student Loan program and parents may borrow under the Federal Direct PLUS program. Individuals participating in these programs borrow money directly from the federal government rather than through lending institutions.

In addition to these need-based programs, Wentworth also participates in the MEFA loan program sponsored by the Massachusetts Educational Financing Authority. Wentworth offers several payment options through payment plans and alternative loan financing.

To apply for financial aid, new students should complete the Free Application for Federal Student Aid (FAFSA) by March 1. Applications received after this date are considered as funds allow.

Faculty

Wentworth's faculty includes 146 full-time and 123 part-time members. The primary responsibility of every faculty member is teaching. Although professors may engage in some research and related work, student development remains the central mission of Wentworth's faculty. Upon entering Wentworth, every student is assigned a faculty adviser.

Student Government

Wentworth's Student Government performs an essential function as the official representative of the student body. Its purposes are to receive and express student opinion, to advance the best interests of the student body with the administration and faculty and with other institutions and associations, to support all extracurricular activities of the student body, and to serve as a bond between the student body and the faculty to foster mutual cooperation and understanding. The Student Government is made up of elected representatives from each class section and the officers elected by the student body at large. The Student Government sponsors social functions and student organizations and serves as an advocate for student concerns.

Admission Requirements

Applicants must be graduates of secondary schools (or have passed the GED test) and must meet specific entrance requirements. All programs require four years of English, a laboratory science, and mathematics through algebra II in a college-preparatory program. Both the electromechanical engineering and the computer science programs require a background in precalculus or trigonometry. All programs require the submission of SAT or ACT scores. International students and transfers are welcome.

Application and Information

Students are admitted to Wentworth for September and January enrollment. Notification of admission is made on a rolling basis. The preferred method for applying is online at http://www.wit.edu/apply. The online application fee is $10. An application form, the application fee, transcripts from the secondary school and any colleges previously attended, SAT or ACT scores, a personal statement, and a letter of recommendation should be sent to:

Admissions Office
Wentworth Institute of Technology
550 Huntington Avenue
Boston, Massachusetts 02115
Phone: 617-989-4000
      800-556-0610 (toll-free)
Fax: 617-989-4010
E-mail: admissions@wit.edu
Web site: http://www.wit.edu

Wentworth Hall.

WESTERN NEW ENGLAND COLLEGE
SPRINGFIELD, MASSACHUSETTS

The College

Western New England College, which was founded in 1919, is a private, independent coeducational institution offering more than thirty undergraduate majors at the baccalaureate level in the Schools of Arts and Sciences, Business, and Engineering. Beginning in fall 2009, Western New England College will admit the first class in the pre-pharmacy program. Students who graduate from this six-year professional program will earn a Doctor of Pharmacy (Pharm.D.) degree. The College offers a unique combined Bachelor of Arts/Juris Doctor program, a six-year biomedical engineering/law program, a five-year bachelor's/M.B.A. or M.S.A. program, and seven graduate degrees. The American Bar Association–accredited School of Law provides full- and part-time programs leading to a Juris Doctor degree and a Master of Law degree. Western New England College also serves part-time working professionals through its continuing education programs offered in Springfield and at six sites throughout the commonwealth.

In its annual "America's Best Colleges" rankings, *U.S. News & World Report* lists Western New England College in the top tier of its North category among colleges and universities that provide a full range of undergraduate and master's degree programs. In addition, Western New England College is featured in *Colleges of Distinction*, a new college guide and Web site profiling some of America's best bets in higher education. Based on the opinions of guidance counselors, educators, and admissions professionals, *Colleges of Distinction* honors colleges that excel in key areas of educational quality.

Western New England College began as a satellite campus of Northeastern University in rented rooms located in the downtown Springfield YMCA. Its mission was to provide a college education for working people who could not afford the time to attend college classes full-time during the day. The high-quality instruction gave "The Springfield Division," as the College was known, a growing reputation, and by 1951, when Northeastern elected to end its satellite program, there was a demand for the institution to continue. That year, Western New England College was incorporated by the Massachusetts Board of Collegiate Authority.

Western New England College is known for providing strong professionally based programs with a solid liberal arts background to prepare students for entry into professional careers or graduate school. There are approximately 2,500 full-time undergraduates, whereas the total enrollment, including part-time undergraduate, graduate, and law students, is about 4,000. Approximately 61 percent of the full-time undergraduates are men, and about 79 percent of the students live on campus. The College annually enrolls students from about thirty-one states; 60 percent come from out of state.

The College has developed a unique holistic Student Development Program that provides a comprehensive educational experience to the student inside and outside of the classroom. In addition to the academic component, other aspects of Learning Beyond the Classroom include personal and social development, career planning, multicultural awareness, physical fitness and health, and artistic and cultural appreciation. The Campus Activities Board is primarily responsible for coordinating a student activities calendar. The Western New England College CareerCenter is staffed with professional career counselors who provide students with the tools they need to obtain internships and succeed professionally—from mock, taped interviews to challenging employment opportunities. The College currently offers students nineteen varsity sports (NCAA Division III) in which to become involved. Men's sports include baseball, basketball, cross-country, football, golf, ice hockey, lacrosse, soccer, tennis, and wrestling. Women's sports include basketball, cross-country, field hockey, lacrosse, soccer, softball, swimming, tennis, and volleyball. Non-NCAA participation sports include men's and women's bowling and martial arts.

The College is accredited by the New England Association of Schools and Colleges; the School of Business is fully accredited by AACSB International; the engineering majors are accredited by the Accreditation Board for Engineering and Technology, Inc. (ABET); the social work major is accredited by the Council on Social Work Education (CSWE); and the School of Law is accredited by the American Bar Association (ABA). Various programs have additional accreditation from specific agencies.

Location

Western New England College's 215-acre campus was developed in a residential section of Springfield, Massachusetts. It is located about 4 miles from downtown Springfield, which is serviced by Greyhound and Peter Pan bus lines, Amtrak, and Bradley International Airport in Windsor Locks, Connecticut. Hartford is just 30 minutes away; Albany, Boston, and Providence are less than 100 miles from the campus; and New York City is a 3-hour drive.

Majors and Degrees

Undergraduate programs offered by the School of Arts and Sciences are majors in biology (concentrations in general and molecular), chemistry, communication (interpersonal and mass media concentrations), computer science, creative writing, criminal justice, economics, education (elementary and secondary), English, forensic biology, forensic chemistry, history, information technology, international studies, law and society, mathematical sciences, philosophy, political science, psychology, social work, and sociology. The pre-pharmacy program will begin in fall 2009.

The School of Business offers degrees in accounting, business information systems, finance, general business, management, marketing, marketing communication/advertising, and sport management.

The School of Engineering offers majors in biomedical engineering, electrical engineering (concentrations in computer and electrical), industrial engineering, and mechanical engineering (concentrations in mechanical and manufacturing).

Specialized programs include secondary teacher certification (biology, business, chemistry, English, history, mathematics, and political science), elementary education certification (English, history, and psychology), and premed and pre-law programs. The College's 3+3 Law Program offers eligible students the opportunity to earn their bachelor's and Juris Doctor degrees from Western New England College School of Law in just six years instead of seven. Western New England College also offers a six-year biomedical engineering/law program. In addition, eligible students may participate in the five-year bachelor's/M.B.A. or M.S.A. programs.

Academic Programs

The College operates on a two-semester calendar and has a limited summer program. Students normally take five courses each semester. Specific information on the various academic programs is available from the Office of Admissions.

Western New England College participates in the College Board's Advanced Placement (AP) Program, College-Level Examination Program (CLEP), and International Baccalaureate (I.B.). Successful completion of these programs may result in the earning of academic credit and the waiving of certain courses.

Profiles and Close-Ups of Other Colleges to Consider

California

UNIVERSITY OF SAN FRANCISCO
San Francisco, California

University of San Francisco is a coed, private, Roman Catholic (Jesuit) university, founded in 1855, offering degrees at the bachelor's, master's, doctoral, and first professional levels and post-master's certificates. It has a 55-acre campus in San Francisco.

Academic Information The faculty has 891 members (43% full-time). The undergraduate student-faculty ratio is 13:1. The library holds 1 million titles and 5,560 serial subscriptions. Special programs include academic remediation, services for learning-disabled students, an honors program, cooperative (work-study) education, study abroad, advanced placement credit, ESL programs, double majors, independent study, distance learning, self-designed majors, summer session for credit, part-time degree programs (daytime, evenings, weekends, summer), external degree programs, adult/continuing education programs, internships, and arrangement for off-campus study with American University, Jackson State University. The most frequently chosen baccalaureate fields are business/marketing, health professions and related sciences, public administration and social services.
Student Body Statistics The student body totals 8,750, of whom 5,459 are undergraduates (1,042 freshmen). 62 percent are women and 38 percent are men. Students come from 49 states and territories and 62 other countries. 76 percent are from California. 8.7 percent are international students.
Expenses for 2009–10 *Application fee:* $55. *Comprehensive fee:* $46,310 includes full-time tuition ($34,430), mandatory fees ($340), and college room and board ($11,540). *College room only:* $7730. *Part-time tuition:* $1225 per credit hour. *Part-time mandatory fees:* $340 per year.
Financial Aid Forms of aid include need-based and non-need-based scholarships, athletic grants, and part-time jobs. The average aided 2007–08 undergraduate received an aid package worth $23,076. The priority application deadline for financial aid is February 1.
Freshman Admission University of San Francisco requires an essay, a high school transcript, a minimum 2.8 high school GPA, 1 recommendation, SAT or ACT scores, and TOEFL scores for international students. A minimum 3.0 high school GPA is recommended. An interview is required for some. The application deadline for regular admission is February 1 and for early action it is November 15.
Transfer Admission The application deadline for admission is rolling.
Entrance Difficulty University of San Francisco assesses its entrance difficulty level as moderately difficult. For the fall 2008 freshman class, 64 percent of the applicants were accepted.
For Further Information Contact Mr. Michael Hughes, Director, University of San Francisco, 2130 Fulton Street, San Francisco, CA 94117-1080. *Phone:* 415-422-6563 or 800-CALLUSF (toll-free out-of-state). *Fax:* 415-422-2217. *E-mail:* admissions@usfca.edu. *Web site:* http://www.usfca.edu/.

See page 164 for the Close-Up.

Florida

BARRY UNIVERSITY
Miami Shores, Florida

Barry University is a coed, private, Roman Catholic university, founded in 1940, offering degrees at the bachelor's, master's, doctoral, and first professional levels and postbachelor's certificates. It has a 122-acre campus in Miami Shores near Miami.

Academic Information The faculty has 636 members (51% full-time). The undergraduate student-faculty ratio is 14:1. The library holds 233,938 titles and 2,880 serial subscriptions. Special programs include academic remediation, services for learning-disabled students, an honors program, study abroad, advanced placement credit, accelerated degree programs, ESL programs, double majors, independent study, distance learning, summer session for credit, part-time degree programs (daytime, evenings, weekends, summer), adult/continuing education programs, internships, and arrangement for off-campus study with St. Thomas Aquinas College, Dominican College of San Rafael. The most frequently chosen baccalaureate fields are business/marketing, education, liberal arts/general studies.
Student Body Statistics The student body totals 8,581, of whom 5,050 are undergraduates (586 freshmen). 68 percent are women and 32 percent are men. Students come from 35 states and territories and 29 other countries. 85 percent are from Florida. 5.1 percent are international students.
Expenses for 2008–09 *Application fee:* $30. *Comprehensive fee:* $34,100 includes full-time tuition ($25,500) and college room and board ($8600). Full-time tuition varies according to program. Room and board charges vary according to board plan. *Part-time tuition:* $765 per credit. Part-time tuition varies according to course load.
Financial Aid Forms of aid include need-based scholarships and athletic grants. The application deadline for financial aid is continuous.
Freshman Admission Barry University requires a high school transcript, a minimum 2.0 high school GPA, SAT or ACT scores, and TOEFL scores for international students. An interview is recommended. An essay is required for some. The application deadline for regular admission is rolling.
Transfer Admission The application deadline for admission is rolling.
Entrance Difficulty Barry University assesses its entrance difficulty level as moderately difficult. For the fall 2008 freshman class, 62 percent of the applicants were accepted.
For Further Information Contact Ms. Magda Castineyra, Director of Undergraduate Admissions, Barry University, Kelly House, 11300 Northeast Second Avenue, Miami Shores, FL 33161. *Phone:* 305-899-3100 or 800-695-2279 (toll-free). *Fax:* 305-899-2971. *E-mail:* admissions@mail.barry.edu. *Web site:* http://www.barry.edu/.

See page 140 for the Close-Up.

New York

CLARKSON UNIVERSITY
Potsdam, New York

Clarkson University is a coed, private university, founded in 1896, offering degrees at the bachelor's, master's, doctoral, and first professional levels. It has a 640-acre campus in Potsdam.

Academic Information The faculty has 217 members (86% full-time), 84% with terminal degrees. The undergraduate student-faculty ratio is 15.3:1. The library holds 309,235 titles, 3,396 serial subscriptions, and 2,095 audiovisual materials. Special programs include services for learning-disabled students, an honors program, cooperative (work-study) education, study abroad, advanced placement credit, accelerated degree programs, ESL programs, double majors, independent study, self-designed majors, summer session for credit, part-time degree programs (daytime, summer), internships, and arrangement for off-campus study with Associated Colleges of the St. Lawrence Valley. The most frequently chosen baccalaureate fields are business/marketing, biological/life sciences, engineering.
Student Body Statistics The student body totals 3,045, of whom 2,593 are undergraduates (735 freshmen). 27 percent are women and 73 percent are men. Students come from 42 states and territories and 25 other countries. 81 percent are from New York. 3.6 percent are international students.

Clarkson University (continued)

Expenses for 2009–10 *Application fee:* $50. *Comprehensive fee:* $44,028 includes full-time tuition ($32,220), mandatory fees ($690), and college room and board ($11,118). *College room only:* $5890. *Part-time tuition:* $1074 per credit.

Financial Aid Forms of aid include need-based and non-need-based scholarships, athletic grants, and part-time jobs. The average aided 2007–08 undergraduate received an aid package worth $23,189. The priority application deadline for financial aid is February 15.

Freshman Admission Clarkson University requires a high school transcript, 2 recommendations, SAT or ACT scores, and TOEFL scores for international students. An interview and SAT Subject Test scores are recommended. The application deadline for regular admission is January 15 and for early decision it is December 1.

Entrance Difficulty Clarkson University assesses its entrance difficulty level as very difficult. For the fall 2008 freshman class, 79 percent of the applicants were accepted.

SPECIAL MESSAGE TO STUDENTS

Social Life Clarkson's 640-acre wooded campus, more than eighty active clubs and organizations, and major cultural and educational events afford enormous extracurricular opportunities for students. The 6-million-acre Adirondack Park is only minutes away, and within 2 hours of campus are Lake Placid and the cosmopolitan Canadian cities of Montreal and Ottawa.

Academic Highlights Academics at Clarkson emphasize rigorous professional preparation; dynamic, real-world learning; flexibility and adaptability; and teamwork that spans disciplines. Clarkson's award-winning programs in engineering, arts, sciences, business, and health sciences also develop communication and collaboration skills, with a focus on practical application of knowledge and creative, open-ended problem solving. Undergraduates customize programs through specialized concentrations and minors that broaden career options. Clarkson's relatively small size encourages personal attention and interactions between students and faculty members, and Clarkson students enjoy extraordinary opportunities to pursue faculty-mentored research. They gain professional experience through internships and co-ops with corporations and government organizations and can broaden their perspectives through a wide range of study-abroad opportunities. The University offers an honors program and an accelerated three-year bachelor's degree.

Interviews and Campus Visits Clarkson strongly recommends that students visit the campus for a tour and a meeting with representatives. Students who visit the campus for an interview with an admission counselor receive a fee-waived voucher for a Clarkson application. Clarkson is located in the friendly community of Potsdam, between the beautiful Adirondack Mountains and the St. Lawrence River. The scenic, open campus features several new buildings, including a state-of-the-art building for business and liberal arts, which features fully networked classrooms and collaborative centers with wireless network access and videoconferencing capabilities and state-of-the-art laboratories, and the centrally located Cheel Student Center, which is a combination student union and multipurpose arena facility. In 2008, the 16,000-square-foot Technology Advancement Center was opened to provide critical laboratory and collaboration space for accelerating the development of research, especially in the fields of renewable energy and clean manufacturing technology. For information about appointments and campus visits, prospective students should call the Office of Undergraduate Admission at 315-268-6480 or 800-527-6577 (toll-free), Monday through Friday 8 to 4:30 or Saturday by appointment. The office is located in Holcroft House on the campus.

For Further Information Write to Mr. Brian Grant, Director of Admission, Clarkson University, P.O. Box 5605, Potsdam, NY 13699-5605. *E-mail:* admission@clarkson.edu. *Web site:* http://www.clarkson.edu.

See page 142 for the Close-Up.

CONCORDIA COLLEGE–NEW YORK
Bronxville, New York

Concordia College–New York is a coed, private, Lutheran, four-year college of Concordia University System, founded in 1881, offering degrees at the associate and bachelor's levels. It has a 33-acre campus in Bronxville near New York City.

Expenses for 2008–09 *Application fee:* $50. *Comprehensive fee:* $32,175 includes full-time tuition ($22,930), mandatory fees ($500), and college room and board ($8745). *College room only:* $4900. Room and board charges vary according to board plan. *Part-time tuition:* varies with course load.

For Further Information Contact Ms. Donna J. Hoyt, Dean of Enrollment, Concordia College–New York, 171 White Plains Road, Bronxville, NY 10708-1998. *Phone:* 914-337-9300 Ext. 2149 or 800-YES-COLLEGE (toll-free). *Fax:* 914-395-4636. *E-mail:* admission@concordia-ny.edu. *Web site:* http://www.concordia-ny.edu/.

See page 144 for the Close-Up.

EUGENE LANG COLLEGE THE NEW SCHOOL FOR LIBERAL ARTS
New York, New York

Eugene Lang College The New School for Liberal Arts is a coed, private, four-year college of The New School, founded in 1978, offering degrees at the bachelor's level. It has a 5-acre campus in New York.

Academic Information The faculty has 143 members (50% full-time), 36% with terminal degrees. The student-faculty ratio is 14:1. The library holds 2 million titles, 42,051 serial subscriptions, and 15,235 audiovisual materials. Special programs include study abroad, advanced placement credit, accelerated degree programs, ESL programs, double majors, independent study, distance learning, self-designed majors, summer session for credit, part-time degree programs, internships, and arrangement for off-campus study with Cooper Union for the Advancement of Science and Art, Bank Street College of Education, Sarah Lawrence College. The most frequently chosen baccalaureate field is liberal arts/general studies.

Student Body Statistics The student body is made up of 1,347 undergraduates (301 freshmen). 68 percent are women and 32 percent are men. Students come from 50 states and territories and 30 other countries. 29 percent are from New York. 4.1 percent are international students.

Expenses for 2008–09 *Application fee:* $50. *Comprehensive fee:* $48,320 includes full-time tuition ($32,350), mandatory fees ($710), and college room and board ($15,260). *College room only:* $12,260. Room and board charges vary according to board plan and housing facility. *Part-time tuition:* $1100 per credit.

Financial Aid Forms of aid include need-based and non-need-based scholarships and part-time jobs. The average aided 2008–09 undergraduate received an aid package worth an estimated $28,432. The application deadline for financial aid is continuous.

Freshman Admission Eugene Lang College The New School for Liberal Arts requires an essay, a high school transcript, 2 recommendations, an interview, SAT or ACT scores, and TOEFL scores for international students. A minimum 3.0 high school GPA is recommended. The application deadline for regular admission is February 1 and for early decision it is November 15.

Transfer Admission The application deadline for admission is May 15.

Entrance Difficulty Eugene Lang College The New School for Liberal Arts assesses its entrance difficulty level as very difficult. For the fall 2008 freshman class, 55 percent of the applicants were accepted.

For Further Information Contact Nicole Curvin, Director of Admissions, Eugene Lang College The New School for Liberal Arts, 65 West 11th Street, New York, NY 10011-8601. *Phone:* 212-229-5665 or 877-528-3321 (toll-free). *Fax:* 212-229-5355. *E-mail:* lang@newschool.edu. *Web site:* http://www.lang.edu/.

See page 146 for the Close-Up.

FORDHAM UNIVERSITY

New York, New York

Fordham University is a coed, private, Roman Catholic (Jesuit) university, founded in 1841, offering degrees at the bachelor's, master's, doctoral, and first professional levels and post-master's certificates (branch locations at Rose Hill and Lincoln Center). It has an 85-acre campus in New York.

Expenses for 2008–09 *Application fee:* $50. *Comprehensive fee:* $48,237 includes full-time tuition ($34,200), mandatory fees ($1057), and college room and board ($12,980). *College room only:* $8560. Full-time tuition and fees vary according to student level. Room and board charges vary according to board plan and location. *Part-time tuition:* $739 per credit hour. Part-time tuition varies according to course load.
For Further Information Contact Mr. Peter Farrell, Director of Admission, Fordham University, Duane Library, 441 East Fordham Road, New York, NY 10458. *Phone:* 718-817-4000 or 800-FORDHAM (toll-free). *Fax:* 718-367-9404. *E-mail:* enroll@fordham.edu. *Web site:* http://www.fordham.edu/.

See page 148 for the Close-Up.

HOFSTRA UNIVERSITY

Hempstead, New York

Hofstra University is a coed, private university, founded in 1935, offering degrees at the bachelor's, master's, doctoral, and first professional levels and post-master's and postbachelor's certificates. It has a 240-acre campus in Hempstead near New York City.

Academic Information The faculty has 1,185 members (46% full-time), 62% with terminal degrees. The undergraduate student-faculty ratio is 14:1. The library holds 1 million titles, 11,229 serial subscriptions, and 15,740 audiovisual materials. Special programs include services for learning-disabled students, an honors program, study abroad, advanced placement credit, accelerated degree programs, Freshman Honors College, ESL programs, double majors, independent study, distance learning, self-designed majors, summer session for credit, part-time degree programs (daytime, evenings, weekends, summer), external degree programs, and internships. The most frequently chosen baccalaureate fields are business/marketing, communications/journalism, psychology.
Student Body Statistics The student body totals 12,333, of whom 8,320 are undergraduates. 52 percent are women and 48 percent are men. Students come from 47 states and territories and 55 other countries. 65 percent are from New York. 1.4 percent are international students.
Expenses for 2008–09 *Application fee:* $70. *Comprehensive fee:* $39,455 includes full-time tuition ($27,600), mandatory fees ($1030), and college room and board ($10,825). *College room only:* $7225. Full-time tuition and fees vary according to course load and program. Room and board charges vary according to board plan and housing facility. *Part-time tuition:* $845 per term. *Part-time mandatory fees:* $155 per term. Part-time tuition and fees vary according to course load and program.
Financial Aid Forms of aid include need-based and non-need-based scholarships, athletic grants, and part-time jobs. The average aided 2008–09 undergraduate received an aid package worth an estimated $16,505.
Freshman Admission Hofstra University requires an essay, a high school transcript, a minimum 2.5 high school GPA, and TOEFL scores for international students. SAT Subject Test scores are recommended. An interview and SAT or ACT scores are required for some. The application deadline for regular admission is rolling and for early action it is December 15.
Entrance Difficulty Hofstra University assesses its entrance difficulty level as moderately difficult; very difficult for Honors College. For the fall 2008 freshman class, 53 percent of the applicants were accepted.
For Further Information Contact Mr. Sunil Samuel, Director of Admissions, Hofstra University, 100 Hofstra University, Hempstead, NY 11549. *Phone:* 516-463-6700 or 800-HOFSTRA (toll-free). *Fax:* 516-463-5100. *E-mail:* admission@hofstra.edu. *Web site:* http://www.hofstra.edu/.

See page 152 for the Close-Up.

SIENA COLLEGE

Loudonville, New York

Siena College is a coed, private, Roman Catholic, four-year college, founded in 1937, offering degrees at the bachelor's level. It has a 164-acre campus in Loudonville.

Expenses for 2008–09 *Application fee:* $50. *One-time mandatory fee:* $250. *Comprehensive fee:* $33,360 includes full-time tuition ($23,750), mandatory fees ($200), and college room and board ($9410). Room and board charges vary according to board plan and housing facility. *Part-time tuition:* $450 per credit hour. *Part-time mandatory fees:* $160 per term.

SPECIAL MESSAGE TO STUDENTS

Social Life Siena's students are active participants in campus life and the community. Siena fields eighteen Division I varsity men's and women's athletic teams, which are enthusiastically supported by the student body. More than 75 percent of Siena students participate in intramural or club athletics ranging from basketball to ice hockey. Siena's Franciscan Center for Service and Advocacy serves as the College's primary vehicle for service with the poor and marginalized of society. Siena students have the opportunity to get involved with the Stage Three Theater productions, work at the campus radio station, or become a member of student senate. Located only a few miles from Albany, the capital of New York, Siena students have access to many cultural and recreational opportunities. Siena is also close to skiing and hiking areas in Vermont, the Berkshires, and New York's Catskill and Adirondack mountains.

Academic Highlights More than 90 percent of Siena's faculty members hold the highest degree achievable in their field; they spend their time teaching and advising undergraduate students. Classes typically have 18–25 students, and students are able to develop meaningful relationships with faculty members, leading to lifelong mentors. Students follow a core liberal arts curriculum that allows them to develop the essential skills of analysis, synthesis, and communication. Siena offers a wealth of internship opportunities in state legislature and government, financial institutions, health-care, research, and communications fields. Study abroad is also popular. Students can pursue internship/study programs in Australia, England, France, Ireland, Italy, and Spain. Students interested in American government can participate in the Washington Semester, interning in the nation's capital and attending classes at American University. Siena offers strong programs for students considering medicine, law, and education as well as career counseling and assistance to all its students.

Interviews and Campus Visits A visit and an interview are strongly recommended. An interview at the Admissions Office provides students and their parents with an opportunity to ask questions about the college and admissions process. It also gives the admissions committee a chance to learn about an applicant in person. A tour with a Siena student ambassador includes visits to classrooms, the library, labs, the chapel, the athletic facility, the dining hall, and residence halls. Siena hosts many visitation programs throughout the year. For more information, prospective students should contact the Admissions Office at 518-783-2423 or 888-AT-SIENA (toll-free). For further information, students should visit http://www.siena.edu.

For Further Information Write to Admissions Office, Siena College, 515 Loudon Road, Loudonville, NY 12211.

See page 158 for the Close-Up.

UTICA COLLEGE
Utica, New York

Utica College is a coed, private, comprehensive institution, founded in 1946, offering degrees at the bachelor's, master's, and first professional levels and postbachelor's certificates. It has a 128-acre campus in Utica.

Academic Information The faculty has 322 members (39% full-time). The undergraduate student-faculty ratio is 11:1. The library holds 185,292 titles, 1,093 serial subscriptions, and 10,033 audiovisual materials. Special programs include academic remediation, services for learning-disabled students, an honors program, cooperative (work-study) education, study abroad, advanced placement credit, accelerated degree programs, double majors, independent study, distance learning, summer session for credit, part-time degree programs (daytime, evenings, weekends, summer), adult/continuing education programs, internships, and arrangement for off-campus study with members of the New York State Visiting Student Program. The most frequently chosen baccalaureate fields are business/marketing, health professions and related sciences, psychology.

Student Body Statistics The student body totals 3,101, of whom 2,502 are undergraduates (574 freshmen). 58 percent are women and 42 percent are men. Students come from 47 states and territories and 21 other countries. 83 percent are from New York. 2 percent are international students.

Expenses for 2008–09 *Application fee:* $40. *Comprehensive fee:* $36,488 includes full-time tuition ($25,538), mandatory fees ($520); and college room and board ($10,430). Full-time tuition and fees vary according to class time and course load. Room and board charges vary according to board plan and housing facility. *Part-time tuition:* $862 per hour. Part-time tuition varies according to class time and course load.

Financial Aid Forms of aid include need-based and non-need-based scholarships and part-time jobs. The average aided 2008–09 undergraduate received an aid package worth an estimated $19,490. The priority application deadline for financial aid is February 15.

Freshman Admission Utica College requires an essay, a high school transcript, a minimum 2.0 high school GPA, 1 recommendation, and TOEFL scores for international students. An interview is recommended. A minimum 3.0 high school GPA and SAT or ACT scores are required for some. The application deadline for regular admission is rolling.

Transfer Admission The application deadline for admission is rolling.

Entrance Difficulty Utica College assesses its entrance difficulty level as moderately difficult; very difficult for physical therapy, occupational therapy, joint health programs. For the fall 2008 freshman class, 74 percent of the applicants were accepted.

For Further Information Contact Mr. Patrick Quinn, Vice President for Enrollment Management, Utica College, 1600 Burrstone Road, Utica, NY 13502. *Phone:* 315-792-3006 or 800-782-8884 (toll-free). *Fax:* 315-792-3003. *E-mail:* admiss@utica.edu. *Web site:* http://www.utica.edu/.

See page 166 for the Close-Up.

Ohio

OHIO WESLEYAN UNIVERSITY
Delaware, Ohio

Ohio Wesleyan University is a coed, private, United Methodist, four-year college, founded in 1842, offering degrees at the bachelor's level. It has a 200-acre campus in Delaware near Columbus.

Academic Information The faculty has 204 members (66% full-time), 78% with terminal degrees. The student-faculty ratio is 12:1. The library holds 441,912 titles and 1,073 serial subscriptions. Special programs include services for learning-disabled students, an honors program, study abroad, advanced placement credit, Freshman Honors College, double majors, independent study, self-designed majors, summer session for credit, part-time degree programs (daytime, summer), internships, and arrangement for off-campus study with Great Lakes Colleges Association,

New York City Arts Program, Wesleyan in Washington, Philadelphia Center. The most frequently chosen baccalaureate fields are biological/life sciences, business/marketing, social sciences.

Student Body Statistics The student body is made up of 1,960 undergraduates (570 freshmen). 53 percent are women and 47 percent are men. Students come from 45 states and territories and 45 other countries. 55 percent are from Ohio. 9.2 percent are international students.

Expenses for 2008–09 *Application fee:* $35. *Comprehensive fee:* $41,970 includes full-time tuition ($33,240), mandatory fees ($460), and college room and board ($8270). *College room only:* $4120. Room and board charges vary according to board plan. *Part-time tuition:* $3620 per course.

Financial Aid Forms of aid include need-based scholarships and part-time jobs. The average aided 2008–09 undergraduate received an aid package worth an estimated $25,103. The application deadline for financial aid is May 1 with a priority deadline of March 1.

Freshman Admission Ohio Wesleyan University requires an essay, a high school transcript, a minimum 2.5 high school GPA, 1 recommendation, SAT or ACT scores, and TOEFL scores for international students. 2 recommendations and an interview are recommended. The application deadline for regular admission is March 1, for early decision it is December 1, and for early action it is December 15.

Transfer Admission The application deadline for admission is May 15.

Entrance Difficulty Ohio Wesleyan University assesses its entrance difficulty level as very difficult; most difficult for honors program. For the fall 2008 freshman class, 63 percent of the applicants were accepted.

For Further Information Contact Ms. Carol DelPropost, Assistant Vice President of Admission and Financial Aid, Ohio Wesleyan University, 61 South Sandusky Street, Delaware, OH 43015. *Phone:* 740-368-3059 or 800-922-8953 (toll-free). *Fax:* 740-368-3314. *E-mail:* cjdelpro@owu.edu. *Web site:* http://www.owu.edu/.

See page 156 for the Close-Up.

Pennsylvania

GROVE CITY COLLEGE
Grove City, Pennsylvania

Grove City College is a coed, private, Presbyterian, four-year college, founded in 1876, offering degrees at the bachelor's level. It has a 150-acre campus in Grove City near Pittsburgh.

Academic Information The faculty has 209 members (67% full-time), 61% with terminal degrees. The student-faculty ratio is 15:1. The library holds 135,093 titles, 300 serial subscriptions, and 2,754 audiovisual materials. Special programs include study abroad, advanced placement credit, double majors, independent study, self-designed majors, summer session for credit, and internships. The most frequently chosen baccalaureate fields are business/marketing, biological/life sciences, education.

Student Body Statistics The student body is made up of 2,499 undergraduates (621 freshmen). 50 percent are women and 50 percent are men. Students come from 44 states and territories and 8 other countries. 48 percent are from Pennsylvania. 0.6 percent are international students.

Expenses for 2008–09 *Application fee:* $50. *Comprehensive fee:* $18,514 includes full-time tuition ($12,074) and college room and board ($6440). Full-time tuition varies according to course load. Room and board charges vary according to housing facility. *Part-time tuition:* $380 per credit.

Financial Aid Forms of aid include need-based and non-need-based scholarships and part-time jobs. The average aided 2008–09 undergraduate received an aid package worth an estimated $6013. The application deadline for financial aid is April 15.

Freshman Admission Grove City College requires an essay, a high school transcript, 2 recommendations, SAT or ACT scores, and TOEFL scores for international students. An interview is recommended. The application deadline for regular admission is February 1 and for early decision it is November 15.

Transfer Admission The application deadline for admission is August 15.

Entrance Difficulty Grove City College assesses its entrance difficulty level as most difficult; moderately difficult for transfers. For the fall 2008 freshman class, 56 percent of the applicants were accepted.

For Further Information Contact Mr. Jeffrey Mincey, Director of Admissions, Grove City College, 100 Campus Drive, Grove City, PA 16127-2104. *Phone:* 724-458-2100. *Fax:* 724-458-3395. *E-mail:* admissions@gcc.edu. *Web site:* http://www.gcc.edu/.

See page 150 for the Close-Up.

MESSIAH COLLEGE
Grantham, Pennsylvania

Messiah College is a coed, private, interdenominational, four-year college, founded in 1909, offering degrees at the bachelor's level. It has a 485-acre campus in Grantham.

Academic Information The faculty has 287 members (60% full-time). The student-faculty ratio is 13:1. The library holds 259,252 titles, 27,936 serial subscriptions, and 19,071 audiovisual materials. Special programs include services for learning-disabled students, an honors program, study abroad, advanced placement credit, accelerated degree programs, Freshman Honors College, ESL programs, double majors, independent study, self-designed majors, summer session for credit, part-time degree programs (daytime), adult/continuing education programs, internships, and arrangement for off-campus study with Christian College Consortium, Council for Christian Colleges and Universities. The most frequently chosen baccalaureate fields are business/marketing, education, health professions and related sciences.

Student Body Statistics The student body is made up of 2,802 undergraduates (678 freshmen). 63 percent are women and 37 percent are men. Students come from 40 states and territories and 35 other countries. 57 percent are from Pennsylvania. 2.6 percent are international students.

Expenses for 2008–09 *Application fee:* $30. *Comprehensive fee:* $33,280 includes full-time tuition ($24,900), mandatory fees ($770), and college room and board ($7610). *College room only:* $4020. Room and board charges vary according to board plan, housing facility, and location. *Part-time tuition:* $1040 per credit.

Financial Aid Forms of aid include need-based and non-need-based scholarships and part-time jobs. The average aided 2008–09 undergraduate received an aid package worth an estimated $16,885.

Freshman Admission Messiah College requires an essay, a high school transcript, 1 recommendation, and TOEFL scores for international students. An interview and SAT or ACT scores are recommended. SAT or ACT scores are required for some. The application deadline for regular admission is rolling.

Entrance Difficulty Messiah College assesses its entrance difficulty level as moderately difficult. For the fall 2008 freshman class, 70 percent of the applicants were accepted.

For Further Information Contact Mr. John Chopka, Vice President for Enrollment Management, Messiah College, PO Box 3005, One College Avenue, Grantham, PA 17027. *Phone:* 717-691-6000 or 800-233-4220 (toll-free). *Fax:* 717-791-2307. *E-mail:* admiss@messiah.edu. *Web site:* http://www.messiah.edu/.

See page 154 for the Close-Up.

Texas

SOUTHERN METHODIST UNIVERSITY
Dallas, Texas

Southern Methodist University is a coed, private university, founded in 1911, affiliated with the United Methodist Church, offering degrees at the bachelor's, master's, doctoral, and first professional levels and postbachelor's certificates. It has a 210-acre campus in Dallas.

Academic Information The faculty has 1,034 members (63% full-time), 71% with terminal degrees. The undergraduate student-faculty ratio is 12:1. The library holds 3 million titles, 11,701 serial subscriptions, and 45,168 audiovisual materials. Special programs include academic remediation, services for learning-disabled students, an honors program, cooperative (work-study) education, study abroad, advanced placement credit, accelerated degree programs, ESL programs, double majors, independent study, distance learning, self-designed majors, summer session for credit, part-time degree programs, adult/continuing education programs, and internships. The most frequently chosen baccalaureate fields are business/marketing, communications/journalism, social sciences.

Student Body Statistics The student body totals 10,965, of whom 6,240 are undergraduates (1,398 freshmen). 54 percent are women and 46 percent are men. Students come from 50 states and territories and 65 other countries. 58 percent are from Texas. 5.6 percent are international students.

Expenses for 2009–10 *Application fee:* $60. *Comprehensive fee:* $47,605 includes full-time tuition ($31,200), mandatory fees ($3960), and college room and board ($12,445). *Part-time tuition:* $1304 per credit hour. *Part-time mandatory fees:* $166 per credit hour.

Financial Aid Forms of aid include need-based scholarships, athletic grants, and part-time jobs. The average aided 2007–08 undergraduate received an aid package worth $26,276. The priority application deadline for financial aid is March 1.

Freshman Admission Southern Methodist University requires an essay, a high school transcript, 1 recommendation, SAT or ACT scores, and TOEFL scores for international students. SAT Subject Test scores are required for some. The application deadline for regular admission is January 15 and for early action it is November 1.

Transfer Admission The application deadline for admission is July 1.

Entrance Difficulty Southern Methodist University assesses its entrance difficulty level as moderately difficult. For the fall 2008 freshman class, 50 percent of the applicants were accepted.

For Further Information Contact Mr. Ron Moss, Director of Admission and Enrollment Management, Southern Methodist University, PO Box 750181, Dallas, TX 75275-0181. *Phone:* 214-768-3417 or 800-323-0672 (toll-free). *Fax:* 214-768-0202. *E-mail:* enrol_serv@smu.edu. *Web site:* http://www.smu.edu/.

See page 160 for the Close-Up.

West Virginia

UNIVERSITY OF CHARLESTON
Charleston, West Virginia

University of Charleston is a coed, private, comprehensive institution, founded in 1888, offering degrees at the associate, bachelor's, master's, and doctoral levels. It has a 40-acre campus in Charleston.

Academic Information The faculty has 143 members (62% full-time), 41% with terminal degrees. The undergraduate student-faculty ratio is 13:1. The library holds 164,457 titles, 14,192 serial subscriptions, and 3,759 audiovisual materials. Special programs include academic remediation, services for learning-disabled students, study abroad, advanced placement credit, accelerated degree programs, ESL programs, double majors, independent study, distance learning, self-designed majors, summer session for credit, part-time degree programs (daytime, evenings, summer), adult/continuing education programs, and internships. The most frequently chosen baccalaureate fields are business/marketing, health professions and related sciences, visual and performing arts.

Student Body Statistics The student body totals 1,398, of whom 1,171 are undergraduates (328 freshmen). 60 percent are women and 40 percent are men. Students come from 35 states and territories and 17 other countries. 69 percent are from West Virginia. 9.2 percent are international students.

Expenses for 2008–09 *Application fee:* $25. *Comprehensive fee:* $31,475 includes full-time tuition ($23,150) and college room and board ($8325). *College room only:* $4550. Room and board charges vary according to board

University of Charleston (continued)

plan and housing facility. *Part-time tuition:* $400 per credit. *Part-time mandatory fees:* $75 per term. Part-time tuition and fees vary according to program.

Financial Aid Forms of aid include need-based and non-need-based scholarships, athletic grants, and part-time jobs. The average aided 2007–08 undergraduate received an aid package worth $20,030.

Freshman Admission University of Charleston requires a high school transcript, a minimum 2.25 high school GPA, SAT or ACT scores, and TOEFL scores for international students. An essay and 3 recommendations are recommended. An interview is required for some. The application deadline for regular admission is rolling.

Transfer Admission The application deadline for admission is rolling.

Entrance Difficulty University of Charleston assesses its entrance difficulty level as moderately difficult. For the fall 2008 freshman class, 67 percent of the applicants were accepted.

For Further Information Contact Mr. Brad Parrish, Vice President for Enrollment, University of Charleston, 2300 MacCorkle Avenue, SE, Charleston, WV 25304. *Phone:* 304-357-4750 or 800-995-GOUC (toll-free). *Fax:* 304-357-4781. *E-mail:* admissions@ucwv.edu. *Web site:* http://www.ucwv.edu/.

See page 162 for the Close-Up.

BARRY UNIVERSITY
MIAMI SHORES, FLORIDA

The University

Barry University is an independent Catholic university. Founded in 1940 by the Dominican Sisters of Adrian, Michigan, the University provides a multicultural student body with an affordable, high-quality education; a caring environment; and a religious dimension, which encourages a commitment to community service. Classes are small, so students receive personal attention from distinguished faculty members and advisers. The student-faculty ratio is 14:1.

The lush, tropical main campus with Spanish-style architecture is located in Miami Shores. The University also offers programs at more than twenty-five additional sites from Tallahassee to Key West. Students come from all compass points, age groups, ethnicities, and faiths, representing nearly all fifty states and eighty countries. Of the more than 8,500 students enrolled, more than 2,700 are full-time undergraduates and nearly 5,500 are graduate and continuing education students.

Barry offers more than sixty undergraduate majors and more than fifty graduate degree programs in the arts and sciences, business, education, health sciences, human performance and leisure sciences, law, podiatric medicine, and social work.

Barry holds membership in twenty honor societies and hosts more than sixty student organizations, including the dance club, gospel choir, the Campus Activities Board, and the *Buccaneer* student newspaper, as well as four fraternities and five sororities. Barry also promotes community service organizations including Best Buddies and Habitat for Humanity.

The University fields twelve intercollegiate athletic teams that participate in the NCAA Division II and the Sunshine State Conference. The Buccaneers have won seven national championships. Nearly 60 percent of Barry's student-athletes achieve grade point averages above 3.0. Intramural sports include basketball, flag football, soccer, softball, and table tennis.

Facilities include the David Brinkley Studio (a full-service digital television production facility), the Monsignor William Barry Library, an extensive library network, multimedia classrooms, and technologically advanced labs. Students gain hands-on professional experience even before graduation, such as helping to provide basic health care for elementary school children, researching marine life in the Caribbean Sea, or editing a local news program.

The 78,000-square-foot R. Kirk Landon Student Union houses the offices of student services and student organizations as well as a bookstore, dining room, snack bar, campus game room, and more. A fully equipped fitness center features weight and cardio equipment. Resident students live in eight air-conditioned residence halls where every room is wired for high-speed Internet access. All students may keep cars on campus. The University's Department of Commuter Affairs serves as a resource center for commuters.

The University is accredited by the Southern Association of Colleges and Schools to award bachelor's, master's, specialist, and doctoral degrees. Barry also holds a number of accreditations from professional organizations for specific programs.

Location

Barry University is in sunny, suburban Miami Shores, Florida, just 5 miles from the ocean and minutes from the dynamic city of Miami. South Florida is an international business, tourism, and entertainment hub with a cosmopolitan, multicultural population, offering a wide range of internship and career options and a vibrant cultural scene. Highlights include Urban Beach Week, the Calle Ocho street festival, the Miami International Book Fair, and the prestigious art fair, Art Basel Miami Beach. The New World Symphony, the Miami International Film Festival, and the Miami City Ballet provide a full season of acclaimed performances. South Florida also hosts the Miami Dolphins football team, the Miami Heat basketball team, the Florida Marlins baseball team, and the Florida Panthers hockey team. The hospitable climate allows for swimming, sailing, scuba diving, golf, tennis, soccer, and other outdoor activities year-round, and the natural beauty of the Florida Keys, Everglades, and coral reefs are just a day trip away.

Majors and Degrees

Barry University offers the Bachelor of Arts degree in advertising, art (art history, ceramics, graphic design, and painting and/or drawing), broadcast communication, communication studies, English (literature and professional writing), general studies, history, international studies, music, philosophy, photography (biomedical/forensic and creative), prelaw, public relations, Spanish (language and literature and translation and interpretation), theater (acting, dance, technical theater), and theology.

The Bachelor of Science degree is offered in accounting, athletic training (premedicine and pre–physical therapy specializations and a five-year seamless B.S. to M.S.), biology (general, marine, and preprofessional), cardiovascular perfusion, chemistry (biochemistry, environmental chemistry, predental, premedical, prepharmacy, and pre-veterinary), computer information sciences, computer science, criminology, elementary education, exercise science (premedical and pre–physical therapy specializations and a five-year seamless B.S. to M.S.), finance, information technology, international business, management, marketing, mathematical sciences (computational, general, and statistics/actuarial science), medical technology, physical education (grades K-12), political science, psychology (industrial/organizational), sociology, and sport management (diving industry, golf industry, and five-year seamless B.S. to M.S.). Business programs also offer five-year seamless bachelor's to master's tracks.

The University also offers the Bachelor of Science in Nursing, the Bachelor of Fine Arts (art and photography), the Bachelor of Music (instrumental performance; sacred music; and voice, opera, and musical theater), and the Bachelor of Social Work.

Minor concentrations are available in specific subject areas as well as in the interdisciplinary areas of Africana studies, film studies, peace studies, and women's studies.

Teaching certification is available for pre-K through primary education, elementary education, exceptional student education, and physical education. A certificate program in the translation and interpretation of Spanish is offered.

Accelerated undergraduate degree programs are offered for working adults through Barry's evening and weekend programs.

Academic Programs

The University operates on a semester plan. The first semester extends from the end of August to mid-December, and the second semester extends from mid-January to early May. Two 6-week sessions are offered during the summer. Students must maintain a minimum cumulative grade point average of 2.0 (or C) and earn a minimum of 120 credits for a degree. Of these 120 credits, 9 must be in philosophy and theology, 9 in communication—oral and written, 9 in humanities and arts, 9 in physical or natural sciences and mathematics, and 9 in social and behavioral sciences. The traditional full-time academic load is 12 to 18 credits each semester and 6 credits each summer term. Candidates for degree programs may elect either a major area of specialization

or a broad liberal arts program and must satisfy all requirements of the program that they choose to follow, including all professional preparation requirements. Exceptionally well-qualified seniors may earn up to 6 hours of graduate credit with the recommendation of the department chairperson and the dean. Internships are required for many majors.

An ELS Language Centers program is available to international students needing to increase language proficiency. The Center for Advanced Learning offers a program designed to assist students with learning disabilities who have the intellectual potential and motivation to complete a four-year degree.

The University also offers an active, interdisciplinary honors program designed to add breadth and depth to the educational experience.

Off-Campus Programs

Barry University offers summer programs abroad. In addition, Barry is a member of the College Consortium for International Studies, enabling students to participate in programs in twenty-five countries offered by member colleges and universities. Barry University students may enroll in Air Force ROTC courses through cross-registration at a nearby university.

Academic Facilities

Students find the high-quality resources they need to support their education at Barry. Campus facilities include the Monsignor William Barry Library, an extensive library network, photography and digital imaging labs, a human performance lab, an athletic training room, a biomechanics lab, a digital television production studio, an academic computing center, multimedia business classrooms, art studios, a performing arts center, a nursing lab, and a cell biology lab as well as several other well-equipped science labs.

Costs

For 2008–09, tuition for full-time undergraduate students for the academic year was $25,500. Student services fees are included in tuition. Room and board costs averaged $8250 (double room). Expenses such as books, supplies, laboratory or other special fees, and transportation are not included in these costs.

Financial Aid

Barry University offers an excellent scholarship and grant program, awarding scholarships each year to students who have demonstrated academic success and promise. These scholarships and grants may be renewed for up to four years as long as the students meet the renewal criteria. Barry need-based grants and athletic scholarships are also available.

Barry also participates in the Federal Pell and Federal Supplemental Educational Opportunity Grant programs, the Federal Perkins Loan Program, the Federal Work-Study Program, the Florida Resident Access Grant Program, the Florida Student Assistance Grant, Florida Bright Futures Scholarships, and the Federal Family Educational Loan Program. Barry awards financial assistance on the basis of financial need and academic excellence. Applicants must submit the Free Application for Federal Student Aid (FAFSA) in order to be considered for aid. Ninety percent of full-time undergraduate students receive assistance from the University. Additional information may be obtained by calling the Office of Financial Aid at 305-899-3673 or 800-495-2279 (toll-free) or by e-mail at finaid@mail.barry.edu.

Faculty

Faculty members are easily accessible to students and are committed to providing individualized attention. The undergraduate faculty members participate in a dynamic academic advisement program. Doctorates are held by 84 percent of full-time faculty members, and the student-faculty ratio is 14:1.

Student Government

The Student Government Association serves as a liaison between the student body and the administration and faculty. All undergraduate students are members of the association, which is governed by an Executive Board comprising 4 members and the Senate, which consists of 7 elected representatives. Six members are elected during the spring semester, and the remaining position (Freshman Senator) is filled early in the fall semester. Unless otherwise specified, meetings of the Senate are open, and students are invited and encouraged to attend the weekly sessions.

Admission Requirements

In reviewing the credentials of students seeking admission, Barry University considers an applicant's composite efforts. Candidates must present the following materials: the completed application form, official high school or college transcripts, and the results of the SAT or ACT.

Application and Information

The University reviews applications as they are completed. Students are advised of their acceptance once the admissions staff has reviewed all required documents. Students may apply any time after completion of the junior year in high school. It is advisable to apply early. The student's completed application form and supporting credentials should be sent to the Office of Admissions. Students may also apply online at http://www.barry.edu/apply.

Ms. Magda Castineyra
Director of Undergraduate Admissions
Kelley House
Barry University
11300 Northeast Second Avenue
Miami Shores, Florida 33161-6695
Phone: 305-899-3100
        800-695-2279 (toll-free)
Fax: 305-899-2971
E-mail: admissions@mail.barry.edu
Web site: http://www.barry.edu

Barry offers an outstanding environment for quiet reflection and study.

CLARKSON UNIVERSITY

POTSDAM, NEW YORK

The University

Founded in 1896, Clarkson stands out among America's private, nationally ranked research institutions because of its dynamic collaborative learning environment, innovative degree and research programs, and unmatched track record for producing leaders and innovators.

The University attracts 3,000 enterprising students from diverse backgrounds (including some 400 graduate students) who thrive in rigorous programs in engineering, arts, sciences, business, and health sciences and in the University's close-knit, residential learning/living community. Clarkson defies convention in the classroom, in its laboratories, and by the impact its graduates have in the world. The University is New York State's highest-ranked small research institution. However, size is Clarkson's advantage—fostering leadership and problem-solving skills and readily affording students and faculty members the flexibility to span the boundaries of traditional academic areas.

Clarkson students also enjoy extraordinary opportunities to pursue faculty-mentored research. They gain professional experience through internships and co-ops with corporations and government organizations and can broaden their perspectives through a wide range of study-abroad opportunities.

Top graduate schools welcome Clarkson graduates to study medicine, law, and other professions. Johns Hopkins, MIT, Princeton, Yale, Caltech, Rice, and Stanford are just some of the schools chosen by Clarkson students.

Clarkson's 98 percent placement rate is among the nation's highest, with the most recent starting salaries averaging more than $52,000. Clarkson is a key recruitment source for many of America's industry leaders, including General Electric, Alcoa, Xerox, Accenture, IBM, and Procter & Gamble. In fact, 1 in 6 Clarkson alumni is already a CEO, president, vice president, or company owner.

Clarkson's active campus also offers a wide variety of extracurricular activities, including more than eighty clubs and interest groups. Students publish a lively campus newspaper and run campus radio and television stations. Active professional and honor societies enrich the campus experience.

There are Division I men's and women's hockey teams, as well as, seventeen Division III intercollegiate athletic teams for women and men. Recreational facilities include a field house and gym with racquetball, basketball, and indoor tennis courts; a state-of-the-art fitness center; and a swimming pool.

Location

Clarkson is located in Potsdam, the quintessential "college town," nestled in the foothills of the northern Adirondack region of New York. The beautiful Northeast corner of the state is the home of the 6-million-acre Adirondack Park. Within 2 hours of the campus are Lake Placid and the cosmopolitan Canadian cities of Montreal and Ottawa.

Majors and Degrees

Undergraduate degree programs offered are aeronautical engineering, American studies, applied mathematics and statistics, Areté (liberal arts/business), biology, biomolecular engineering, biomolecular science, management, chemical engineering, chemistry, civil engineering, communication, computer engineering, computer science, digital arts and sciences, electrical engineering, engineering and management, environmental engineering, environmental health science, environmental science and policy, financial information and analysis, global supply chain management, history, humanities, information systems and business processes, innovation and entrepreneurship, liberal studies, mathematics, mechanical engineering, physical therapy (pre–physical therapy leading to a doctorate), physics, political science, psychology, social sciences, and software engineering.

First-year students who are still deciding on a major may begin in a general program in business studies, engineering studies, science studies, or university studies.

Clarkson offers a University honors program, a three-year bachelor's degree option, a five-year B.S./M.S. in chemistry/biochemistry, a five-year B.S./M.B.A., and preprofessional programs in dentistry, law, medicine, physical therapy, and veterinary science.

Academic Programs

Clarkson's historic strengths in business, engineering, liberal arts, and science remain at the core of the curriculum. These programs have also been combined into cutting-edge, cross-disciplinary majors: biomolecular science, digital arts and sciences, environmental science and policy, information technology, interdisciplinary engineering and management, and software engineering.

A dynamic, hands-on approach to learning is one of the hallmarks of a Clarkson education. Clarkson students learn about business by actually starting a business. They conduct scientific research alongside distinguished faculty mentors in state-of-the-art laboratories. The University's undergraduate research program has produced 19 Goldwater Scholars since the highly competitive national scholarship program was launched in 1986.

National rankings and honors include the following: among the 125 "Best National Universities–Doctoral," *U.S. News & World Report,* 2009; among the "Best Undergraduate Engineering Programs," *U.S. News & World Report,* 2009; among the "Top 20 Wired Campuses," in *PC Magazine* and the *Princeton Review* 2007; the Supply Chain Management Program ranks thirteenth in the nation, *U.S. News & World Report,* 2009; and among the best business schools in the nation, the *Princeton Review's Best 282 Business Schools,* 2007 edition. The undergraduate program in innovation and entrepreneurship is ranked number twenty-two among 700 U.S. higher educational institutions by the *Princeton Review* and *Entrepreneur* magazine, 2006.

Clarkson was also ranked among the top 100 graduate schools in environmental engineering and civil engineering by *U.S. News & World Report's* "Best Graduate Programs," 2009.

In addition, Clarkson's award-winning Student Projects for Engineering Experience and Design (SPEED) program promotes multidisciplinary, project-based extracurricular learning opportunities for more than 400 undergraduates annually. Some fifteen design teams compete in national and regional collegiate competitions that involve design and analysis, teamwork, and communication skills.

Off-Campus Programs

Students benefit from the resources of the Associated Colleges of the St. Lawrence Valley, which comprises Clarkson University, St. Lawrence University, SUNY Canton, and SUNY Potsdam. Benefits for students include opportunities to participate in activities ranging from clubs to concerts, interlibrary exchange, and cross-

registration that allows students to pursue two courses per year at member colleges at no extra cost.

Academic Facilities

The University's 640-acre wooded campus is the site of forty-six buildings that comprise more than 1.2-million square feet of assignable space. Dedicated exclusively to instructional programs are more than 375,000 square feet, including some 54,000 square feet of traditional classrooms and more than 168,000 square feet assigned as laboratory areas. In the Center for Advanced Materials Processing (a New York State Center for Advanced Technology), there are seventy state-of-the-art research labs, including many related to nanotechnology and environmental research. Others include a multidisciplinary engineering and project laboratory for team-based projects, such as the mini-Baja and Formulae SAE racers, a robotics laboratory, a high-voltage lab, electron microscopy, a Class 10 clean room, a polymer fabrication lab, crystal growth labs, and a structural testing lab. School of Arts and Sciences facilities include a virtual-reality laboratory, the Clarkson Open Source Institute, a molecular design laboratory, a human brain electrophysiology laboratory, and other specialized facilities. In 2008, a 16,000-square-foot Technology Advancement Center was opened.

Bertrand H. Snell Hall houses the School of Business and the School of Arts and Sciences administrative offices as well as fully networked classrooms and study spaces and collaborative centers that feature wireless network access and videoconferencing capabilities. The facility includes three academic centers, which are available to all students: the Shipley Center for Innovation, the Center for Global Competitiveness, and the Eastman Kodak Center for Excellence in Communication. The Center for Health Sciences at Clarkson is a regional center of excellence for education, treatment, and research in physical rehabilitation and other health sciences.

Costs

Tuition was $30,320 for the 2008–09 year, room (2-person) was $5586, and the meal plan was $4026. Student fees totaled $690. In addition, students usually spend about $2000 annually on books, supplies, travel, and personal expenses.

Financial Aid

The University offers a variety of scholarships and loans, including state and federal student loans, state scholarships and awards, individual scholarships, federal grants, and federal work-study programs.

Faculty

Clarkson's 190 full-time faculty members teach undergraduate and graduate classes, with graduate students assisting only in undergraduate lab sciences. With an excellent student-faculty ratio of 15:1, undergraduates benefit from regular interaction with the school's faculty members and small class sizes (especially at the upper levels). The University attracts teacher/scholars who are also highly regarded scholars in their fields. 96 percent hold a doctorate.

Student Government

The Student Senate and the Interfraternity Council combine to form the student government at Clarkson University. The former supervises all extracurricular activities (except athletics) and has responsibility for the allocation of student activity funds and for other appropriate business. The latter prescribes standards and rules for fraternities. Students are involved in the formation of University policies through membership, with faculty and staff representatives, on all important committees.

Admission Requirements

Clarkson recommends that prospective students follow a challenging secondary school curriculum that includes mathematics, science, and English. Candidates for entrance to the Wallace H. Coulter School of Engineering or students pursuing a degree in the sciences or an interdisciplinary engineering and management degree should have successfully completed secondary school courses in physics and chemistry. All candidates for admission are required to take the SAT or ACT. SAT Subject Tests are optional. The high school record is the most important factor in an admission decision. International students for whom English is a second language must submit a minimum TOEFL score of 550 (paper-based) or 212 (computer-based). All applicants must include a personal statement of 250 to 500 words describing a special interest, experience, or achievement.

Students achieving scores of 4 or better on the College Board's Advanced Placement examinations are considered for advanced placement and credit in virtually all academic areas. Advanced standing is most common in English, mathematics, and science.

An early decision plan is offered on a "first-choice" basis; this plan does not prohibit the student from making other applications, but it does commit the student to withdrawing other applications if accepted at Clarkson.

Although not required, a personal interview with a member of the Office of Admission is highly recommended, especially for early decision candidates. Interviews on campus should be arranged by letter or telephone at least one week prior to the intended visit. The Office of Admission is open Monday through Friday, from 8 a.m. to 4:30 p.m., and Saturday by appointment. The University welcomes visitors to the campus and makes arrangements, as requested, for families to tour and meet with academic and other departments on campus.

Application and Information

Office of Undergraduate Admission
Holcroft House
Clarkson University
P.O. Box 5605
Potsdam, New York 13699-5605
Phone: 315-268-6480
        800-527-6577 (toll-free)
Fax: 315-268-7647
E-mail: admission@clarkson.edu
Web site: http://www.clarkson.edu

Clarkson is a leader in project-based learning, providing students with strong communication skills, leadership ability, and technological skill in their fields.

CONCORDIA COLLEGE–NEW YORK

BRONXVILLE, NEW YORK

The College

Founded in 1881, Concordia College–New York is a four-year, coeducational institution offering a Christ-centered, value-oriented liberal arts education for lives of service to church and community. Part of the Concordia University System, Concordia is affiliated with the Lutheran Church–Missouri Synod.

Students come from twenty-seven states and thirty-four countries worldwide; 60 percent are women. As members of a close-knit community, Concordia students are mentored by a dedicated faculty and staff, most of whom live within a 10-minute walk of the campus. Students develop lifelong relationships as they prepare for fulfilling lives and careers. During their time at Concordia, students are encouraged to reach their full academic, spiritual, athletic, and artistic potential.

Two-thirds of the students live on campus, forming an active, close-knit community involved in all aspects of college life— student organizations, athletics, community outreach, and performance ensembles. From daily chapel to servant events, spiritual life activities invite students to put faith into practice.

Residence halls include Sieker, Romoser, Rippe, and Bohm. Other facilities include Feth Hall, the campus's main administration building and one of several classroom sites, the Commons (dining hall), the Music Building, and Ressmeyer, Koepchen, and Ward— several historic houses adjacent to campus that serve as student housing. The College also owns a number of homes throughout the community, enabling faculty and staff members to live near campus.

The multipurpose room on the main level of Schoenfeld Campus Center is used for musical and dramatic performances and can be converted to a gymnasium for intramural sports. The lower level of Schoenfeld includes the Brickyard Grille and Snack Bar, the Coop Store, the Campus Bookstore, the television lounge, the game room, and the student mailroom.

The Meyer Athletic Center includes a full-size gymnasium, a weight room, a fitness and sports training center, squash courts, indoor and outdoor tennis courts, and baseball, soccer, and softball fields.

The Concordia Clippers are members of the NCAA Division II and compete in the East Coast Conference in men's baseball, basketball, cross-country, soccer, and tennis and women's basketball, cross-country, soccer, softball, tennis, and volleyball.

Concordia College is accredited by the Commission on Higher Education of the Middle States Association of Colleges and Schools and registered by the New York State Education Department.

Location

Concordia's 33-acre campus is set in the small, affluent village of Bronxville. Bronxville is only 1 square mile in size and is home to 7,000 inhabitants, including diplomats, corporate executives, lawyers, and a wide range of other professionals. From the Bronxville train station, it is just under 30 minutes to Grand Central Station in the heart of New York City.

Concordia is the right place for students who participate in their education, want to be involved in lots of activities, seek a broad-based education, want to be part of a Christian community, and want to be near New York City.

Majors and Degrees

Concordia offers Bachelor of Arts (B.A.) and Bachelor of Science (B.S.) degrees. The B.A. is offered in biology (with tracks in health, environmental, and research), education (NCATE-accredited, with tracks in early childhood, childhood, and middle childhood generalist), English (with tracks in literature and writing), liberal studies (with tracks in art, biblical languages, English, history, math, music, new media, psychology, religion, and sociology), and social sciences (with tracks in history, international studies, psychology, and sociology).

The B.S. is offered in business (with tracks in international management and Certified Financial Planning®) and social work (with a track in family life ministry). The social work program is CSWE-accredited and allows for advanced standing in the Master of Social Work graduate degree program.

The College also offers a Fellows Program (honors); Lutheran Teaching Diploma; the Concordia Connection, a support program for students with a diagnosed learning disability; and an English as a second language program. The College also offers preprofessional studies programs (deaconess, law, medicine, and seminary).

Academic Programs

At Concordia, students are immersed in a learning environment that sparks the imagination and provides the skills to build a future. The curriculum emphasizes an interdisciplinary, hands-on approach to academics grounded by a strong foundation of the liberal arts. What students learn in the classroom is connected to the real world through exciting experiential learning opportunities.

To graduate, students must complete the Concordia Distinctive (the College's highly regarded core curriculum), the program of study, and general studies requirements, integrated with field experience and internships in Westchester County and the New York area. All these components together are known as The Concordia Experience.

Concordia operates on a two-semester calendar. A minimum of 122 completed semester hours is required to earn the bachelor's degree.

The Concordia Fellows Program (honors) is open via application to all students who demonstrate high academic achievement. Fellows are enriched through a variety of unique academic experiences, seminars, and travel.

Concordia offers an intensive English as a second language (ESL) program, serving students at a variety of proficiency levels. The ESL program is housed on campus and serves both matriculated and nonmatriculated students.

The Concordia Connection Program is for students with diagnosed learning differences. Support services are provided to qualified students who meet regular admission requirements but need specific assistance in order to maximize their academic success. Space in this program is quite limited and additional fees are assessed.

Concordia also offers an Adult Education Program with Accelerated Degree Programs for adult students over age 25. Degrees are offered in behavioral sciences (B.A.), business administration (B.S.), and liberal studies (A.A.).

Off-Campus Programs

Study abroad and international travel experiences are available. Students may study abroad for a semester (through AHA International) or join a Concordia faculty-led tour during the month of May.

Concordia is part of the national Concordia University System, which is made up of ten colleges and universities affiliated with the Lutheran Church–Missouri Synod. Students may enroll for up to one year at any of these sister institutions.

Academic Facilities

Concordia's quintessential college campus is designed around the work of the College's first campus architect, Edward L. Tilton—an award-winning architect of Ellis Island. Inside these historical buildings, students have access to some of the finest technology and performing arts resources around. A perfect blend of old and new, Concordia's facilities reflect its history and its future. Students and faculty and staff members alike take pride in a safe, clean, and inviting campus. Simply put, Concordia College's facilities help nourish students' minds, bodies, and spirits.

The Donald A. Krenz Academic Center on the top floor of the library contains technology-enhanced classrooms, including the eighty-two-seat Pietruski Auditorium, a forty-eight-seat classroom overlooking the quad, a twenty-station computer teaching room, and the Darlene Hedin Krenz New Media Center designed for electronic and digital media instruction. Fully handicapped accessible, the center is also home to the OSilas Art Gallery, the Yeager Collection of original autographs of American financial leaders, a spacious student lounge, and the campus Information Technology Services department.

Sommer Center for Worship and the Performing Arts includes a recital/lecture hall with tiered seating for 315 and the College's Chapel. Private rehearsal rooms for individual and ensemble, vocal, instrumental, and organ practice adjoin the recital hall. The recital hall has hosted recording sessions for artists such as Itzhak Perlman, Yehudi Menuhin, and Harry Connick Jr., as well as the Concordia Choir.

Scheele Memorial Library offers support and assistance in the academic pursuits of the Concordia College community. The library provides an online catalog to search its own resources as well as those of forty-two other colleges. In addition, the library subscribes to more than twenty databases, which are available for both on- and off-campus use. The library also houses the Curriculum Materials Center for education students; the Information Commons, complete with computer Internet access; a computerized writing center; and group study rooms.

Brunn-Maier Science Hall contains a full range of science laboratories and general classrooms.

Stein Hall houses individual practice studios and an electric piano laboratory. Stein Hall is home to the Concordia Conservatory—the College's music conservatory serving both students and the surrounding community.

Costs

Tuition and fees for the 2008–09 academic year are $22,930. Room and board charges are $8745. Costs are the same for in-state, out-of-state, and transfer students.

Financial Aid

Awards, merit scholarships, Lutheran grants and scholarships, need-based financial aid, and more make Concordia a valuable and affordable investment. Ninety-three percent of the students receive some form of financial aid, totaling over $8.25 million. To be considered, students must file the Free Application for Federal Student Aid (FAFSA). Concordia's FAFSA code is 002709.

Faculty

Concordia College's faculty members are dedicated and talented; over 75 percent hold the highest degrees in their respective fields of study. The 16:1 student-faculty ratio enables students and faculty members to interact on a very personal level. In classes and labs, students see professors up front, not teaching assistants.

Student Government

All full-time students are members of the Student Government Association (SGA) and elect its representatives each spring. The SGA organizes and supports a host of campus events and provides a voice for all student concerns.

Admission Requirements

Concordia College–New York is proud to be a member of the Common Application and Universal College Application. Applications are evaluated using a holistic selection process. Admission to the College is based upon a wide range of criteria designed to identify a student body with integrity, high academic standards, and serious educational and personal goals. Applicants are considered on the basis of academic record, class rank, test scores, essay, and recommendations. In order to be considered for first-year admission, students should submit the $50 application fee ($100 for international students), application for admission (available at http://www.commonapp.org or http://www.universalcollegeapp.com), official high school transcripts, SAT or ACT scores, school report form (part of the application), supplemental application (part of the application), a written personal statement, and an optional activity/volunteer resume. In addition, transfer students must submit official transcripts from all colleges and universities attended plus SAT or ACT scores (if they have earned fewer than 28 college credits).

Prospective students are encouraged to visit the campus and meet with a faculty member in their area of interest. Open house preview day events are regularly scheduled; Concordia is also happy to arrange individual visits. Campus visit scholarships of $500 are awarded upon enrollment after an official campus visit.

Application and Information

The application priority deadline is March 15, with a rolling/space-available policy thereafter. The transfer application deadline is July 15. Requests for information and applications should be addressed to:

Office of Admission
Concordia College
171 White Plains Road
Bronxville, New York 10708
Phone: 914-337-9300 Ext. 2155
       800-YES-COLLEGE (937-2655; toll-free)
Fax: 914-395-4636
E-mail: admission@concordia-ny.edu
Web site: http://www.concordia-ny.edu

At Concordia College, students benefit from the 16:1 student-faculty ratio and the dedication of the faculty members.

EUGENE LANG COLLEGE
THE NEW SCHOOL FOR LIBERAL ARTS
NEW YORK, NEW YORK

The College

Eugene Lang College is the undergraduate liberal arts division of The New School, a leading university in New York City with a tradition of innovative learning. Eugene Lang College offers all the benefits of a small and supportive college as well as the full range of opportunities found in a university setting. At Lang, rigorous academic programs are closely connected with all that New York City has to offer: its wealth of music, theater, and arts; its vibrant international community; its history; and its energy.

Eugene Lang students are encouraged to participate in the creation and direction of their education. The desire to explore and the freedom to imagine shared by students and faculty members contribute to a distinctive academic community.

Eugene Lang College students currently come from forty-five states and thirteen countries. The ratio of men to women is approximately 2:3. About 45 percent of the College's 985 students come from outside the New York metropolitan area; 4 percent hold foreign citizenship and 23 percent are members of minority groups. The student body is composed of both residential and day students. The university operates residence halls within walking distance of classes; incoming freshmen and transfer students are given housing priority within these facilities, and housing is guaranteed for the first year for new students. Great diversity in interests and aspirations is found among the students. Through the Office of Student Services, students produce a student newspaper and an award-winning literary magazine. They organize and participate in dramatic, musical, and artistic events through the "Lang in the City Program," as well as numerous political, social, and cultural organizations at the university and throughout New York City.

The New School was founded in 1919 by such notable scholars and intellectuals as John Dewey, Alvin Johnson, and Thorstein Veblen. It has long been a home for leading artists, educators, and public figures. For example, the university was the first institution of higher learning to offer college-level courses in fields such as black culture and race, taught by W. E. B. DuBois, and psychoanalysis, taught by Freud's disciple Sandor Ferenczi. Among the world-famous artists and performers who have taught at The New School are Martha Graham, Aaron Copland, and Thomas Hart Benton. Today, such noted scholars as Robert Heilbroner, Eric Hobsbawm, Jerome Bruner, and Rayna Rapp are among the hundreds of university faculty members accessible to Eugene Lang College students.

The other divisions of the university are The New School for General Studies, which offers nearly 1,000 credit and noncredit courses to students each semester and awards the B.A., B.S., M.A., M.S., and M.F.A. degrees; The New School for Social Research, which grants M.A. and Ph.D. degrees; Milano The New School for Management and Urban Policy, which awards the M.S. and Ph.D. degrees; Parsons The New School for Design, one of the oldest and most influential art schools in the country; Mannes College The New School for Music, a renowned classical conservatory; The New School for Jazz and Contemporary Music; and The New School for Drama. The total university enrollment in 2008–09 was approximately 9,900 degree-seeking students.

Location

The university is located in New York City's Greenwich Village, which historically has been a center for intellectual and artistic life. This legendary New York City neighborhood of town houses and tree-lined streets offers students a friendly and stimulating environment. Over and above the resources of Greenwich Village, New York City offers virtually unlimited cultural, artistic, recreational, and intellectual resources that make it one of the world's great cities.

Majors and Degrees

Eugene Lang College awards the Bachelor of Arts degree in the arts, culture and media; economics; environmental studies; history; interdisciplinary science; liberal arts; literary studies; philosophy; and psychology. In addition, students are encouraged to pursue an internship, where appropriate.

Students may apply to a five-year, dual-degree B.A./B.F.A. program in conjunction with Parsons The New School for Design or The New School for Jazz and Contemporary Music. Students may also apply for the accelerated B.A./M.A. option offered in conjunction with the university's graduate divisions.

Academic Programs

By actively participating in the process of their education, Eugene Lang College students gain the knowledge to make informed choices about the direction of their studies with the help of their advisers and peers.

Small seminar classes serve as the focus of the academic program at the College. The maximum class size is 20 students. Classes are in-depth, interdisciplinary inquiries into topics or issues selected each semester by the College's outstanding faculty. Most important, the classes engage participants in the study of primary texts, rather than textbooks, and emphasize dialogue between teacher and student as a mode of learning. Here, not only is intellectual curiosity fostered by the small classes, but a genuine sense of community develops as well.

Freshmen are required to take one writing course and three other seminars of their choice in each of their first two semesters at the College. Upper-level students create their programs by selecting seminars from the College's curriculum, or they may combine offerings of the College with courses and workshops offered by The New School for General Study, The New School for Social Research, Milano The New School for Management and Urban Policy, and Parsons The New School for Design.

The College operates on a semester calendar; the first semester runs from September through mid-December, and the second runs from late January through mid-May. Students generally earn 16 credits per semester; a minimum of 120 credits is required for graduation.

Off-Campus Programs

Eugene Lang College recognizes the immense value of work undertaken beyond the classroom. The College arranges appropriate projects—internships with private and nonprofit organizations—that serve to strengthen the connection between theoretical work in the classroom and practical work on the job. Sophomores and juniors have the option of spending a year on a

sponsored exchange with Sarah Lawrence College and the University of Amsterdam. Other exchanges, both in the United States and abroad, are available.

Academic Facilities

Eugene Lang College is located on 11th Street between Fifth and Sixth Avenues in Greenwich Village. The university includes twelve academic buildings, including a student center, the University Computing Center with IBM and Macintosh stations, a 500-seat auditorium, art galleries, studios for the fine arts, classrooms, a writing center, and faculty offices. Eugene Lang College students have full and easy access to the Raymond Fogelman Library and the Adam and Sophie Gimbel Design Library. In addition, the university participates in the South Manhattan Library Consortium. Together, the libraries in the consortium house approximately 3 million volumes covering all the traditional liberal arts disciplines and the fine arts.

Costs

Tuition and fees for the 2008–09 academic year were $32,700. Room and board cost approximately $12,500, depending upon the student's choice of specific meal plan and dormitory accommodations.

Financial Aid

Students are encouraged to apply for aid by filing the Free Application for Federal Student Aid (FAFSA) and requesting that a copy of the need analysis report be sent to The New School (FAFSA code number 002780). Qualified College students are eligible for all federal and state financial aid programs in addition to university gift aid. University aid is awarded on the basis of need and merit and is part of a package consisting of both gift aid (grants and/or scholarships) and a self-help component (loans and Federal Work-Study Program awards). Aid is renewable each year as long as need continues and students maintain satisfactory academic standing at the College. Special attention is given to continuing students who have done exceptionally well.

Faculty

At Eugene Lang College, the faculty-student ratio is 1:10. Class size ranges from 10 to 20 students. Faculty members are graduates of outstanding colleges and universities and represent a wide variety of academic disciplines; 95 percent hold Ph.D.'s. College faculty members also serve as academic advisers, who are selected carefully in order to ensure thoughtful supervision of students' programs and academic progress.

Well-known faculty members from other divisions of the university teach at the College on a regular basis. In addition, every semester, the College hosts distinguished scholars and writers as visiting faculty and guest lecturers who further enrich the academic program of the College and the university.

Student Government

There is a student union at the College, which is an organized vehicle for student expression and action as well as a means of funding student projects and events. Students are encouraged to express their views and concerns about academic policies and community life through regular student-faculty member meetings.

Admission Requirements

Eugene Lang College welcomes admission applications from students of diverse racial, ethnic, religious, and political backgrounds whose past performance and academic and personal promise make them likely to gain from and add to the College community. The College seeks students who combine inquisitiveness and seriousness of purpose with the ability to engage in a distinctive, rigorous liberal arts program. Each applicant to the College is judged individually; the Admissions Committee, which renders all admission decisions, considers both academic qualifications and the personal, creative, and intellectual qualities of each applicant. A strong academic background, including a college-preparatory program, is recommended. An applicant's transcript; teacher and counselor recommendations; SAT, ACT, or SAT Subject Test scores; and personal essays are all taken into consideration. In addition, an interview, a tour of university facilities, and a visit to Eugene Lang College seminars are optional but highly recommended.

High school students for whom the College is their first choice are strongly encouraged to apply as early decision candidates and are notified early of an admission decision. Early entrance is an option for qualified high school juniors who wish to enter college prior to high school graduation. Candidates for early entrance must submit two teacher recommendations.

Students who have successfully completed one full year or more at another accredited institution may apply as transfer candidates. If accepted, transfer students may enter upper-level seminars and pursue advanced work. International students may apply for admission as freshmen or transfers by submitting a regular application to the College. If English is spoken as a second language, TOEFL scores are required. The New York Connection Program invites students from other colleges to Eugene Lang College for a semester and incorporates an internship into their studies.

Students interested in applying for the combined B.A./B.F.A. degree program in fine arts or jazz studies are encouraged to apply for admission as freshmen to these special five-year programs. In addition to the admission requirements outlined above, a home exam and a portfolio are required for fine arts, and an audition is required for jazz studies.

Application and Information

Freshmen, transfers, and visiting students may apply for either the September (fall) or January (spring) semester. To apply for admission to the College, students must request an application packet and submit the required credentials and a $50 application fee by the appropriate deadline. The application fee may be waived in accordance with the College Board's Fee Waiver Service. For the semester beginning in January, the required credentials must be submitted by November 15, with notification by December 15. For the September semester, early decision candidates must submit the required credentials by November 15, with notification by December 15. For freshman candidates applying for general admission and freshman early entrants, the deadline is February 1, with notification by April 1. For transfers and visiting students, the deadline is rolling to May 15, with notification rolling until July 1. For further information, students should contact:

Nicole Curvin
Director of Admissions
Eugene Lang College The New School for Liberal Arts
72 Fifth Avenue, Second Floor
New York, New York 10011
Phone: 212-229-5665
Fax: 212-229-5355
E-mail: lang@newschool.edu
Web site: http://www.newschool.edu/lang

FORDHAM UNIVERSITY
NEW YORK, NEW YORK

The University

Fordham, the Jesuit University of New York, offers a distinctive educational experience that is rooted in the nearly 500-year-old Jesuit tradition of intellectual rigor and personal respect for the individual. A Fordham education blends a challenging curriculum with the resources, culture and energy of New York City—a unique combination by any measure.

The University enrolls approximately 14,600 students, of whom 7,994 are undergraduates. Fordham has four undergraduate colleges and six graduate and professional schools. In addition to its full-time undergraduate programs, the University offers part-time undergraduate study at Fordham College of Liberal Studies and through two summer sessions.

Fordham features two residential campuses: Rose Hill, on 85 green, leafy acres adjacent to the New York Botanical Garden and the Bronx Zoo; and Lincoln Center, a cosmopolitan campus in the cultural heart of Manhattan, which features a twenty-story complex that provides apartment-style living and great city views. Both campuses are easily accessible by public and private transportation. Enjoying the academic and student life of both is convenient with the University's Ram Van service, which operates between the two campuses.

The University has an extensive athletics program consisting of twenty-three varsity sports and numerous club and intramural sports. Murphy Field is the heart of intramural and recreational sports at Fordham, hosting softball, soccer, and flag football games. The Vincent T. Lombardi Memorial Center provides facilities for basketball, squash, swimming and diving, tennis, track, and water polo.

Location

As the Jesuit University of New York, Fordham offers its students the unparalleled academic, cultural, and recreational advantages of one of the world's great cities. Fordham draws students from across the country who want to live and learn while immersed in the diversity and opportunity of a global capital. More than 2,600 corporations and organizations—from the United Nations to Fortune 500 companies—offer valuable work experience to Fordham interns. New York City not only provides extraordinary internship possibilities and career advantages, but also a never-ending list of things to see and do—from Broadway theater, museums and music to major league sports or a bike ride through Central Park.

Majors and Degrees

Fordham offers undergraduates more than fifty majors. Fordham College at Rose Hill provides programs of study leading to the B.A. or B.S. in African and African American studies, American studies, anthropology, art history, biological sciences, chemistry, classical civilization, classical languages (Latin and Greek), communication and media studies, comparative literature, computer and information sciences, economics, engineering physics, English, French, French studies, general science, German, German studies, history, international political economy, Italian, Italian studies, Latin American and Latino studies, mathematics, mathematics/economics, medieval studies, Middle East studies, music, philosophy, physics, political science,

psychology, religious studies, social work, sociology, Spanish, Spanish studies, theology, urban studies, visual arts, and women's studies.

Also located at the Rose Hill campus, the College of Business Administration offers programs leading to majors, minors, concentrations, or specializations in accounting, accounting information services, applied accounting and finance, business administration, business economics, business law and ethics, communication and media management, e-business, entrepreneurship, finance, human resource management, information systems, management of information and communication systems, management systems, marketing, and public accountancy. The G.L.O.B.E. Program (Global Learning Opportunities and Business Experiences) provides business students with an international study option that incorporates course offerings in language, culture, and history with business.

Special programs at Rose Hill include a cooperative engineering program, double majors or individualized majors, interdisciplinary studies, a B.S./M.B.A. program, numerous joint masters degree programs (dual degree), 3-3 law and honors programs. Preprofessional programs are offered in architecture, dentistry, law, medicine, and veterinary medicine, and a program for teacher certification is offered in elementary and secondary education.

At Fordham College at Lincoln Center students choose from the B.A. in African and African American studies, anthropology, art history, classical civilization, classical languages (Latin and Greek), communication and media studies, comparative literature, computer science, dance, economics, English, French, French studies, German, German studies, history, information science, international studies, Italian, Italian studies, Latin American and Latino studies, mathematics, mathematics/economics, medieval studies, Middle East studies, music, natural science, philosophy, political science, psychology, religious studies, social science, social work, sociology, Spanish, Spanish studies, theater, theology, urban studies, visual arts, and women's studies. Special programs at Fordham College at Lincoln Center include options in the performing arts (including a B.F.A. in dance with The Ailey School), creative writing, double majors or individualized majors, independent study, an honors program, and interdisciplinary studies. Preprofessional studies are offered in dentistry, health, and law. A teacher certification program is offered in elementary and secondary education.

Academic Programs

Students in all undergraduate colleges pursue a common core curriculum designed to provide them with the breadth of knowledge that marks the educated person. The core involves foundational courses chosen from groups of academic disciplines: history, philosophy, theology, natural sciences, social sciences, languages, and literature. In every core course, students think, speak, write, and act in fundamentally new ways, with a broadened appreciation of human values and a deepened commitment to the human community.

Off-Campus Programs

Reflecting the values-centered education that is a Fordham hallmark, more than 1,300 students engage in community

service each year, locally and in distant corners of the world. The Global Outreach program is an ambitious international service program designed for students to live and work in communities of need. The University also provides access to yearlong, semester-long and summer study-abroad programs in more than fifty countries on six continents including La Sorbonne in Paris and American University in Cairo.

Academic Facilities

The outstanding libraries on the two campuses have combined holdings of more than 2.2 million volumes and more than 49,920 electronic and print periodicals. On the Rose Hill campus, the William D. Walsh Family Library, which serves the entire Fordham community, has seating for more than 1,500 and a state-of-the-art Electronic Information Center, as well as media production laboratories, studios, and auditoriums. Students also have access to the vast library facilities of New York City, neighboring universities, and the various specialized collections maintained by numerous local museums and other institutions. Among laboratory facilities utilized by undergraduates are Mulcahy Hall (chemistry), Larkin Hall (biology), and Freeman Hall (physics and biology). The University has more than forty buildings that provide ample space for smart classrooms, science laboratories, theaters, and athletic facilities.

Costs

At the Rose Hill and Lincoln Center campuses, undergraduate costs for the 2008–09 academic year were $34,200 for tuition and fees, and averaged $12,980 for room and board. Chemistry, physics, and biology fees were approximately $50 per laboratory course. Nominally priced meals are available in cafeterias on each campus. Such incidentals as transportation and laundry vary in cost. There is no difference in fees for out-of-state students.

Financial Aid

More than 90 percent of the entering students enroll with aid from Fordham as well as from outside sources. Among the major aid programs are Federal Pell Grants, Federal Supplemental Educational Opportunity Grants, Federal Perkins Loans, work grants sponsored by both the government and the University, and University grants-in-aid. Outside sources of aid include state scholarships, the New York State Tuition Assistance Program (TAP), privately sponsored scholarships, state government loan programs, and deferred-payment programs. The University also offers academic merit scholarships ranging from $10,000 to the full cost of tuition and room. Applicants for aid must submit the Free Application for Federal Student Aid (FAFSA) and the College Scholarship Service (CSS) PROFILE. Please direct inquiries to Fordham's Office of Undergraduate Admission or Office of Student Financial Services.

Faculty

The University has a full-time faculty of 704 and a student-faculty ratio of 12:1. Most members of the undergraduate faculty also teach at the graduate level, and 96 percent of the full-time faculty members hold doctoral or other terminal degrees.

Student Government

The traditional student governing body at Fordham has been the United Student Government, composed of undergraduates attending the University.

Admission Requirements

Admission is based on academic performance, class rank (if available), secondary school recommendations, and SAT or ACT scores. Extracurricular activities and essays are also factors in the evaluation process. Religious preference, physical handicap, race, or ethnic origin is not considered. Out-of-state students are encouraged to apply. More than 85 percent of the students accepted for the freshman class ranked in the top quarter of their secondary school class. The middle 50 percent combined SAT score for students entering in fall 2008 was 1200–1330. Recommended are 22 high school units, including 4 in English, 3 in mathematics, 3 in science, 2 in social studies, 2 in foreign language, 2 in history, and 6 electives. For regular admission, the SAT or the ACT should be taken no later than the January preceding entrance. Candidates for early action should complete the examinations by October of their senior year. The University participates in the College Board's Advanced Placement Program. Personal interviews are not required.

Application and Information

Application may be made for either September or January enrollment. The regular decision application deadline is January 15 for fall admission. The completed application, the secondary school report, the results of the SAT or ACT, and an application fee of $50 (check or money order made payable to Fordham University) should be submitted by this date. All financial aid forms are due by February 1. Students are notified on or about April 1. Candidates for Early Action should apply by November 1 and receive notification by December 25. Transfer students must apply by December 1 for spring admission or by June 1 for fall admission.

For additional details and application forms, students should contact:

Peter Farrell
Director of Admission
Fordham University
Duane Library
441 East Fordham Road
Bronx, New York 10458

Phone: 800-FORDHAM (367-3426)
E-mail: enroll@fordham.edu
Web site: http://www.fordham.edu

Members of the class of 2008 join Fordham's distinguished alumni family of more than 120,000.

GROVE CITY COLLEGE

GROVE CITY, PENNSYLVANIA

The College

The beautifully landscaped campus of Grove City College (GCC) stretches more than 150 acres and includes twenty-seven neo-Gothic buildings valued at more than $100 million. The campus is considered one of the loveliest in the nation. While the College has changed to meet the needs of the society it serves, its basic philosophy has remained unchanged since its founding in 1876. It is a Christian liberal arts and sciences institution of ideal size and dedicated to the principle of providing the highest-quality education at the lowest possible cost. Wishing to remain truly independent and to retain its distinctive qualities as a private school governed by private citizens (trustees), it is one of the very few colleges in the country that does not accept any state or federal monies. It is informally affiliated with the Presbyterian Church (U.S.A.) but not narrowly denominational; the College believes that to be well educated a student should be exposed to the central ideas of the Christian faith. A 20-minute chapel program offered Tuesday and Thursday mornings, along with a Sunday evening worship service, challenges students in their faith. Sixteen chapel services per semester are required out of fifty opportunities. Religious organizations and activities exist to provide fellowship and spiritual growth.

Grove City students generally come from middle-income families. The greatest number comes from Pennsylvania, Ohio, New Jersey, Virginia, and New York, although forty-two states and eleven other countries were represented in 2007–08. Eighty-six percent of the women and 70 percent of the men in the most recent freshman class ranked in the top fifth of their high school class. Their average SAT combined score was 1268 (combining only the critical reading and math scores); the average ACT composite score was 28.

Ninety-three percent of the 2,500 students live in separate men's and women's residence halls. All others are regular commuters or married students. A full program of cultural, professional, athletic, and social activities is offered. An arena, Crawford Auditorium, and the J. Howard Pew Fine Arts Center are used for athletics, concerts, movies, plays, and lectures. The Physical Learning Center is one of the finest among the nation's small colleges and includes an eight-lane bowling alley, two swimming pools, handball/racquetball courts, playing surfaces, fitness rooms with free weights, aerobic equipment and Cybex machines, an indoor three-lane running track, and the basketball arena. A Student Union, which includes an eatery, mailroom, bookstore, and commuters' lounge, and Ketler Recreation Lounge are also available. There are more than 100 organizations and special interest groups, including local fraternities and sororities. No alcohol or drugs are permitted on campus. The athletic activities include an extensive intramural, club, and varsity sports program that provides nineteen intercollegiate teams that compete at the NCAA Division III level for men and women.

The College's well-established placement services, ranked recently by *The Princeton Review* in the top 20 in the nation, are used constantly by students who are interested in business and industrial employment and by those seeking educational positions in the teaching field. A complete file of personal data, scholastic records, and recommendations is prepared for each registrant. These files are available to the scores of prospective employers who visit the campus annually to interview the graduating seniors. One of Grove City's strengths is placing students in business, industrial, and teaching positions, as well as in professional institutions such as medical schools.

Location

Grove City, a town of 8,000 people, is 60 miles north of Pittsburgh. Convenient to I-79 and I-80, Grove City is only a day's drive from Chicago, New York City, Toronto, and Washington, D.C. The municipal airport has a 3,500-foot runway, and there is bus service to Pittsburgh.

Majors and Degrees

Grove City College offers undergraduate degrees in liberal arts, sciences, engineering, and music. The Bachelor of Arts is offered with majors in Christian thought, communication studies, economics, English, history, modern language (French and Spanish), philosophy, political science, psychology, secondary education, and sociology. Preprofessional students in law or theology usually earn the B.A. degree. Interdisciplinary major programs are also available for qualified students.

The Bachelor of Science is granted with majors in accounting, applied physics, applied physics/computer, biochemistry, biology, business management, chemistry, computer information systems, computer science, early childhood education, elementary education, entrepreneurship, financial management, industrial management, international business, marketing management, mathematics, molecular biology, and psychology. Preprofessional students often select one of these majors for dentistry, medicine, or other health fields.

The Bachelor of Science in Electrical and Computer Engineering degree is also offered. The Bachelor of Science in Mechanical Engineering major provides for mechanical systems design and/or thermal systems design. The electrical and computer and mechanical engineering programs are accredited by the Engineering Accreditation Commission of the Accreditation Board for Engineering and Technology, Inc. (ABET).

The Bachelor of Music degree is awarded to those who major in music. Programs may also include concentrations in business, education, performing arts, or religion.

Academic Programs

Grove City College's goal is to assist young men and women in developing as complete individuals—academically, spiritually, and physically. The general education requirements provide all students with a high level of cultural literacy and communication skills. They include 40–52 semester hours of courses with emphases in the humanities, social sciences, and natural sciences; in quantitative and logical reasoning; and in science, faith, and technology, as well as a language requirement for nonengineering and science majors. Degree candidates must also complete the requirements in their field of concentration, physical education, electives, and convocation. To graduate, a student must have completed 128 semester hours (132 hours for electrical engineering) plus 4 convocation credits. Seventy-eight percent of those entering as freshmen stay and receive a diploma in four years.

A distinctive liberal arts–engineering program includes engineering courses plus courses in the humanities to provide students with a well-grounded preparation for entering the engineering field, as well as the civic and cultural life of society. The economics program exposes students to all economic philosophies, yet strongly advocates economic freedoms and free markets.

Grove City follows the early semester calendar plan. Academic credit may be granted to incoming freshmen on the basis of

scores on appropriate Advanced Placement tests, International Baccalaureate tests, or College-Level Examination Program tests. Honors courses, independent study, seminars, and the opportunity for juniors to study abroad for credit are also offered.

Academic Facilities

The Hall of Arts and Letters opened in 2003. This state-of-the-art teaching facility features a 200-seat lecture hall, forty classrooms (including multimedia-equipped rooms and tiered "case study" rooms), eighty faculty offices, the Early Education Center, the Curriculum Library, and language, computer, and video production labs.

The College library houses 158,000 books and 270,000 microfilm/microfiche units. Modern, well-equipped laboratories for biology, chemistry, engineering, and physics are available, as are facilities for language and piano studies.

The Weir C. Ketler Technological Learning Center consists of forty microcomputers and three big-screen projection systems and houses the help desk and repair center that support the student technology initiative. All freshmen receive their own tablet PC.

The J. Howard Pew Fine Arts Center has art, photography, and music studios; a rehearsal hall; a little theater; a museum; an art gallery; music practice rooms; and an auditorium and stage large enough to accommodate the most elaborate drama productions and concerts. An addition completed in 2002 contains additional classrooms, practice rooms, and a 188-seat recital hall.

Costs

As a relatively small, financially sound college, Grove City is able to charge an unusually low tuition in comparison to other independent institutions of similar quality. The 2008–09 annual tuition charge is $12,074 for all degrees. The cost of a tablet PC for all freshmen is included in the tuition fees. There is no comprehensive fee. Part-time tuition is $380 per credit. Room and board are $6440. Expenses for books, laundry, transportation, and personal needs vary considerably with the lifestyle of the individual.

Financial Aid

Because the College's tuition charges are low, every student, in effect, receives significant financial assistance. Sixty-two percent of the freshmen receive additional aid from GCC. Students applying for financial assistance must complete Grove City College's financial aid form. Job opportunities are available both on and off campus.

Faculty

The focus of the Grove City faculty members is on teaching students, although many members are involved with research and writing. Ninety percent of the faculty members hold doctorates. Most of the administrative staff members also teach part-time in various departments. The student-faculty ratio is approximately 15:1. Faculty members emphasize teaching and attention to the students' individual needs; they also participate extensively in the College's extracurricular programs.

Student Government

The Student Government Association provides an opportunity for direct student interaction with the faculty members and administration in matters relating to campus activities. Students serve on regular College committees (library, publications, religious activities, and student activities) and also on the Men's and Women's Governing Board and the Discipline Committee.

Admission Requirements

The College seeks academically qualified students without regard to race, color, sex, religion, or national or ethnic origin. An applicant for admission should be a high school graduate with the following recommended units: English, 4; foreign language, 3; mathematics, 3; history, 2; and science, 2. Engineering, science, and mathematics majors should have 4 units each in both mathematics and science. Auditions are required for music majors. An interview is highly recommended, especially for those who live within a day's drive (400 miles).

Transfer students may receive advanced standing if they have been in good standing at their previous institutions and have maintained a minimum grade point average of 2.0 (on a 4.0 scale).

Application and Information

A regular admission applicant should take the SAT or ACT by October or November of the senior year in high school. The application should include scores on the SAT (preferred) or the ACT, a high school transcript, references, a recommendation from the student's principal or counselor, and a nonrefundable application fee of $50. An application may be submitted after the eleventh grade. An early decision applicant should take the entrance test in the eleventh grade, visit the College for an interview, and submit the application by November 15; notification of the admission decision is mailed on December 15. Approved early decision applicants must accept by January 15 and submit a nonrefundable deposit of $200.

Applicants seeking regular decision must submit the completed application and supporting documents by February 1 of their senior year. Notification of the admission decision is mailed on March 15. Students who are offered admission should reply as soon as possible, but no later than May 1, and include a nonrefundable deposit of $200. Applications received after February 1 are considered as space permits. The College receives three applications for every freshman vacancy.

Additional information may be obtained from:

Jeffrey C. Mincey
Director of Admissions
Grove City College
100 Campus Drive
Grove City, Pennsylvania 16127-2104

Phone: 724-458-2100
Fax: 724-458-3395
E-mail: admissions@gcc.edu
Web site: http://www.gcc.edu

A view of the campus at Grove City College.

HOFSTRA UNIVERSITY

HEMPSTEAD, NEW YORK

The University

Hofstra University is a dynamic, private university where students find their edge to succeed in more than 140 undergraduate and 155 graduate programs of study. With an outstanding faculty, advanced technological resources, and state-of-the-art facilities, Hofstra enjoys a growing national reputation. Yet the average class size is just 22, and the student-to-faculty ratio is 14:1. Professors teach small classes that emphasize interaction, critical thinking, and analysis.

Six undergraduate colleges at Hofstra offer students a broad array of academic offerings. Major University divisions are Hofstra College of Liberal Arts and Sciences; the School of Communication; the Frank G. Zarb School of Business; the School of Education, Health, and Human Services; Honors College; and New College for Interdisciplinary Studies.

Hofstra's student body is diverse, with students on the main campus representing forty-seven states and territories and sixty-eight countries. Total enrollment at Hofstra is about 12,400, with 7,631 full-time undergraduates.

Residential facilities accommodate more than 4,000 students in thirty-seven modern residence halls. Hofstra is 100 percent program accessible to persons with disabilities. Necessary services are provided for students with physical, learning, and/or psychological disabilities who meet the University's academic requirements for admission.

Hofstra has a vibrant campus life, with more than 180 student clubs and organizations, about thirty local and national fraternities and sororities, eighteen NCAA Division I athletic teams for men and women, and more than 500 cultural events on campus each year.

Recreational and athletic facilities include a 15,000-seat stadium, a 5,000-seat arena, a 1,600-seat field turf soccer stadium, and a new field hockey stadium. Students can also take advantage of a physical fitness center, a swim center with an indoor Olympic-sized swimming pool and high-dive area, a softball stadium, and a recreation center offering a multipurpose gymnasium, an indoor track, a fully equipped weight room, spacious locker rooms, a cardio area, and mirrored aerobics/martial arts room. Extensive recreational and intramural sports are also available.

Location

A nationally recognized arboretum, Hofstra's distinctive 240-acre campus is situated just 25 miles east of New York City. Students have easy access by train or car to the incredible cultural resources of New York City as well as the corporate headquarters of some of the world's leading companies, where many students secure internships that lead to future careers. The surrounding Long Island area offers world-class beaches and parks, golf courses, fine dining, and theaters. Long Island's Nassau Veterans Memorial Coliseum is just minutes from Hofstra's campus and hosts the NHL's New York Islanders and numerous concerts and cultural events each year.

Majors and Degrees

The Bachelor of Arts (B.A.) is awarded in African studies, American studies, anthropology, art history, Asian studies, audio/radio, biology, chemistry, Chinese, Chinese studies, classics, comparative literature and languages, computer science, creative arts, dance, drama, early childhood and childhood education (with dual major in another discipline), early childhood education (with dual major in another discipline), economics, elementary education (with dual major in another discipline), engineering science, English, English education, film studies and production, fine arts, foreign language education (French, German, Italian, Russian, Spanish), French, geography, geology, German, global studies, Hebrew, history, humanities, Ibero-American studies, interdisciplinary studies, Italian, Jewish studies, journalism, labor studies, Latin, Latin American and

Caribbean studies, liberal arts, linguistics, mass media studies, math education, mathematical economics, mathematics, music, natural sciences, philosophy, physics, political science, psychology, public relations, religion, Russian, science education (biology, chemistry, Earth science, physics), social sciences, social studies education, sociology, Spanish, speech communication and rhetorical studies, speech-language-hearing sciences, University Without Walls, urban ecology, video/television, and women's studies.

The Bachelor of Business Administration (B.B.A.) is awarded in accounting, business, business education, entrepreneurship, finance, information technology, international business, legal studies in business, management, and marketing.

The Bachelor of Science (B.S.) is offered in applied physics, athletic training, biochemistry, biology, business economics, chemistry, community health, computer engineering, computer science, computer science and mathematics, electrical engineering, environmental resources, exercise specialist studies, fine arts, forensic science, geology, health education, health science, industrial engineering, mathematical business economics, mathematics, mechanical engineering, music, physician assistant studies, physics, University Without Walls, technology and public policy, urban ecology, video/television, video/television and business, and video/television and film.

The Bachelor of Science in Education (B.S.Ed.) is offered with specializations in dance, fine arts, music, and physical education.

The Bachelor of Engineering (B.E.) is offered in engineering science with specializations in biomedical engineering and civil engineering.

The Bachelor of Fine Arts (B.F.A.) is awarded in theater arts with specializations in performance and production.

A combined Bachelor of Arts/Juris Doctor (B.A./J.D.) is awarded in engineering science/law.

Academic Programs

Requirements for graduation vary among schools and majors. A liberal arts core curriculum is an integral part of all areas of concentration. The University calendar is organized on a traditional semester system, including one January session and three summer sessions. Some divisions offer part-time programs during the day and evening and on weekends.

Hofstra offers many innovative programs designed to meet the needs of its diverse student body. These include Honors College, New College for Interdisciplinary Studies, Legal Education Accelerated Program, and First-Year Connections.

Honors College provides a rich academic and extracurricular experience for students who show both the potential and the desire to excel. Honors students can elect to study in any of the University's undergraduate programs; these students are involved in all fields of advanced study, including premedicine, prelaw, engineering, business, communication and media arts, humanities, and social sciences.

New College for Interdisciplinary Studies offers innovative block scheduling. The Legal Education Accelerated Program allows students to earn both a B.A. and a J.D. in just six years. First-Year Connections, an integrated academic and social program, helps first-year students connect to each other and all the resources and opportunities of the University.

Off-Campus Programs

Hofstra extends learning beyond the classroom through an active internship program and many study-abroad opportunities. The internship program takes advantage of the proximity of New York City, allowing students to gain on-the-job experience in areas such as finance, business, media, advertising, and entertainment.

Hofstra sponsors study-abroad programs in the Czech Republic, England, France, Greece, Ireland, Italy and Spain, as well as in Ecuador, Jamaica, Japan, and Mexico. Previous international locales have included Australia, Austria, Belgium, China, Germany, the Netherlands, Russia, Singapore, South Korea, Taiwan, Ukraine, and the West Indies. Students wishing to pursue such study should contact the appropriate program director or the International Off-Campus Education program. Other overseas opportunities are organized by faculty members as part of credit-bearing courses. Recent courses have been held in China, Egypt, Greece, and Mexico.

Academic Facilities

Hofstra's libraries contain more than 1.2 million print volumes and provide 24 hours a day, seven days a week electronic access to more than 47,000 journals and 33,000 books. There are special units for periodicals, reserve books, government documents, curriculum materials, special collections, and microfilm.

Hofstra University's Student Computing Services provides students with a multitude of resources and learning opportunities. The Hofstra computer network provides individual accounts for all students for Internet, e-mail, and about 200 networked software programs. Almost 1,600 PC, Macintosh, and UNIX workstations are available to students in the various labs and classrooms on campus. The labs are staffed, and one computer lab is open 24 hours a day, seven days a week. All campus workstations have high-speed Internet access, and there are numerous wireless hotspots on campus. All resident students are provided with Internet and e-mail access from their residence hall rooms.

Other facilities include art galleries, an arboretum, an accredited museum, bird sanctuary, writing center, career center, cultural center, language lab, technology lab, six theaters, dance studios and performing arts classrooms, and a rooftop observatory with powerful telescopes. The state-of-the-art facilities in Hofstra's School of Communication include a 24-hour, student-operated radio station, one of the largest noncommercial television broadcast facilities in the Northeast, audio production studios, a film/video screening room, film editing rooms, and a cutting-edge converged newsroom and multimedia classroom. C. V. Starr Hall, home to the Zarb School of Business, features one of the most advanced academic trading rooms in the nation, complete with Bloomberg terminals and Internet access at every student seat. The innovative School of Education, health and human services building, Hagedorn Hall, is a completely wireless environment featuring assessment centers for child observation and mock counseling and interactive Smart Boards in many classrooms.

Costs

The annual cost of tuition and fees at Hofstra University for 2008–09 for a full-time undergraduate student was $28,630. The average housing and meal plan was $12,560. Books and supplies cost approximately $1000; personal expenses and transportation generally amount to $2640. For the full tuition and fees schedule, students should visit http://www.hofstra.edu/tuition.

Financial Aid

To help students achieve their educational goals, Hofstra University offers several financial aid options. Hofstra awarded nearly $60 million in financial assistance in 2008–09, and 83 percent of all Hofstra students received some type of financial aid, including nearly 90 percent of first-year students. For more detailed information, students should visit http://www.hofstra.edu/FinancialAid.

Faculty

Hofstra has 1,185 faculty members, including 551 full-time members; 90 percent of the full-time faculty member holds the highest degree in their fields. The faculty is dedicated to excellence in teaching, scholarship, and research, and many have been recognized with the nation's highest academic honors, including membership in the American Academy of Arts and Sciences, Fulbright and Guggenheim Fellowships, and Emmy Awards. The student-faculty ratio is 14:1. The average class size is 22. All classes are taught by faculty members who are accessible to students outside the classroom; no courses are taught by graduate assistants.

Student Government

The Student Government Association is a student-run governing body that supervises and coordinates all student activities and serves as a liaison with the faculty and administration. The Student Government Association sends representatives to the committees of the University Senate. A judicial board has responsibility for promoting justice in the conduct of student affairs.

Admission Requirements

Hofstra is a competitive institution that seeks to enroll students who demonstrate academic ability, intellectual curiosity, and the motivation to be successful and contribute to the campus community. Careful consideration is given to a student's high school record, types of courses taken, SAT or ACT scores, letters of recommendation, extracurricular involvement, and the personal essay. The most competitive applicants will have followed a rigorous college preparatory curriculum within their high school and will have taken advantage of honors and advanced placement level courses where appropriate. The Office of Admission prefers to see a high school curriculum which includes 4 years of English, 3 to 4 years of social studies, 2 to 3 years of foreign language, 3 years of mathematics, and 3 years of science. Prospective engineering majors need at least 4 years of mathematics, 1 year of chemistry, and 1 year of physics. Campus visits are strongly recommended. Hofstra accepts applications from first-year, transfer, and international students.

The University offers an early action plan for students whose first choice is Hofstra. There are two early action periods: when submitted by November 15, notification is made to the student by December 15; when submitted by December 15, notification is made to the student by January 15. Students applying for regular decision are considered on a rolling basis.

First-year applicants must submit an application, $70 application fee, high school transcript, SAT or ACT scores, personal essay and letter of recommendation. Hofstra accepts applications via mail or online and participates in the Common Application; the online application fee is $50.

Application and Information

Hofstra University
Office of Admission
100 Hofstra University
Hempstead, New York 11549-1000
Phone: 516-463-6700
      800-HOFSTRA (toll-free)
Fax: 516-463-5100
Web site: http://www.hofstra.edu
E-mail: admission@hofstra.edu

MESSIAH COLLEGE
GRANTHAM, PENNSYLVANIA

The College

Messiah College is a place where students' minds are strengthened in unison with their character, where there is no separation between intellectual and spiritual life, and where students can make the connection between what they think and what they believe. At Messiah College, students are encouraged to engage both their heads and their hearts to pursue a higher education and discover their calling.

A Christian college of the liberal and applied arts and sciences, Messiah College takes its mission seriously: to educate men and women toward maturity of intellect, character, and Christian faith to prepare them for lives of service and reconciliation in church and society. More than 2,800 students from forty states, twenty-three countries, and several denominations choose to take on the rigors of academic pursuit while strengthening their faith and putting it into meaningful action.

Alumni and faculty members include a Rhodes Scholar, a Marshall Scholar, a Truman Scholar, and several Fulbright Fellowship and award recipients. In addition, Messiah has been listed for more than ten consecutive years on the Templeton Foundation's "Honor Roll of Character-Building Colleges."

At Messiah College, more than 86 percent of students live on campus, creating a vibrant community life and lasting friendships. More than sixty extracurricular activities, from national honor societies to special interest clubs to service and outreach teams, allow students the opportunity to enhance their classroom experiences and hone their leadership and team skills. In fact, in a recent year, students volunteered more than 60,000 hours in service and mission projects. Student government, the yearbook, the student-run weekly newspaper, the College radio station, theatrical productions, traveling musical groups, Habitat for Humanity, and residence hall activities are among the many opportunities offered by Messiah College for students to get involved.

Messiah encourages fitness for the body, mind, and spirit, offering active club and recreational sports programs as well as fielding twenty-two intercollegiate sports teams: eleven for men and eleven for women. Several of the NCAA Division III teams attain national rankings each year. In 2006, 2005, 2004, 2002, and 2000, the men's soccer team won the national championship. In 2005, the women's soccer team won the national championship; the team was a national runner-up in 2007. In 2005, the women's field hockey team was a national finalist. *USA Today* not only recognized the College for the success of its teams on the field, but also ranked Messiah fifth in the country for its high graduation rate of student athletes in Division III. Top-notch athletics facilities include a competition-size indoor pool, a diving pool, two gymnasiums, an artificial-turf field-hockey field, a weight-training center, exercise machines, a human-performance laboratory, competition tennis courts, a demonstration tennis court, and an indoor track as well as an expansive soccer stadium, manicured baseball and softball diamonds, a high ropes course, a fitness trail, and an outdoor track and field stadium.

Location

Located just 12 miles southwest of the state capital, Harrisburg, Messiah College's beautiful 471-acre campus provides an ideal setting for outdoor recreation, with easy access to urban centers such as Baltimore, Philadelphia, and Washington, D.C. Students enjoy picnics and canoeing on the Yellow Breeches Creek, which passes through the campus. The thriving suburban environment of central Pennsylvania affords students the opportunity to participate in the cultural, internship, and service options provided by the state capital and other major East Coast urban hubs.

Majors and Degrees

Messiah College awards both Bachelor of Arts and Bachelor of Science degrees in more than sixty majors: accounting, adventure education, art education, art history, athletic training, biblical and religious studies, biochemistry and molecular biology, biology, biopsychology, broadcasting, business administration, business information systems, chemistry, Christian ministries, communication, computer science, criminal justice, early childhood education (N–3), economics, elementary education (K–6), engineering, English, entrepreneurship, environmental science, environmental studies, family and consumer sciences education, French, German, health and exercise science, health and physical education (K–12), history, human development and family science, human resource management, humanities, international business, journalism, marketing, mathematics, music, nursing, nutrition and dietetics, nutrition science, philosophy, physics, politics, psychology, religion, social work, sociology, Spanish, Spanish business, sport management, studio art, and theater. Individualized majors are also available.

Students may also pursue teaching certification in art, biology and environmental education, chemistry, early childhood education, elementary education, elementary and special education, English, environmental education, French, German, health and physical education, mathematics, music education, social studies, and Spanish.

Preprofessional programs of study include allied health, dentistry, medicine, physical therapy, and veterinary science.

In addition, students may choose from sixty different minors that include coaching, African American religion and culture, peace and conflict, urban studies, and prelaw.

Academic Programs

Messiah's unique approach to academics combines a solid liberal arts foundation with study in one (or more) academic major. In addition to courses required in their major, students complete required general courses in writing, the sciences, the arts, language and culture, Christian faith, and physical education as well as electives to broaden their understanding and skills.

The College's academic year consists of two semesters, fall and spring, with a monthlong January term offering concentrated study in a single course or numerous cross-cultural trips to expand horizons. The College Honors Program, independent study, service learning, and internships enrich students' academic studies.

U.S. News & World Report has repeatedly ranked Messiah College among the top ten best colleges in the Northern Comprehensive Colleges–Bachelor's category. More important, Messiah's approach allows students to seek top-quality higher education to equip them for a higher calling. Ninety-nine percent of Messiah graduates are employed full-time, attending graduate school, or in voluntary service within six months of graduation. In 2006, Messiah's accounting program ranked seventh in the nation for the percentage of students who passed the CPA exam on their first attempt. That same year, 100 percent of nursing graduates passed the National Council Licensure Examination for registered nurses on their first attempt.

Off-Campus Programs

Through the College's EpiCenter (experiential learning center), Messiah students have many opportunities for off-campus study. In fact, the *Open Doors Report* ranked Messiah ninth among the nation's undergraduate institutions in sending students to study abroad.

In addition to a satellite campus in conjunction with Temple University in Philadelphia, students may also study in the following semester-long programs: American Studies Program (Washington, D.C.), AuSable Institute of Environmental Studies (Michigan), Australia Studies Centre (Sydney, Australia), Central American Study and Service, China Studies Program, Creation Care Study Program,

Jerusalem University College, Latin American Studies Program (Costa Rica), Los Angeles Film Studies Center, Oxford Semester (England), Russian Studies Program, Middle East Studies Program, Oregon Extension, and International Business Institute (Europe and Russia).

Messiah students may also participate in the Brethren Colleges Abroad program in locations such as China, Ecuador, England, France, Germany, Greece, Japan, and Spain. Annual cross-cultural study tours to locales such as the Bahamas, Greece, Guatemala, and Israel provide additional educational opportunities during January or summer terms.

Academic Facilities

Messiah College is committed to providing modern academic facilities with state-of-the-art technology and equipment for students in all fields of study. In addition to a library with more than 300,000 volumes and access to information, literature, and publications from around the globe, academic buildings include a new science center; a renovated and expanded nursing hall; a hall of engineering, mathematics, and business; a fine arts center; and a sports center, all constructed or renovated within the last twenty years. Two new facilities opened in fall 2003: a 95,000-square-foot academic building and a 35,000-square-foot student union. More than 500 computers in various academic and residence hall labs are connected to a campuswide network, along with fully wired residence hall rooms, enabling students to have access to research and important communication.

Costs

Tuition and fees for 2008–09 totaled $24,900, and room and board average $7610. Additional fees total $770.

Financial Aid

Keeping a Messiah education affordable for all students who desire it continues to be a high priority for the College. Tuition, room, and board costs remain competitive, with costs at about the average of comparable four-year private colleges in Pennsylvania. Financial aid counselors help students and families find available resources and create aid packages designed to meet their needs. In addition to federal and state grants and loans and on-campus employment programs, Messiah students benefit from about $20 million in institutional merit scholarships and need-based aid. About 97 percent of Messiah students receive financial aid, with the average annual award per recipient (from all sources of aid) being nearly $18,500. Students should apply for institutional aid by the March 1 deadline for the following fall semester.

The College also offers both a semester and a monthly payment plan, allowing students and their families to choose the payment option most suitable to their needs.

Faculty

Professors, not teaching assistants, teach all classes at Messiah College. Representing nearly 150 graduate schools in five countries as well as a variety of denominational affiliations, more than 70 percent of the professors have earned the terminal degree in their field. While Messiah's faculty members are serious scholars who pursue original research, present findings, and publish widely, they are first and foremost committed to teaching. Chosen for their scholarship, Christian commitment, and teaching ability, Messiah's 172 full-time and more than 191 part-time faculty members lead by example, encouraging students to dig deeper, seek truth, pursue academic excellence, and grow in all areas of their lives. A low student-faculty ratio of 13:1 enables professors and students to forge close relationships while learning from each other.

Student Government

The self-governing Messiah College Student Government Association (SGA) is the vital force behind many campus activities. SGA also provides student services such as outreach opportunities, social events, and book sales. Encouraging trial by peers rather than the College administration, the student judicial council hears cases of rule violations on a regular basis. Messiah also values student input for critical College decisions, inviting student representatives to sit on almost every standing and ad hoc committee on campus.

Admission Requirements

Messiah College seeks student applicants who are serious about their intellectual, spiritual, and personal development—those who strive to excel in many areas of their life and who will make a contribution to the campus community. Transfer, international, and ethnic minority students are highly encouraged to apply.

Selective in its admissions policy, the College examines academic achievement, extracurricular involvement, leadership skills, and Christian service. More than 30 percent of last year's freshman class ranked in the top 10 percent of their high school class. Forty-one were valedictorians or salutatorians, 3 were National Merit Scholars, 19 percent had SAT scores of more than 1300, and 21 percent had ACT scores of more than 28.

Applicants should have taken at least 4 years of English, 3 years of mathematics, 2 years each of science and social studies, and 6 electives, preferably 2 in a foreign language. A large majority of students accepted at Messiah College exceed these minimum requirements. Students should take the SAT or the ACT by January of their senior year in high school. The Write Choice option, where a required interview replaces the standardized test score, is available to students who rank in the upper 20 percent of their high school class. One Christian Life recommendation is required. Students are invited to attend on-campus information sessions and tours.

Application and Information

Messiah College makes admissions decisions on a rolling basis beginning September 15 prior to the student's senior year. The Admissions Office is open weekdays from 8 to 5. For more information, to arrange a campus tour and an interview, or to request a catalog and application, students should contact:

Admissions Office
Box 3005
Messiah College
One College Avenue
Grantham, Pennsylvania 17027
Phone: 717-691-6000
    800-233-4220 (toll-free)
Fax: 717-691-2307
E-mail: admiss@messiah.edu
Web site: http://www.messiah.edu

Messiah's faculty members mentor and prepare students to excel in their professions.

OHIO WESLEYAN UNIVERSITY

DELAWARE, OHIO

The University

"We inspire you. You change the world." These words are Ohio Wesleyan's charge to its students, and the University provides the tools to help them achieve that goal. A unique blend of liberal arts learning and preprofessional preparation sets Ohio Wesleyan University (OWU) apart. Founded by the United Methodist Church in 1842, the University is strongly committed to education for leadership and service, to fusing theory and practice, and to confronting specific issues of long-range public importance.

A selective, residential institution, Ohio Wesleyan is home to approximately 1,850 undergraduates, with a nearly equal number of men and women. Students come to Ohio Wesleyan from forty-seven states and fifty countries; most live on the attractive 200-acre campus. Housing options include six large residence halls; several small living units (SLUs), such as the Creative Arts House, the Modern Foreign Languages House, and the Peace and Justice House; and seven fraternity houses. The five sorority houses are nonresidential.

There is a wide range of cocurricular activities. Students initiate discussion groups, service projects, and intramural athletics. Other activities include the nation's oldest independent student newspaper; cultural- and ethnic-interest groups such as the Student Union on Black Awareness (SUBA) and SANGAM and VIVA (which promote an understanding of the cultures of South Asia and Latin America, respectively); the College Republicans and College Democrats; and prelaw and premed clubs. In the course of a year, students may enjoy more than 100 concerts, plays, dance programs, films, exhibits, and speakers. The Department of Theatre and Dance stages four major productions and much additional studio work each year, while the Music Department sponsors four large performance groups and a variety of smaller ensembles. The impressive Hamilton-Williams Campus Center is the hub of cocurricular life on campus.

There are twenty-three Division III varsity athletic teams—eleven for men and eleven for women; sailing is a coed sport. In 2007–08, the University won the North Coast Athletic Conference (NACA) All-Sports Trophy for the second consecutive time and the eighth time overall, posting top-3 finishes in seven of the nine spring sports and winning championships in baseball, golf, women's lacrosse, men's outdoor track and field, and men's and women's indoor track and field. The Bishops finished in the top 5 in nineteen of the twenty-two sports in which the NCAC offers championships.

Intramural programs are extensive, and all students have access to racquet sports, swimming, and weight-lifting facilities in the Branch Rickey Physical Education Center. Fitness equipment and health services are housed in the 7,000-square-foot Health and Wellness Center, conveniently located in Stuyvesant Hall. Off-campus opportunities for backpacking, boating, camping, golf, skiing, and swimming are abundant.

Location

Delaware combines the small-town pace and maple-lined streets of the county seat (population 31,000) with easy access to the state capital, Columbus, the fifteenth-largest city in America. Thirty minutes south of the campus, Columbus provides rich internship opportunities, international research centers, fine dining and shopping, and cultural events that complement those on campus.

Majors and Degrees

With ninety-three different courses of study, Ohio Wesleyan offers the Bachelor of Arts in accounting; ancient, medieval, and Renaissance studies; astronomy; biological sciences (botany, genetics, microbiology, and zoology); chemistry; computer science; economics (including accounting, international business, and management); education (elementary and secondary licensure in seventeen areas); English literature and writing; fine arts; French; geography; geology; German; history; humanities-classics; journalism; mathematics; music (applied or history/literature); philosophy; physical education; physics; politics and government; psychology; religion; sociology/anthropology; Spanish; and theater and dance. Interdisciplinary majors include Black world studies, East Asian studies, environmental studies, international studies, Latin American studies, neuroscience, urban studies, and women's and gender studies, as well as prelaw and premedicine. Students also may design majors in topical, period, or regional studies.

Two professional degrees are awarded: the Bachelor of Fine Arts in art history, arts education, and studio art, and the Bachelor of Music in music education and performance. Combined-degree (generally 3-2) programs are offered in engineering, medical technology, optometry, and physical therapy. Ohio Wesleyan is one of only eleven colleges in the United States that has a 3-2 engineering program with the California Institute of Technology.

Academic Programs

Ohio Wesleyan provides opportunities for students to acquire not only depth in a major area but also knowledge about their cultural past through the insight provided by a broad liberal arts curriculum. At Ohio Wesleyan, education is placed in a context of values, and students are encouraged to develop the intellectual skills of effective communication, independent and logical thought, and creative problem solving. To these ends, students are required to demonstrate competence in English composition and a foreign language (often through placement testing) and to complete distributional study in the natural and social sciences, the humanities, and the arts. With few exceptions, the major requires the completion of eight to fifteen courses. Many students double major or take more than one minor in addition to their major, and self-designed majors are not uncommon. Thirty-four courses are required for graduation.

Advanced placement is available with or without credit. Under the four-year honors program, even first-year students may be named Merit Scholars and work individually with faculty mentors on research, directed readings, or original creative work. Undergraduate students frequently present their research to prestigious societies such as the American Society for Microbiology, the American Microscopy Society, and the American Ornithologists' Union and many other nationally recognized professional organizations. Upperclass students also are encouraged to participate in independent study. Phi Beta Kappa is only one of the twenty-six scholastic honorary societies with chapters on campus.

The objectives of an Ohio Wesleyan education are crystallized in the distinctive Sagan National Colloquium, a program focused annually on one issue of compelling public importance. The 2008 Colloquium is titled "Cultivating a Green Campus: Promoting sustainability and environmental understanding on the OWU campus and the Delaware community." Through speakers, seminars, and student-led initiatives, the colloquium stimulates campuswide dialogue and encourages students to discover not only what they think about the issue but also why they think as they do and how to make important decisions based on their beliefs.

Off-Campus Programs

Full-semester internships and apprenticeships, as well as programs of advanced research, are available to students. Many are approved by the Great Lakes Colleges Association, Inc. (GLCA), a highly regarded academic consortium of twelve independent institutions. Programs include the Philadelphia Center, the GLCA New York Arts Program, and the Oak Ridge Science Semester. Other cooperative arrangements include the Newberry Library Program, Wesleyan in Washington, and the Drew University United Nations Semester. Students also conduct research locally at the U.S. Department of Agriculture (USDA) Laboratories in Delaware, the nearby Columbus Zoo, The Wilds, and several other sites. The Summer Science Research Program offers selected students the opportunity for an intensive, ten-week one-to-one research experience with a faculty member. The program concludes with a symposium at which research results are presented to the entire campus.

Ohio Wesleyan has been long committed to education for a global society. The curriculum has an international perspective, and a significant portion of the student body is drawn from other countries. In

fact, OWU has the highest percentage of international students among undergraduate, bachelor's-degree-granting colleges in the state of Ohio and the fourteenth-highest percentage among similar colleges in the United States. Domestic students are offered a wide variety of opportunities to study abroad. Students can arrange individual projects, but formal programs are offered in more than twenty countries. These include Ohio Wesleyan's affiliation with the University of Salamanca in Spain as well as programs in Mexico, Ireland, Central Europe, Turkey, Africa, China, England, India/Nepal, Japan, Russia, and others.

Academic Facilities

The Beeghly Library houses more than 550,000 holdings, one of the largest collections in the country for a private university of Ohio Wesleyan's size. The library's federal documents depository is among the nation's oldest and largest, providing an additional 200,000 reference publications. Beeghly Library also offers the Online Computer Library Center's most advanced cataloging system. The collection is enhanced by OhioLINK and CONSORT membership. An Internet Café within the Beeghly Library provides students with a 24-hour study area. The café has eight computer workstations and wireless capabilities and serves Starbucks coffee and other assorted sandwiches and snacks.

The comprehensive academic computing system is accessible to students 24 hours per day, and all residence hall rooms are wired for campus network and global Internet access. The latest generation of wireless communication allows students to work online anywhere on the campus.

The Conrades-Wetherell Science Center includes a 145,000-square-foot three-level building that houses a wide variety of state-of-the-art instrumentation, including a scanning electron microscope and scanning and transmission electron microscopes, all for undergraduate use. Located in the Science Center is the Hobson Science Library, which consolidates all of OWU's science holdings. The University has a state-of-the-art Geographic Information Systems Computer Laboratory.

The R.W. Corns Building houses the Woltemade Center for Economics, Business, and Entrepreneurship; the Department of Economics; the Sagan Academic Resource Center, which includes the Writing Resource Center, the Academic Skills Center, and the Quantitative Skills Center; and Information Systems.

Perkins Observatory features a 32-inch reflecting telescope and two smaller instruments, while an on-campus student observatory includes a 9.5-in refracting telescope. Two University wilderness preserves cover a total of 100 acres. Other special facilities include the multi-stage Chappelear Drama Center; Sanborn Hall, home to the Music Department, Jemison Auditorium, and the Kinnison Music Library; and the 1,100-seat Gray Chapel, which houses the largest of only six Klais concert organs in the United States.

Costs

The general fee for 2008–09 is $41,970. This amount covers tuition and fees ($33,700) and room and board ($8270). Books and personal expenses average $1100. Nominal fees are charged for some studio art courses, off-campus study, private music lessons for students who are not majoring in music, and student teaching.

Financial Aid

Nearly all first-year students who demonstrate need are awarded aid packages that include grant, loan, and employment assistance from Ohio Wesleyan and the standard federal and state programs (such as Federal Pell Grant, Federal Stafford Student Loan, Federal Perkins Loan, and Federal Work-Study). More than two thirds of the students receive some form of need-based aid, and another quarter receive merit- or non-need-based aid. More than 75 percent of all aid is provided by grants and scholarships. On the average, students on financial aid at Ohio Wesleyan receive more scholarship and grant assistance and rely less on loan support than do students at most other institutions.

Several merit scholarship programs, some worth as much as full tuition per year; private loan programs; and flexible payment plans are available without regard to financial need. This year, more than 140 enrolling first-year students received merit awards.

Faculty

The full-time faculty numbers 137, providing a student-faculty ratio of approximately 12:1. Nearly 100 percent of the full-time faculty members hold the highest degree in their fields. Although committed first to teaching and advising, most faculty members maintain active research programs and publish important articles and books. Some members of the faculty are practicing artists whose contributions include the creation and exhibition of original works of art and theater.

Student Government

Students have a significant voice in the government of campus life. The Wesleyan Council on Student Affairs formulates basic policy. Students also sit on judicial boards and nine faculty committees and are represented at all meetings of the Board of Trustees.

Admission Requirements

The admission process is competitive. Each prospective student's application is individually reviewed. Although the applicant's academic record is the most important factor, followed closely by teacher and counselor evaluations and SAT or ACT scores, many other aspects are considered, such as evidence of creativity, community service, and leadership. A sixteen-course preparatory program is required. Four units of English and 3 each of mathematics, social studies, science, and foreign language are recommended, but variations of this program are considered. SAT Subject Tests are not required but may qualify students for advanced placement. Candidates for the Bachelor of Music degree must audition (tapes are accepted). Early action, early decision, and transfer admission are offered. Campus interviews are strongly recommended but not required. For the 2008–09 school year, approximately 4,200 applications were received; about 65 percent of the applicants gained admission.

Application and Information

Students are urged to complete the application process as early as possible in the senior year of secondary school, especially if they are applying for financial aid. Once complete credentials (application, transcript, recommendations, and SAT or ACT scores) are received, decisions are made on a rolling basis after January 1. The student's response is required by May 1. The deadline for early decision application is December 1; the deadline for early action application is December 15. Notification is given within four weeks. After April 1, students are admitted on a space-available, rolling admission basis.

For further information, students should contact:

Office of Admission
Ohio Wesleyan University
Delaware, Ohio 43015
Phone: 740-368-3020
       800-922-8953 (toll-free)
Fax: 740-368-3314
E-mail: owuadmit@owu.edu
Web site: http://www.owu.edu

The Hamilton-Williams Campus Center is a magnificent meeting place for the campus community.

SIENA COLLEGE
LOUDONVILLE, NEW YORK

The College

Siena College is a four-year, coeducational, independent liberal arts college with a Franciscan and Catholic tradition. It is a community of 3,000 full-time students that offers undergraduate degrees in business, liberal arts, and sciences. Student-focused professors are at the heart of a supportive and challenging learning community that allows students to realize their potential and prepares them for careers and an active leadership role in their communities. Founded by the Franciscan Friars in 1937, Siena seeks to develop the potential for extraordinary achievement. It welcomes all races and creeds and prides itself on the care and concern for the intellectual, spiritual, ethical, and social growth of all students.

Approximately 80 percent of the College's students live on campus. Siena offers traditional residence halls, suites, and town-house units. When Siena students are not in class, they have plenty to do. More than sixty clubs and organizations are active each year. The Franciscan Center for Service and Advocacy is the College's primary vehicle for service with and among the poor and marginalized and offers service to Habitat for Humanity, soup kitchens, and teaching in religious education programs. More than 70 percent of the student body is involved in some type of athletic program. The College offers eighteen Division I intercollegiate sports, club teams, and intramurals. Siena also provides numerous student support services, including counseling, tutoring, health services, peer counseling, and a career center. Popular activities include the Stage III Theatre, the student newspaper, the radio station, the yearbook, the Rugby Club, the Black and Latino Student Union, and Model United Nations.

Siena College's Marcelle Athletic Complex features a field house with an elevated running track, racquetball and squash courts, an aerobics/dance studio, and an area with exercise and other weight-training equipment. Serra Hall, the dining hall on campus, underwent a $4.5-million renovation during the summer of 2006.

Siena provides additional learning and cultural experiences outside of its academic programs to its students and the wider community. Examples of these efforts include the Martin Luther King Jr. Lecture Series, the Niebuhr Institute of Religion and Culture, and the Sister Thea Bowman Center for Women.

Siena has developed a number of cooperative and special programs. In addition to the college-wide honors program, Siena offers a premed program with Albany Medical College; a five-year M.B.A. program with Clarkson University, Union University, and Pace University; a seven-year accelerated predental program with Boston University; a 3-2 engineering program in cooperation with Clarkson University, Catholic University, Rensselaer Polytechnic Institute, Manhattan College, SUNY at Binghamton, and Western New England College; and the Washington Semester at American University.

Location

Siena's 166-acre campus is ideally located in Loudonville, a residential community 2 miles north of Albany, the capital of New York. With eighteen colleges in the area, there is a wide variety of activities off campus. The Times Union Center hosts performances by major concert artists and professional sporting events. Within 50 miles are the Adirondacks, the Berkshires, and the Catskill Mountains, providing outdoor recreation throughout the year. Montreal, New York City, and Boston are less than 3 hours away. With all of the professional, cultural, and recreational opportunities the Capital Region offers, many Siena graduates choose to begin their careers here.

Majors and Degrees

The College offers bachelor's degrees in the following areas: accounting, actuarial studies, American studies, biochemistry, biology, chemistry, classics, computational science, computer science, creative arts, economics, English, environmental studies, finance, French, history, marketing and management, mathematics, philosophy, physics, political science, psychology, religious studies, social work, sociology, and Spanish. In addition, the College offers forty-six minors and certificate programs.

Academic Programs

A strong liberal arts core forms the basis for all of Siena's programs. All students take courses within a broad core requirement: 30 hours in the humanities and social sciences (including a 6-credit freshman foundations course), 9 hours in mathematics and science (with 3 of these in a natural science), and 3 hours in creative arts. Students must also maintain a minimum cumulative index of 2.0 and earn at least a C in every major field concentration course. Within the major, students must take a minimum of 30 credits, with no more than 39 credits counting toward the degree requirements. A total of 120 hours is required to qualify for a bachelor's degree.

Students may get credit for prior work by taking standardized college proficiency exams with the approval of the head of the department in the discipline to be examined. A total of 18 credits may be obtained this way. Siena offers honors courses in English, history, philosophy, and political science. ROTC affiliation is available at Siena in a U.S. Army unit, and an Air Force ROTC unit is available at a nearby college through cross-registration.

Off-Campus Programs

Siena students have the opportunity to spend a semester or a year studying abroad. Programs directly affiliated with the College include Siena at Regent's College, London; the Siena in London Internship Experience; the Siena semester at the Centre d'Études Franco-Américain de Management in Lyon, France; and the Center for Cross-Cultural Studies in Seville,

Spain. In addition, programs are available for all majors everywhere on the globe. International study is typically pursued during the junior year.

Locally, internships are available through government, business, and nonprofit organizations on a two- or three-day-a-week basis, enabling students to continue with their course work at the same time. Many students are offered jobs by their internship organization upon graduation.

In addition, through the Hudson Mohawk Association of Colleges and Universities (which comprises the eighteen colleges in the area), cross-registration is possible at such institutions as the College of Saint Rose, Rensselaer Polytechnic Institute, Skidmore College, Union College, and the University at Albany, State University of New York.

Academic Facilities

The Standish Library collection of more than 321,000 volumes consists of books, journals, microforms, compact discs, videocassettes, and a growing number of electronic information sources. More than 6,000 volumes are added annually, and 1,600 serial subscriptions are currently maintained, with electronic access to thousands of additional journals. In 2004, Siena completed the renovation of Siena Hall, a high-technology teaching and learning center. It is also home to Siena's Hickey Financial Technology Center. The Hickey Center provides Siena's students the opportunity to trade stocks, bonds, cash, and currency in a virtual environment and provides students with access to leading sources of financial data.

All academic and residential buildings are interconnected with a high-speed Ethernet network connected via fiber optics. This network backbone runs at 10 and 100 Mbps. Every student residence space includes a 10 Mbps connection point to access the College's network and the Internet. The network includes more than 2,500 ports. The computer facilities are accessible 24 hours a day, seven days a week. Numerous computers are available throughout the campus for student use.

Costs

Tuition at Siena remains reasonable, helping the College to provide an education of fine quality at moderate cost. For 2008–09, tuition is $23,750 and room and board are $9410. There are lab fees for accounting, natural sciences, languages, and some fine arts and psychology courses. Miscellaneous fees may account for about $600 per year.

Financial Aid

Siena is committed to providing personal attention to every student's financial needs, recognizing that each situation is different. More than 86 percent of students receive financial aid. Federal programs that Siena students may qualify for include Federal Pell Grants, Federal Supplemental Educational Opportunity Grants, Federal Perkins Loans, Federal Stafford Student Loans, and Federal PLUS loans. Residents of New York State may receive Tuition Assistance Program and aid for part-time Federal Work-Study Program awards. Financial need is determined by the Free Application for Federal Student Aid and, where applicable, the state version of the supplemental Financial Aid Form. Aid is usually awarded in a package combining scholarships or grants, loans, and a job. Students who remain in good academic standing have their aid renewed.

Faculty

Siena's faculty members are committed to teaching. Student concerns and development are at the heart of the curriculum. Nine out of every 10 full-time faculty members hold the highest degree awarded in their field. The student-faculty ratio of 14:1 helps to develop interaction with students, as does the fact that Siena professors teach labs. Students are assigned a faculty adviser to help in the planning of their course of study.

Student Government

The Student Senate oversees student involvement in academic and social life and interprets students' attitudes, opinions, and rights for the faculty and administration. It charters all student organizations and provides funds for many through fees collected by the College. The governing board is made up of officers and representatives of all four classes and of the commuting students. Elections are held in April for the following year, except for freshmen, who are elected in September.

Admission Requirements

Siena seeks bright, articulate people who will take advantage of the opportunities available at the College. Academic standards are demanding but not threatening. The average SAT score of accepted students is 1125. The high school curriculum, activities, recommendations, and campus visit all affect the final decision. Students seeking degrees in the science or business division should be well versed in mathematics. Those interested in American studies, English, history, or philosophy are likely to find a working knowledge of a foreign language very helpful.

Application and Information

The deadline for the submission of a regular application is March 1 of a student's senior year in high school. Decisions are sent starting in mid-March. Siena also offers an early decision and an early action program. Early applications should be submitted before December 1. Candidates are notified by January 1. Presidential Scholar candidates must apply by January 15.

Transfer students must apply by December 1 for the spring semester or by June 1 for the fall semester. Generally, transfers are expected to have a cumulative average of at least 2.5. A minimum of 30 semester hours and half of the credits for the major must be earned at Siena. A maximum of 66 credits may be transferred from accredited two-year institutions. Credit is given only for courses that are similar in content, level, and scope to those at Siena.

For more information, students should contact:

Admissions Office
Siena College
515 Loudon Road
Loudonville, New York 12211
Phone: 518-783-2423
      888-AT-SIENA (toll-free)
E-mail: admit@siena.edu
Web site: http://www.siena.edu

SOUTHERN METHODIST UNIVERSITY
DALLAS, TEXAS

The University

Southern Methodist University (SMU) is a small, caring academic community in the heart of a vibrant city, where excellence is the standard and the goal is helping students succeed. SMU prepares students for life and leadership in the twenty-first century by educating them to meet the challenges of a rapidly changing world, intellectually equipping them for lifelong learning, and preparing them for successful careers. The broad-based curriculum provides a strong foundation in the humanities and sciences. SMU's four undergraduate schools offer nearly eighty majors in business, engineering, the arts, and humanities and sciences. Learning at SMU includes opportunities for mentoring relationships, internships, leadership development, research experience, international study, and community service.

Founded in 1911, SMU welcomes students of every religion, race, color, ethnic origin, and economic status. Students come from all fifty states and more than ninety countries. Total University enrollment is 10,829; 6,176 are undergraduates. Sixty percent of all undergraduate lecture sections have fewer than 25 students. Academically promising students are invited into the University Honors Program.

The life of a student's education is enriched at SMU, where there are nearly 180 student activities and organizations. From debate club to intramural sports, campus events to marching band, academic interests to community service, students have many options. There are also a large number of academic honorary societies.

SMU hosts more than 400 public arts events each year. The world-renowned Willis M. Tate Distinguished Lecture Series brings guests, such as Secretary of State Colin Powell, actor Julie Andrews, and former President George Bush to campus. SMU is a member of the National Collegiate Athletic Association and participates in Conference USA, Division I-A. Seventeen Division I-A teams include basketball, football, golf, soccer, swimming/diving, and tennis and women's cross-country, equestrian, rowing, track and field, and volleyball.

SMU offers fourteen residence halls and living communities, including an honors hall, a fine arts community, and a service-learning house. First-year students are required to live on campus, except in special circumstances. Residence halls have local phone service, voice mail, Ethernet computer connections, Internet and e-mail, air conditioning, and community computer and lounge areas. Main campus, including the residence halls, also offers students free wireless Internet access.

Location

SMU's parklike campus, located north of downtown Dallas in a traditional and upscale residential neighborhood, features Georgian-style architecture and enjoys a pleasant Sun Belt climate. Dallas, often ranked as one of the world's most livable cities, is home to more than 6,000 corporate headquarters and offers outstanding opportunities for internships and future employment. A convenient light rail and bus system is located near the campus.

Majors and Degrees

SMU offers nearly eighty degrees through its four undergraduate schools, with flexible options such as double majors, minors, and dual degrees. Dedman College offers a Bachelor of Arts (B.A.) degree with a major in a department of the College and a Bachelor of Science (B.S.) degree with a major in mathematics, a natural science, or selected social sciences. The College also offers two part-time multidisciplinary evening degrees: the Bachelor of Humanities (B.Hum.) and the Bachelor of Social Science (B.Soc.Sci.). The Cox School of Business awards the Bachelor of Business Administration (B.B.A.) degree. The Meadows School of Arts awards the Bachelor of Fine Arts (B.F.A.) in art, art history, dance, and theater; the Bach-

elor of Arts (B.A.) in advertising, art history, cinema-television, journalism, music, corporate communications and public affairs; and the Bachelor of Music (B.M.) degrees. The School of Engineering offers the Bachelor of Arts (B.A.) degree in computer science and the Bachelor of Science (B.S.) degree in the fields of computer engineering, computer science, electrical engineering, environmental engineering, management science, and mechanical engineering, with specializations and biomedical and premed options.

Academic Programs

All undergraduates enter SMU through Dedman College. The College provides the University's general education curriculum, which is designed to help students develop analytical and communication skills, the ability to explore ethical issues, and a broad understanding of the world. The curriculum includes courses in such categories as cultural formation, perspectives, human diversity, and information technology. Students who know their career interest can select courses in their planned major while in Dedman College. Students majoring in the humanities, mathematics, the natural sciences, and the social or behavioral sciences remain in Dedman College. Requirements for graduation vary according to the major program.

SMU grants both credit and advanced placement for satisfactory completion of Advanced Placement (AP) courses in high school. Credit up to 6 semester hours is given for each course in which a score of 4 or 5 was earned; 12 to 14 hours of credit can be granted for foreign languages with a score of 4 or 5. SMU also gives credit for departmental examination. Credit also is awarded for scores from 5 to 7 on higher-level exams in transferable subjects for the International Baccalaureate. Credit is not awarded for subsidiary-level exams. High school students may earn dual credit by attending off-campus colleges. A maximum of 32 advanced credits can be awarded. The academic year at SMU is composed of two semesters, plus an optional summer session that comprises two 5-week terms. A May term is also available.

Off-Campus Programs

SMU Study Abroad offers thirty-three programs in Australia, China, Denmark, Egypt, France, Germany, Great Britain, Italy, Japan, Mexico, Russia, South Africa, Southeast Asia, Spain, and Taiwan. SMU-in-Taos is the University's summer campus in northern New Mexico.

Academic Facilities

Newer facilities include the Meadows Museum of Art, which houses one of the world's largest collections of Spanish art; an addition to the Fondren Library Center; the Dedman Life Sciences Building; the Lindsey Embrey Engineering Building; and the Gerald R. Ford Stadium and Paul B. Loyd Jr. All-Sports Center. SMU's Dedman Center for Lifetime Sports recently expanded to offer students more new and renovated indoor and outdoor facilities.

SMU libraries contain more than 3 million volumes. Fondren Library contains a catalog of all holdings and major works of a general nature. Other collections are located in the Science Information Center, the Underwood Law Library, the Bridwell Library (a component of Perkins School of Theology), Hamon Arts Library, DeGolyer Library, and the Business Information Center. The Altshuler Learning Enhancement Center, known as the A-LEC, offers students individual tutoring, study groups, and techniques to enhance study and time management skills and test-taking strategies.

SMU has high-quality facilities campuswide, including specialized laboratories in the Dallas Seismological Observatory and the electron microscopy laboratory. The Institute for the Study of Earth and Man houses specialized laboratories for archeology, ethnology, geology, and physical anthropology. The Dedman Life Sciences Build-

ing and the Junkins Electrical Engineering Building feature state-of-the-art research, teaching, and computer labs.

Costs

The comprehensive fee for full-time undergraduate students for the 2008–09 academic year was $43,295. This amount included tuition and fees totaling $33,170 and a room and board charge of $10,125. SMU offers a monthly payment plan and other resources and plans to help students manage their investment in a college education.

Financial Aid

About 78 percent of first-year students receive some form of financial assistance. The SMU financial aid program includes University, state, and federal scholarships; merit- and need-based scholarships; grants; part-time jobs; payment plans; and/or low-interest loans. Most students who demonstrate financial need are awarded an aid package that combines SMU funds with government resources. The University assists all qualified students who cannot afford an SMU education. Financial aid decisions are based on academic performance and financial need. Accepted students interested in federal or state financial aid must file the Free Application for Federal Student Aid (FAFSA). SMU's code is 003136. Students may file online at http://www.fafsa.ed.gov. Students should complete the FAFSA by February 15 to receive primary consideration.

Students who also wish to be considered for SMU need-based assistance must complete the College Scholarship Service Financial Aid PROFILE (CSS PROFILE) in addition to the FAFSA. The PROFILE is available online at http://profileonline.collegeboard.com.

Financial aid, such as grants, low-interest loans, and campus employment, is also available to transfer students who demonstrate financial need based on the FAFSA and the CSS PROFILE, both of which should be filed each year. SMU offers transfer students a range of merit scholarships. For details, students should contact a transfer admission counselor at the phone number listed in this description.

SMU's merit-based scholarships have been named among the best in the United States by *America's Best College Scholarships 2001*. SMU's most prestigious scholarship programs include the President's Scholars, the Nancy Ann and Ray L. Hunt Leadership Scholars, SMU Distinguished Scholars, University Scholars, and International Baccalaureate (IB) Scholars. National Merit Scholarships are available only to finalists who name SMU as their first college choice. Students must apply for merit scholarships by January 15.

Faculty

The undergraduate student-faculty ratio is 12:1, which allows students to interact closely with faculty members. Sixty percent of all undergraduate lecture sections have fewer than 25 students. Almost 90 percent of the full-time faculty members hold a Ph.D. or the highest degrees in their field. Regular, full-time faculty members teach most undergraduate classes (74 percent). SMU has more than 500 full-time faculty members.

Student Government

The SMU Student Senate is a comprehensive governing body that meets weekly to initiate and facilitate action on student affairs. The Senate is composed of 4 student body officers, 40 senators, and ten committees.

Admission Requirements

The Office of Admission bases selection of applicants on several criteria: the strength of the high school program and the grades received, SAT or ACT scores, teacher and counselor recommendations, an essay, and optional input from parents and peers. Applicants should present a college-preparatory program and are expected to complete a minimum of 4 years of English, 3 of mathematics (including algebra I and II and plane geometry), 3 of a natural science (including two lab sciences), 3 of social studies, and 2 of a foreign language. SMU places value on personal accomplishment, and an attempt is made to get to know the individual and the academic record beyond standardized scores.

Although the average GPA of successful transfer applicants who have completed 30 or more transferable hours is considerably higher than a 2.7 GPA (on a 4.0 scale), applicants with a GPA below this threshold are not typically successful in gaining admission. Candidates with a transferable GPA below 2.0 are not admitted to the University. For all candidates who have completed 30 or more college hours, the Admission Committee considers the rigorous nature of the courses attempted; in particular, applicants should have completed at least one course in English composition, a lab science, a math course beyond college algebra, and a course pertaining to the intended major. The committee weighs overall academic performance as well as evidence of recent improvement. For some applicants, the high school performance is also a factor. Candidates with fewer than 30 hours are considered on an individual basis and may be required to submit additional information, including high school records.

As a privately endowed institution, SMU has no limits on enrollment based solely on geography, and it makes no distinctions in tuition, fees, or other costs based on the home state of the student. Southern Methodist University does not discriminate on the basis of race, color, religion, national origin, sex, age, disability, or veteran status. SMU's commitment to equal opportunity includes nondiscrimination on the basis of sexual orientation.

Application and Information

Students should apply soon after completing the junior year of high school. Online applications are available at http://www.smu.edu/apply. The nonbinding early action deadline is November 1, with notification by December 31. For regular decision and priority merit scholarship application consideration, the deadline is January 15, with notification by March 15. SMU offers a spring decision deadline of March 15 on a space-available basis.

Transfer application deadlines are April 1 for the summer term entry, June 1 for fall term and merit scholarship consideration, and November 1 for spring term (including scholarship applicants).

For admission information, students should contact:

Division of Enrollment Services
Southern Methodist University
P.O. Box 750181
Dallas, Texas 75275-0181
Phone: 214-768-2058
      800-323-0672 (toll-free)
E-mail: ugadmission@smu.edu
Web site: http://www.smu.edu/admission/

Dallas Hall is the landmark building of SMU, reflecting the neo-Georgian architecture of the campus.

UNIVERSITY OF CHARLESTON
CHARLESTON, WEST VIRGINIA

The University

The University of Charleston (UC) strives to educate each student for a life of productive work, enlightened living, and community involvement. The University is very serious about its responsibility to provide students with the knowledge, abilities, and character necessary for them to have successful careers and to be productive and active citizens.

Founded in 1888 and formerly known as Morris Harvey College, the University of Charleston acquired its new name in 1979 to signify its importance as the leading higher education opportunity in the capital. Today, UC proudly represents the capital city of Charleston and the surrounding Kanawha Valley. Currently, approximately 1,400 students representing thirty-five states and twenty countries enjoy the University's 40-acre riverfront campus overlooking the State Capitol Complex and the beautiful city of Charleston.

The University has received numerous national accolades for its outstanding quality and educational approach. In September 2007, the University of Charleston was recognized as the national leader in outcomes-based learning and student assessment by the *New York Times Magazine*. The University also was ranked number 1 in the nation for 2007 by the Collegiate Learning Assessment (CLA), which also showed that UC students show the largest learning gain from freshman to sophomore year among all schools in the CLA report. The University of Charleston has been recognized as a national model for the Freshman-Year Experience, which includes faculty mentoring, university transitions, and living/learning communities. In addition, *U.S. News & World Report* placed UC in the top 20 in the Baccalaureate Colleges in the South category and as the Top Ranked Comprehensive College in West Virginia in its "Best Colleges for 2007" rankings. Students at UC also score among the highest in the country on the National Survey of Student Engagement.

The UC educational program focuses on "Learning Your Way." Students are the focus at UC. The academic program allows them to demonstrate what they have learned in order to earn the credits necessary for graduation. Students are expected to demonstrate knowledge and skills in the areas of communication, critical thinking, citizenship, ethical practice, science, and creativity. These attributes are integrated with knowledge and skills in a chosen field of study. Future employers and graduate schools consistently seek and employ college graduates with these abilities, and it is imperative that all University graduates have a strong foundation in these skills. Therefore, the University of Charleston has designed this program to help students master the knowledge and skills that are necessary for success.

Students are also encouraged to demonstrate mastery and earn credits at their own pace. Many students earn more than the traditional 15–18 credits per semester and graduate within three years, double major, or earn a master's degree quicker than at other schools.

Housing facilities for residential students are very modern and student friendly. Brotherton Hall was built in 2000 and houses 220 students; New Hall, built in 2003, houses 183 students; and Middle Hall, built in 2005 and 2006, houses 240 students. An expansion was completed for Middle Hall in August 2006 to accommodate increased student housing numbers, allowing the campus to house approximately 700 students.

Because the University believes that students learn from their involvement in community and campus activities, students are strongly encouraged to participate in one or more of the forty cocurricular organizations found at the University. There are academic clubs, publications, fraternities, sororities, religious organizations, intramural sports, honorary societies, drama clubs, cheerleading, chorus and band programs, and many student leadership organizations. The new Morrison Fitness Center opened in January 2007 and houses modern exercise equipment, weight systems, and classrooms for dance, yoga, Tae Kwon Do, or other activities. The University's Welch Colleague program integrates student involvement, the academic curriculum, community service, and leadership. The Community Service program provides opportunities for students to participate both on campus and in the Charleston area through opportunities like Habitat for Human-

ity. In addition, there are numerous civic, political, social, and charitable organizations easily accessible in the community.

The varsity sports program for men and women has become one of the University's most valuable assets. Men and women may participate in basketball, cheerleading, soccer, and tennis. Men may also participate in baseball, football, and golf and women in crew, cross-country, softball, track and field, and volleyball. The University's athletic teams compete in Division II of the NCAA. In recent years, men's and women's teams have been contenders in the WVIAC tournaments, with several teams winning conference championships and attending national championship tournaments. The women's basketball team participated in the Elite 8 in 2005 and 2006, and the men's football team had the largest one-season turnaround in conference history in 2005. UC athletics won the President's and Commissioner's Cups in 2006–07, signifying the top athletic teams in the WVIAC Conference.

The University of Charleston is accredited by the North Central Association of Colleges and Schools, National Council for Accreditation of Teacher Education, National Athletic Trainers Association, Commission on the Accreditation of Allied Health Education Programs–Athletic Training, Joint Review Committee on Education in Radiological Technology, and the National League for Nursing Accrediting Commission. The University holds a variety of professional recognitions, approvals, and memberships, including the International Assembly of Collegiate Business Education, West Virginia Academy of Sciences, Interior Design Educator's Council, and the American Council on Education.

The University offers master's degrees in business administration: an Executive M.B.A. and a plus-one M.B.A. for full-time study, one year beyond the bachelor's degree. A new Graduate School of Business is scheduled to open in fall 2008 with an emphasis on experiential learning and an enhanced master's program for outstanding students. The University of Charleston School of Pharmacy, which offers the University's first doctoral-level program, opened in fall 2006.

Location

Charleston, West Virginia's vibrant state capital, is a cultural, social, political, and economic hub. Located in the Kanawha Valley near the foothills of the Appalachian Mountains, it offers scenic tranquility as well as the convenience and excitement of a modern city. With a metropolitan population of 200,000, Charleston has grown to be West Virginia's finest city. Accessibility to the city is quite easy via plane, car, bus, and train. A large civic center, historic sites, libraries, movie theaters, shopping malls, and a symphony orchestra are all highlights of the Charleston business district. The rapport between the University and the community is excellent, and many events are cosponsored annually.

Downtown Charleston, just a short ride from the campus by campus shuttle or city bus, offers the kind of social and cultural opportunities that can be found only in a large city. In addition, fishing, hunting, horseback riding, waterskiing, snow skiing, mountain biking, and white-water rafting are just a few of the many recreational activities to be found within a short distance of the campus.

Majors and Degrees

The University of Charleston offers undergraduate degree programs through its various divisions: the Morris Harvey Division of Arts and Sciences, the Herbert Jones Division of Business, and the Bert Bradford Division of Health Sciences.

The Morris Harvey Division of Arts and Sciences offers the Bachelor of Arts degree with the following majors: art, communications, education (various certifications), general studies, interior design, political science, and psychology. The Bachelor of Science degree is offered with majors in biology, chemistry, and a biology/chemistry preprofessional program focused on the health sciences. The Division of Arts and Sciences is also home to the popular Pre-Pharmacy program. This program is segmented into the Pre-Pharmacy Scholars track and the Traditional Pre-Pharmacy track. Students who excel in this unique program have preferential entry into the Pharm.D. program.

The Jones Division of Business offers Bachelor of Science degree programs in accounting, sports administration, business administration, and finance.

The Division of Health Sciences offers the Bachelor of Science degree in athletic training, nursing, and radiologic science. An Associate of Arts degree in nursing is also offered at the University.

Students may pursue directed independent study and internships in most majors. Army ROTC is offered to interested men and women.

Academic Programs

Candidates for a bachelor's degree from UC are required to complete a minimum of 120 semester hours and have a cumulative grade point average of at least 2.0 on all college work attempted. This must include 30 hours in upper division courses; demonstration of learning in the required outcomes of communication, critical thinking, ethical practice, creativity, science, and citizenship; and advanced work leading to a major in a department or a division. The minimum requirement for an associate degree is 60 semester hours and a cumulative grade point average of at least a 2.0 on all college work attempted, including completion of a prescribed program of general education and specialized work in a department.

The University follows a semester academic calendar and offers summer terms for students who wish to accelerate their college program.

Academic Facilities

A large number of support facilities and programs supplement the various academic opportunities at the University of Charleston. The Schoenbaum Library serves as the center of the learning experience. Located in the technologically advanced Clay Tower Building, the library has a collection of more than 120,000 books, 200,000 microforms, and 3,600 audiovisual items. More than 8,000 journal titles are available either in print or electronically and are accessible from any Web-enabled computer, on or off campus. In addition, numerous specialized collections, CD-ROM-based electronic indexes, and online electronic search services are at the students' disposal for specialized research and study. The library also offers wireless technology and laptop computer check-out.

The University has numerous computer labs for student and faculty use: the Cabot Apple Lab, the IBM-PC combination classroom labs, an IBM-PC network lab, and an IBM-PC open lab. Wireless access is also available on much of the campus, including the scenic riverbank. The Learning Support Center provides a variety of services and classes to help students achieve academic, personal, and professional success. The Communication Resource Center provides support for students and faculty members through consultation services, workshops, and electronic access to a variety of writing resources.

The Clay Tower Building houses state-of-the-art science, technology, and information resource facilities. Riggleman Hall, the main college building, houses classrooms, a 976-seat auditorium and stage, education and language laboratories, the Carleton Varney Department of Art and Design, and administrative offices.

Costs

For the 2007–08 academic year, tuition was $22,050, and room (double occupancy) and board were $7930, for a total of $29,980. This does not include the cost of books, supplies, or other incidental charges.

Financial Aid

The University of Charleston provides generous financial assistance that may include a combination of scholarships, grants, loans, and work-study. In 2007–08, more than 90 percent of full-time students received some form of financial aid. Special academic scholarships and grants are awarded to outstanding full-time students. The University also offers grants to qualified athletes and to students who are involved in leadership, community service, band, school newspaper, or vocal music.

Faculty

The University has 61 full-time and 38 part-time undergraduate faculty members. At the University of Charleston, faculty members pro-vide academic, career, and in some cases, personal advice to students. They encourage active learning through collaborative projects and faculty/student research. Small classes through a 13:1 faculty-student ratio allow for individual attention for students.

Student Government

The Student Government Association is a policymaking body composed of students representing most campus organizations and student classes. Both the Student Government Association and the University believe that students should have the privilege, along with the faculty and administration, of participating in the governance of the University.

Admission Requirements

Admission to the University of Charleston is based on the academic records and potential for leadership and involvement. A qualified applicant's credentials must strongly suggest ability and motivation to succeed in higher education and in the University community. Candidates for admission must present a transcript of work from an accredited secondary school showing at least 16 academic units, grades indicating intellectual ability and promise, and proof of graduation or a GED. The pattern of courses should show purpose and continuity and furnish a background for the liberal learning outcomes curriculum offered by the University.

Since the unique and student-friendly curriculum emphasizes communication, critical thinking, and citizenship, secondary school courses should emphasize courses in English, mathematics, sciences, and social sciences. Candidates are also required to submit scores on the ACT or SAT. Students must have an above-average academic profile that includes a minimum 2.25 academic grade point average and a minimum ACT composite score of 19 or SAT score (combined math and critical reading) of 900. Applicants for admission are considered on an individual basis without regard to race, religion, geographic origin, or handicap. Letters of recommendation and a personal visit to the campus scheduled with the Office of Admissions are highly recommended.

Application and Information

For more information, interested students should contact:

Office of Admissions
University of Charleston
2300 MacCorkle Avenue, SE
Charleston, West Virginia 25304
Phone: 304-357-4750
      800-995-GO UC (4682) (toll-free)
Fax: 304-357-4781
E-mail: admissions@ucwv.edu
Web site: http://www.ucwv.edu

The Clay Tower Building houses state-of-the-art science facilities and a library with lounges overlooking the Kanawha River. The campus is directly across the river from the State Capitol.

UNIVERSITY OF SAN FRANCISCO

SAN FRANCISCO, CALIFORNIA

The University

From its beginnings as a one-room schoolhouse, founded in 1855 by the Jesuits, the University of San Francisco (USF) has developed into one of the premier Catholic universities on the West Coast. Throughout its history, USF has been committed to preparing students to improve the world in which they live. With more than 9,000 undergraduate and graduate students, the University has remained faithful to the Jesuit tradition and has maintained its small class size and low student-faculty ratio. Its programs in the arts, the sciences, business, education, nursing, and law foster a love of learning grounded by the challenge to serve society.

USF is one of the most diverse university campuses in the United States. Living and learning with a student body that consists of students from all fifty states and sixty-nine other countries is a unique opportunity. All new incoming freshman and sophomore students under the age of 21 are required to live on the campus, unless living with their parents. More than 90 percent of the incoming freshmen and 55 percent of all undergraduates live on-campus.

The University offers five on-campus residence halls, two on-campus apartment-style residences, and one off-campus traditional residence hall. Gillson and Hayes-Healy house freshmen, while Phelan and Lone Mountain are for sophomores and upperclass students. Fromm Hall is the only all-female residence hall. Located just twelve blocks from the USF campus, Pedro Arrupe Hall is the off-campus traditional residence hall offered to sophomore and upperclass students. Loyola Village is a student residential community that features apartment-style living for students who are 21 or over or in their junior year. Most rooms in residence halls are doubles, with some single rooms available for upperclass students. Fulton House is located adjacent to USF and provides a "home" living environment for 12 upperclass students. Each residence hall has laundry facilities, study/computer rooms, television lounges, and 24-hour front desks.

On the campus, students have access to various University facilities. The Koret Health and Recreation Center is an exciting complex that provides facilities for exercise, racquetball, court games, weight training, personal training, and various aquatic activities in an Olympic-size pool. Tai Chi, yoga, hip-hop, and spinning are just some of the classes offered at Koret. Outdoor adventures include horseback riding, sailing, and sea kayaking. Intramural and club sports are offered in the fall and spring semesters and include basketball, boxing, flag football, fencing, karate, lacrosse, rugby, and co-ed volleyball. NCAA Division I sports include baseball, basketball, cross-country, golf, soccer, tennis, track and field, and women's volleyball.

Dining facilities are located all over campus and are within walking distance of the residence halls and classrooms. Located on the main campus, The Market Café offers a food court experience with a variety of choices, including global, vegan, homestyle classics, and vegetarian options. Other dining options include Outtakes Café, Jamba Juice, Crossroads coffeehouse, Club Ed, and Kendrick Café at the Law School.

Undergraduates keep busy by participating in nearly 100 on-campus, student-run associations, fraternities and sororities, honor societies, and clubs, such as the USF Rugby Club and Los Locos, a club that supports USF athletics. Among these clubs are the oldest continuously performing theater group west of the Mississippi River, an award-winning FM radio station, an award-winning weekly newspaper, and a literary magazine.

For students interested in giving back to the community, the Office of Service-Learning and Community Action forms a partnership between the local community and USF. Students may participate in community service activities that include preparing meals for the homeless, tutoring underprivileged children, habitat restoration, and annual events such as AIDS Walk San Francisco.

Location

The University of San Francisco is located on a stunning 58-acre campus in a residential neighborhood just minutes from downtown San Francisco, the Financial District, Fisherman's Wharf, and the Pacific Ocean. The hilltop campus, renowned for its beautiful landscaping, borders the 1,000-acre Golden Gate Park and offers spectacular panoramic views of the city. The dynamic city of San Francisco keeps students entertained with concerts, the ballet, opera, museum exhibits, theater, and sporting events. Because of the diversity and geographical compactness of San Francisco, students find research facilities, opportunities for community involvement, and employment experiences that cannot be matched by most cities.

Majors and Degrees

The College of Arts and Sciences offers both B.A. and B.S. degrees. Majors include architecture and community design, art history/art management, biology, chemistry, communication studies, comparative literature and culture, computer science, design, economics, economics B.A.-M.A. (five-year program), English, environmental science, environmental studies, exercise and sports science, fine arts, French studies, history, international and development economics B.A.-M.A. (five-year program), Japanese studies, Latin American studies, mathematics, media studies, performing arts and social justice, philosophy, physics, physics/engineering, politics, psychology, sociology, Spanish, theology/religious studies, undeclared arts, undeclared science, and visual arts. The McLaren College of Business offers Bachelor of Business Administration degrees in accounting, business administration, entrepreneurship, finance, hospitality industry management, international business, management, and marketing. The School of Nursing offers a four-year Bachelor of Science in Nursing for qualified high school graduates and for second-baccalaureate candidates.

USF has sixty minors and offers unique programs that enhance the learning experience at USF. Special programs include the Catholic Studies interdisciplinary minor, Asia Pacific Studies B.A.-M.A. (five-year program); ethnic studies; film studies; Honors Program in the Humanities; Intensive English Program; journalism; Judaic studies; Middle East studies; neuroscience; 4+3 dual degrees in law, military science, premedical, and other pre-professional health studies; Saint Ignatius Institute Program; and a five-year dual degree Teacher Preparation Program that results in teacher certification at the elementary or secondary level.

Academic Programs

The University of San Francisco is committed to providing students with the essentials of a well-rounded education. A baccalaureate degree is issued upon the successful completion of a 128-unit curriculum. The curriculum consists of 44 units of core courses chosen from six specified categories in addition to 80–85 units that are divided among departmental major requirements and electives. An honors program is available for selected superior students seeking a strong academic challenge. The academic year is based on the two-semester system, with a summer session and a winter intersession also available.

In an effort to encourage high school students to move rapidly into the study of subjects now customarily reserved for colleges, the University of San Francisco honors advanced placement credits, as certified by the College Board's Advanced Placement Program tests. The University also cooperates with the College-Level Examination Program (CLEP). Students intending to earn such credit must take the CLEP examinations prior to registering at the University for their freshman courses.

The USF Pre-Professional Health Committee serves to guide and recommend students to medical and dental professional health schools as well as to schools for pharmacy, optometry, veterinary medicine, and podiatry. A student may complete the premedical or other pre-health science requirements as part of, or in addition to, the requirements of an academic major. The Pre-Professional Health Committee assists students with the application process, develops a professional file for each student, collects and mails recommendations to professional schools, conducts interviews in preparation for application, and endorses approved candidates via a committee letter of recommendation sent to all professional schools selected by the student.

Academic Facilities

The Western New England campus contains twenty major buildings and is situated on 215 acres. Classes are held in five classroom-laboratory buildings, which contain more than sixty-five classrooms. The D'Amour Library contains 110,000 volumes, with access to more than 15,000 titles via the Internet, and has wireless access for all students to use. The library is also home to the College's state-of-the-art television studio, the highlight of the 2005 $1.9-million renovation. The College is committed to providing students with access to a wide range of computing hardware and software. The College has a campus-wide network linking all buildings to hundreds of PCs in public areas, including the Churchill Hall Lab, the D'Amour Library, the Writing and Math Centers, the Accounting Lab, the School of Law, and the Engineering Labs. In addition, the School of Engineering has a large number of microcomputers, graphic plotters, and other peripherals that may be used to support the laboratory programs. All College residence hall rooms are wired for Internet access and are cable-TV ready. In addition, each semester, faculty members and students use the Manhattan Virtual Classroom, which was developed by Western New England College, to provide safe and secure file transport between faculty members, students, campus organizations, and informal groups.

Costs

Tuition and fees for the 2007–08 academic year for the School of Engineering were $27,034 for commuting students and $37,032 for residential students. For the Schools of Business and Arts and Science, tuition and fees were $25,942 for commuting students and $35,940 for residential students.

Financial Aid

Western New England College offers comprehensive programs of financial assistance to students who demonstrate financial need. The programs include merit- and need-based scholarships, grants, loans, and on-campus employment. Students seeking financial aid must submit the Free Application for Federal Student Aid (FAFSA) and a copy of the federal income tax return and W-2 form. Approximately 90 percent of Western New England College students annually receive assistance.

Faculty

Western New England College has a faculty of 164 full-time instructors, of whom 92 percent have received their terminal degrees. The College also has adjunct instructors, who share important specialized information with the students. The Western New England College School of Law has a distinguished legal faculty numbering 38 full-time and adjunct instructors.

The ratio of students to faculty members is 15:1. The average class size is 20, and students have ample opportunity to meet with faculty members outside of class.

Admission Requirements

Applicants must have graduated from an approved secondary school or have obtained a General Educational Development (GED) credential. The minimum units of high school preparation should include 4 units of English, 2 units of mathematics, 1 unit of laboratory science, and 1 unit of U.S. history. Applicants to the School of Business and those who wish to major in chemistry, computer science, forensic biology, forensic chemistry, or mathematics are required to present 3 units of mathematics. Prospective engineering students must present 1 unit of physics or 1 unit of chemistry as well as 4 units of mathematics.

Application and Information

Admission is offered to students on a rolling basis for all programs. However, students are encouraged to apply early in order to receive complete consideration for admission, financial aid, and housing. Students must submit the Western New England College application, SAT or ACT scores, an official secondary school transcript, and a recommendation from a guidance counselor or teacher. International students can substitute the Test of English as a Foreign Language (TOEFL) for the SAT or ACT. American students for whom English is not the first language are encouraged to submit TOEFL scores. Transfer students must also submit official transcripts for any collegiate work. An essay is not required, but essays and personal statements are welcome. Notification of acceptance begins in late fall.

For further information, students should contact:

Office of Admission
Western New England College
1215 Wilbraham Road
Springfield, Massachusetts 01119-2684
Phone: 413-782-1321
      800-325-1122 Ext. 1321 (toll-free)
Fax: 413-782-1777
E-mail: ugradmis@wnec.edu
Web site: http://www.wnec.edu

Students enjoy the beautiful and spacious Western New England College campus.

The St. Ignatius Institute has an integrated core curriculum based on the great books of Western civilization and an emphasis upon the great works of Christianity. Any undergraduate student at the University, regardless of major, may take courses through the Institute to meet general education requirements. The University also offers Army ROTC. ROTC scholarships are available for qualified applicants and continuing students.

Off-Campus Programs

The University of San Francisco's Center for Global Education has numerous study-abroad programs available to students with junior standing and a cumulative minimum GPA of 3.0. Exchanges with Jesuit universities include locations in Japan, Mexico, China, Spain, Philippines, El Salvador, and Chile. USF's St. Ignatius Institute program includes an exchange with Oxford University in England. Affiliations with other Jesuit universities make travel to other countries possible, e.g., Gonzaga University's study-abroad program in Florence, Italy, and Loyola University of Chicago's program in Rome. USF is also an associate member of the Institute of European and Asian Studies, which offers programs in Durham and London, England; Paris, Dijon, and Nantes, France; Berlin and Freiburg, Germany; Vienna, Austria; Madrid and Salamanca, Spain; Milan, Italy; Tokyo and Nagoya, Japan; Moscow, Russia; Adelaide and Canberra, Australia; Beijing, China; and Singapore. Numerous other study-abroad opportunities are also available. USF assists students in selecting a location, applying to programs, making financial arrangements, registering for academic credit, securing a passport and visa, and making travel plans.

Academic Facilities

University of San Francisco students have access to Gleeson Library's more than 1.8 million holdings and Harney Science Center, which houses the Computer Center, Applied Math Laboratory, the Institute of Chemical Biology, and the Physics Research Laboratories. Cowell Hall, the base for nursing classes and the Nursing Skills Laboratory, also includes the Instructional Media Center. Students also have access to Phelan Hall, the home of KUSF, the University's FM radio station, and *The Foghorn*, the official campus newspaper. Malloy Hall, headquarters for the McLaren College of Business, houses an additional computer laboratory and special seminar rooms. Kalmanovitz Hall, the new home for humanities and social sciences, features state-of-the-art classrooms, a rooftop sculpture garden, and seventeen laboratories for language, writing, media, and psychology.

Costs

Tuition for the 2008–09 school year was $34,519. Room and board were $11,130 for the academic year. Books, travel, and other expenses are about $4200 per year.

Financial Aid

A wide variety of scholarships, grants, loans, and work-study programs are available at the University. Domestic students who wish to be considered for financial aid must submit the Free Application for Federal Student Aid (FAFSA) by February 1. More than two thirds of all USF students receive some type of financial aid. There are also many on- and off-campus jobs available.

The University Scholars Program is available to new domestic freshman applicants who have an exceptional cumulative GPA, SAT combined score, or ACT composite score. Scholars are awarded a non-need-based scholarship that pays a significant percentage of the cost of tuition for four years of undergraduate study. To remain eligible, University Scholars are expected to maintain a minimum GPA of 3.25. Eligible students are identified during the admission process and must apply under early action by the November 15 deadline.

Faculty

The University has a faculty of 371 full-time and 526 part-time members; 92 percent of the full-time faculty members hold doctoral degrees. The University of San Francisco fosters a close relationship between students and faculty members. This is reflected in the small size of classes, the low student-faculty ratio, and the faculty members' availability for advising. Classes are not taught by student teachers or teachers' assistants.

Student Government

All undergraduates are members of the Associated Students of the University of San Francisco (ASUSF). ASUSF is the official representative body of undergraduate students at USF. The ASUSF government has three functions: to represent the official student viewpoint, to recommend policies, and to fund activities and services. ASUSF consists of three branches: the executive branch, the Student Senate, and the Student Court. The Senate comprises an executive board and student senators.

Admission Requirements

The University seeks students who are sincerely interested in pursuing a well-rounded education. The admission process is selective, and each application is reviewed individually. To enhance the quality and diversity of its student body, the University of San Francisco encourages men and women of all races, nationalities, and religious beliefs to apply. Eligibility is based on high school course work and GPA, the application essay, an academic and personal recommendation, and satisfactory test scores. Domestic applicants are required to submit SAT or ACT test scores with writing. International applicants are generally required to submit TOEFL or IELTS test scores; however, if an international applicant submits SAT or ACT test scores, the TOEFL or IELTS may be waived.

Application and Information

A completed application includes the application form, the application fee, a personal essay, all academic transcripts, test scores, and one letter of recommendation. For the fall semester, the application deadlines are November 15 for early action and January 15 for regular action.

Inquiries should be addressed to:

Office of Undergraduate Admission
University of San Francisco
2130 Fulton Street
San Francisco, California 94117-1046
Phone: 415-422-6563
       800-CALL-USF (toll-free outside California)
Fax: 415-422-2217
E-mail: admission@usfca.edu
Web site: http://www.usfca.edu

St. Ignatius Church, where freshman convocation and all graduation ceremonies are performed by each college.

UTICA COLLEGE
UTICA, NEW YORK

The College

A private, independent college founded in 1946, Utica College (UC) is known for its excellent academic programs, outstanding faculty members, personal attention, and diversity among students. The hallmarks of Utica College's academic programs are the integration of liberal and professional studies and a strong emphasis on internships, research, and other experiential learning opportunities, but UC is best known for the close, personal relationship students have with both faculty and staff members. Approximately 3,000 undergraduate and graduate students attend UC, including men and women from a wide variety of socioeconomic and cultural backgrounds as well as older students, veterans, and students with disabilities. While most students come from New York, New England, and the Middle Atlantic States, students are drawn to UC from all parts of the United States, and there is a growing international student population.

Academic programs of note include accounting-CPA, economic crime investigation, education, the health sciences, journalism, management, psych–child life, and public relations. Utica College also offers a robust study-abroad program as well as an honors program.

Utica College is located on a modern, 128-acre campus on the southwestern edge of Utica, New York. Its facilities include an academic complex where most classes are held, the Frank E. Gannett Memorial Library, seven residence halls, an athletic center, a 1,200-seat stadium, and numerous athletic fields.

Half of UC's students live on campus in residence halls that feature a variety of housing options, modern amenities, and lounges for studying or relaxing with friends. Freshmen primarily live in North and South Halls, which offer mostly double-occupancy rooms. Campus dining services provide a wide variety of options, including American and international cuisines, vegetarian meals, a large salad bar, and lighter fare such as burgers and pizza.

Whether students live on or off campus, they can take advantage of more than eighty student organizations—all devoted to such interests as community service, fraternities and sororities, music, theater, and politics as well as major-related clubs that provide opportunities for students to organize career-related events. Students can write for the student newspaper, work at the College's radio station, submit entries for the College's literary magazine, or work on the yearbook. Events throughout the year give students opportunities to enjoy lectures, concerts, poetry readings, art exhibits, plays, and nationally recognized speakers.

Utica College offers twenty-one NCAA Division III varsity sports, including men's baseball, basketball, cross-country, football, ice hockey, lacrosse, soccer, swimming and diving, and tennis; women's basketball, cross-country, field hockey, ice hockey, lacrosse, soccer, softball, swimming and diving, tennis, volleyball, and water polo; and coed golf. UC also offers club sports and a wide variety of intramural opportunities. Utica College is a member of the Empire 8 Athletic Conference, the Eastern College Athletic Conference, and the New York State Women's Collegiate Athletic Association. Nearly a third of all UC students participate in at least one Division III intercollegiate sport, and more than 45 percent are active in intramural or nonvarsity club sports.

Athletic facilities include a 1,200-seat multisport stadium with a state-of-the-art field turf synthetic grass playing surface; the Clark Athletic Center, which contains a large gymnasium, racquetball courts, a swimming pool, saunas, a recently renovated 6,400-square-foot free-weight room and fully equipped fitness facility, and numerous outdoor fields and courts. Ice hockey games are played at the downtown Utica Memorial Auditorium, which features pro-style hockey locker rooms and training facilities.

Graduate degrees are available in business administration, criminal justice administration, economic crime management, education, health-care administration, liberal studies, occupational therapy, and physical therapy.

Location

The city of Utica is located in the heart of the historic Mohawk Valley in the center of New York State. Just 90 miles west of Albany and 50 miles east of Syracuse, Utica has a thriving arts community, beautiful parks, and expanding shopping centers featuring national retailers. There are numerous recreational facilities, including a municipal ski slope and a world-class golf course less than a mile from the Utica College campus. Other nearby recreational opportunities include tennis, swimming, boating, fishing, hiking, and camping.

Majors and Degrees

Utica College offers undergraduate degree programs in accounting, accounting-CPA, biochemistry, biology, business economics, chemistry, communication arts, computer science, construction management, criminal justice, criminal justice–economic crime investigation, cybersecurity and information assurance, economics, English, foreign language, geoscience, gerontology, government and politics, health studies, health studies–human behavior, health studies–management, history, international studies, journalism studies, liberal studies, management, mathematics, nursing, occupational therapy, philosophy, physical therapy, physics, psychology, psychology–child life, public relations, public relations/journalism studies, risk management and insurance, sociology and anthropology, and therapeutic recreation.

Students interested in the occupational therapy or physical therapy major can earn a bachelor's degree in health studies with direct entry into UC's graduate programs, as long as academic requirements are met. Utica College offers a master's degree in occupational therapy and a doctorate in physical therapy (D.P.T.).

Students may minor in anthropology, chemistry, communication arts, computer science, creative writing, economics, English language, film studies, French, gender studies, geoscience, gerontology, government, history, human rights advocacy, literature, management, mathematics, philosophy, psychology, recreation leadership, sociology, Spanish, theater, and writing.

Preprofessional programs include dentistry, law, medicine, optometry, podiatry, and veterinary medicine. Special programs are available in teacher education, gerontology, engineering, and joint health professions.

Academic Programs

Students may choose from thirty-seven undergraduate majors and twenty-seven minors in a wide variety of fields as well as accelerated programs, independent study, cooperative education, field placements, and internships. Utica College also offers a rapidly growing education program; students wishing to pursue a career in teaching choose either a liberal arts major (to teach elementary education) or a major in their intended field (to teach at the secondary level).

For those students who are undecided, the Academic Support Services Center provides academic advising and career counseling, and Career Services offers students opportunities to explore career options.

To earn a bachelor's degree, students must complete a minimum of 120 to 128 credits, satisfy major and major-related requirements, and complete any special program requirements. In addition, all Utica College students, regardless of their major, must complete a liberal arts core program as part of the degree requirements.

Utica College operates on a semester system, with the fall term beginning in late August and ending shortly before Christmas, and the spring term beginning in late January and ending in early May. Summer and winter sessions offer students opportunities to accelerate their studies or take classes for which they have no time during the regular academic year.

First-year seminar offers freshmen and transfer students opportunities to earn academic credit while learning how to make the transition to college. Utica College offers the Higher Education Opportunity Program (HEOP), the Collegiate Science and Technology Entry Program (CSTEP), and a Summer Institute, which serves as an academic bridge between high school and college.

Off-Campus Programs

Studying abroad gives students opportunities to widen their global perspectives. Utica College is proud to participate in exchange programs with universities in Spain, Italy, Poland, Finland, Hungary, Peru, Scotland, and Wales. Students may also study at American College in Dublin in Ireland. UC students are also eligible to participate in Syracuse University's Division of International Programs Abroad. This arrangement allows students to study in Madrid, Strasbourg, Florence, London, and Hong Kong.

Students are encouraged to complete internships and field placements to gain professional experience with businesses and organizations while they are earning college credit. Utica College's cooperative education program allows students to earn money while gaining professional experience.

Academic Facilities

The Frank E. Gannett Memorial Library includes a collection of some 200,000 volumes, 1,200 serial subscriptions, hundreds of online journals, and a microform collection of more than 60,000 journals, newspapers, and books. The library is fully automated and shares a local system with Mid-York Library System. It is also a member of OCLC, a bibliographic database through which it is possible to locate and borrow interlibrary loan items from local, regional, national, and international libraries. Located on the lower level of the library are the Media Center, computer labs, the Edith Langley Barrett Fine Art Gallery, and a large concourse—the site of special events, such as musical recitals, receptions, and guest lectures.

Classes, laboratories, and faculty offices are primarily located in an academic complex comprises five buildings: Hubbard Hall, White Hall, Gordon Science Center, F. Eugene Romano Hall, and the Faculty Center. Other offices are located in DePerno Hall.

F. Eugene Romano Hall, the first phase of Utica College's new science and technology complex, opened in summer 2007 and provides state-of-the-art classroom, laboratory, and clinical space in addition to modern technology for students majoring in physical therapy, occupational therapy, and nursing. The second phase of the science and technology project is a new building for economic crime and justice studies, scheduled to be completed in November 2008. The final phase will provide modern facilities for the natural sciences.

Named in honor of one of UC's most celebrated faculty members, Professor Emeritus of Public Relations Raymond Simon, UC's state-of-the-art high-definition broadcast facility provides a hands-on learning environment for the next generation of media professionals.

Utica College maintains eight academic computer laboratories with both IBM-compatible and Macintosh computers, including two portable wireless laptop laboratories. Students have additional Internet access in the Pioneer Café and in all student residence hall rooms. Other resources include the Academic Support Services Center, the Math/Science Center, and the Writing Center.

Costs

For 2008–09, tuition is $25,538; room and board costs are $10,430. Student activity and technology fees cost $520. Books and supplies average $900 per year.

Financial Aid

The College is recognized as a best buy in education and works to control costs and keep its education affordable. The average financial aid package for 2007–08 freshmen was $24,802. About two thirds of that aid came from grants and a third from loans and/or jobs. More than 90 percent of the freshmen received a financial aid package. At the same time, UC awarded numerous merit scholarships to students with outstanding grades and test scores.

Almost every federal and state financial aid program is available through Utica College. Students apply for institutional and governmental financial aid by filing the Free Application for Federal Student Aid (FAFSA) by February 15. In addition, UC offers three different deferred-payment programs that spread payments over the academic year.

Faculty

Utica College's faculty is diverse, energetic, accomplished, and devoted to their students. The vast majority have earned their Ph.D. or other terminal degree, and while many are involved in research, the primary focus of faculty members is teaching. The typical class size is 20 students, the student-faculty ratio is 15:1, and all faculty members are involved in assisting students with their academic planning.

Student Government

One of Utica College's strongest traditions is student participation in the College's governance structure. Students may serve on a number of student governing bodies, and students also serve on all standing committees of the College.

Admission Requirements

Utica College admits students who can best benefit from the educational opportunities the College offers. The Admission Committee gives each application individual attention, and the potential for a student's success at UC is measured primarily by an evaluation of past academic performance, scholastic ability, and personal characteristics. Freshman applicants must have completed 16 academic units, including 4 years of English. Students should follow a college-preparatory program, including 3 units of mathematics, 3 units of science, 2 units of foreign language, and 3 units of social studies.

Application and Information

Students may apply for fall, spring, or summer admission. Materials required include a completed Utica College application form, official high school or college transcripts, and a $40 application fee. Utica College prefers, but does not require, SAT or ACT scores, with the exception of the programs listed below. A personal interview for all applications is strongly suggested.

Occupational therapy, physical therapy, nursing, and joint health professions program applicants must submit SAT or ACT scores, a preferred letter of clinical recommendation if applicable, and a personal statement. International students must complete the international student application form. The application fee is waived for students who apply to HEOP or CSTEP; however, SAT or ACT scores are required to be considered for either program.

The College conducts a rolling admissions program; however certain programs do have application deadlines. For students applying to the occupational therapy or physical therapy programs, the joint health professions program, or for academic achievement awards, the application deadline is January 15. For students applying to the nursing program, the preferred application deadline is February 1. The application deadline for the HEOP program is January 15. Students should note that a tuition deposit of $200 is required by April 1 to secure a place in the HEOP program.

Additional admissions information can be found online at http://www.utica.edu/enrollment/admission/international.htm or http://www.utica.edu/enrollment/admission/transfer/htm or http://www.utica.edu/academic/honorsprogram.htm.

Inquiries should be sent to:

Director of Admissions
Utica College
1600 Burrstone Road
Utica, New York 13502-4892

Phone: 315-792-3006
       800-782-8884 (toll-free)
E-mail: admiss@utica.edu
Web site: http://www.utica.edu

The Addison Miller White Hall Plaza.

Indexes

Majors and Degrees

Accounting

Albertus Magnus Coll, CT	B
Assumption Coll, MA	B
Atlantic Union Coll, MA	B
Babson Coll, MA	B
Barry U, FL	B
Bay Path Coll, MA	B
Bentley U, MA	B
Boston Coll, MA	B
Bridgewater State Coll, MA	B
Bryant U, RI	B
Castleton State Coll, VT	B
Central Connecticut State U, CT	B
Champlain Coll, VT	A,B
Clarkson U, NY	B
Coll of St. Joseph, VT	A,B
Coll of the Holy Cross, MA	B
Eastern Connecticut State U, CT	B
Endicott Coll, MA	B
Fairfield U, CT	B
Fisher Coll, MA	A
Fitchburg State Coll, MA	B
Franklin Pierce U, NH	B
Gordon Coll, MA	B
Grove City Coll, PA	B
Hofstra U, NY	B
Husson U, ME	A,B
Johnson State Coll, VT	A,B
Lasell Coll, MA	B
Lyndon State Coll, VT	B
Messiah Coll, PA	B
New England Coll, NH	B
Nichols Coll, MA	B
Northeastern U, MA	B
Ohio Wesleyan U, OH	B
Plymouth State U, NH	B
Providence Coll, RI	B
Quinnipiac U, CT	B
Rhode Island Coll, RI	B
Roger Williams U, RI	B
Saint Joseph Coll, CT	B
Saint Michael's Coll, VT	B
Salem State Coll, MA	B
Salve Regina U, RI	B
Simmons Coll, MA	B
Southern Connecticut State U, CT	B
Southern Methodist U, TX	B
Southern New Hampshire U, NH	A,B
Stonehill Coll, MA	B
Suffolk U, MA	B
U of Bridgeport, CT	B
U of Charleston, WV	A,B
U of Connecticut, CT	B
U of Hartford, CT	B
The U of Maine at Augusta, ME	B
U of Maine at Machias, ME	B
U of Maine at Presque Isle, ME	B
U of Massachusetts Amherst, MA	B
U of Massachusetts Dartmouth, MA	B
U of New Haven, CT	B
U of Rhode Island, RI	B
U of San Francisco, CA	B
U of Southern Maine, ME	B
Utica Coll, NY	B
Western Connecticut State U, CT	B
Western New England Coll, MA	B

Accounting and Business/Management

Babson Coll, MA	B
Mitchell Coll, CT	B

Accounting and Computer Science

Husson U, ME	B
Southern New Hampshire U, NH	B

Accounting and Finance

Albertus Magnus Coll, CT	B
Babson Coll, MA	B
Southern New Hampshire U, NH	B

Accounting Related

Bentley U, MA	B

Accounting Technology and Bookkeeping

Bryant U, RI	B

Acting

Bard Coll at Simon's Rock, MA	B
Barry U, FL	B
Bennington Coll, VT	B
Emerson Coll, MA	B
Hampshire Coll, MA	B
Hofstra U, NY	B
Johnson State Coll, VT	B
Keene State Coll, NH	B
U of Connecticut, CT	B
U of Hartford, CT	B

Actuarial Science

Bryant U, RI	B
Hofstra U, NY	B
Quinnipiac U, CT	B
U of Connecticut, CT	B
Worcester Polytechnic Inst, MA	B

Administrative Assistant and Secretarial Science

Salem State Coll, MA	B

Adult and Continuing Education

Atlantic Union Coll, MA	B
Fisher Coll, MA	A
Franklin Pierce U, NH	B
U of San Francisco, CA	B

Adult Health Nursing

Worcester State Coll, MA	B

Advertising

Barry U, FL	B
Emerson Coll, MA	B
Franklin Pierce U, NH	B

Quinnipiac U, CT	B
Southern Methodist U, TX	B
Southern New Hampshire U, NH	B
Western New England Coll, MA	B

Aeronautical/Aerospace Engineering Technology

Northeastern U, MA	B

Aerospace, Aeronautical and Astronautical Engineering

Clarkson U, NY	B
Massachusetts Inst of Technology, MA	B
Worcester Polytechnic Inst, MA	B

African American/Black Studies

Amherst Coll, MA	B
Bard Coll at Simon's Rock, MA	B
Bates Coll, ME	B
Brandeis U, MA	B
Brown U, RI	B
Colby Coll, ME	B
Dartmouth Coll, NH	B
Hampshire Coll, MA	B
Harvard U, MA	B
Mount Holyoke Coll, MA	B
Northeastern U, MA	B
Ohio Wesleyan U, OH	B
Rhode Island Coll, RI	B
Simmons Coll, MA	B
Smith Coll, MA	B
Southern Methodist U, TX	B
Suffolk U, MA	B
Tufts U, MA	B
U of Massachusetts Amherst, MA	B
U of Massachusetts Boston, MA	B
U of Rhode Island, RI	B
Wellesley Coll, MA	B
Wesleyan U, CT	B
Wheaton Coll, MA	B
Yale U, CT	B

African Studies

Bowdoin Coll, ME	B
Connecticut Coll, CT	B
Dartmouth Coll, NH	B
Hofstra U, NY	B
Marlboro Coll, VT	B
Wellesley Coll, MA	B
Wheaton Coll, MA	B
Yale U, CT	B

Agribusiness

U of Maine, ME	B
Vermont Tech Coll, VT	A

Agricultural and Domestic Animals Services Related

Sterling Coll, VT	A,B

Agricultural and Horticultural Plant Breeding

Sterling Coll, VT	A,B

Agricultural Animal Breeding

Sterling Coll, VT	A,B

Agricultural/Biological Engineering and Bioengineering

U of Maine, ME	B

Agricultural Business and Management

Bard Coll at Simon's Rock, MA	B
Sterling Coll, VT	B

Agricultural Business and Management Related

Sterling Coll, VT	B

Agricultural Communication/Journalism

Sterling Coll, VT	B

Agricultural Economics

U of Connecticut, CT	B
U of Maine, ME	B
U of Massachusetts Amherst, MA	B

Agricultural Production Related

Sterling Coll, VT	A,B

Agricultural Public Services Related

Sterling Coll, VT	A,B

Agricultural Teacher Education

Sterling Coll, VT	B
U of Connecticut, CT	B
U of New Hampshire, NH	B

Agriculture

Sterling Coll, VT	A,B
U of Connecticut, CT	B
U of Vermont, VT	B

Agriculture and Agriculture Operations Related

Sterling Coll, VT	A,B

Agronomy and Crop Science

U of Connecticut, CT	B
U of Vermont, VT	B

Airline Pilot and Flight Crew

Bridgewater State Coll, MA	B

Air Traffic Control

Daniel Webster Coll, NH	B

Allied Health Diagnostic, Intervention, and Treatment Professions Related

Hofstra U, NY	B
U of Connecticut, CT	B

Alternative and Complementary Medicine Related

Johnson State Coll, VT	B

American Government and Politics

Bennington Coll, VT	B

A—associate degree; B—bachelor's degree

Bridgewater State Coll, MA	B
Hampshire Coll, MA	B
Rivier Coll, NH	B

American History
Bennington Coll, VT	B
Hampshire Coll, MA	B
Keene State Coll, NH	B

American Indian/Native American Studies
Dartmouth Coll, NH	B
Hampshire Coll, MA	B

American Literature
Bard Coll at Simon's Rock, MA	B
Bennington Coll, VT	B
Castleton State Coll, VT	B
Clarkson U, NY	B
Hampshire Coll, MA	B
Middlebury Coll, VT	B

American Native/Native American Education
Bard Coll at Simon's Rock, MA	B

American Studies
Amherst Coll, MA	B
Atlantic Union Coll, MA	B
Bard Coll at Simon's Rock, MA	B
Bates Coll, ME	B
Bennington Coll, VT	B
Brandeis U, MA	B
Brown U, RI	B
Clarkson U, NY	B
Colby Coll, ME	B
Connecticut Coll, CT	B
Emmanuel Coll, MA	B
Fairfield U, CT	B
Franklin Pierce U, NH	B
Hampshire Coll, MA	B
Hofstra U, NY	B
Keene State Coll, NH	B
Lesley U, MA	B
Marlboro Coll, VT	B
Middlebury Coll, VT	B
Mount Holyoke Coll, MA	B
Mount Ida Coll, MA	B
Providence Coll, RI	B
Roger Williams U, RI	B
Saint Joseph Coll, CT	B
Saint Michael's Coll, VT	B
Salve Regina U, RI	B
Smith Coll, MA	B
Stonehill Coll, MA	B
Trinity Coll, CT	B
Tufts U, MA	B
U of Connecticut, CT	B
U of Massachusetts Boston, MA	B
U of Massachusetts Lowell, MA	B
U of New England, ME	B
Wellesley Coll, MA	B
Wesleyan U, CT	B
Western Connecticut State U, CT	B
Wheaton Coll, MA	B
Williams Coll, MA	B
Yale U, CT	B

Ancient/Classical Greek
Amherst Coll, MA	B
Boston Coll, MA	B
Dartmouth Coll, NH	B
Mount Holyoke Coll, MA	B
Smith Coll, MA	B
U of New Hampshire, NH	B
U of Vermont, VT	B
Wellesley Coll, MA	B

Wheaton Coll, MA	B
Yale U, CT	B

Ancient Studies
Bates Coll, ME	B
Bowdoin Coll, ME	B
Mount Holyoke Coll, MA	B
Ohio Wesleyan U, OH	B
Wheaton Coll, MA	B

Animal Genetics
Dartmouth Coll, NH	B
Ohio Wesleyan U, OH	B
Worcester Polytechnic Inst, MA	B

Animal Health
Sterling Coll, VT	A,B

Animal/Livestock Husbandry and Production
Sterling Coll, VT	A,B
U of Connecticut, CT	A

Animal Nutrition
Sterling Coll, VT	A,B

Animal Physiology
U of Connecticut, CT	B

Animal Sciences
Becker Coll, MA	A
Hampshire Coll, MA	B
Sterling Coll, VT	A,B
U of Connecticut, CT	A,B
U of Maine, ME	B
U of Massachusetts Amherst, MA	B
U of New Hampshire, NH	A,B
U of Rhode Island, RI	B
U of Vermont, VT	B

Animal Sciences Related
Sterling Coll, VT	A,B

Animal Training
Becker Coll, MA	A
Sterling Coll, VT	B

Animation, Interactive Technology, Video Graphics and Special Effects
Bennington Coll, VT	B
Champlain Coll, VT	A,B
Hampshire Coll, MA	B
ITT Tech Inst, Woburn, MA	B
Massachusetts Coll of Art and Design, MA	B
Mount Ida Coll, MA	B
The New England Inst of Art, MA	B
U of Hartford, CT	B

Anthropology
Amherst Coll, MA	B
Bard Coll at Simon's Rock, MA	B
Bates Coll, ME	B
Bennington Coll, VT	B
Bowdoin Coll, ME	B
Brandeis U, MA	B
Brown U, RI	B
Central Connecticut State U, CT	B
Colby Coll, ME	B
Coll of the Holy Cross, MA	B
Connecticut Coll, CT	B
Dartmouth Coll, NH	B
Eugene Lang Coll The New School for Liberal Arts, NY	B
Franklin Pierce U, NH	B
Green Mountain Coll, VT	B

Hampshire Coll, MA	B
Harvard U, MA	B
Hofstra U, NY	B
Johnson State Coll, VT	B
Marlboro Coll, VT	B
Massachusetts Inst of Technology, MA	B
Mount Holyoke Coll, MA	B
Northeastern U, MA	B
Ohio Wesleyan U, OH	B
Rhode Island Coll, RI	B
Roger Williams U, RI	B
Salve Regina U, RI	B
Smith Coll, MA	B
Southern Connecticut State U, CT	B
Southern Methodist U, TX	B
Trinity Coll, CT	B
Tufts U, MA	B
U of Connecticut, CT	B
U of Maine, ME	B
U of Maine at Farmington, ME	B
U of Massachusetts Amherst, MA	B
U of Massachusetts Boston, MA	B
U of New Hampshire, NH	B
U of Rhode Island, RI	B
U of Southern Maine, ME	B
U of Vermont, VT	B
Wellesley Coll, MA	B
Wesleyan U, CT	B
Western Connecticut State U, CT	B
Wheaton Coll, MA	B
Williams Coll, MA	B
Yale U, CT	B

Anthropology Related
Bridgewater State Coll, MA	B

Apparel and Accessories Marketing
U of Rhode Island, RI	B

Apparel and Textiles
Framingham State Coll, MA	B
U of Rhode Island, RI	B

Applied Art
Franklin Pierce U, NH	B
School of the Museum of Fine Arts, Boston, MA	B
U of Maine at Presque Isle, ME	A

Applied Economics
Plymouth State U, NH	B
Southern Methodist U, TX	B
U of Rhode Island, RI	B
U of San Francisco, CA	B
Western New England Coll, MA	B

Applied Horticulture
Sterling Coll, VT	A,B
U of Connecticut, CT	A
The U of Maine at Augusta, ME	A
U of New Hampshire, NH	A

Applied Horticulture/ Horticultural Business Services Related
U of Massachusetts Amherst, MA	A

Applied Mathematics
Bard Coll at Simon's Rock, MA	B
Brown U, RI	B

Clarkson U, NY	B
Harvard U, MA	B
Hofstra U, NY	B
Marlboro Coll, VT	B
Quinnipiac U, CT	B
Salem State Coll, MA	B
U of Connecticut, CT	B
U of Massachusetts Lowell, MA	B
U of New Haven, CT	B
Worcester Polytechnic Inst, MA	B
Yale U, CT	B

Applied Mathematics Related
Keene State Coll, NH	B

Aquaculture
U of New England, ME	B

Arabic
Dartmouth Coll, NH	B

Archeology
Bowdoin Coll, ME	B
Bridgewater State Coll, MA	B
Brown U, RI	B
Dartmouth Coll, NH	B
Franklin Pierce U, NH	B
Tufts U, MA	B
Wellesley Coll, MA	B
Wesleyan U, CT	B
Yale U, CT	B

Architectural Drafting and CAD/CADD
Benjamin Franklin Inst of Technology, MA	A

Architectural Engineering
Tufts U, MA	B

Architectural Engineering Technology
Benjamin Franklin Inst of Technology, MA	A
U of Hartford, CT	B
Vermont Tech Coll, VT	A,B
Wentworth Inst of Technology, MA	A

Architectural History and Criticism
Brown U, RI	B
Roger Williams U, RI	B

Architectural Technology
Fitchburg State Coll, MA	B
The U of Maine at Augusta, ME	A

Architecture
Bennington Coll, VT	B
Boston Architectural Coll, MA	B
Connecticut Coll, CT	B
Keene State Coll, NH	B
Massachusetts Coll of Art and Design, MA	B
Massachusetts Inst of Technology, MA	B
Northeastern U, MA	B
Roger Williams U, RI	B
Smith Coll, MA	B
U of San Francisco, CA	B
Wellesley Coll, MA	B
Wentworth Inst of Technology, MA	B
Yale U, CT	B

Architecture Related
Mount Holyoke Coll, MA	B

Area, Ethnic, Cultural, and Gender Studies Related

Bennington Coll, VT	B
Connecticut Coll, CT	B
Mount Holyoke Coll, MA	B
Sterling Coll, VT	B

Area Studies Related

Bridgewater State Coll, MA	B
Hofstra U, NY	B

Art

Albertus Magnus Coll, CT	B
Amherst Coll, MA	B
Anna Maria Coll, MA	B
Atlantic Union Coll, MA	B
Bates Coll, ME	B
Bowdoin Coll, ME	B
Brown U, RI	B
Castleton State Coll, VT	B
Central Connecticut State U, CT	B
Colby Coll, ME	B
Coll of the Atlantic, ME	B
Connecticut Coll, CT	B
Eastern Connecticut State U, CT	B
Emmanuel Coll, MA	B
Fairfield U, CT	B
Framingham State Coll, MA	B
Franklin Pierce U, NH	B
Gordon Coll, MA	B
Green Mountain Coll, VT	B
Hampshire Coll, MA	B
Johnson State Coll, VT	B
Lesley U, MA	B
Marlboro Coll, VT	B
Massachusetts Coll of Liberal Arts, MA	B
Mount Holyoke Coll, MA	B
New England Coll, NH	B
Northeastern U, MA	B
Plymouth State U, NH	B
Rivier Coll, NH	A,B
Roger Williams U, RI	B
Saint Michael's Coll, VT	B
Salem State Coll, MA	B
School of the Museum of Fine Arts, Boston, MA	B
Simmons Coll, MA	B
Smith Coll, MA	B
Suffolk U, MA	A
Trinity Coll, CT	B
U of Charleston, WV	B
U of Maine, ME	B
U of Maine at Farmington, ME	B
U of Maine at Machias, ME	B
U of Maine at Presque Isle, ME	B
U of Massachusetts Boston, MA	B
U of New Hampshire, NH	B
U of Rhode Island, RI	B
U of San Francisco, CA	B
U of Southern Maine, ME	B
Wesleyan U, CT	B
Western Connecticut State U, CT	B
Westfield State Coll, MA	B
Yale U, CT	B

Art History, Criticism and Conservation

Albertus Magnus Coll, CT	B
Bard Coll at Simon's Rock, MA	B
Boston Coll, MA	B
Bowdoin Coll, ME	B
Brandeis U, MA	B
Bridgewater State Coll, MA	B
Brown U, RI	B
Clark U, MA	B
Colby Coll, ME	B
Coll of the Holy Cross, MA	B
Connecticut Coll, CT	B
Dartmouth Coll, NH	B
Fairfield U, CT	B
Hampshire Coll, MA	B
Harvard U, MA	B
Hofstra U, NY	B
Marlboro Coll, VT	B
Massachusetts Coll of Art and Design, MA	B
Messiah Coll, PA	B
Middlebury Coll, VT	B
Mount Holyoke Coll, MA	B
New England Coll, NH	B
Ohio Wesleyan U, OH	B
Providence Coll, RI	B
Rhode Island Coll, RI	B
Roger Williams U, RI	B
Saint Joseph Coll, CT	B
Salve Regina U, RI	B
Smith Coll, MA	B
Southern Connecticut State U, CT	B
Southern Methodist U, TX	B
Trinity Coll, CT	B
Tufts U, MA	B
U of Connecticut, CT	B
U of Hartford, CT	B
U of Maine, ME	B
U of Massachusetts Amherst, MA	B
U of Massachusetts Dartmouth, MA	B
U of Rhode Island, RI	B
U of San Francisco, CA	B
U of Vermont, VT	B
Wellesley Coll, MA	B
Wesleyan U, CT	B
Wheaton Coll, MA	B
Williams Coll, MA	B
Yale U, CT	B

Artificial Intelligence and Robotics

Hampshire Coll, MA	B

Arts Management

Massachusetts Coll of Liberal Arts, MA	B
Simmons Coll, MA	B
U of Hartford, CT	B
U of San Francisco, CA	B

Art Teacher Education

Anna Maria Coll, MA	B
Assumption Coll, MA	B
Bridgewater State Coll, MA	B
Central Connecticut State U, CT	B
Franklin Pierce U, NH	B
Hofstra U, NY	B
Johnson State Coll, VT	B
Massachusetts Coll of Art and Design, MA	B
Messiah Coll, PA	B
Ohio Wesleyan U, OH	B
Plymouth State U, NH	B
Rhode Island Coll, RI	B
Saint Michael's Coll, VT	B
Salem State Coll, MA	B

School of the Museum of Fine Arts, Boston, MA	B
Southern Connecticut State U, CT	B
U of Maine, ME	B
U of Maine at Presque Isle, ME	B
U of Massachusetts Dartmouth, MA	B
U of Southern Maine, ME	B
U of Vermont, VT	B

Art Therapy

Albertus Magnus Coll, CT	B
Anna Maria Coll, MA	B
Emmanuel Coll, MA	B
Lesley U, MA	B
Ohio Wesleyan U, OH	B

Asian American Studies

Hampshire Coll, MA	B

Asian History

Hampshire Coll, MA	B

Asian Studies

Amherst Coll, MA	B
Bard Coll at Simon's Rock, MA	B
Bennington Coll, VT	B
Bowdoin Coll, ME	B
Clark U, MA	B
Coll of the Holy Cross, MA	B
Dartmouth Coll, NH	B
Hampshire Coll, MA	B
Hofstra U, NY	B
Marlboro Coll, VT	B
Mount Holyoke Coll, MA	B
Tufts U, MA	B
U of San Francisco, CA	B
U of Vermont, VT	B
Wheaton Coll, MA	B
Williams Coll, MA	B

Asian Studies (East)

Bates Coll, ME	B
Brandeis U, MA	B
Brown U, RI	B
Colby Coll, ME	B
Connecticut Coll, CT	B
Harvard U, MA	B
Marlboro Coll, VT	B
Middlebury Coll, VT	B
Ohio Wesleyan U, OH	B
Simmons Coll, MA	B
Smith Coll, MA	B
Wellesley Coll, MA	B
Wesleyan U, CT	B
Yale U, CT	B

Asian Studies (South)

Brown U, RI	B

Asian Studies (Southeast)

Tufts U, MA	B

Astronomy

Amherst Coll, MA	B
Bennington Coll, VT	B
Dartmouth Coll, NH	B
Marlboro Coll, VT	B
Mount Holyoke Coll, MA	B
Ohio Wesleyan U, OH	B
Smith Coll, MA	B
Tufts U, MA	B
U of Massachusetts Amherst, MA	B
Wellesley Coll, MA	B
Wesleyan U, CT	B
Wheaton Coll, MA	B

Williams Coll, MA	B
Yale U, CT	B

Astronomy and Astrophysics Related

Harvard U, MA	B

Astrophysics

Connecticut Coll, CT	B
Marlboro Coll, VT	B
Ohio Wesleyan U, OH	B
Wellesley Coll, MA	B
Williams Coll, MA	B
Yale U, CT	B

Athletic Training

Bridgewater State Coll, MA	B
Castleton State Coll, VT	B
Central Connecticut State U, CT	B
Endicott Coll, MA	B
Hofstra U, NY	B
Johnson State Coll, VT	B
Keene State Coll, NH	B
Lyndon State Coll, VT	B
Merrimack Coll, MA	B
Messiah Coll, PA	B
Northeastern U, MA	B
Plymouth State U, NH	B
Quinnipiac U, CT	B
Sacred Heart U, CT	B
Southern Connecticut State U, CT	B
U of Charleston, WV	B
U of Maine at Presque Isle, ME	B
U of New England, ME	B
U of New Hampshire, NH	B
U of Southern Maine, ME	B
U of Vermont, VT	B

Atmospheric Sciences and Meteorology

Lyndon State Coll, VT	B
Plymouth State U, NH	B
Western Connecticut State U, CT	B

Atomic/Molecular Physics

Harvard U, MA	B

Audio Engineering

Berklee Coll of Music, MA	B
U of Hartford, CT	B

Audiology and Speech-Language Pathology

Emerson Coll, MA	B
Hofstra U, NY	B
Northeastern U, MA	B
Southern Connecticut State U, CT	B

Auditing

Babson Coll, MA	B

Automobile/Automotive Mechanics Technology

Benjamin Franklin Inst of Technology, MA	A,B

Automotive Engineering Technology

Benjamin Franklin Inst of Technology, MA	A,B
Vermont Tech Coll, VT	A

Aviation/Airway Management

Bridgewater State Coll, MA	B
Salem State Coll, MA	B

A—associate degree; B—bachelor's degree

Baking and Pastry Arts
Southern New Hampshire U, NH — A

Banking and Financial Support Services
Husson U, ME — B
Providence Coll, RI — B

Behavioral Sciences
Brown U, RI — B
Coll of St. Joseph, VT — B
Granite State Coll, NH — A,B
Hampshire Coll, MA — B
Marlboro Coll, VT — B
Northeastern U, MA — B
Tufts U, MA — B
U of Maine at Fort Kent, ME — B
U of Maine at Machias, ME — B
U of Maine at Presque Isle, ME — B

Biblical Studies
Boston Baptist Coll, MA — A,B
Marlboro Coll, VT — B
Messiah Coll, PA — B
Zion Bible Coll, MA — B

Bilingual and Multilingual Education
U of Maine at Fort Kent, ME — B
U of San Francisco, CA — B

Biochemistry
Bates Coll, ME — B
Boston Coll, MA — B
Bowdoin Coll, ME — B
Brandeis U, MA — B
Bridgewater State Coll, MA — B
Brown U, RI — B
Central Connecticut State U, CT — B
Clarkson U, NY — B
Clark U, MA — B
Colby Coll, ME — B
Connecticut Coll, CT — B
Dartmouth Coll, NH — B
Eastern Connecticut State U, CT — B
Emmanuel Coll, MA — B
Fairfield U, CT — B
Grove City Coll, PA — B
Hampshire Coll, MA — B
Harvard U, MA — B
Hofstra U, NY — B
Marlboro Coll, VT — B
Merrimack Coll, MA — B
Messiah Coll, PA — B
Middlebury Coll, VT — B
Mount Holyoke Coll, MA — B
Northeastern U, MA — B
Providence Coll, RI — B
Quinnipiac U, CT — B
Regis Coll, MA — B
Sacred Heart U, CT — B
Saint Joseph Coll, CT — B
Saint Michael's Coll, VT — B
Simmons Coll, MA — B
Smith Coll, MA — B
Southern Methodist U, TX — B
Stonehill Coll, MA — B
Suffolk U, MA — B
Trinity Coll, CT — B
U of Maine, ME — B
U of Massachusetts Boston, MA — B
U of New England, ME — B
U of New Hampshire, NH — B

U of Vermont, VT — B
Wellesley Coll, MA — B
Wesleyan U, CT — B
Wheaton Coll, MA — B
Worcester Polytechnic Inst, MA — B

Biochemistry/Biophysics and Molecular Biology
Harvard U, MA — B
U of Massachusetts Amherst, MA — B

Bioinformatics
Wheaton Coll, MA — B

Biological and Biomedical Sciences Related
U of New Hampshire, NH — B

Biological and Physical Sciences
Castleton State Coll, VT — B
Coll of the Atlantic, ME — B
Hampshire Coll, MA — B
Keene State Coll, NH — B
Lyndon State Coll, VT — B
Mitchell Coll, CT — A
Quinnipiac U, CT — B
Sterling Coll, VT — A,B
U of Massachusetts Amherst, MA — B
Worcester State Coll, MA — B

Biology/Biological Sciences
Albertus Magnus Coll, CT — B
Amherst Coll, MA — B
Assumption Coll, MA — B
Atlantic Union Coll, MA — B
Bard Coll at Simon's Rock, MA — B
Barry U, FL — B
Bates Coll, ME — B
Bay Path Coll, MA — B
Bennington Coll, VT — B
Boston Coll, MA — B
Bowdoin Coll, ME — B
Brandeis U, MA — B
Bridgewater State Coll, MA — B
Brown U, RI — B
Castleton State Coll, VT — B
Central Connecticut State U, CT — B
Clarkson U, NY — B
Clark U, MA — B
Colby Coll, ME — B
Coll of the Atlantic, ME — B
Coll of the Holy Cross, MA — B
Connecticut Coll, CT — B
Curry Coll, MA — B
Dartmouth Coll, NH — B
Eastern Connecticut State U, CT — B
Emmanuel Coll, MA — B
Fairfield U, CT — B
Fitchburg State Coll, MA — B
Framingham State Coll, MA — B
Franklin Pierce U, NH — B
Gordon Coll, MA — B
Green Mountain Coll, VT — B
Grove City Coll, PA — B
Hampshire Coll, MA — B
Harvard U, MA — B
Hofstra U, NY — B
Husson U, ME — B
Johnson State Coll, VT — B
Keene State Coll, NH — B
Marlboro Coll, VT — B

Massachusetts Coll of Liberal Arts, MA — B
Massachusetts Inst of Technology, MA — B
Merrimack Coll, MA — B
Messiah Coll, PA — B
Middlebury Coll, VT — B
Mount Holyoke Coll, MA — B
Mount Ida Coll, MA — B
New England Coll, NH — B
Northeastern U, MA — B
Ohio Wesleyan U, OH — B
Plymouth State U, NH — B
Providence Coll, RI — B
Quinnipiac U, CT — B
Regis Coll, MA — B
Rhode Island Coll, RI — B
Rivier Coll, NH — B
Roger Williams U, RI — B
Sacred Heart U, CT — B
Saint Joseph Coll, CT — B
Saint Michael's Coll, VT — B
Salem State Coll, MA — B
Salve Regina U, RI — B
Simmons Coll, MA — B
Smith Coll, MA — B
Southern Connecticut State U, CT — B
Southern Methodist U, TX — B
Stonehill Coll, MA — B
Suffolk U, MA — B
Trinity Coll, CT — B
Tufts U, MA — B
U of Bridgeport, CT — B
U of Charleston, WV — B
U of Connecticut, CT — B
U of Hartford, CT — B
U of Maine, ME — B
The U of Maine at Augusta, ME — A
U of Maine at Farmington, ME — B
U of Maine at Fort Kent, ME — B
U of Maine at Machias, ME — B
U of Maine at Presque Isle, ME — B
U of Massachusetts Amherst, MA — B
U of Massachusetts Boston, MA — B
U of Massachusetts Dartmouth, MA — B
U of Massachusetts Lowell, MA — B
U of New England, ME — B
U of New Hampshire, NH — B
U of New Hampshire at Manchester, NH — A
U of New Haven, CT — B
U of Rhode Island, RI — B
U of San Francisco, CA — B
U of Southern Maine, ME — B
U of Vermont, VT — B
Utica Coll, NY — B
Wellesley Coll, MA — B
Wesleyan U, CT — B
Western Connecticut State U, CT — B
Western New England Coll, MA — B
Westfield State Coll, MA — B
Wheaton Coll, MA — B
Williams Coll, MA — B
Worcester Polytechnic Inst, MA — B
Worcester State Coll, MA — B
Yale U, CT — B

Biology/Biotechnology Laboratory Technician
Northeastern U, MA — B
Suffolk U, MA — B
U of New Haven, CT — B
Worcester Polytechnic Inst, MA — B

Biology Teacher Education
Assumption Coll, MA — B
Bridgewater State Coll, MA — B
Fitchburg State Coll, MA — B
Hofstra U, NY — B
Husson U, ME — B
Johnson State Coll, VT — B
Keene State Coll, NH — B
Messiah Coll, PA — B
Ohio Wesleyan U, OH — B
Rhode Island Coll, RI — B
Rivier Coll, NH — B
Sacred Heart U, CT — B
Salve Regina U, RI — B
U of Charleston, WV — B
U of Maine, ME — B
U of Maine at Farmington, ME — B
U of Maine at Machias, ME — B
Utica Coll, NY — B

Biomedical/Medical Engineering
Benjamin Franklin Inst of Technology, MA — A
Brown U, RI — B
Hofstra U, NY — B
Massachusetts Inst of Technology, MA — B
Trinity Coll, CT — B
U of Connecticut, CT — B
U of Hartford, CT — B
U of Rhode Island, RI — B
Western New England Coll, MA — B
Worcester Polytechnic Inst, MA — B
Yale U, CT — B

Biomedical Sciences
Bridgewater State Coll, MA — B
Brown U, RI — B
Suffolk U, MA — B
U of Maine, ME — B
U of New England, ME — B
Worcester Polytechnic Inst, MA — B

Biomedical Technology
Benjamin Franklin Inst of Technology, MA — A
Suffolk U, MA — B

Biophysics
Brandeis U, MA — B
Brown U, RI — B
Clarkson U, NY — B
Suffolk U, MA — B
U of Connecticut, CT — B

Biopsychology
Hampshire Coll, MA — B
Messiah Coll, PA — B

Biostatistics
Emmanuel Coll, MA — B

Biotechnology
Bay Path Coll, MA — B
Clarkson U, NY — B
Endicott Coll, MA — B
Fitchburg State Coll, MA — B
Plymouth State U, NH — B

U of Massachusetts Boston, MA	B	Nichols Coll, MA	A,B	Hofstra U, NY	B	**Cell and Molecular Biology**	
U of Southern Maine, ME	B	Northeastern U, MA	B	Johnson State Coll, VT	B	Bennington Coll, VT	B
Worcester State Coll, MA	B	Ohio Wesleyan U, OH	B	Landmark Coll, VT	A	Bridgewater State Coll, MA	B
		Plymouth State U, NH	B	Massachusetts Inst of		Connecticut Coll, CT	B
Botany/Plant Biology		Providence Coll, RI	A,B	Technology, MA	B	Harvard U, MA	B
Bennington Coll, VT	B	Quinnipiac U, CT	B	Nichols Coll, MA	B		
Coll of the Atlantic, ME	B	Rhode Island Coll, RI	B	Northeastern U, MA	B	**Cell Biology and Anatomical**	
Connecticut Coll, CT	B	Rivier Coll, NH	A,B	Plymouth State U, NH	B	**Sciences Related**	
Hampshire Coll, MA	B	Roger Williams U, RI	A,B	Regis Coll, MA	B	U of Connecticut, CT	B
Marlboro Coll, VT	B	Saint Joseph Coll, CT	B	Rhode Island Coll, RI	B	Yale U, CT	B
Ohio Wesleyan U, OH	B	Saint Michael's Coll, VT	B	Southern Methodist U, TX	B		
U of Maine, ME	B	Salem State Coll, MA	B	U of Bridgeport, CT	A	**Cell Biology and Histology**	
U of New Hampshire, NH	B	Salve Regina U, RI	A,B	U of Connecticut, CT	B	Clarkson U, NY	B
U of Vermont, VT	B	Simmons Coll, MA	B	U of Maine, ME	B	Colby Coll, ME	B
		Southern Connecticut State U,		U of Massachusetts Dartmouth,		Marlboro Coll, VT	B
Broadcast Journalism		CT	B	MA	B	U of Maine, ME	B
Barry U, FL	B	Southern Methodist U, TX	B	U of San Francisco, CA	B	Worcester Polytechnic Inst,	
Emerson Coll, MA	B	Southern New Hampshire U,		Western New England Coll,		MA	B
Hofstra U, NY	B	NH	A,B	MA	B		
Mitchell Coll, CT	B	Stonehill Coll, MA	B			**Ceramic Arts and Ceramics**	
Ohio Wesleyan U, OH	B	Suffolk U, MA	B	**Business/Corporate**		Bard Coll at Simon's Rock, MA	B
Quinnipiac U, CT	B	U of Charleston, WV	A,B	**Communications**		Bennington Coll, VT	B
Suffolk U, MA	B	U of Hartford, CT	B	Babson Coll, MA	B	Coll of the Atlantic, ME	B
		U of Maine, ME	B	Bentley U, MA	B	Franklin Pierce U, NH	B
Building/Construction		The U of Maine at Augusta,				Hofstra U, NY	B
Finishing, Management, and		ME	A,B	**Business, Management, and**		Maine Coll of Art, ME	B
Inspection Related		U of Maine at Fort Kent, ME	A,B	**Marketing Related**		Marlboro Coll, VT	B
Wentworth Inst of Technology,		U of Maine at Machias, ME	B	Bentley U, MA	B	Massachusetts Coll of Art and	
MA	A	U of Maine at Presque Isle,		Bridgewater State Coll, MA	B	Design, MA	B
		ME	B	Messiah Coll, PA	B	Providence Coll, RI	B
Business Administration and		U of Massachusetts Amherst,		Southern New Hampshire U,		Salve Regina U, RI	B
Management		MA	B	NH	B	School of the Museum of Fine	
Anna Maria Coll, MA	A,B	U of Massachusetts Boston,		Utica Coll, NY	B	Arts, Boston, MA	B
Assumption Coll, MA	B	MA	B	Wentworth Inst of Technology,		U of Hartford, CT	B
Atlantic Union Coll, MA	B	U of Massachusetts Lowell, MA	B	MA	B	U of Massachusetts Dartmouth,	
Babson Coll, MA	B	U of New England, ME	B			MA	B
Barry U, FL	B	U of New Hampshire, NH	A,B	**Business/Managerial**			
Bay Path Coll, MA	B	U of New Hampshire at		**Economics**		**Chemical Engineering**	
Becker Coll, MA	B	Manchester, NH	A,B	Albertus Magnus Coll, CT	B	Brown U, RI	B
Bentley U, MA	A,B	U of New Haven, CT	B	Bentley U, MA	B	Clarkson U, NY	B
Boston Coll, MA	B	U of Phoenix–Boston Campus,		Boston Coll, MA	B	Massachusetts Inst of	
Bridgewater State Coll, MA	B	MA	B	Emmanuel Coll, MA	B	Technology, MA	B
Bryant U, RI	B	U of Phoenix–Central		Green Mountain Coll, VT	B	Northeastern U, MA	B
Castleton State Coll, VT	B	Massachusetts Campus, MA	B	Grove City Coll, PA	B	Tufts U, MA	B
Central Connecticut State U,		U of Rhode Island, RI	B	Hofstra U, NY	B	U of Connecticut, CT	B
CT	B	U of San Francisco, CA	B	Merrimack Coll, MA	B	U of Maine, ME	B
Champlain Coll, VT	A,B	U of Southern Maine, ME	B	Messiah Coll, PA	B	U of Massachusetts Amherst,	
Clarkson U, NY	B	U of Vermont, VT	B	Ohio Wesleyan U, OH	B	MA	B
Clark U, MA	B	Utica Coll, NY	B	Quinnipiac U, CT	B	U of Massachusetts Lowell, MA	B
Coll of St. Joseph, VT	A,B	Vermont Tech Coll, VT	A,B	Rhode Island Coll, RI	B	U of New Hampshire, NH	B
Curry Coll, MA	B	Western Connecticut State U,		Sacred Heart U, CT	B	U of New Haven, CT	A,B
Eastern Connecticut State U,		CT	B	Salem State Coll, MA	B	U of Rhode Island, RI	B
CT	B	Western New England Coll,		Southern Connecticut State U,		Worcester Polytechnic Inst,	
Emmanuel Coll, MA	B	MA	B	CT	B	MA	B
Endicott Coll, MA	B	Westfield State Coll, MA	B	U of Hartford, CT	B	Yale U, CT	B
Fairfield U, CT	B	Worcester Polytechnic Inst,		U of Maine at Farmington, ME	B		
Fisher Coll, MA	A,B	MA	B	U of New Haven, CT	B	**Chemical Engineering**	
Fitchburg State Coll, MA	B	Worcester State Coll, MA	B	Utica Coll, NY	B	**Technology**	
Franklin Pierce U, NH	B					U of Hartford, CT	B
Gordon Coll, MA	B	**Business Administration,**		**Business Teacher Education**			
Grove City Coll, PA	B	**Management and Operations**		Hofstra U, NY	B	**Chemical Physics**	
Hofstra U, NY	B	**Related**		Ohio Wesleyan U, OH	B	Bowdoin Coll, ME	B
Husson U, ME	A,B	Babson Coll, MA	B	Salem State Coll, MA	B		
Johnson State Coll, VT	A,B	Becker Coll, MA	B	Suffolk U, MA	B	**Chemistry**	
Keene State Coll, NH	B	Hofstra U, NY	B	U of Maine at Fort Kent, ME	B	Albertus Magnus Coll, CT	B
Landmark Coll, VT	A	U of Charleston, WV	B	U of Maine at Machias, ME	B	Amherst Coll, MA	B
Lasell Coll, MA	B			Utica Coll, NY	B	Assumption Coll, MA	B
Lesley U, MA	B	**Business/Commerce**				Bard Coll at Simon's Rock, MA	B
Maine Maritime Academy, ME	B	Castleton State Coll, VT	A	**CAD/CADD Drafting/Design**		Barry U, FL	B
Massachusetts Coll of Liberal		Champlain Coll, VT	A,B	**Technology**		Bates Coll, ME	B
Arts, MA	B	Eastern Connecticut State U,		ITT Tech Inst, Woburn, MA	A	Bennington Coll, VT	B
Messiah Coll, PA	B	CT	B			Boston Coll, MA	B
Mitchell Coll, CT	B	Fisher Coll, MA	A	**Canadian Studies**		Bowdoin Coll, ME	B
Mount Ida Coll, MA	B	Framingham State Coll, MA	B	Sterling Coll, VT	B	Brandeis U, MA	B
New England Coll, NH	B	Granite State Coll, NH	A	U of Vermont, VT	B	Bridgewater State Coll, MA	B
		Hampshire Coll, MA	B			Brown U, RI	B
				Cartography		Castleton State Coll, VT	A
				Salem State Coll, MA	B		

A—associate degree; B—bachelor's degree

Central Connecticut State U, CT — B
Clarkson U, NY — B
Clark U, MA — B
Colby Coll, ME — B
Coll of the Holy Cross, MA — B
Connecticut Coll, CT — B
Dartmouth Coll, NH — B
Emmanuel Coll, MA — B
Fairfield U, CT — B
Framingham State Coll, MA — B
Gordon Coll, MA — B
Grove City Coll, PA — B
Hampshire Coll, MA — B
Harvard U, MA — B
Hofstra U, NY — B
Husson U, ME — B
Keene State Coll, NH — B
Marlboro Coll, VT — B
Massachusetts Coll of Pharmacy and Health Sciences, MA — B
Massachusetts Inst of Technology, MA — B
Merrimack Coll, MA — B
Messiah Coll, PA — B
Middlebury Coll, VT — B
Mount Holyoke Coll, MA — B
Northeastern U, MA — B
Ohio Wesleyan U, OH — B
Plymouth State U, NH — B
Providence Coll, RI — B
Quinnipiac U, CT — B
Regis Coll, MA — B
Rhode Island Coll, RI — B
Rivier Coll, NH — B
Roger Williams U, RI — B
Saint Joseph Coll, CT — B
Saint Michael's Coll, VT — B
Salem State Coll, MA — B
Salve Regina U, RI — B
Simmons Coll, MA — B
Smith Coll, MA — B
Southern Connecticut State U, CT — B
Southern Methodist U, TX — B
Stonehill Coll, MA — B
Suffolk U, MA — B
Trinity Coll, CT — B
Tufts U, MA — B
U of Charleston, WV — B
U of Connecticut, CT — B
U of Hartford, CT — B
U of Maine, ME — B
U of Massachusetts Amherst, MA — B
U of Massachusetts Boston, MA — B
U of Massachusetts Dartmouth, MA — B
U of Massachusetts Lowell, MA — B
U of New England, ME — B
U of New Hampshire, NH — B
U of New Haven, CT — B
U of Rhode Island, RI — B
U of San Francisco, CA — B
U of Southern Maine, ME — B
U of Vermont, VT — B
Utica Coll, NY — B
Wellesley Coll, MA — B
Wesleyan U, CT — B
Western Connecticut State U, CT — B
Western New England Coll, MA — B
Wheaton Coll, MA — B
Williams Coll, MA — B
Worcester Polytechnic Inst, MA — B
Worcester State Coll, MA — B
Yale U, CT — B

Chemistry Related
Bridgewater State Coll, MA — B
Connecticut Coll, CT — B
Dartmouth Coll, NH — B
Keene State Coll, NH — B
U of Massachusetts Dartmouth, MA — B

Chemistry Teacher Education
Assumption Coll, MA — B
Hofstra U, NY — B
Husson U, ME — B
Keene State Coll, NH — B
Messiah Coll, PA — B
Ohio Wesleyan U, OH — B
Rhode Island Coll, RI — B
Rivier Coll, NH — B
Sacred Heart U, CT — B
U of Maine, ME — B
Utica Coll, NY — B

Child Development
Albertus Magnus Coll, CT — B
Bennington Coll, VT — B
Hampshire Coll, MA — B
Lasell Coll, MA — B
Lesley U, MA — B
Mitchell Coll, CT — A,B
Mount Ida Coll, MA — B
Quinnipiac U, CT — B
Saint Joseph Coll, CT — B
Southern New Hampshire U, NH — B
Tufts U, MA — B
U of Maine, ME — B
Wheelock Coll, MA — B

Chinese
Bard Coll at Simon's Rock, MA — B
Bates Coll, ME — B
Bennington Coll, VT — B
Connecticut Coll, CT — B
Dartmouth Coll, NH — B
Hofstra U, NY — B
Middlebury Coll, VT — B
Trinity Coll, CT — B
Tufts U, MA — B
U of Massachusetts Amherst, MA — B
U of Vermont, VT — B
Wellesley Coll, MA — B
Williams Coll, MA — B
Yale U, CT — B

Chinese Studies
Bard Coll at Simon's Rock, MA — B

Christian Studies
Gordon Coll, MA — B

Cinematography and Film/Video Production
Bennington Coll, VT — B
Emerson Coll, MA — B
Fitchburg State Coll, MA — B
Hampshire Coll, MA — B
Keene State Coll, NH — B
Massachusetts Coll of Art and Design, MA — B
Middlebury Coll, VT — B
Quinnipiac U, CT — B
Sacred Heart U, CT — B

School of the Museum of Fine Arts, Boston, MA — B
U of Hartford, CT — B

City/Urban, Community and Regional Planning
Bridgewater State Coll, MA — B
Massachusetts Inst of Technology, MA — B
Plymouth State U, NH — B
Salem State Coll, MA — B
U of New Hampshire, NH — B
U of San Francisco, CA — B
Westfield State Coll, MA — B

Civil Engineering
Brown U, RI — B
Clarkson U, NY — B
Hofstra U, NY — B
Massachusetts Inst of Technology, MA — B
Merrimack Coll, MA — B
Northeastern U, MA — B
Southern Methodist U, TX — B
Tufts U, MA — B
United States Coast Guard Academy, CT — B
U of Connecticut, CT — B
U of Hartford, CT — B
U of Maine, ME — B
U of Massachusetts Amherst, MA — B
U of Massachusetts Dartmouth, MA — B
U of Massachusetts Lowell, MA — B
U of New Hampshire, NH — B
U of New Haven, CT — B
U of Rhode Island, RI — B
U of Vermont, VT — B
Worcester Polytechnic Inst, MA — B

Civil Engineering Technology
Central Connecticut State U, CT — B
U of Massachusetts Lowell, MA — A
U of New Hampshire, NH — A
Vermont Tech Coll, VT — A
Wentworth Inst of Technology, MA — B

Classical, Ancient Mediterranean and Near Eastern Studies and Archaeology
Bowdoin Coll, ME — B

Classics
Wheaton Coll, MA — B

Classics and Languages, Literatures and Linguistics
Albertus Magnus Coll, CT — B
Amherst Coll, MA — B
Assumption Coll, MA — B
Boston Coll, MA — B
Bowdoin Coll, ME — B
Brandeis U, MA — B
Brown U, RI — B
Clark U, MA — B
Colby Coll, ME — B
Coll of the Holy Cross, MA — B
Connecticut Coll, CT — B
Dartmouth Coll, NH — B
Harvard U, MA — B
Hofstra U, NY — B
Marlboro Coll, VT — B
Middlebury Coll, VT — B
Mount Holyoke Coll, MA — B

Ohio Wesleyan U, OH — B
Saint Michael's Coll, VT — B
Smith Coll, MA — B
Trinity Coll, CT — B
Tufts U, MA — B
U of Connecticut, CT — B
U of Maine, ME — B
U of Massachusetts Amherst, MA — B
U of Massachusetts Boston, MA — B
U of New Hampshire, NH — B
U of Rhode Island, RI — B
U of Southern Maine, ME — B
U of Vermont, VT — B
Wellesley Coll, MA — B
Wesleyan U, CT — B
Wheaton Coll, MA — B
Williams Coll, MA — B
Yale U, CT — B

Clinical Laboratory Science/ Medical Technology
Atlantic Union Coll, MA — B
Barry U, FL — B
Rhode Island Coll, RI — B
Salem State Coll, MA — B
Salve Regina U, RI — B
Suffolk U, MA — B
U of Connecticut, CT — B
U of Hartford, CT — B
U of Maine, ME — B
U of Massachusetts Dartmouth, MA — B
U of Massachusetts Lowell, MA — B
U of New England, ME — B
U of New Hampshire, NH — B
U of Rhode Island, RI — B
U of Vermont, VT — B
Western Connecticut State U, CT — B

Clinical/Medical Laboratory Assistant
The U of Maine at Augusta, ME — A

Clinical/Medical Laboratory Technology
Barry U, FL — B
Northeastern U, MA — B
U of Maine at Presque Isle, ME — A

Clinical Nutrition
Messiah Coll, PA — B

Clinical Psychology
Franklin Pierce U, NH — B
Husson U, ME — B
Keene State Coll, NH — B

Cognitive Psychology and Psycholinguistics
Bard Coll at Simon's Rock, MA — B
Brown U, RI — B
Dartmouth Coll, NH — B
Hampshire Coll, MA — B
Massachusetts Inst of Technology, MA — B
Wellesley Coll, MA — B
Yale U, CT — B

Cognitive Science
Hampshire Coll, MA — B
U of Connecticut, CT — B

Commercial and Advertising Art
Albertus Magnus Coll, CT — B

Champlain Coll, VT — A,B
Clark U, MA — B
Curry Coll, MA — B
Emmanuel Coll, MA — B
Franklin Pierce U, NH — B
Keene State Coll, NH — B
Lasell Coll, MA — B
Lyndon State Coll, VT — B
Massachusetts Coll of Art and Design, MA — B
Mitchell Coll, CT — A
Newbury Coll, MA — A
Northeastern U, MA — B
Rivier Coll, NH — B
Salem State Coll, MA — B
Simmons Coll, MA — B
Suffolk U, MA — A,B
U of Massachusetts Dartmouth, MA — B
U of New Haven, CT — A,B

Communication and Journalism Related
Champlain Coll, VT — A,B
Quinnipiac U, CT — B

Communication and Media Related
Champlain Coll, VT — A,B
Eugene Lang Coll The New School for Liberal Arts, NY — B
Green Mountain Coll, VT — B
Roger Williams U, RI — B
Southern New Hampshire U, NH — B

Communication Disorders
Bridgewater State Coll, MA — B
Emerson Coll, MA — B
U of Maine, ME — B
U of Massachusetts Amherst, MA — B
U of Rhode Island, RI — B
U of Vermont, VT — B
Worcester State Coll, MA — B

Communication Disorders Sciences and Services Related
U of New Hampshire, NH — B

Communication/Speech Communication and Rhetoric
Barry U, FL — B
Boston Coll, MA — B
Bridgewater State Coll, MA — B
Bryant U, RI — B
Central Connecticut State U, CT — B
Clarkson U, NY — B
Eastern Connecticut State U, CT — B
Emerson Coll, MA — B
Emmanuel Coll, MA — B
Fairfield U, CT — B
Fitchburg State Coll, MA — B
Gordon Coll, MA — B
Hampshire Coll, MA — B
Hofstra U, NY — B
Keene State Coll, NH — B
Lasell Coll, MA — B
Lyndon State Coll, VT — A
Merrimack Coll, MA — B
Messiah Coll, PA — B
Northeastern U, MA — B
Plymouth State U, NH — B
Regis Coll, MA — B
Rhode Island Coll, RI — B

Rivier Coll, NH — B
Southern Connecticut State U, CT — B
Stonehill Coll, MA — B
U of Connecticut, CT — B
U of Hartford, CT — B
U of Maine, ME — B
U of Massachusetts Amherst, MA — B
U of New Hampshire, NH — B
U of New Haven, CT — A,B
U of Rhode Island, RI — B
U of San Francisco, CA — B
U of Southern Maine, ME — B
Utica Coll, NY — B
Western Connecticut State U, CT — B
Western New England Coll, MA — B
Westfield State Coll, MA — B
Worcester State Coll, MA — B

Communications Technologies and Support Services Related
Framingham State Coll, MA — B
Lesley U, MA — B

Communications Technology
Salve Regina U, RI — B

Community Health and Preventive Medicine
Hofstra U, NY — B
Tufts U, MA — B
U of Massachusetts Lowell, MA — B

Community Health Services Counseling
Western Connecticut State U, CT — B
Worcester State Coll, MA — B

Community Organization and Advocacy
Hampshire Coll, MA — B
Providence Coll, RI — B
U of Massachusetts Boston, MA — B
U of New Hampshire, NH — A

Comparative Literature
Brandeis U, MA — B
Brown U, RI — B
Clark U, MA — B
Coll of the Holy Cross, MA — B
Dartmouth Coll, NH — B
Hampshire Coll, MA — B
Harvard U, MA — B
Hofstra U, NY — B
Marlboro Coll, VT — B
New England Coll, NH — B
Salem State Coll, MA — B
Simmons Coll, MA — B
Smith Coll, MA — B
Trinity Coll, CT — B
U of Massachusetts Amherst, MA — B
U of Rhode Island, RI — B
Wellesley Coll, MA — B

Computer and Information Sciences
Anna Maria Coll, MA — B
Assumption Coll, MA — B
Bard Coll at Simon's Rock, MA — B
Bennington Coll, VT — B
Bentley U, MA — B
Boston Coll, MA — B

Bryant U, RI — B
Castleton State Coll, VT — B
Central Connecticut State U, CT — B
Champlain Coll, VT — A,B
Clarkson U, NY — B
Eastern Connecticut State U, CT — B
Fairfield U, CT — B
Fisher Coll, MA — A
Fitchburg State Coll, MA — B
Framingham State Coll, MA — B
Grove City Coll, PA — B
Keene State Coll, NH — A,B
Massachusetts Coll of Liberal Arts, MA — B
Regis Coll, MA — B
Rhode Island Coll, RI — B
Roger Williams U, RI — B
Southern New Hampshire U, NH — A,B
Suffolk U, MA — B
U of Charleston, WV — A,B
U of Hartford, CT — B
The U of Maine at Augusta, ME — A,B
U of Massachusetts Boston, MA — B
U of Massachusetts Dartmouth, MA — B
U of New Hampshire, NH — B
U of New Haven, CT — B
U of Rhode Island, RI — B
U of San Francisco, CA — B
U of Vermont, VT — B
Utica Coll, NY — B
Wentworth Inst of Technology, MA — B
Worcester Polytechnic Inst, MA — B
Worcester State Coll, MA — B
Yale U, CT — B

Computer and Information Sciences and Support Services Related
Hofstra U, NY — B
Keene State Coll, NH — B

Computer and Information Systems Security
Champlain Coll, VT — A,B
ITT Tech Inst, Woburn, MA — B

Computer Engineering
Brown U, RI — B
Clarkson U, NY — B
Fairfield U, CT — B
Franklin W. Olin Coll of Engineering, MA — B
Hofstra U, NY — B
Merrimack Coll, MA — B
Northeastern U, MA — B
Southern Methodist U, TX — B
Trinity Coll, CT — B
Tufts U, MA — B
U of Bridgeport, CT — B
U of Connecticut, CT — B
U of Hartford, CT — B
U of Maine, ME — B
U of Massachusetts Amherst, MA — B
U of Massachusetts Dartmouth, MA — B
U of Massachusetts Lowell, MA — B
U of New Hampshire, NH — B

U of New Haven, CT — B
U of Rhode Island, RI — B
Worcester Polytechnic Inst, MA — B

Computer Engineering Technology
Benjamin Franklin Inst of Technology, MA — A
Central Connecticut State U, CT — B
ITT Tech Inst, Woburn, MA — A
Northeastern U, MA — B
U of Hartford, CT — A
Vermont Tech Coll, VT — A,B
Wentworth Inst of Technology, MA — B

Computer Graphics
Bard Coll at Simon's Rock, MA — B
Becker Coll, MA — B
Champlain Coll, VT — A,B
Coll of the Atlantic, ME — B
Hampshire Coll, MA — B
School of the Museum of Fine Arts, Boston, MA — B

Computer/Information Technology Services Administration Related
Champlain Coll, VT — A,B
Endicott Coll, MA — B

Computer Management
Champlain Coll, VT — A,B
Grove City Coll, PA — B
New England Coll, NH — B

Computer Programming
Castleton State Coll, VT — A
Franklin Pierce U, NH — B
Husson U, ME — B

Computer Programming (Specific Applications)
Husson U, ME — B

Computer Science
Amherst Coll, MA — B
Bard Coll at Simon's Rock, MA — B
Barry U, FL — B
Benjamin Franklin Inst of Technology, MA — A
Bennington Coll, VT — B
Boston Coll, MA — B
Bowdoin Coll, ME — B
Brandeis U, MA — B
Bridgewater State Coll, MA — B
Brown U, RI — B
Clarkson U, NY — B
Clark U, MA — B
Colby Coll, ME — B
Coll of the Holy Cross, MA — B
Connecticut Coll, CT — B
Daniel Webster Coll, NH — B
Dartmouth Coll, NH — B
Endicott Coll, MA — B
Fitchburg State Coll, MA — B
Franklin Pierce U, NH — B
Gordon Coll, MA — B
Hampshire Coll, MA — B
Harvard U, MA — B
Hofstra U, NY — B
Lyndon State Coll, VT — A
Marlboro Coll, VT — B
Massachusetts Coll of Liberal Arts, MA — B

A—associate degree; B—bachelor's degree

Massachusetts Inst of Technology, MA	B
Messiah Coll, PA	B
Middlebury Coll, VT	B
Mount Holyoke Coll, MA	B
Northeastern U, MA	B
Ohio Wesleyan U, OH	B
Plymouth State U, NH	B
Providence Coll, RI	B
Quinnipiac U, CT	B
Regis Coll, MA	B
Rivier Coll, NH	A,B
Roger Williams U, RI	B
Saint Michael's Coll, VT	B
Salem State Coll, MA	B
Simmons Coll, MA	B
Smith Coll, MA	B
Southern Connecticut State U, CT	B
Southern Methodist U, TX	B
Stonehill Coll, MA	B
Suffolk U, MA	B
Trinity Coll, CT	B
Tufts U, MA	B
U of Bridgeport, CT	B
U of Connecticut, CT	B
U of Maine, ME	B
U of Maine at Farmington, ME	B
U of Maine at Fort Kent, ME	A,B
U of Massachusetts Amherst, MA	B
U of Massachusetts Lowell, MA	B
U of New Haven, CT	A
U of San Francisco, CA	B
U of Southern Maine, ME	B
U of Vermont, VT	B
Wellesley Coll, MA	B
Wesleyan U, CT	B
Western Connecticut State U, CT	B
Western New England Coll, MA	B
Westfield State Coll, MA	B
Wheaton Coll, MA	B
Williams Coll, MA	B
Worcester Polytechnic Inst, MA	B

Computer Software and Media Applications Related

Champlain Coll, VT	B
ITT Tech Inst, Woburn, MA	A
U of Massachusetts Boston, MA	B

Computer Software Engineering

Champlain Coll, VT	B
Clarkson U, NY	B
Fairfield U, CT	B
Vermont Tech Coll, VT	A,B

Computer Systems Analysis

U of Vermont, VT	B

Computer Systems Networking and Telecommunications

Champlain Coll, VT	A,B

Computer Teacher Education

Keene State Coll, NH	B
Utica Coll, NY	B

Computer Technology/ Computer Systems Technology

Benjamin Franklin Inst of Technology, MA	A

Conservation Biology

Sterling Coll, VT	B
U of Maine at Machias, ME	B

Construction Engineering

Clarkson U, NY	B

Construction Engineering Technology

Fitchburg State Coll, MA	B
Roger Williams U, RI	B
U of Maine, ME	B
Vermont Tech Coll, VT	A

Construction Management

Central Connecticut State U, CT	B
Vermont Tech Coll, VT	A,B
Wentworth Inst of Technology, MA	B

Consumer Economics

U of Rhode Island, RI	B

Consumer Merchandising/ Retailing Management

Lasell Coll, MA	B
Newbury Coll, MA	A
Salem State Coll, MA	B
Simmons Coll, MA	B

Corrections

Northeastern U, MA	B

Corrections and Criminal Justice Related

Roger Williams U, RI	B
Southern New Hampshire U, NH	B

Counseling Psychology

Emmanuel Coll, MA	B
Lesley U, MA	B

Counselor Education/School Counseling and Guidance

Franklin Pierce U, NH	B

Crafts, Folk Art and Artisanry

Bridgewater State Coll, MA	B
Hampshire Coll, MA	B

Creative Writing

Bard Coll at Simon's Rock, MA	B
Bennington Coll, VT	B
Brandeis U, MA	B
Bridgewater State Coll, MA	B
Brown U, RI	B
Champlain Coll, VT	B
Colby Coll, ME	B
Dartmouth Coll, NH	B
Emerson Coll, MA	B
Eugene Lang Coll The New School for Liberal Arts, NY	B
Fitchburg State Coll, MA	B
Franklin Pierce U, NH	B
Green Mountain Coll, VT	B
Hampshire Coll, MA	B
Hofstra U, NY	B
Johnson State Coll, VT	B
Marlboro Coll, VT	B
Massachusetts Inst of Technology, MA	B
New England Coll, NH	B
Ohio Wesleyan U, OH	B
Roger Williams U, RI	B
Southern Methodist U, TX	B
Southern New Hampshire U, NH	B
Trinity Coll, CT	B
U of Maine at Farmington, ME	B

U of Maine at Machias, ME	B
U of Maine at Presque Isle, ME	A
Western New England Coll, MA	B

Criminal Justice/Law Enforcement Administration

Albertus Magnus Coll, CT	B
Bay Path Coll, MA	B
Castleton State Coll, VT	A,B
Champlain Coll, VT	A,B
Coll of St. Joseph, VT	A,B
Curry Coll, MA	B
Fisher Coll, MA	A
Franklin Pierce U, NH	B
Granite State Coll, NH	B
Mitchell Coll, CT	A,B
Mount Ida Coll, MA	B
New England Coll, NH	B
Roger Williams U, RI	A,B
Sacred Heart U, CT	B
Salem State Coll, MA	B
Salve Regina U, RI	B
Suffolk U, MA	A,B
The U of Maine at Augusta, ME	B
U of Maine at Fort Kent, ME	A
U of Maine at Presque Isle, ME	A,B
U of Massachusetts Lowell, MA	B
U of New Haven, CT	B
Utica Coll, NY	B

Criminal Justice/Police Science

Husson U, ME	A,B
Northeastern U, MA	B
U of Hartford, CT	B
U of New Haven, CT	A
Western Connecticut State U, CT	B

Criminal Justice/Safety

Anna Maria Coll, MA	B
Becker Coll, MA	B
Bridgewater State Coll, MA	B
Champlain Coll, VT	A,B
Endicott Coll, MA	B
Fisher Coll, MA	A
Fitchburg State Coll, MA	B
Granite State Coll, NH	B
Husson U, ME	A,B
Lasell Coll, MA	B
Messiah Coll, PA	B
Mitchell Coll, CT	B
Northeastern U, MA	B
Plymouth State U, NH	B
Quinnipiac U, CT	B
Rhode Island Coll, RI	B
The U of Maine at Augusta, ME	A
U of Massachusetts Boston, MA	B
Western New England Coll, MA	B
Westfield State Coll, MA	B
Worcester State Coll, MA	B

Criminology

Barry U, FL	B
Castleton State Coll, VT	B
Central Connecticut State U, CT	B
Husson U, ME	B
Rivier Coll, NH	B
Stonehill Coll, MA	B

U of Massachusetts Dartmouth, MA	B
U of New Hampshire, NH	B
U of Southern Maine, ME	B

Crop Production

Sterling Coll, VT	A,B
U of Massachusetts Amherst, MA	A

Culinary Arts

Newbury Coll, MA	A
Southern New Hampshire U, NH	A

Culinary Arts Related

Newbury Coll, MA	B

Cultural Resource Management and Policy Analysis

Hampshire Coll, MA	B
Sterling Coll, VT	B

Cultural Studies

Bard Coll at Simon's Rock, MA	B
Clark U, MA	B
Eugene Lang Coll The New School for Liberal Arts, NY	B
Hampshire Coll, MA	B
Marlboro Coll, VT	B
Ohio Wesleyan U, OH	B
Yale U, CT	B

Curriculum and Instruction

Albertus Magnus Coll, CT	B

Cytotechnology

Barry U, FL	B
Salve Regina U, RI	B
U of Connecticut, CT	B

Dairy Husbandry and Production

Sterling Coll, VT	A,B
U of Vermont, VT	B

Dairy Science

U of New Hampshire, NH	B
Vermont Tech Coll, VT	A

Dance

Amherst Coll, MA	B
Bard Coll at Simon's Rock, MA	B
Bennington Coll, VT	B
The Boston Conservatory, MA	B
Connecticut Coll, CT	B
Eugene Lang Coll The New School for Liberal Arts, NY	B
Hampshire Coll, MA	B
Hofstra U, NY	B
Johnson State Coll, VT	B
Keene State Coll, NH	B
Marlboro Coll, VT	B
Middlebury Coll, VT	B
Mount Holyoke Coll, MA	B
Rhode Island Coll, RI	B
Roger Williams U, RI	B
Smith Coll, MA	B
Southern Methodist U, TX	B
Trinity Coll, CT	B
U of Hartford, CT	B
U of Massachusetts Amherst, MA	B
Wesleyan U, CT	B
Wheaton Coll, MA	B

Demography and Population

Hampshire Coll, MA	B

Dental Assisting

The U of Maine at Augusta, ME	A

Dental Hygiene

Massachusetts Coll of Pharmacy and Health Sciences, MA	B
Mount Ida Coll, MA	A
Northeastern U, MA	B
U of Bridgeport, CT	A,B
The U of Maine at Augusta, ME	A,B
U of New England, ME	A,B
U of New Haven, CT	A,B
Vermont Tech Coll, VT	A,B

Design and Applied Arts Related

Hofstra U, NY	B
U of Massachusetts Dartmouth, MA	B

Design and Visual Communications

Bennington Coll, VT	B
Central Connecticut State U, CT	B
Champlain Coll, VT	A,B
Endicott Coll, MA	B
Hampshire Coll, MA	B
U of Hartford, CT	B
U of Massachusetts Dartmouth, MA	B

Developmental and Child Psychology

Bard Coll at Simon's Rock, MA	B
Bay Path Coll, MA	B
Bridgewater State Coll, MA	B
Castleton State Coll, VT	B
Eastern Connecticut State U, CT	B
Emmanuel Coll, MA	B
Fitchburg State Coll, MA	B
Hampshire Coll, MA	B
Keene State Coll, NH	B
Marlboro Coll, VT	B
Mount Ida Coll, MA	B
Quinnipiac U, CT	B
Suffolk U, MA	B
Tufts U, MA	B
Utica Coll, NY	B

Development Economics and International Development

Brown U, RI	B
Clark U, MA	B
Hampshire Coll, MA	B
U of Vermont, VT	B

Diesel Mechanics Technology

Vermont Tech Coll, VT	A

Dietetics

Keene State Coll, NH	B
Labouré Coll, MA	A
Simmons Coll, MA	B
U of Connecticut, CT	B
U of New Haven, CT	B
U of Vermont, VT	B

Digital Communication and Media/Multimedia

Champlain Coll, VT	A,B
Clarkson U, NY	B
Fitchburg State Coll, MA	B
Hampshire Coll, MA	B

Southern New Hampshire U, NH	B
Wellesley Coll, MA	B

Directing and Theatrical Production

Bennington Coll, VT	B
Hampshire Coll, MA	B
Hofstra U, NY	B
Keene State Coll, NH	B

Divinity/Ministry

Atlantic Union Coll, MA	A,B
Grove City Coll, PA	B
Providence Coll, RI	A,B

Dog/Pet/Animal Grooming

Becker Coll, MA	A

Drafting and Design Technology

Benjamin Franklin Inst of Technology, MA	A
U of Maine, ME	B

Drama and Dance Teacher Education

Bridgewater State Coll, MA	B
Emerson Coll, MA	B
Johnson State Coll, VT	B
Ohio Wesleyan U, OH	B
Salve Regina U, RI	B

Dramatic/Theater Arts

Albertus Magnus Coll, CT	B
Amherst Coll, MA	B
Bard Coll at Simon's Rock, MA	B
Barry U, FL	B
Bates Coll, ME	B
Bennington Coll, VT	B
Boston Coll, MA	B
The Boston Conservatory, MA	B
Brandeis U, MA	B
Bridgewater State Coll, MA	B
Brown U, RI	B
Castleton State Coll, VT	B
Clark U, MA	B
Colby Coll, ME	B
Coll of the Holy Cross, MA	B
Connecticut Coll, CT	B
Dartmouth Coll, NH	B
Emerson Coll, MA	B
Eugene Lang Coll The New School for Liberal Arts, NY	B
Fairfield U, CT	B
Fitchburg State Coll, MA	B
Franklin Pierce U, NH	B
Hampshire Coll, MA	B
Hofstra U, NY	B
Johnson State Coll, VT	B
Marlboro Coll, VT	B
Messiah Coll, PA	B
Middlebury Coll, VT	B
Mount Holyoke Coll, MA	B
New England Coll, NH	B
Northeastern U, MA	B
Ohio Wesleyan U, OH	B
Plymouth State U, NH	B
Quinnipiac U, CT	B
Regis Coll, MA	B
Rhode Island Coll, RI	B
Roger Williams U, RI	B
Sacred Heart U, CT	B
Saint Michael's Coll, VT	B
Salem State Coll, MA	B
Salve Regina U, RI	B
Smith Coll, MA	B

Southern Connecticut State U, CT	B
Southern Methodist U, TX	B
Suffolk U, MA	B
Trinity Coll, CT	B
Tufts U, MA	B
U of Connecticut, CT	B
U of Hartford, CT	B
U of Maine, ME	B
U of Maine at Farmington, ME	B
U of Maine at Machias, ME	B
U of Massachusetts Amherst, MA	B
U of Massachusetts Boston, MA	B
U of New Hampshire, NH	B
U of Southern Maine, ME	B
U of Vermont, VT	B
Wellesley Coll, MA	B
Wesleyan U, CT	B
Western Connecticut State U, CT	B
Westfield State Coll, MA	B
Wheaton Coll, MA	B
Williams Coll, MA	B
Yale U, CT	B

Dramatic/Theater Arts and Stagecraft Related

U of Connecticut, CT	B

Drawing

Bard Coll at Simon's Rock, MA	B
Bennington Coll, VT	B
Coll of the Atlantic, ME	B
Hampshire Coll, MA	B
Lyme Academy Coll of Fine Arts, CT	B
Marlboro Coll, VT	B
New England Coll, NH	B
Providence Coll, RI	B
Rivier Coll, NH	B
Salem State Coll, MA	B
School of the Museum of Fine Arts, Boston, MA	B
U of Hartford, CT	B
U of San Francisco, CA	B

Early Childhood Education

Becker Coll, MA	B
Bennington Coll, VT	B
Bridgewater State Coll, MA	B
Champlain Coll, VT	A
Curry Coll, MA	B
Eastern Connecticut State U, CT	B
Endicott Coll, MA	B
Fitchburg State Coll, MA	B
Granite State Coll, NH	A,B
Hampshire Coll, MA	B
Hofstra U, NY	B
Keene State Coll, NH	B
Messiah Coll, PA	B
Mitchell Coll, CT	B
Mount Ida Coll, MA	B
Ohio Wesleyan U, OH	B
Plymouth State U, NH	B
Rhode Island Coll, RI	B
Saint Joseph Coll, CT	B
Salve Regina U, RI	B
Southern Connecticut State U, CT	B
Southern New Hampshire U, NH	B
Stonehill Coll, MA	B
U of Hartford, CT	B

U of Maine at Farmington, ME	B
U of Vermont, VT	B
Wheelock Coll, MA	A
Worcester State Coll, MA	B

East Asian Languages

Hampshire Coll, MA	B
Smith Coll, MA	B

East Asian Languages Related

Dartmouth Coll, NH	B

Ecology

Bard Coll at Simon's Rock, MA	B
Barry U, FL	B
Bennington Coll, VT	B
Clarkson U, NY	B
Clark U, MA	B
Connecticut Coll, CT	B
Dartmouth Coll, NH	B
Franklin Pierce U, NH	B
Hampshire Coll, MA	B
Marlboro Coll, VT	B
Sterling Coll, VT	A,B
Tufts U, MA	B
U of Connecticut, CT	B
U of Maine, ME	B
U of Maine at Machias, ME	B
U of New Haven, CT	B
Yale U, CT	B

Ecology, Evolution, Systematics and Population Biology Related

Hofstra U, NY	B
Sterling Coll, VT	B

E-Commerce

Champlain Coll, VT	A,B
Clarkson U, NY	B
U of Phoenix–Central Massachusetts Campus, MA	B

Econometrics and Quantitative Economics

Bowdoin Coll, ME	B
Hofstra U, NY	B
Southern Methodist U, TX	B
U of Rhode Island, RI	B

Economics

Albertus Magnus Coll, CT	B
Amherst Coll, MA	B
Assumption Coll, MA	B
Babson Coll, MA	B
Barry U, FL	B
Bates Coll, ME	B
Boston Coll, MA	B
Bowdoin Coll, ME	B
Brandeis U, MA	B
Bridgewater State Coll, MA	B
Brown U, RI	B
Bryant U, RI	B
Central Connecticut State U, CT	B
Clark U, MA	B
Colby Coll, ME	B
Coll of the Atlantic, ME	B
Coll of the Holy Cross, MA	B
Connecticut Coll, CT	B
Dartmouth Coll, NH	B
Eastern Connecticut State U, CT	B
Emmanuel Coll, MA	B
Eugene Lang Coll The New School for Liberal Arts, NY	B
Fairfield U, CT	B
Fitchburg State Coll, MA	B

A—associate degree; B—bachelor's degree

Framingham State Coll, MA	B
Franklin Pierce U, NH	B
Gordon Coll, MA	B
Grove City Coll, PA	B
Hampshire Coll, MA	B
Harvard U, MA	B
Hofstra U, NY	B
Keene State Coll, NH	B
Marlboro Coll, VT	B
Massachusetts Inst of Technology, MA	B
Merrimack Coll, MA	B
Messiah Coll, PA	B
Middlebury Coll, VT	B
Mount Holyoke Coll, MA	B
Nichols Coll, MA	B
Northeastern U, MA	B
Ohio Wesleyan U, OH	B
Providence Coll, RI	B
Quinnipiac U, CT	B
Rhode Island Coll, RI	B
Saint Joseph Coll, CT	B
Saint Michael's Coll, VT	B
Salem State Coll, MA	B
Salve Regina U, RI	B
Simmons Coll, MA	B
Smith Coll, MA	B
Southern Connecticut State U, CT	B
Southern Methodist U, TX	B
Southern New Hampshire U, NH	B
Stonehill Coll, MA	B
Suffolk U, MA	B
Trinity Coll, CT	B
Tufts U, MA	B
U of Connecticut, CT	B
U of Hartford, CT	B
U of Maine, ME	B
U of Massachusetts Amherst, MA	B
U of Massachusetts Boston, MA	B
U of Massachusetts Dartmouth, MA	B
U of Massachusetts Lowell, MA	B
U of New Hampshire, NH	B
U of Rhode Island, RI	B
U of San Francisco, CA	B
U of Southern Maine, ME	B
U of Vermont, VT	B
Utica Coll, NY	B
Wellesley Coll, MA	B
Wesleyan U, CT	B
Western Connecticut State U, CT	B
Western New England Coll, MA	B
Westfield State Coll, MA	B
Wheaton Coll, MA	B
Williams Coll, MA	B
Worcester Polytechnic Inst, MA	B
Worcester State Coll, MA	B
Yale U, CT	B

Economics Related

Bard Coll at Simon's Rock, MA	B
U of Hartford, CT	B

Education

Albertus Magnus Coll, CT	B
Atlantic Union Coll, MA	B
Barry U, FL	B
Becker Coll, MA	B
Bennington Coll, VT	B
Brandeis U, MA	B

Brown U, RI	B
Clark U, MA	B
Coll of the Atlantic, ME	B
Curry Coll, MA	B
Emmanuel Coll, MA	B
Eugene Lang Coll The New School for Liberal Arts, NY	B
Fitchburg State Coll, MA	B
Framingham State Coll, MA	B
Franklin Pierce U, NH	B
Hampshire Coll, MA	B
Hebrew Coll, MA	B
Johnson State Coll, VT	B
Lasell Coll, MA	B
Lesley U, MA	B
Massachusetts Coll of Liberal Arts, MA	B
New England Coll, NH	B
Northeastern U, MA	B
Ohio Wesleyan U, OH	B
Quinnipiac U, CT	B
Rivier Coll, NH	B
Sacred Heart U, CT	B
Saint Michael's Coll, VT	B
Salem State Coll, MA	B
Simmons Coll, MA	B
Smith Coll, MA	B
Southern New Hampshire U, NH	B
Suffolk U, MA	B
Trinity Coll, CT	B
U of Charleston, WV	B
U of Maine, ME	B
U of Maine at Fort Kent, ME	B
U of Maine at Machias, ME	B
U of Maine at Presque Isle, ME	B
U of San Francisco, CA	B
U of Vermont, VT	B
Westfield State Coll, MA	B
Wheelock Coll, MA	B

Educational, Instructional, and Curriculum Supervision

Sterling Coll, VT	B

Educational/Instructional Media Design

U of Maine, ME	B

Educational Leadership and Administration

Sterling Coll, VT	B
U of San Francisco, CA	B

Education (K–12)

New England Coll, NH	B
Ohio Wesleyan U, OH	B
U of Maine, ME	B
U of Maine at Fort Kent, ME	B

Education (Multiple Levels)

Connecticut Coll, CT	B
Hofstra U, NY	B
Ohio Wesleyan U, OH	B
Rhode Island Coll, RI	B

Education Related

Mount Holyoke Coll, MA	B
Sterling Coll, VT	B

Education (Specific Subject Areas) Related

Plymouth State U, NH	B
U of New Hampshire, NH	B

Electrical and Electronic Engineering Technologies Related

Benjamin Franklin Inst of Technology, MA	A
Grove City Coll, PA	B

Electrical and Power Transmission Installation

Benjamin Franklin Inst of Technology, MA	A

Electrical, Electronic and Communications Engineering Technology

Benjamin Franklin Inst of Technology, MA	A
ITT Tech Inst, Woburn, MA	B
U of Hartford, CT	A,B
U of Maine, ME	B
U of Massachusetts Dartmouth, MA	B
U of Massachusetts Lowell, MA	A
U of New Hampshire, NH	B
U of New Hampshire at Manchester, NH	B
Vermont Tech Coll, VT	A
Wentworth Inst of Technology, MA	B

Electrical, Electronics and Communications Engineering

Brown U, RI	B
Central Connecticut State U, CT	B
Clarkson U, NY	B
Fairfield U, CT	A
Grove City Coll, PA	B
Hofstra U, NY	B
Massachusetts Inst of Technology, MA	B
Merrimack Coll, MA	B
Northeastern U, MA	B
Southern Methodist U, TX	B
Suffolk U, MA	B
Trinity Coll, CT	B
Tufts U, MA	B
United States Coast Guard Academy, CT	B
U of Connecticut, CT	B
U of Hartford, CT	B
U of Maine, ME	B
U of Massachusetts Amherst, MA	B
U of Massachusetts Dartmouth, MA	B
U of Massachusetts Lowell, MA	B
U of New Hampshire, NH	B
U of New Haven, CT	B
U of Rhode Island, RI	B
U of Southern Maine, ME	B
U of Vermont, VT	B
Western New England Coll, MA	B
Worcester Polytechnic Inst, MA	B
Yale U, CT	B

Electromechanical Technology

Vermont Tech Coll, VT	B

Electroneurodiagnostic/ Electroencephalographic Technology

Labouré Coll, MA	A

Elementary Education

Albertus Magnus Coll, CT	B

Assumption Coll, MA	B
Atlantic Union Coll, MA	B
Barry U, FL	B
Bay Path Coll, MA	B
Becker Coll, MA	B
Bennington Coll, VT	B
Boston Coll, MA	B
Bridgewater State Coll, MA	B
Central Connecticut State U, CT	B
Champlain Coll, VT	B
Clark U, MA	B
Coll of St. Joseph, VT	B
Coll of the Atlantic, ME	B
Connecticut Coll, CT	B
Curry Coll, MA	B
Eastern Connecticut State U, CT	B
Emmanuel Coll, MA	B
Endicott Coll, MA	B
Fitchburg State Coll, MA	B
Franklin Pierce U, NH	B
Gordon Coll, MA	B
Green Mountain Coll, VT	B
Grove City Coll, PA	B
Hampshire Coll, MA	B
Hofstra U, NY	B
Husson U, ME	B
Johnson State Coll, VT	B
Keene State Coll, NH	B
Lasell Coll, MA	B
Lesley U, MA	B
Lyndon State Coll, VT	B
Merrimack Coll, MA	B
Messiah Coll, PA	B
New England Coll, NH	B
Northeastern U, MA	B
Ohio Wesleyan U, OH	B
Plymouth State U, NH	B
Rhode Island Coll, RI	B
Rivier Coll, NH	B
Roger Williams U, RI	B
Sacred Heart U, CT	B
Saint Joseph Coll, CT	B
Saint Michael's Coll, VT	B
Salem State Coll, MA	B
Salve Regina U, RI	B
Simmons Coll, MA	B
Southern Connecticut State U, CT	B
Southern New Hampshire U, NH	B
Stonehill Coll, MA	B
Suffolk U, MA	B
Tufts U, MA	B
U of Charleston, WV	B
U of Connecticut, CT	B
U of Hartford, CT	B
U of Maine, ME	B
U of Maine at Farmington, ME	B
U of Maine at Fort Kent, ME	B
U of Maine at Machias, ME	B
U of Maine at Presque Isle, ME	B
U of New England, ME	B
U of Rhode Island, RI	B
U of San Francisco, CA	B
U of Vermont, VT	B
Utica Coll, NY	B
Western Connecticut State U, CT	B
Western New England Coll, MA	B
Westfield State Coll, MA	B
Wheelock Coll, MA	B
Worcester State Coll, MA	B

Energy Management and Systems Technology
Fitchburg State Coll, MA — B
Sterling Coll, VT — B

Engineering
Barry U, FL — B
Bates Coll, ME — B
Brown U, RI — B
Clarkson U, NY — B
Clark U, MA — B
Daniel Webster Coll, NH — A
Dartmouth Coll, NH — B
Franklin W. Olin Coll of Engineering, MA — B
Harvard U, MA — B
Maine Maritime Academy, ME — B
Massachusetts Maritime Academy, MA — B
Messiah Coll, PA — B
Mount Holyoke Coll, MA — B
Northeastern U, MA — B
Roger Williams U, RI — B
Trinity Coll, CT — B
Tufts U, MA — B
U of Hartford, CT — B
U of Massachusetts Amherst, MA — B
U of New Haven, CT — B

Engineering/Industrial Management
Massachusetts Maritime Academy, MA — B
U of Massachusetts Lowell, MA — B
U of Vermont, VT — B
Worcester Polytechnic Inst, MA — B

Engineering Mechanics
Fairfield U, CT — B
Worcester Polytechnic Inst, MA — B

Engineering Physics
Brown U, RI — B
Connecticut Coll, CT — B
Dartmouth Coll, NH — B
Fairfield U, CT — B
Providence Coll, RI — B
Tufts U, MA — B
U of Connecticut, CT — B
U of Maine, ME — B
U of Massachusetts Boston, MA
Worcester Polytechnic Inst, MA — B
Yale U, CT — B

Engineering Related
Massachusetts Maritime Academy, MA — B
Ohio Wesleyan U, OH — B
Tufts U, MA — B
U of Connecticut, CT — B
Wentworth Inst of Technology, MA — B
Worcester Polytechnic Inst, MA — B

Engineering Science
Daniel Webster Coll, NH — A
Hofstra U, NY — B
Merrimack Coll, MA — A
Ohio Wesleyan U, OH — B
Smith Coll, MA — B

Tufts U, MA — B
Yale U, CT — B

Engineering Technologies Related
Keene State Coll, NH — A
U of Hartford, CT — B

Engineering Technology
Benjamin Franklin Inst of Technology, MA — A
Maine Maritime Academy, ME — B
Massachusetts Maritime Academy, MA — B
U of Hartford, CT — B
U of Maine, ME — B

English
Albertus Magnus Coll, CT — B
Amherst Coll, MA — B
Anna Maria Coll, MA — B
Assumption Coll, MA — B
Barry U, FL — B
Bates Coll, ME — B
Bennington Coll, VT — B
Boston Coll, MA — B
Bowdoin Coll, ME — B
Brandeis U, MA — B
Bridgewater State Coll, MA — B
Brown U, RI — B
Bryant U, RI — B
Central Connecticut State U, CT — B
Clark U, MA — B
Colby Coll, ME — B
Coll of St. Joseph, VT — B
Coll of the Atlantic, ME — B
Coll of the Holy Cross, MA — B
Connecticut Coll, CT — B
Curry Coll, MA — B
Dartmouth Coll, NH — B
Eastern Connecticut State U, CT — B
Emmanuel Coll, MA — B
Endicott Coll, MA — B
Eugene Lang Coll The New School for Liberal Arts, NY — B
Fairfield U, CT — B
Fitchburg State Coll, MA — B
Framingham State Coll, MA — B
Franklin Pierce U, NH — B
Gordon Coll, MA — B
Green Mountain Coll, VT — B
Grove City Coll, PA — B
Hampshire Coll, MA — B
Harvard U, MA — B
Hofstra U, NY — B
Johnson State Coll, VT — B
Keene State Coll, NH — B
Lesley U, MA — B
Lyndon State Coll, VT — B
Marlboro Coll, VT — B
Massachusetts Coll of Liberal Arts, MA — B
Massachusetts Inst of Technology, MA — B
Merrimack Coll, MA — B
Messiah Coll, PA — B
Middlebury Coll, VT — B
Mount Holyoke Coll, MA — B
Mount Ida Coll, MA — B
New England Coll, NH — B
Nichols Coll, MA — B
Northeastern U, MA — B
Ohio Wesleyan U, OH — B
Plymouth State U, NH — B

Providence Coll, RI — B
Quinnipiac U, CT — B
Regis Coll, MA — B
Rhode Island Coll, RI — B
Rivier Coll, NH — B
Roger Williams U, RI — B
Saint Joseph Coll, CT — B
Saint Michael's Coll, VT — B
Salem State Coll, MA — B
Salve Regina U, RI — B
Simmons Coll, MA — B
Smith Coll, MA — B
Southern Connecticut State U, CT — B
Southern Methodist U, TX — B
Southern New Hampshire U, NH — B
Stonehill Coll, MA — B
Suffolk U, MA — B
Trinity Coll, CT — B
Tufts U, MA — B
U of Bridgeport, CT — B
U of Connecticut, CT — B
U of Hartford, CT — B
U of Maine, ME — B
U of Maine at Farmington, ME — B
U of Maine at Fort Kent, ME — B
U of Maine at Machias, ME — B
U of Maine at Presque Isle, ME — B
U of Massachusetts Amherst, MA — B
U of Massachusetts Boston, MA — B
U of Massachusetts Dartmouth, MA — B
U of Massachusetts Lowell, MA — B
U of New England, ME — B
U of New Hampshire, NH — B
U of New Hampshire at Manchester, NH — B
U of New Haven, CT — B
U of Rhode Island, RI — B
U of San Francisco, CA — B
U of Southern Maine, ME — B
U of Vermont, VT — B
Utica Coll, NY — B
Wellesley Coll, MA — B
Wesleyan U, CT — B
Western Connecticut State U, CT — B
Western New England Coll, MA — B
Westfield State Coll, MA — B
Wheaton Coll, MA — B
Williams Coll, MA — B
Worcester State Coll, MA — B
Yale U, CT — B

English as a Second/Foreign Language (Teaching)
Simmons Coll, MA — B

English Composition
Bard Coll at Simon's Rock, MA — B
Bennington Coll, VT — B
Hampshire Coll, MA — B

English Language and Literature Related
Burlington Coll, VT — B
Emmanuel Coll, MA — B
Harvard U, MA — B
Hofstra U, NY — B
The U of Maine at Augusta, ME — B

English/Language Arts Teacher Education
Anna Maria Coll, MA — B
Assumption Coll, MA — B
Barry U, FL — B
Bridgewater State Coll, MA — B
Fitchburg State Coll, MA — B
Hofstra U, NY — B
Johnson State Coll, VT — B
Keene State Coll, NH — B
Lyndon State Coll, VT — A
Messiah Coll, PA — B
Rhode Island Coll, RI — B
Rivier Coll, NH — B
Sacred Heart U, CT — B
Salve Regina U, RI — B
Southern New Hampshire U, NH — B
U of Maine, ME — B
U of Maine at Farmington, ME — B
U of Maine at Fort Kent, ME — B
U of Maine at Machias, ME — B
U of Vermont, VT — B
Utica Coll, NY — B

English Literature (British and Commonwealth)
Bennington Coll, VT — B
Hampshire Coll, MA — B
Hofstra U, NY — B

Entomology
U of New Hampshire, NH — B

Entrepreneurial and Small Business Related
Babson Coll, MA — B

Entrepreneurship
Babson Coll, MA — B
Clarkson U, NY — B
Grove City Coll, PA — B
Hofstra U, NY — B
Messiah Coll, PA — B
Northeastern U, MA — B
Quinnipiac U, CT — B
U of Hartford, CT — B
U of Maine at Machias, ME — B
U of Vermont, VT — B

Environmental Biology
Bennington Coll, VT — B
Bridgewater State Coll, MA — B
Coll of the Atlantic, ME — B
Fitchburg State Coll, MA — B
Franklin Pierce U, NH — B
Hampshire Coll, MA — B
Marlboro Coll, VT — B
Plymouth State U, NH — B
Sacred Heart U, CT — B
Sterling Coll, VT — B
Suffolk U, MA — B
U of Charleston, WV — B
Westfield State Coll, MA — B

Environmental Design/Architecture
Boston Architectural Coll, MA — B
Coll of the Atlantic, ME — B
Hampshire Coll, MA — B
Sterling Coll, VT — B
U of Massachusetts Amherst, MA — B

Environmental Education
Coll of the Atlantic, ME — B
Johnson State Coll, VT — B
U of Maine at Machias, ME — B

A—associate degree; B—bachelor's degree

Environmental/Environmental Health Engineering

Clarkson U, NY	B
Hofstra U, NY	B
Massachusetts Inst of Technology, MA	B
Massachusetts Maritime Academy, MA	B
Southern Methodist U, TX	B
Tufts U, MA	B
U of Connecticut, CT	B
U of Hartford, CT	B
U of New Hampshire, NH	B
U of Vermont, VT	B
Worcester Polytechnic Inst, MA	B
Yale U, CT	B

Environmental Health

Clarkson U, NY	B
U of Southern Maine, ME	B

Environmental Science

Anna Maria Coll, MA	B
Assumption Coll, MA	B
Bennington Coll, VT	B
Brown U, RI	B
Colby Coll, ME	B
Eastern Connecticut State U, CT	B
Hampshire Coll, MA	B
Massachusetts Coll of Liberal Arts, MA	B
Massachusetts Coll of Pharmacy and Health Sciences, MA	B
Massachusetts Maritime Academy, MA	B
Messiah Coll, PA	B
New England Coll, NH	B
Roger Williams U, RI	B
Saint Joseph Coll, CT	B
Saint Michael's Coll, VT	B
Trinity Coll, CT	B
U of Charleston, WV	B
U of Maine, ME	B
U of Massachusetts Amherst, MA	B
U of Massachusetts Lowell, MA	B
U of New England, ME	B
U of New Hampshire, NH	B
U of San Francisco, CA	B
U of Vermont, VT	B
Wheaton Coll, MA	B

Environmental Studies

Amherst Coll, MA	B
Bard Coll at Simon's Rock, MA	B
Bates Coll, ME	B
Bennington Coll, VT	B
Bowdoin Coll, ME	B
Brandeis U, MA	B
Brown U, RI	B
Castleton State Coll, VT	B
Clarkson U, NY	B
Colby Coll, ME	B
Coll of the Atlantic, ME	B
Coll of the Holy Cross, MA	B
Connecticut Coll, CT	B
Curry Coll, MA	B
Dartmouth Coll, NH	B
Emmanuel Coll, MA	B
Endicott Coll, MA	B
Franklin Pierce U, NH	B
Green Mountain Coll, VT	B
Hampshire Coll, MA	B
Harvard U, MA	B

Hofstra U, NY	B
Johnson State Coll, VT	B
Keene State Coll, NH	B
Lesley U, MA	B
Marlboro Coll, VT	B
Massachusetts Maritime Academy, MA	B
Messiah Coll, PA	B
Middlebury Coll, VT	B
Mitchell Coll, CT	B
Mount Holyoke Coll, MA	B
New England Coll, NH	B
Northeastern U, MA	B
Ohio Wesleyan U, OH	B
Simmons Coll, MA	B
Southern Methodist U, TX	B
Southern New Hampshire U, NH	B
Sterling Coll, VT	A,B
Stonehill Coll, MA	B
Suffolk U, MA	B
Tufts U, MA	B
U of Connecticut, CT	B
U of Maine at Farmington, ME	B
U of Maine at Fort Kent, ME	B
U of Maine at Machias, ME	B
U of Maine at Presque Isle, ME	B
U of New England, ME	B
U of Rhode Island, RI	B
U of San Francisco, CA	B
U of Southern Maine, ME	B
U of Vermont, VT	B
Wellesley Coll, MA	B
Wesleyan U, CT	B
Worcester Polytechnic Inst, MA	B
Yale U, CT	B

Equestrian Studies

Mount Ida Coll, MA	B
U of Massachusetts Amherst, MA	A

Ethics

Bridgewater State Coll, MA	B
Hampshire Coll, MA	B

Ethnic, Cultural Minority, and Gender Studies Related

Bard Coll at Simon's Rock, MA	B
Burlington Coll, VT	B
Connecticut Coll, CT	B
Saint Michael's Coll, VT	B
Sterling Coll, VT	B
Stonehill Coll, MA	B
Wellesley Coll, MA	B
Williams Coll, MA	B
Yale U, CT	B

European History

Bennington Coll, VT	B
Hampshire Coll, MA	B
Keene State Coll, NH	B

European Studies

Amherst Coll, MA	B
Bard Coll at Simon's Rock, MA	B
Bennington Coll, VT	B
Brandeis U, MA	B
Marlboro Coll, VT	B
Middlebury Coll, VT	B
Mount Holyoke Coll, MA	B
Salem State Coll, MA	B
Southern Methodist U, TX	B
U of New Hampshire, NH	B
U of Vermont, VT	B

European Studies (Central and Eastern)

Bowdoin Coll, ME	B
Connecticut Coll, CT	B
Marlboro Coll, VT	B
Middlebury Coll, VT	B
Salem State Coll, MA	B
Wesleyan U, CT	B

Evolutionary Biology

Bennington Coll, VT	B
Coll of the Atlantic, ME	B
Dartmouth Coll, NH	B
Hampshire Coll, MA	B
Harvard U, MA	B
Yale U, CT	B

Exercise Physiology

Fitchburg State Coll, MA	B

Experimental Psychology

Hampshire Coll, MA	B
Keene State Coll, NH	B
Marlboro Coll, VT	B
Tufts U, MA	B

Facilities Planning and Management

Fitchburg State Coll, MA	B

Family and Community Services

Messiah Coll, PA	B

Family and Consumer Economics Related

Saint Joseph Coll, CT	B

Family and Consumer Sciences/Human Sciences

Framingham State Coll, MA	B
Saint Joseph Coll, CT	B

Family/Community Studies

Curry Coll, MA	B
U of Maine at Machias, ME	B

Family Systems

Connecticut Coll, CT	B

Farm and Ranch Management

Sterling Coll, VT	B

Fashion/Apparel Design

Fisher Coll, MA	A
Lasell Coll, MA	B
Massachusetts Coll of Art and Design, MA	B
Mount Ida Coll, MA	B

Fashion Merchandising

Fisher Coll, MA	B
Lasell Coll, MA	B
Mount Ida Coll, MA	B
Newbury Coll, MA	A
The New England Inst of Art, MA	B
Southern New Hampshire U, NH	A
U of Bridgeport, CT	A

Fiber, Textile and Weaving Arts

Massachusetts Coll of Art and Design, MA	B
U of Massachusetts Dartmouth, MA	B

Film/Cinema Studies

Bennington Coll, VT	B
Boston Coll, MA	B
Brandeis U, MA	B

Brown U, RI	B
Burlington Coll, VT	A,B
Clark U, MA	B
Connecticut Coll, CT	B
Curry Coll, MA	B
Dartmouth Coll, NH	B
Emerson Coll, MA	B
Hampshire Coll, MA	B
Keene State Coll, NH	B
Marlboro Coll, VT	B
Mount Holyoke Coll, MA	B
Quinnipiac U, CT	B
Rhode Island Coll, RI	B
Sacred Heart U, CT	B
School of the Museum of Fine Arts, Boston, MA	B
Southern Methodist U, TX	B
U of Hartford, CT	B
U of Vermont, VT	B
Wellesley Coll, MA	B
Wesleyan U, CT	B
Yale U, CT	B

Film/Video and Photographic Arts Related

Fairfield U, CT	B
School of the Museum of Fine Arts, Boston, MA	B
Wellesley Coll, MA	B

Finance

Albertus Magnus Coll, CT	B
Babson Coll, MA	B
Barry U, FL	B
Bentley U, MA	B
Boston Coll, MA	B
Bridgewater State Coll, MA	B
Bryant U, RI	B
Castleton State Coll, VT	B
Central Connecticut State U, CT	B
Clarkson U, NY	B
Fairfield U, CT	B
Fitchburg State Coll, MA	B
Franklin Pierce U, NH	B
Grove City Coll, PA	B
Hofstra U, NY	B
Husson U, ME	B
Lasell Coll, MA	B
Merrimack Coll, MA	B
New England Coll, NH	B
Nichols Coll, MA	B
Northeastern U, MA	B
Providence Coll, RI	B
Quinnipiac U, CT	B
Rhode Island Coll, RI	B
Roger Williams U, RI	B
Salem State Coll, MA	B
Salve Regina U, RI	B
Simmons Coll, MA	B
Southern Connecticut State U, CT	B
Southern Methodist U, TX	B
Stonehill Coll, MA	B
Suffolk U, MA	B
U of Bridgeport, CT	B
U of Charleston, WV	B
U of Connecticut, CT	B
U of Hartford, CT	B
U of Maine, ME	B
U of Massachusetts Amherst, MA	B
U of Massachusetts Dartmouth, MA	B
U of New Haven, CT	B
U of Rhode Island, RI	B
U of San Francisco, CA	B

Western Connecticut State U,
CT — B
Western New England Coll,
MA — B

Finance and Financial Management Services Related
Babson Coll, MA — B
Bryant U, RI — B
Hofstra U, NY — B
Southern Methodist U, TX — B

Financial Planning and Services
Southern Methodist U, TX — B
The U of Maine at Augusta,
ME — A,B

Fine Arts Related
Burlington Coll, VT — B
School of the Museum of Fine
Arts, Boston, MA — B
U of Hartford, CT — B
U of Massachusetts Dartmouth,
MA — B

Fine/Studio Arts
Albertus Magnus Coll, CT — B
Amherst Coll, MA — B
The Art Inst of Boston at
Lesley U, MA — B
Bard Coll at Simon's Rock, MA — B
Bennington Coll, VT — B
Boston Coll, MA — B
Bowdoin Coll, ME — B
Brandeis U, MA — B
Bridgewater State Coll, MA — B
Brown U, RI — B
Clark U, MA — B
Colby Coll, ME — B
Coll of the Holy Cross, MA — B
Dartmouth Coll, NH — B
Emmanuel Coll, MA — B
Endicott Coll, MA — B
Fairfield U, CT — B
Franklin Pierce U, NH — B
Green Mountain Coll, VT — B
Hampshire Coll, MA — B
Hofstra U, NY — B
Johnson State Coll, VT — B
Keene State Coll, NH — B
Marlboro Coll, VT — B
Massachusetts Coll of Art and
Design, MA — B
Merrimack Coll, MA — B
Messiah Coll, PA — B
Middlebury Coll, VT — B
Mount Holyoke Coll, MA — B
New England Coll, NH — B
New Hampshire Inst of Art,
NH — B
Ohio Wesleyan U, OH — B
Plymouth State U, NH — B
Providence Coll, RI — B
Rhode Island Coll, RI — B
Rivier Coll, NH — B
Salve Regina U, RI — B
School of the Museum of Fine
Arts, Boston, MA — B
Smith Coll, MA — B
Southern Connecticut State U,
CT — B
Southern Methodist U, TX — B
Stonehill Coll, MA — B
Trinity Coll, CT — B
U of Connecticut, CT — B
U of Maine, ME — B

The U of Maine at Augusta,
ME — A,B
U of Maine at Presque Isle,
ME — B
U of Massachusetts Amherst,
MA — B
U of Massachusetts Lowell, MA — B
U of New Hampshire, NH — B
U of New Hampshire at
Manchester, NH — A
U of New Haven, CT — B
U of San Francisco, CA — B
U of Vermont, VT — B
Wellesley Coll, MA — B
Wesleyan U, CT — B
Wheaton Coll, MA — B
Williams Coll, MA — B

Fire Protection and Safety Technology
U of New Haven, CT — A,B

Fire Protection Related
U of New Haven, CT — B

Fire Science
Anna Maria Coll, MA — B
Providence Coll, RI — A,B
Vermont Tech Coll, VT — A

Fishing and Fisheries Sciences and Management
Sterling Coll, VT — A,B
U of Rhode Island, RI — B

Fluid/Thermal Sciences
Worcester Polytechnic Inst,
MA — B

Folklore
Marlboro Coll, VT — B

Food Science
Framingham State Coll, MA — B
U of Maine, ME — B
U of Massachusetts Amherst,
MA — B

Food Service Systems Administration
U of New Hampshire, NH — A
U of New Haven, CT — A

Foods, Nutrition, and Wellness
Hampshire Coll, MA — B
Simmons Coll, MA — B
U of Maine, ME — B
U of Maine at Presque Isle,
ME — A
U of Rhode Island, RI — B

Foreign Languages and Literatures
Assumption Coll, MA — B
Bard Coll at Simon's Rock, MA — B
Bennington Coll, VT — B
Eugene Lang Coll The New
School for Liberal Arts, NY — B
Framingham State Coll, MA — B
Gordon Coll, MA — B
Massachusetts Inst of
Technology, MA — B
Rhode Island Coll, RI — B
Roger Williams U, RI — B
Stonehill Coll, MA — B
U of Hartford, CT — B
U of Maine, ME — B
U of Massachusetts Lowell, MA — B
Utica Coll, NY — B

Foreign Languages Related
Yale U, CT — B

Foreign Language Teacher Education
Hofstra U, NY — B
Ohio Wesleyan U, OH — B
Rhode Island Coll, RI — B
Rivier Coll, NH — B
U of Maine, ME — B
U of Vermont, VT — B

Forensic Psychology
Bay Path Coll, MA — B

Forensic Science and Technology
Becker Coll, MA — B
Champlain Coll, VT — B
Hofstra U, NY — B
Mount Ida Coll, MA — B
U of New Haven, CT — B

Forest Engineering
U of Maine, ME — B

Forest/Forest Resources Management
Sterling Coll, VT — A,B

Forest Resources Production and Management
Sterling Coll, VT — A,B

Forestry
Sterling Coll, VT — A,B
U of Maine, ME — B
U of Maine at Fort Kent, ME — A
U of Massachusetts Amherst,
MA — B
U of New Hampshire, NH — B
U of Vermont, VT — B

Forestry Related
Sterling Coll, VT — A,B

Forestry Technology
U of Maine at Fort Kent, ME — A
U of New Hampshire, NH — A

Forest Sciences and Biology
Sterling Coll, VT — A,B

French
Albertus Magnus Coll, CT — B
Amherst Coll, MA — B
Assumption Coll, MA — B
Bard Coll at Simon's Rock, MA — B
Barry U, FL — B
Bates Coll, ME — B
Bennington Coll, VT — B
Boston Coll, MA — B
Bowdoin Coll, ME — B
Brandeis U, MA — B
Brown U, RI — B
Central Connecticut State U,
CT — B
Clark U, MA — B
Colby Coll, ME — B
Coll of the Holy Cross, MA — B
Connecticut Coll, CT — B
Dartmouth Coll, NH — B
Fairfield U, CT — B
Gordon Coll, MA — B
Grove City Coll, PA — B
Hofstra U, NY — B
Keene State Coll, NH — B
Marlboro Coll, VT — B
Merrimack Coll, MA — B
Messiah Coll, PA — B

Middlebury Coll, VT — B
Mount Holyoke Coll, MA — B
Northeastern U, MA — B
Ohio Wesleyan U, OH — B
Plymouth State U, NH — B
Providence Coll, RI — B
Rhode Island Coll, RI — B
Rivier Coll, NH — B
Saint Michael's Coll, VT — B
Salve Regina U, RI — B
Simmons Coll, MA — B
Smith Coll, MA — B
Southern Connecticut State U,
CT — B
Southern Methodist U, TX — B
Suffolk U, MA — B
Trinity Coll, CT — B
Tufts U, MA — B
U of Connecticut, CT — B
U of Maine, ME — B
U of Maine at Fort Kent, ME — B
U of Massachusetts Amherst,
MA — B
U of Massachusetts Boston,
MA — B
U of Massachusetts Dartmouth,
MA — B
U of New Hampshire, NH — B
U of Rhode Island, RI — B
U of San Francisco, CA — B
U of Southern Maine, ME — B
U of Vermont, VT — B
Wellesley Coll, MA — B
Wesleyan U, CT — B
Williams Coll, MA — B
Yale U, CT — B

French Language Teacher Education
Assumption Coll, MA — B
Hofstra U, NY — B
Keene State Coll, NH — B
Messiah Coll, PA — B
Ohio Wesleyan U, OH — B
Rhode Island Coll, RI — B
Salve Regina U, RI — B
U of Maine, ME — B
U of Maine at Fort Kent, ME — B

French Studies
Bard Coll at Simon's Rock, MA — B
Brown U, RI — B
Smith Coll, MA — B
U of New Hampshire, NH — B
Wellesley Coll, MA — B
Wheaton Coll, MA — B

Funeral Service and Mortuary Science
Mount Ida Coll, MA — A,B

Gay/Lesbian Studies
Bennington Coll, VT — B
Hampshire Coll, MA — B
Trinity Coll, CT — B

General Studies
Albertus Magnus Coll, CT — B
Burlington Coll, VT — A
Castleton State Coll, VT — A
Daniel Webster Coll, NH — B
Eastern Connecticut State U,
CT — A,B
Fairfield U, CT — B
Fisher Coll, MA — A
Johnson State Coll, VT — A
Keene State Coll, NH — A

A—associate degree; B—bachelor's degree

Landmark Coll, VT	A
Ohio Wesleyan U, OH	B
Providence Coll, RI	B
Southern New Hampshire U, NH	B
U of Bridgeport, CT	A
U of Charleston, WV	B
U of Connecticut, CT	B
U of Hartford, CT	A
The U of Maine at Augusta, ME	B
U of Maine at Farmington, ME	B
U of Maine at Fort Kent, ME	A
U of Maine at Machias, ME	B
U of Massachusetts Amherst, MA	B
U of New Hampshire, NH	B
U of New Haven, CT	A

Genetics
Ohio Wesleyan U, OH	B

Geochemistry
Bowdoin Coll, ME	B
Bridgewater State Coll, MA	B
Brown U, RI	B
U of Maine at Farmington, ME	B

Geography
Bard Coll at Simon's Rock, MA	B
Bridgewater State Coll, MA	B
Central Connecticut State U, CT	B
Clark U, MA	B
Dartmouth Coll, NH	B
Fitchburg State Coll, MA	B
Framingham State Coll, MA	B
Hofstra U, NY	B
Keene State Coll, NH	B
Middlebury Coll, VT	B
Mount Holyoke Coll, MA	B
Ohio Wesleyan U, OH	B
Plymouth State U, NH	B
Rhode Island Coll, RI	B
Salem State Coll, MA	B
Southern Connecticut State U, CT	B
U of Connecticut, CT	B
U of Maine at Farmington, ME	B
U of Massachusetts Amherst, MA	B
U of New Hampshire, NH	B
U of Southern Maine, ME	B
U of Vermont, VT	B
Worcester State Coll, MA	B

Geography Related
Bridgewater State Coll, MA	B

Geography Teacher Education
Fitchburg State Coll, MA	B
Rhode Island Coll, RI	B

Geological and Earth Sciences/Geosciences Related
Bridgewater State Coll, MA	B
Utica Coll, NY	B
Yale U, CT	B

Geological/Geophysical Engineering
Tufts U, MA	B

Geology/Earth Science
Amherst Coll, MA	B
Bard Coll at Simon's Rock, MA	B
Bates Coll, ME	B
Boston Coll, MA	B
Bowdoin Coll, ME	B
Bridgewater State Coll, MA	B

Brown U, RI	B
Castleton State Coll, VT	B
Central Connecticut State U, CT	B
Clark U, MA	B
Colby Coll, ME	B
Dartmouth Coll, NH	B
Hampshire Coll, MA	B
Harvard U, MA	B
Hofstra U, NY	B
Keene State Coll, NH	B
Massachusetts Inst of Technology, MA	B
Middlebury Coll, VT	B
Mount Holyoke Coll, MA	B
Northeastern U, MA	B
Ohio Wesleyan U, OH	B
Salem State Coll, MA	B
Smith Coll, MA	B
Southern Connecticut State U, CT	B
Southern Methodist U, TX	B
Tufts U, MA	B
U of Connecticut, CT	B
U of Maine, ME	B
U of Maine at Farmington, ME	B
U of Maine at Presque Isle, ME	B
U of Massachusetts Amherst, MA	B
U of Massachusetts Boston, MA	B
U of New Hampshire, NH	B
U of Rhode Island, RI	B
U of Southern Maine, ME	B
U of Vermont, VT	B
Wellesley Coll, MA	B
Wesleyan U, CT	B
Western Connecticut State U, CT	B
Williams Coll, MA	B

Geophysics and Seismology
Boston Coll, MA	B
Bowdoin Coll, ME	B
Brown U, RI	B
Southern Methodist U, TX	B

German
Amherst Coll, MA	B
Bard Coll at Simon's Rock, MA	B
Bates Coll, ME	B
Boston Coll, MA	B
Bowdoin Coll, ME	B
Brandeis U, MA	B
Brown U, RI	B
Central Connecticut State U, CT	B
Colby Coll, ME	B
Coll of the Holy Cross, MA	B
Dartmouth Coll, NH	B
Fairfield U, CT	B
Gordon Coll, MA	B
Harvard U, MA	B
Hofstra U, NY	B
Marlboro Coll, VT	B
Messiah Coll, PA	B
Middlebury Coll, VT	B
Mount Holyoke Coll, MA	B
Northeastern U, MA	B
Ohio Wesleyan U, OH	B
Smith Coll, MA	B
Southern Connecticut State U, CT	B
Southern Methodist U, TX	B
Trinity Coll, CT	B
Tufts U, MA	B

U of Connecticut, CT	B
U of Maine, ME	B
U of Massachusetts Amherst, MA	B
U of Massachusetts Boston, MA	B
U of New Hampshire, NH	B
U of Rhode Island, RI	B
Wellesley Coll, MA	B
Wesleyan U, CT	B
Wheaton Coll, MA	B
Williams Coll, MA	B
Yale U, CT	B

Germanic Languages
Bennington Coll, VT	B
Hampshire Coll, MA	B

German Language Teacher Education
Hofstra U, NY	B
Messiah Coll, PA	B
Ohio Wesleyan U, OH	B

German Studies
Bard Coll at Simon's Rock, MA	B
Brown U, RI	B
Coll of the Holy Cross, MA	B
Connecticut Coll, CT	B
Mount Holyoke Coll, MA	B
Smith Coll, MA	B
Wellesley Coll, MA	B
Wheaton Coll, MA	B

Gerontology
Quinnipiac U, CT	B
U of Massachusetts Boston, MA	B

Graphic Communications
Roger Williams U, RI	B

Graphic Design
Albertus Magnus Coll, CT	B
Anna Maria Coll, MA	B
The Art Inst of Boston at Lesley U, MA	B
Becker Coll, MA	B
Bridgewater State Coll, MA	B
Champlain Coll, VT	A,B
Curry Coll, MA	B
Emmanuel Coll, MA	B
Fitchburg State Coll, MA	B
Hampshire Coll, MA	B
Lasell Coll, MA	B
Maine Coll of Art, ME	B
Mount Ida Coll, MA	B
The New England Inst of Art, MA	B
Regis Coll, MA	B
Salve Regina U, RI	B
School of the Museum of Fine Arts, Boston, MA	B
Southern New Hampshire U, NH	B
U of Bridgeport, CT	B
U of San Francisco, CA	B

Greenhouse Management
Sterling Coll, VT	A,B

Health and Physical Education
Castleton State Coll, VT	B
Johnson State Coll, VT	B
Keene State Coll, NH	B
Lyndon State Coll, VT	B
New England Coll, NH	B
Plymouth State U, NH	B
U of Massachusetts Boston, MA	B

U of San Francisco, CA	B
Wesleyan U, CT	B

Health and Physical Education Related
Bridgewater State Coll, MA	B
Regis Coll, MA	B
U of New England, ME	B

Health/Health-Care Administration
Albertus Magnus Coll, CT	B
Brandeis U, MA	B
Newbury Coll, MA	B
New England Coll, NH	B
Northeastern U, MA	B
Providence Coll, RI	B
Roger Williams U, RI	B
Stonehill Coll, MA	B
U of Connecticut, CT	B
U of New England, ME	B
U of New Hampshire, NH	B
U of Rhode Island, RI	B

Health Information/Medical Records Administration
Labouré Coll, MA	A

Health Information/Medical Records Technology
Fisher Coll, MA	A

Health/Medical Preparatory Programs Related
Utica Coll, NY	B

Health/Medical Psychology
Bridgewater State Coll, MA	B
Massachusetts Coll of Pharmacy and Health Sciences, MA	

Health Occupations Teacher Education
U of Maine at Farmington, ME	B

Health Professions Related
Massachusetts Coll of Pharmacy and Health Sciences, MA	B
U of Charleston, WV	A,B
U of New England, ME	B
Worcester State Coll, MA	B

Health Science
Castleton State Coll, VT	B
Fisher Coll, MA	A
Johnson State Coll, VT	B
Merrimack Coll, MA	B
Northeastern U, MA	B
U of Hartford, CT	A,B
U of New England, ME	B
U of Southern Maine, ME	B

Health Services/Allied Health/Health Sciences
Anna Maria Coll, MA	B
Fisher Coll, MA	A
Hofstra U, NY	B

Health Teacher Education
Bridgewater State Coll, MA	B
Curry Coll, MA	B
Hofstra U, NY	B
Ohio Wesleyan U, OH	B
Rhode Island Coll, RI	B
Salem State Coll, MA	B
U of Charleston, WV	B
U of Maine, ME	B
U of Maine at Farmington, ME	B

U of Maine at Presque Isle, ME   B
Western Connecticut State U, CT   B

Hebrew
Brandeis U, MA   B
Dartmouth Coll, NH   B
Hofstra U, NY   B

Hispanic American, Puerto Rican, and Mexican American/ Chicano Studies
Boston Coll, MA   B
Brown U, RI   B
Connecticut Coll, CT   B
Dartmouth Coll, NH   B
Hampshire Coll, MA   B
Hofstra U, NY   B
Southern Methodist U, TX   B
U of Southern Maine, ME   B
Wheaton Coll, MA   B.

Historic Preservation and Conservation
Roger Williams U, RI   B
Salve Regina U, RI   B

History
Albertus Magnus Coll, CT   B
Amherst Coll, MA   B
Anna Maria Coll, MA   B
Assumption Coll, MA   B
Barry U, FL   B
Bates Coll, ME   B
Bennington Coll, VT   B
Bentley U, MA   B
Boston Coll, MA   B
Bowdoin Coll, ME   B
Brandeis U, MA   B
Bridgewater State Coll, MA   B
Brown U, RI   B
Bryant U, RI   B
Castleton State Coll, VT   B
Central Connecticut State U, CT   B
Clarkson U, NY   B
Clark U, MA   B
Colby Coll, ME   B
Coll of St. Joseph, VT   B
Coll of the Holy Cross, MA   B
Connecticut Coll, CT   B
Curry Coll, MA   B
Dartmouth Coll, NH   B
Eastern Connecticut State U, CT   B
Emmanuel Coll, MA   B
Eugene Lang Coll The New School for Liberal Arts, NY   B
Fairfield U, CT   B
Fitchburg State Coll, MA   B
Framingham State Coll, MA   B
Franklin Pierce U, NH   B
Gordon Coll, MA   B
Green Mountain Coll, VT   B
Grove City Coll, PA   B
Hampshire Coll, MA   B
Harvard U, MA   B
Hofstra U, NY   B
Johnson State Coll, VT   B
Keene State Coll, NH   B
Lasell Coll, MA   B
Marlboro Coll, VT   B
Massachusetts Coll of Liberal Arts, MA   B

Massachusetts Inst of Technology, MA   B
Merrimack Coll, MA   B
Messiah Coll, PA   B
Middlebury Coll, VT   B
Mount Holyoke Coll, MA   B
New England Coll, NH   B
Nichols Coll, MA   B
Northeastern U, MA   B
Ohio Wesleyan U, OH   B
Plymouth State U, NH   B
Providence Coll, RI   B
Quinnipiac U, CT   B
Regis Coll, MA   B
Rhode Island Coll, RI   B
Rivier Coll, NH   B
Roger Williams U, RI   B
Saint Joseph Coll, CT   B
Saint Michael's Coll, VT   B
Salem State Coll, MA   B
Salve Regina U, RI   B
Simmons Coll, MA   B
Smith Coll, MA   B
Southern Connecticut State U, CT   B
Southern Methodist U, TX   B
Southern New Hampshire U, NH   B
Stonehill Coll, MA   B
Suffolk U, MA   B
Trinity Coll, CT   B
Tufts U, MA   B
U of Charleston, WV   B
U of Connecticut, CT   B
U of Hartford, CT   B
U of Maine, ME   B
U of Maine at Farmington, ME   B
U of Maine at Machias, ME   B
U of Massachusetts Amherst, MA   B
U of Massachusetts Boston, MA   B
U of Massachusetts Dartmouth, MA   B
U of Massachusetts Lowell, MA   B
U of New England, ME   B
U of New Hampshire, NH   B
U of New Hampshire at Manchester, NH   B
U of New Haven, CT   B
U of Rhode Island, RI   B
U of San Francisco, CA   B
U of Southern Maine, ME   B
U of Vermont, VT   B
Utica Coll, NY   B
Wellesley Coll, MA   B
Wesleyan U, CT   B
Western Connecticut State U, CT   B
Western New England Coll, MA   B
Westfield State Coll, MA   B
Wheaton Coll, MA   B
Williams Coll, MA   B
Worcester Polytechnic Inst, MA   B
Worcester State Coll, MA   B
Yale U, CT   B

History and Philosophy of Science and Technology
Hampshire Coll, MA   B
Harvard U, MA   B
Worcester Polytechnic Inst, MA   B

History of Philosophy
Marlboro Coll, VT   B

History Related
Bridgewater State Coll, MA   B
Harvard U, MA   B

History Teacher Education
Anna Maria Coll, MA   B
Assumption Coll, MA   B
Fitchburg State Coll, MA   B
Johnson State Coll, VT   B
Keene State Coll, NH   B
Ohio Wesleyan U, OH   B
Rhode Island Coll, RI   B
Sacred Heart U, CT   B
Salve Regina U, RI   B
U of Maine, ME   B
U of Maine at Machias, ME   B
Utica Coll, NY   B

Holocaust and Related Studies
Hampshire Coll, MA   B

Horse Husbandry/Equine Science and Management
Becker Coll, MA   B
Sterling Coll, VT   B
Vermont Tech Coll, VT   A,B

Horticultural Science
Sterling Coll, VT   B
U of Connecticut, CT   A,B
U of New Hampshire, NH   B
U of Vermont, VT   B

Hospitality Administration
Becker Coll, MA   B
Champlain Coll, VT   A,B
Endicott Coll, MA   B
Fisher Coll, MA   B
Husson U, ME   B
Johnson State Coll, VT   B
Southern New Hampshire U, NH   B
U of Massachusetts Amherst, MA   B
U of New Hampshire, NH   B
U of New Haven, CT   B

Hospitality Administration Related
Champlain Coll, VT   A,B
Mitchell Coll, CT   B

Hospitality and Recreation Marketing
Champlain Coll, VT   A,B

Hotel/Motel Administration
Becker Coll, MA   B
Champlain Coll, VT   A,B
Lasell Coll, MA   B
Mount Ida Coll, MA   B
U of Maine at Machias, ME   B
U of New Haven, CT   B
U of San Francisco, CA   B

Human Development and Family Studies
Boston Coll, MA   B
Connecticut Coll, CT   B
Hampshire Coll, MA   B
Lesley U, MA   B
Mitchell Coll, CT   B
U of Connecticut, CT   B
U of Maine, ME   B
U of New Hampshire, NH   B
U of Rhode Island, RI   B

U of Vermont, VT   B
Wheelock Coll, MA   B

Human Ecology
Coll of the Atlantic, ME   B
Connecticut Coll, CT   B
Sterling Coll, VT   A,B

Humanities
Albertus Magnus Coll, CT   B
Bennington Coll, VT   B
Clarkson U, NY   B
Eugene Lang Coll The New School for Liberal Arts, NY   B
Fisher Coll, MA   A
Hampshire Coll, MA   B
Hofstra U, NY   B
Holy Apostles Coll and Seminary, CT   A,B
Johnson State Coll, VT   B
Lesley U, MA   B
Marlboro Coll, VT   B
Messiah Coll, PA   B
Mitchell Coll, CT   B
Newbury Coll, MA   A
Ohio Wesleyan U, OH   B
Plymouth State U, NH   B
Providence Coll, RI   B
Southern Methodist U, TX   B
Suffolk U, MA   B
U of Bridgeport, CT   B
U of Massachusetts Amherst, MA   B
U of New Hampshire, NH   B
U of New Hampshire at Manchester, NH
Wesleyan U, CT   B
Worcester Polytechnic Inst, MA   B
Yale U, CT   B

Human Nutrition
U of Massachusetts Amherst, MA   B

Human Resources Management
Boston Coll, MA   B
Clarkson U, NY   B
Messiah Coll, PA   B
Newbury Coll, MA   B
Nichols Coll, MA   B
Northeastern U, MA   B
Quinnipiac U, CT   B
U of Massachusetts Dartmouth, MA   B

Human Resources Management and Services Related
Albertus Magnus Coll, CT   B
Becker Coll, MA   B

Human Services
Albertus Magnus Coll, CT   B
Anna Maria Coll, MA   B
Burlington Coll, VT   B
Cambridge Coll, MA   B
Champlain Coll, VT   A,B
Coll of St. Joseph, VT   A,B
Endicott Coll, MA   B
Fisher Coll, MA   B
Fitchburg State Coll, MA   B
Lasell Coll, MA   B
Lesley U, MA   B
Merrimack Coll, MA   B
Mount Ida Coll, MA   B

A—associate degree; B—bachelor's degree

Northeastern U, MA — B
Quinnipiac U, CT — B
Suffolk U, MA — B
U of Bridgeport, CT — B
U of Hartford, CT — B
The U of Maine at Augusta, ME — A
U of Maine at Fort Kent, ME — A
U of Maine at Machias, ME — B
U of Rhode Island, RI — B

Hydrology and Water Resources Science
U of New Hampshire, NH — B

Illustration
The Art Inst of Boston at Lesley U, MA — B
Hampshire Coll, MA — B
Lyme Academy Coll of Fine Arts, CT — B
School of the Museum of Fine Arts, Boston, MA — B
U of Bridgeport, CT — B
U of San Francisco, CA — B

Industrial and Organizational Psychology
Bridgewater State Coll, MA — B
Clarkson U, NY — B
Eastern Connecticut State U, CT — B
Fitchburg State Coll, MA — B

Industrial Arts
U of Southern Maine, ME — B

Industrial Design
Massachusetts Coll of Art and Design, MA — B
U of Bridgeport, CT — B
Wentworth Inst of Technology, MA — B

Industrial Engineering
Hofstra U, NY — B
Northeastern U, MA — B
Tufts U, MA — B
U of Connecticut, CT — B
U of Massachusetts Amherst, MA — B
U of Rhode Island, RI — B
U of Vermont, VT — B
Western New England Coll, MA — B
Worcester Polytechnic Inst, MA — B

Industrial Technology
Central Connecticut State U, CT — B
Fitchburg State Coll, MA — B
U of Massachusetts Lowell, MA — B

Information Resources Management
Clarkson U, NY — B

Information Science/Studies
Albertus Magnus Coll, CT — A,B
Barry U, FL — B
Champlain Coll, VT — A,B
Husson U, ME — A,B
Johnson State Coll, VT — A,B
Lasell Coll, MA — B
Messiah Coll, PA — B
Northeastern U, MA — B
Quinnipiac U, CT — B
Regis Coll, MA — B
Rivier Coll, NH — A,B

Saint Michael's Coll, VT — B
Salve Regina U, RI — B
Southern Methodist U, TX — B
Suffolk U, MA — B
U of Bridgeport, CT — B
U of Charleston, WV — B
U of New Haven, CT — B
U of San Francisco, CA — B
U of Vermont, VT — B
Westfield State Coll, MA — B
Worcester Polytechnic Inst, MA — B

Information Technology
Bryant U, RI — B
Curry Coll, MA — B
Plymouth State U, NH — B
Sacred Heart U, CT — B
Simmons Coll, MA — B
U of Massachusetts Boston, MA — B
U of Massachusetts Lowell, MA — A
U of New Hampshire, NH — B
U of Phoenix–Boston Campus, MA — B
U of Phoenix–Central Massachusetts Campus, MA — B
Vermont Tech Coll, VT — A,B

Inorganic Chemistry
Hampshire Coll, MA — B

Insurance
U of Connecticut, CT — B
U of Hartford, CT — B

Intercultural/Multicultural and Diversity Studies
Hampshire Coll, MA — B

Interdisciplinary Studies
Albertus Magnus Coll, CT — B
Amherst Coll, MA — B
Bard Coll at Simon's Rock, MA — B
Bentley U, MA — B
Boston Coll, MA — B
Bowdoin Coll, ME — B
Clarkson U, NY — B
Clark U, MA — B
Colby Coll, ME — B
Coll of the Atlantic, ME — B
Connecticut Coll, CT — B
Emerson Coll, MA — B
Emmanuel Coll, MA — B
Lasell Coll, MA — B
Lesley U, MA — A
Marlboro Coll, VT — B
Massachusetts Coll of Liberal Arts, MA — B
Merrimack Coll, MA — B
Smith Coll, MA — B
Suffolk U, MA — A,B
Trinity Coll, CT — B
U of Bridgeport, CT — B
U of Hartford, CT — B
U of Maine at Farmington, ME — B
U of Massachusetts Dartmouth, MA — B
U of Rhode Island, RI — B
U of San Francisco, CA — B
U of Vermont, VT — B
Wesleyan U, CT — B
Worcester Polytechnic Inst, MA — B

Interior Architecture
Boston Architectural Coll, MA — B
U of New Haven, CT — A,B

Interior Design
Becker Coll, MA — B
Endicott Coll, MA — B
Mount Ida Coll, MA — B
The New England Inst of Art, MA — B
Suffolk U, MA — B
U of Bridgeport, CT — B
U of Massachusetts Amherst, MA — B
Wentworth Inst of Technology, MA — B

Intermedia/Multimedia
Bennington Coll, VT — B
Champlain Coll, VT — A,B
Emerson Coll, MA — B
Hampshire Coll, MA — B
Maine Coll of Art, ME — B
Massachusetts Coll of Art and Design, MA — B
School of the Museum of Fine Arts, Boston, MA — B
U of Massachusetts Dartmouth, MA — B
Worcester Polytechnic Inst, MA — B

International Agriculture
Sterling Coll, VT — B

International Business/Trade/Commerce
Albertus Magnus Coll, CT — B
Assumption Coll, MA — B
Babson Coll, MA — B
Barry U, FL — B
Bridgewater State Coll, MA — B
Bryant U, RI — B
Central Connecticut State U, CT — B
Champlain Coll, VT — A,B
Clarkson U, NY — B
Fairfield U, CT — B
Fitchburg State Coll, MA — B
Grove City Coll, PA — B
Hampshire Coll, MA — B
Hofstra U, NY — B
Husson U, ME — B
Lasell Coll, MA — B
Maine Maritime Academy, ME — B
Massachusetts Maritime Academy, MA — B
Merrimack Coll, MA — B
Messiah Coll, PA — B
Newbury Coll, MA — B
Northeastern U, MA — B
Ohio Wesleyan U, OH — B
Quinnipiac U, CT — B
Roger Williams U, RI — B
Sacred Heart U, CT — B
Southern New Hampshire U, NH — B
Stonehill Coll, MA — B
U of Bridgeport, CT — B
U of New Haven, CT — B
U of Rhode Island, RI — B
U of San Francisco, CA — B
Utica Coll, NY — B

International Economics
Albertus Magnus Coll, CT — B
Hampshire Coll, MA — B
Marlboro Coll, VT — B
Suffolk U, MA — B

International Finance
Babson Coll, MA — B

International/Global Studies
Assumption Coll, MA — B
Bennington Coll, VT — B
Brandeis U, MA — B
Central Connecticut State U, CT — B
Colby Coll, ME — B
Emmanuel Coll, MA — B
Endicott Coll, MA — B
Hampshire Coll, MA — B
Providence Coll, RI — B
Roger Williams U, RI — B
Saint Joseph Coll, CT — B
Sterling Coll, VT — B
U of Hartford, CT — B
U of Maine at Farmington, ME — B
Western New England Coll, MA — B

International Public Health
Hampshire Coll, MA — B

International Relations and Affairs
Barry U, FL — B
Bennington Coll, VT — B
Bridgewater State Coll, MA — B
Brown U, RI — B
Bryant U, RI — B
Clark U, MA — B
Colby Coll, ME — B
Connecticut Coll, CT — B
Fairfield U, CT — B
Gordon Coll, MA — B
Hampshire Coll, MA — B
Marlboro Coll, VT — B
Middlebury Coll, VT — B
Mount Holyoke Coll, MA — B
Northeastern U, MA — B
Ohio Wesleyan U, OH — B
Quinnipiac U, CT — B
Regis Coll, MA — B
Sacred Heart U, CT — B
Simmons Coll, MA — B
Southern Methodist U, TX — B
Stonehill Coll, MA — B
Trinity Coll, CT — B
Tufts U, MA — B
U of Bridgeport, CT — B
U of Maine, ME — B
U of Maine at Presque Isle, ME — B
U of Southern Maine, ME — B
Utica Coll, NY — B
Wellesley Coll, MA — B
Wheaton Coll, MA — B

Investments and Securities
Babson Coll, MA — B

Islamic Studies
Wellesley Coll, MA — B

Italian
Albertus Magnus Coll, CT — B
Assumption Coll, MA — B
Bennington Coll, VT — B
Boston Coll, MA — B
Brown U, RI — B
Central Connecticut State U, CT — B
Coll of the Holy Cross, MA — B
Connecticut Coll, CT — B
Dartmouth Coll, NH — B
Fairfield U, CT — B
Hofstra U, NY — B
Marlboro Coll, VT — B
Middlebury Coll, VT — B

Mount Holyoke Coll, MA	B
Northeastern U, MA	B
Providence Coll, RI	B
Smith Coll, MA	B
Southern Connecticut State U, CT	B
Southern Methodist U, TX	B
Trinity Coll, CT	B
U of Connecticut, CT	B
U of Massachusetts Amherst, MA	
U of Massachusetts Boston, MA	B
U of Rhode Island, RI	B
Wellesley Coll, MA	B
Wesleyan U, CT	B
Yale U, CT	B

Italian Studies

Brown U, RI	B
Connecticut Coll, CT	B
U of Vermont, VT	B
Wellesley Coll, MA	B
Wheaton Coll, MA	B

Japanese

Bates Coll, ME	B
Bennington Coll, VT	B
Connecticut Coll, CT	B
Dartmouth Coll, NH	B
Middlebury Coll, VT	B
Trinity Coll, CT	B
U of Massachusetts Amherst, MA	B
U of Vermont, VT	B
Wellesley Coll, MA	B
Williams Coll, MA	B
Yale U, CT	B

Japanese Studies

U of San Francisco, CA	B

Jazz/Jazz Studies

Bard Coll at Simon's Rock, MA	B
Bennington Coll, VT	B
Berklee Coll of Music, MA	B
Hofstra U, NY	B
Johnson State Coll, VT	B
New England Conservatory of Music, MA	B
U of Hartford, CT	B

Jewish/Judaic Studies

Bennington Coll, VT	B
Brown U, RI	B
Clark U, MA	B
Hampshire Coll, MA	B
Hebrew Coll, MA	B
Hofstra U, NY	B
Mount Holyoke Coll, MA	B
Trinity Coll, CT	B
Tufts U, MA	B
U of Hartford, CT	B
U of Massachusetts Amherst, MA	B
Wellesley Coll, MA	B
Yale U, CT	B

Journalism

Barry U, FL	B
Bennington Coll, VT	B
Castleton State Coll, VT	B
Curry Coll, MA	B
Emerson Coll, MA	B
Eugene Lang Coll The New School for Liberal Arts, NY	B
Franklin Pierce U, NH	B
Hofstra U, NY	B

Johnson State Coll, VT	B
Keene State Coll, NH	B
Lyndon State Coll, VT	B
Messiah Coll, PA	B
New England Coll, NH	B
Northeastern U, MA	B
Ohio Wesleyan U, OH	B
Quinnipiac U, CT	B
Sacred Heart U, CT	B
Saint Michael's Coll, VT	B
Salem State Coll, MA	B
Southern Connecticut State U, CT	B
Southern Methodist U, TX	B
Suffolk U, MA	B
U of Bridgeport, CT	B
U of Connecticut, CT	B
U of Maine, ME	B
U of Massachusetts Amherst, MA	B
U of Rhode Island, RI	B
Utica Coll, NY	B
Western New England Coll, MA	B

Journalism Related

Champlain Coll, VT	B

Kindergarten/Preschool Education

Anna Maria Coll, MA	B
Atlantic Union Coll, MA	A,B
Barry U, FL	B
Bay Path Coll, MA	B
Boston Coll, MA	B
Champlain Coll, VT	A,B
Curry Coll, MA	B
Eastern Connecticut State U, CT	B
Fisher Coll, MA	A
Franklin Pierce U, NH	B
Grove City Coll, PA	B
Lasell Coll, MA	B
Lesley U, MA	B
Northeastern U, MA	B
Ohio Wesleyan U, OH	B
Rivier Coll, NH	A,B
Sacred Heart U, CT	B
Saint Joseph Coll, CT	B
Salem State Coll, MA	B
Simmons Coll, MA	B
Tufts U, MA	B
U of Vermont, VT	B
Westfield State Coll, MA	B
Wheelock Coll, MA	B

Kinesiology and Exercise Science

Barry U, FL	B
Becker Coll, MA	B
Bridgewater State Coll, MA	B
Castleton State Coll, VT	B
Fitchburg State Coll, MA	B
Gordon Coll, MA	B
Johnson State Coll, VT	B
Lasell Coll, MA	B
Messiah Coll, PA	B
Sacred Heart U, CT	B
Salem State Coll, MA	B
U of Massachusetts Lowell, MA	B
U of New England, ME	B
U of New Hampshire, NH	B
U of Vermont, VT	B

Kinesiotherapy

Bridgewater State Coll, MA	B

Knowledge Management

Framingham State Coll, MA	B

Labor and Industrial Relations

U of Maine, ME	B
U of Massachusetts Boston, MA	B

Labor Studies

Hampshire Coll, MA	B
Hofstra U, NY	B
Rhode Island Coll, RI	B

Landscape Architecture

Boston Architectural Coll, MA	B
Coll of the Atlantic, ME	B
U of Connecticut, CT	B
U of Massachusetts Amherst, MA	B
U of Rhode Island, RI	B

Landscaping and Groundskeeping

U of Maine, ME	B
U of Massachusetts Amherst, MA	A
Vermont Tech Coll, VT	A

Land-Use Planning and Management

Sterling Coll, VT	B

Latin

Amherst Coll, MA	B
Bard Coll at Simon's Rock, MA	B
Boston Coll, MA	B
Dartmouth Coll, NH	B
Hofstra U, NY	B
Marlboro Coll, VT	B
Mount Holyoke Coll, MA	B
Smith Coll, MA	B
Tufts U, MA	B
U of Maine, ME	B
U of New Hampshire, NH	B
U of Vermont, VT	B
Wellesley Coll, MA	B
Wheaton Coll, MA	B
Yale U, CT	B

Latin American Studies

Assumption Coll, MA	B
Bard Coll at Simon's Rock, MA	B
Bennington Coll, VT	B
Bowdoin Coll, ME	B
Brandeis U, MA	B
Brown U, RI	B
Burlington Coll, VT	B
Colby Coll, ME	B
Connecticut Coll, CT	B
Dartmouth Coll, NH	B
Hampshire Coll, MA	B
Marlboro Coll, VT	B
Middlebury Coll, VT	B
Mount Holyoke Coll, MA	B
Ohio Wesleyan U, OH	B
Rhode Island Coll, RI	B
Smith Coll, MA	B
Southern Methodist U, TX	B
U of Connecticut, CT	B
U of Rhode Island, RI	B
U of San Francisco, CA	B
U of Vermont, VT	B
Wellesley Coll, MA	B
Wesleyan U, CT	B
Yale U, CT	B

Latin Teacher Education

Assumption Coll, MA	B
Ohio Wesleyan U, OH	B

Legal Assistant/Paralegal

Anna Maria Coll, MA	A,B
Champlain Coll, VT	A,B
Fisher Coll, MA	A
Husson U, ME	A,B
Newbury Coll, MA	A
Quinnipiac U, CT	B
Roger Williams U, RI	B
Suffolk U, MA	A,B

Legal Professions and Studies Related

Roger Williams U, RI	B
U of Massachusetts Boston, MA	B

Legal Studies

Amherst Coll, MA	B
Bay Path Coll, MA	B
Becker Coll, MA	B
Bridgewater State Coll, MA	B
Burlington Coll, VT	B
Coll of the Atlantic, ME	B
Hampshire Coll, MA	B
Lasell Coll, MA	B
Newbury Coll, MA	B
Quinnipiac U, CT	B
Rivier Coll, NH	B
Suffolk U, MA	B
U of Hartford, CT	A,B
U of Massachusetts Amherst, MA	B
U of New Haven, CT	A,B
Western New England Coll, MA	B

Liberal Arts and Sciences and Humanities Related

Bennington Coll, VT	B
Hofstra U, NY	B
Mitchell Coll, CT	B
Southern Methodist U, TX	B
Southern New Hampshire U, NH	A
U of Massachusetts Amherst, MA	B

Liberal Arts and Sciences/ Liberal Studies

Albertus Magnus Coll, CT	A,B
Anna Maria Coll, MA	B
Bard Coll at Simon's Rock, MA	A
Barry U, FL	B
Bay Path Coll, MA	B
Becker Coll, MA	B
Bennington Coll, VT	B
Bentley U, MA	B
Champlain Coll, VT	B
Clarkson U, NY	B
Coll of St. Joseph, VT	A,B
Coll of the Atlantic, ME	B
Daniel Webster Coll, NH	A
Emmanuel Coll, MA	B
Endicott Coll, MA	A
Eugene Lang Coll The New School for Liberal Arts, NY	B
Fairfield U, CT	A
Fisher Coll, MA	A
Fitchburg State Coll, MA	B
Framingham State Coll, MA	B
Franklin Pierce U, NH	B
Granite State Coll, NH	A,B
Green Mountain Coll, VT	B

A—associate degree; B—bachelor's degree

Hampshire Coll, MA	B	U of New Hampshire, NH	B	Southern Methodist U, TX	B	Mitchell Coll, CT	B

Hampshire Coll, MA — B
Harvard U, MA — B
Hofstra U, NY — B
Husson U, ME — B
Johnson State Coll, VT — A,B
Landmark Coll, VT — A
Lasell Coll, MA — B
Lesley U, MA — B
Massachusetts Inst of
  Technology, MA — B
Merrimack Coll, MA — A
Middlebury Coll, VT — B
Mitchell Coll, CT — A,B
Mount Ida Coll, MA — B
New England Coll, NH — A
Northeastern U, MA — B
Providence Coll, RI — A,B
Quinnipiac U, CT — B
Regis Coll, MA — B
Rhode Island Coll, RI — B
Rivier Coll, NH — A,B
Roger Williams U, RI — A,B
Saint Joseph Coll, CT — B
Salem State Coll, MA — B
Salve Regina U, RI — A,B
Southern Connecticut State U,
  CT — A,B
Sterling Coll, VT — A,B
Suffolk U, MA — B
U of Hartford, CT — A
U of Maine, ME — B
The U of Maine at Augusta,
  ME — A
U of Maine at Farmington, ME — B
U of Maine at Fort Kent, ME — A,B
U of Maine at Presque Isle,
  ME — A,B
U of Massachusetts Dartmouth,
  MA — B
U of Massachusetts Lowell, MA — B
U of New England, ME — B
U of New Hampshire at
  Manchester, NH — A
U of New Haven, CT — B
U of Rhode Island, RI — B
U of San Francisco, CA — B
U of Vermont, VT — B
Utica Coll, NY — B
Western Connecticut State U,
  CT — A,B
Western New England Coll,
  MA — A,B
Westfield State Coll, MA — B

Library Assistant
The U of Maine at Augusta,
  ME — A

Library Science
Southern Connecticut State U,
  CT — B
The U of Maine at Augusta,
  ME — B

Linguistics
Brandeis U, MA — B
Brown U, RI — B
Dartmouth Coll, NH — B
Hampshire Coll, MA — B
Harvard U, MA — B
Hofstra U, NY — B
Marlboro Coll, VT — B
Massachusetts Inst of
  Technology, MA — B
Northeastern U, MA — B
U of Connecticut, CT — B
U of Massachusetts Amherst,
  MA — B

U of New Hampshire, NH — B
U of Southern Maine, ME — B
Wellesley Coll, MA — B
Yale U, CT — B

Linguistics of ASL and Other Sign Languages
Hampshire Coll, MA — B

Literature
Bard Coll at Simon's Rock, MA — B
Barry U, FL — B
Castleton State Coll, VT — B
Coll of the Atlantic, ME — B
Coll of the Holy Cross, MA — B
Eugene Lang Coll The New
  School for Liberal Arts, NY — B
Franklin Pierce U, NH — B
Grove City Coll, PA — B
Johnson State Coll, VT — B
Marlboro Coll, VT — B
Ohio Wesleyan U, OH — B
Quinnipiac U, CT — B
Salem State Coll, MA — B
Williams Coll, MA — B
Yale U, CT — B

Livestock Management
Sterling Coll, VT — A,B

Logistics and Materials Management
Clarkson U, NY — B
Maine Maritime Academy, ME — B
Northeastern U, MA — B

Management Information Systems
Albertus Magnus Coll, CT — B
Anna Maria Coll, MA — B
Babson Coll, MA — B
Barry U, FL — B
Boston Coll, MA — B
Bridgewater State Coll, MA — B
Central Connecticut State U,
  CT — B
Clarkson U, NY — B
Eastern Connecticut State U,
  CT — B
Fairfield U, CT — B
Hofstra U, NY — B
Husson U, ME — A,B
Johnson State Coll, VT — A,B
Nichols Coll, MA — B
Northeastern U, MA — B
Rhode Island Coll, RI — B
Roger Williams U, RI — B
Salem State Coll, MA — B
Simmons Coll, MA — B
Suffolk U, MA — B
U of Connecticut, CT — B
U of Hartford, CT — B
U of Maine, ME — B
U of Massachusetts Dartmouth,
  MA — B
U of Rhode Island, RI — B
U of San Francisco, CA — B
Western Connecticut State U,
  CT — B
Western New England Coll,
  MA — B
Worcester Polytechnic Inst,
  MA — B

Management Science
Cambridge Coll, MA — B
Fitchburg State Coll, MA — B
Granite State Coll, NH — B
Northeastern U, MA — B

Southern Methodist U, TX — B
United States Coast Guard
  Academy, CT — B
U of Connecticut, CT — B
U of Massachusetts Lowell, MA — A
U of Phoenix–Boston Campus,
  MA — B
U of Phoenix–Central
  Massachusetts Campus, MA — B

Manufacturing Engineering
Clarkson U, NY — B
Hofstra U, NY — B
U of Connecticut, CT — B

Manufacturing Technology
Central Connecticut State U,
  CT — B
Fitchburg State Coll, MA — B

Marine Biology and Biological Oceanography
Barry U, FL — B
Brown U, RI — B
Coll of the Atlantic, ME — B
Maine Maritime Academy, ME — B
Northeastern U, MA — B
Roger Williams U, RI — B
Salem State Coll, MA — B
Suffolk U, MA — B
U of Connecticut, CT — B
U of Maine, ME — B
U of Maine at Machias, ME — B
U of New England, ME — B
U of New Haven, CT — B
U of Rhode Island, RI — B

Marine Science/Merchant Marine Officer
Maine Maritime Academy, ME — B
Massachusetts Maritime
  Academy, MA — B
Salem State Coll, MA — B

Maritime Science
Coll of the Atlantic, ME — B
Massachusetts Maritime
  Academy, MA — B

Marketing/Marketing Management
Albertus Magnus Coll, CT — B
Assumption Coll, MA — B
Babson Coll, MA — B
Barry U, FL — B
Bay Path Coll, MA — B
Becker Coll, MA — B
Bentley U, MA — B
Boston Coll, MA — B
Bridgewater State Coll, MA — B
Bryant U, RI — B
Castleton State Coll, VT — B
Central Connecticut State U,
  CT — B
Champlain Coll, VT — A,B
Clarkson U, NY — B
Daniel Webster Coll, NH — A
Emerson Coll, MA — B
Fairfield U, CT — B
Fisher Coll, MA — B
Fitchburg State Coll, MA — B
Franklin Pierce U, NH — B
Grove City Coll, PA — B
Hofstra U, NY — B
Husson U, ME — B
Johnson State Coll, VT — B
Lasell Coll, MA — B
Merrimack Coll, MA — B
Messiah Coll, PA — B

Mitchell Coll, CT — B
Mount Ida Coll, MA — B
New England Coll, NH — B
Nichols Coll, MA — B
Northeastern U, MA — B
Plymouth State U, NH — B
Providence Coll, RI — B
Quinnipiac U, CT — B
Rhode Island Coll, RI — B
Roger Williams U, RI — B
Sacred Heart U, CT — B
Salem State Coll, MA — B
Simmons Coll, MA — B
Southern Connecticut State U,
  CT — B
Southern Methodist U, TX — B
Southern New Hampshire U,
  NH — A,B
Stonehill Coll, MA — B
Suffolk U, MA — B
U of Charleston, WV — B
U of Connecticut, CT — B
U of Hartford, CT — B
U of Maine at Machias, ME — B
U of Massachusetts Amherst,
  MA — B
U of Massachusetts Dartmouth,
  MA — B
U of New Haven, CT — B
U of Rhode Island, RI — B
U of San Francisco, CA — B
Western Connecticut State U,
  CT — B
Western New England Coll,
  MA — B

Marketing Related
Babson Coll, MA — B
Western New England Coll,
  MA — B

Marketing Research
Newbury Coll, MA — B
Salve Regina U, RI — B

Mass Communication/Media
Albertus Magnus Coll, CT — B
Anna Maria Coll, MA — B
Barry U, FL — B
Bentley U, MA — B
Champlain Coll, VT — A,B
Clark U, MA — B
Curry Coll, MA — B
Emerson Coll, MA — B
Emmanuel Coll, MA — B
Endicott Coll, MA — B
Fisher Coll, MA — B
Franklin Pierce U, NH — B
Grove City Coll, PA — B
Hampshire Coll, MA — B
Hofstra U, NY — B
Massachusetts Inst of
  Technology, MA — B
New England Coll, NH — B
Northeastern U, MA — B
Quinnipiac U, CT — B
Salem State Coll, MA — B
Simmons Coll, MA — B
Suffolk U, MA — B
U of Bridgeport, CT — B
U of Maine, ME — B
U of New Hampshire at
  Manchester, NH — B
U of San Francisco, CA — B
U of Southern Maine, ME — B
Western New England Coll,
  MA — B
Worcester State Coll, MA — B

Mass Communications
Mitchell Coll, CT — B

Materials Engineering
Brown U, RI — B
Clarkson U, NY — B
Massachusetts Inst of Technology, MA — B
U of Connecticut, CT — B
Worcester Polytechnic Inst, MA — B

Materials Science
Clarkson U, NY — B
Worcester Polytechnic Inst, MA — B

Mathematics
Albertus Magnus Coll, CT — B
Amherst Coll, MA — B
Assumption Coll, MA — B
Bard Coll at Simon's Rock, MA — B
Barry U, FL — B
Bates Coll, ME — B
Bennington Coll, VT — B
Bentley U, MA — B
Boston Coll, MA — B
Bowdoin Coll, ME — B
Brandeis U, MA — B
Bridgewater State Coll, MA — B
Brown U, RI — B
Castleton State Coll, VT — B
Central Connecticut State U, CT — B
Clarkson U, NY — B
Clark U, MA — B
Colby Coll, ME — B
Coll of the Holy Cross, MA — B
Connecticut Coll, CT — B
Dartmouth Coll, NH — B
Eastern Connecticut State U, CT — B
Emmanuel Coll, MA — B
Fairfield U, CT — B
Fitchburg State Coll, MA — B
Framingham State Coll, MA — B
Franklin Pierce U, NH — B
Gordon Coll, MA — B
Grove City Coll, PA — B
Hampshire Coll, MA — B
Harvard U, MA — B
Hofstra U, NY — B
Johnson State Coll, VT — B
Keene State Coll, NH — B
Lyndon State Coll, VT — B
Marlboro Coll, VT — B
Massachusetts Coll of Liberal Arts, MA — B
Massachusetts Inst of Technology, MA — B
Merrimack Coll, MA — B
Messiah Coll, PA — B
Middlebury Coll, VT — B
Mount Holyoke Coll, MA — B
Nichols Coll, MA — B
Northeastern U, MA — B
Ohio Wesleyan U, OH — B
Plymouth State U, NH — B
Providence Coll, RI — B
Quinnipiac U, CT — B
Rhode Island Coll, RI — B
Rivier Coll, NH — B
Roger Williams U, RI — B
Saint Joseph Coll, CT — B
Saint Michael's Coll, VT — B
Salem State Coll, MA — B

Salve Regina U, RI — B
Simmons Coll, MA — B
Smith Coll, MA — B
Southern Connecticut State U, CT — B
Southern Methodist U, TX — B
Stonehill Coll, MA — B
Suffolk U, MA — B
Trinity Coll, CT — B
Tufts U, MA — B
U of Bridgeport, CT — B
U of Connecticut, CT — B
U of Hartford, CT — B
U of Maine, ME — B
U of Maine at Farmington, ME — B
U of Massachusetts Amherst, MA — B
U of Massachusetts Boston, MA — B
U of Massachusetts Dartmouth, MA — B
U of Massachusetts Lowell, MA — B
U of New England, ME — B
U of New Hampshire, NH — B
U of New Haven, CT — B
U of Rhode Island, RI — B
U of San Francisco, CA — B
U of Southern Maine, ME — B
U of Vermont, VT — B
Utica Coll, NY — B
Wellesley Coll, MA — B
Wesleyan U, CT — B
Western Connecticut State U, CT — B
Western New England Coll, MA — B
Westfield State Coll, MA — B
Wheaton Coll, MA — B
Williams Coll, MA — B
Worcester Polytechnic Inst, MA — B
Worcester State Coll, MA — B
Yale U, CT — B

Mathematics and Computer Science
Bennington Coll, VT — B
Bowdoin Coll, ME — B
Brown U, RI — B
Hampshire Coll, MA — B
Hofstra U, NY — B
Massachusetts Inst of Technology, MA — B
Sacred Heart U, CT — B
Yale U, CT — B

Mathematics and Statistics Related
Hofstra U, NY — B
U of Hartford, CT — B
U of New Hampshire, NH — B

Mathematics Teacher Education
Albertus Magnus Coll, CT — B
Assumption Coll, MA — B
Castleton State Coll, VT — B
Fitchburg State Coll, MA — B
Hofstra U, NY — B
Johnson State Coll, VT — B
Keene State Coll, NH — B
Lyndon State Coll, VT — B
Messiah Coll, PA — B
Ohio Wesleyan U, OH — B
Regis Coll, MA — B
Rhode Island Coll, RI — B

Rivier Coll, NH — B
Sacred Heart U, CT — B
Salve Regina U, RI — B
U of Maine, ME — B
U of Maine at Farmington, ME — B
U of Maine at Fort Kent, ME — B
U of Maine at Machias, ME — B
U of New Hampshire, NH — B
U of Vermont, VT — B
Utica Coll, NY — B

Mechanical Engineering
Brown U, RI — B
Clarkson U, NY — B
Fairfield U, CT — A
Franklin W. Olin Coll of Engineering, MA — B
Grove City Coll, PA — B
Hofstra U, NY — B
Massachusetts Inst of Technology, MA — B
Northeastern U, MA — B
Southern Methodist U, TX — B
Trinity Coll, CT — B
Tufts U, MA — B
United States Coast Guard Academy, CT — B
U of Connecticut, CT — B
U of Hartford, CT — B
U of Maine, ME — B
U of Massachusetts Amherst, MA — B
U of Massachusetts Dartmouth, MA — B
U of Massachusetts Lowell, MA — B
U of New Hampshire, NH — B
U of New Haven, CT — B
U of Rhode Island, RI — B
U of Vermont, VT — B
Western New England Coll, MA — B
Worcester Polytechnic Inst, MA — B
Yale U, CT — B

Mechanical Engineering/ Mechanical Technology
Benjamin Franklin Inst of Technology, MA — A
Central Connecticut State U, CT — B
Northeastern U, MA — B
U of Maine, ME — B
U of Massachusetts Lowell, MA — A
U of New Hampshire, NH — B
U of New Hampshire at Manchester, NH — B
Vermont Tech Coll, VT — A
Wentworth Inst of Technology, MA — B

Mechanical Engineering Technologies Related
Grove City Coll, PA — B
U of Hartford, CT — B

Medical Laboratory Technology
U of New England, ME — B

Medical Microbiology and Bacteriology
Ohio Wesleyan U, OH — B
Quinnipiac U, CT — B
U of Maine, ME — B
U of New Hampshire, NH — B
U of Rhode Island, RI — B

U of Vermont, VT — B
Worcester Polytechnic Inst, MA — B

Medical Radiologic Technology
Labouré Coll, MA — A
Massachusetts Coll of Pharmacy and Health Sciences, MA — B
U of Hartford, CT — B
U of Vermont, VT — B

Medicinal and Pharmaceutical Chemistry
Worcester Polytechnic Inst, MA — B

Medieval and Renaissance Studies
Brown U, RI — B
Coll of the Holy Cross, MA — B
Connecticut Coll, CT — B
Marlboro Coll, VT — B
Mount Holyoke Coll, MA — B
Ohio Wesleyan U, OH — B
Smith Coll, MA — B
Southern Methodist U, TX — B
Wellesley Coll, MA — B
Wesleyan U, CT — B

Mental and Social Health Services and Allied Professions Related
The U of Maine at Augusta, ME — A,B

Mental Health/Rehabilitation
Tufts U, MA — B
U of Maine at Farmington, ME — B

Metal and Jewelry Arts
Bard Coll at Simon's Rock, MA — B
Hofstra U, NY — B
Maine Coll of Art, ME — B
Massachusetts Coll of Art and Design, MA — B
School of the Museum of Fine Arts, Boston, MA — B
U of Massachusetts Dartmouth, MA — B

Microbiology
U of Massachusetts Amherst, MA — B
U of Vermont, VT — B

Middle School Education
Albertus Magnus Coll, CT — B
Assumption Coll, MA — B
Bennington Coll, VT — B
Champlain Coll, VT — B
Clark U, MA — B
Coll of the Atlantic, ME — B
Fitchburg State Coll, MA — B
Gordon Coll, MA — B
Johnson State Coll, VT — B
Lesley U, MA — B
Merrimack Coll, MA — B
Ohio Wesleyan U, OH — B
Sacred Heart U, CT — B
U of Vermont, VT — B

Modern Greek
Marlboro Coll, VT — B
Mount Holyoke Coll, MA — B
Tufts U, MA — B

A—associate degree; B—bachelor's degree

Modern Languages

Clark U, MA	B
Grove City Coll, PA	B
Marlboro Coll, VT	B
Middlebury Coll, VT	B
Northeastern U, MA	B
Rivier Coll, NH	B
Saint Michael's Coll, VT	B
Suffolk U, MA	B
Trinity Coll, CT	B
U of Maine, ME	B
U of Southern Maine, ME	B

Molecular Biology

Assumption Coll, MA	B
Brown U, RI	B
Central Connecticut State U, CT	B
Clarkson U, NY	B
Clark U, MA	B
Colby Coll, ME	B
Connecticut Coll, CT	B
Dartmouth Coll, NH	B
Grove City Coll, PA	B
Marlboro Coll, VT	B
Middlebury Coll, VT	B
U of Maine, ME	B
U of Vermont, VT	B
Wesleyan U, CT	B
Western New England Coll, MA	B
Worcester Polytechnic Inst, MA	B
Yale U, CT	B

Molecular Genetics

U of Vermont, VT	B

Movement Therapy and Movement Education

U of Vermont, VT	B

Multicultural Education

Hampshire Coll, MA	B

Multi/Interdisciplinary Studies Related

Anna Maria Coll, MA	B
Bates Coll, ME	B
Bentley U, MA	B
Brandeis U, MA	B
Burlington Coll, VT	B
Cambridge Coll, MA	B
Central Connecticut State U, CT	B
Connecticut Coll, CT	B
Dartmouth Coll, NH	B
Hofstra U, NY	B
Keene State Coll, NH	B
Messiah Coll, PA	B
Mount Holyoke Coll, MA	B
Ohio Wesleyan U, OH	B
Plymouth State U, NH	B
Providence Coll, RI	A
Regis Coll, MA	B
Roger Williams U, RI	B
Southern Methodist U, TX	B
Sterling Coll, VT	A,B
Stonehill Coll, MA	B
U of Connecticut, CT	B
U of Hartford, CT	B
U of Massachusetts Amherst, MA	
U of Massachusetts Boston, MA	B
U of New Hampshire, NH	B
Yale U, CT	B

Museum Studies

Coll of the Atlantic, ME	B
Connecticut Coll, CT	B
Regis Coll, MA	B

Music

Amherst Coll, MA	B
Anna Maria Coll, MA	B
Assumption Coll, MA	B
Bard Coll at Simon's Rock, MA	B
Bates Coll, ME	B
Bennington Coll, VT	B
Berklee Coll of Music, MA	B
Boston Coll, MA	B
The Boston Conservatory, MA	B
Bowdoin Coll, ME	B
Brandeis U, MA	B
Bridgewater State Coll, MA	B
Brown U, RI	B
Castleton State Coll, VT	B
Central Connecticut State U, CT	B
Clark U, MA	B
Colby Coll, ME	B
Coll of the Atlantic, ME	B
Coll of the Holy Cross, MA	B
Connecticut Coll, CT	B
Dartmouth Coll, NH	B
Fairfield U, CT	B
Franklin Pierce U, NH	B
Gordon Coll, MA	B
Grove City Coll, PA	B
Hampshire Coll, MA	B
Harvard U, MA	B
Hebrew Coll, MA	B
Hofstra U, NY	B
Johnson State Coll, VT	B
Marlboro Coll, VT	B
Massachusetts Inst of Technology, MA	B
Messiah Coll, PA	B
Middlebury Coll, VT	B
Mount Holyoke Coll, MA	B
Northeastern U, MA	B
Ohio Wesleyan U, OH	B
Plymouth State U, NH	B
Providence Coll, RI	B
Rhode Island Coll, RI	B
Saint Michael's Coll, VT	B
Salve Regina U, RI	B
Simmons Coll, MA	B
Smith Coll, MA	B
Southern Connecticut State U, CT	B
Southern Methodist U, TX	B
Trinity Coll, CT	B
Tufts U, MA	B
U of Bridgeport, CT	B
U of Connecticut, CT	B
U of Hartford, CT	B
U of Maine, ME	B
The U of Maine at Augusta, ME	A,B
U of Maine at Farmington, ME	B
U of Maine at Machias, ME	B
U of Massachusetts Amherst, MA	
U of Massachusetts Boston, MA	B
U of Massachusetts Dartmouth, MA	
U of Massachusetts Lowell, MA	B
U of New Hampshire, NH	B
U of New Haven, CT	B
U of Rhode Island, RI	B
U of Southern Maine, ME	B
U of Vermont, VT	B

Wellesley Coll, MA	B
Wesleyan U, CT	B
Western Connecticut State U, CT	B
Westfield State Coll, MA	B
Wheaton Coll, MA	B
Williams Coll, MA	B
Worcester Polytechnic Inst, MA	B
Yale U, CT	B

Music History, Literature, and Theory

Bennington Coll, VT	B
Eugene Lang Coll The New School for Liberal Arts, NY	B
Hofstra U, NY	B
Keene State Coll, NH	B
Marlboro Coll, VT	B
New England Conservatory of Music, MA	B
Northeastern U, MA	B
Simmons Coll, MA	B
U of Hartford, CT	B
U of Vermont, VT	B

Music Management and Merchandising

Berklee Coll of Music, MA	B
Grove City Coll, PA	B
Hofstra U, NY	B
Johnson State Coll, VT	B
Northeastern U, MA	B
U of Hartford, CT	B
U of New Haven, CT	B

Musicology and Ethnomusicology

Bennington Coll, VT	B
Brown U, RI	B
Hampshire Coll, MA	B

Music Performance

Anna Maria Coll, MA	B
Bennington Coll, VT	B
Berklee Coll of Music, MA	B
Gordon Coll, MA	B
Grove City Coll, PA	B
Hampshire Coll, MA	B
Hofstra U, NY	B
Johnson State Coll, VT	B
Keene State Coll, NH	B
New England Conservatory of Music, MA	B
Ohio Wesleyan U, OH	B
Rhode Island Coll, RI	B
Southern Methodist U, TX	B
U of Hartford, CT	B
U of Massachusetts Amherst, MA	B
U of Massachusetts Lowell, MA	B
U of Rhode Island, RI	B
U of Southern Maine, ME	B
U of Vermont, VT	B
Western Connecticut State U, CT	B

Music Related

Brown U, RI	B
Connecticut Coll, CT	B
Keene State Coll, NH	B
U of Hartford, CT	B

Music Teacher Education

Anna Maria Coll, MA	B
Berklee Coll of Music, MA	B
The Boston Conservatory, MA	B
Bridgewater State Coll, MA	B
Castleton State Coll, VT	B

Central Connecticut State U, CT	B
Connecticut Coll, CT	B
Gordon Coll, MA	B
Grove City Coll, PA	B
Hofstra U, NY	B
Johnson State Coll, VT	B
Keene State Coll, NH	B
Messiah Coll, PA	B
Ohio Wesleyan U, OH	B
Plymouth State U, NH	B
Providence Coll, RI	B
Rhode Island Coll, RI	B
Salve Regina U, RI	B
Southern Methodist U, TX	B
U of Charleston, WV	B
U of Connecticut, CT	B
U of Hartford, CT	B
U of Maine, ME	B
U of Rhode Island, RI	B
U of Southern Maine, ME	B
U of Vermont, VT	B
Western Connecticut State U, CT	B

Music Theory and Composition

Bard Coll at Simon's Rock, MA	B
Bennington Coll, VT	B
Berklee Coll of Music, MA	B
The Boston Conservatory, MA	B
Hofstra U, NY	B
Keene State Coll, NH	B
New England Conservatory of Music, MA	B
Southern Methodist U, TX	B
U of Hartford, CT	B
U of Rhode Island, RI	B
Western Connecticut State U, CT	B

Music Therapy

Anna Maria Coll, MA	B
Berklee Coll of Music, MA	B
Southern Methodist U, TX	B

Natural Resource Economics

U of New Hampshire, NH	B

Natural Resources and Conservation Related

Sterling Coll, VT	A,B
U of New Hampshire, NH	B

Natural Resources/Conservation

Hampshire Coll, MA	B
Marlboro Coll, VT	B
Sterling Coll, VT	A,B
U of Connecticut, CT	B
U of New Hampshire, NH	B
U of Rhode Island, RI	B
U of Vermont, VT	B

Natural Resources/Conservation Related

Sterling Coll, VT	A,B

Natural Resources Management

Green Mountain Coll, VT	B
Massachusetts Maritime Academy, MA	B
Sterling Coll, VT	A,B

Natural Resources Management and Policy

Clark U, MA	B
Johnson State Coll, VT	B
Sterling Coll, VT	A,B

U of Maine, ME — B
U of Massachusetts Amherst, MA — B
U of Rhode Island, RI — B

Natural Sciences
Atlantic Union Coll, MA — B
Bard Coll at Simon's Rock, MA — B
Castleton State Coll, VT — B
Coll of the Atlantic, ME — B
Hampshire Coll, MA — B
Hofstra U, NY — B
Lesley U, MA — B
Marlboro Coll, VT — B
Sterling Coll, VT — A,B
U of Maine, ME — B

Naval Architecture and Marine Engineering
Maine Maritime Academy, ME — A,B
Massachusetts Maritime Academy, MA — B
United States Coast Guard Academy, CT — B

Near and Middle Eastern Studies
Brandeis U, MA — B
Brown U, RI — B
Dartmouth Coll, NH — B
Harvard U, MA — B
Smith Coll, MA — B
U of Massachusetts Amherst, MA — B
Wellesley Coll, MA — B

Neurobiology and Neurophysiology
Harvard U, MA — B

Neuroscience
Amherst Coll, MA — B
Bates Coll, ME — B
Bowdoin Coll, ME — B
Brandeis U, MA — B
Brown U, RI — B
Clark U, MA — B
Colby Coll, ME — B
Connecticut Coll, CT — B
Emmanuel Coll, MA — B
Hampshire Coll, MA — B
Massachusetts Inst of Technology, MA — B
Middlebury Coll, VT — B
Mount Holyoke Coll, MA — B
Ohio Wesleyan U, OH — B
Smith Coll, MA — B
Stonehill Coll, MA — B
Trinity Coll, CT — B
Wellesley Coll, MA — B

Nonprofit Management
Clarkson U, NY — B

Nuclear Engineering
Massachusetts Inst of Technology, MA — B
Worcester Polytechnic Inst, MA — B

Nuclear Medical Technology
Barry U, FL — B
Massachusetts Coll of Pharmacy and Health Sciences, MA — B
Salem State Coll, MA — B
U of Vermont, VT — B

Nursing Administration
U of San Francisco, CA — B

Nursing (Licensed Practical/Vocational Nurse Training)
Vermont Tech Coll, VT — A

Nursing (Registered Nurse Training)
Anna Maria Coll, MA — A,B
Atlantic Union Coll, MA — A,B
Barry U, FL — B
Becker Coll, MA — A,B
Boston Coll, MA — B
Castleton State Coll, VT — A
Central Connecticut State U, CT — B
Central Maine Medical Center Coll of Nursing and Health Professions, ME — A
Curry Coll, MA — B
Endicott Coll, MA — B
Fairfield U, CT — B
Fitchburg State Coll, MA — B
Framingham State Coll, MA — B
Husson U, ME — B
Labouré Coll, MA — A
Massachusetts Coll of Pharmacy and Health Sciences, MA — B
Messiah Coll, PA — B
Quinnipiac U, CT — B
Regis Coll, MA — A,B
Rhode Island Coll, RI — B
Rivier Coll, NH — A,B
Sacred Heart U, CT — B
Saint Joseph Coll, CT — B
Salem State Coll, MA — B
Salve Regina U, RI — B
Simmons Coll, MA — B
Southern Connecticut State U, CT — B
U of Charleston, WV — A,B
U of Connecticut, CT — B
U of Hartford, CT — B
U of Maine, ME — B
The U of Maine at Augusta, ME — A,B
U of Maine at Fort Kent, ME — B
U of Massachusetts Amherst, MA — B
U of Massachusetts Boston, MA — B
U of Massachusetts Dartmouth, MA — B
U of Massachusetts Lowell, MA — B
U of New England, ME — A,B
U of New Hampshire, NH — B
U of Rhode Island, RI — B
U of San Francisco, CA — B
U of Southern Maine, ME — B
U of Vermont, VT — B
Utica Coll, NY — B
Vermont Tech Coll, VT — A
Western Connecticut State U, CT — B
Worcester State Coll, MA — B

Nursing Related
Northeastern U, MA — B
U of Massachusetts Dartmouth, MA — B

Nursing Science
U of New Hampshire at Manchester, NH — B

Nutrition Sciences
Hampshire Coll, MA — B
Saint Joseph Coll, CT — B
U of Connecticut, CT — B
U of New Hampshire, NH — B
U of Vermont, VT — B

Occupational Health and Industrial Hygiene
Clarkson U, NY — B

Occupational Safety and Health Technology
Keene State Coll, NH — B
U of New Haven, CT — A,B

Occupational Therapy
Bay Path Coll, MA — B
Husson U, ME — B
Quinnipiac U, CT — B
Sacred Heart U, CT — B
U of Hartford, CT — B
U of New England, ME — B
U of New Hampshire, NH — B

Ocean Engineering
U of Rhode Island, RI — B

Oceanography
Coll of the Atlantic, ME — B

Oceanography (Chemical and Physical)
Maine Maritime Academy, ME — B
United States Coast Guard Academy, CT — B

Office Management
Babson Coll, MA — B

Operations Management
Babson Coll, MA — B
Boston Coll, MA — B
Clarkson U, NY — B
U of Massachusetts Dartmouth, MA — B
Wentworth Inst of Technology, MA — B

Operations Research
Babson Coll, MA — B
United States Coast Guard Academy, CT — B

Opticianry
Benjamin Franklin Inst of Technology, MA — A

Organic Chemistry
Hampshire Coll, MA — B

Organizational Behavior
Brown U, RI — B
U of San Francisco, CA — B

Organizational Communication
Assumption Coll, MA — B

Ornamental Horticulture
U of Maine, ME — B
Vermont Tech Coll, VT — A

Painting
Bard Coll at Simon's Rock, MA — B
Bennington Coll, VT — B
Hampshire Coll, MA — B
Hofstra U, NY — B
Lyme Academy Coll of Fine Arts, CT — B
Maine Coll of Art, ME — B
Massachusetts Coll of Art and Design, MA — B

Nutrition Sciences (cont.)
Providence Coll, RI — B
Rivier Coll, NH — B
Salve Regina U, RI — B
School of the Museum of Fine Arts, Boston, MA — B
U of Hartford, CT — B
U of Massachusetts Dartmouth, MA — B
U of San Francisco, CA — B

Parks, Recreation and Leisure
Bridgewater State Coll, MA — B
Gordon Coll, MA — B
Green Mountain Coll, VT — B
Johnson State Coll, VT — B
Lyndon State Coll, VT — B
Messiah Coll, PA — B
New England Coll, NH — B
Salem State Coll, MA — B
Southern Connecticut State U, CT — B
Sterling Coll, VT — B
U of Maine at Machias, ME — B
U of Maine at Presque Isle, ME — A,B
Westfield State Coll, MA — B

Parks, Recreation and Leisure Facilities Management
Franklin Pierce U, NH — B
Lyndon State Coll, VT — B
New England Coll, NH — B
Sterling Coll, VT — B
U of Connecticut, CT — B
U of Maine, ME — B
U of Maine at Machias, ME — B
U of New Hampshire, NH — B
U of Vermont, VT — B

Parks, Recreation, and Leisure Related
New England Coll, NH — B
Plymouth State U, NH — B

Pathology/Experimental Pathology
U of Connecticut, CT — B

Peace Studies and Conflict Resolution
Bennington Coll, VT — B
Clark U, MA — B
Hampshire Coll, MA — B
Wellesley Coll, MA — B

Pharmacology and Toxicology Related
Massachusetts Coll of Pharmacy and Health Sciences, MA — B

Pharmacy
Massachusetts Coll of Pharmacy and Health Sciences, MA — B
Northeastern U, MA — B
Simmons Coll, MA — B
U of Connecticut, CT — B
U of Rhode Island, RI — B

Pharmacy, Pharmaceutical Sciences, and Administration Related
Massachusetts Coll of Pharmacy and Health Sciences, MA — B
U of Connecticut, CT — B

A—associate degree; B—bachelor's degree

Philosophy

Albertus Magnus Coll, CT — B
Amherst Coll, MA — B
Assumption Coll, MA — B
Bard Coll at Simon's Rock, MA — B
Barry U, FL — B
Bates Coll, ME — B
Bennington Coll, VT — B
Bentley U, MA — B
Boston Coll, MA — B
Bowdoin Coll, ME — B
Brandeis U, MA — B
Bridgewater State Coll, MA — B
Brown U, RI — B
Castleton State Coll, VT — B
Central Connecticut State U, CT — B
Clark U, MA — B
Colby Coll, ME — B
Coll of the Atlantic, ME — B
Coll of the Holy Cross, MA — B
Connecticut Coll, CT — B
Curry Coll, MA — B
Dartmouth Coll, NH — B
Eugene Lang Coll The New School for Liberal Arts, NY — B
Fairfield U, CT — B
Gordon Coll, MA — B
Green Mountain Coll, VT — B
Grove City Coll, PA — B
Hampshire Coll, MA — B
Harvard U, MA — B
Hofstra U, NY — B
Holy Apostles Coll and Seminary, CT — A,B
Marlboro Coll, VT — B
Massachusetts Coll of Liberal Arts, MA — B
Massachusetts Inst of Technology, MA — B
Merrimack Coll, MA — B
Messiah Coll, PA — B
Middlebury Coll, VT — B
Mount Holyoke Coll, MA — B
New England Coll, NH — B
Northeastern U, MA — B
Ohio Wesleyan U, OH — B
Plymouth State U, NH — B
Providence Coll, RI — B
Rhode Island Coll, RI — B
Roger Williams U, RI — B
Saint Joseph Coll, CT — B
Saint Michael's Coll, VT — B
Salve Regina U, RI — B
Simmons Coll, MA — B
Smith Coll, MA — B
Southern Connecticut State U, CT — B
Southern Methodist U, TX — B
Stonehill Coll, MA — B
Suffolk U, MA — B
Trinity Coll, CT — B
Tufts U, MA — B
U of Connecticut, CT — B
U of Hartford, CT — B
U of Maine, ME — B
U of Massachusetts Amherst, MA — B
U of Massachusetts Boston, MA — B
U of Massachusetts Dartmouth, MA — B
U of Massachusetts Lowell, MA — B
U of New Hampshire, NH — B
U of Rhode Island, RI — B
U of San Francisco, CA — B
U of Southern Maine, ME — B
U of Vermont, VT — B
Utica Coll, NY — B
Wellesley Coll, MA — B
Wesleyan U, CT — B
Western New England Coll, MA — B
Wheaton Coll, MA — B
Williams Coll, MA — B
Worcester Polytechnic Inst, MA — B
Yale U, CT — B

Philosophy and Religious Studies Related

U of Maine at Farmington, ME — B
Wheaton Coll, MA — B

Philosophy Related

U of Massachusetts Boston, MA — B

Photographic and Film/Video Technology

U of Hartford, CT — B

Photography

Albertus Magnus Coll, CT — B
The Art Inst of Boston at Lesley U, MA — B
Bard Coll at Simon's Rock, MA — B
Barry U, FL — B
Bennington Coll, VT — B
Bridgewater State Coll, MA — B
Burlington Coll, VT — B
Fitchburg State Coll, MA — B
Hampshire Coll, MA — B
Hofstra U, NY — B
Maine Coll of Art, ME — B
Marlboro Coll, VT — B
Massachusetts Coll of Art and Design, MA — B
New England Coll, NH — B
The New England Inst of Art, MA — A,B
Rivier Coll, NH — B
Salem State Coll, MA — B
Salve Regina U, RI — B
School of the Museum of Fine Arts, Boston, MA — B
U of Hartford, CT — B
The U of Maine at Augusta, ME — A
U of Massachusetts Dartmouth, MA — B

Physical Education Teaching and Coaching

Barry U, FL — B
Bridgewater State Coll, MA — B
Castleton State Coll, VT — B
Central Connecticut State U, CT — B
Eastern Connecticut State U, CT — B
Endicott Coll, MA — B
Hofstra U, NY — B
Husson U, ME — B
Johnson State Coll, VT — B
Keene State Coll, NH — B
Lyndon State Coll, VT — B
Messiah Coll, PA — B
Mitchell Coll, CT — A
New England Coll, NH — B
Ohio Wesleyan U, OH — B
Rhode Island Coll, RI — B
Salem State Coll, MA — B
U of Connecticut, CT — B
U of Maine, ME — B
U of Maine at Presque Isle, ME — B
U of Massachusetts Boston, MA — B
U of Rhode Island, RI — B
U of San Francisco, CA — B
U of Vermont, VT — B

Physical Sciences

Bennington Coll, VT — B
Hampshire Coll, MA — B
Lyndon State Coll, VT — B
Mitchell Coll, CT — A
Saint Michael's Coll, VT — B
Westfield State Coll, MA — B
Worcester State Coll, MA — B

Physical Sciences Related

Worcester Polytechnic Inst, MA — B

Physical Therapy

Husson U, ME — B
Merrimack Coll, MA — B
Northeastern U, MA — B
Quinnipiac U, CT — B
Sacred Heart U, CT — B
Simmons Coll, MA — B
U of Connecticut, CT — B
U of Hartford, CT — B
U of New England, ME — B

Physician Assistant

Hofstra U, NY — B
Quinnipiac U, CT — B
U of New England, ME — B

Physics

Amherst Coll, MA — B
Bard Coll at Simon's Rock, MA — B
Bates Coll, ME — B
Bennington Coll, VT — B
Boston Coll, MA — B
Bowdoin Coll, ME — B
Brandeis U, MA — B
Bridgewater State Coll, MA — B
Brown U, RI — B
Central Connecticut State U, CT — B
Clarkson U, NY — B
Clark U, MA — B
Colby Coll, ME — B
Coll of the Holy Cross, MA — B
Curry Coll, MA — B
Dartmouth Coll, NH — B
Fairfield U, CT — B
Gordon Coll, MA — B
Grove City Coll, PA — B
Hampshire Coll, MA — B
Harvard U, MA — B
Hofstra U, NY — B
Marlboro Coll, VT — B
Massachusetts Coll of Liberal Arts, MA — B
Massachusetts Inst of Technology, MA — B
Messiah Coll, PA — B
Middlebury Coll, VT — B
Mount Holyoke Coll, MA — B
Northeastern U, MA — B
Ohio Wesleyan U, OH — B
Rhode Island Coll, RI — B
Saint Michael's Coll, VT — B
Smith Coll, MA — B
Southern Connecticut State U, CT — B
Southern Methodist U, TX — B
Stonehill Coll, MA — B
Suffolk U, MA — B
Trinity Coll, CT — B
Tufts U, MA — B
U of Connecticut, CT — B
U of Hartford, CT — B
U of Maine, ME — B
U of Massachusetts Amherst, MA — B
U of Massachusetts Boston, MA — B
U of Massachusetts Dartmouth, MA — B
U of Massachusetts Lowell, MA — B
U of New Hampshire, NH — B
U of Rhode Island, RI — B
U of San Francisco, CA — B
U of Southern Maine, ME — B
U of Vermont, VT — B
Utica Coll, NY — B
Wellesley Coll, MA — B
Wesleyan U, CT — B
Wheaton Coll, MA — B
Williams Coll, MA — B
Worcester Polytechnic Inst, MA — B
Yale U, CT — B

Physics Related

Bridgewater State Coll, MA — B

Physics Teacher Education

Connecticut Coll, CT — B
Hofstra U, NY — B
Husson U, ME — B
Ohio Wesleyan U, OH — B
Rhode Island Coll, RI — B
Utica Coll, NY — B

Physiological Psychology/Psychobiology

Quinnipiac U, CT — B
Simmons Coll, MA — B
U of New England, ME — B
Wheaton Coll, MA — B

Piano and Organ

Barry U, FL — B
Bennington Coll, VT — B
Berklee Coll of Music, MA — B
The Boston Conservatory, MA — B
New England Conservatory of Music, MA — B
Southern Methodist U, TX — B

Plant Protection and Integrated Pest Management

Sterling Coll, VT — A,B

Plant Sciences

Hampshire Coll, MA — B
Sterling Coll, VT — B
U of Maine, ME — B
U of Massachusetts Amherst, MA — B
U of New Hampshire, NH — B
U of Vermont, VT — B

Plant Sciences Related

Sterling Coll, VT — A,B

Playwriting and Screenwriting

Bard Coll at Simon's Rock, MA — B
Bennington Coll, VT — B
Emerson Coll, MA — B
Hampshire Coll, MA — B

Political Communication

Emerson Coll, MA — B

Political Science and Government

Albertus Magnus Coll, CT	B
Amherst Coll, MA	B
Anna Maria Coll, MA	B
Assumption Coll, MA	B
Bard Coll at Simon's Rock, MA	B
Barry U, FL	B
Bates Coll, ME	B
Bennington Coll, VT	B
Boston Coll, MA	B
Bowdoin Coll, ME	B
Bridgewater State Coll, MA	B
Brown U, RI	B
Central Connecticut State U, CT	B
Clarkson U, NY	B
Clark U, MA	B
Colby Coll, ME	B
Coll of the Holy Cross, MA	B
Connecticut Coll, CT	B
Curry Coll, MA	B
Dartmouth Coll, NH	B
Eastern Connecticut State U, CT	B
Emmanuel Coll, MA	B
Eugene Lang Coll The New School for Liberal Arts, NY	B
Fairfield U, CT	B
Fitchburg State Coll, MA	B
Framingham State Coll, MA	B
Franklin Pierce U, NH	B
Gordon Coll, MA	B
Grove City Coll, PA	B
Hampshire Coll, MA	B
Harvard U, MA	B
Hofstra U, NY	B
Johnson State Coll, VT	B
Keene State Coll, NH	B
Marlboro Coll, VT	B
Massachusetts Coll of Liberal Arts, MA	B
Massachusetts Inst of Technology, MA	B
Merrimack Coll, MA	B
Messiah Coll, PA	B
Middlebury Coll, VT	B
Mount Holyoke Coll, MA	B
New England Coll, NH	B
Northeastern U, MA	B
Ohio Wesleyan U, OH	B
Plymouth State U, NH	B
Providence Coll, RI	B
Quinnipiac U, CT	B
Regis Coll, MA	B
Rhode Island Coll, RI	B
Rivier Coll, NH	B
Roger Williams U, RI	B
Saint Michael's Coll, VT	B
Salem State Coll, MA	B
Salve Regina U, RI	B
Simmons Coll, MA	B
Smith Coll, MA	B
Southern Connecticut State U, CT	B
Southern Methodist U, TX	B
Southern New Hampshire U, NH	B
Stonehill Coll, MA	B
Suffolk U, MA	B
Trinity Coll, CT	B
Tufts U, MA	B
United States Coast Guard Academy, CT	B
U of Connecticut, CT	B
U of Hartford, CT	B
U of Maine, ME	B
U of Maine at Farmington, ME	B
U of Maine at Presque Isle, ME	B
U of Massachusetts Amherst, MA	B
U of Massachusetts Boston, MA	B
U of Massachusetts Dartmouth, MA	B
U of Massachusetts Lowell, MA	B
U of New England, ME	B
U of New Hampshire, NH	B
U of New Haven, CT	B
U of Rhode Island, RI	B
U of San Francisco, CA	B
U of Southern Maine, ME	B
U of Vermont, VT	B
Utica Coll, NY	B
Wellesley Coll, MA	B
Wesleyan U, CT	B
Western Connecticut State U, CT	B
Western New England Coll, MA	B
Westfield State Coll, MA	B
Wheaton Coll, MA	B
Williams Coll, MA	B
Yale U, CT	B

Political Science and Government Related

Brandeis U, MA	B
Regis Coll, MA	B

Polymer/Plastics Engineering

U of Massachusetts Lowell, MA	B

Portuguese

Marlboro Coll, VT	B
Smith Coll, MA	B
U of Massachusetts Amherst, MA	B
U of Massachusetts Dartmouth, MA	B
Yale U, CT	B

Pre-Dentistry Studies

Albertus Magnus Coll, CT	B
Atlantic Union Coll, MA	B
Barry U, FL	B
Clarkson U, NY	B
Clark U, MA	B
Franklin Pierce U, NH	B
Grove City Coll, PA	B
Hampshire Coll, MA	B
Hofstra U, NY	B
Ohio Wesleyan U, OH	B
Quinnipiac U, CT	B
Rhode Island Coll, RI	B
Rivier Coll, NH	B
Sacred Heart U, CT	B
Saint Michael's Coll, VT	B
Salem State Coll, MA	B
Simmons Coll, MA	B
U of Bridgeport, CT	B
U of Hartford, CT	B
U of Massachusetts Amherst, MA	B
U of New England, ME	B
U of San Francisco, CA	B
Utica Coll, NY	B

Pre-Law Studies

Albertus Magnus Coll, CT	B
Atlantic Union Coll, MA	B

Babson Coll, MA	B
Bard Coll at Simon's Rock, MA	B
Barry U, FL	B
Bay Path Coll, MA	B
Bennington Coll, VT	B
Champlain Coll, VT	B
Clarkson U, NY	B
Clark U, MA	B
Curry Coll, MA	B
Franklin Pierce U, NH	B
Grove City Coll, PA	B
Hampshire Coll, MA	B
Hofstra U, NY	B
Lasell Coll, MA	B
Marlboro Coll, VT	B
Newbury Coll, MA	B
New England Coll, NH	B
Ohio Wesleyan U, OH	B
Quinnipiac U, CT	B
Rhode Island Coll, RI	B
Rivier Coll, NH	B
Saint Michael's Coll, VT	B
Salem State Coll, MA	B
Simmons Coll, MA	B
Smith Coll, MA	B
Suffolk U, MA	B
U of Bridgeport, CT	B
Utica Coll, NY	B

Premedical Studies

Albertus Magnus Coll, CT	B
Atlantic Union Coll, MA	B
Bard Coll at Simon's Rock, MA	B
Barry U, FL	B
Bennington Coll, VT	B
Clarkson U, NY	B
Clark U, MA	B
Coll of the Holy Cross, MA	B
Franklin Pierce U, NH	B
Grove City Coll, PA	B
Hampshire Coll, MA	B
Hofstra U, NY	B
Johnson State Coll, VT	B
Marlboro Coll, VT	B
Massachusetts Coll of Pharmacy and Health Sciences, MA	B
Ohio Wesleyan U, OH	B
Quinnipiac U, CT	B
Rhode Island Coll, RI	B
Rivier Coll, NH	B
Sacred Heart U, CT	B
Saint Michael's Coll, VT	B
Salem State Coll, MA	B
Simmons Coll, MA	B
Smith Coll, MA	B
U of Bridgeport, CT	B
U of Hartford, CT	B
U of Maine, ME	B
U of Maine at Machias, ME	B
U of Massachusetts Amherst, MA	B
U of New England, ME	B
U of San Francisco, CA	B
Utica Coll, NY	B

Prenursing Studies

Hampshire Coll, MA	B

Pre-Pharmacy Studies

Barry U, FL	B
Hampshire Coll, MA	B
U of Charleston, WV	B
U of Connecticut, CT	B
Western New England Coll, MA	B

Pre-Theology/Pre-Ministerial Studies

Ohio Wesleyan U, OH	B

Pre-Veterinary Studies

Albertus Magnus Coll, CT	B
Atlantic Union Coll, MA	B
Barry U, FL	B
Becker Coll, MA	B
Clarkson U, NY	B
Clark U, MA	B
Coll of the Atlantic, ME	B
Franklin Pierce U, NH	B
Grove City Coll, PA	B
Hampshire Coll, MA	B
Hofstra U, NY	B
Marlboro Coll, VT	B
Ohio Wesleyan U, OH	B
Quinnipiac U, CT	B
Rhode Island Coll, RI	B
Rivier Coll, NH	B
Sacred Heart U, CT	B
Saint Michael's Coll, VT	B
Salem State Coll, MA	B
U of Bridgeport, CT	B
U of Hartford, CT	B
U of Maine, ME	B
U of Massachusetts Amherst, MA	B
U of San Francisco, CA	B
Utica Coll, NY	B

Printmaking

Bard Coll at Simon's Rock, MA	B
Bennington Coll, VT	B
Maine Coll of Art, ME	B
Massachusetts Coll of Art and Design, MA	B
School of the Museum of Fine Arts, Boston, MA	B
U of Hartford, CT	B
U of San Francisco, CA	B

Professional Studies

Champlain Coll, VT	B
Coll of St. Joseph, VT	B

Psychology

Albertus Magnus Coll, CT	B
Amherst Coll, MA	B
Anna Maria Coll, MA	B
Assumption Coll, MA	B
Atlantic Union Coll, MA	B
Bard Coll at Simon's Rock, MA	B
Barry U, FL	B
Bates Coll, ME	B
Bay Path Coll, MA	B
Becker Coll, MA	B
Bennington Coll, VT	B
Boston Coll, MA	B
Bowdoin Coll, ME	B
Brandeis U, MA	B
Bridgewater State Coll, MA	B
Brown U, RI	B
Bryant U, RI	B
Burlington Coll, VT	B
Cambridge Coll, MA	B
Castleton State Coll, VT	B
Central Connecticut State U, CT	B
Clarkson U, NY	B
Clark U, MA	B
Colby Coll, ME	B
Coll of St. Joseph, VT	B
Coll of the Atlantic, ME	B
Coll of the Holy Cross, MA	B
Connecticut Coll, CT	B

A—associate degree; B—bachelor's degree

Curry Coll, MA | B
Dartmouth Coll, NH | B
Eastern Connecticut State U, CT | B
Emmanuel Coll, MA | B
Endicott Coll, MA | B
Eugene Lang Coll The New School for Liberal Arts, NY | B
Fairfield U, CT | B
Fisher Coll, MA | A
Fitchburg State Coll, MA | B
Framingham State Coll, MA | B
Franklin Pierce U, NH | B
Gordon Coll, MA | B
Green Mountain Coll, VT | B
Grove City Coll, PA | B
Hampshire Coll, MA | B
Harvard U, MA | B
Hofstra U, NY | B
Johnson State Coll, VT | B
Keene State Coll, NH | B
Lasell Coll, MA | B
Lyndon State Coll, VT | B
Marlboro Coll, VT | B
Massachusetts Coll of Liberal Arts, MA | B
Merrimack Coll, MA | B
Messiah Coll, PA | B
Middlebury Coll, VT | B
Mitchell Coll, CT | B
Mount Holyoke Coll, MA | B
Mount Ida Coll, MA | B
New England Coll, NH | B
Nichols Coll, MA | B
Northeastern U, MA | B
Ohio Wesleyan U, OH | B
Plymouth State U, NH | B
Providence Coll, RI | B
Quinnipiac U, CT | B
Regis Coll, MA | B
Rhode Island Coll, RI | B
Rivier Coll, NH | B
Roger Williams U, RI | B
Saint Joseph Coll, CT | B
Saint Michael's Coll, VT | B
Salem State Coll, MA | B
Salve Regina U, RI | B
Simmons Coll, MA | B
Smith Coll, MA | B
Southern Connecticut State U, CT | B
Southern Methodist U, TX | B
Southern New Hampshire U, NH | B
Stonehill Coll, MA | B
Suffolk U, MA | B
Trinity Coll, CT | B
Tufts U, MA | B
U of Bridgeport, CT | B
U of Charleston, WV | B
U of Connecticut, CT | B
U of Hartford, CT | B
U of Maine, ME | B
U of Maine at Farmington, ME | B
U of Maine at Machias, ME | B
U of Massachusetts Amherst, MA | B
U of Massachusetts Boston, MA | B
U of Massachusetts Dartmouth, MA | B
U of Massachusetts Lowell, MA | B
U of New England, ME | B
U of New Hampshire, NH | B
U of New Hampshire at Manchester, NH | B

U of New Haven, CT | B
U of Rhode Island, RI | B
U of San Francisco, CA | B
U of Southern Maine, ME | B
U of Vermont, VT | B
Utica Coll, NY | B
Wellesley Coll, MA | B
Wesleyan U, CT | B
Western Connecticut State U, CT | B
Western New England Coll, MA | B
Westfield State Coll, MA | B
Wheaton Coll, MA | B
Williams Coll, MA | B
Worcester State Coll, MA | B
Yale U, CT | B

Psychology Related
Burlington Coll, VT | B
U of New England, ME | B

Psychology Teacher Education
Ohio Wesleyan U, OH | B

Public Administration
Fisher Coll, MA | B
Northeastern U, MA | B
Ohio Wesleyan U, OH | B
Plymouth State U, NH | B
Rhode Island Coll, RI | B
Roger Williams U, RI | B
Southern New Hampshire U, NH | B
Stonehill Coll, MA | B
Suffolk U, MA | B
U of Maine, ME | B
The U of Maine at Augusta, ME | A,B
U of Maine at Fort Kent, ME | B
U of Maine at Machias, ME | B
U of New Haven, CT | B
U of San Francisco, CA | B

Public Administration and Social Service Professions Related
U of Massachusetts Boston, MA | B

Public Health
Southern Connecticut State U, CT | B
Tufts U, MA | B

Public Health Education and Promotion
Hampshire Coll, MA | B
Plymouth State U, NH | B

Public Policy Analysis
Anna Maria Coll, MA | B
Coll of the Atlantic, ME | B
Simmons Coll, MA | B
Southern Methodist U, TX | B
Suffolk U, MA | B
Trinity Coll, CT | B
U of Charleston, WV | B
U of Rhode Island, RI | B

Public Relations
Southern Methodist U, TX | B

Public Relations, Advertising, and Applied Communication Related
Champlain Coll, VT | A,B
Southern New Hampshire U, NH | B
U of Vermont, VT | B

Public Relations/Image Management
Barry U, FL | B
Castleton State Coll, VT | B
Champlain Coll, VT | A,B
Curry Coll, MA | B
Emerson Coll, MA | B
Hofstra U, NY | B
New England Coll, NH | B
Quinnipiac U, CT | B
Regis Coll, MA | B
Salem State Coll, MA | B
Simmons Coll, MA | B
Southern Methodist U, TX | B
Suffolk U, MA | B
Utica Coll, NY | B
Western New England Coll, MA | B

Publishing
Emerson Coll, MA | B

Radio and Television
Barry U, FL | B
Castleton State Coll, VT | B
Curry Coll, MA | B
Emerson Coll, MA | B
Franklin Pierce U, NH | B
Hofstra U, NY | B
Lyndon State Coll, VT | B
Messiah Coll, PA | B
Newbury Coll, MA | A
Northeastern U, MA | B
Sacred Heart U, CT | B

Radio and Television Broadcasting Technology
Emerson Coll, MA | B
Lyndon State Coll, VT | A
The New England Inst of Art, MA | A,B
Worcester State Coll, MA | B

Radiologic Technology/ Science
Champlain Coll, VT | A,B
Coll of St. Joseph, VT | A,B
Massachusetts Coll of Pharmacy and Health Sciences, MA | B
Quinnipiac U, CT | B
Regis Coll, MA | A
Suffolk U, MA | B
U of Charleston, WV | B

Radio, Television, and Digital Communication Related
Emerson Coll, MA | B
Hofstra U, NY | B
Mitchell Coll, CT | B
Sacred Heart U, CT | B

Range Science and Management
Sterling Coll, VT | A,B

Reading Teacher Education
Lyndon State Coll, VT | B

Real Estate
U of Connecticut, CT | B

Recording Arts Technology
U of Hartford, CT | B

Rehabilitation and Therapeutic Professions Related
Assumption Coll, MA | B
U of Maine at Farmington, ME | B

Rehabilitation Therapy
Northeastern U, MA | B
U of Maine at Farmington, ME | B

Religious Education
Hebrew Coll, MA | B
Messiah Coll, PA | B

Religious/Sacred Music
Hebrew Coll, MA | B

Religious Studies
Albertus Magnus Coll, CT | B
Amherst Coll, MA | B
Atlantic Union Coll, MA | A,B
Bard Coll at Simon's Rock, MA | B
Bates Coll, ME | B
Bowdoin Coll, ME | B
Brown U, RI | B
Colby Coll, ME | B
Coll of the Holy Cross, MA | B
Connecticut Coll, CT | B
Dartmouth Coll, NH | B
Emmanuel Coll, MA | B
Eugene Lang Coll The New School for Liberal Arts, NY | B
Fairfield U, CT | B
Grove City Coll, PA | B
Hampshire Coll, MA | B
Harvard U, MA | B
Hofstra U, NY | B
Holy Apostles Coll and Seminary, CT | A,B
Marlboro Coll, VT | B
Merrimack Coll, MA | B
Messiah Coll, PA | B
Middlebury Coll, VT | B
Mount Holyoke Coll, MA | B
Ohio Wesleyan U, OH | B
Saint Joseph Coll, CT | B
Saint Michael's Coll, VT | B
Salve Regina U, RI | B
Smith Coll, MA | B
Southern Methodist U, TX | B
Stonehill Coll, MA | B
Trinity Coll, CT | B
U of Bridgeport, CT | B
U of San Francisco, CA | B
U of Vermont, VT | B
Wellesley Coll, MA | B
Wesleyan U, CT | B
Wheaton Coll, MA | B
Williams Coll, MA | B
Yale U, CT | B

Resort Management
Green Mountain Coll, VT | B
Mitchell Coll, CT | B

Respiratory Care Therapy
U of Hartford, CT | B
Vermont Tech Coll, VT | A

Restaurant/Food Services Management
U of San Francisco, CA | B

Retailing
Southern New Hampshire U, NH | B

Robotics
Worcester Polytechnic Inst, MA | B

Romance Languages
Albertus Magnus Coll, CT | B
Bowdoin Coll, ME | B
Dartmouth Coll, NH | B
Hampshire Coll, MA | B

Harvard U, MA	B
Marlboro Coll, VT	B
Merrimack Coll, MA	B
Mount Holyoke Coll, MA	B
Tufts U, MA	B
U of Maine, ME	B
Wesleyan U, CT	B

Romance Languages Related

Merrimack Coll, MA	A,B
Mount Holyoke Coll, MA	B

Russian

Amherst Coll, MA	B
Bates Coll, ME	B
Boston Coll, MA	B
Bowdoin Coll, ME	B
Brandeis U, MA	B
Coll of the Holy Cross, MA	B
Dartmouth Coll, NH	B
Hofstra U, NY	B
Middlebury Coll, VT	B
Northeastern U, MA	B
Smith Coll, MA	B
Trinity Coll, CT	B
Tufts U, MA	B
U of Massachusetts Boston, MA	B
U of New Hampshire, NH	B
U of Vermont, VT	B
Wellesley Coll, MA	B
Wesleyan U, CT	B
Wheaton Coll, MA	B
Williams Coll, MA	B
Yale U, CT	B

Russian Studies

Boston Coll, MA	B
Brown U, RI	B
Colby Coll, ME	B
Coll of the Holy Cross, MA	B
Dartmouth Coll, NH	B
Marlboro Coll, VT	B
Middlebury Coll, VT	B
Mount Holyoke Coll, MA	B
Smith Coll, MA	B
Tufts U, MA	B
U of Massachusetts Amherst, MA	B
U of Southern Maine, ME	B
U of Vermont, VT	B
Wellesley Coll, MA	B
Wesleyan U, CT	B
Wheaton Coll, MA	B
Yale U, CT	B

Sales, Distribution and Marketing

Babson Coll, MA	B
Champlain Coll, VT	A,B
Husson U, ME	B
Quinnipiac U, CT	B

Sanskrit and Classical Indian Languages

Harvard U, MA	B

Scandinavian Studies

Sterling Coll, VT	B

Science Teacher Education

Assumption Coll, MA	B
Castleton State Coll, VT	B
Coll of the Atlantic, ME	B
Grove City Coll, PA	B
Hofstra U, NY	B
Keene State Coll, NH	B
Lyndon State Coll, VT	B

Rhode Island Coll, RI	B
Sacred Heart U, CT	B
U of Charleston, WV	B
U of Maine, ME	B
U of Maine at Farmington, ME	B
U of Maine at Machias, ME	B
U of Maine at Presque Isle, ME	B
U of Vermont, VT	B

Science Technologies Related

Bridgewater State Coll, MA	B

Science, Technology and Society

Colby Coll, ME	B
Hampshire Coll, MA	B
Massachusetts Inst of Technology, MA	B
Wesleyan U, CT	B
Worcester Polytechnic Inst, MA	B

Sculpture

Bard Coll at Simon's Rock, MA	B
Bennington Coll, VT	B
Hampshire Coll, MA	B
Lyme Academy Coll of Fine Arts, CT	B
Maine Coll of Art, ME	B
Marlboro Coll, VT	B
Massachusetts Coll of Art and Design, MA	B
School of the Museum of Fine Arts, Boston, MA	B
U of Hartford, CT	B
U of Massachusetts Dartmouth, MA	B

Secondary Education

Albertus Magnus Coll, CT	B
Assumption Coll, MA	B
Atlantic Union Coll, MA	B
Bennington Coll, VT	B
Boston Coll, MA	B
Champlain Coll, VT	B
Clark U, MA	B
Coll of St. Joseph, VT	B
Coll of the Atlantic, ME	B
Connecticut Coll, CT	B
Eastern Connecticut State U, CT	B
Emmanuel Coll, MA	B
Fitchburg State Coll, MA	B
Franklin Pierce U, NH	B
Green Mountain Coll, VT	B
Grove City Coll, PA	B
Hampshire Coll, MA	B
Hofstra U, NY	B
Johnson State Coll, VT	B
Keene State Coll, NH	B
Lesley U, MA	B
Merrimack Coll, MA	B
New England Coll, NH	B
Nichols Coll, MA	B
Ohio Wesleyan U, OH	B
Providence Coll, RI	B
Rhode Island Coll, RI	B
Rivier Coll, NH	B
Roger Williams U, RI	B
Sacred Heart U, CT	B
Saint Joseph Coll, CT	B
Saint Michael's Coll, VT	B
Salve Regina U, RI	B
Simmons Coll, MA	B
Southern Connecticut State U, CT	B

Suffolk U, MA	B
Tufts U, MA	B
U of Hartford, CT	B
U of Maine, ME	B
U of Maine at Farmington, ME	B
U of Maine at Presque Isle, ME	B
U of Rhode Island, RI	B
U of San Francisco, CA	B
U of Vermont, VT	B
Utica Coll, NY	B
Western Connecticut State U, CT	B
Western New England Coll, MA	B

Security and Protective Services Related

Massachusetts Maritime Academy, MA	B

Sign Language Interpretation and Translation

Northeastern U, MA	B
U of New Hampshire at Manchester, NH	B

Slavic Languages

Boston Coll, MA	B
Connecticut Coll, CT	B
Harvard U, MA	B

Slavic Studies

Connecticut Coll, CT	B

Small Business Administration

Babson Coll, MA	B
Husson U, ME	B

Social and Philosophical Foundations of Education

Hampshire Coll, MA	B

Social Psychology

Bennington Coll, VT	B
U of New England, ME	B

Social Sciences

Albertus Magnus Coll, CT	B
Bennington Coll, VT	B
Castleton State Coll, VT	B
Central Connecticut State U, CT	B
Clarkson U, NY	B
Daniel Webster Coll, NH	B
Eugene Lang Coll The New School for Liberal Arts, NY	B
Fisher Coll, MA	A
Hampshire Coll, MA	B
Harvard U, MA	B
Hofstra U, NY	B
Holy Apostles Coll and Seminary, CT	A,B
Keene State Coll, NH	B
Lesley U, MA	B
Lyndon State Coll, VT	B
Marlboro Coll, VT	B
Newbury Coll, MA	A
Plymouth State U, NH	B
Providence Coll, RI	B
Quinnipiac U, CT	B
Rhode Island Coll, RI	B
Roger Williams U, RI	B
Salem State Coll, MA	B
Southern Methodist U, TX	B
Southern New Hampshire U, NH	B
Suffolk U, MA	B

U of Bridgeport, CT	B
The U of Maine at Augusta, ME	A
U of Maine at Fort Kent, ME	B
U of Massachusetts Boston, MA	B
U of Southern Maine, ME	B
Utica Coll, NY	B
Wesleyan U, CT	B
Western Connecticut State U, CT	B
Worcester Polytechnic Inst, MA	B

Social Sciences Related

Connecticut Coll, CT	B
Mount Holyoke Coll, MA	B
Plymouth State U, NH	B
Roger Williams U, RI	B
U of Massachusetts Amherst, MA	B
U of New England, ME	B

Social Science Teacher Education

Johnson State Coll, VT	B
Lyndon State Coll, VT	B
Rhode Island Coll, RI	B
Rivier Coll, NH	B
Sacred Heart U, CT	B
U of Maine at Farmington, ME	B
U of Maine at Fort Kent, ME	B
U of Maine at Machias, ME	B
Utica Coll, NY	B

Social Studies Teacher Education

Castleton State Coll, VT	B
Hofstra U, NY	B
Johnson State Coll, VT	B
Keene State Coll, NH	B
Messiah Coll, PA	B
Ohio Wesleyan U, OH	B
Rhode Island Coll, RI	B
Southern New Hampshire U, NH	B
U of Charleston, WV	B
U of Maine, ME	B
U of Vermont, VT	B
Utica Coll, NY	B

Social Work

Albertus Magnus Coll, CT	B
Anna Maria Coll, MA	B
Bridgewater State Coll, MA	B
Castleton State Coll, VT	B
Central Connecticut State U, CT	B
Champlain Coll, VT	A,B
Eastern Connecticut State U, CT	B
Franklin Pierce U, NH	B
Gordon Coll, MA	B
Messiah Coll, PA	B
Plymouth State U, NH	B
Providence Coll, RI	B
Regis Coll, MA	B
Rhode Island Coll, RI	B
Sacred Heart U, CT	B
Saint Joseph Coll, CT	B
Salem State Coll, MA	B
Salve Regina U, RI	B
Southern Connecticut State U, CT	B
Suffolk U, MA	A,B
U of Maine, ME	B

A—associate degree; B—bachelor's degree

U of Maine at Presque Isle, ME B
U of Massachusetts Boston, MA B
U of New Hampshire, NH B
U of Southern Maine, ME B
U of Vermont, VT B
Western Connecticut State U, CT B
Western New England Coll, MA B
Westfield State Coll, MA B
Wheelock Coll, MA B

Sociobiology
Tufts U, MA B

Sociology
Albertus Magnus Coll, CT B
Amherst Coll, MA B
Anna Maria Coll, MA B
Assumption Coll, MA B
Bard Coll at Simon's Rock, MA B
Barry U, FL B
Bates Coll, ME B
Bennington Coll, VT B
Boston Coll, MA B
Bowdoin Coll, ME B
Brandeis U, MA B
Bridgewater State Coll, MA B
Brown U, RI B
Castleton State Coll, VT B
Central Connecticut State U, CT B
Clarkson U, NY B
Clark U, MA B
Colby Coll, ME B
Coll of the Holy Cross, MA B
Connecticut Coll, CT B
Curry Coll, MA B
Dartmouth Coll, NH B
Eastern Connecticut State U, CT B
Emmanuel Coll, MA B
Eugene Lang Coll The New School for Liberal Arts, NY B
Fairfield U, CT B
Fitchburg State Coll, MA B
Framingham State Coll, MA B
Franklin Pierce U, NH B
Gordon Coll, MA B
Green Mountain Coll, VT B
Grove City Coll, PA B
Hampshire Coll, MA B
Harvard U, MA B
Hofstra U, NY B
Johnson State Coll, VT B
Keene State Coll, NH B
Lasell Coll, MA B
Marlboro Coll, VT B
Massachusetts Coll of Liberal Arts, MA B
Merrimack Coll, MA B
Messiah Coll, PA B
Middlebury Coll, VT B
Mount Holyoke Coll, MA B
Newbury Coll, MA A
New England Coll, NH B
Northeastern U, MA B
Ohio Wesleyan U, OH B
Providence Coll, RI B
Quinnipiac U, CT B
Regis Coll, MA B
Rhode Island Coll, RI B
Rivier Coll, NH B
Roger Williams U, RI B
Saint Joseph Coll, CT B

Saint Michael's Coll, VT B
Salem State Coll, MA B
Salve Regina U, RI B
Simmons Coll, MA B
Smith Coll, MA B
Southern Connecticut State U, CT B
Southern Methodist U, TX B
Stonehill Coll, MA B
Suffolk U, MA B
Trinity Coll, CT B
Tufts U, MA B
U of Connecticut, CT B
U of Hartford, CT B
U of Maine, ME B
U of Maine at Farmington, ME B
U of Maine at Presque Isle, ME B
U of Massachusetts Amherst, MA B
U of Massachusetts Boston, MA B
U of Massachusetts Dartmouth, MA B
U of Massachusetts Lowell, MA B
U of New England, ME B
U of New Hampshire, NH B
U of Rhode Island, RI B
U of San Francisco, CA B
U of Southern Maine, ME B
U of Vermont, VT B
Utica Coll, NY B
Wellesley Coll, MA B
Wesleyan U, CT B
Western Connecticut State U, CT B
Western New England Coll, MA B
Westfield State Coll, MA B
Wheaton Coll, MA B
Williams Coll, MA B
Worcester State Coll, MA B
Yale U, CT B

Soil Science and Agronomy
Hampshire Coll, MA B
Sterling Coll, VT A,B
U of Maine, ME B
U of New Hampshire, NH B

Soil Sciences Related
Sterling Coll, VT A,B

Solar Energy Technology
Sterling Coll, VT A,B

South Asian Languages
Yale U, CT B

Spanish
Albertus Magnus Coll, CT B
Amherst Coll, MA B
Anna Maria Coll, MA B
Assumption Coll, MA B
Bard Coll at Simon's Rock, MA B
Barry U, FL B
Bates Coll, ME B
Bennington Coll, VT B
Boston Coll, MA B
Bowdoin Coll, ME B
Bridgewater State Coll, MA B
Brown U, RI B
Castleton State Coll, VT B
Central Connecticut State U, CT B
Clark U, MA B
Colby Coll, ME B
Coll of the Holy Cross, MA B
Connecticut Coll, CT B

Dartmouth Coll, NH B
Eastern Connecticut State U, CT B
Emmanuel Coll, MA B
Endicott Coll, MA B
Fairfield U, CT B
Gordon Coll, MA B
Grove City Coll, PA B
Hofstra U, NY B
Keene State Coll, NH B
Marlboro Coll, VT B
Merrimack Coll, MA B
Messiah Coll, PA B
Middlebury Coll, VT B
Mount Holyoke Coll, MA B
Northeastern U, MA B
Ohio Wesleyan U, OH B
Plymouth State U, NH B
Providence Coll, RI B
Quinnipiac U, CT B
Regis Coll, MA B
Rhode Island Coll, RI B
Rivier Coll, NH B
Saint Joseph Coll, CT B
Saint Michael's Coll, VT B
Salve Regina U, RI B
Simmons Coll, MA B
Smith Coll, MA B
Southern Connecticut State U, CT B
Southern Methodist U, TX B
Suffolk U, MA B
Trinity Coll, CT B
Tufts U, MA B
U of Connecticut, CT B
U of Maine, ME B
U of Massachusetts Amherst, MA B
U of Massachusetts Boston, MA B
U of Massachusetts Dartmouth, MA B
U of New Hampshire, NH B
U of Rhode Island, RI B
U of San Francisco, CA B
U of Vermont, VT B
Wellesley Coll, MA B
Wesleyan U, CT B
Western Connecticut State U, CT B
Williams Coll, MA B
Worcester State Coll, MA B
Yale U, CT B

Spanish and Iberian Studies
Bard Coll at Simon's Rock, MA B

Spanish Language Teacher Education
Assumption Coll, MA B
Connecticut Coll, CT B
Hofstra U, NY B
Keene State Coll, NH B
Messiah Coll, PA B
Ohio Wesleyan U, OH B
Rhode Island Coll, RI B
Salve Regina U, RI B
U of Maine, ME B

Special Education
Barry U, FL B
Bridgewater State Coll, MA B
Curry Coll, MA B
Fitchburg State Coll, MA B
Gordon Coll, MA B
Green Mountain Coll, VT B
Lesley U, MA B
Lyndon State Coll, VT B

New England Coll, NH B
Providence Coll, RI B
Rhode Island Coll, RI B
Rivier Coll, NH B
Saint Joseph Coll, CT B
Salve Regina U, RI B
Simmons Coll, MA B
Southern Connecticut State U, CT B
Tufts U, MA B
U of Connecticut, CT B
U of Hartford, CT B
U of Maine at Farmington, ME B
Westfield State Coll, MA B
Wheelock Coll, MA B

Special Education (Early Childhood)
U of Vermont, VT B

Special Education (Emotionally Disturbed)
U of Maine at Farmington, ME B

Special Education (Mentally Retarded)
U of Maine at Farmington, ME B

Special Education Related
Keene State Coll, NH B
U of Hartford, CT B

Special Education (Specific Learning Disabilities)
U of Maine at Farmington, ME B

Special Education (Speech or Language Impaired)
Emerson Coll, MA B

Special Products Marketing
Newbury Coll, MA A

Speech and Rhetoric
Bates Coll, ME B
Emerson Coll, MA B

Speech-Language Pathology
Emerson Coll, MA B

Speech/Theater Education
U of Maine, ME B

Speech Therapy
Emerson Coll, MA B

Sport and Fitness Administration/Management
Anna Maria Coll, MA B
Barry U, FL B
Becker Coll, MA B
Bridgewater State Coll, MA B
Daniel Webster Coll, NH B
Eastern Connecticut State U, CT B
Endicott Coll, MA B
Fitchburg State Coll, MA B
Franklin Pierce U, NH B
Husson U, ME B
Johnson State Coll, VT B
Lyndon State Coll, VT B
Messiah Coll, PA B
Mitchell Coll, CT B
Mount Ida Coll, MA B
New England Coll, NH B
Nichols Coll, MA B
Sacred Heart U, CT B
Salem State Coll, MA B
Southern New Hampshire U, NH B

U of Massachusetts Amherst, MA — B
U of New England, ME — B
Western New England Coll, MA — B

Statistics
Clarkson U, NY — B
Harvard U, MA — B
Mount Holyoke Coll, MA — B
Ohio Wesleyan U, OH — B
Southern Methodist U, TX — B
U of Connecticut, CT — B
U of Vermont, VT — B

Structural Biology
U of Connecticut, CT — B

Structural Engineering
Clarkson U, NY — B

Substance Abuse/Addiction Counseling
Coll of St. Joseph, VT — B
Keene State Coll, NH — A
Rhode Island Coll, RI — B

Surveying Engineering
U of Maine, ME — B

Survey Technology
U of Maine, ME — B

System Administration
Champlain Coll, VT — B

System, Networking, and LAN/WAN Management
Champlain Coll, VT — A,B
ITT Tech Inst, Woburn, MA — A

Systems Engineering
Maine Maritime Academy, ME — B
Providence Coll, RI — B
U of Maine, ME — B

Systems Science and Theory
Yale U, CT — B

Technical and Business Writing
Champlain Coll, VT — B
Clarkson U, NY — B
U of Hartford, CT — B
Worcester Polytechnic Inst, MA — B

Technical Teacher Education
Rhode Island Coll, RI — B

Technology/Industrial Arts Teacher Education
Central Connecticut State U, CT — B
Fitchburg State Coll, MA — B
Keene State Coll, NH — B
Rhode Island Coll, RI — B
Westfield State Coll, MA — B

Telecommunications
Champlain Coll, VT — A,B

Telecommunications Technology
Vermont Tech Coll, VT — A

Textile Sciences and Engineering
U of Massachusetts Dartmouth, MA — B

Theater Design and Technology
Bard Coll at Simon's Rock, MA — B
Bennington Coll, VT — B
Emerson Coll, MA — B
Fitchburg State Coll, MA — B
Johnson State Coll, VT — A
Keene State Coll, NH — B
U of Connecticut, CT — B

Theater Literature, History and Criticism
Bard Coll at Simon's Rock, MA — B
Bennington Coll, VT — B
Bowdoin Coll, ME — B
Hampshire Coll, MA — B
Keene State Coll, NH — B
U of Connecticut, CT — B

Theology
Anna Maria Coll, MA — B
Assumption Coll, MA — B
Atlantic Union Coll, MA — B
Barry U, FL — B
Boston Coll, MA — B
Providence Coll, RI — B
U of San Francisco, CA — B

Therapeutic Recreation
Northeastern U, MA — B
U of Southern Maine, ME — A,B
Utica Coll, NY — B

Tourism and Travel Services Management
Becker Coll, MA — B
Champlain Coll, VT — A,B
Fisher Coll, MA — A
Johnson State Coll, VT — B
Lasell Coll, MA — B
Newbury Coll, MA — A
Salem State Coll, MA — B
Southern New Hampshire U, NH — B
U of Maine at Machias, ME — B

Tourism and Travel Services Marketing
Champlain Coll, VT — A,B

Tourism Promotion
Champlain Coll, VT — A,B

Tourism/Travel Marketing
Mitchell Coll, CT — B

Toxicology
Clarkson U, NY — B

Trade and Industrial Teacher Education
Fitchburg State Coll, MA — B
U of Southern Maine, ME — B

Transportation Management
Bridgewater State Coll, MA — B

Transportation Technology
Maine Maritime Academy, ME — A,B

Turf and Turfgrass Management
U of Massachusetts Amherst, MA — A
U of Rhode Island, RI — B

Ukraine Studies
Bard Coll at Simon's Rock, MA — B

Urban Studies/Affairs
Albertus Magnus Coll, CT — B
Brown U, RI — B
Connecticut Coll, CT — B
Eugene Lang Coll The New School for Liberal Arts, NY — B
Hampshire Coll, MA — B
Ohio Wesleyan U, OH — B
Tufts U, MA — B
U of Connecticut, CT — B
Worcester State Coll, MA — B

Veterinary/Animal Health Technology
The U of Maine at Augusta, ME — A

Veterinary Sciences
Becker Coll, MA — B

Veterinary Technology
Becker Coll, MA — A
Mount Ida Coll, MA — A,B
Vermont Tech Coll, VT — A

Violin, Viola, Guitar and Other Stringed Instruments
Bennington Coll, VT — B
Berklee Coll of Music, MA — B
The Boston Conservatory, MA — B
New England Conservatory of Music, MA — B

Visual and Performing Arts
Assumption Coll, MA — B
Bard Coll at Simon's Rock, MA — B
Bennington Coll, VT — B
Brown U, RI — B
Eastern Connecticut State U, CT — B
Emerson Coll, MA — B
Hampshire Coll, MA — B
Harvard U, MA — B
Johnson State Coll, VT — B
Massachusetts Coll of Liberal Arts, MA — B
Providence Coll, RI — B
U of Maine at Machias, ME — B
U of San Francisco, CA — B

Visual and Performing Arts Related
Bard Coll at Simon's Rock, MA — B
Maine Coll of Art, ME — B
Providence Coll, RI — B
School of the Museum of Fine Arts, Boston, MA — B
U of New Haven, CT — B

Voice and Opera
Barry U, FL — B
Bennington Coll, VT — B
Berklee Coll of Music, MA — B
The Boston Conservatory, MA — B
New England Conservatory of Music, MA — B
Southern Methodist U, TX — B

Water, Wetlands, and Marine Resources Management
Sterling Coll, VT — B
U of New Hampshire, NH — B

Web/Multimedia Management and Webmaster
Champlain Coll, VT — A,B
ITT Tech Inst, Woburn, MA — A
The New England Inst of Art, MA — B

Web Page, Digital/Multimedia and Information Resources Design
Champlain Coll, VT — A,B
ITT Tech Inst, Woburn, MA — A
The New England Inst of Art, MA — B
Quinnipiac U, CT — B

Wildlife and Wildlands Science and Management
Sterling Coll, VT — A,B
U of Maine, ME — B
U of Massachusetts Amherst, MA — B
U of New Hampshire, NH — B
U of Rhode Island, RI — B

Wildlife Biology
Coll of the Atlantic, ME — B
Sterling Coll, VT — B
U of Vermont, VT — B

Wind/Percussion Instruments
Berklee Coll of Music, MA — B
The Boston Conservatory, MA — B
New England Conservatory of Music, MA — B

Women's Studies
Amherst Coll, MA — B
Bard Coll at Simon's Rock, MA — B
Bates Coll, ME — B
Bennington Coll, VT — B
Bowdoin Coll, ME — B
Brandeis U, MA — B
Brown U, RI — B
Clark U, MA — B
Colby Coll, ME — B
Connecticut Coll, CT — B
Curry Coll, MA — B
Dartmouth Coll, NH — B
Eugene Lang Coll The New School for Liberal Arts, NY — B
Fisher Coll, MA — A
Hampshire Coll, MA — B
Harvard U, MA — B
Hofstra U, NY — B
Marlboro Coll, VT — B
Middlebury Coll, VT — B
Mount Holyoke Coll, MA — B
Northeastern U, MA — B
Ohio Wesleyan U, OH — B

A—associate degree; B—bachelor's degree

Rhode Island Coll, RI — B
Saint Joseph Coll, CT — B
Simmons Coll, MA — B
Smith Coll, MA — B
Suffolk U, MA — B
Trinity Coll, CT — B
Tufts U, MA — B
U of Connecticut, CT — B
U of Maine, ME — B
U of Maine at Farmington, ME — B
U of Massachusetts Amherst, MA — B

U of Massachusetts Boston, MA — B
U of Massachusetts Dartmouth, MA — B
U of New Hampshire, NH — B
U of Rhode Island, RI — B
U of Southern Maine, ME — B
U of Vermont, VT — B
Wellesley Coll, MA — B
Wesleyan U, CT — B
Wheaton Coll, MA — B

Williams Coll, MA — B
Yale U, CT — B

Wood Science and Wood Products/Pulp and Paper Technology
U of Maine, ME — B
U of Massachusetts Amherst, MA — B

Youth Ministry
Gordon Coll, MA — B

Zoology/Animal Biology
Bennington Coll, VT — B
Coll of the Atlantic, ME — B
Hampshire Coll, MA — B
Ohio Wesleyan U, OH — B
U of Maine, ME — B
U of New Hampshire, NH — B
U of Rhode Island, RI — B
U of Vermont, VT — B

Athletic Programs and Scholarships

Archery
U of New Hampshire, NH	M, W
Yale U, CT	M, W

Badminton
Colby Coll, ME	M, W
Dartmouth Coll, NH	M, W
U of Hartford, CT	M, W
U of New Hampshire, NH	M, W

Baseball
Albertus Magnus Coll, CT	M
Amherst Coll, MA	M
Anna Maria Coll, MA	M
Assumption Coll, MA	M
Babson Coll, MA	M
Barry U, FL	M(s)
Bates Coll, ME	M
Becker Coll, MA	M
Bentley U, MA	M(s)
Boston Coll, MA	M
Bowdoin Coll, ME	M
Brandeis U, MA	M
Bridgewater State Coll, MA	M
Brown U, RI	M
Bryant U, RI	M
Castleton State Coll, VT	M
Central Connecticut State U, CT	M(s)
Clarkson U, NY	M
Clark U, MA	M
Colby Coll, ME	M
Coll of St. Joseph, VT	M
Coll of the Holy Cross, MA	M
Connecticut Coll, CT	M
Curry Coll, MA	M
Daniel Webster Coll, NH	M
Dartmouth Coll, NH	M
Eastern Connecticut State U, CT	M
Emerson Coll, MA	M
Endicott Coll, MA	M
Fairfield U, CT	M(s)
Fisher Coll, MA	M
Fitchburg State Coll, MA	M
Framingham State Coll, MA	M
Franklin Pierce U, NH	M(s)
Gordon Coll, MA	M
Grove City Coll, PA	M
Harvard U, MA	M
Hofstra U, NY	M(s)
Husson U, ME	M
Keene State Coll, NH	M
Landmark Coll, VT	M
Lasell Coll, MA	M
Lyndon State Coll, VT	M
Massachusetts Coll of Liberal Arts, MA	M
Massachusetts Inst of Technology, MA	M
Massachusetts Maritime Academy, MA	M
Merrimack Coll, MA	M
Messiah Coll, PA	M
Middlebury Coll, VT	M
Mitchell Coll, CT	M
Mount Ida Coll, MA	M

Newbury Coll, MA	M
New England Coll, NH	M
Nichols Coll, MA	M
Northeastern U, MA	M(s)
Ohio Wesleyan U, OH	M
Plymouth State U, NH	M
Quinnipiac U, CT	M(s)
Rhode Island Coll, RI	M
Rivier Coll, NH	M
Roger Williams U, RI	M
Sacred Heart U, CT	M(s)
Saint Michael's Coll, VT	M
Salem State Coll, MA	W
Salve Regina U, RI	M
Southern Connecticut State U, CT	M(s)
Southern Methodist U, TX	M
Southern New Hampshire U, NH	M(s)
Stonehill Coll, MA	M(s)
Suffolk U, MA	M
Trinity Coll, CT	M
Tufts U, MA	M
United States Coast Guard Academy, CT	M
U of Bridgeport, CT	M(s)
U of Charleston, WV	M(s)
U of Connecticut, CT	M(s)
U of Hartford, CT	M(s)
U of Maine, ME	M(s)
U of Maine at Farmington, ME	M
U of Maine at Presque Isle, ME	M
U of Massachusetts Amherst, MA	M(s)
U of Massachusetts Boston, MA	M
U of Massachusetts Dartmouth, MA	M
U of Massachusetts Lowell, MA	M(s)
U of New Hampshire, NH	M
U of New Haven, CT	M(s)
U of Rhode Island, RI	M(s)
U of San Francisco, CA	M(s)
U of Southern Maine, ME	M
Utica Coll, NY	M
Vermont Tech Coll, VT	M
Wentworth Inst of Technology, MA	M
Wesleyan U, CT	M
Western Connecticut State U, CT	M
Western New England Coll, MA	M
Westfield State Coll, MA	M
Wheaton Coll, MA	M
Williams Coll, MA	M
Worcester Polytechnic Inst, MA	M
Worcester State Coll, MA	M
Yale U, CT	M

Basketball
Albertus Magnus Coll, CT	M, W
Amherst Coll, MA	M, W
Anna Maria Coll, MA	M, W
The Art Inst of Boston at Lesley U, MA	M, W
Assumption Coll, MA	M(s), W(s)
Babson Coll, MA	M, W
Bard Coll at Simon's Rock, MA	M, W

Barry U, FL	M(s), W(s)
Bates Coll, ME	M, W
Bay Path Coll, MA	W
Becker Coll, MA	M, W
Bentley U, MA	M(s), W(s)
Boston Coll, MA	M(s), W(s)
Bowdoin Coll, ME	M, W
Brandeis U, MA	M, W
Bridgewater State Coll, MA	M, W
Brown U, RI	M, W
Bryant U, RI	M(s), W(s)
Castleton State Coll, VT	M, W
Central Connecticut State U, CT	M(s), W(s)
Clarkson U, NY	M, W
Clark U, MA	M, W
Colby Coll, ME	M, W
Coll of St. Joseph, VT	M, W
Coll of the Holy Cross, MA	M(s), W(s)
Connecticut Coll, CT	M, W
Curry Coll, MA	M, W
Daniel Webster Coll, NH	M, W
Dartmouth Coll, NH	M, W
Eastern Connecticut State U, CT	M, W
Emerson Coll, MA	M, W
Emmanuel Coll, MA	M, W
Endicott Coll, MA	M, W
Fairfield U, CT	M(s), W(s)
Fisher Coll, MA	M, W
Fitchburg State Coll, MA	M, W
Framingham State Coll, MA	M, W
Franklin Pierce U, NH	M(s), W(s)
Gordon Coll, MA	M, W
Green Mountain Coll, VT	M, W
Grove City Coll, PA	M, W
Hampshire Coll, MA	M, W
Harvard U, MA	M, W
Hofstra U, NY	M(s), W(s)
Husson U, ME	M, W
Johnson State Coll, VT	M, W
Keene State Coll, NH	M, W
Landmark Coll, VT	M, W
Lasell Coll, MA	M, W
Lesley U, MA	M, W
Lyndon State Coll, VT	M, W
Maine Maritime Academy, ME	M, W
Massachusetts Coll of Liberal Arts, MA	M, W
Massachusetts Inst of Technology, MA	M, W
Merrimack Coll, MA	M(s), W(s)
Messiah Coll, PA	M, W
Middlebury Coll, VT	M, W
Mitchell Coll, CT	M, W
Mount Holyoke Coll, MA	W
Mount Ida Coll, MA	M, W
Newbury Coll, MA	M, W
New England Coll, NH	M, W
Nichols Coll, MA	M, W
Northeastern U, MA	M(s), W(s)
Ohio Wesleyan U, OH	M, W
Plymouth State U, NH	M, W
Providence Coll, RI	M(s), W(s)
Quinnipiac U, CT	M(s), W(s)

M—for men; W—for women; (s)—scholarship offered

Regis Coll, MA	M, W
Rhode Island Coll, RI	M, W
Rivier Coll, NH	M, W
Roger Williams U, RI	M, W
Sacred Heart U, CT	M(s), W(s)
Saint Joseph Coll, CT	W
Saint Michael's Coll, VT	M(s), W(s)
Salem State Coll, MA	M, W
Salve Regina U, RI	M, W
Simmons Coll, MA	W
Smith Coll, MA	W
Southern Connecticut State U, CT	M(s), W(s)
Southern Methodist U, TX	M(s), W(s)
Southern New Hampshire U, NH	M(s), W(s)
Stonehill Coll, MA	M(s), W(s)
Suffolk U, MA	M, W
Trinity Coll, CT	M, W
Tufts U, MA	M, W
United States Coast Guard Academy, CT	M, W
U of Bridgeport, CT	M(s), W(s)
U of Charleston, WV	M(s), W(s)
U of Connecticut, CT	M(s), W(s)
U of Hartford, CT	M(s), W(s)
U of Maine, ME	M(s), W(s)
The U of Maine at Augusta, ME	M(s), W(s)
U of Maine at Farmington, ME	M, W
U of Maine at Fort Kent, ME	M, W
U of Maine at Machias, ME	M, W
U of Maine at Presque Isle, ME	M, W
U of Massachusetts Amherst, MA	M(s), W(s)
U of Massachusetts Boston, MA	M, W
U of Massachusetts Dartmouth, MA	M, W
U of Massachusetts Lowell, MA	M(s), W(s)
U of New England, ME	M, W
U of New Hampshire, NH	M(s), W(s)
U of New Haven, CT	M(s), W(s)
U of Rhode Island, RI	M(s), W(s)
U of San Francisco, CA	M(s), W(s)
U of Southern Maine, ME	M, W
U of Vermont, VT	M(s), W(s)
Utica Coll, NY	M, W
Vermont Tech Coll, VT	M, W
Wellesley Coll, MA	W
Wentworth Inst of Technology, MA	M, W
Wesleyan U, CT	M, W
Western Connecticut State U, CT	M, W
Western New England Coll, MA	M, W
Westfield State Coll, MA	M, W
Wheaton Coll, MA	M, W
Wheelock Coll, MA	M, W
Williams Coll, MA	M, W
Worcester Polytechnic Inst, MA	M, W
Worcester State Coll, MA	M, W
Yale U, CT	M, W

Bowling

Bryant U, RI	M, W
Sacred Heart U, CT	W(s)
Stonehill Coll, MA	M, W
United States Coast Guard Academy, CT	M, W
U of Rhode Island, RI	W
Western New England Coll, MA	M, W

Cheerleading

Babson Coll, MA	W
Bard Coll at Simon's Rock, MA	M, W
Becker Coll, MA	M, W
Boston Coll, MA	M, W
Bryant U, RI	M, W
Castleton State Coll, VT	M, W
Dartmouth Coll, NH	M, W
Eastern Connecticut State U, CT	W
Endicott Coll, MA	W
Gordon Coll, MA	M, W
Grove City Coll, PA	W

Massachusetts Inst of Technology, MA	M, W
Merrimack Coll, MA	W
Mount Ida Coll, MA	M, W
Plymouth State U, NH	M, W
Providence Coll, RI	W
Regis Coll, MA	M, W
Rivier Coll, NH	M, W
Roger Williams U, RI	W
Sacred Heart U, CT	W
Saint Michael's Coll, VT	M, W
Southern Connecticut State U, CT	M, W
Southern Methodist U, TX	M(s), W(s)
Southern New Hampshire U, NH	M, W
Stonehill Coll, MA	M, W
U of Charleston, WV	W(s)
U of Massachusetts Amherst, MA	M, W
U of Massachusetts Dartmouth, MA	W
U of New Haven, CT	M, W
U of Rhode Island, RI	M
U of Southern Maine, ME	M, W
U of Vermont, VT	M, W
Western Connecticut State U, CT	W
Westfield State Coll, MA	W

Crew

Amherst Coll, MA	M, W
The Art Inst of Boston at Lesley U, MA	W
Assumption Coll, MA	M, W
Barry U, FL	W(s)
Bates Coll, ME	M, W
Boston Coll, MA	W(s)
Bowdoin Coll, ME	M, W
Brandeis U, MA	M
Brown U, RI	M, W
Clark U, MA	M, W
Colby Coll, ME	M, W
Coll of the Holy Cross, MA	M, W
Connecticut Coll, CT	M, W
Dartmouth Coll, NH	M, W
Endicott Coll, MA	M, W
Fairfield U, CT	M(s), W(s)
Franklin Pierce U, NH	M, W
Harvard U, MA	M, W
Lesley U, MA	W
Massachusetts Inst of Technology, MA	M, W
Massachusetts Maritime Academy, MA	M, W
Mount Holyoke Coll, MA	W
Northeastern U, MA	M(s), W(s)
Roger Williams U, RI	M, W
Sacred Heart U, CT	W(s)
Simmons Coll, MA	W
Smith Coll, MA	W
Southern Methodist U, TX	W(s)
Trinity Coll, CT	M, W
Tufts U, MA	M, W
United States Coast Guard Academy, CT	M, W
U of Charleston, WV	M(s), W(s)
U of Connecticut, CT	W
U of Massachusetts Amherst, MA	W(s)
U of Massachusetts Lowell, MA	M, W
U of New Hampshire, NH	M, W
U of Rhode Island, RI	M, W(s)
U of Vermont, VT	M, W
Wellesley Coll, MA	W
Wentworth Inst of Technology, MA	M, W
Wesleyan U, CT	M, W
Williams Coll, MA	M, W
Worcester Polytechnic Inst, MA	M, W
Worcester State Coll, MA	W
Yale U, CT	M, W

Cross-Country Running

Albertus Magnus Coll, CT	M, W
Amherst Coll, MA	M, W
Anna Maria Coll, MA	M

The Art Inst of Boston at Lesley U, MA	M, W
Assumption Coll, MA	M, W
Babson Coll, MA	M, W
Bard Coll at Simon's Rock, MA	M, W
Bates Coll, ME	M, W
Bay Path Coll, MA	W
Bentley U, MA	M(s), W(s)
Boston Coll, MA	M(s), W(s)
Bowdoin Coll, ME	M, W
Brandeis U, MA	M, W
Bridgewater State Coll, MA	M, W
Brown U, RI	M, W
Bryant U, RI	M, W
Castleton State Coll, VT	M, W
Central Connecticut State U, CT	M(s), W(s)
Clarkson U, NY	M, W
Clark U, MA	M, W
Colby Coll, ME	M, W
Coll of the Holy Cross, MA	M, W
Connecticut Coll, CT	M, W
Curry Coll, MA	W
Daniel Webster Coll, NH	M, W
Dartmouth Coll, NH	M, W
Eastern Connecticut State U, CT	M, W
Emerson Coll, MA	M, W
Emmanuel Coll, MA	M, W
Endicott Coll, MA	M, W
Fairfield U, CT	M(s), W(s)
Fitchburg State Coll, MA	M, W
Framingham State Coll, MA	M, W
Franklin Pierce U, NH	M, W
Gordon Coll, MA	M, W
Green Mountain Coll, VT	M, W
Grove City Coll, PA	M, W
Harvard U, MA	M, W
Hofstra U, NY	M(s), W(s)
Johnson State Coll, VT	M, W
Keene State Coll, NH	M, W
Landmark Coll, VT	M, W
Lasell Coll, MA	M, W
Lesley U, MA	M, W
Lyndon State Coll, VT	M, W
Maine Maritime Academy, ME	M, W
Massachusetts Coll of Liberal Arts, MA	M, W
Massachusetts Inst of Technology, MA	M, W
Massachusetts Maritime Academy, MA	M, W
Merrimack Coll, MA	M, W(s)
Messiah Coll, PA	M, W
Middlebury Coll, VT	M, W
Mitchell Coll, CT	M, W
Mount Holyoke Coll, MA	W
Mount Ida Coll, MA	W
Newbury Coll, MA	M, W
New England Coll, NH	M, W
Northeastern U, MA	M(s), W(s)
Ohio Wesleyan U, OH	M, W
Providence Coll, RI	M(s), W(s)
Quinnipiac U, CT	M(s), W(s)
Rhode Island Coll, RI	M, W
Rivier Coll, NH	M, W
Roger Williams U, RI	M, W
Sacred Heart U, CT	M(s), W(s)
Saint Joseph Coll, CT	W
Saint Michael's Coll, VT	M, W
Salem State Coll, MA	M, W
Salve Regina U, RI	M, W
Smith Coll, MA	W
Southern Connecticut State U, CT	M(s), W(s)
Southern Methodist U, TX	W(s)
Southern New Hampshire U, NH	M(s), W(s)
Stonehill Coll, MA	M(s), W(s)
Suffolk U, MA	M, W
Trinity Coll, CT	M, W
Tufts U, MA	M, W

United States Coast Guard Academy, CT	M, W
U of Bridgeport, CT	M, W
U of Charleston, WV	M(s), W(s)
U of Connecticut, CT	M(s), W(s)
U of Hartford, CT	M(s), W(s)
U of Maine, ME	M(s), W(s)
U of Maine at Farmington, ME	M, W
U of Maine at Machias, ME	M, W
U of Maine at Presque Isle, ME	M, W
U of Massachusetts Amherst, MA	M(s), W(s)
U of Massachusetts Boston, MA	M, W
U of Massachusetts Dartmouth, MA	M, W
U of Massachusetts Lowell, MA	M(s), W(s)
U of New England, ME	M, W
U of New Hampshire, NH	M(s), W(s)
U of New Haven, CT	M(s), W(s)
U of Rhode Island, RI	M(s), W(s)
U of San Francisco, CA	M(s), W(s)
U of Southern Maine, ME	M, W
U of Vermont, VT	M(s), W(s)
Wellesley Coll, MA	W
Wesleyan U, CT	M, W
Western New England Coll, MA	M, W
Westfield State Coll, MA	M, W
Wheaton Coll, MA	M, W
Wheelock Coll, MA	M, W
Williams Coll, MA	M, W
Worcester Polytechnic Inst, MA	M, W
Worcester State Coll, MA	M, W
Yale U, CT	M, W

Equestrian Sports

Amherst Coll, MA	M, W
Bates Coll, ME	M, W
Becker Coll, MA	M, W
Bowdoin Coll, ME	M, W
Brown U, RI	W
Castleton State Coll, VT	M, W
Colby Coll, ME	M, W
Connecticut Coll, CT	M, W
Dartmouth Coll, NH	M, W
Endicott Coll, MA	M, W
Fairfield U, CT	M, W
Mount Holyoke Coll, MA	W
Mount Ida Coll, MA	W
Ohio Wesleyan U, OH	M, W
Roger Williams U, RI	M, W
Sacred Heart U, CT	W(s)
Salve Regina U, RI	M, W
Smith Coll, MA	W
Southern Methodist U, TX	W(s)
Stonehill Coll, MA	W(s)
U of Massachusetts Dartmouth, MA	W
U of Rhode Island, RI	M, W
U of Vermont, VT	M, W
Wesleyan U, CT	M, W
Williams Coll, MA	M, W
Yale U, CT	M, W

Fencing

Amherst Coll, MA	M, W
Bard Coll at Simon's Rock, MA	M, W
Bates Coll, ME	M, W
Boston Coll, MA	M, W
Bowdoin Coll, ME	M, W
Brandeis U, MA	M, W
Brown U, RI	M, W
Central Connecticut State U, CT	M, W
Colby Coll, ME	M, W
Dartmouth Coll, NH	M, W
Hampshire Coll, MA	M, W
Harvard U, MA	M, W
Massachusetts Inst of Technology, MA	M, W
Sacred Heart U, CT	M, W(s)
Southern Methodist U, TX	M, W

Trinity Coll, CT	M, W
Tufts U, MA	W
U of New Hampshire, NH	M, W
U of Vermont, VT	M, W
Wellesley Coll, MA	W
Yale U, CT	M, W

Field Hockey

Amherst Coll, MA	W
Anna Maria Coll, MA	W
Assumption Coll, MA	W
Babson Coll, MA	W
Bates Coll, ME	W
Bay Path Coll, MA	W
Becker Coll, MA	W
Bentley U, MA	W(s)
Boston Coll, MA	W(s)
Bowdoin Coll, ME	W
Brandeis U, MA	W
Bridgewater State Coll, MA	W
Brown U, RI	W
Bryant U, RI	W
Castleton State Coll, VT	W
Clark U, MA	W
Colby Coll, ME	W
Coll of the Holy Cross, MA	W
Connecticut Coll, CT	W
Daniel Webster Coll, NH	W
Dartmouth Coll, NH	W
Eastern Connecticut State U, CT	W
Endicott Coll, MA	W
Fairfield U, CT	W(s)
Fitchburg State Coll, MA	W
Framingham State Coll, MA	W
Franklin Pierce U, NH	W(s)
Gordon Coll, MA	W
Harvard U, MA	W
Hofstra U, NY	W(s)
Husson U, ME	W
Keene State Coll, NH	W
Lasell Coll, MA	W
Massachusetts Inst of Technology, MA	W
Merrimack Coll, MA	W(s)
Messiah Coll, PA	W
Middlebury Coll, VT	W
Mount Holyoke Coll, MA	W
New England Coll, NH	W
Nichols Coll, MA	W
Northeastern U, MA	W(s)
Ohio Wesleyan U, OH	W
Plymouth State U, NH	W
Providence Coll, RI	W(s)
Quinnipiac U, CT	W(s)
Regis Coll, MA	W
Sacred Heart U, CT	W(s)
Saint Michael's Coll, VT	W
Salem State Coll, MA	W
Salve Regina U, RI	W
Simmons Coll, MA	W
Smith Coll, MA	W
Southern Connecticut State U, CT	W(s)
Stonehill Coll, MA	W(s)
Tufts U, MA	W
U of Connecticut, CT	W(s)
U of Maine, ME	W(s)
U of Maine at Farmington, ME	W
U of Massachusetts Amherst, MA	W(s)
U of Massachusetts Dartmouth, MA	W
U of Massachusetts Lowell, MA	W(s)
U of New England, ME	W
U of New Hampshire, NH	W(s)
U of Southern Maine, ME	W
U of Vermont, VT	W(s)
Utica Coll, NY	W
Wellesley Coll, MA	W

Wesleyan U, CT	W
Western Connecticut State U, CT	W
Western New England Coll, MA	W
Westfield State Coll, MA	W
Wheaton Coll, MA	W
Wheelock Coll, MA	W
Williams Coll, MA	W
Worcester Polytechnic Inst, MA	W
Worcester State Coll, MA	W
Yale U, CT	W

Football

Amherst Coll, MA	M
Anna Maria Coll, MA	M
Assumption Coll, MA	M
Bates Coll, ME	M
Becker Coll, MA	M
Bentley U, MA	M(s)
Boston Coll, MA	M(s)
Bowdoin Coll, ME	M
Bridgewater State Coll, MA	M
Brown U, RI	M
Bryant U, RI	M
Central Connecticut State U, CT	M
Colby Coll, ME	M, W
Coll of the Holy Cross, MA	M
Curry Coll, MA	M
Dartmouth Coll, NH	M
Endicott Coll, MA	M
Fitchburg State Coll, MA	M
Framingham State Coll, MA	M
Grove City Coll, PA	M
Harvard U, MA	M
Hofstra U, NY	M(s)
Husson U, ME	M
Maine Maritime Academy, ME	M
Massachusetts Inst of Technology, MA	M
Massachusetts Maritime Academy, MA	M
Merrimack Coll, MA	M
Middlebury Coll, VT	M
Mount Ida Coll, MA	M
Nichols Coll, MA	M
Northeastern U, MA	M(s)
Ohio Wesleyan U, OH	M
Plymouth State U, NH	M
Sacred Heart U, CT	M(s)
Salve Regina U, RI	M
Southern Connecticut State U, CT	M(s)
Southern Methodist U, TX	M(s)
Stonehill Coll, MA	M(s)
Trinity Coll, CT	M
Tufts U, MA	M
United States Coast Guard Academy, CT	M
U of Charleston, WV	M(s)
U of Connecticut, CT	M(s)
U of Maine, ME	M(s)
U of Massachusetts Amherst, MA	M(s)
U of Massachusetts Dartmouth, MA	M
U of New Hampshire, NH	M(s)
U of New Haven, CT	M(s)
U of Rhode Island, RI	M(s)
Utica Coll, NY	M
Wesleyan U, CT	M
Western Connecticut State U, CT	M
Western New England Coll, MA	M
Westfield State Coll, MA	M
Williams Coll, MA	M
Worcester Polytechnic Inst, MA	M
Worcester State Coll, MA	M
Yale U, CT	M

Golf

Amherst Coll, MA	M, W
Anna Maria Coll, MA	M
Assumption Coll, MA	M

M—for men; W—for women; (s)—scholarship offered

College	
Babson Coll, MA	M
Barry U, FL	M(s), W(s)
Bates Coll, ME	M, W
Becker Coll, MA	M
Bentley U, MA	M
Boston Coll, MA	M(s), W(s)
Bowdoin Coll, ME	M, W
Brandeis U, MA	M
Brown U, RI	M, W
Bryant U, RI	M, W
Castleton State Coll, VT	M
Central Connecticut State U, CT	M(s), W(s)
Clarkson U, NY	M
Colby Coll, ME	M, W
Coll of the Holy Cross, MA	M, W
Daniel Webster Coll, NH	M, W
Dartmouth Coll, NH	M, W
Emerson Coll, MA	M, W
Emmanuel Coll, MA	M
Endicott Coll, MA	M, W
Fairfield U, CT	M(s), W(s)
Franklin Pierce U, NH	M, W
Gordon Coll, MA	M, W
Green Mountain Coll, VT	M
Grove City Coll, PA	M, W
Harvard U, MA	M, W
Hofstra U, NY	M(s), W(s)
Husson U, ME	M, W
Johnson State Coll, VT	M
Massachusetts Coll of Liberal Arts, MA	M
Massachusetts Inst of Technology, MA	M
Messiah Coll, PA	M
Middlebury Coll, VT	M, W
Mitchell Coll, CT	M, W
Mount Holyoke Coll, MA	W
Newbury Coll, MA	M, W
Nichols Coll, MA	M
Ohio Wesleyan U, OH	M
Providence Coll, RI	M, W
Quinnipiac U, CT	M(s)
Rhode Island Coll, RI	M
Rivier Coll, NH	M, W
Sacred Heart U, CT	M(s), W(s)
Saint Michael's Coll, VT	M
Salem State Coll, MA	M
Southern Methodist U, TX	M(s), W(s)
Southern New Hampshire U, NH	M
Stonehill Coll, MA	M, W
Suffolk U, MA	M
Trinity Coll, CT	M
Tufts U, MA	M
United States Coast Guard Academy, CT	M, W
U of Charleston, WV	M(s)
U of Connecticut, CT	M(s)
U of Hartford, CT	M(s), W(s)
The U of Maine at Augusta, ME	M, W
U of Maine at Farmington, ME	M
U of Maine at Fort Kent, ME	M, W
U of Maine at Presque Isle, ME	M
U of Massachusetts Dartmouth, MA	M
U of New England, ME	M
U of New Hampshire, NH	M, W
U of New Haven, CT	M(s)
U of Rhode Island, RI	M(s)
U of San Francisco, CA	M(s), W(s)
U of Southern Maine, ME	M, W
Utica Coll, NY	M, W
Vermont Tech Coll, VT	M, W
Wellesley Coll, MA	W
Wentworth Inst of Technology, MA	M
Wesleyan U, CT	M
Western New England Coll, MA	M
Westfield State Coll, MA	M, W
Williams Coll, MA	M, W
Worcester State Coll, MA	M
Yale U, CT	M, W

Gymnastics

College	
Brown U, RI	W
Dartmouth Coll, NH	M, W
Massachusetts Inst of Technology, MA	M, W
Rhode Island Coll, RI	W
Southern Connecticut State U, CT	W(s)
U of Bridgeport, CT	W(s)
U of New Hampshire, NH	W(s)
U of Vermont, VT	M, W
Yale U, CT	W

Ice Hockey

College	
Amherst Coll, MA	M, W
Assumption Coll, MA	M
Babson Coll, MA	M, W
Bates Coll, ME	M, W
Becker Coll, MA	M
Bentley U, MA	M(s)
Boston Coll, MA	M(s), W(s)
Bowdoin Coll, ME	M, W
Brown U, RI	M, W
Bryant U, RI	M
Castleton State Coll, VT	M, W
Clarkson U, NY	M(s), W(s)
Colby Coll, ME	M, W
Coll of the Holy Cross, MA	M(s), W(s)
Connecticut Coll, CT	M, W
Curry Coll, MA	M
Daniel Webster Coll, NH	M, W
Dartmouth Coll, NH	M, W
Emerson Coll, MA	M
Endicott Coll, MA	M
Fairfield U, CT	M, W
Fitchburg State Coll, MA	M
Framingham State Coll, MA	M
Franklin Pierce U, NH	M
Harvard U, MA	M, W
Massachusetts Inst of Technology, MA	M, W
Merrimack Coll, MA	M(s)
Middlebury Coll, VT	M, W
New England Coll, NH	M, W
Nichols Coll, MA	M, W
Northeastern U, MA	M(s), W(s)
Ohio Wesleyan U, OH	M, W
Plymouth State U, NH	M, W
Providence Coll, RI	M(s), W(s)
Quinnipiac U, CT	M(s), W(s)
Sacred Heart U, CT	M(s), W
Saint Michael's Coll, VT	M, W
Salem State Coll, MA	M
Salve Regina U, RI	M, W
Southern Methodist U, TX	M
Southern New Hampshire U, NH	M
Stonehill Coll, MA	M
Suffolk U, MA	M
Trinity Coll, CT	M, W
Tufts U, MA	M
United States Coast Guard Academy, CT	M
U of Connecticut, CT	M(s), W(s)
U of Maine, ME	M(s), W(s)
U of Maine at Farmington, ME	M
U of Massachusetts Amherst, MA	M(s)
U of Massachusetts Boston, MA	M
U of Massachusetts Dartmouth, MA	M
U of Massachusetts Lowell, MA	M(s)
U of New Hampshire, NH	M(s), W(s)
U of Rhode Island, RI	M, W
U of Southern Maine, ME	M, W
U of Vermont, VT	M(s), W(s)
Utica Coll, NY	M, W
Wentworth Inst of Technology, MA	M
Wesleyan U, CT	M, W
Western New England Coll, MA	M
Westfield State Coll, MA	M
Williams Coll, MA	M, W
Worcester State Coll, MA	M
Yale U, CT	M, W

Lacrosse

College	
Amherst Coll, MA	M, W
Anna Maria Coll, MA	M, W
Assumption Coll, MA	M, W
Babson Coll, MA	M, W
Bates Coll, ME	M, W
Becker Coll, MA	M, W
Bentley U, MA	M(s), W(s)
Boston Coll, MA	W(s)
Bowdoin Coll, ME	M, W
Brandeis U, MA	M, W
Bridgewater State Coll, MA	M, W
Brown U, RI	M, W
Bryant U, RI	M, W
Castleton State Coll, VT	M, W
Central Connecticut State U, CT	M, W(s)
Clarkson U, NY	M, W
Clark U, MA	M
Colby Coll, ME	M, W
Coll of the Holy Cross, MA	M, W
Connecticut Coll, CT	M, W
Curry Coll, MA	M, W
Daniel Webster Coll, NH	M, W
Dartmouth Coll, NH	M, W
Eastern Connecticut State U, CT	M, W
Emerson Coll, MA	M, W
Endicott Coll, MA	M, W
Fairfield U, CT	M(s), W(s)
Fitchburg State Coll, MA	W
Framingham State Coll, MA	W
Franklin Pierce U, NH	M, W
Gordon Coll, MA	M, W
Green Mountain Coll, VT	M, W
Harvard U, MA	M, W
Hofstra U, NY	M(s), W(s)
Husson U, ME	M, W
Johnson State Coll, VT	W
Keene State Coll, NH	M, W
Lasell Coll, MA	M, W
Lyndon State Coll, VT	M
Maine Maritime Academy, ME	M
Massachusetts Inst of Technology, MA	M, W
Massachusetts Maritime Academy, MA	M
Merrimack Coll, MA	M, W(s)
Messiah Coll, PA	M, W
Middlebury Coll, VT	M, W
Mitchell Coll, CT	M
Mount Holyoke Coll, MA	W
Mount Ida Coll, MA	M, W
New England Coll, NH	M, W
Nichols Coll, MA	M, W
Ohio Wesleyan U, OH	M, W
Plymouth State U, NH	M, W
Providence Coll, RI	M(s)
Quinnipiac U, CT	M(s), W(s)
Regis Coll, MA	M, W
Rhode Island Coll, RI	W
Roger Williams U, RI	M, W
Sacred Heart U, CT	M(s), W(s)
Saint Joseph Coll, CT	W
Saint Michael's Coll, VT	M, W
Salve Regina U, RI	M, W
Smith Coll, MA	W
Southern Connecticut State U, CT	W(s)
Southern Methodist U, TX	M
Southern New Hampshire U, NH	M(s), W(s)
Stonehill Coll, MA	M, W(s)
Trinity Coll, CT	M, W
Tufts U, MA	M, W
United States Coast Guard Academy, CT	M, W
U of Bridgeport, CT	W

Lacrosse

U of Connecticut, CT	W
U of Hartford, CT	M(s)
U of Maine at Farmington, ME	M, W
U of Maine at Machias, ME	M, W
U of Massachusetts Amherst, MA	M(s), W(s)
U of Massachusetts Boston, MA	M
U of Massachusetts Dartmouth, MA	M, W
U of New England, ME	M, W
U of New Hampshire, NH	M, W(s)
U of New Haven, CT	W(s)
U of Rhode Island, RI	M, W
U of Southern Maine, ME	M, W
U of Vermont, VT	M(s), W(s)
Utica Coll, NY	M, W
Wellesley Coll, MA	W
Wentworth Inst of Technology, MA	M
Wesleyan U, CT	M, W
Western Connecticut State U, CT	M, W
Western New England Coll, MA	M, W
Westfield State Coll, MA	M, W
Wheaton Coll, MA	M, W
Williams Coll, MA	M, W
Worcester State Coll, MA	W
Yale U, CT	M, W

Racquetball

Bard Coll at Simon's Rock, MA	M, W
Bryant U, RI	M, W
Nichols Coll, MA	M, W
Providence Coll, RI	M, W
U of Hartford, CT	M, W

Riflery

Bowdoin Coll, ME	M, W
Massachusetts Inst of Technology, MA	M, W
Massachusetts Maritime Academy, MA	M, W
United States Coast Guard Academy, CT	M, W
U of New Hampshire, NH	M, W
Wentworth Inst of Technology, MA	M, W
Yale U, CT	M, W

Rock Climbing

Keene State Coll, NH	M, W
Landmark Coll, VT	M, W
Marlboro Coll, VT	M, W
U of New Hampshire, NH	M, W

Rugby

Amherst Coll, MA	M, W
Babson Coll, MA	M, W
Bates Coll, ME	M, W
Bowdoin Coll, ME	M, W
Brandeis U, MA	M, W
Brown U, RI	M, W
Bryant U, RI	M, W
Castleton State Coll, VT	M, W
Colby Coll, ME	M, W
Connecticut Coll, CT	W
Dartmouth Coll, NH	M, W
Fairfield U, CT	M, W
Nichols Coll, MA	M, W
Ohio Wesleyan U, OH	M, W
Providence Coll, RI	M, W
Roger Williams U, RI	M
Saint Michael's Coll, VT	M, W
Salve Regina U, RI	M
Southern Connecticut State U, CT	M, W
Southern Methodist U, TX	M, W
Stonehill Coll, MA	M, W
Trinity Coll, CT	M, W
United States Coast Guard Academy, CT	M, W
U of Hartford, CT	M, W
U of Massachusetts Dartmouth, MA	M, W
U of New Hampshire, NH	M, W
U of Rhode Island, RI	M, W

U of Vermont, VT	M, W
Wellesley Coll, MA	W
Wentworth Inst of Technology, MA	M, W
Wesleyan U, CT	M, W
Williams Coll, MA	M, W
Yale U, CT	M, W

Sailing

Amherst Coll, MA	M, W
Bates Coll, ME	M, W
Boston Coll, MA	M, W
Bowdoin Coll, ME	M, W
Brandeis U, MA	M, W
Brown U, RI	M, W
Colby Coll, ME	M, W
Connecticut Coll, CT	M, W
Dartmouth Coll, NH	M, W
Endicott Coll, MA	M, W
Fairfield U, CT	M, W
Harvard U, MA	M, W
Maine Maritime Academy, ME	M, W
Massachusetts Inst of Technology, MA	M, W
Massachusetts Maritime Academy, MA	M, W
Mitchell Coll, CT	M, W
Ohio Wesleyan U, OH	M, W
Providence Coll, RI	M, W
Roger Williams U, RI	M, W
Salve Regina U, RI	M, W
Simmons Coll, MA	W
Trinity Coll, CT	M, W
Tufts U, MA	M, W
United States Coast Guard Academy, CT	M, W
U of New Hampshire, NH	M, W
U of Rhode Island, RI	M, W
U of Southern Maine, ME	M, W
U of Vermont, VT	M, W
Wellesley Coll, MA	W
Wesleyan U, CT	M, W
Williams Coll, MA	M, W
Yale U, CT	M, W

Skiing (Cross-Country)

Bates Coll, ME	M, W
Bowdoin Coll, ME	M, W
Clarkson U, NY	M, W
Colby Coll, ME	M, W
Connecticut Coll, CT	M, W
Dartmouth Coll, NH	M, W
Harvard U, MA	M, W
Massachusetts Inst of Technology, MA	M, W
Middlebury Coll, VT	M, W
Saint Michael's Coll, VT	M, W
U of Maine at Fort Kent, ME	M, W
U of New Hampshire, NH	M(s), W(s)
U of Vermont, VT	M(s), W(s)
Wesleyan U, CT	M, W
Williams Coll, MA	M, W
Yale U, CT	M, W

Skiing (Downhill)

Amherst Coll, MA	M, W
Babson Coll, MA	M, W
Bates Coll, ME	M, W
Boston Coll, MA	M, W
Bowdoin Coll, ME	M, W
Brandeis U, MA	M, W
Brown U, RI	M, W
Castleton State Coll, VT	M, W
Clarkson U, NY	M, W
Colby Coll, ME	M, W
Connecticut Coll, CT	M, W
Dartmouth Coll, NH	M, W
Fairfield U, CT	M, W
Green Mountain Coll, VT	M, W
Harvard U, MA	M, W

Keene State Coll, NH	M, W
Massachusetts Inst of Technology, MA	M, W
Middlebury Coll, VT	M, W
Plymouth State U, NH	M, W
Saint Michael's Coll, VT	M, W
Smith Coll, MA	W
Trinity Coll, CT	M, W
U of Maine at Fort Kent, ME	M, W
U of Massachusetts Amherst, MA	M(s), W(s)
U of New Hampshire, NH	M(s), W(s)
U of Rhode Island, RI	M, W
U of Vermont, VT	M(s), W(s)
Wellesley Coll, MA	W
Wesleyan U, CT	M, W
Williams Coll, MA	M, W
Worcester State Coll, MA	M, W
Yale U, CT	M, W

Soccer

Albertus Magnus Coll, CT	M, W
Amherst Coll, MA	M, W
Anna Maria Coll, MA	M, W
The Art Inst of Boston at Lesley U, MA	M, W
Assumption Coll, MA	M, W
Babson Coll, MA	M, W
Bard Coll at Simon's Rock, MA	M, W
Barry U, FL	M(s), W(s)
Bates Coll, ME	M, W
Bay Path Coll, MA	W
Becker Coll, MA	M, W
Benjamin Franklin Inst of Technology, MA	M
Bennington Coll, VT	M, W
Bentley U, MA	M(s), W(s)
Boston Coll, MA	M(s), W(s)
Bowdoin Coll, ME	M, W
Brandeis U, MA	W
Bridgewater State Coll, MA	M, W
Brown U, RI	M, W
Bryant U, RI	M, W
Castleton State Coll, VT	M, W
Central Connecticut State U, CT	M(s), W(s)
Clarkson U, NY	M, W
Clark U, MA	M, W
Colby Coll, ME	M, W
Coll of St. Joseph, VT	M, W
Coll of the Holy Cross, MA	M(s), W(s)
Connecticut Coll, CT	M, W
Curry Coll, MA	M, W
Daniel Webster Coll, NH	M, W
Dartmouth Coll, NH	M, W
Eastern Connecticut State U, CT	M, W
Emerson Coll, MA	M, W
Emmanuel Coll, MA	M, W
Endicott Coll, MA	M, W
Fairfield U, CT	M(s), W(s)
Fisher Coll, MA	M, W
Fitchburg State Coll, MA	M, W
Framingham State Coll, MA	M, W
Franklin Pierce U, NH	M(s), W(s)
Franklin W. Olin Coll of Engineering, MA	M, W
Gordon Coll, MA	M, W
Green Mountain Coll, VT	M, W
Grove City Coll, PA	M, W
Hampshire Coll, MA	M, W
Harvard U, MA	M, W
Hofstra U, NY	M(s), W(s)
Husson U, ME	M, W
Johnson State Coll, VT	M, W
Keene State Coll, NH	M, W
Landmark Coll, VT	M, W
Lasell Coll, MA	M, W
Lesley U, MA	M, W

M—for men; W—for women; (s)—scholarship offered

Lyndon State Coll, VT	M, W
Maine Maritime Academy, ME	M, W
Marlboro Coll, VT	M, W
Massachusetts Coll of Liberal Arts, MA	M, W
Massachusetts Inst of Technology, MA	M, W
Massachusetts Maritime Academy, MA	M
Merrimack Coll, MA	M, W(s)
Messiah Coll, PA	M, W
Middlebury Coll, VT	M, W
Mitchell Coll, CT	M, W
Mount Holyoke Coll, MA	W
Mount Ida Coll, MA	M, W
Newbury Coll, MA	M
New England Coll, NH	M, W
Nichols Coll, MA	M, W
Northeastern U, MA	M(s), W(s)
Ohio Wesleyan U, OH	M, W
Plymouth State U, NH	M, W
Providence Coll, RI	M(s), W(s)
Quinnipiac U, CT	M(s), W(s)
Regis Coll, MA	M, W
Rhode Island Coll, RI	M, W
Rivier Coll, NH	M, W
Roger Williams U, RI	M, W
Sacred Heart U, CT	M(s), W(s)
Saint Joseph Coll, CT	W
Saint Michael's Coll, VT	M, W
Salem State Coll, MA	M, W
Salve Regina U, RI	M, W
Simmons Coll, MA	W
Smith Coll, MA	W
Southern Connecticut State U, CT	M(s), W(s)
Southern Methodist U, TX	M(s), W(s)
Southern New Hampshire U, NH	M(s), W(s)
Stonehill Coll, MA	M(s), W(s)
Suffolk U, MA	M
Trinity Coll, CT	M, W
Tufts U, MA	M, W
United States Coast Guard Academy, CT	M, W
U of Bridgeport, CT	M(s), W(s)
U of Charleston, WV	M(s), W(s)
U of Connecticut, CT	M(s), W(s)
U of Hartford, CT	M(s), W(s)
U of Maine, ME	M(s), W(s)
The U of Maine at Augusta, ME	W(s)
U of Maine at Farmington, ME	M, W
U of Maine at Fort Kent, ME	M, W
U of Maine at Machias, ME	M, W
U of Maine at Presque Isle, ME	M, W
U of Massachusetts Amherst, MA	M(s), W(s)
U of Massachusetts Boston, MA	M, W
U of Massachusetts Dartmouth, MA	M, W
U of Massachusetts Lowell, MA	M
U of New England, ME	M, W
U of New Hampshire, NH	M(s), W(s)
U of New Haven, CT	M(s), W(s)
U of Rhode Island, RI	M(s), W(s)
U of San Francisco, CA	M(s), W(s)
U of Southern Maine, ME	M, W
U of Vermont, VT	M(s), W(s)
Utica Coll, NY	M, W
Vermont Tech Coll, VT	M, W
Wellesley Coll, MA	W
Wentworth Inst of Technology, MA	M, W
Wesleyan U, CT	M, W
Western Connecticut State U, CT	M, W
Western New England Coll, MA	M, W
Westfield State Coll, MA	M, W
Wheaton Coll, MA	M, W
Wheelock Coll, MA	M, W
Williams Coll, MA	M, W
Worcester Polytechnic Inst, MA	M, W
Worcester State Coll, MA	M, W
Yale U, CT	M, W

Softball

Albertus Magnus Coll, CT	W
Amherst Coll, MA	W
Anna Maria Coll, MA	W
The Art Inst of Boston at Lesley U, MA	W
Assumption Coll, MA	W
Babson Coll, MA	W
Barry U, FL	W(s)
Bates Coll, ME	W
Bay Path Coll, MA	W
Becker Coll, MA	W
Bentley U, MA	W(s)
Boston Coll, MA	W(s)
Bowdoin Coll, ME	W
Brandeis U, MA	W
Bridgewater State Coll, MA	W
Brown U, RI	W
Bryant U, RI	W
Castleton State Coll, VT	W
Central Connecticut State U, CT	W(s)
Clark U, MA	W
Colby Coll, ME	W
Coll of St. Joseph, VT	W
Coll of the Holy Cross, MA	W
Curry Coll, MA	W
Daniel Webster Coll, NH	W
Dartmouth Coll, NH	W
Eastern Connecticut State U, CT	W
Emerson Coll, MA	W
Emmanuel Coll, MA	W
Endicott Coll, MA	W
Fairfield U, CT	W(s)
Fisher Coll, MA	W
Fitchburg State Coll, MA	W
Framingham State Coll, MA	W
Franklin Pierce U, NH	W(s)
Gordon Coll, MA	W
Green Mountain Coll, VT	W
Grove City Coll, PA	W
Harvard U, MA	W
Hofstra U, NY	W(s)
Husson U, ME	W
Johnson State Coll, VT	W
Keene State Coll, NH	W
Landmark Coll, VT	W
Lasell Coll, MA	W
Lesley U, MA	W
Lyndon State Coll, VT	W
Maine Maritime Academy, ME	W
Massachusetts Coll of Liberal Arts, MA	W
Massachusetts Inst of Technology, MA	W
Massachusetts Maritime Academy, MA	W
Merrimack Coll, MA	W(s)
Messiah Coll, PA	W
Middlebury Coll, VT	W
Mitchell Coll, CT	W
Mount Ida Coll, MA	W
Newbury Coll, MA	W
New England Coll, NH	W
Nichols Coll, MA	W
Ohio Wesleyan U, OH	W
Plymouth State U, NH	W
Providence Coll, RI	W(s)
Quinnipiac U, CT	W(s)
Regis Coll, MA	W
Rhode Island Coll, RI	W
Rivier Coll, NH	W
Roger Williams U, RI	W
Sacred Heart U, CT	W(s)
Saint Joseph Coll, CT	W
Saint Michael's Coll, VT	W
Salem State Coll, MA	W
Salve Regina U, RI	W
Simmons Coll, MA	W
Smith Coll, MA	W

Southern Connecticut State U, CT	W(s)
Southern New Hampshire U, NH	W(s)
Stonehill Coll, MA	W(s)
Suffolk U, MA	W
Trinity Coll, CT	W
Tufts U, MA	W
United States Coast Guard Academy, CT	W
U of Bridgeport, CT	W(s)
U of Charleston, WV	W(s)
U of Connecticut, CT	W(s)
U of Hartford, CT	W(s)
U of Maine, ME	W(s)
U of Maine at Farmington, ME	W
U of Maine at Presque Isle, ME	W
U of Massachusetts Amherst, MA	W(s)
U of Massachusetts Boston, MA	W
U of Massachusetts Dartmouth, MA	W
U of New England, ME	W
U of New Hampshire, NH	W
U of New Haven, CT	W(s)
U of Rhode Island, RI	W(s)
U of San Francisco, CA	M, W
U of Southern Maine, ME	W
Utica Coll, NY	W
Wellesley Coll, MA	W
Wentworth Inst of Technology, MA	W
Wesleyan U, CT	W
Western Connecticut State U, CT	W
Western New England Coll, MA	W
Westfield State Coll, MA	W
Wheaton Coll, MA	W
Wheelock Coll, MA	W
Williams Coll, MA	W
Worcester Polytechnic Inst, MA	W
Worcester State Coll, MA	W
Yale U, CT	W

Squash

Amherst Coll, MA	M, W
Bates Coll, ME	M, W
Bowdoin Coll, ME	M, W
Brandeis U, MA	M
Brown U, RI	M, W
Bryant U, RI	M, W
Colby Coll, ME	M, W
Connecticut Coll, CT	M, W
Dartmouth Coll, NH	M, W
Harvard U, MA	M, W
Massachusetts Inst of Technology, MA	M
Middlebury Coll, VT	W
Mount Holyoke Coll, MA	W
Smith Coll, MA	W
Trinity Coll, CT	M, W
Tufts U, MA	M, W
U of Hartford, CT	M, W
Wellesley Coll, MA	W
Wesleyan U, CT	M, W
Williams Coll, MA	M, W
Yale U, CT	M, W

Swimming and Diving

Amherst Coll, MA	M, W
Assumption Coll, MA	W
Babson Coll, MA	M, W
Bard Coll at Simon's Rock, MA	M, W
Bates Coll, ME	M, W
Bentley U, MA	M(s), W(s)
Boston Coll, MA	M(s), W(s)
Bowdoin Coll, ME	M, W
Brandeis U, MA	M, W
Bridgewater State Coll, MA	M, W
Brown U, RI	M, W
Bryant U, RI	M, W
Central Connecticut State U, CT	W(s)
Clarkson U, NY	M, W
Clark U, MA	M, W

College	
Colby Coll, ME	M, W
Coll of the Holy Cross, MA	M, W
Connecticut Coll, CT	M, W
Dartmouth Coll, NH	M, W
Eastern Connecticut State U, CT	W
Fairfield U, CT	M(s), W(s)
Gordon Coll, MA	M, W
Grove City Coll, PA	M, W
Harvard U, MA	M, W
Husson U, ME	W
Keene State Coll, NH	M, W
Massachusetts Inst of Technology, MA	M, W
Messiah Coll, PA	M, W
Middlebury Coll, VT	M, W
Mount Holyoke Coll, MA	W
Northeastern U, MA	W(s)
Ohio Wesleyan U, OH	M, W
Plymouth State U, NH	W
Providence Coll, RI	M(s), W(s)
Regis Coll, MA	M, W
Roger Williams U, RI	M, W
Sacred Heart U, CT	W(s)
Saint Joseph Coll, CT	W
Saint Michael's Coll, VT	M, W
Simmons Coll, MA	W
Smith Coll, MA	W
Southern Connecticut State U, CT	M(s), W(s)
Southern Methodist U, TX	M(s), W(s)
Trinity Coll, CT	M, W
Tufts U, MA	M, W
United States Coast Guard Academy, CT	M, W
U of Bridgeport, CT	M, W(s)
U of Charleston, WV	M(s), W(s)
U of Connecticut, CT	M(s), W(s)
U of Maine, ME	M, W(s)
U of Massachusetts Amherst, MA	M(s), W(s)
U of Massachusetts Dartmouth, MA	M, W
U of Massachusetts Lowell, MA	M(s)
U of New England, ME	W
U of New Hampshire, NH	W(s)
U of Rhode Island, RI	W(s)
U of Vermont, VT	W(s)
Utica Coll, NY	M, W
Wellesley Coll, MA	W
Wesleyan U, CT	M, W
Western Connecticut State U, CT	W
Western New England Coll, MA	W
Westfield State Coll, MA	W
Wheaton Coll, MA	M, W
Williams Coll, MA	M, W
Worcester Polytechnic Inst, MA	M, W
Yale U, CT	M, W

Table Tennis

College	
Dartmouth Coll, NH	M, W
U of Vermont, VT	M, W
Yale U, CT	M

Tennis

College	
Albertus Magnus Coll, CT	M, W
Amherst Coll, MA	M, W
Anna Maria Coll, MA	M, W
Assumption Coll, MA	M, W
Babson Coll, MA	M, W
Barry U, FL	M(s), W(s)
Bates Coll, ME	M, W
Bay Path Coll, MA	W
Becker Coll, MA	M, W
Bentley U, MA	M(s), W(s)
Boston Coll, MA	M(s), W(s)
Bowdoin Coll, ME	M, W
Brandeis U, MA	M, W
Bridgewater State Coll, MA	M, W
Brown U, RI	M, W
Bryant U, RI	M, W
Castleton State Coll, VT	M, W
Clark U, MA	M, W
Colby Coll, ME	M, W
Coll of the Holy Cross, MA	M, W
Connecticut Coll, CT	M, W
Curry Coll, MA	M, W
Dartmouth Coll, NH	M, W
Emerson Coll, MA	M, W
Emmanuel Coll, MA	W
Endicott Coll, MA	M, W
Fairfield U, CT	M(s), W(s)
Franklin Pierce U, NH	M(s), W(s)
Gordon Coll, MA	M, W
Green Mountain Coll, VT	M
Grove City Coll, PA	M, W
Harvard U, MA	M, W
Hofstra U, NY	M(s), W(s)
Husson U, ME	W
Johnson State Coll, VT	M, W
Lyndon State Coll, VT	M, W
Massachusetts Coll of Liberal Arts, MA	W
Massachusetts Inst of Technology, MA	M, W
Merrimack Coll, MA	M, W(s)
Messiah Coll, PA	M, W
Middlebury Coll, VT	M, W
Mount Holyoke Coll, MA	W
Mount Ida Coll, MA	W
Newbury Coll, MA	M, W
Nichols Coll, MA	M, W
Northeastern U, MA	M(s)
Ohio Wesleyan U, OH	M, W
Plymouth State U, NH	W
Providence Coll, RI	W(s)
Quinnipiac U, CT	M(s), W(s)
Regis Coll, MA	W
Rhode Island Coll, RI	M, W
Roger Williams U, RI	M, W
Sacred Heart U, CT	M(s), W(s)
Saint Joseph Coll, CT	W
Saint Michael's Coll, VT	M, W
Salem State Coll, MA	M, W
Salve Regina U, RI	M, W
Simmons Coll, MA	W
Smith Coll, MA	W
Southern Methodist U, TX	M(s), W(s)
Southern New Hampshire U, NH	M(s), W(s)
Stonehill Coll, MA	M(s), W(s)
Suffolk U, MA	M, W
Trinity Coll, CT	M, W
Tufts U, MA	M, W
United States Coast Guard Academy, CT	M, W
U of Charleston, WV	M(s), W(s)
U of Connecticut, CT	M(s), W(s)
U of Hartford, CT	M(s), W(s)
U of Maine at Farmington, ME	M, W
U of Massachusetts Amherst, MA	W(s)
U of Massachusetts Boston, MA	M, W
U of Massachusetts Dartmouth, MA	M, W
U of Massachusetts Lowell, MA	M(s), W(s)
U of New Hampshire, NH	M, W(s)
U of New Haven, CT	W(s)
U of Rhode Island, RI	W(s)
U of San Francisco, CA	M(s), W(s)
U of Southern Maine, ME	M, W
Utica Coll, NY	M, W
Wellesley Coll, MA	W
Wentworth Inst of Technology, MA	M, W
Wesleyan U, CT	M, W
Western Connecticut State U, CT	M, W
Western New England Coll, MA	M, W
Wheaton Coll, MA	M, W
Wheelock Coll, MA	M
Williams Coll, MA	M, W
Worcester State Coll, MA	W
Yale U, CT	M, W

Track and Field

College	
Amherst Coll, MA	M, W
Assumption Coll, MA	M, W
Babson Coll, MA	M, W
Bates Coll, ME	M, W
Bentley U, MA	M(s), W(s)
Boston Coll, MA	M(s), W(s)
Bowdoin Coll, ME	M, W
Brandeis U, MA	M, W
Bridgewater State Coll, MA	M, W
Brown U, RI	M, W
Bryant U, RI	M, W
Central Connecticut State U, CT	M(s), W(s)
Colby Coll, ME	M, W
Coll of the Holy Cross, MA	M, W
Connecticut Coll, CT	M, W
Dartmouth Coll, NH	M, W
Eastern Connecticut State U, CT	M, W
Emerson Coll, MA	W
Emmanuel Coll, MA	W
Fairfield U, CT	M, W
Fitchburg State Coll, MA	M, W
Gordon Coll, MA	M, W
Grove City Coll, PA	M, W
Harvard U, MA	M, W
Keene State Coll, NH	M, W
Lasell Coll, MA	M, W
Massachusetts Inst of Technology, MA	M, W
Massachusetts Maritime Academy, MA	M, W
Merrimack Coll, MA	M, W
Messiah Coll, PA	M, W
Middlebury Coll, VT	M, W
Mount Holyoke Coll, MA	W
Nichols Coll, MA	M, W
Northeastern U, MA	M(s), W(s)
Ohio Wesleyan U, OH	M, W
Providence Coll, RI	M(s), W(s)
Quinnipiac U, CT	M(s), W(s)
Regis Coll, MA	M, W
Rhode Island Coll, RI	M, W
Roger Williams U, RI	M, W
Sacred Heart U, CT	M(s), W(s)
Salem State Coll, MA	M, W
Salve Regina U, RI	W
Simmons Coll, MA	W
Smith Coll, MA	W
Southern Connecticut State U, CT	M(s), W(s)
Southern Methodist U, TX	W
Stonehill Coll, MA	M(s), W(s)
Trinity Coll, CT	M, W
Tufts U, MA	M, W
United States Coast Guard Academy, CT	M, W
U of Charleston, WV	M(s), W(s)
U of Connecticut, CT	M(s), W(s)
U of Hartford, CT	M, W
U of Maine, ME	M(s), W(s)
U of Massachusetts Amherst, MA	M(s), W(s)
U of Massachusetts Boston, MA	M, W
U of Massachusetts Dartmouth, MA	M, W
U of Massachusetts Lowell, MA	M(s), W(s)
U of New Hampshire, NH	M(s), W(s)
U of New Haven, CT	M(s), W(s)
U of Rhode Island, RI	M(s), W(s)
U of San Francisco, CA	W(s)
U of Southern Maine, ME	M, W
U of Vermont, VT	M(s), W(s)
Wellesley Coll, MA	W
Wesleyan U, CT	M, W
Westfield State Coll, MA	M, W
Wheaton Coll, MA	M, W
Williams Coll, MA	M, W

M—for men; W—for women; (s)—scholarship offered

Worcester Polytechnic Inst, MA	M, W
Worcester State Coll, MA	M, W
Yale U, CT	M, W

Ultimate Frisbee

Amherst Coll, MA	M, W
Bates Coll, ME	M, W
Bowdoin Coll, ME	M, W
Bryant U, RI	M, W
Burlington Coll, VT	M, W
Colby Coll, ME	M, W
Connecticut Coll, CT	M, W
Dartmouth Coll, NH	M, W
Franklin W. Olin Coll of Engineering, MA	M, W
Hampshire Coll, MA	M, W
Ohio Wesleyan U, OH	M, W
Southern Connecticut State U, CT	M, W
Stonehill Coll, MA	M, W
Trinity Coll, CT	M, W
U of Maine at Farmington, ME	M, W
U of New Hampshire, NH	M, W
U of Vermont, VT	M, W
Wellesley Coll, MA	W
Yale U, CT	M, W

Volleyball

Albertus Magnus Coll, CT	M, W
Amherst Coll, MA	M, W
Anna Maria Coll, MA	W
The Art Inst of Boston at Lesley U, MA	M, W
Assumption Coll, MA	W
Babson Coll, MA	W
Barry U, FL	W(s)
Bates Coll, ME	M, W
Bay Path Coll, MA	W
Becker Coll, MA	W
Bentley U, MA	W(s)
Boston Coll, MA	W(s)
Bowdoin Coll, ME	M, W
Brandeis U, MA	W
Bridgewater State Coll, MA	W
Brown U, RI	M, W
Bryant U, RI	W
Burlington Coll, VT	M, W
Castleton State Coll, VT	W
Central Connecticut State U, CT	W(s)
Clarkson U, NY	M, W
Clark U, MA	W
Colby Coll, ME	M, W
Coll of the Holy Cross, MA	W
Connecticut Coll, CT	M, W
Daniel Webster Coll, NH	M, W
Dartmouth Coll, NH	M, W
Eastern Connecticut State U, CT	W
Emerson Coll, MA	M, W
Emmanuel Coll, MA	M, W
Endicott Coll, MA	M, W
Fairfield U, CT	M, W(s)
Framingham State Coll, MA	W
Franklin Pierce U, NH	W(s)
Gordon Coll, MA	W

Green Mountain Coll, VT	W
Grove City Coll, PA	W
Harvard U, MA	M, W
Hofstra U, NY	W(s)
Husson U, ME	W
Johnson State Coll, VT	W
Keene State Coll, NH	W
Lasell Coll, MA	M, W
Lesley U, MA	M, W
Lyndon State Coll, VT	W
Maine Maritime Academy, ME	W
Massachusetts Inst of Technology, MA	M, W
Massachusetts Maritime Academy, MA	W
Merrimack Coll, MA	M, W(s)
Messiah Coll, PA	W
Middlebury Coll, VT	W
Mitchell Coll, CT	W
Mount Holyoke Coll, MA	W
Mount Ida Coll, MA	M, W
Newbury Coll, MA	M, W
Nichols Coll, MA	M, W
Northeastern U, MA	W(s)
Ohio Wesleyan U, OH	M, W
Plymouth State U, NH	M, W
Providence Coll, RI	M, W(s)
Quinnipiac U, CT	W(s)
Regis Coll, MA	M, W
Rhode Island Coll, RI	W
Rivier Coll, NH	M, W
Roger Williams U, RI	M, W
Sacred Heart U, CT	M(s), W(s)
Saint Joseph Coll, CT	W
Saint Michael's Coll, VT	W
Salem State Coll, MA	W
Salve Regina U, RI	W
Simmons Coll, MA	W
Smith Coll, MA	W
Southern Connecticut State U, CT	W(s)
Southern Methodist U, TX	W(s)
Southern New Hampshire U, NH	W(s)
Stonehill Coll, MA	M, W(s)
Suffolk U, MA	W
Trinity Coll, CT	W
Tufts U, MA	W
United States Coast Guard Academy, CT	W
U of Bridgeport, CT	W(s)
U of Charleston, WV	W(s)
U of Connecticut, CT	W(s)
U of Hartford, CT	M, W(s)
U of Maine, ME	W(s)
U of Maine at Farmington, ME	W
U of Maine at Fort Kent, ME	W
U of Maine at Machias, ME	W
U of Maine at Presque Isle, ME	W
U of Massachusetts Boston, MA	W
U of Massachusetts Dartmouth, MA	W
U of Massachusetts Lowell, MA	W(s)
U of New England, ME	W
U of New Hampshire, NH	M, W(s)
U of New Haven, CT	M(s), W(s)
U of Rhode Island, RI	M, W(s)
U of San Francisco, CA	M, W(s)

U of Southern Maine, ME	W
U of Vermont, VT	M, W
Utica Coll, NY	W
Vermont Tech Coll, VT	M, W
Wellesley Coll, MA	W
Wentworth Inst of Technology, MA	M, W
Wesleyan U, CT	M, W
Western Connecticut State U, CT	W
Western New England Coll, MA	W
Westfield State Coll, MA	W
Wheaton Coll, MA	W
Williams Coll, MA	M, W
Worcester Polytechnic Inst, MA	W
Worcester State Coll, MA	M, W
Yale U, CT	M, W

Water Polo

Amherst Coll, MA	M, W
Bates Coll, ME	M, W
Bowdoin Coll, ME	M, W
Bridgewater State Coll, MA	M, W
Brown U, RI	M, W
Colby Coll, ME	M, W
Connecticut Coll, CT	M, W
Dartmouth Coll, NH	M, W
Grove City Coll, PA	W
Harvard U, MA	M, W
Massachusetts Inst of Technology, MA	M
Trinity Coll, CT	M, W
United States Coast Guard Academy, CT	M
U of Vermont, VT	M, W
Utica Coll, NY	W
Wesleyan U, CT	M
Williams Coll, MA	M, W
Worcester Polytechnic Inst, MA	M, W
Yale U, CT	M, W

Wrestling

Amherst Coll, MA	M, W
Bridgewater State Coll, MA	M
Brown U, RI	M
Bryant U, RI	M
Dartmouth Coll, NH	M
Harvard U, MA	M
Hofstra U, NY	M(s)
Massachusetts Inst of Technology, MA	M
Messiah Coll, PA	M
Plymouth State U, NH	M
Rhode Island Coll, RI	M
Roger Williams U, RI	M
Sacred Heart U, CT	M(s)
Southern Methodist U, TX	M
Trinity Coll, CT	M
United States Coast Guard Academy, CT	M
U of New Hampshire, NH	M
U of Southern Maine, ME	M
Wesleyan U, CT	M
Western New England Coll, MA	M
Williams Coll, MA	M
Worcester Polytechnic Inst, MA	M
Yale U, CT	M

ROTC Programs

Anna Maria Coll, MA	AF(c)
Assumption Coll, MA	A(c), AF(c)
Babson Coll, MA	A(c), N(c), AF(c)
Barry U, FL	A(c), AF(c)
Bay Path Coll, MA	A(c), AF(c)
Becker Coll, MA	A(c), N(c), AF(c)
Bentley U, MA	A(c), AF(c)
Boston Coll, MA	A(c), N(c), AF(c)
Brandeis U, MA	A(c), AF(c)
Bridgewater State Coll, MA	A(c), AF(c)
Brown U, RI	A(c)
Bryant U, RI	A
Castleton State Coll, VT	A(c)
Central Connecticut State U, CT	A(c), AF(c)
Champlain Coll, VT	A(c)
Clarkson U, NY	A, AF
Clark U, MA	A(c), N(c), AF(c)
Colby Coll, ME	A(c)
Coll of the Holy Cross, MA	A(c), N, AF(c)
Curry Coll, MA	A(c)
Daniel Webster Coll, NH	A(c), AF(c)
Dartmouth Coll, NH	A(c)
Eastern Connecticut State U, CT	A(c), AF(c)
Emmanuel Coll, MA	A(c)
Endicott Coll, MA	A(c), AF(c)
Fairfield U, CT	A(c), AF(c)
Fisher Coll, MA	A(c)
Fitchburg State Coll, MA	AF(c)
Framingham State Coll, MA	A(c)
Franklin Pierce U, NH	A(c), AF(c)
Gordon Coll, MA	A(c), AF(c)
Grove City Coll, PA	A(c)
Hampshire Coll, MA	A(c)
Harvard U, MA	A(c), N(c), AF(c)
Hofstra U, NY	A
Husson U, ME	A(c), N(c)
Johnson State Coll, VT	A(c)
Keene State Coll, NH	AF(c)
Lyndon State Coll, VT	AF(c)
Maine Maritime Academy, ME	A, N
Massachusetts Inst of Technology, MA	A, N, AF
Massachusetts Maritime Academy, MA	A(c), N
Merrimack Coll, MA	AF(c)
Middlebury Coll, VT	A(c)
Mount Holyoke Coll, MA	A(c), AF(c)
New England Coll, NH	A(c), AF(c)
Nichols Coll, MA	A(c)
Northeastern U, MA	A, N(c), AF(c)
Ohio Wesleyan U, OH	A(c), AF(c)
Plymouth State U, NH	A(c), AF(c)
Providence Coll, RI	A
Quinnipiac U, CT	A(c), AF(c)
Rhode Island Coll, RI	A(c)
Rivier Coll, NH	AF(c)
Roger Williams U, RI	A(c)
Sacred Heart U, CT	A
Saint Michael's Coll, VT	A(c), AF(c)
Salem State Coll, MA	A(c), AF(c)
Salve Regina U, RI	A(c)
Simmons Coll, MA	A(c)
Smith Coll, MA	A(c), AF(c)
Southern Connecticut State U, CT	A(c), AF(c)
Southern Methodist U, TX	A, AF(c)
Southern New Hampshire U, NH	A(c), AF(c)
Stonehill Coll, MA	A
Suffolk U, MA	A(c)
Trinity Coll, CT	A(c)
Tufts U, MA	A(c), N(c), AF(c)
U of Bridgeport, CT	A
U of Charleston, WV	A
U of Connecticut, CT	A, AF
U of Hartford, CT	A(c), AF(c)
U of Maine, ME	A, N
The U of Maine at Augusta, ME	A(c), N(c), AF(c)
U of Massachusetts Amherst, MA	A, AF
U of Massachusetts Dartmouth, MA	A(c)
U of Massachusetts Lowell, MA	AF
U of New England, ME	A(c)
U of New Hampshire, NH	A, AF
U of New Hampshire at Manchester, NH	A(c), AF(c)
U of Rhode Island, RI	A
U of San Francisco, CA	A, AF(c)
U of Southern Maine, ME	A(c), AF(c)
U of Vermont, VT	A
Utica Coll, NY	A, AF(c)
Vermont Tech Coll, VT	A(c)
Wellesley Coll, MA	A(c), AF(c)
Wentworth Inst of Technology, MA	A(c), AF(c)
Wesleyan U, CT	AF(c)
Western Connecticut State U, CT	A(c), AF(c)
Western New England Coll, MA	A, AF(c)
Westfield State Coll, MA	A(c), AF(c)
Wheaton Coll, MA	A(c)
Worcester Polytechnic Inst, MA	A, N(c), AF
Worcester State Coll, MA	A(c), N(c), AF(c)
Yale U, CT	A(c), AF(c)

A—Army; N—Navy; AF—Air Force; (c)—available through a cooperating host institution

Alphabetical Listing of Colleges and Universities

In this index, the page locations of the **Profiles** are printed in regular type, **Profiles** with **Special Messages to Students** in *italics*, and **Close-Ups** in **bold type**.

Alphabetical Listing of Colleges and Universities

Peterson's
Book Satisfaction Survey

Give Us Your Feedback

Thank you for choosing Peterson's as your source for personalized solutions for your education and career achievement. Please take a few minutes to answer the following questions. Your answers will go a long way in helping us to produce the most user-friendly and comprehensive resources to meet your individual needs.

When completed, please tear out this page and mail it to us at:

Publishing Department
Peterson's, a Nelnet company
2000 Lenox Drive
Lawrenceville, NJ 08648

You can also complete this survey online at **www.petersons.com/booksurvey.**

1. **What is the ISBN of the book you have purchased? (The ISBN can be found on the book's back cover in the lower right-hand corner.)** _____

2. **Where did you purchase this book?**
   - ❑ Retailer, such as Barnes & Noble
   - ❑ Online reseller, such as Amazon.com
   - ❑ Petersons.com
   - ❑ Other (please specify) _____

3. **If you purchased this book on Petersons.com, please rate the following aspects of your online purchasing experience on a scale of 4 to 1 (4 = Excellent and 1 = Poor).**

	4	3	2	1
Comprehensiveness of Peterson's Online Bookstore page	❑	❑	❑	❑
Overall online customer experience	❑	❑	❑	❑

4. **Which category best describes you?**
   - ❑ High school student
   - ❑ Parent of high school student
   - ❑ College student
   - ❑ Graduate/professional student
   - ❑ Returning adult student
   - ❑ Teacher
   - ❑ Counselor
   - ❑ Working professional/military
   - ❑ Other (please specify) _____

5. **Rate your overall satisfaction with this book.**

Extremely Satisfied	Satisfied	Not Satisfied
❑	❑	❑

6. Rate each of the following aspects of this book on a scale of 4 to 1 (4 = Excellent and 1 = Poor).

	4	3	2	1
Comprehensiveness of the information	❑	❑	❑	❑
Accuracy of the information	❑	❑	❑	❑
Usability	❑	❑	❑	❑
Cover design	❑	❑	❑	❑
Book layout	❑	❑	❑	❑
Special features (e.g., CD, flashcards, charts, etc.)	❑	❑	❑	❑
Value for the money	❑	❑	❑	❑

7. This book was recommended by:
- ❑ Guidance counselor
- ❑ Parent/guardian
- ❑ Family member/relative
- ❑ Friend
- ❑ Teacher
- ❑ Not recommended by anyone—I found the book on my own
- ❑ Other (please specify) _____

8. Would you recommend this book to others?

Yes	Not Sure	No
❑	❑	❑

9. Please provide any additional comments.

_____

_____

_____

_____

_____

Remember, you can tear out this page and mail it to us at:

Publishing Department
Peterson's, a Nelnet company
2000 Lenox Drive
Lawrenceville, NJ 08648

or you can complete the survey online at **www.petersons.com/booksurvey.**

Your feedback is important to us at Peterson's, and we thank you for your time!

If you would like us to keep in touch with you about new products and services, please include your e-mail address here: _____